Cambridge Studies in Chinese History, Literature and Institutions
General Editors
Patrick Hanan and Denis Twitchett

TUN-HUANG POPULAR NARRATIVES

Other books in the series

GLEN DUDBRIDGE: The *Hsi-yu Chi*: A Study of Antecedents to the Sixteenth-Century Chinese Novel

STEPHEN FITZGERALD: China and the Overseas Chinese: A Study of Peking's Changing Policy 1949–70

CHRISTOPHER HOWE: Wage Patterns and Wage Policy in Modern China, 1919–1972

RAY HUANG: Taxation and Government Finance in Sixteenth-Century Ming China

DIANA LARY: Region and Nation: The Kwangsi Clique in Chinese Politics, 1925–37

CHI-YUN CHEN: Hsün Yüeh (A.D. 148–209): The Life and Reflections of an Early Medieval Confucian

DAVID R. KNECHTGES: The Han Rhapsody: A Study of the *Fu* of Yang Hsiung (53 B.C.–A.D. 18)

J. Y. WONG: Yeh Ming-ch'en: Viceroy of Liang Kuang (1852–8)

LI-LI CH'EN: Master Tung's Western Chamber Romance (*Tung hsi-hsiang chu-kung-tiao*): a Chinese *Chantefable*

DONALD HOLZMAN: Poetry and Politics: The Life and Works of Juan Chi (A.D. 210–63)

C. A. CURWEN: Taiping Rebel: The Deposition of Li Hsiu-cheng

P. B. EBREY: The Aristocratic Families of Early Imperial China: A Case Study of the Po-Ling Ts'ui Family

HILARY J. BEATTIE: Land and Lineage in China: A Study of T'ung-Ch'eng County, Anhwei, in the Ming and Ch'ing Dynasties

WILLIAM T. GRAHAM: The Lament for the South: Yü Hsin's 'Ai Chiang-nan fu'

HANS BIELENSTEIN: The Bureaucracy of Han Times

MICHAEL R. GODLEY: The Mandarin-Capitalists from Nanyang: Overseas Chinese Enterprise in the Modernization of China 1893–1911

CHARLES BACKUS: The Nan-chao Kingdom and T'ang China's Southwestern Frontier

Tun-huang popular narratives

VICTOR H. MAIR

Assistant Professor of Oriental Studies,
University of Pennsylvania

CAMBRIDGE UNIVERSITY PRESS

CAMBRIDGE
LONDON NEW YORK NEW ROCHELLE
MELBOURNE SYDNEY

CAMBRIDGE UNIVERSITY PRESS
Cambridge, New York, Melbourne, Madrid, Cape Town, Singapore, São Paulo

Cambridge University Press
The Edinburgh Building, Cambridge CB2 8RU, UK

Published in the United States of America by Cambridge University Press, New York

www.cambridge.org
Information on this title: www.cambridge.org/9780521247610

First published 1983
This digitally printed version 2007

A catalogue record for this publication is available from the British Library

Library of Congress Catalogue Card Number: 83–1939

ISBN 978-0-521-24761-0 hardback
ISBN 978-0-521-03983-3 paperback

Meinem Vater
dem geheiligten Weisen der Drehbank

CONTENTS

	List of illustrations	*page* viii
	Preface	ix
	Introduction	1
1	**Śāriputra**	31
	Transformation on the Subduing of Demons, One Scroll	
2	**Maudgalyāyana**	87
	Transformation Text on Mahāmaudgalyāyana Rescuing His Mother from the Underworld, With Pictures, One Scroll, With Preface	
3	**Wu Tzu-hsü**	123
	[The Story of Wu Tzu-hsü]	
4	**Chang I-ch'ao**	167
	[Transformation Text on Chang I-ch'ao]	
	Usages and symbols	172
	Notes on the texts	174
	References	312
	Index	319

ILLUSTRATIONS

1 Beginning of the Śāriputra illustrated transformation scroll (ms P4524) *page* x
2 'Transformation Text on the Subduing of Demons, One Scroll' (ms formerly in possession of Hu Shih), end portion 30
3 'Transformation Text on Mahāmaudgalyāyana Rescuing his Mother from the Underworld, With Pictures, One Scroll, With Preface' (ms S2614) 86
4 The story of Wu Tzu-hsü (ms S328) 122
5 Chang I-ch'ao transformation text (ms P2962) 166
6 'Fasting Siddhārtha', dating from the Kuchān era (second to third century, I.E.), from Sīkri, now kept in the Lahore Museum 204
7 From a wall-painting in the Shiffahrtshöhle at Qyzil in Central Asia, now kept at the Museum für Völkerkunde 205
8 Details from the left and right sides of the back wall of cave 8 at Tun-huang 221

The reproduction of the Maudgalyāyana ms (fig. 3) is published here by courtesy of the British Library Board. The plate of the Wu Tzu-hsü scroll (fig. 4), also in the British Library, is from M. A. Stein, *Serindia* (Oxford, 1921), p. 918 (no. CLXVI). The Śāriputra manuscript (fig. 2) is reproduced from a set of photostatic copies kept in the Library of Congress. The Śāriputra illustrated scroll (fig. 1) is from a photograph prepared expressly for this book by the Bibliothèque Nationale. The photograph of the Chang I-ch'ao transformation text (fig. 5) has also been provided by the Bibliothèque Nationale.

PREFACE

There are many persons to whom thanks are due for the help and encouragement given to me during the writing of this book. I should first like to thank Professor Patrick D. Hanan. Not only did he introduce me to the serious study of Tun-huang popular literature but he has consistently given me expert guidance during all phases of the writing of the book. Professor James R. Hightower read over portions of the early drafts and made numerous corrections. I have benefited immeasurably from the high standards of accuracy and scholarship which he demands of his students.

My debt to Professor Masatoshi Nagatomi is particularly great for his able assistance on matters of Buddhist doctrine and Indian languages. I was especially privileged to be able to consult Professor L. S. Yang. His vast fund of knowledge in many areas and his great skill in reading T'ang colloquial Chinese have rescued me from many impasses. Thanks are also due to Mr George Potter and Miss Deborah White who have helped me obtain the materials necessary to carry on my research without interruption.

Kate Owen and Elizabeth O'Beirne-Ranelagh of the Cambridge University Press deserve special thanks for many good and sensible solutions to difficult problems. They made the editing of this book a pleasure instead of a predicament. I am also grateful to the designers and typesetters who, though faced with unusual specifications, have created such an attractive printed product.

I am indebted to my colleagues, Joseph Miller, Barbara Ruch, Nathan Sivin, and Barbara Herrnstein Smith, for their careful criticism of the Introduction. I am also grateful to my wife, Li-ching, for the many sacrifices she has endured, and to my son, Thomas Krishna, who has been most understanding and sympathetic throughout. It goes without saying that all the good waves coming from Ohio (Athens, Canton, Kent, and Columbus) gave me the strength required to complete this work.

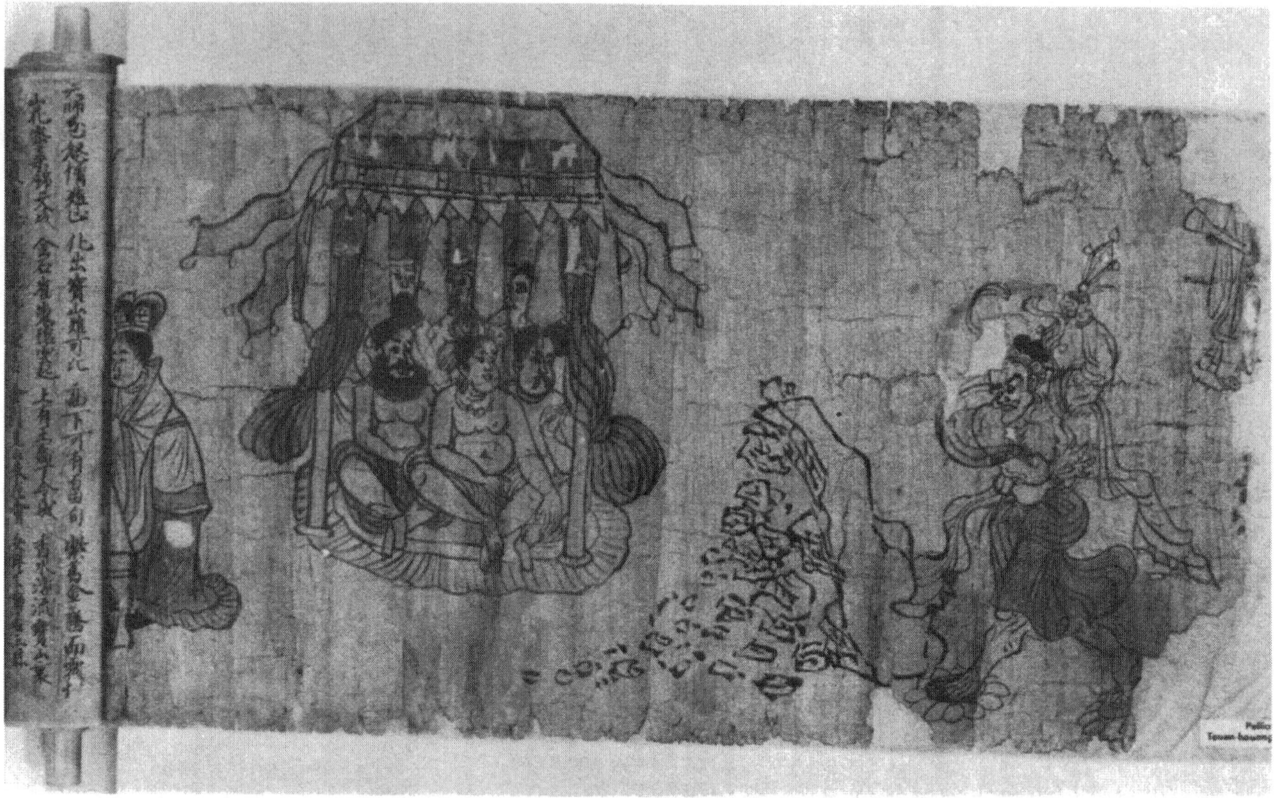

1. Beginning of the Śāriputra illustrated transformation scroll (ms P4524).

INTRODUCTION

General remarks

In the first decade of this century, a hoard of manuscripts was discovered in a small room connected to the side of a cave shrine at Tun-huang in the province of Kansu in northwestern China. For students of literature, among the most important texts found there was a group of narratives written in semicolloquial Chinese. These texts deal with both religious (mostly Buddhist) and secular themes and represent the earliest known examples of the alternating prose–verse (*chantefable*, prosimetric) narrative style in China. They are of the utmost importance in understanding the development of a wide variety of popular literary genres, including various types of fiction, drama, and recitatives or chants. However, due to the difficult language in which these texts are written, far less attention has been paid to them than they deserve.

The purpose of the present work is to understand as much as possible of four representative texts. These are the Śāriputra, Maudgalyāyana, and Chang I-ch'ao transformation texts and the Tun-huang story about Wu Tzu-hsü. It is my hope that competent literary historians will thereby be stimulated to examine closely the entire corpus of Tun-huang popular literature and to incorporate it as a fundamental topic in future discussions of the origin and evolution of vernacular literary forms. I have myself completed research on several basic questions regarding these texts and plan to publish the results of my work (entitled *T'ang Transformations*) in the near future. In particular, I have investigated the precise meaning of the problematic terms *pien* 變 and *pien-wen* 變文 which occur on some of the manuscripts as generic designations, Indian influences on the growth of popular narrative in China, and analogues in other Asian countries. To avoid duplication with *Transformations*, theoretical and historical discussion of *pien-wen* will only briefly be touched on here.

The meaning of *pien-wen*

Since the discovery of the Tun-huang manuscripts, numerous explanations of the term *pien-wen* have been put forward by scholars studying these texts. As we shall see in our discussion of the *pien-wen* corpus below, there is much disagreement about just what belongs therein. A large part of that disagreement stems from the lack of a precise understanding of the word *pien*. There is no ambiguity about *wen* since it simply means 'text'. The problem lies with *pien* whose basic signification is 'alter' but which has a broad range of extended meanings. Among the more common renditions of *pien-wen* are 'alternating text', 'popularization' (i.e. popularized text), and 'text relating a marvellous/strange incident'. Those who advance the 'alternating text' interpretation stress one formal characteristic of these prosimetric narratives, namely the alternation between prose and verse sections. This view has largely been discredited because, among other reasons, it is hard to justify the extraction of the stipulated meaning from the word *pien* standing by itself. The idea that *pien-wen* are 'popularizations' is still very prevalent and is the meaning intended by most modern scholars who write on this subject. But this explanation ignores the demonstrably strong Buddhist connotations of the term and, furthermore, requires some such forced interpretation as the following: 'changed [from a canonical sūtra to a popular narrative] text' or 'changed [from literary language text to colloquial language] text'. The third major explanation of *pien-wen* mentioned above is much closer to the actual meaning of the term as it would have been understood by the T'ang (618–907) and Five Dynasties (907–959) individuals who wrote it as a generic designation on certain Tun-huang manuscripts. Modern scholars who advance this explanation legitimately refer to such Japanese expressions as *hen-na koto* 変な事 ('unusual event') and Six Dynasties (222–589) occurrences of *pien* where it seems to mean something like *ch'i* 奇 ('strange') or *i* 異 ('uncommon'). Yet close, philological analysis[1] of the word *pien* as it is employed in numerous Buddhist texts and, more importantly, in the *pien-wen* themselves, reveals that the contemporary (late ninth through early tenth centuries) usage of the term was derived from Buddhist sources. Any explanation of *pien* as it applies to Tun-huang popular narratives must take into account its Buddhist connotations.

The *pien* of *pien-wen* is etymologically related to a Buddhist technical term meaning 'transformation'. 'Transformation' here implies the coming or bringing into being (i.e. into illusory reality, Skt. *māyā*) of a scene or deity. The creative agent who causes the transformational manifestation

[1] This has been carried out in my forthcoming *T'ang Transformations* and will not be repeated here. *Transformations* also provides documentation for all other statements herein and an account of previous studies on the *pien-wen* genre. For abbreviated references to works cited, see the References.

may be a Buddha, a Bodhisattva, or a saint such as Maudgalyāyana or Śāriputra. Highly skilled storytellers and actors – with the help of visual aids, gestures, and music – were also thought to be able to replicate transformational acts of creation. The ultimate religious purpose of such transformations was the release of all sentient beings from the vicious cycle of death and rebirth (*saṃsāra*). By hearing and viewing these transformations and reflecting upon them, the individual could become enlightened. Therefore, it is permissible to refer to *pien-wen* in English as 'transformation text' and the related visual art form, *pien-hsiang* 變相, as 'transformation tableau'.

The philosophical basis for the concept of 'transformation' can readily be traced to its Indian sources. One of the most important ideas relating to this concept is expressed by a Sanskrit term indicating a changed state, *nirmāṇa* (Pāli *nimmāna*), which also can mean 'a magical creation'.[2] The Sanskrit term *nirmāṇa-rati* (*lo pien-hua* 樂變化) thus means 'enjoying magical creations' and one expression for a transformationally manifested image is *nirmāṇa-nirbhāsa* (inadequately rendered in the Chinese version of the *Gaṇḍavyuha* as 'reflected/shadowy image', *ying-hsiang* 影像).

Though originally alien to China, the Buddhistic notion of transformation proved fascinating to the Chinese people. In later popular culture, enormous delight was taken in the constantly shifting series of transformational guises adopted by the likes of Monkey in the novel, *Journey to the West*, by Wu Ch'eng-en 吳承恩 (fl. *c.* 1500–*c.* 1582). It is no accident that the performance of magic came to be known as *pien mo-shu* 變魔術 or *pien hsi-fa* 變戲法. Contemporary descriptions of the entertainers who told these T'ang and Five Dynasties transformation tales indicate that audiences were impressed by the manifestations evoked during their performances. Through singing, dancing, gestures, painted scrolls, shadow projections, and picturesque language, the performers recreated magically the characters and events in their stories.[3]

[2] Cf. '*Dharmasya nirmāṇam ivopaviṣṭam*' (Aśvaghoṣa's *Buddhacarita-kāvya-sūtra*, x.19): '[The Boddhisattva] sitting like a magic-image of dharma', i.e., a 'picture' of Dharma. Johnston: 'magically projected by Dharma'. Weller: '*wie eine übernatürliche Schöpfung des Gesetzes*'. Tibetan: *chos kyi sprul pa*. From Franklin Edgerton, *Buddhist Hybrid Sanskrit Grammar and Dictionary*, vol. II (New Haven, 1953), p. 302. The corresponding passage in the Chinese translation (*Fo so hsing tsan ching* 佛所行讚經) by Dharmarakṣa (414–21) accurately reads *yu jo fa-hua-shen* 猶若法化身 (Ta4.19c). The translation of the *Buddhacarita* (*Fo pen-hsing chi ching* 佛本行集經) by Jñānagupta (587) gives *ju chu fa-se hsiang hu-jan erh hua-hsien* 如諸法色像/忽然而化現 (Ta4.71c).

[3] See Matsumoto Eiichi 松本栄一, *Tonkō-ga no kenkyū* 敦煌画の研究 (Tokyo, 1937), vol. II, plate 54, for the sort of rough illustrations that may have been worked up rapidly to accompany the presentation of transformations.

Corpus

There is no agreement on how many *pien-wen* manuscripts exist. Estimates vary from around eighteen to over eight thousand! Such latitude obviously indicates that the terminology for dealing with Tun-huang literature remains in a chaotic state. The main reason why no consensus has been reached on the number of extant *pien-wen* is because no strict guidelines have been established for identifying the formal features of this genre. For some scholars, *pien-wen* signifies any noncanonical, nondocumentary literary text recovered from Tun-huang. Such a definition includes poetry of various types. Other scholars stipulate that a *pien-wen* be a popular narrative (in the broadest sense of the term) text from Tun-huang. The range of possibilities is still further narrowed by those who hold that it must be written in prosimetric form. Most students of Chinese popular literature recognize approximately eighty texts (those found in *Tun-huang pien-wen chi* (Peking, 1957), hereafter T) as legitimate representatives of the *pien-wen* genre. But when this body of texts is carefully examined, it is apparent that it embraces a disparate assortment of literary styles and forms. It would be extremely difficult, if not impossible, to formulate a rigorous definition of *pien-wen* on the basis of this group of eighty texts.

A reasonable means for determining which texts are *pien-wen* and which are not is to examine and analyse those manuscripts that bear original titles designating them as *pien* or *pien-wen* and then extrapolate from this data the features of the genre. Very little contemporary evidence outside of the texts themselves sheds light on what the people of the T'ang and Five Dynasties periods conceived a *pien-wen* to be. Contemporary literary references to *pien-wen* tell us little more than that the oral antecedents of this genre were popular throughout China.

There is no essential, exclusive link between Tun-huang and *pien-wen*. The chief connection is the fortuitous one (dependent upon exigencies of climate and historical event) that the manuscripts happened to be preserved and discovered in Tun-huang. Some scholars view Tun-huang literary forms as if they were provincial in nature and thus not generally pertinent to the study of Chinese literature. But many of the manuscripts recovered from Tun-huang were copied down in far-distant parts of China and brought there by travellers. Similarly, although the Chin period (1115–1234) *Liu Chih-yüan Medley* 劉知遠諸宮調 was unearthed in the Gobi desert, we know that the printing blocks for it were cut in Shansi. The multitude of texts discovered in Japan (often in temples) is another case in point which demonstrates the mobility of Chinese popular literary texts.

Hence, 'Tun-huang *pien-wen*' simply implies '*pien-wen* discovered at Tun-huang', not '*pien-wen* peculiar to Tun-huang'.[4]

Several features identify the overwhelming majority of texts designated on the manuscripts as *pien* or *pien-wen*. They are narratives written in prosimetric style, the verse portions chiefly heptasyllabic. They deal with both secular and religious themes but all are written in semicolloquial language.

Another important fact was brought out by Umezu Jirō and Naba Toshisada many years ago but has not been much noticed outside of Japan: *pien-wen* have an intimate relationship to pictures. In *Transformations*, I demonstrate that the antecedent of *pien-wen* was actually a type of picture storytelling transmitted to China through Central Asia from India and having analogues in southeast Asian countries. Picture storytellers in ancient India included *śaubhikas*, *yamapaṭas*, *maṅkhas*, and *pratimādhāriṇs*. In modern India, these traditions survived well into the twentieth century in the performances of the *killēkyatas*, *katbus*, *cītrakathīs*, *citrakārs*, *paṭuās*, *paṛ bhopos*, and many others.[5] It is probable that, in Central Asia, the Uighurs referred to pictures used in narrative storytelling as *körünč*. The same Indian traditions which passed through Central Asia into China and became *pien* also were transmitted to Indonesia where they are known as *wayang bèbèr*. An early Ming (1368–1661) traveller to Indonesia witnessed a performance of *wayang bèbèr* (dramatic storytelling utilizing a picture scroll or series of individual scenes on cards) and declared that it was just like Chinese 'expository tales' (*p'ing-hua* 評話). This is evidence that oral *p'ing-hua* was a type of storytelling with pictures and a direct descendant of *pien*. In Japan, the Sino-Indian picture storytelling tradition, known as 'picture explanation' (*etoki* 繪解), still survives to this day.

With regard to the relationship between *pien-wen* and pictures, I should like here only to analyse the formulaic expression occurring before verse passages that is a characteristic feature of almost all these texts. Indeed, in *Transformations*, I argue that this formula can be used as an identifying feature of manuscripts which lack titles specifically designating them as

[4] Judging from the rhyme classes compiled from the verse portions of the transformation texts and sūtra lectures (see Lo, *Studies*, 445–596), some of the Tun-huang texts display slight regional specificity (similar to the dialect of the city of Ch'ang-an during the T'ang). But this is a common phenomenon of Chinese popular literature from ancient times to the present day and cannot be used to classify an entire genre as being unique to a given locality. On the basis of rhyme variation alone, we can say only that there exist regional variants of a given genre.

[5] Detailed information on these types of storytellers may be found in *Transformations*.

pien-wen. The basic formula is 'Please look at the place where XX [occurs], how does it go?' (*ch'ieh k'an XX ch'u, jo-wei ch'en shuo?* 且看XX處若爲陳說).[6] The usage of *ch'u* 處 ('place') in the formula derives from the practice of picture storytellers pointing to a specific spot on their paintings when narrating the events it depicts. In time, the force of the word weakened so that it came to function simply as a sign of narrative rather than visual locus, parallel to clauses ending in *shih* 時 ('time') indicating narrative moment in other Tun-huang texts. It would appear that this verse-introductory formula in the written transformation texts was a stylized attempt to capture a distinctive feature of oral performances.

Given the criteria outlined above, we obtain a corpus of around eighteen to twenty-one extant *pien-wen*. Since there are multiple copies (with some variations) of several texts, only seven stories are actually represented.[7] This grouping is based on a definition that can be no more rigorous than T'ang and Five Dynasties usage itself. On the other hand, for the term *pien-wen* to have any meaningful signification, we ought to distinguish it from other types of popular literature which were discovered at Tun-huang and which bear titles identifying them by designations other than *pien-wen*. These include 'lyric text' (*tz'u-wen* 詞文), 'rhapsody' or 'rhyme-prose' (*fu* 賦), 'tale' (*chuan* 傳), 'story' (*hua* 話), 'canto' (*ch'ü*[*-tzu-tz'u*] 曲[子詞]), 'poem' (*shih* 詩), 'text' (*shu* 書), 'discussion' (*lun* 論), 'dialogue' (*tz'u* 詞), 'eulogy' or 'hymn' (*tsan* 讚), '[apocryphal] sūtra' (*ching* 經), 'seat-settling text' or 'introit' (*ya-tso-wen* 押座文), 'conditional origins' or '[founding] legend' (*yüan-ch'i* 緣起, Skt. *pratītya-samutpāda*, or simply *yüan* 緣, Skt. *pratyaya*, *nidāna*), 'causation' (*yin-yüan* 因緣, Skt. *hetupratyaya*, *avadāna*), 'cantillation' (*yin* 吟), 'account' (*chi* 記), and 'sūtra lecture' (*chiang-ching-wen* 講經文).

It is particularly important to differentiate sūtra lectures from transformation texts. Sūtra lectures are line-by-line (occasionally word-by-word) explications of canonical scripture; transformation texts are prosimetric narratives whose sources are more often folk tales and legends than scripture. Depending on the circumstances (whether a cantor or other assistant is present), sūtra lectures are distinguished by formulaic expressions such as 'Please sing/intone/chant' or 'Let us sing' or 'I shall begin to sing' (*ch'ang chiang-lai* 唱將來, *ch'ang k'an-k'an* 唱看看, etc.) before the quoted scripture passage; transformation texts generally possess the verse-introductory formula described above and in the appendix. Sūtra lectures were part of religious services known as 'popular lectures' or 'lectures for

[6] For a more detailed discussion of this formula, see the appendix, pp. 27–8.

[7] A list of these pieces, with a discussion of certain problems relating to them, may be found in *Transformations*. If the doubtful cases are included in the total count, there are at most twenty-eight texts and twelve stories represented.

the laity' (*su-chiang* 俗講) that have a history stretching back to the Six Dynasties period; transformation texts are written versions of folk entertainments that were current during the eighth, ninth, and tenth centuries. And so on. T'ang usage is consistent; *chiang-ching-wen* were not thought by people of the ninth and tenth centuries to be a type of *pien-wen* nor vice versa.

The prosimetric form of *pien-wen* and of many other Tun-huang popular narratives calls for a brief discussion of the relationship between prose and verse in these texts. The proportion of verse to prose in Tun-huang popular narratives varies. Some are entirely in verse (e.g., the stories about Tung Yung 董永 and about the capture of Chi Pu 季布) and others are wholly prose (e.g., the tales of Han P'eng 韓朋, Ch'iu Hu 秋胡, 'Catch Tiger' Han 韓擒虎, and of Emperor T'ai-tsung 太宗 entering hell). Still others include only an incidental quoted poem (e.g., the accounts of Wizard Yeh Ching-neng 葉淨能 and the eminent monk Hui-yüan 惠遠). In the prosimetric narratives, there are two basic patterns for the relationship between prose and verse. In the first pattern, the verse is an integral component of the narrative structure; it helps to carry the story forward. Examples of this type are the story of Wu Tzu-hsü 伍子胥 and the Maudgalyāyana 目連 transformation text. The former, incidentally, uses verse sparingly while the latter, like Yüan period (1260–1367) drama, relies heavily upon it. The second pattern introduces most of the essential narrative content in the prose passages and utilizes the verse chiefly to recapitulate or embellish. Here the verse serves to emphasize certain aspects of the action or heighten the emotions of the actors. The Śāriputra and Chang I-ch'ao transformation texts fall under this category. The division between these two patterns is not rigid and most narratives share elements of both. With very few exceptions, the verse portions of Tun-huang popular narratives are heptasyllabic, the rhymes falling at the end of every second line. One rhyme may continue for several dozen couplets or may change after every half-dozen or so. The prose is highly conversational in some of the narratives while, in others, it exhibits pronounced euphuistic parallelism. I have tried to convey these stylistic differences in my translations by various means such as typographical arrangement and number of syllables per line.

Scribes and performers

One of the issues that has most intrigued scholars working with *pien-wen* is who wrote them down and why? Earlier students[8] had suggested that

[8] For references on this and other points in these paragraphs, see *Transformations* and 'Inventory'.

they were promptbooks for the performers who presented the stories recorded on them before an audience. It was widely assumed that the performers were monks who used the *pien-wen* to attract crowds into the temples where they could then be instructed in more serious religious matters. But recent research by folklorists and students of oral epic has shown that storytellers seldom employ promptbooks.[9] There is, in any case, no proof that the written *pien-wen* were meant for this purpose. Serious doubt has also been cast on the assumption that professional religious (i.e. ordained Buddhist monks) functioned as entertainers.[10] The matter is altogether different with regard to sūtra lectures. There is strong evidence that some of the Tun-huang *chiang-ching-wen* were referred to by lecturers who were ordained Buddhist monks.

Information gleaned from contemporary literary sources, examination of parallel picture storytelling traditions in other societies, and internal evidence of the manuscripts themselves now allow us to determine with a high degree of probability that *pien-wen* were not promptbooks for use during performance. An example of internal evidence that corroborates this interpretation is a question that was recorded in the Śāriputra transformation text. After Śāriputra conjures up a mighty warrior-god, we read the following: 'What was the appearance of his Diamond Deity?' (T382.16).[11] This seems not to be strictly rhetorical but rather to be a perfunctory 'question to the audience'. This question provides evidence that these texts were at a remove from promptbooks intended for use in performance. Rather, they would seem to be meta-texts[12] in the process of evolving into literary texts. Such disruptions of the oral narrative would be most likely to have occurred extemporaneously. The more removed from actual oral performance, the greater is the likelihood for many devices which constitute elements of the 'simulated context'[13] in pseudo-oral

[9] See, for example, René Louis, 'L'épopée française est carolingienne', *Coloquios de Roncesvalles, Agosto, 1955* (Saragossa, Publications of the Faculties of Philosophy and Letters, 2nd ser. no. 18, 1956), 327–460 (esp. 452). Louis maintains that no *jongleur* steeped in the oral tradition would have worked from a written text.

[10] In conversation on March 14, 1981 and in a letter dated April 25, 1981, Stephen H. West informed me that he has data showing that many popular entertainers who passed themselves off as monks really were not. I also address this issue in *Transformations*.

[11] For abbreviations see 'Usages and symbols', 'Notes on the texts' and 'References'. Page references to T are given in bold figures in the text.

[12] As used by Eugene Eoyang in 'Word of Mouth: Oral Storytelling in the *Pien-wen*' (Bloomington, Indiana, Indiana University Ph.D. dissertation, 1971), this refers to written texts that bear clear marks of oral composition.

[13] An analytical concept presented by Patrick Hanan in his 'The Nature of Ling Meng-ch'u's Fiction', in Andrew Plaks, ed., *Chinese Narrative: Critical and Theoretical Essays* (Princeton, 1977), pp. 85–114.

written narratives. The converse of this does not hold true, i.e. total absence of such devices does *not* constitute proof of orality. Proof that a given text was intended for performance always requires additional evidence external to the text itself. For example, there may be a colophon attached or an independent record stating the circumstances (date, place, etc.) of the performance. Or there may be historical and cross-cultural evidence available which confirms that a given genre is customarily employed for performance. Failing this, caution should be exercised in labelling any written or printed text as 'oral literature'.

The colophon of one religious *pien-wen* tells us that it was copied for pious reasons. In the majority of instances that we can verify from the Tun-huang manuscripts, the scribes and copyists were lay students studying in monastery schools. Their curriculum embraced both secular and religious subjects. There is no evidence that the lay students themselves performed transformations. Certainly a vital oral storytelling tradition (known simply as 'unrolling/unfolding/turning transformation [scrolls]', *chuan-pien* 轉變, referring to the pictures displayed before the audience) lay behind the *pien-wen* manuscripts. The performers were primarily entertainers and not ordained monks. We know, for example, that singing girls from Szechwan performed transformations on the streets and in the banquet halls of Ch'ang-an during the T'ang period. Their main assets were their picture scrolls, their beauty, and their voices. That entertainers and storytellers frequently gathered around the temples to perform was as true of the T'ang period[14] as it was of the first part of this century[15] and in Taiwan today. But this does not mean that they themselves were religious specialists.

Transformation storytelling was a product of popular culture and, on occasion, was even attacked by the Buddhist establishment who wished to maintain good relations with the government. This is ironic, of course, because famous poets such as Po Chü-i 白居易 (772–846) and Emperor Hsüan-tsung 玄宗 (for dates see the next section) himself enjoyed a good transformation performance from time to time. But ambivalent reception has been the frequent fate of folk and popular culture in China from the beginning of recorded history.

Dating

It has generally been assumed that the Tun-huang popular narratives date from the late T'ang and Five Dynasties periods. This impression, however, is due primarily to the fact that the dates given in surviving

[14] See Sun Ch'i 孫棨 (*c.* 789–881), *Account of the Northern Quarter* 北里志.
[15] See Mao Tun 矛盾 (*b.* 1896), 'Spring Silkworms' 春蠶.

colophons fall within that time range. The colophons, however, are of little value in establishing date of authorship because they generally mention only the time when a given copy was made. As an example of the sort of close textual examination that can determine when a text was originally composed, the date of the Śāriputra transformation text will be briefly considered.

On T361.12, Emperor Hsüan-tsung is referred to by a lengthy title. The literary historian Cheng Chen-to (1898–1958) proposed, on the basis of this title, that the Śāriputra transformation text in which it occurs must have been written during Hsüan-tsung's reign.[16] Sceptics, however, have declared rightly that the title may have been employed retroactively. A closer look, nevertheless, compels us not to abandon the evidence of the title. When we turn to the *T'ang hui yao* 唐會要, a collection of important documents relating to the T'ang dynasty, we find that Hsüan-tsung held this title only for a little over a year and that the titles given him before and after differ by just a word or two.

> On March 22, 742, [Hsüan-tsung] was given the honorific title Emperor Sage in Civil Affairs and Divine in Military Matters of the Epochal Beginning and Heavenly Treasure Reign-Periods. On June 13, 748, he was given the honorific title Emperor of the Epochal Beginning and Heavenly Treasure Reign-Periods Who Is Sage in Civil Affairs and Divine in Military Matters and Who Responds to the Way. On July 23, 749, he was given the honorific title Emperor of the Epochal Beginning and Great Heavenly-cum-Earthly Treasure Reign-Periods Who Is Sage in Civil Affairs and Divine in Military Matters and Who Responds to the Way.
> 天寶元年二月十一日又加尊號開元天寶聖文神武皇帝。七載五月十三日又加尊號開元天寶聖文神武應道皇帝。八載閏六月五日又加尊號開元天地大寶聖文神武應道皇帝。[17]

It seems highly improbable that anyone writing long after 749 would have remembered this title which was used for such an exceptionally short length of time. It is far more likely that Hsüan-tsung's temple name ('Original Progenitor' 元宗) or his posthumous title ('Greatly Sage and Greatly Perspicacious Filial Emperor of the Utmost Way' 至道大聖大明孝皇帝) would have been used. Still, we must agree with the sceptics that this alone does not settle the date of authorship.

If we look at the previous line in T, we notice the statement that it has

[16] Cheng, *Popular*, 225.
[17] *T'ang hui yao* (1884 edn), p. 1.7a.

been 'more than several hundred years'[18] since the *Vajracchedikā-prajñā-pāramitā-sūtra* was transmitted to China and translated. What is most interesting is that the manuscript S4398v has a variant reading,[19] 'more than four hundred years'. The language is imprecise and may mean something like 'approximately four hundred years'. Now the first translation of this sūtra into Chinese is that by Kumārajīva (344–413) – Ta no. 235. Thus the amount of time specified makes it virtually certain that this transformation text was, indeed, originally composed around the time of Hsüan-tsung. That the connection between Hsüan-tsung and the *Vajracchedikā-sūtra* was not made carelessly is obvious from the well-known fact that the emperor himself was especially devoted to it. Tun-huang manuscript PK9802 is a 'Hymn on the *Vajra(cchedikā)-sūtra*' which includes the lines:

> Listen to this song about the *Vajra(cchedikā)-prajñā(-pāramitā-sūtra)*,
> The Epochal Beginning Emperor personally annotated it himself.
>
> 聽唱金剛般若詞
> 開元皇帝親自註[20]

P2721 is a more complete version of the same hymn.[21]

From contemporary references, we learn that the Maudgalyāyana transformation was already well-known by the literati in the year 825. On the basis of language and parallels to certain apocryphal Chinese Buddhist sūtras, I would place its writing no later than 800. Most of the extant manuscripts, however, are from approximately a century later.

The date of the Chang I-ch'ao transformation text is a rather straightforward matter. Because of dates mentioned within the text itself, we know that it could not have been written before 856. The physical characteristics of the manuscript and comparison with the language and style of other texts lead me to believe that it could not have been written down much later than 870.

The question of establishing a date for the Wu Tzu-hsü story is much more difficult than for the preceding three texts. I should like here to attempt an approximate date on the basis of internal evidence alone. On T18.10, the expression 'Dragon of Good Prospect' occurs in somewhat unusual circumstances. This may provide us with a highly tentative *terminus a quo* for the story inasmuch as this expression was also the name of a reign period during the T'ang (707–709, of the Emperor Chung-tsung

[18] See Śāriputra line 78n1.
[19] See Śāriputra line 78n2.
[20] *Tsa-lu*, 54.
[21] *To-so* no. 40, p. 189. See also P2094 and D296.

中宗) and so may have suggested itself to the author. On T19.3, there is an apparent reference to crimson and green silk being presented to military officers. I have discussed this passage in some detail in Wu line 1032n. It may point to a practice that was codified in the year 716. A similar reference on T25.15 (see Wu line 1498n) to the award of scarlet silk and golden fish pouches (worn at the waist as a sign of official rank) indicates the year 721. The mention of 'present-day Ch'eng-fu District' 今城父縣 on T21.11 would have been most likely during the years 636–884. On the basis of these bits of information alone, we may presume that the Tun-huang Wu Tzu-hsü story was *originally* composed sometime around the year 720. Lionel Giles dates one of the fragments (S6331) to the seventh century,[22] but we may revise this to the eighth. Nonetheless, the mature style of the bulk of the text as copied on S328 seems characteristic of the late T'ang. The fact that there are four separate manuscripts with noticeable variants guarantees that the story was popular enough to have been copied many times. Furthermore, if the story first took shape in the Kiangsu – Anhwei – Chekiang region, as David Johnson asserts, there would have been ample opportunity for literary improvement and polish as it made its way across the breadth of China to Tun-huang. My tentative conclusions are that what we now know as the Tun-huang version of the Wu Tzu-hsü story was composed in southeast China near the end of the first quarter of the eighth century and gradually spread to other parts of China during the second half of the eighth century and the first half of the ninth. Along the way, it absorbed elements of the Buddhist narrative tradition (a slight adaptation to the prosimetric form, a significant amount of Buddhistic language, etc.) and was repeatedly copied and revised. The text given in T and translated here is a composite one made up of four disparate renditions of the story. That they can now be fused fairly smoothly together indicates, in all likelihood, that they derive from a single parent.

Sources

The chief sources of the texts translated in this book are identified in the notes to the text, in the studies listed in the References, and in *Transformations*.

It is possible to identify many of the ultimate sources of material which found its way into Tun-huang popular narratives.[23] *The Chronicle of Tso*, *Records of the Grand Historian*, *History of the Han*, the Buddhist *Tripiṭaka*, and so forth, often contain parallels to the stories presented in the Tun-huang popular narratives. More important, however, and much more diffi-

[22] Giles, *Chinese Manuscripts from Tunhuang*, p. 240a.
[23] See, for example, Lo, *Studies*, 14–353.

cult to determine, is the mechanism whereby materials from classical sources found their way into these popular narratives.

In the process of popularization there are numerous participants. This naturally complicates the process. It would have been impossible for an illiterate or minimally literate singing girl who performed the Wang Chao-chün 王昭君 transformation to read the *History of the Han* or the *Miscellaneous Accounts of the Western Capital* 西京雜記. And yet she utilized materials that ultimately had their source in these works. How did she learn them? Probably somewhat in this fashion. Our singing girl may have been apprenticed for a time, perhaps only in a very informal way, to a more experienced performer. The same goes for her teacher and, before that, her teacher's teacher. Like her, they must all have had little education. They would have heard from their friends and relatives bits and pieces of the story as it occurred in the history books. Their friends and relatives, in turn, would probably have picked up this information from the local savant, often a 'failed B.A.', as it were, who served as the village schoolmaster. Another point at which material from the literate tradition could have entered was during the transcribing of the transformation text. Someone had to write down the transformation. The best candidates would have had the rudiments of classical learning. The fact that their writing is full of errors, however, indicates that they were not highly educated. In this process of popularization, there were many chances for distortion and adaptation of the literary sources. Naturally, elements of legend, myth, and folklore could have been integrated into the story at any time by any individual who transmitted it. That the particular version of the Wang Chao-chün transformation text which survived at Tun-huang has a significant admixture of Turkish lore reflects the area of its currency but does not tell us anything definite about the place of its composition.

Relationship to drama

Students of Chinese literature generally accept the crucial importance of Tun-huang popular narratives for the development of fiction in China. According to Jaroslav Průšek, 'In their style and diction they are the predecessors of the later popular short stories.'[24] Much less frequently, it

[24] Průšek, *Chinese History and Literature* (Dordrecht, 1970), p. 240. Y. W. Ma has recently written an important article calling for greater precision in pronouncements about the direct influence of *pien-wen* on later storytelling. See his 'The Beginnings of Professional Storytelling in China: A Critique of Current Theories and Evidence' that is part of the *Études d'histoire et de littérature offertes au Professeur Jaroslav Průšek*, Bibliothèque de l'Institut des Hautes Études Chinoises vol. XXIV (Paris, 1976), pp. 227–45. His remarks are in harmony with the main assertion of this section, i.e., that the influence of transformations on popular literature is more likely to be evident in the area of oral performing arts than upon written narratives such as *hua-pen* 話本.

has been suggested that they may have been instrumental in the development of drama in China.[25] Yet rarely is there much conviction behind such suggestions. Indeed, one often encounters outright denial that transformation texts and related genres decisively influenced early drama. Why so, in spite of the fact that, in matters of detail, it is possible to demonstrate specific influences?[26] There are three major objections.

The first objection to such influence denies that the alternating spoken and sung form (present in virtually all Chinese drama before the twentieth century) of transformation texts represented anything new on the Chinese scene. Jen Pan-t'ang, in his *T'ang Theatricals*, makes just such an assertion.[27] Unable to point to any definite texts which would give credence to his claim, Jen is reduced to complaining that modern scholars are too historically minded. He asserts that it is natural for people to speak and natural for them to sing, ergo it is natural for them to speak and sing:

> *Actually, these two things, speaking and singing, like drinking and eating, are innate to human beings. Among China's ancient arts, they had long ago developed separately. If the two are brought together into one new form, it is no different from people's eating and drinking at the same meal. This is something which is absolutely normal and natural. If the Indian people could do this, surely our own people could have done the same. Did our people have to wait for the Buddhist tradition of speaking and singing to open the way for them and to guide them before they could eat and drink at the same meal, before they could speak and sing in the same performance?*[28]

Yet it is not immediately obvious that all peoples possess alternating sung and spoken narrative forms. Nor is there anything shameful in not having such forms.[29]

Jen is by no means alone in his efforts to disavow *pien-wen* influence upon the theatre. Wang Wen-ts'ai 王文才 speaks of a 'folk *pien-wen*' which he says preceded even the sūtra lectures (*chiang-ching-wen*) and originally

[25] One scholar who does posit a strong, formative influence of transformations on the development of Chinese drama is T'ien Shih-lin 田士林. See his *Outline History of the Development of Chinese Theatre* 中國戲劇發展史略 (Taipei, 1972), especially chapter 2, section 2, pp. 41–4, 'From *pien-wen* to Medleys and Drum Tales' 從變文到諸宮調鼓子詞.

[26] See *Transformations* and the annotations in this book.

[27] Jen Pan-t'ang 任半塘, *T'ang hsi-nung* 唐戲弄 (Peking, 1958), pp. 904–5.

[28] *Ibid.*, p. 905 (emphasis in the original).

[29] Two collections of studies which give, in my estimation, a more accurate description of the early theatre on the basis of known manuscripts and specific textual references are Feng Yüan-chün 馮沅君, *Ku-chü shuo-hui* 古劇說彙 (Peking, 1956) and Hu Chi 胡忌, *Sung Chin tsa-chü k'ao* 宋金雜劇考 (Peking, 1959). Unfortunately, neither Feng nor Hu gives serious consideration to the role of transformations in the development of Chinese drama.

consisted only of sung parts.[30] Later, so he says, these pure-song 'folk *pien-wen*' came in contact with the Buddhist forms and took on prose passages. But this does not deny that the Buddhist lecture and story forms were the first popular literary works in China to employ alternating prose and verse passages for narrative purposes.[31]

In an attempt to find a Chinese precedent for the prosimetric form, Ch'eng I-chung 程毅中 links *pien-wen* with the Ch'in (249–207 B.I.E. (Before International Era)) and Han (206–8 B.I.E.) *tsa-fu* 雜賦 ('miscellaneous rhapsodies'), but concedes[32] that the *fu* simply was not an alternating narrative form composed of prose and verse. Rather, it was a species of descriptive writing located somewhere between the two. Ch'eng, like Wang Wen-ts'ai, also speculates on the possibility of 'folk *pien-wen*' that were supposedly not called *pien-wen* until the Buddhist storytelling and sūtra lecture forms became popular.[33]

While the existence of non-Buddhist, pre-T'ang prosimetric narrative forms in China is dubious, India, from an early age, has been fond of narrations which are advanced through alternations of prose and verse (*gadya* and *padya*). Sanskrit even has a name, *campū*, for a particular type of composition which signifies this form.[34] Many of the most famous Buddhist sūtras, such as the *Saddharmapuṇḍarika*, *Lalitavistara*, *Vajracchedikā*, and *Jātakamālā*, consist of both prose and verse. The fourth century I.E. Allahabad Stone Pillar inscription (Hariṣeṇa's panegyric of Samudragupta) consists of prose and verse passages.[35] Prose and poetry were used also in the forerunners of classical Indian drama.[36] It was common to use prose in Sanskrit plays for ordinary speech and verse was used where concentrated expression and heightened emotion were desired.[37] This statement would be equally applicable to *pien-wen* and to Yüan (1260–1367) drama. Aśvaghoṣa (first or second century I.E.), the

[30] This he does in his preface to Jen Erh-pei 任二北 (Jen Pan-t'ang) *Initial Researches on Tun-huang Cantos* 敦煌曲初探 (Shanghai, 1954), pp. 4–5. On p. 14 of the same preface, Wang himself admits that the term 'folk *pien-wen*' is speculative and so he is careful to see that it always has quotation marks around it.

[31] For more information on these matters, see Ch'en Ju-heng 陳汝衡, *History of Storytelling* 說書史話 (Peking, 1958), pp. 7–10.

[32] 'Some Investigations Concerning *pien-wen*' 關於變文的幾點探索, *Wen-hsüeh i-ch'an tseng-k'an* 文學遺產增刊 (Peking, 1962), vol. X, pp. 80–101 (p. 83).

[33] *Ibid.*, p. 86.

[34] *Kāvyādarśa*, 31; *Sāhityadarpana*, vi, 336, as cited in Monier Monier-Williams, *A Sanskrit–English Dictionary* (Berkeley, 1976), p. 389a.

[35] See Gaurinath Sastri, *A Concise History of Classical Sanskrit Literature* (Oxford, 1960), p. 55.

[36] A. Berriedale Keith, *The Sanskrit Drama* (Oxford, 1924), p. 90.

[37] Balwant Gargi, *Theatre in India* (New York, 1962), pp. 17–18.

author of the famous *Buddhacarita-kāvya-sūtra* and the first Indian playwright for whom manuscripts are available, employed the alternating form in many of his works.

Jen Pan-t'ang's second objection[38] to the theory of the influence of transformation texts upon drama is in the assertion that Chinese plays, since at least the Han period, possessed a story line. Yet none of the documents relating to the earliest Chinese theatrical entertainments reflect more than the most rudimentary outline of an incident as their 'plot'. It is undeniable that theatrical entertainment did exist in China at an early age. Chang Heng's 張衡 'Rhapsody on the Western Capital' 西京賦 portrays the theatre during the Han as little more than singing and dancing, acrobatics and magic, mime and burlesque. The very earliest entertainers, such as Entertainer Meng (*yu* Meng 優孟) who appears in the 'Biographies of Jesters' ('Ku-chi lieh-chuan' 滑稽列傳) of the *Record of the Grand Historian* (*Shih-chi* 史記), were not so much thespians as court jesters. Entertainer Meng himself, for example, is most famous for his flawless impersonation of Sun Shu-ao 孫叔敖, a wise minister of the king of Ch'u during the Spring and Autumn period (722–481 B.I.E.). And, before the entertainers, there were shamans or mediums such as Shaman Hsien (*wu* Hsien 巫咸) and Shaman Yang (*wu* Yang 巫陽) in the *Songs of the South* (*Ch'u-tz'u* 楚辭), whom some have adduced as proof of the existence of drama in ancient China. But, though the shaman may have presented a spectacular show, his primary business was the worship of the gods and the exorcizing of unwanted spirits, and not portraying stories.

Later, there is the 'Big Mask' 大面 or 代面, which was introduced during the Northern Ch'i 北齊 period (550–577) when foreign influence was strong. The actor in this skit plays Lan Ling 蘭陵, a very handsome warrior who would wear a hideous mask when he went into battle because he thought his appearance too feminine. The important aspects of this performance were its dance and visual qualities. The actor wore a purple robe, a gold seal dangled at his waist, and he held a whip in his hand. Called *ryō-ō* 陵王 in Japan, this dance is one of the best-known of the *bugaku* 舞樂 repertoire. The important elements of the performance are the music (especially the entrance and exit percussion and flute pieces called *ranjō* 亂聲), the grotesque mask worn by the actor, and the heroic, military gestures and dance movements.[39]

Again, with the 'Shake Head' (?) (*po-t'ou* 撥頭) which is derived from

[38] Jen Pan-t'ang, *T'ang hsi-nung*, pp. 43–4.

[39] There is a photograph of a modern performance of *ryō-ō* in Robert Garfias, *Dances of the Japanese Imperial Household* (New York, 1959), unpaginated. See also Masataro Togi, *Gagaku*, tr. Don Kenney (New York, 1971), plates 8, 43, 101, and 177.

Central Asia, there is but the barest outline of a story-incident. It is also written 鉢頭, 缽頭, 秡頭, 髮頭, 馬頭 and 拔頭. The profusion of variant transliterations certifies that it is most probably derived from a foreign word. But the consistency of the second syllable and the fact that several of these combinations have meaning when translated show that the people who coined them were trying to make sense of the sounds. Most critics, following Wang Kuo-wei 王國維, declare that *po-t'ou* is the transliteration of the name of an obscure Indian kingdom. Since this has not been securely established, however, there is room for my own very hesitant suggestion that in the minds of Chinese the term may have been associated with the Buddhist and Taoist practice of self-flagellation described by Lien-sheng Yang.[40] The penitent would wallow in the mud, scream loudly, and pummel himself. As recorded in seventh-century Pure-Land texts, it served as a form of confession. The possible connection with dramatic performances called 'Shake Head' (?) which I propose is that this practice, called *tzu-pu* 自搏 by Taoists and *tzu-p'u* 自撲 by Buddhists, is described in the 'Eight Aspects Transformation' (*Pa-hsiang pien* 八相變) thus: 'His hair dishevelled and shaking his head [?], he fell upon the ground and pummelled himself' 散髮 拔頭 渾塠 自撲 (T337.10).[41] The violent self-incriminations of this practice would certainly fit the contemporary descriptions of the 'Shake Head' (?) play. T'ang sources[42] reveal that this 'Shake Head' (?) act depicted how a young man killed a tiger which had devoured his father. The main action shows the son climbing a hill which has eight turns to recover his father's body. The music that accompanied the performance, appropriately, consisted of eight repetitions. But, again, the visual aspects were the most important element of the act. The performer, in tears, wore white clothing (mourner's garb) and his hair was dishevelled. 'Shake Head' (?) (*batō* 拔頭), which is also preserved in Japan as a court dance, is a sort of pantomimic, symbolic ballet that does not rely upon the spoken word.[43]

Other early theatrical performances included 'Tottering Lady' 踏搖娘

[40] See Wu line 352n.

[41] Compare also T7, last line but one; T707.8; and T741, last line but one.

[42] 'Treatise on Music' 音樂志 in *Old T'ang History* 斐普賢 and in Tuan An-chieh's 段安節 *Yüeh-fu tsa-lu* 樂府雜錄 as quoted in P'ei P'u-hsien 斐普賢, *Researches into Sino-Indian Literary Relationships* 中印文學關係研究 (Taipei, 1959), p. 29.

[43] For a résumé of conjectures about the name, see Martin Gimm's meticulously annotated *Das Yüeh-fu Tsa-lu des Tuan An-chieh* (Wiesbaden, 1966), pp. 184–6. For illustrations of *batō*, see Togi, *Gagaku*, plates 1, 63, 179, and 162–9 (a series of photographs showing the dancer Hayashi Tamio dressing for a *batō* performance). For the types of masks used in the 'Lan Ling' and 'Shake Head' (?) performances, see also plates 7 AB and 8 AB in Hsiang Ta 向達, *Ch'ang-an during the T'ang Period and the Civilization of the Western Regions* 唐代長安與西域文明 (Peking, 1957).

from Northern Chou 北周 (557–581) which showed a drunken husband beating his wife. It was also called 'Su Chung-lang' 蘇中郎, the name of the husband. Another performance was 'The Adjutant' 參軍戲 which consisted of the public humiliation of an officer who had stolen silks from the royal storehouses and may have involved some humorous repartee.[44]

Not long before the appearance of transformations in China, it is reported that, during the reign (604–617) of Emperor Yang-ti 煬帝 of the Sui, festivities were held on the fifteenth night of the first month of each year in which a multitude of entertainers was involved. The common people rushed to witness these amusements in droves. Liu Yü 柳彧, a respected official, protested the unseemliness of female impersonators and men wearing masks of beasts. The acts were described as loud, bizarre, and endless, the costumes too gaudy, the music too raucous, and the temporary stages either too broad or too high. Liu Yü was particularly upset that men and women of all classes mingled freely in this setting. And yet, there is no mention of what could properly be termed drama.[45]

Another type of performance that is frequently mentioned as evidence that Chinese drama from an early age was concerned with the portrayal of a story is the puppet show. But the term itself has so many variant orthographical forms (窟礧子, 魁礧, 傀儡, 魁櫑, 窟磊, 魁壘, 魁擂, 滙磊, 傀磊子, 苟利子, 加[嘉]禮戲) that it must undoubtedly have been transliterated from a foreign tongue. Many of the actors, jugglers, and mimes who flooded the T'ang capital hailed from Kucha in eastern Turkestan. They brought with them the Turkish word for marionette which Laufer traces to medieval Greek (via the Slavs and Byzantium)[46] and whose sound

[44] See Aoki Masaru 青木正児, *An Introduction to Yüan Drama* 元人雜劇序說 (Tokyo, 1937), p. 1. This work has been translated by Sui Shu-sen 隋樹森 as 元人雜劇概說 (Peking, 1957). The above discussion is based largely on Shionoya On 鹽谷溫, *Kokuyaku Gen kyoku sen* 國譯元曲選 (Tokyo, 1940), pp. 11–14 and Chou I-po 周貽白, *Chung-kuo hsi-chü shih chiang-tso* 中國戲劇史講座 (Peking, 1958), pp. 1–17. A. E. Zucker, *The Chinese Theater* (Boston, 1925), chapter 1, covers the same material but less precisely. I have also used Martin Gimm, *Das Yüeh-fu Tsa-lu*, chapter 7.

[45] 'Biography of Liu Yü', in Wei Cheng (580–643) *et al.*, eds., *History of Sui* 隋書 (K'ai-ming edn), p. 2496.4.

[46] Berthold Laufer, *Oriental Theatricals*, Field Museum Guide part 1 (Chicago, 1923), p. 39, has a picture of two clay figures representing the sort of performers who may have brought the first puppets with them to China. In his preface to W. Grube and E. Krebs, *Chinesische Schattenspiele* (Munich, 1915), p. xvi, Laufer gives the medieval Greek for puppet as *χούχλα* and the Turkish (Osman.) as *quqla*. Cf. also the Russian word *kukl'i* ('doll'). The earliest reference to puppets in Indian literature occurs in the *Mahābhārata*, for which see E. P. Horrowitz, *The Indian Theatre* (London, 1912), p. 155. Although the problem is too complicated to go into here in detail, it is probable that India was the home of the puppet play (see *Transformations* for discussion and references) and that migrating gypsies were responsible for spreading it over the Eurasian land mass.

is close to the seventh-century pronunciation of the Chinese names for puppet listed above.

Lo Chin-t'ang has demonstrated that there is no solid evidence of puppets in China before the Chin 晉 (265–420). And the Chin mention (*Lieh-tzu*, 'Questions of T'ang' 湯問) sounds suspiciously like a passage in the *Sheng-ching* 生經 (*Jātaka*) which consists of stories about the lives and deeds of the Buddha and his disciples. It was translated about 285 by Dharmarakṣa who was, perhaps significantly, a monk from Tun-huang and was, in fact, known as the 'Tun-huang Bodhisattva'. This date would put it well before the compilation of *Lieh-tzu* by Chang Chan 張湛 (fl. 370). Both the passage in *Lieh-tzu* and that in the *Sheng-ching* deal with the craft of an artisan who created a superbly life-like puppet. And both related a king's angry reaction when the puppet eyes one of his courtesans.[47]

Shadow figures, while apparently indigenous to China, were originally not used for dramatic purposes at all but as a magical means to summon the 'shades' of the departed. The first mention of such shadows is in the twenty-eighth fascicle of *Records of the Grand Historian*[48] and relates to the year 121 B.I.E. when Emperor Wu, who had lost one of his favourite wives, was obsessed by the desire to see her again. His desire was satisfied by a necromancer, Shao Weng 少翁, who was able to project her image on a transparent screen. But it was not until the Sung period, more than a thousand years later, that the shadow play came to be used as a means of telling a story – chiefly narratives related to the Three Kingdoms cycle of stories.[49]

There is, then, no convincing evidence that Chinese theatricals were seriously concerned with relating a story at a date earlier than the introduction of transformations (early T'ang). The Indian literary tradition, however, had long since made story an integral part of drama. Bharata, in his *Treatise on Dramaturgy* (*Nāṭya Śāstra*, *c.* second century I.E., but parts go back at least three or four hundred years earlier), has the God Brahmā speak:

> I will create the lore of drama which promotes dharma [virtue], material gain, and fame, which will show for posterity all activities, which is enriched with the ideas of all branches of knowledge and

[47] Lo Chin-t'ang 羅錦堂, 'The Origins of the Puppet Show' 傀儡戲的由來, *Continent Magazine* 大陸雜誌, 41.12 (December 31, 1970), 3–5. Lo's article is based on an earlier study in English by Dschi Hiän-lin entitled 'Lieh-tzu and Buddhist Sūtras: A Note on the Author of Lieh-tzu and the Date of Its Composition' in *Studia Serica*, 9.1 (1950), 18–32.
[48] Ssu-ma Ch'ien (145–86 B.I.E.), *Shih-chi* 史記 (K'ai-ming edn), p. 113.4.
[49] See Laufer, *Oriental Theatricals*, pp. 36–7.

presents all the arts; I shall create it, *along with the story required for its theme*, with its teachings and the summary of its topics. I.14–15[50]

That legitimate theatre had developed very early in India is evident from the fact that the great grammarian, Pāṇini (fourth century B.I.E.), cites aphorisms on acting. Kauṭiliya, Chief Minister of Chandragupta (fourth century B.I.E.), in the *Arthaśāstra* gives an account of theatrical companies being taxed when travelling between various states and describes academies for dancing, singing, and acting.[51]

Indian dramaturgy did have a direct influence upon the Chinese theatre. Wang Kuo-wei discusses the Southern Sung (1127–1279) *hsi-wen* 戲文 as having had its source in Wen-chou 溫州 near the Chekiang coast (east-central China) and as having been influenced by Indian drama.[52] Yang Yin-shen declares that the *hsi-wen* is the first genuine drama in China and reports that a fragment of Kālidāsa's *Śakuntalā* was discovered in the temple known as Kuo-ch'ing ssu 國淸寺 on T'ien-t'ai Mountain 天台山 near Wen-chou, the birthplace of *hsi-wen*.[53] Some similarities between Indian and Chinese drama include: a division according to class between those who spoke genteel (Sanskrit) language and those who spoke common language (Prakrits); set names for each role, e.g. the supporting female role was *datta*, the military man was *sena*, hermits were *ghanta*; terms of address comparable to *yüan-wai* 員外, *hsiang-kung* 相公, etc.; maids and government servants with stock names like Ch'un-mei 春梅 and Mei-hsiang 梅香 on the one hand and Chang Ch'ien 張千 and Li Wan 李萬 on the other; an emphasis on dance and prescribed gestures; a tendency to draw upon well-known stories for the raw material of the play; the 'wedge', a brief extra act that could be inserted into a play; and, of course, the alternating sung–spoken form.

In the north, as I have shown above, Chinese theatrical entertainments lacked a strong sense of story before the appearance of the dramatic recitation forms which we know as sūtra lectures and transformations. An early Ch'ing writer, Mao Ch'i-ling 毛奇齡 (1623–1716), has pointed out this deficiency in the early Chinese theatre:

[50] See William Theodore De Bary, *et al.*, *Sources of Indian Tradition* (New York, 1958), p. 267. The italics are mine.
[51] See Gargi, *Theatre in India*, p. 17.
[52] *Sung Yüan hsi-ch'ü k'ao* 宋元戲曲考, in *Hsi-ch'ü lun-wen chi* 戲曲論文集 (Peking, 1957), p. 123.
[53] Yang Yin-shen 楊蔭深, *An Outline of Chinese Popular Literature* 中國俗文學概論 (Taipei, 1961), *Su-wen-hsüeh ts'ung-k'an* 俗文學叢刊, 1st ser., no. 7, p. 49.

> In ancient times, song and dance did not relate to each other. The singer did not dance and the dancer did not sing. Even the words of the dance melody did not necessarily correspond to the dancer's performance. But, from the creation of the songs 'Briar Branch Lyric' and 'Lotus Flower Twirl' by people of the T'ang, the import of what the dancer enacted and what the singer expressed came slightly to correspond with each other. Yet there was still no story or substance. It was not until the end of the Sung that the king of An-ting Commandery, Chao Ling-chih 安定郡王趙令畤, wrote a drum-song in the *shang* mode as a score for the 'West Chamber Tale'[54] which was composed purely on the basis of the story. Yet there were still no acting and spoken parts intermingled with the tunes until the reign of Chang-tsung 章宗 (1190–1208) of the Chin dynasty. It was then that Master Tung 董解元,[55] though we do not know who he was, must have written his lyric with string accompaniment on the West Chamber story 西廂搊彈詞. This work had both spoken parts and cantos. There was one person who plucked a stringed instrument as well as spoke and sang ...[56]

The 'lyric with string accompaniment' we now know as a medley (*chu-kung-tiao* 諸宮調). Mao Ch'i-ling, of course, had no way of knowing about transformations and so was unable to discuss their role in the development of drama during the T'ang and Sung. Instead, to fill the very obvious gap which the absence of transformations left, he adduced a rather undramatic drum-song. The latter, in spite of the fact that it has both the prosimetric form of transformations and a definite story line, is an art piece rather than a type of dramatic entertainment. It is appropriate for Mao to mention the medley of Master Tung because this piece belongs to a genre that relates directly to the tradition of transformations. Still more appropriate, however, would have been a reference to the folkish *Liu Chih-yüan Medley* since it resembles the *pien-wen* in its style and even in its language. Here, again, Mao could not have known about this text because it was only discovered in 1907–1908 in Karakhoto by the Russian explorer, Petr Kuz'mich Kozlov.

Writing before Mao Ch'i-ling, Wang Chi-te 王驥德 (?–1623) had already noticed the difference between the early theatrics and later drama:

[54] The 'West Chamber Tale' 西廂傳奇 is a reference to 'The Story of Ying-ying' by Yüan Chen 元稹, 鶯鶯傳. For the drum-song, see 'The Butterfly Falls in Love with a Flower (in *shang* mode)' 商調蝶戀花 by Chao Ling-chih, *tzu* Te-lin 德麟, in *Collection of Classical Fiction by T'ang Authors* 唐人傳奇小說 (Taipei, 1972 and 1975), pp. 145–50.

[55] Master Tung is listed in the *Record of Ghosts* 錄鬼簿 (Peking, 1957), p. 6.

[56] The passage translated is from Mao's *Hsi-ho tz'u-hua* 西河詞話 and may be found in T'ang Kuei-chang 唐圭璋, ed., *Tz'u-hua ts'ung-pien* 詞話叢編 (Nanking, 1935), *ts'e* 4, p. 2.4a.

> The ancient thespians were primarily concerned with repartee and wit in order to make people laugh. They were not yet actors, such as we have today, who act out on the stage both sung and spoken parts. Furthermore, everything was created impromptu by the thespians themselves. They were not accustomed to ready-made scripts such as we have today ... It was not until the Yüan [1260–1367] that drama was enacted as it is today.[57]

We see that perceptive literary historians of the Ming and Ch'ing periods had identified the lack of a definite story line as an obstacle to the formation of full-blown drama.

It would appear that transformation texts and their oral antecedents in the Buddhist narrative tradition were instrumental, though not entirely responsible, for the increasing attention given to story in T'ang and Sung drama. We know from contemporary accounts, for example, that one of the most lively, long-lasting, and crowd-pleasing dramatic performances of the Sung period was the staging of the Maudgalyāyana story. This is to be expected because the transformation texts presenting the same story evidently were equally well received during the T'ang and Five Dynasties periods. The transformation text, though basically a narrative form, presented its story dramatically. This was true neither of the classical tale (*ch'uan-ch'i* 傳奇), which I consider to be strictly a narrative form, nor of its derivatives.

The third (and most widespread) objection to the idea of the influence of transformations upon the theatre in China is that Chinese drama predominantly uses either lyrics (*tz'u* 詞) or cantos (*ch'ü* 曲) for its sung parts whereas transformation texts rely almost exclusively on verse of various fixed line lengths, principally seven syllables (similar to the metrical portions of sūtras known as *gāthā* 偈 and actually thus identified on one manuscript). If this theoretical objection could be obviated, it would be possible to point to a direct, formal progression from T'ang transformations to Sung 'court texts' (*yüan-pen* 院本) to Chin medleys to the Yüan drama (*tsa-chü* 雜劇).

It so happens that the mid-T'ang, when transformation texts came into prominence, was the very time at which transitional forms of poetry that were no longer true *shih* 詩 (having a fixed line length) nor yet fully formed *tz'u* 詞 (having varying line lengths) began to emerge.[58] Yin Fa-lu states that *tz'u* arose among entertainers and musicians much earlier than written

[57] See *Ch'ü lü* 曲律 (preface 1610), *chüan* 3, p. 86, in *Tseng-pu ch'ü-yüan ssu-chi* 增補曲苑絲集 (1932), *ts'e* 3.

[58] See Cheng Ch'ien 鄭騫, *From 'shih' to 'ch'ü'* 從詩到曲 (Taipei, 1961), p. 103.

records indicate.[59] The mid-T'ang *tz'u* patterns differed only slightly from five-, six-, and seven-syllable quatrain (*chüeh-chü* 絕句, a type of *shih*) forms. Liu Yü-hsi 劉禹錫, for example, wrote forty-one *tz'u* employing seven different tunes which were almost indistinguishable from seven-syllable *chüeh-chü* and were probably called *tz'u* only because they were sung to current tunes. Po Chü-i's '*tz'u*' were of a similar nature. Several decades later, Wen T'ing-yün 溫庭筠 and Wei Chuang 韋莊, whose works are included in the *Hua-chien chi* 花間集, employed a much larger variety of tunes and line lengths.

Glen William Baxter has explained the process whereby *shih* may have evolved into *tz'u* or were adapted to their patterns.[60] Interpolated words or sounds (called *ho-sheng* 和聲, *hsü-sheng* 虛聲, *fan-sheng* 泛聲, or *san-sheng* 散聲 and comparable to the Yüan *ch'ü* 元曲 'padding words' 襯字) could be used to fill out a line.[61] Words could be dropped or melisma employed to shorten a line. Given this information, I doubt that the entertainers who performed transformations confined themselves to wooden recitation of line after line after line of seven-syllable verse. Unfortunately, only one piece of formal musical notation was found among the Tun-huang manuscripts (P3808). Several manuscripts (though none are genuine transformation texts) have musical notations written above the verse but these have not yet been deciphered.

On the basis of the foregoing discussion, it seems fair to say that China long possessed the elements necessary for drama (song, dance, music, costume, repartee, mime, gesture); that transformations and related genres current during the T'ang and Five Dynasties periods acted as catalysts which put all of these constituents in a ferment; that there were subsidiary stages in the reaction (*chu-kung-tiao*, *yüan-pen*, Sung *tsa-chü* 雜劇 ('variety plays')); that the products of this reaction were Yüan drama and its successor forms, and that there were many by-products (*pao-chüan* 寶卷, *t'an-tz'u* 彈詞, *hua-pen* 話本, *p'ing-hua* 評話, *t'an-ch'ang yin-yüan* 彈唱因緣, *ch'ang-ching-tz'u* 唱京詞, *ch'ang-shua-ling* 唱耍令, *ch'ang-po pu-tuan* 唱撥不斷, *ch'ang-chuan* 唱賺, etc.). Clearly, the T'ang and Five Dynasties periods witnessed a fundamental revolution in the dramatic arts. From that time forward, story became an essential ingredient of the theatre and the prosimetric form a fundamental characteristic of dramatic presentation. Transformation performances, it would seem, were at the very centre of this revolution.

[59] Yin Fa-lu 陰法魯, in his preface to Wang Chung-min 王重民, *Tun-huang ch'ü-tzu-tz'u chi* 敦煌曲子詞集 (Shanghai, 1954), second edn, pp. 2–3.

[60] In his 'Metrical Origins of the *tz'u*', *HJAS*, 16.1 (June 1953), 108–45.

[61] *Ibid.*, p. 125.

The sociolinguistics of popular Buddhism

The correspondence in language between the recorded sayings of the early Zen masters (Ch'an *yü-lu* 禪語錄) which begin to appear in the ninth century and the Tun-huang popular narratives is an important topic, both for students of language and for students of literature. Studies on the language of the Zen masters bring out striking differences with standard literary Chinese of the same period.[62] One scholar has boldly stated that 'the earliest written colloquial language (*pai-hua-wen* 白話文)' is to be found in 'the recorded sayings of the Zen sect'.[63] This is a bit of an overstatement since a few elements of colloquial language are already evident in Buddhist translations from the Eastern Han period (6–220) onward. What we need to ask now is *why* the Tun-huang narratives and the Zen records are so like each other in their use of demotic language. What is the relationship, sociological or otherwise, between the two? What forces were at work to bring about such drastic modifications of the written language during the T'ang period? Is it simply fortuitous that Buddhist or Buddhist-related manuscripts represent by far the largest number of vernacular texts to have survived from the T'ang period? Or may it be that the spread of Buddhism in China was the cause of profound social and linguistic changes? Finally, and more particularly, how do we account for the increasing polysyllabism of words as represented in colloquial texts? Is this phenomenon – which is of great importance since both the written and the spoken language of the twentieth century exhibit it to a marked degree – to be explained solely on the basis of the internal dynamics (e.g. dimunition of the phonemic inventory) of Chinese itself? These questions must be exhaustively studied if we are to understand fully the development of the Chinese language. There are far more questions to be asked than answers to be given. Yet it would seem apparent from many of the annotations in this book that Indic languages had a massive impact on the vocabulary and even on the grammar and syntax of Chinese. Intensive linguistic research is necessary to determine precisely how Sanskrit cases and tenses were approximated in the developing Chinese language. Chinese metrics and phonology from the Six Dynasties onwards offer similarly fruitful areas of investigation.

Szechwan and beyond

References to Szechwan (southwest China) abound in Tun-huang popular literature. A number of these have been pointed out in the anno-

[62] See Henri Maspéro, 'Sur quelques textes anciens de Chinois parlé', *BEFEO*, 14(1914), 1–36 and Kao Ming-k'ai 高名凱, 'T'ang-tai ch'an-chia yü-lu so chien te yü-fa ch'eng-fen' 唐代禪家語錄所見的語法成分, *Yen-ching hsüeh-pao* 燕京學報, 34 (1948), 49–84 which is a supplement to Maspéro's article.

[63] Kao, 'T'ang-tai ch'an-chia yü-lu', p. 51.

tations to the story of Wu Tzu-hsü. For example, one curious feature of the 'medicine poem' is that a large number of the medicines named refer particularly to products of the Szechwan area. Indeed, Wu Tzu-hsü falsely claims to have been born there.[64]

The first part of manuscript P2249v consists of a short set of practice characters. The words ramble on from Mahāmaudgalyāyana to the title of a sūtra and go on to include the name of a Buddhist monk from Ch'eng-tu in Szechwan who has written a eulogy, as well as the title of a children's schoolbook:大目乾連.往生淨土經.成都府大意沙門.藏川述讚.開蒙要訓. That this list from Tun-huang idly names a monk from Szechwan is not without significance.

It is thought-provoking that it is also in Tun-huang and Szechwan that we find the earliest lyric (*tz'u*) and canto (*ch'ü* 曲) collections. In attempting to formulate a comprehensive framework within which the remarkable literary developments of the T'ang period may be discussed, it would seem that special consideration need be given to the links between Tun-huang and the Szechwan area as well as to the relations of these two areas with peoples and places beyond such as Tibet, Central Asia, India, and Iran.

Going in the opposite direction, there is also a need for investigations of the relationship between Tun-huang popular narratives and other East Asian literary traditions. Japanese scholars have already contributed much in this area of investigation. And a start has been made for Korea by Minn Yong-gyu 閔永珪.[65] Minn presents materials that show the similarities in language and content between an apocryphal Korean sūtra on Maudgalyāyana and the Tun-huang transformation text which is translated in this book.

No matter whether we are dealing with Ch'ang-an, Tun-huang, Szechwan, Korea, Japan, or Khotan, India is always a constant presence in the background of popular Buddhist literature. It is impossible now to reconstruct fully the milieu in which this literature took shape. That it was pervaded by Indian ideas is evident from the fact that even a secular tale such as the Tun-huang Wu Tzu-hsü story is full of Buddhist imagery and language. For example, on T12.14b, it speaks of 'the mighty transforming power (*prabhāva*) of all deities (*devas*)' 諸天威力化. During his flight (T4.13), Wu Tzu-hsü is said to be 'trusting his karma and in accordance with conditioning causes (*pratyaya*)' 信業隨緣. Upon learning the sad news of her father's and brother's deaths (T8.1a), his sister asks what sins

[64] Also see T222.4, 12, 13, T224.4, 10, 12, 13, T227.7, 11, 13, T228.1, 3, T267.9, T420.3, T618.12, etc.

[65] 'On the Twenty-third Volume of the *Worin Sokpo*' 月印釋譜第二十三殘卷, *Dong Bang Hak Chi* 東方學志, 6 (June 1963), 1–18 plus 36 plates.

she has committed 'over the vast reaches of time (*kalpas*)' 曠大刼來. When Wu Tzu-hsü takes leave of his sister (T8.6a), the manuscript P2794v writes that he 'uttered a *gāthā* and said "Take good care of yourself!"' 説偈稱好住. That purely Chinese stories could be modified by the addition of Indian elements is obvious in Indra's guarding over the boy Shun because he is a filial son (T13.7–8). We have only begun to scratch the surface of the impact of the Indian tradition upon Chinese popular literature.

Choice of texts

Some readers may find the Tun-huang popular narratives crude and simple. Their influence on later fiction and drama, however, can hardly be overstressed. They represent the only surviving primary evidence of a widespread and flourishing world of popular entertainment during the T'ang and Five Dynasties periods. They also exhibit a certain literary appeal. In spite of obvious infelicities, these stories make exciting reading and are capable of exerting a powerful effect upon a sympathetic audience.

Apart from my own preferences, there are sound reasons for choosing these four texts for translation and annotation. By the standards outlined in the section on 'Corpus' above, three of the texts are genuine *pien-wen* and one, the Wu Tzu-hsü story, is not. Two of the texts translated are historical and two are religious. Of the historical stories, one is from an ancient period and the other deals with a contemporary hero. As for the religious stories, a literary historian has said that 'the most fascinating and certainly the most popular of the Buddhist tales is "Great Mu-lien Rescuing His Mother from the Hades"'.[66] And, most students will agree, the Śāriputra transformation text is the *pièce de résistance* of all Tun-huang popular literature. Finally, the four texts presented here are representative in that they display formal features typical of many other Tun-huang popular narratives. Judging from the dates of these texts[67] and others that I have examined, the Wu Tzu-hsü type of story arose shortly after genuine *pien-wen* became popular. It is a hybrid of traditional Chinese historical and legendary narrative forms (e.g. *Wu Yüeh ch'un-ch'iu* 吳越春秋 and *Yüeh chüeh shu* 越絕書) with Buddhist storytelling models.[68] Stories of this type did not supplant the *pien-wen* but continued to be produced side by side with them until about the end of the Five Dynasties period.

[66] Wu-chi Liu, *An Introduction to Chinese Literature* (Bloomington, 1966), p. 152.

[67] See the section above on 'Dating'.

[68] See the section above on 'Szechwan and beyond' for explicit evidence of Indic influence on the Tun-huang Wu Tzu-hsü story.

End of a genre?

There remains the difficult and complicated question of why the *pien-wen* appear to have died out so abruptly and totally at the beginning of the Sung period. It is beyond the scope of this introduction to do adequate justice to this important problem. I can here only mention two possibilities for consideration and refer my reader for additional information to *Transformations*.

The first thing that must be taken into account is the generally introspective attitude that prevailed during the eleventh and twelfth centuries. The inward-looking orientation of the Sung neo-Confucians was already presaged in the anti-Buddhist polemics of Han Yü 韓愈 (768–824). It is natural that a move to obliterate such an obviously Buddhist-sounding name as *pien-wen* would have taken shape in such an atmosphere. The deliberate Sinicization of foreign titles can be seen as early as the reign of T'ang Hsüan-tsung when a tune known as 'The Brahman' 婆羅門 overnight became the famous 'Rainbow Skirt and Feathered Blouse' 霓裳羽衣. The second factor to consider is that *pien-wen* did not actually die out but that they had become so thoroughly absorbed into the popular literary tradition that they were no longer identifiable as a discrete form. Viewed in this fashion, we may say that *pien-wen* have survived to this very century though under various guises.

Although there is much more that could be said by way of introduction to Tun-huang popular narratives, I am anxious to allow my readers the chance to savour these delightful stories for themselves. Those who find this introduction inadequate may perhaps find more satisfaction in *Transformations*.

Appendix

Interpretation of the characteristic *pien-wen* verse-introductory formula ('Please look at the place where XX [happens], how does it go?' *ch'ieh k'an xx ch'u, jo-wei ch'en-shuo?* 且看xx處若爲陳說) has baffled students of the genre for a long time. I have already explained the meaning of *ch'u* (on p. 6), but *jo-wei* requires separate treatment.[1] This expression always has interrogative force in T'ang-Yüan popular literature.[2] However, certain variations of the latter part of

[1] By example from Indian literature, we might expect something like 'this is how it goes' (*evam uktam*) for the last four characters. Cf. also Skt. *evam-vācaka* (*shuo ju tz'u* 說如此) in the *Abhidharmakośa-vyākhyā* and *evaṃ-vādin* (*ju shih shuo* 如是說) in the *Laṇkāvatara-sūtra*. The usual classical Buddhist Chinese for 'how' (Skt. *katham*) is *ju ho* 如何. See Wogihara Unrai [Ogiwara Unrai] 荻原雲來 and Tsuji Naoshirō 辻直四郎, ed., (*Kan'yaku taishō*) *Bon-wa daijiten* (漢譯對照) 梵和大辭典(Tokyo, 1968), pp. 299b and 311b.

[2] See the entries in Iriya, *Index*, 24; Chang Hsiang's exhaustive note 97–98; *Tsu-t'ang chi*, I.119.6, I.123.6, I.126.1, I.127.8–9, III.114.14, IV.17.2, and IV.28.2; and *Yu-hsien k'u*, 14, 23, 26, and 28.

the formula, particularly those which occur in the 'Transformation on the Han General Wang Ling' (*Han chiang Wang Ling pien* 漢將王陵變, T36–46), lead me to believe that the interrogative force of *jo-wei* as used in the *pien-wen* verse-introductory formula is extremely weak.

Variations of standard formula

Daggers mark textual variants.

1. 'place' (*ch'u* 處): T86.12, T114.6, T115.6, T371.11, T716.7,† T719.3, T720.6, T721.14, T723.14, T725.14, T726.9, T728.8, T729.11, T730.8, T731.7, T733.11, T737.3, T738.3, T741.10.
2. 'how' (*jo-wei* 若爲): T381.14.
3. 'place, how?' (*ch'u, jo-wei* 處若爲): T91.10, T95.2, T100.16, T122.6, T365.12, T368.11, T370.11, T375.15, T378.15, T380.5, 16, T383.3, T384.4, T385.3, T387.4, T388.2, 16, T716.7.†
4. 'place, how shall we present it?' (*ch'u, jo-wei ch'en* 處若爲陳): T364.7.†
5. 'place, how shall we describe it?' (*ch'u, jo-wei ch'en-shuo* 處若爲陳說): T41.3, T46.12, T88.11, T90.4, T94.2, T102.4, T104.16, T105.15, T123.11, T124.13, T126.1, T364.7,† T767.12. Without *ch'u* 處: T43.6, T373.4, T374.14.
6. 'then is the beginning of the transformation [scroll]' (*pien shih pien ch'u* 便是變初): T36.11, a very special case which is discussed separately in *Transformations*.
7. 'place, attentively we shall describe it' (*ch'u chin wei ch'en-shuo* 處謹爲陳說): T38.10.
8. 'and we turn [the picture scroll] to explain it' (*erh wei chuan shuo* 而爲轉說): T39.11, T45.10.
9. 'whereupon we describe it' (*sui wei ch'en-shuo* 遂爲陳說): T42.3.
10. 'place, there is this presentation' (*ch'u yu wei ch'en* 處有爲陳): T99.15.

A given transformation text generally shows a predilection or even exclusive preference for one or another of these variations, e.g., Maudgalyāyana prefers number one and Śāriputra prefers number three. Note that, in a large number of cases, *jo-wei* is altogether absent. In other cases, only *wei* 爲 is present, preceded by a conjunction or adverb. Both Yang Shu-ta 5.91 and P'ei Hsüeh-hai 557 give *jo* 若 = *erh* 而. *Jo-wei* 若爲 and *erh-wei* 而爲 may well have nearly the same force. When *jo-wei* does occur, although we must render it as an interrogative, we should also understand that it is perfunctory and only vestigially constitutes a so-called 'question to the audience'. Mechanical questions of weakened interrogative force such as 'how should I put it?' or 'how should I say it?' would seem to represent the closest approximation to this formula.

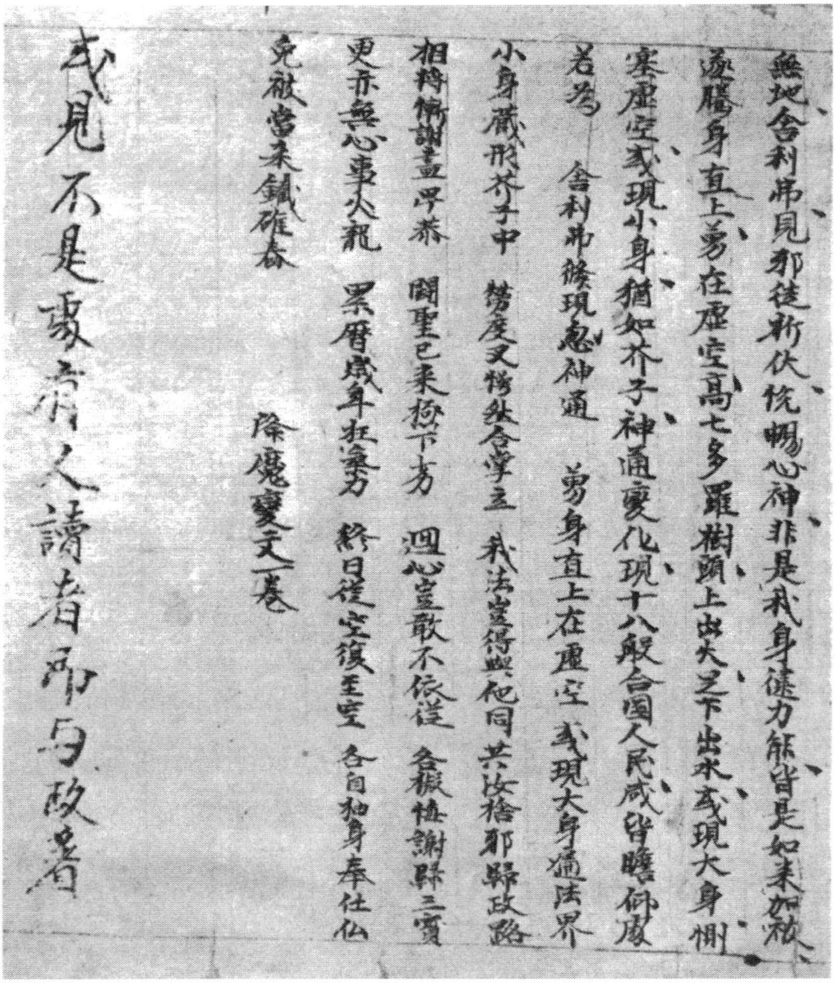

無地舍利弗見邪徒新伏悅暢心神非是我身德力能皆是如來加被
遂騰身直上踴在虛空高七多羅樹頭上出火足下出水或現大身滿
塞虛空或現小身猶如芥子神通變化現十八般合國人民咸皆瞻仰處
若為 舍利弗條現急神通 踴身直上在虛空 或現大身遍法界
小身藏形芥子中 勞度叉稽首合掌立 我法豈得與他同 共投捨邪歸政路
相將儀謝盡浮恭 闔聖已來極下方 迴心豈敢不依從 合掌懺謝歸三寶
更亦無心事火龍 累劫歲身狂妄方 終日從空復至空 各自知身奉仕仏
免被當來鑊碓舂
降魔變文一卷
或見不是處有人讀者即與政著

2. ‘Transformation Text on the Subduing of Demons, One Scroll’ (ms formerly in possession of Hu Shih), end portion.

1

ŚĀRIPUTRA

Transformation on the Subduing of Demons, One Scroll

And so we have heard:
The Tathāgata has explained the Law
To people as countless as the sands of the Ganges;
The Bodhisattvas have transmitted the sūtras
Through thousands upon thousands of worlds.
It all began in the Deer Park,
Passed to the five first converts,
And ended beneath the twin trees,
With the subjugation of the ten Brāhman students.
When he expounded his subtle message, the waves of the river of desire were stilled,
When he discoursed upon Wisdom, the mountain of affliction was toppled;
He conjoined in their true origin the three points of Alpha,
Cleansed mankind of the six impurities of sense.

Consequently,
Within the great city of Śrāvastī,
His compassionate regard was aroused so that he saved all living beings;
In the midst of the garden of the elder Anāthapiṇḍada,
He carried the lamp of knowledge and transmitted the seal of the Law.

The Tathāgata,
Donning his clothes and taking his alms-bowl,
Strode forth early in the mornings,
And promptly at the time for his noon meal
Returned to his own lodgings.
His begging for food extended the karma of blessed virtue,
He manifested – at various levels – his impartial compassion.
His going barefoot displayed the merit of keeping the rules,
Spreading his mat, he settled into meditation and calmed his thoughts.

Subsequently,
Men and deities venerated him and gathered round him,
The dragon-spirits were respectful and listened to him joyfully.

Subhūti
Bore himself with dignity when he appeared at assemblies,
He straightened his robes and was ardently sincere;
Wishing to promote discussions on formlessness,
He would bring up questions about which he had doubts.
As a result, he was
Declared by the Master to be unusual,
Praised by the Buddha as being 'Virtuous'.

Whereupon,
The mystic gate was opened wide,
The fund of meaning broadly revealed.
Those who heard the sūtras were caused to have
Correctly oriented quadruple hearts,
Radiantly bright quintuple eyes.

The four fruits completely banished the illusions regarding the ego,
The three virtues roamed freely on the eightfold noble path.

The essential nature of the four mental states such as ego and personality came to be understood as totally vacuous. The six types of sensations ended by being completely annihilated.

Of the presentation of the Law by stages,
Even a portion is considerable;
Though one reaches the end of space in all ten directions,
Its measure cannot be known.
When the various distinguishing marks are seen as nondistinctive,
The Dharma-body of the Tathāgata may be seen;
When life is equated with the unborn,
The levelling of true and false is obtained.

But then,
Though the seven treasures of the great chiliacosm be exhausted,
When set against the four terms, they are of utterly no consequence;
Later, for all living beings in the five periods of decay,
There will be transcendence as soon as they hear the Law.

Afterwards, one should renounce even the Law itself so that the raft of attachment will be sunk. Merge ego and not-I in the recognition of the unreality of unreality. Blot out the distinction between right and wrong with the supranoumenal. In the sphere unsullied by the six sense perceptions, convene perfect wisdom. But even if sought for through the six types of comprehension, it will be found that all the myriad forms are embraced by wisdom.

The Buddhas of the past, present, and future
Are born from this sūtra;
The supremely perfect wisdom
Is derived from this sūtra.

Adding to this the fact that it holds within it all and sundry teachings, we may allow that it is the principal item in the entire sacred canon.

Since this sūtra was transmitted to China and translated, it has already been more than several hundred years. Although it was intoned over a wide area and there was a profusion of commentaries and sub-commentaries, yet there was still concern that their meaning was not in accord with the holy mind and that their principles were opposed to the central way.

Humbly do we observe:

His Highness, the Sage Han Court Ruler of our Great T'ang Dynasty during the Incipient Origin and Heavenly Treasure Reign-periods, Emperor Sage in Civil Affairs and Divine in Military Matters Who Responds to the Way,

Whose civilizing influence surpasses that of a thousand ages,
Whose fame exceeds that of the hundred kings:
Who, in learning, mastered the essence of the Five Classics,
Who, in valour, broke the courage of the Nine Barbarians.
Over the eight directions his effortless civilizing influence is concentrated,
In every quarter men sing of his influence so like that of Yao and Shun.

What is more, in addition to his pervasive influence, he often spread the Three Teachings. [**362**] Sometimes, by

Searching into Confucianism and Taoism,
He would probe these doctrines to their very sources;
In explicating the Buddhist religion,
His sentences were deep, his perception far-reaching.

The Imperial
Grace gushed out with the fountain of the ocean;
His Heavenly Vision was as bright as the sun and the moon.
Because of this, Taoist teachings were resurrected;
Due to it, the Buddhist Law was re-refulgent.

Above the monasteries in precious groves,
Pleasant palms vied to unfold their leaves;
Within the gardens of esotericism,
There were copious dharma-clouds which nourished extensively.

Now, however, as to the title *Vajracchedikā-prajñā-pāramitā-sūtra*: *Vajra(cchedikā)*, 'diamond', is a metaphor for hardness and sharpness; *prajñā* is the appellation of wisdom; *pāra* is 'getting to the other shore', the full name being [*pāra*]*mitā*; *sūtra*, finally, has the meaning of 'threaded together' – which signifies goodness and uprightness. Therefore it is called *Vajracchedikā-prajñā-pāramitā-sūtra*.

When the World-Honoured One of the great enlightenment was in the Jetavana Park at Śrāvastī, he proclaimed this sūtra which was the beginning of our esoteric canon.

The four orders gathered round him,
A host of immortals supported him;
The sky rained down the four divine flowers,
Clouds spread across the eight regions.
How ineffable is the wonderful power of the Tathāgata!

Sudatta was a charitable man, fond of providing for the destitute and the impoverished. Thus, because of his actions, he came to be known as Anāthapiṇḍada, the Benefactor.

He spread out his gold to purchase land,
On which he constructed a monastery garden,
Where he invited the Buddha and a company of monks to reside.
For this, his name was entered in the scriptures.

Prince Jetā, observing Sudatta's respect for the Law, donated trees and, together with him, built the park. And because a ruler's position is more weighty than that of his subject, in naming the park, precedence was given to him. The details of the matter are presented in the following text.

In ancient times, there was a great kingdom in southern India called Śrāvastī. The King's

Majesty shook the whole world,
Fame swept the eight directions;
The three borders were calm,
The four frontiers were clear.

A capable prime minister helped govern the kingdom,
His name was Sudatta.

In his mind, he perfected secret policy,
In an instant, he fathomed the crux of the moment.
Men dubbed him Pillar of the Kingdom,
His moral purchase was as important as salt and pepper is for cooking.
But always he harboured heterodox views,
And he did not, as yet, respect the Three Precious Ones.

He did not covet a more exalted position,
His mind was content with refinement and cultivation.

There were in Sudatta's home several sons, the youngest of whom had not taken a wife. On the occasion of a festival banquet, all of a sudden he thought to himself: 'Our family as it is now lacks nothing. Throughout the kingdom, we are praised and honoured. My youngest son has not yet been capped and married. It is only right that the ceremony should be performed at the proper time. If our own kingdom does not have a suitable match, I shall send a messenger abroad to fetch one.'

That very day, he issued instructions to his servants whereby they were to open his storehouses and take from them

One thousand ounces of gold,
Several bracelets of white jade,
Soft brocades and light gauzes –
A thousand lengths, ten thousand bolts.
One hundred stout elephants
Set out on that very day.

'To settle this matter, you must be on your way!
Even when the stars come out at night, you should not tarry.
The only condition is that you succeed,
Do not be niggardly with my riches.
Should you gratify my son's wishes,
A handsome reward awaits you on the day of your return!'

The leave-taking over, the emissary promised to fulfil his duty and started on his journey at once.

Day and night he sped on his way,
And soon arrived at his destination.
He cruised the streets and coursed the alleys,
With eyes attentive and ears alert.
While he was walking,
He chanced to come upon Ānanda begging for food.
In his whole life, Sudatta had never seen the like of him,

And was astounded by his uncommonness.
Ānanda held a staff in one hand and a basin in the other;
Raising his voice, he begged for food.

Humi's family respected the ten commandments. They were always cordial to the Buddha and to Buddhist monks. Young and old were of the same mind in that they all venerated the Three Precious Ones.

Although the youngest daughter dwelt in the seclusion of the women's quarters,
As soon as she heard the sound of someone begging for food,
– Her respect, to be sure, was most profound –
She swiftly ran outside the gate.
She threw herself upon the ground in an attitude of utmost reverence,
Paying respectful obedience to Ānanda.
She inquired about his evangelistic exertions,
And offered salutations to Śākyamuni.

The emissary
Caught a fleeting glimpse of her profile,
– She was of peerless mien –
Hsi-shih could not be compared with her divine form, **[363]**
Luo-p'u is not to be ranked with her dazzling beauty.

He wanted to rush straight ahead and examine her closely but he feared that this would be in violation of etiquette. So, dragging his feet, he withdrew and casually asked one of the neighbours: 'Whose residence is this? Its woods now dense, now scattered –

In front they have set an entrance with impressive gate-posts left and right,
Outside it are rows of long lances and spears.
Its splendid towers and ornate chambers,
So very like those of a royal palace;
Its singing girls, ponds, and terraces,
Are all quite different from those in the houses of commoners.'

'Haven't you heard, sir,' asked the neighbour, 'of the honoured premier whose name is Humi? He assists in the ancestral temple of the royal family and enjoys a daily salary of ten thousand coins. Except for the sovereign, he is the most highly esteemed person in the realm. He is consulted about even the most minute details of the rules for the government of the kingdom.'

Hearing these words left the emissary in an astonished frame of mind. Again he inquired of the neighbour:

'It is most fortunate for me
To have encountered a man of such excellent parts.
But one thing I have not learned about the Premier's family is:
How many children has he?
I am a traveller from a far-off land,
Commissioned to come here as its emissary;
Do not, sir, refuse to tarry a while,
Tell me briefly about the circumstances of the Premier's family.'

The neighbour replied:
'The Premier's daughters
Are altogether three in number.
Two have already been given away to royal descendants,
One is now at home, unwed.
Her delightful manner and pleasant beauty
Are without peer throughout the land;
Her deportment and chaste purity
Are paragons for all time.'

When the emissary heard these words,
He was immeasurably relieved.
At once, he communicated this information
By dispatching a letter.
The emissary was conducted inside
Where he offered greetings and paid his respects.
He did not express the feelings in the corners of his heart,
But only reached the stage of exchanging pleasantries.
They observed the protocol governing host and guest,
And held meetings which lasted several days;
But in the deliberations on the marriage,
No promise was granted.

The elder, Humi, suddenly of a night,
Began to make a great hustle and bustle;
He swept and washed the rooms and chambers,
Put in order the courts and the yards.
With scented plaster, he coated and spread,
Making extraordinarily fancy decorations.
Around each courtyard, banners were hung,
In every room, rugs and mats were spread.

When the elder, Sudatta, saw that Humi had risen so early,
He could not find ease for sleep.

When he further saw the fancy decorations being laid out,
He was intrigued and asked what was behind it all:
'Is this for a marriage ceremony?
Or is it because you are going to request the presence of the King?
Why is there such a great hustle and bustle?
And why such elegant arrangements?'

The elder replied:
'I do this neither because of a ceremony,
Nor am I planning to request the King's presence.
My intention is to invite the Buddha and company of monks,
And to make offerings to them with a pure heart.'

Sudatta, by nature, was well-disposed to learning.
Now that he had once come close to a Buddhist monk,
And suddenly heard the name of Buddha being uttered,
He broke out into a profuse sweat all over his body.

Sudatta asked:
'What divine manifestations does the Buddha possess?
What powers do the Buddhist monks possess?
When I hear their names, it makes me
Break out in a shivering sweat.
In what place do they dwell?
Be so kind as to tell me the particulars.
I regret that I long followed false ways,
And did not know the correct path;
Now I am filled with deep desire and earnest longing,
And wish that you would explain the Buddha's origin.'

'The Buddha,' replied Humi, 'is no ordinary person. He is the son of Śuddhodana, King of Kapilavastu.
His ancestors, one after the other,
Held the kingship for a thousand generations;
The numerous pages of their history are full of honour and glory –
They are, then, descendants of peacock and phoenix.'

When Sudatta heard this,
He was startled and shaken;
The feeling of intense yearning
Would not leave his heart.
He wished that Humi would reveal the Buddha's whereabouts,
For he wanted to look upon the Honoured One's countenance.

'The Buddha is not far from here now,' Humi responded to the elder, Sudatta. 'He's just at Vulture Peak where he reigns over the eight spirit realms and elucidates the principles of the three conveyances to nirvāṇa. It is already night, now, but if you leave tomorrow morning, there will still be plenty of time.'

Sudatta, having heard of the power of the Buddha,
Slept restlessly.
With anxious sincerity and ardent longing,
All his thoughts were fixed on the compassionate Honoured One.

The Tathāgata, to give recognition to this single-mindedness,
Proceeded to release radiant beams of illumination;
Heaven and earth were flooded with light,
As though with the brilliance of a thousand suns.
When Sudatta suddenly **[364]** saw this brightness,
He thought that it must have been dawn;
He followed the light straight to the city-gate,
The bolts and locks of which were still unopened.

Sudatta thus came to know of the Buddha's awe-inspiring strength,
Which caused his feelings of admiration to double.
Thinking of the Tathāgata,
He moaned and sighed,
Saying:

§'Past tall towers and high buildings, I go down to the double gates,
In the morning mist, I walk along the road, but it is blocked – I pace to and fro;
I think earnestly of the Honoured One's countenance, yet I cannot see him,
Fretting, I gaze up at the wall, but have not the strength to climb it.
I ever regret that I was born and lived in a land of false views,
And was not granted a wisdom-club to smash the mountain of error;
May the compassionate Honoured One confer acceptance upon me,
§With all my heart, I wait eagerly to worship his honoured visage.'

Sudatta's lamentation had come to an end,
But the Tathāgata's celestial ear heard it all from afar;
He knows the minds of others intuitively,
A distance of ten thousand miles presents not the slightest hindrance.

Again he released a divine light of illumination,
Causing the city-gates suddenly to open of themselves.

Sudatta, seeing that the gates were open,
Followed the light directly to the place where Buddha was.
He circled round him more than several dozen times, until his single-minded energy was exhausted. Then he intently and reverently looked upon the Honoured One's visage.

Here is the place where his joy and sorrow commingled. How does it go?

§Sudatta's Buddha-heart suddenly awakened to enlightenment,
From his eyes fell tears in thousands of streams.
'Your disciple was born and lived in a land of false views,
All day long accumulating bad karma and serving the King of Devils.
I humbly beseech you, Celestial Teacher, to receive my request,
§Send down your spiritual influence to Śrāvastī by making a bridge of me.'

The Buddha knew that Sudatta's roots of goodness were already mature,
That he was worthy of being transformed and would be easy to train;
So he responded at once by acceding to Sudatta's wishes,
Granting him the request which he had made.

Then the Buddha called to the elder, Sudatta:
'I am the Lord of the three cosmological realms –
All-conquering and honoured above all,
Whether in motion or at rest, I am self-composed.
Deities and dragons are my attendants and guards,
Brahmā stands at my left hand,
Indra goes ahead to lead the way.
Immortals crowd into all the empty spaces,
The four orders race like clouds along the streets and roads.

'You must
Build temples and towers on a grand scale,
Construct numerous halls and chambers.
The disciples of my teaching are now quite numerous,
Their living quarters should not be made too small.

'As for yourself,
Since you have long been schooled in non-Buddhist doctrine,
You are not familiar with our rules and precepts.
Take our Śāriputra as your guide,
Ask him about the regulations, one by one.'

Sudatta thus was granted his request,
And, what is more, found a saintly being as his guide.

At once, they selected two stout elephants,
On top of which were mounted roofed boxes.
Before many days had passed,
They arrived at the city of Śrāvastī.
Whereupon Sudatta followed along with the sainted one,
And went about methodically selecting a site for the monastery garden;
First they went outside the city-wall to the east,
And saw in the distance a park.
In it, there were ever so many flowers and trees,
And exceedingly fine ponds and pavilions.
Sudatta took hold of his whip and went forward,
Inquiring of the monk, Śāriputra;
'Is this park suitable or not?'

Śāriputra replied to the elder:
'Although the park is quite nice,
There is far too much onion and garlic;
The vile stench reeks to high heaven,
The holy and the wise could not bear to dwell here.'

Sudatta turned his elephants around,
And went back to the west of the city-wall.
He raised his eyes and suddenly saw a park,
The woods of which were twice as fine as those of the previous one.

Sudatta **[365]** took on a serious expression and crossed his fingers,
Then inquired of the monk, Śāriputra:
'Since you said that the last one was not good enough,
I wonder whether this park will be suitable for dwelling?'

Śāriputra replied to the elder:
'This place used to be a horse market,
Many living beings were slaughtered here
There is a noxious stench of blood and fetid flesh –
In truth, it too is unsuitable for dwelling.'

Reining in their horses, they turned their cart around,
Then travelled to the north of the city-wall;
Again, they saw another garden,
Whose woods grew lushly.

Sudatta inquired of the monk:
'Is this park suitable or not?'

Śāriputra replied to the elder:
'Although the park is quite nice,
Its woods are too rambling.
There are too many wine-shops and bawdy-houses
Which stupefy the minds of sentient beings,
And nourish the root of the ocean of misery.
This place will not do –
We must make another selection!'

The elder had successively visited three different sites,
But the honoured one said that all were unsuitable,
That the Buddha had no affinity with these places,
Or that they had produced too many karmic hindrances.

Sudatta was abashed, ill at ease,
And altogether perplexed.
Disconsolate, he turned the cart around,
And, again, continued the selection process by going south of the city.
When they were neither too close to nor too far from the city,
They gazed down the road they were on,
And suddenly saw a garden,
The vegetation of which was uncommonly luxuriant.
During the months of spring and the days of summer,
Its appearance was one of fragrance and freshness;
At the turn of winter and the beginning of autumn,
The lingering flowers continued to flourish.
Lush, lush grasses spewed forth greenness,
Bright, brilliant flowers opened in redness.
– A thousand kinds of ponds and pavilions,
Ten thousand types of fruits and herbs –
A delicate fragrance was wafted against the nostrils,
Chattering birds sang together harmoniously.
When the trees waved in the wind, they displayed the names of the Three Jewels;
When the sacred bells reverberated, they sounded the end of suffering.
Propitious peacocks and fortunate phoenixes
Competed in flaunting the brilliance of their plumage;
Fairy girls and elfin boys
Vied in performing their 'Music of Lasting Life'.

When the elder saw this park and its gardens,
It perfectly fitted his expectations;
So he quickly assumed a serious look,
And inquired of the monk:
'The previous three places
Were all declared unsuitable;
Now there is just this park –
I wonder whether it is to your liking?'

Śāriputra replied to the elder:
'I am a man of minor spiritual achievements,
My doctrinal strength is trifling;
Wait while I enter into meditation and observe it,
Then we can know whether it is good or evil.'

Śāriputra
Collected his spirits and entered meditation.
He gathered his thoughts for a moment,
Looked over this park and its pavilions,
And found absolutely nothing inauspicious.
Hundreds and thousands of Buddhas in the past
Had all once dwelt within it;
Here they expounded the Law and redeemed men
Countless in number as the dust and sand.

Seeing that this was the case, Śāriputra
Danced with pleasure in body and soul.
He smiled, then his face creased in a grin,
As he informed the elder, Sudatta:
'This park, not only in the present age
Is fit for our Teacher to dwell in,
But throughout the millennium, one thousand Tathāgatas
Shall all come to dwell within it.
It is most highly auspicious,
And utterly without imperfection;
If a monastery-park is to be constructed,
This is the only acceptable site.'

Here is the place where Śāriputra and the elder are holding their discussion – how is it?

§Since the elder had been granted divine protection,
He awoke instantly from all of his delusions;
Following Śāriputra, he set about building a seminary,

§With the intention of inviting the Tathāgata to elucidate the four terms.
They went successively to three sides of the city but there was no place fit to dwell,
The elder was disconsolate and his will began to waver;
Pondering the problem, he mounted his elephant and proceeded forward,
Then suddenly saw a park with flourishing fruits and flowers. **[366]**
Sudatta and Śāriputra were mounted on their white elephants,
On they went to the south of the city and there gazed into the distance;
Suddenly they saw several thousand groves composed of treasured trees,
Unusual varieties of flowers blossomed in unparalleled beauty.
Auspicious clouds formed a propitious canopy and filled all space,
White phoenixes and blue-green peacocks soared through the air.
Sudatta gasped in wonderment at such prodigiousness,
Looking reverently toward his honoured visage, he asked the monk about it.
Śāriputra turned to face Sudatta and replied to him:
'Rarely does one encounter a park so marvellous as this;
Holy bells echo each other amidst the groves of trees,
In the air, immortals hold the implements of worship.
Earlier Buddhas had dwelt here peacefully in the past,
Saving countless billions of living beings on a grand scale;
Possessed of wisdom and divine power which is ineffable,
It was in this place that the Tathāgatas expounded the Law.'
Sudatta was greatly astonished when he heard all of this:
'It is rare in this kingdom to behold a park and pavilions so fine as these,
But we still do not know who the real proprietor is –
Through which of all possible stratagems will we succeed in buying them?
All men cherish those things in the world which are the finest;
It is hard to expect anything from someone who does not intend to sell.'
For quite a long time he muttered to himself discontentedly;
His mind in a perplexed whirl and feeling all abashed,
He called the gardener to him and asked courteously:
'At the present time, who is the owner of this park?
I have urgent business today, and it is essential that I see him,
Tell me all the particulars immediately! Do not delay!'
The gardener crossed his fingers in respect, then disclosed all the particulars:
'The park's owner, who is both wealthy and honoured, is no ordinary person;

§He is the present Crown Prince, the occupant of the Eastern Palace,
Who comes here daily to inspect the park himself and then goes back. [**367**]
But he hasn't been here now for some three or four days,
And so we have redoubled our fixing and trimming beyond what is usual;
The owner of the park, with whom you wish to be acquainted,
§Is none other than the son of our sovereign, Prasenajit.'

Sudatta addressed the monk:
'Is this park suitable or not?'

Śāriputra replied to the elder:
'Not only is this park a place which our Original Teacher,
Śākyamuni, will love and enjoy,
In the past, Buddhas numerous as the dust and the sand
Also dwelt within it.
Men who are laden with defilements
Become pure and clean when they walk over this ground.
Divine bells and heavenly music
Often sound without being performed or struck.
Heavenly flowers of exotic fragrance
Compete riotously, then descend in disorder.'

'Return to your own place for the time being, Śāriputra,
In a moment I shall go to the Eastern Palace;
There, with all courtesy, I shall pry and probe
In an effort to determine whether we can obtain it or not.
If he declares that he is willing to sell,
I'll not haggle over how high the price is;
If he is adamant in refusing,
Then, out of convenience, I'll just have to resort to ruse.
Even if I exhaust one thousand stratagems and ten thousand plans,
I shall not rest until it is ours!'

The leave-taking completed, Sudatta set out at once,
And went directly to the gate of the Eastern Palace.
Though it was not the proper hour,
He straightaway entered to call on the Royal Heir.

When the Crown Prince saw from a distance that he was an important minister,
He quickly descended the steps of his throne to receive him.

The Crown Prince said:
'You, sir, are an important minister, a mainstay of our kingdom,
Often have you served as an official of my Lord;
On account of what urgent matter
Have you come so suddenly to see me at this unaccustomed hour?'

Sudatta wanted to explain everything straightforwardly,
But he found it somewhat difficult to put in words;
For the moment, he employed cunning language
In his reply to the Heir-Apparent:

'Yesterday, as I was out touring,
I chanced to come upon Your Highness's park;
From afar, I saw pandemonium breaking loose,
And flocks of strange birds crying.
So I reined in my horse to observe what was happening,
When suddenly I felt my spirits tremble with fear;
The ponds dried up and the arbours withered,
Flowers faded and fruits became few.
If Your Highness does not believe what I have been saying,
You may send a runner there to observe the actual state of affairs.'

When the Crown Prince heard these words,
He was exceedingly astonished:
'I purchased this park myself,
And have kept it all these years.
In the spring months, there are soft willows,
Whose weeping switches spread fresh greenness all around;
On summer days, there are cherry-apples,
Which shine brilliantly across the pavilioned ponds.
All this suffices to dissolve my cares and release my sorrows,
It gladdens my heart and gives joy to my soul;
Now, sir, you unexpectedly utter these words –
Should they not be considered stuff and nonsense?'

Sudatta composed his facial expression,
Then replied to the Crown Prince:
'Crown Prince! You are most highly respected and honoured,
The Heir-Apparent to a kingdom;
Your lowly servant waits upon you beneath the jade steps of your throne,
I am an arm of flesh to the royal house.
How could I possibly make false accusations?

That would be as grave as issuance of forged proclamations.
If I ever engaged in the slightest prevarication,
How would I be able to keep from losing my head?
If Your Highness still does not believe,
You may betake yourself there to view it personally,
And verify whether what I have said is true;
This will exonerate the honesty of your humble servant.'

The Crown Prince said:
'You, sir, are a loyal minister,
Who would not engage in unfounded hyperbole;
If there really exists such a state of affairs,
What should be done to suppress and exorcise these baneful spirits?'

Sudatta replied to the Crown Prince:
'If something begins to behave strangely,
It must be sold off to another person.
Your Highness should post notices at the four city-gates,
Stating that the park is offered for sale.
"Many mouths can melt metal" –
The evil portents will naturally disperse.
If someone decides to purchase it,
Demand a high price;
Namely: he should cover the ground everywhere with gold,
And the branches of the trees must be completely filled with silver coins.
The people of the world attach great importance to riches,
Rest assured that no one will be willing to buy it.'

The Crown Prince listened to what he said,
And consented to proceed accordingly;
That very day, the notices were written,
And attached to the four gates of the city-wall.

Sudatta's secret plans having been brought to a successful issue,
He departed from the Crown Prince.
Then he proceeded to the four city-gates,
Where he tore down the notices;
Directly he entered the Eastern Palace,
And went to see the Crown Prince.

The Crown Prince could not reconcile himself **[368]** to this state of affairs,

So he mounted his horse and went out of the city
To see personally for himself.
Following along behind Sudatta,
He went straight to the very park,
Gazing around in every direction,
The park was just as it always had been;
Scrutinizing the four sides,
There was nothing whatsoever which was strange.
So he sought out the person who oversaw the garden and asked him,
But he said that there had been no developments at all.

The Crown Prince then grew angry,
And reproached the great minister, Sudatta:
'You, sir, ought to strive on behalf of our society,
Instead, you are intent on banding together with foreign kingdoms.
Your machinations create dissension between ruler and ruled,
And cause division between father and son;
The demise of our House and the destruction of the kingdom
Shall both be charged to you, sir!
Now,
One who is a gentleman,
In his private capacity is utterly filial.
And in public life is utterly loyal;
His manner is one of deference and circumspection,
He is frugal and emulates correct patterns.
In this way,
He preserves his emoluments and rank,
And prolongs his fortune and honour.
How can a disloyal minister be countenanced?
In uttering words which damage his credibility,
Not only does he himself court misfortune and invite disaster,
But he also brings infamy upon his ancestors.
I will inform His Grace of this in a memorial,
So that you, sir, shall be banished and deprived of a place of haven.

'Rise and fall, glory and disgrace,
Are determined in the space of a breath.
"Proximate to power but performing poorly" –
"One who covets the occupancy of high position" –
"And who accepts the emoluments of office without doing the work" –
Now this, sir, is precisely what you are!

It is imperative that I memorialize the throne,
That you be punished ten thousand times over!'

At that time, they acted in disregard of circumstances because of their constitutions;
They feared neither loss of life nor shades of death.
The two of them, prince and minister, raced along,
Each intent upon seeing the King.

The Heavenly King Śūdra,
High in the sky, heard what they were saying,
And thought to himself:
'If I do not admonish these men,
A good work will run into difficulty.'

So he made his heavenly form invisible,
By transforming himself into an old man,
With hoary temple and white moustache;
Holding in his hand a supple staff,
He rushed directly in front of the Crown Prince's horse.
Raising his voice, he called out,
Then went forward and detained the princely son:
'There are principles which govern good and evil –
What is the use of all this noisy quarrelling?
Relationships of status are naturally governed by ceremony,
Considerations of position must prescribe to a pattern;
How can you block the streets and cut off the alleys,
Shouting so vehemently and so loudly?
Let each of you tell his own version,
Making sure that it be based on the truth.
Even the Son of Heaven attended the Three Old Ones;
The ancients cared for the old and begged their advice.
Do not avail yourselves of foolish fabrication and empty verbiage,
For this will disrupt the government.
I shall make a decision in accordance with justice,
But I can only hope that the evidence I take will not be distorted.'

The Crown Prince dismounted;
Unwilling to countenance the circumstances of his deception,
He outlined in detail the source of his discontent.
His testimony to the old man was: '. . . and so forth and so on'.

When the old man heard what the Crown Prince said,
He upbraided the great minister, Sudatta –

Cited a thousand types of disobedience,
And instanced a hundred kinds of error.
Glaring with eyes full of rage,
He harshly scolded the great minister, Sudatta,
And released the anger in the Crown Prince's heart.

Here is the place where the obstruction of a good work is avoided – how is it?

§When the Crown Prince saw that there was nothing strange about the park,
He knew at once that Sudatta had been engaging in deception.
'You, sir, who were once a loyal minister, have been indulging in wild talk,
For your own convenience, you have tricked me out of my park;
I shall draft a memorial and present it to the King to take action,
He'll have you chopped in two in a moment – your life shall not be preserved!'
While the two were wrangling on and on with no end of their words,
They suddenly happened upon the Heavenly King, Śūdra;
On his face, which was tinged with red, there were thousands of wrinkles, **[369]**
The rheumy tears in his eyes flowed as though from a fountain.
He leaned upon his thousand-year-old staff made of elder,
And, trembling and shaky, went up to the Crown Prince to greet him:
'This is the place where the Heir-Apparent holds his banquets,
It is but inches away from the august countenance of the King himself.
A gentleman, because he is cordial, contends with others only where virtue is an issue,
A man of wisdom does not rely on the vociferousness of his words;
If something is wrong, tell me – old man that I am – all about it,
I'll make an impartial judgement without interjecting any bias.'
The Crown Prince crossed his fingers in greeting and addressed the old man:
'Listen a moment without getting upset while I make myself clear.
My position is that of Crown Prince, the Heir to the Throne;
In my coming and going, I am always accompanied by half a regiment.
Sudatta, the minister, is lacking in thoughtfulness and wisdom,
He fails to maintain the decorum of superior and inferior, ruler and ruled;
Inexplicably, he has swindled me by devising a nefarious scheme,

§Whereby he conveniently desires to carry out the usurpation of the realm.
I hope that you will be so kind, old man, as to look into this closely,
And determine who is at fault in having made reckless statements about bad omens.'
When the elderly man heard this, he lowered his voice and said angrily:
'I used to hear it said that you were a loyal subject –
But now your speech is at sixes and sevens and without any standard,
Your prime ministership and ordering of the common people is a mockery.
Why must you babble about the appearance of bad omens? –
Because of your mendacious attitude, your deeds have become unseemly;
Based on these crimes of yours, it will be hard to forgive you,
When the King learns of this, he'll have you severed at the waist and pulverized.'
Then the elderly man spoke amiably to the Crown Prince:
'When a ruler of men gives his word, it is not fitting to go back on it.
Better that you ask a price so exorbitant no one can pay it,
Than act contrary to human feeling by saying you'll sell it then not sell.
I have seen many things during the course of my long life,
With straightforward words of reproof, I have made an impartial ruling; **[370]**
From now on, try to get along together and avoid dissension,
§As ruler and subject, you should be attentive to supporting and serving each other.'

Sudatta addressed the old man with these words:
'How can "one hand clap by itself"?
Two hands must be struck together before a sound is produced;
One sentence may be enough to bring about the downfall of a country,
Enormous losses may result from discrepancies of a hairbreadth.
In ancient times, one word of promise
Outweighed a thousand pieces of gold and was unwavering;
To say something is "as easy as turning over one's palm",
But to restrain oneself is more difficult than uprooting a mountain.
How could you first say one thing and then be inconsistent in what you said later?
You, Crown Prince, put up the notices,
Declaring yourself that you would sell the park;

Yet when I tore down the notices and tried to make a deal,
Then you said you would not sell.'

The elderly man's real intention
Was to be partial to the minister Sudatta;
But, in order to mollify the Crown Prince's feelings,
He gnashed his teeth in anger at Sudatta.
Sudatta's composure turned to dismay,
So he withdrew several steps away;
Thereupon the old man invited the Crown Prince to come forward:
'Aged as I am and though I occupy a subservient position,
Nevertheless, I am sixty years old and have an ear for truth;
Even the Sovereign attended the Five Gerontions,
And Confucius made inquiries when he was in the ancestral temple.
"A family depends on its eldest sons,
A kingdom relies on its loyal ministers."
"Boats are able to move about because of water,
The lips enclose the teeth but are also dependent on them;
If the lips are too thin, the teeth will be exposed,
If the water dries up, the boat will stop."
When there is only a ruler but no subjects,
What may the kingdom's altars depend on to stand secure?
It is well-known that, when one has offended another's feelings or carelessly provoked him,
The only thing that can be done is for the two to make amends in private.
A family at peace can raise silkworms in winter,
But it is essential that all of their comings and goings be governed by etiquette.
Your park, Crown Prince, must be very broad,
And its woods most dense;
Have him spread gold over the entire surface of the ground,
And fill all the branches of the trees with silver coins.
If he is made to empty his storehouses and exhaust his coffers,
There is no expectation that he will be willing to buy it;
Thus the terms of the agreement will not be met,
And the park will remain in your hands.'

The Crown Prince listened to what he said,
Then decided to follow his instructions;
So he turned to the great minister, Sudatta,
And demanded this price which would be so hard to pay.

Sudatta immediately consented to his behest,
Not even bothering to haggle over the amount;
On the very spot and facing each other, they discussed the terms,
Then proceeded to draw up a contract at once;
Many guarantees were attached,
And heavy fines were fixed for breach of contract.
Fearful that the Crown Prince might change his mind –
That he would restrain his earlier impulse and not carry out the bargain –
Sudatta immediately proceeded to open his storehouses,
And removed from them the finest red and yellow gold.
He chose one hundred stout elephants,
Had them loaded and sent off at once.
Unexpectedly, they were assisted by divine power,
In a moment they had reached the edges;
But for some few remaining steps,
The greater portion was almost covered.

Look at the place where the gold is being spread – how is it?

§Sudatta accepted the judgement of the elderly man,
And quickly assumed a happy look because it suited his own wishes;
He proceeded to select stout elephants from his stables,
Then opened his storerooms and loaded them only with the finest gold.
Piled high like so many lofty peaks, it was all safely transported,
Then spread everywhere thickly so that not even a needle could have been inserted.
The members of the entire household, be they of high or low standing,
Joined in extolling this labour with sounds of 'Great Wisdom';
In an instant, they had finished spreading the gold everywhere –
§Truly are divine power and perspicacious wisdom of great profundity! **[371]**

Sudatta had almost completed the spreading of the gold,
And estimated that the amount required for the remaining work was not much;
But he was discomfitted as he contemplated this in his mind,
Considering which storehouse he should open.
As he was deeply pondering,
The Crown Prince became suspicious,
And declared to Sudatta, the elder:
'If your heart has grown hesitant,

It's not too late to change your mind;
You embarked upon the fulfilment of this task,
For what reason do you now delay?'

Sudatta said:
'If the flesh of my body were used to cover the ground,
Even that toil I would not shirk –
How much less from expending these trifling and insignificant riches?
Dare I be parsimonious toward the Buddha?
Rarely does a Buddha-age occur,
An eternity might pass before one befalls;
If I be not earnest and absolutely sincere,
Regret later on would be to no avail!'

The Crown Prince said:
'Now you, sir, hold wealth as lightly as though it were dirt,
And value virtue as if it were a gem;
You are determined to buy this park,
To what use do you intend to put it?'

Sudatta said:
'Now the reason why I am buying it,
Is for a very special purpose;
Yesterday, on account of a marriage I was arranging,
It was my good fortune to meet the Great Sage.
His father's title is Śuddhodana,
His mother was called Māyā.
Exceptionally, he achieved self-enlightenment,
Learning it neither from men nor gods;
Through precocity, he achieved self-awareness.
His transformation-body is sixteen feet in height;
Behind his neck is a halo of light,
Which is as bright as a thousand suns,
Making it quite difficult to approach him.
Furthermore, he is capable of overwhelming heaven and earth,
And can cause men and other beings to be pacified.
He can transmute mountain and river,
Without actualizing the form of his coming and going;
He can swallow air and inhale fire,
Without the slightest harm to the tiniest hair on his body.
Should dangers press upon a person,
If his name is uttered, they will dissolve forthwith.

'What I have done just now is roughly to relate his virtues,
Summarizing as I spoke;
Were I fully to proclaim the capabilities of the Great Sage,
It would be difficult to exhaust them even after numerous aeons.'

When the Crown Prince heard what he said,
Shivers of sweat trickled from his skin.
'If there truly is virtue so mighty as this,
My deepest wish is that I may bow to him in worship.
As to the remaining part which has not yet been covered,
I request that you terminate your labours;
And as for the silver coins on the trees,
I myself will take care of that.'

'The lord sings and his subjects harmonize' –
Which nicely accords with the rules of rationality.
'When you see a worthy, you should think of emulating him' –
Which perfectly matches the usages of the former sages.
Of one heart and of one mind,
Together they constructed the monastery garden.
Is this not a case of
'The boat and the water rely on each other' –
'Those in the same vessel help one another'?

Having finished their pondering,
At once they followed along with Śāriputra,
Pacing across from east to west,
Making a tour from south to north.
Suddenly they saw a colony of ants,
Which swarmed over the ground as it went along,
Its numbers impossible to count.
When Śāriputra saw these ants,
He smiled, then his face creased in a grin.

This is the place where he explains antecedent causes to Sudatta and Jetā:

§Sudatta was successful in buying the Crown Prince's park,
He jumped for joy in body and soul, so boundless were his feelings;
At once, he invited Śāriputra to enter the park.
They measured and paced as they looked over the premises.
But before they had completed a circuit of inspection,
They suddenly happened upon a colony of ants.
Śāriputra turned his head and declared to Sudatta:

§'Observe these creatures which are of the category of bad karma;
At the time when the Buddha Vipaśyin appeared in the world,
They had long since received their ant-bodies and were born in this place. **[372]**
Now, today, they will encounter another Buddha – Śākyamuni,
This time, they will surely be relieved of their evil circumstances;
He will grant them the ten commandments and the three formulas of refuge,
And will, in addition, bestow upon them the sweet dew of perfect wisdom;
After this, there will be for them eternal renunciation,
They will be reborn among the deities in the company of disciples.'
The elder, Sudatta, resolved to construct the monastery garden,
With lecture halls, courts, and temples all complete;
Above in the Tuṣita heaven, there was a great burst of music,
From afar, he visualized himself being reborn there.
Having finished the spreading of the gold, he looked upward with feelings of reverence,
Then, with a sense of urgency, felt compelled to build the likes of a monastery garden;
He spared neither his gems and jewels nor his gold and silver,
And put up notices summoning the most skilled artisans of the land.
'Neath the tower of the triple gate, they sculptured figures bearing thunderbolts,
In each court, they were instructed to paint icons in bright colours;
The side-rooms, the spirit chambers, and the corridors,
When looked at, could remove delusions which lead to disaster.
Zithers and dulcimers were hung from the tips of the four corners,
When the wind blew, ten thousand separate sounds issued loud and clear;
There were also pan-pipes and flutes together with some harps,
As well as brass cymbals and lutes which stood facing chimes.
The high seat from which the lectures on the Law were given was adorned with jewels,
Ox-head sandal-wood burned in the censers as a form of worship;
The nine classes of incarnate beings came here to be born in accordance with their vows,
Sweetly singing cuckoos glided about in the air above.
While Sudatta, the elder, piously constructed these spirit rooms,
The various Buddhas and Bodhisattvas looked on from space;
The Crown Prince Jetā annunciated a solemn resolve,
§Vowing to attain by degrees the germ of perfect wisdom.

After Sudatta had completed the purchase of the park,
He and the Crown Prince set off on their return;
Suddenly, in the middle of their path,
They encountered the Six Heretical Masters.
Without asking for any details,
The Masters became angry as soon as they caught a glimpse of the others:
'The Crown Prince is the heir to the throne of a kingdom, **[373]**
In his comings and goings, he should be escorted by half a regiment;
The elder occupies the honourable position of prime minister,
An official who assists in the administration of the State.
How can you defame the kingdom by having such slight regard for yourselves,
Going about like this with no more than ten mounted attendants?
Granted that
Yao left unhewn the beams of his house,
But this was to proclaim his renown for frugality;
Shun allowed no mutton in his cooking-pot,
But this was to save by eliminating the evil of luxurious habits.
Furthermore,
Long tassels and broad sleeves
May yet serve to certify the dignity of a powerful kingdom;
Golden pillars and jade steps
Are manifest praise of the glory of earlier kings.
This is merely what is recorded in the ancient writings,
And not our own arrogant assumptions.
For what reason
Do you go rushing about so hurriedly,
And so careless of your person as to ride horseback?
Is it that you wish to plan for the good of the State,
Or do you have some ulterior motive?
It is imperative that we draw up a memorial and present it to the King,
We must solicit from him a royal decree.'

Please look where they are questioning about the particulars. How does it go?

§'The Crown Prince is the second most honoured person in the kingdom,
When he leaves or enters, the hundred officers should make adequate preparation;
For what reason are your mounted attendants no more than ten?
And why do you loose your reins and come here all unequipped?

§Try to tell me about it as truthfully as you can;
Whether good or bad, you must not avoid mentioning anything.'
The Crown Prince dismounted and reported to his honoured teachers:
'Don't you gentlemen know that Sudatta has purchased my park?
He intends to invite the Tathāgata to come here to expound the Law,
Out of admiration, my own feelings have made me, too, take refuge in the Buddha.
Just now, we witnessed the completion of the business of spreading the gold,
And that is why we are now returning to the palace.
Every single word I have said is according to the truth,
I have opened my heart and bared my mind to you hoping you will be clearly informed.'
When the Six Masters heard these words, they could not stop laughing.
'Gautama's illusory tricks are incomparable,
His beautiful words and honeyed tongue swindle the people.
Seven days after he was born, his mother suddenly died;
He was unable to stay settled in the exquisite halls and ornate towers,
So he abandoned his father and fled into the depths of the mountains.
The words which he utters are designated as "sūtras",
And he boasts to himself that his body is made of gold and is absolutely unique;
Should he come to this kingdom, it would do harm to the people,
We cannot, with open eyes, adopt these perfidious ways! **[374]**
Tomorrow morning, we shall draft a memorial and present it to the sovereign,
The merits and demerits of this case must all be reported to His Majesty;
Having nothing to do, they impulsively grab at this drivel from the nose of an ox –
§How can it be compared with the water from our rivers and seas?'

When the Six Masters heard of the invitation to the Buddha to come and dwell,
They angrily took it to heart;
Their cheeks puffed up and their jowls raised,
They arched their eyebrows abruptly,
Gnashed their teeth and bared their gums –
They were extraordinarily irate!

§'We would rather give our lives once for a worthy cause,
Than be willing to live twice ignominiously.
Our students are all being enticed away from us,

§We shall be driven off and left without a way to survive;
Everywhere we go, we shall be ridiculed,
All the day long we shall be reviled by others.
If even emperors and kings are submitting to them,
How much more will the commoners and the vulgar masses!
How shall we make known our present indignation?
§We must register our complaint in the presence of the King!'

The Six Masters, in great haste,
Bounded forward with great strides;
Quickly they ran to the dragon court,
And beat the drum for announcing grievances.
The King sent a representative,
Who asked them what this stemmed from;
The Six Masters sobbed and choked till their voices became hoarse,
For a long while they only moaned but could not speak.

They addressed the great King:
'We have heard that, ever since the creation of heaven and earth,
There have been those who rule and those who are ruled;
It is like the immaculate light of the sun and the moon,
In that all depend on the transforming influence of the sovereign.
As a result, today those in the eight directions are your suppliants,
And everyone within the four seas comes to you as a guest.
Only there is a rebellious son and a villainous minister,
Who seek to subvert the government of your kingdom;
They cherish evil and embrace treachery,
But are not attentive to what the people are singing in their songs.
He is covetously ensconced in the honourable position of prime minister,
And idly enjoys an official salary of ten thousand bushels of grain.
We have heard that treacherous ministers destroyed the Six Kingdoms,
And that treacherous women cause fighting among the six relations;
As for Jetā and Sudatta,
This is, now, precisely what they are!
Whoever heard of failing to inform the throne
While enticing a foreign deity to enter from abroad?!
He confounds the common people with his illusions,
And styles himself "the Buddha".
He is unfilial to his parents
In that he consistently fails to repay their kindness;
He is disrespectful to his sovereign

In that he contravenes the propriety required of a subject.
He is not diligent about production,
But is quick to shave the head of anyone he meets.
He makes absurd statements about heaven and hell,
And pursues topics that no one has verified –
If he should come to this place,
We only fear that he will harm the kingdom and bring ruin to the royal house.
Now, as your subjects, we have opened our hearts and bared our minds,
In humble expectation that Your Grace will look closely into this matter.'

Please look where the Tathāgata is being accused. How does it go?

§'The Crown Prince of the royal family is honoured throughout the kingdom,
It is improper for him to introduce from abroad a foreign deity;
The rebellious minister, Sudatta, is the ringleader,
His agitation and defamatiom disturb the integrity of the government. **[375]**
Merely because of Gautama's many illusory tricks,
He has become both disloyal and unfilial in the service of his Ruler;
Neither does he pay court to his King nor does he worship his parents,
Though he belittles men of honour and high rank, he respects those who are stupid.
It is our humble wish that you, great King, will take out your precious mirror,
§And, today, turn its light upon this minister so that you may closely examine him.'

§After the Six Masters had made their plaint, again they petitioned the throne,
This time with backs bent obsequiously and heads lowered:
'The supernatural powers which we possess,
Were accumulated over a long period of many, many years;
Our miracles and revelations are of a thousand different kinds,
The entire kingdom recognizes our skill.
Mindful of our meritorious achievements,
One by one they follow us as teachers and receive our instructions;
Today, oh King, we who are undistinguished do petition you,
§Earnestly expecting that Your Heavenly Grace will grant us protection.'

§Once again, the Six Masters petitioned the King saying:
'We, your subjects, today have a matter which we shall truthfully explain;
Your villainous minister and rebellious son have set up a conspiracy,
We worry that the kingdom will be destroyed and its people annihilated.
Sudatta's original idea was to invite a foreign deity,
It was his broad intention to effect weird apparitions in the city;
That this would defeat our government and laws is not to be marvelled at –
His invitation to this vile deity from afar is exceedingly base.
This man is despicable and cannot be relied upon;
§It is our humble wish, oh discerning ruler, that you will closely examine him.'

The King said to the monks:
'Please present the evidence carefully,
You must not proceed too precipitately;
We, then, shall inquire into the roots of the matter,
And examine the facts of the case.
If there have been any errors because of irregularities,
Both of them will definitely be put to death ten thousand times over!'

The King issued orders to his representatives,
Whereby they captured Sudatta alive;
And, together with
The Crown Prince Jetā,
Confined him in gyves.

Here is the place where, immediately, the inquiry into the causes begins – how is it?

§The King questioned Sudatta: 'What was your purpose in doing this?
You impulsively purchased the park and turned it into a monastery; **[376]**
Because you intended to invite Gautama to come to this place,
The Six Masters say that disastrous portents have arisen.
We dwell deep within the palace and were totally unaware of this,
So you, sir, must tell us the whole story, omitting nothing;
How can Gautama be compared with this Six Master of mine,
§Who emulates good models and responds to praiseworthy affairs?'

§The august King sits in state in his palace of crystal,
Robes draped and arms folded in the inner precincts of his palace, he faces directly south;

§Splendid literary men attend to geomantic problems,
§Gallant soldiers holding precious fans provide a cooling breeze.

§Sudatta is taken by surprise and questioned about the roots of this affair.
'For what reason have we not seen you these several days?
I have also heard that you have introduced a foreign deity from abroad,
§In my estimation, your crime, sir, will be difficult to absolve.'

§Sudatta made his plaint to the King, addressing him thus:
'Your subject has served 'neath your jade steps for many long months and years;
I have poured out my feelings and opened my heart to you, being ever attentive,
Never have I engaged in the slightest prevarication.
If you were to take these heretics and stand them next to the Tathāgata,
This would be comparable to comparing tares with excellent grain;
The Buddha-body is colossal, being sixteen feet in height,
While the heretics are as childishly small as a firefly's light.
The waters of the four great oceans can be contained in the tip of one of his hairs,
A five-coloured divine light is emitted from his mouth;
He is constantly preceded by Brahmā, Śakra, and the four Heavenly Kings,
The eight spirit realms all follow along after him.
How can you take a toad which has worked itself into a sweat,
§And dare to pit it against the great and sage unicorn?'

The King listened to these eulogies of praise,
And, still ignorant of the roots of the matter,
Proceeded to call Sudatta forward:
'You, sir, must be genuine and true,
No dissembling will be permitted;
Glory and disgrace, rise and fall,
Are determined in the lapse of a moment.
We are the sovereign of a kingdom,
We reign over ten thousand principalities;
You, sir, must maintain your honesty and preserve your loyalty,
No flippancy nor fickleness will be permitted!
Once the Son of Heaven is angered,
He is capable of strewing the ground with countless corpses,
So that the blood flows for a thousand miles.

Of which family and clan is the Buddha? [**377**]
What was the status of his forebears?
In his studies, whom has he consulted?
What moral power resides in his person?
You must not hide anything –
Tell us the whole and truthful story.
In the event that there is the slightest dissemblance,
Your body will swiftly face the provisions of the law.'

Sudatta addressed the throne:
'Among the Tathāgata's ancestors,
There appeared no less than a thousand universal kings;
They succeeded one another like leaves on a branch,
Their honour and glory were unceasing.
From his forefathers to his father,
All have occupied the honoured position of "Lord of Ten Thousand Chariots";
Their sons were outstanding, their grandsons splendid,
And each was styled the direct descendant of peacocks and phoenixes.
His father's title is Śuddhodana –
He occupies the most honoured position among the eight kingdoms;
His mother was called Māyā –
She was recognized throughout Inḍịạ as peerless.
The Tathāgata
Was born in a south Indian kingdom,
And grew up in the city of Kapilavastu;
From his birth to his death,
From his death to his rebirth,
There is nothing which he did not effect –
There is nothing which he did not achieve –
There is nothing which he did not undergo –
There is nothing which he did not experience.
He grew up in the palace of Śuddhodana,
And was called by the name Siddhārtha.
When he passed the age of nineteen,
He awoke to an understanding of life and death;
Before he had reached twenty,
He escaped by leaping over the walls of the palace.
Beneath the tree of wisdom he sat,
Uncontaminated by mundane sentiments;
Year after year, he performed diligent austerities,

Until he was disfigured by emaciation.
All that he ate during the day was sesame and grain,
He eked out his life a day at a time;
Crows and magpies nested on the top of his head,
Raising their fledglings until they were full-grown.
His hair was like a tangled thicket,
His neck seemed but a nail or a pin;
His ribs were like the rafters of a dilapidated house,
His eyes were like stars at the bottom of a well.
So lean and weak was his body,
That it had the appearance of a hungry ghost;
But with the building up of merit and the accumulation of virtue,
The Way to Perfect Wisdom was attained.

'His transformation-body is sixteen feet in height,
Behind his neck is a radiant light;
On his chest is inscribed a swastika,
Which stands out clearly and distinctly.
He has the distinctive mark of a long and broad tongue,
His forehead is broad and has a flat appearance;
He has the breast of a Lion King,
His hair grows in spirals like conch shells.
The Tathāgata at-nir without dying,
He tained-vāṇa without being born.
Though you stir him up, he is not muddied,
Let him settle and right away he is clear;
Though you put him in a gloomy place, he feels no dark,
He will illuminate himself and right away become bright.
When you look at him, you cannot see his body,
When you listen to him, you cannot hear his voice;
He is high without being lofty,
And low without falling flat.
He can transform rivers and oceans into kumiss,
And can convert the vast earth into a glass-crystal.
When he plucks up Mount Sumeru,
He registers it in ounces and pounds;
He can cut through the four seas
Transforming them into dry trenches.
Eyes closed, he can transport himself ten thousand miles away,
Eyes open, he stops right at once.
When he manifests his great body,

It extends over the whole of the world;
Or if he manifests his minor body,
He can hide his shape within a tiny particle of dust.
When the Tathāgata
Takes up his knife to cut, he does it not with a vengeance,
In spreading a medicinal application, he is not jocular;
Finding something does not make him happy,
Losing something does not make him sad.
In the midst of a great crowd, he is unaware of the commotion,
Sitting alone by himself, he does not feel isolated;
His two hearts, the collected and the distracted, have coalesced in one rudiment,
They exist in close juxtaposition and on an equal standing.
He can separate his body into a billion parts,
Everywhere observing abstinential duties.
One of his names is Siddhārtha,
A second title is the Tathāgata;
He is the teacher of gods and men,
Who is possessed of all wisdom.
Four times has he been born in the triple-world –
He is all-conquering and most highly honoured.

'Today I have briefly described his abilities,
But many *kalpas* would be exhausted before completing his praises,
Oh, Your Highness!'
When the King heard these words,
He was so delighted that he could hardly bear it:
'Although, sir, you have extolled his moral powers,
You still have not demonstrated this in a concrete fashion;
It will be necessary to have a face-to-face trial,
Then we can determine who is right and who is wrong.
He whom you, sir, take as your teacher –
Can he stand up to our Six Master Monk or not?' **[378]**

Sudatta addressed the throne in these words:
'"A thousand-pound cross-bow
Is not to be launched by a little mouse";
"A hundred-foot fiery furnace
Does not burn hotter because of a tiny hair."
We need not avail ourselves of the Great and Holy Heavenly Teacher,
For the youngest of his disciples
Will be able to stand up against them.'

The King asked:
'Who is this disciple,
That can face our Six Master Monk?'

Sudatta addressed the great King in these words:
'The Buddha's disciple
Is no one other
Than Śāriputra.'

The King said:
'Śāriputra
Is the nephew of our Six Master Monk.
It is only recently that he left home to become a monk,
His knowledge of the Law is shallow;
If you count up his meritorious practice,
It has not gone on for very long.
Age and youth cannot stand shoulder to shoulder,
How can he face our Six Master Monk?'

'Although Yen Ying was small,
He could make plans against rapacious officials.
"One who is possessed of moral power need not rely on advanced age,
He who is without wisdom toils in vain though he live to a hundred";
Fabricating falsities
Is not so good as taking truth for a touchstone.
Gold may be refined one hundred times,
Yet the quality of its sheen will become more brilliant;
If lead and tin are placed in a furnace,
They will immediately turn into ashes.
I humbly hope that you will make a clear pronouncement of your commands –
Gathering together on a grand scale your entire body of courtiers and proclaiming to them
That there shall be a great contest,
After which it will be possible to establish the winners and the losers.
If Six Master is victorious,
I deserve to be beheaded ten thousand times over;
And have all the members of my family become public property.'

Thereupon the King decreed to his subordinates:
'You must swiftly make arrangements –
On the eighth day of the coming month,

A religious arena is to be constructed south of the city.
If the Buddhists are the stronger,
I and the people of my entire kingdom,
Shall all be converted to Buddhism;
If there is the slightest slip or error,
The two of you must both be executed.'

When Sudatta received this royal decree,
He became extremely depressed and troubled at heart;
So he returned home at once,
Where he knit his brows and screwed up his cheeks.

Śāriputra
Saw how depressed and worried he was,
And how his features had changed;
At once, a gasp of surprise escaped him,
And, feeling perplexed, he asked:
'For what reason, elder, are you so depressed and worried?
Why is your appearance so changed?'

Sudatta said:
'Today, I went to the court,
Where I personally received the King's explicit decree;
It has been ordered that,
On the eighth of the coming month,
A religious arena be constructed south of the city.
Each side is to demonstrate its supernatural powers,
Whereby it will be determined who is superior.
If the Buddhists are victorious,
The King, together with his subjects, intends to turn to the Buddha in all sincerity;
If Six Master is the stronger,
The Crown Prince and I, who am so insignificant,
Will both be executed.
Now, I am just an ordinary person of shallow wisdom,
Who has not yet fathomed the depths of your sagacity;
May you be so kind as to show compassion toward my predicament –
I hope that you will extend to me your prestige and power.'

Here is the place where Śāriputra indulges in braggadocio so as to comfort Sudatta in his grief – how is it?

§Sudatta addressed Śāriputra in the following words:
'The decree orders that, on the eighth of the coming month, **[379]**

§A great religious arena is to be constructed south of the city,
Where each side will display all sorts of supernatural powers.
The King himself will go there in person to examine their ability,
And will consult in detail with his functionaries to determine who wins and who loses;
May you be so kind, oh monk, as to express your feelings –
You must run through once an elucidation of this predicament.'
With a smile on his face, Śāriputra replied to Sudatta:
'All erroneous notions must be totally extirpated!
For the heretics to have a contest of supernatural powers with me,
Is like taking a fish and giving it to an oṭṭẹr;
The bright moon has never seen comparison with the light of a firefly,
You cannot talk about the waters of the sea in terms of pẹc̣ḳs and pinches.
Yet again, it will be the same as late spring ice melting in the summer sun,
Or like comparing sawdust with gold which can be refined hundreds of times.
These followers of heterodox ways are all so much chaff –
As soon as a big wind arises, there is no gathering them up;
Certainly, now, I shall take the upper hand in subduing these demons,
§And will have them all converted so that they become Bodhisattvas.'

Śāriputra smiled, then his face creased in a grin,
As he informed Sudatta:
'Now, although I am but a minor sage,
Nevertheless, I do have access to high places;
If it is only a question of revealing what is correct and repressing what is false,
It is decidedly a small matter.
Even the billions in the host of the Scourge of Heaven,
Who crowd into all the empty spaces,
Cannot move the tiniest hair on my body;
How much less, then, will this little gnat of a Six Master
Be able to stand against me!
Now I "sharpen my knife and feed my horse",
Accumulating only the merit of practising my artifice;
There is no need to resort to procrastination,
Indeed, it is necessary to proceed with dispatch!
You, Sudatta, should petition the King again,
To the effect that the eighth is too late;

"The rabbit has entered the dog's hole" –
Who can wait when the food is on the table?
We should get this show on the road right away tomorrow;
Request that the date of the eighth be moved up.'

Thereupon, Sudatta made another petition to the King,
And the King went along with his request;
He instructed his subordinates:
'Tonight, just before daybreak,
The preparations must all be completed.
The religious arena of the Buddhists
Must be provided by you, sirs;
Whatever the Six Masters require,
I, myself, will supply.
Tomorrow, at the crack of dawn,
The contest must begin promptly.'

When the instructions of the King's decree were finished,
Sudatta immediately returned;
Upon reaching his home,
He was unable to find Śāriputra.
Sudatta clapped his hands with a gasp of surprise.
'Disastrous!' he called out.
'For such a terrible misfortune to happen!
He agreed to tomorrow's contest of skill,
But today he pulled foot and slipped away;
Granting that he may have reckoned the situation to be hopeless,
It still does not seem right that he treat us this way.
On behalf of the Law,
I would gladly be content to lay down my life;
But, as for the Crown Prince,
For what crime should he be executed?'

Hurriedly, he set out in pursuit,
Without knowing which way Śāriputra's trail led;
He asked at every intersection,
But no one knew where he had gone.
At last, he met a lad with nine head of cattle,
And detained him so as to ask **[380]** this question:
'When you went out to the pastures,
Did you meet one of our monks or not?'

The lad bowed as he replied:
'Grandpa,
Yesterday as I was drivin' the cattle lookin' for grass,
I happened t' come t' the side of Sev'n Mile Creek;
I saw a bald little fellow there,
Who had a red shirt thrown over his shoulders.
He was sittin' up straight under a tree asleepin',
Dunno what sort he is –
You can go yourself t' look at 'im, grandpa.'

When the elder, Sudatta, heard what he said,
He knew right away it was the person he was after;
Of the people inside this kingdom,
There was no one else whose head was shaved.
Sudatta raced his chariot as fast as the horses could run,
And soon he arrived at the bank of Seven Mile Creek.
He went directly beneath the banyan tree;
Motioning aside his attendants,
He crossed his fingers and went forward,
Addressing the monk in these words:
'I, your disciple, have personally heard the royal decree –
Its restrictions are quite severe;
You yourself pushed the time ahead,
And agreed to have the contest of skills tomorrow.
How can you not know the difference between urgency and leisureliness?
You have come to this place,
Not recognizing when to relax and when to be busy.
You've actually run off to this place to sit and sleep!
If there is the slightest remissness,
Two men will lose their lives;
Even if it is allowed that I am culpable,
How can you, oh Monk, look on in silence?'

This is the place where Sudatta confers with Śāriputra – how is it?

§The elder brought his palms together in greeting and addressed his spiritual master:
'I, your disciple, am ignorant and unenlightened,
But I did not shirk from spreading my gold to buy the park,
And, now, the heretics are treating me with bitter cruelty.
I, your disciple, personally followed your instructions,

§So that Raudrākṣa wishes to have a battle of spiritual might.
I am apprehensive now that, halfway through, this predicament has arisen,
It is because of this that I am depressed and worried and that I knit my brows.'
Śāriputra listened to what Sudatta was saying,
Then, through self-reflection, proceeded to enter a deep state of meditation.
He cleansed his spirit and calmed his thoughts in peaceful contemplation,
Overcoming false notions and bringing a halt to all wrong views,
The six marauding senses, though ranging everywhere, could not contaminate him;
Yet, when he was about to realize the ineffability of mind-control,
He was repeatedly concerned by the inferiority of his acquired doctrinal strength,
§And humbly wished that the Tathāgata would protect and support him.

Śāriputra did not stir from where he was sitting;
He exercised his supernatural power,
And swiftly reached the peak of Vulture Mountain;
Tears of sadness flowing like rain,
And sobbing until his voice grew hoarse,
He circled round the World-Honoured
More than several dozen times.

This is the place where he hopes that the Great Sage's awe-inspiring majesty will be bestowed upon him – how is it? [**381**]

§Crying sadly, Śāriputra addressed the King of the Law:
'You, oh Tathāgata, enjoined me to construct monks' quarters;
Before I could show my sincerity by completing the building and decoration,
Six Master and his crowd behaved quite insufferably.
I, your disciple, am a small man and my spiritual powers are inferior,
May you extend to me your protective regard and lend me the light of your majesty;
If I should be successful in subduing them readily,
They shall all be redeemed and made to join the ranks of the company of monks.'
'You need not be sad,' the Buddha told Śāriputra,
'This is because your acquired doctrinal strength is meagre.'

§Thereupon he summoned Ānanda to come close by his side.
'Take down from the clothes rack the patch-robe of our monastic order;
Through aeons of time, you shall always be employed in the subduing of demons,
With this, one need not toil in the exercise of supernatural power and wisdom.
Take my gold-embroidered cassock with you when you depart,
Infinite beneficent deities will guard and protect you;
One look at it and all the demon kings will be overthrown,
§Its undefiled, underlying nature is witness to unconditionalness.'

Śāriputra
Suddenly awoke from meditation;
Neither to the left nor to the right did he see anyone,
He saw only the great minister Sudatta.

He was accompanied by the eight spirit realms,
Who supported him front and back,
And circled about him on all four sides.
Titans
Holding the sun and moon went ahead to lead the way;
Heavenly musicians
Grasping swords and spears followed behind.
At that time,
The wind master made the winds blow,
The rain master made the rains fall;
This dampened the din and dust of the world,
And smoothed the way of the doctrine.
The kings of spirits wielded their cudgels,
Diamond deities held their thunderbolts;
The most capable and brave were selected,
And lined up in columns and rows.
Afterwards, they
Blew Conches of the Law,
Beat Drums of the Law,
Flourished their swords and spears,
Flaunted their wrathful majesty.
They moved like galloping thunder,
Walked as though they were spreading clouds.
There were also
The elephant king from the Himalayas,
And the lion with golden hair;

It rolled its eyes and raised its brows,
Opened wide its jaws and gnashed its teeth;
It bristled its furry coat,
Shook its head and wagged its tail.
The weapons reflected to the sky,
Spears and lances enwrapped the earth.

They matched abilities, each wishing to demonstrate his awe-inspiring majesty, and to bestow it upon the great disciple of our Tathāgata – how is it?

§Śāriputra bid his farewell to the assembled hosts,
On this very day, he promptly set forth on his journey.
The Heavenly King Virūpākṣa held a golden banner,
Dhṛtarāṣṭra carried a jade insignia of office; **[382]**
Their armour and weapons, even their whole bodies were entirely of gold,
Their swords and arrows, in vast profusion, used exclusively iron.
The Black-Faced Diamond Deity had a mulberry-coloured complexion,
The Fire-Headed Diamond Deity glared unceasingly;
Bells and drums sounded with a deafening roar which shook the heavens,
There was a bright and auspicious aura of glistening purity.
Heavenly immortals scattered beautiful flowers in space,
There were continuous sounds of hymns in praise of the Buddha;
From the top of the demon-subduing thunderbolt a fiery light shone forth,
Beside the sword of knowledge and wisdom, frost and snow glimmered.
His only wish was that the many Buddhas would show their compassion,
So that, before long, all the flags of heterodoxy would be torn down.
In the time it took to flex his finger, his spiritual power
§Took him instantaneously to the gates of the royal city.

When King Prasenajit saw Śāriputra,
He at once decreed to his assembled courtiers:
'Each of you must be attentive!
The Buddhists are to sit on the east side,
The Six Masters on the western edge;
We shall sit at the northern rim,
The officials and commoners on the south side.
Regarding the two possibilities of victory and defeat,
Each must be clearly recorded.
If the Six Master Monks win,

Beat the golden drum and lay down a golden tally;
If the Buddhists are the stronger,
Strike the golden bell and mark up a score for them.
Each is to remain in his own place,
But may show his stuff as he pleases.'

Śāriputra, self-composed, ascended the Lion platform with slow steps. Raudrākṣa settled himself amidst gem-studded curtains, closely supported by his followers. Having ascended the gem-encrusted platform, Śāriputra sat there like a King of Lions. Speaking in an elegant voice, he told the spectators on all four sides: 'Now, within the Buddhist Law, we do not affirm that the mind has a permanent identity. We reveal what is correct and repress what is false; relying on this, we establish ourselves. Whatever transformations Raudrākṣa can come up with, let him show his stuff as he pleases!'

When Six Master heard these words,
He immediately conjured up a precious mountain,
Several leagues in height;
It had lofty pinnacles of blue-green jade
And soaring crests of whitest silver;
Its peak trespassed on the Milky Way,
On it there were groves of bamboo and fragrant grasses.
To the east and the west were the sun and the moon,
To the north and the south were Orion and Lucifer.
There were also
Pine trees which reached to the sky,
And countless strands of vines and creeping plants.
On its peak a hermit peacefully dwelled,
As well as many immortals out seeing the sights;
Some rode on cranes, others mounted dragons,
Strains of immortal music twining about them.
There were none among those present who did not gasp in amazement,
All of the spectators acclaimed and praised it.

Though Śāriputra saw the mountain, in his mind he was completely undaunted. In the space of an instant, he suddenly conjured up a Diamond Deity. What was the appearance of his Diamond Deity? Well, the head of his Diamond Deity [**383**] was round like the heavens and only the circling skies themselves would do for a canopy. His feet were ten thousand miles square, and only the great earth itself could serve as a pedestal. His eyebrows were as bushy as the twin summits of a wooded mountain. His mouth opened wide as the broad rivers and oceans.

In his hand, he held a jewelled mace,
From the top of the mace, flames leaped to the sky;
As soon as he pointed the mace at the mountain of evil,
It instantaneously broke into pieces.
The mountain flowers withered and fell,
The bamboos and trees disappeared.

All the officials praised this marvel with one voice,
The spectators on all four sides readily shouted their approval.

Therefore, in telling of the place where the adamantine mace of wisdom breaks the mountain of evil, how is it?

§Six Master was so enraged that his emotions were hard to quell,
He conjured up a precious mountain that would be difficult to match;
Its precipitous cliffs were all of several leagues in height,
There were purple creepers and golden vines which covered the ground.
The mountain flowers and dense foliage formed an embroidered pattern,
From soaring crests made of golden rocks, blue-green clouds arose;
On its top, there were the hermits Wang Ch'iao and Ting Ling-wei,
In the recesses of this precious mountain, fragrant waters flowed.
Flying immortals continuously scattered beautiful flowers,
All of which filled the great King who looked on from afar with pleasure.
Śāriputra watched as the mountain was introduced into the assembly,
But sat there self-composed and motionless, deep in meditation.
Instantaneously, he conjured up a great Diamond Deity,
With high brows, a broad forehead, and a body bulging with muscles;
In his hand, he held a diamond mace from which fire shot up to heaven,
Which caused the mountain of evil to break in pieces as soon as he pointed at it.
The heretics sobbed and wailed till their voices became hoarse,
§While the spectators swiftly and unanimously shouted their approval.

Thereupon,
The Potentate was surprised,
And all the spectators were delighted.
Since he was not equal to his opponent this time,
Everyone wondered what the next miracle would be.

Then the elder, Sudatta, proceeded to strike the big bell. Holding a gold medal in his hand, he reported to the King, asking him for the score marker.

When Six Master saw that his precious mountain had been toppled, his rage towered to heaven. His anger heightened, he reported to the King: 'Now, there will never be a day when my supernatural transformations are exhausted. Although my first round was unequal to his, I'm sure I'll gain the victory with this next manifestation.'

Suddenly, Raudrākṣa conjured up a water-buffalo in the midst of the assembly. His buffalo had sparkling horns which startled the heavens. Its four hoofs were like Damascus swords. A hanging dewlap trailed on the ground. Its twin pupils [**384**] were as bright as the sun and the moon. It bellowed once – thunder rumbled and lightning crackled. The spectators gasped in amazement, and everyone said that the heretics had taken the lead.

Although Śāriputra saw this buffalo, his expression remained unchanged. Suddenly, he conjured up a lion whose ferocity was not to be challenged. His lion had

A mouth like a mountain gorge,
A body similar to a snow-covered mountain,
Eyes comparable to shooting stars,
And teeth like cold steel.
With a rousing roar,
It leaped right into the middle of the arena.
When the water-buffalo saw the lion,
It lost pluck and knelt on the ground.

Then the lion

First seized the buffalo's nape,
Next snapped its spinal column;
Before the lion was able to devour it,
The buffalo's body broke into pieces.

The Potentate gasped with surprise,
The officials and commoners were taken aback.

This is the place where Six Master trembled in horror and where the Crown Prince could not contain himself for joy – how is it?

§In the presence of the King himself, Six Master was enraged,
So he conjured up a water-buffalo which was really impressive;
It leaped right into the middle of the arena, startling the spectators,
Sharpening its horns by digging them in the ground, its bellow reached to the heavens.

§The heretics simultaneously shouted, 'Bravo!
The citizens will now be made to transmit our doctrine.'
Seated on his dais, Śāriputra was unperturbed,
All because his knowledge and wisdom were quite immeasurable;
He rearranged his clothing and, having collected his thoughts,
Conjured up an imperatorial King of Lions.
When it roared, the lion's eyes flashed as though they were lightning or stars,
Its tapered teeth and pointed claws cut as sharply as frost;
Waving its tail so as to display its heroic mettle,
It went forward and directly seized the water-buffalo, injuring it.
The buffalo soon dissolved under the ripping and slashing of the lion,
Even its bones were devoured so that the buffalo completely disappeared.
In both of the first two rounds, the Buddhists were victorious,
§The heretics, at their wit's end, were at a loss for a plan.

Since Six Master had twice shown himself unequal to Śāriputra,
His expression more and more became one of embarrassment;
Forcing himself to put on a bold face,
He conjured up a pond in the midst of the assembly.
Its four banks were adorned with the seven types of jewels,
And its bottom was covered with golden sand.
Drifting duckweed and leaves of the water-chestnut
Competed with each other to spread the surface with green;
Supple willows and lotuses in blossom
Encircled the charming pool in a nebulous blur.

Śāriputra saw how wonderful the pond was,
But still he did not show any sign of alarm;
He conjured up a white elephant king.
Its body was enormous,
Its eyes like the sun and the moon;
There were six tusks in its mouth,
And from each tusk burst seven lotus blossoms.
On top of the flowers **[385]** there were seven heavenly maidens,
Holding musical instruments in their hands,
And singing to the accompaniment of strings;
Their voices were elegantly refreshing,
Their gestures were sinuously alluring.

The elephant moved with slow and dignified steps,
It entered directly into the middle of the pond;
It trampled east and trod west,

Turned north then whirled to the south.
With its trunk, it sucked up the water,
Until the water was all dried up.
The banks collapsed in puffs of dust,
As it turned into a dry land.

Thereupon Six Master went pale,
And the spectators all gasped with surprise.

This is the place where the officials of the entire country simultaneously exclaim in wonder – how is it?

§The banks of his pond were made of the seven types of jewels,
Cornelian and coral competed in lustrousness;
Fish leaped above the pond, crisscrossing every which way,
Tortoises, turtles, terrapins and water-lizards scrambled about in chaos.
The lotus blossoms in the water shined with a brilliant light,
None there were among the spectators who did not feel surprised;
The heretics exclaimed in self-satisfaction: 'It's really marvellous!
Just wait and see if we don't show 'em who's who in this round!'
Śāriputra raised his eyes and looked off toward the south,
Then conjured up a huge, six-tusked elephant which emitted a fragrance;
As it walked along, its appearance was like a snowy mountain in motion,
Its body was so enormous that it would have been difficult to measure.
From out of its mouth, there burgeoned six sharply jagged tusks,
And each one of the tusks was several hundred feet high.
On top of every tusk there were seven lotus blossoms,
Inside the blossoms were maidens of incomparable beauty;
They plucked zithers and lutes and sang to their own string accompaniment,
Their elegantly refreshing voices echoed harmoniously.
Together they hymned the paradise of Amida Buddha,
Hand in hand, they did but encourage men of like mind to go there.
The elephant then waded into the middle of the pond,
It trampled and trod east and west and on the banks as well;
With its trunk, it sucked up the water until the pond was completely dry,
§Causing Six Master to choke with the vexation which filled his breast.

Six Master lost again and again,
Which made him increasingly heart-stricken;
'It's strange how today I'm not up to him,
Just the opposite of my dreams last night.'

The colour of his face was flushed and flaxen,
His lips and mouth were extraordinarily parched;
His stomach was as hot **[386]** as boiling soup,
His innards ached as though a knife were being turned in them.
'Although Gautama is a fierce wolf,
He won't be able to fend off a pack of biting dogs.
Śāriputra has little knowledge and less plans,
He's just an amateur, showing off in front of an expert;
If I succeed in beating him this round,
I'll be able to break through and wipe out even what went before.'

Unwilling to endure insult,
He swiftly conjured up a poisonous dragon.
Clouds of smoke billowed from its mouth,
Darkening the sky by blocking out the sun;
When it raised its brows or blinked its eyes,
The earth trembled and thunder roared;
Flashes of lightning made things now dark, now light,
Ominous clouds first spread out, then rolled back.
It startled the spectators on all four sides,
And terrified the commoners;
The entire kingdom watched the dragon,
Marvelling at its monstrousness.

Śāriputra sat self-composedly on his bejewelled platform,
Feeling not in the least perturbed.
He conjured up a golden-winged King of Birds,
With rare feathers and unusual bones.
Flapping its wings, it rose,
Concealing the light of the sun and the moon;
Its claws and spurs were long and slender,
No different from a sword of Toledo.
From up in space, it dived straight down,
Like a shooting star out of the skies;
Watching the poisonous dragon from afar,
It attacked its prey repeatedly.

'Although it's not enough to make a full meal, at least it will do for a snack.' First the bird pecked out the eyes of the dragon, then it gobbled up the four legs. After two swipes of its beak, there were not even any bones left. Six Master trembled with fright and gasped in alarm. His mind was in a muddle.

§That day, Six Master gradually became more and more frustrated,
Bitterly resentful and not knowing what to do, he had nowhere to tụṛṇ;
Although he forced himself to go on putting up resistance,
He had a premonition that he would be defeated in the end.
Again, he conjured up the body of a poisonous dragon,
Clouds of smoke billowed from its mouth and its breast was full of ire;
Thunder rumbled and roared – the sky was darkened by haze,
The sound of the rising claps and peals was like that of a fiery explosion.
Those in the arena were so frightened that they gasped with alarm,
In groups of twos, they looked at one another and simultaneously called out 'Bravo!'
Śāriputra observed the arrival of the poisonous dragon,
Then proceeded to cause the appearance of a golden-winged bird with rare plumage;
It was no trouble at all for the bird to rip and slash the dragon from head to tail,
When it started to eat, it began by pecking out the brains;
The muscles and bones broke into pieces and became fine dust,
Leaving Six Master without knowing what he ought to say.
The awe-inspiring power of the Three Precious Ones is unfathomable,
§The King of Demons shudders and is beset with vexation.

The King said:
'Six Master Monk, you boast behind the scenes,
How you have a thousand different kinds of tricks;
But when you are examined face-to-face in front of someone,
You are incapable of anything.
Whatever supernatural power you still have,
You must use it to make your transformation appear at once!'

Six Master forced himself to pluck up his courage,
Then reported to the [**387**] King:
'Within our doctrine,
There will never, after all, be a day when our spiritual transformations are exhausted.'
Suddenly, in the midst of those assembled,
He conjured up two monsters.
Their appearance was repulsive,
Their bodies all contorted;
Their faces were more blue than the sky,
Their eyes were redder than rubies.
Fire issued from their mouths,

Smoke snorted from their nostrils;
When they ran, they were like streaks of lightning,
When they sped, it was as though they were whirlwinds.
They raised their brows and blinked their eyes,
Throwing terror into the assembly.
The spectators all got goose pimples,
But Śāriputra alone was self-possessed. Śāriputra hesitated while he considered what to do. Before long, Vaiśravaṇa appeared in front of the King with a leap.

His awe-inspiring majesty was splendiferous,
His armour and weapons were bright and shiny;
Earth deities supported his feet,
And a precious sword hung at his waist.

This is the place where the two monsters, after taking one look at him, incessantly beg for their lives – how is it?

§Six Master himself claimed that he was incomparable,
So he conjured up a pair of yellow-headed monsters;
Their pates were of such a strange sort, their carcasses so ugly,
That they terrified the people on all four sides, filling them with dread.
While Śāriputra pondered the problem for a moment and considered what to do,
Vaiśravana the Heavenly King arrived on his own;
The Heavenly King made a circling survey, his eyes glaring with rage,
The two monsters were so stupefied that they threw themselves on the ground.
That day, the heretics were an army of defeated demons,
Six Master, his courage shaken, was completely at wit's end;
Whereas Śāriputra, who put his trust in the Compassionate One,
Exercised his spiritual power with magnanimous patience.
When an ass or a mule with a heavy load sets out on a distant journey,
It begins to wonder whether it can be compared to the scale of a dragon;
Only, because his mind was confused, he strayed off on a minor by-way,
§And had to be converted so that he could take refuge inside the gate of Buddhism.

Although Six Master had lost five rounds,
He still would not surrender.
'Let's just give it another try,
Our belated merits will offset our previous errors.
In the event that I make a mistake and lose again,
I shall willingly bow down and commit myself to them.'

Having finished with his reflections,
Suddenly, in the midst of the assembly,
He conjured up a great tree.
Its leafy limbs were so dense,
They blocked out the sun and reached to the clouds;
Its soaring trunk and spreading branches
Were a full ten thousand fathoms in height.
Auspicious fowl and birds of good omen
Sang harmoniously from everywhere on its leafy limbs;
Its green leaves and fragrant flowers
Abruptly made it dark for several miles around.
At that time, among the spectators,
There were none who refrained from gasping in surprise.

Suddenly, Śāriputra conjured up a God of Wind in the midst of the assembly:
Crossing his fingers in greeting, he came forward,
And addressed Six Master Monk:
'Even a great chiliacosm of worlds
Could be blown away on a moment's notice without difficulty;
How much less should this little wisp of a tree **[388]**
Dare to stand in the path of my wind!'
After completing this declaration,
He opened up his bag of wind and let it blow.
Thereupon, the earth rolled up like a carpet,
Rocks were pulverized into dust;
Limbs and branches were scattered in every direction,
There was not even anything left of the trunk.

This is the place where the heretics have no place to hide and where all those assembled readily shouted their approval – how is it?

§Six Master lost again and again, five times in a row,
But, once more, he conjured up a tree in front of the King;
From its top to its bottom, it was all of several leagues,
Its limbs and branches were luxuriant and flourishing.
Śāriputra's doctrinal power, however, was beyond conception,
His supernatural powers of transformation were really marvellous;
He bid farewell to the Buddha and came here expressly to subdue the heretics,
One gust after another, he set a series of strong winds blowing.
The sound of the spirit king calling was like the roar of thunder,

§It was a long serpent plucking at the tree and leaving not a branch;
In the twinkling of an eye, it had completely disintegrated,
Bereft of support, the heretics were blown about by the wind,
Six Master was blown upon so hard that his feet left the ground,
His censer and thurible were sent flying by the wind;
His gem-encrusted platform leaned so precariously that it nearly toppled,
The heretics, frightened and anxious, together held it up.
In groups of twos, everyone judged Six Master to be inferior,
§How can a mustard seed be compared to Mount Sumeru?

Then the King addressed Six Master Monk:
'Day after day, we have
Vainly given you our respect,
Been munificent with our jade and silk,
Wastefully expended our kingdom's wealth.
Thus is it known that genuine gold and worthless fool's gold
Can be assayed by examining with the eye;
When dragons and snakes are mixed together,
Only then can their abilities be distinguished.
You have exhausted your strength and depleted your power,
You have been the loser in everything;
The final outcome is that you must hang your head in humiliation,
And bend to him in submission.
And no more empty prating about ego and individuality!
– Nor talk of heaven and tales of earth!'

When Six Master heard what the King said,
All he could do was give his assent and comply.
His face was tinged with shame,
There was no place for him to hide.

Śāriputra saw that the heathens had been chastened which made him delighted and pleased. 'It's not that I am strong or capable. Everything is due to the assistance of the Tathāgata.' Then, springing straight up, he leaped into space. He went as high as seven palmyra trees. Fire issued from the top of his head; water issued from the bottom of his feet. When he manifested his major body, it packed all space. When he manifested his minor body, it was a though it were a mustard seed. His supernatural transformations were manifested in eighteen different categories.

This is the place where the people of the entire kingdom all look up to him with reverence – how is it? **[389]**

§Quite suddenly, Śāriputra manifested his supernatural power,
Propelling himself straight up into empty space above;
When he manifested his major body, it spread over the whole universe,
His minor body could be concealed within a mustard seed.
Raudrākṣa stood there in amazement with his palms joined together:
'How can my doctrine be considered similar to theirs?
Together with you, I will abandon evil and return to the correct path,
I will be contrite and utterly self-effacing in my reverence.
In our contest of skills, I was far and away the more contemptible,
How dare I not rely upon and follow him with repentant heart?'
So each of them determined to confess his regret and take refuge in the Three Jewels,
They no longer had the heart to wait upon the fiery dragon.
For many years in succession, they had wasted their energy,
They had spent whole days going from emptiness and back to emptiness again;
But each of them was able to extricate himself and serve the Buddha,
§And thus was able to avoid being pounded with an iron pestle in the future.

Transformation Text on the Subduing of Demons, One Scroll

If anyone who reads this sees a part which is incorrect, I pray that he will correct it forthwith.

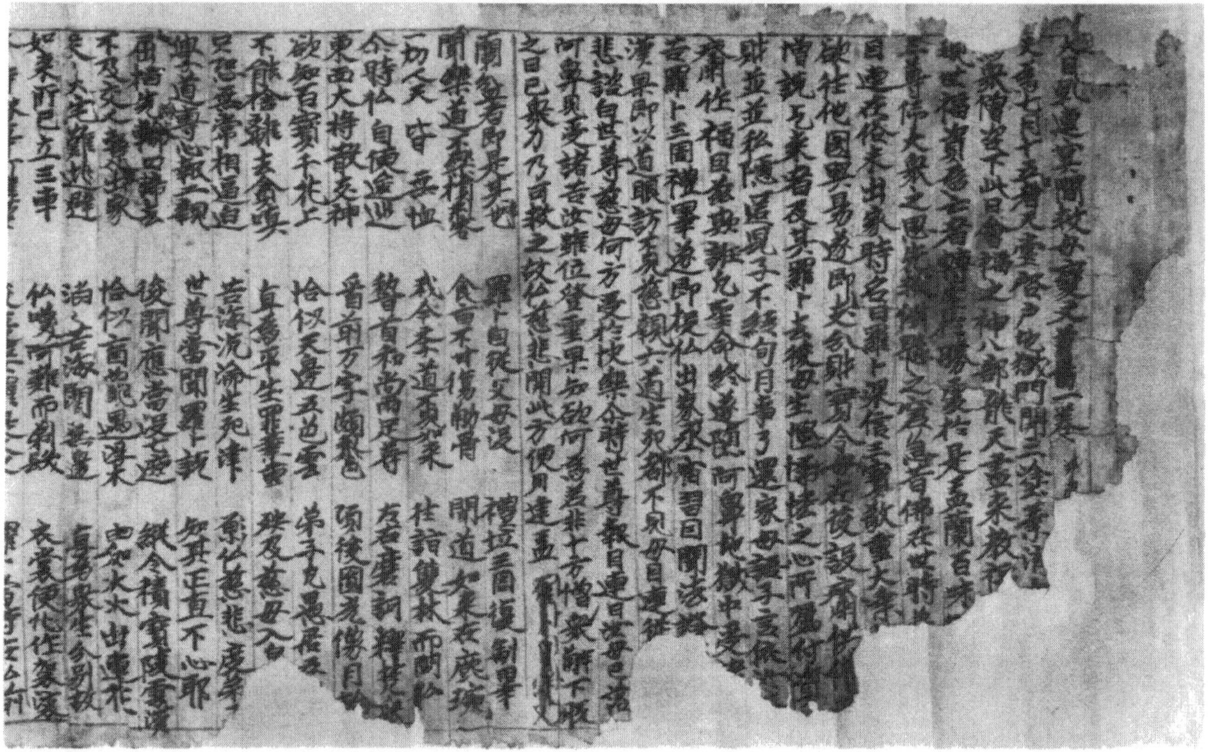

3. 'Transformation Text on Mahāmaudgalyāyana Rescuing his Mother from the Underworld, With Pictures, One Scroll, With Preface' (ms S2614).

2

MAUDGALYĀYANA

Transformation Text on Mahāmaudgalyāyana Rescuing His Mother from the Underworld, With Pictures, One Scroll, With Preface

Now, on the fifteenth day of the seventh month, the heavens open their doors and the gates of the hells are flung wide. The three mires dissipate, the ten virtues increase. Because this is the day when the company of monks end their summer retreat, the deity who confers blessings and the eight classes of supernatural beings all come to convey blessings. Those who undertake to make offerings to them in the present world will have a supply of blessings and those who are dead will be reborn in a superlative place. Therefore, a purgatorian feast is spread before the Three Honoured Ones who, through the grace of their welcoming the great assembly, put a priority upon saving those who are distressed by hanging in limbo.

Long ago, when the Buddha was in the world, he had a disciple who was styled Maudgalyāyana. When he was still a layman and had not yet left home to become a monk, his name was Turnip. He believed deeply in the Three Precious Ones, and had a high regard for Salvationism. Once he wanted to go to another country to engage in trade. So he disposed of his wealth, ordering his mother later on to arrange for vegetarian food to be provided for the many members of the Buddhist Trinity and the numerous beggars who would come. But after Turnip departed, his mother became stingy and hid away for herself all the riches which had been entrusted to her.

Before many months had elapsed, the son had completed his business and returned home. 'As you had charged me,' the mother said to her son, 'I held vegetarian feasts which shall bring us blessings.' Thus did she deceive commoners and saints so that, when her life came to an end, she fell into the Avīci Hell where she endured much harsh suffering.

After Turnip finished observing the three full years of mourning, he immediately surrendered himself to the Buddha and left home to become a monk. Having inherited the good deeds of his former lives, he actualized these inherent causes by paying heed to the Law and attaining arhatship. Whereupon he sought his mother in the six paths of transmigration with his unlimited vision, but nowhere did he see her.

Maudgalyāyana awoke from meditation full of sadness. 'In which place is my dear mother enjoying happiness?' he inquired of the World-Honoured.

The World-Honoured then informed Maudgalyāyana: 'Your mother has already dropped down into the Avīci hell, where she is now undergoing much suffering. Although you have attained the fruit of the saintly life, your knowledge will be to no avail. You can save her only if you employ the might of the assembly on the day when the companies of monks in all directions disband at the end of the summer retreat.' Therefore, the Buddha in his compassion instituted this expedient method. This, then, is the story of how the purgatorian offerings were founded.

§From the time when Turnip's father and mother had passed away,
After three full years of ceremonial sorrow, the period of mourning came to an end;
Listening to music did not make him happy – his appearance became emaciated,
Eating fine foods gave him no pleasure – he wasted away to skin and bones.
But then he heard that the Tathāgata was in the Deer Park,
Where he comforted and cared for all men and deities; **[715]**
'Now I shall study the Way and seek the Tathāgata!'
And so he journeyed to the twin trees to visit the Buddha.
At that time, the Buddha came immediately to receive him,
The monk prostrated himself before him who is most honoured among men and deities;
To his right and left were the mighty Indra and Brahmā with their hosts,
To his east and west were the great generals and other sundry spirits.
The sauvastika on the front of his breast had a crystalline glow,
The halo behind his neck was like the disc of the moon;
Don't you know, the hundreds of gems and the thousands of flowers on his throne,
Were just like the five-coloured clouds at the edge of the horizon.
'I, your disciple, am a mediocre person who is limited by his desires,
Neither can I renounce nor free myself from desire and anger;

§Just because the sinful karma of my whole life was of such enormity,
It extended to my dear mother, causing her to enter the gates of Hades.
I only fear that impermanence will press upon her,
And that she will sink in the ocean of misery beside the ford of births and deaths;
May you, oh Buddha, show compassion by saving your disciple,
Allowing me to concentrate on studying the Way so that I may repay my parents.'
As soon as the World-Honoured heard what Turnip was saying,
He knew that he was upright and was not being deceitful;
He began by enumerating and explaining the doctrine of the Four Noble Truths,
Then lectured him on the necessity of avoiding the seven rebellious acts.
Even though one amasses so much treasure that it towers to the Milky Way,
This is not as good as urgently to persuade others to leave home and become monks;
It is precisely the same as a blind turtle bumping into a floating log,
Or yet like a lotus blossom issuing from a great expanse of water.
It is difficult to escape from a house which is wrapped in flames,
The raging sea of misery is so broad that it has no shores;
Just for the reason that all living beings are different,
The Tathāgata established three types of conveyances to nirvāṇa.
The Buddha summoned Ānanda to perform the tonsure,
And his clothing was then exchanged for a monk's cassock; **[716]**
Instantaneously, Maudgalyāyana achieved sainthood,
And subsequently he received the commandments for monks.
During the time that Turnip was there in front of the Buddha,
Incense smoke curled up in wreaths from a golden censer;
The fabulous forest shook by the six kinds of earthquakes moved heaven and earth,
The four divine flowers were wafted on the air and scattered through the clear skies.
A thousand sorts of elegant brocades were spread on the couches and seats,
Ten thousand styles of pearled banners hung in the air.
The Buddha himself proclaimed: 'Now you are my disciple!'
§And he styled him 'Mighty Maudgalyāyana of Supernatural Power'.

At that moment, Maudgalyāyana achieved sainthood beneath the twin trees. How did it happen like this? It is just as in the *Lotus Sūtra*:

'The prodigal son first received his worth, then later was cleansed of his impurities.' This is precisely the same in that he first obtained the fruit of sainthood and afterwards engaged in the study of the Way.

Look at the place where Maudgalyāyana sits meditating deep in the mountains – how is it?

§After Maudgalyāyana's beard and hair had been shaved away,
Right away he took himself into the depths of the mountains;
It was a remote and quiet place where there was no one else,
Right away, he contemplated unreality and sat in meditation.
He sat in meditation and contemplated unreality, learning good and evil,
He subdued his mind, he settled his mind, until nothing more adhered to it;
Facing a mirror, its image was clear and unwavering,
And all the while he pressed his right foot down upon his left foot.
    He sat with his body erect on a large rock,
    And with his tongue touching the roof of his mouth;
    White bones became for him completely empty,
    His breathings no longer were intertwined.
Just at that time, a herd of deer stopped to drink in the woods,
They drew near to the clear pool and looked across its waters;
Beneath the bright moon in front of the courtyard, he listened to religious discourses,
Under the pines on the green hills, he sat meditating.
The lake air on the horizon was like coloured clouds,
The watchtowers on the green hills outside the frontier were visible; **[717]**
The autumn wind soughed as it passed through the centre of the forest,
Yellow leaves drifted down and floated on the water.
Maudgalyāyana sat reposefully in a state of incorporeality,
Gradually he cultivated his internal and external experiential mind;
By realizing discipleship, he occupied his hoped-for position,
He entered and left the mountains as freely as he pleased.
    Maudgalyāyana awoke from abstract meditation,
    Then swiftly exercised his supernatural power;
    His coming was quick as a thunderclap,
    His going seemed like a gust of wind.
    Wild geese honked at the hunter's darts,
    Grey hawks escaped from nets and cages;
    The mist in the centre of the pond was greenish,
    The sky was clear, the distant road was red.
    With his supernatural power, he gained freedom,

§So he hurled up his begging-bowl and leaped into space;
Thereupon, instantaneously,
He ascended to the heavenly palace of Brahmā.
In an instant, Maudgalyāyana arrived at the heavenly court,
All that he heard in his ears was the sound of music and drums;
Red towers were faintly reflected on the golden halls,
A profusion of green lattices opened on white jade walls.
With his metal-ringed staff, he knocked at the gate three or four times,
Unaware of the tears which were crisscrossing his breast;
An elder came out from within to have a talk with him,
He brought his palms together and began to speak of his sincere filiality.
'I wonder if you know me?' he inquired of the elder,
'I, a poor monk, am an inhabitant of Jambūdvīpa.
When I was still young, I was bereft of my father and mother;
Although our family was quite wealthy, it was lacking in sons and grandsons,
I was orphaned and, furthermore, had no future before me.
The dear mother of this poor monk was styled Nīladhi, **[718]**
My father's name was Śūlakṣaṇa;
All his life was spent in doing kind and charitable works,
After he died, it would have been fitting for him to be reborn in this heaven.
This is such a delightfully splendid and charming place,
Just gazing at it brings happiness to the hearts of men;
Bells and drums resound in harmony with elegant music,
§The sound of harps being strummed is also loud and clear.

§'How sad it is that they never relaxed from their parental chores!
The affection she showed in nursing me is not easily forgotten;
I wonder whether they have been peaceful and well since leaving me,
§And that is why I am now searching for them in this place.'

§When the elder heard these words, he seemed to be sympathetic,
But his mind was in a whirl and he spoke haltingly:
'I, your disciple, had a son in Jambūdvīpa,
But I wasn't aware that he had left home to become a monk.
Do not blame me, Your Reverence, if I question you closely,
There are so many different types of people in the world;
As I observed you speaking for the first time, I took you for a stranger,
But now that I reflect upon it, I am somewhat nonplussed.
Among laymen, there are many people who have the same name and surname,

§And there are hundreds of types of faces which are similar;
Your appearance and disposition are familiar,
But then when I think about it, I cannot place you.
If, oh Teacher, you insist on seeking to be recognized,
§Please tell me some more about your family matters.'

Maudgalyāyana went to the palaces of heaven in search of his father. He arrived at a gate where he met an elder. 'When I was young,' he informed the elder, 'my name was Turnip. After my parents died, I surrendered myself to the Buddha and left home to become a monk. My whiskers and hair were shaved off and I was given the title "Mahāmaudgalyāyana, Pre-eminent in Supernatural Power".'

When the elder heard him say his childhood name, he knew right away that it was his son. 'We have long been separated. Have you been well?'

After Turnip–Maudgalyāyana had been acknowledged by his dear father and had inquired about how he was getting along, he asked: 'In what place is my dear mother enjoying happiness?'

The elder replied to Turnip: 'Your mother's activities while she was alive **[719]** were different from mine. I practised the ten virtues and the five commandments, so that, after I died, my soul was reborn in heaven. Throughout her life, your mother committed a large number of sins and, at the end of her days, she fell into hell. If you search for mother along the infernal paths of Jambūdvīpa, you'll soon find out where she has gone.'

After hearing these words, Maudgalyāyana took leave of the elder. He vanished and descended to Jambūdvīpa. There he searched for his mother along the infernal paths but could not find her. However, he did see eight or nine men and women wandering about aimlessly with nothing to do.

This is the place where he goes forward and asks the reasons for this situation:

§'Please do not pay me any reverence.
Who are you, my good friends,
That have all gathered here in this place –
Wandering about aimlessly with not a thing to do,
Roaming around outside the walls of the city?
I, who am a humble monk, only arrived here today,
To my mind, it is really quite extraordinary.'
The men and women answered the reverend one with these words:

§'It's only because we had the same name and same surname as someone else,
Our names were mixed up with theirs and so we were escorted here;
The interrogation lasted just four or five days,
We were judged "not guilty" and released to return to our homes.
Long since sent to the grave by our wives and sons,
Our solitary bodies were flung into the wilderness;
On all four sides, there were neither relatives nor companions,
Foxes, wolves, crows, and magpies competed to divide us up.
Our houses fell into disrepair leaving us with no place to take refuge,
We appealed to the King of the Underworld with plaintive voices;
His judgement was that we be released as wandering ghosts with nothing to do,
Having received this supplemental verdict, what more is there to say?
Today, we have already been cut off from the road of births and deaths,
Once the gates of Hades slam shut, they never open again.
Though there be a thousand kinds of food placed on our grave-mounds,
How can they alleviate the hunger in our stomachs?
All our wailing and weeping, in the end, will be to no avail,
In vain do they trouble themselves to make folded paper money. **[720]**
Take a message to the sons and daughters in our homes telling them:
§"We entreat you to save us from infernal suffering by performing good deeds." '

Maudgalyāyana waited a long while before speaking. 'I wonder whether you know of a Lady Nīladhi?'

'None of us know her,' the men and women replied.

'Where does the Great King Yama dwell?' Maudgalyāyana continued with his questioning.

'Reverend sir!' the men and women replied. 'If you walk several steps farther toward the north, you'll see in the distance a tower with triple gates where there are thousands and ten thousands of stalwart soldiers, all holding swords and cudgels. That is the gate of the Great King Yama.'

Upon hearing these words, Maudgalyāyana walked several steps farther toward the north. From there he could see the tower with its triple gates into which stalwart soldiers were driving countless sinners. Maudgalyāyana went forward and made inquiries but could not find his mother so he sat by the side of the road and cried loudly. When he had finished crying, he went forward again and was taken in to see the King by functionaries.

This is the place where Maudgalyāyana is led in by the gatekeepers to see the Great King who asks him his business:

§When the Great King saw Maudgalyāyana enter,
He quickly joined his palms in salutation and was about to stand up:
'What is your reason for coming here, reverend sir?'
Hurriedly, he bowed respectfully from behind his table.
'Your coming here embarrasses me, oh Exemplar!
I, your disciple, am situated here in this infernal region,
Where I flog sinners to determine whether they shall remain dead or be reborn;
Although I do not recognize you, reverend sir,
It was long ago that I had heard of your name.
It must be either that the Buddha has sent you here on a mission,
Or that there is some private family business;
The Lord of Mount T'ai's verdicts are, in the end, difficult to alter,
For all were sanctioned by heaven's bureaucrats and earth's pen-pushers.
A sinner's karmic retribution is in accord with conditional causation,
Who is there that could rescue them on the spur of the moment?
Fetid blood and congealed fats stink through the Long Night,
Leaving an offensive stain on your clothing which is so pure.
These infernal paths are no place for you to spend much time,
It is my humble wish that you, oh Exemplar, make an early departure.'
Maudgalyāyana replied to him as best as he could: **[721]**
'Perhaps you may be aware, oh Great King,
That I, poor monk, had a father and mother who, when alive,
Day and night observed the laws of abstinence, never eating after noon?
Based on their behaviour while in the World of Mankind,
After their deaths, they should have been reborn in the Pure Land.
My father alone is dwelling in the mansions of heaven,
But I cannot locate my dear mother in any of the heavens;
In my estimation, she should not even have passed through hell,
My only fear is that she may have been unjustly punished by High Heaven.
I have followed her traces to the edges of heaven and earth,
Filled with sorrowful vexation, I heave a long sigh;
If she has come to this realm because of her karmic retribution,
§Perhaps you, oh Great King, would have been made aware of it.'

When Maudgalyāyana had finished speaking, the Great King then summoned him to the upper part of the hall. There he was given audience with Kṣitigarbha Bodhisattva to whom he quickly paid obeisance.

'Have you come here in search of your mother?'

'Yes,' replied Maudgalyāyana, 'I am searching for my mother.'

'In the days when your mother was still alive, she committed a large number of sins. So limitless and boundless were they that she must have fallen into hell. Would you please come forward? My duty-officers will be here in just a moment.'

The King then summoned his karma-watcher, fate-investigator, and book-keeper who came immediately.

'The name of this reverend monk's mother is Lady Nīladhi. How long has it been since she died?'

The karma-watcher replied to the Great King: 'Three years have already passed since Lady Nīladhi died. The legal records of the criminal proceedings against her are all in the case-book of the Commandant of Mount T'ai, who is Recorder for the Bureau of the Underworld.'

The King summoned the two Good and Evil Boys and told them to examine the books at Mount T'ai to find out which hell Lady Nīladhi was in.

'Reverend sir,' the Great King said, 'Follow along with the Boys. If you ask the General of the Five Ways, you should be able to find out where she has gone.'

After Maudgalyāyana had heard these words, he took leave of the Great King and went out. He walked several steps and soon came to the banks of the Wathellwedo River. There he saw numberless sinners taking off their clothes and hanging them on trees. There were many sounds of loud crying by those who wished to cross but could not. Distraught and apprehensive, they clustered in groups of threes and fours. They held their heads as they wept and wailed.

This is the place where Maudgalyāyana asks them the reason for this:

§The waters of the Wathellwedo River flow swiftly to the west,
Broken stones and precipitous crags obstruct the road they walk on;
They take off their clothes and hang them on the sides of tree branches,
Pursued, they are not allowed to stand still for even a moment. **[722]**
At the edge of the river, when they hear their names being called out,
They are unaware of the tears which are drenching their breasts;
Today, at last, they know that their bodies have really died,
They stand next to trees in pairs and weep sorrowfully for a long time.
'When I was alive, I was in thrall to my prized possessions,
I went out in a golden four-in-hand carriage with crimson wheels;
Saying that it would never change in ten thousand ages,

§Who would have thought that it long ago was transformed into dust?
Oh! Alas and alack! What pain there is inside my heart!
In vain have my white bones been buried in a tall tumulus.
My sons and grandsons ride the dragon-horses in the southern stables,
My wives and concubines use the scented carriage outside the northern window.'
Their many mouths all said the same thing – 'It is inexpressible!'
Long did they sigh but all their complaining went for nought;
Every person who commits sins will fall into hell,
He who does good will certainly be reborn in heaven.
Now each must follow his own circumstantial karma,
It is certain that it will be difficult to meet again later on;
They grasp each other's hands and repeatedly enjoin, 'You must cheer up!'
Looking back, they wipe away their tears as they look longingly at one another.
In their ears, all they hear are cries of 'Hurry along!'
As they are driven forward by the thousands and ten thousands;
On the river's southern bank, ox-head guards hold their truncheons,
At the water's northern edge, hell's gaolers raise their pitchforks.
The eyes of the people in the water are filled with distress,
The tears of those who are on the banks flow copiously;
If only they had known earlier that they were to sink in a place of hardship,
§Now all they can do is regret that they had not done good works while they were still alive.

Maudgalyāyana asked a man who was beneath a tree at the side of the Wathellwedo River:

§'Heaven's Mansions and Hell's Halls are not insubstantial;
It goes without saying that Heaven punishes those who do evil,
The minions of the underworld also promptly join in prosecution. **[723]**
This poor monk's dear mother did not accumulate goodness,
So that her lost soul fell into the three mires leading to hell;
I have heard tell that she has been taken inside hell,
All I want to ask is whether or not you have any news of her?'
As all the sinners looked at Maudgalyāyana the teacher,
Together they wept mournfully and knitted their brows:
'It is only recently in time that we, your disciples, died,
Truly, we do not know of your dear mother, reverend sir.
While we were alive, we committed numerous sins,

§Now, today, that we endure such suffering, we at last begin to feel regret;
Even though one has wives and concubines enough to fill the mountains and rivers,
Who among them would be willing to die in his place?
Whenever you are able to depart from the underworld gates,
Inform those sons and grandsons of ours who are still at home
That it is unnecessary to make coffins and caskets of white jade,
And that gold is spent in vain when it is buried in the grave.
Endless sorrow and sighs of resentment are ultimately to no avail,
For we hear not the sacred drum-music and songs to string accompaniment;
If they wish to obliterate the suffering of the dead,
§Nothing is better than cultivating blessedness to save these souls from darkness.'

'When you go back, reverend sir, pass this news to all men. Instruct them to create blessings whereby they may save the dead. Except for the Buddha and him alone, there is no other way to be saved. We wish, reverend sir, that you achieve perfect wisdom and nirvāṇa which, even on ordinary occasions, is not concealed and that it will serve as a conveyance for all living beings. May your blade of knowledge be assiduously sharpened and not be obstructed by the forest of moral affliction. Thus will your awe-inspiring mind be active everywhere throughout the world and so realize the great vow of all the buddhas. If we are to escape from this joyless place, it will be due to the universal bestowal of your compassionate regard, reverend sir.'

After Maudgalyāyana heard this, he went forward once again and, within a short period of time, he arrived at the seat of the General of the Five Ways.

This is the place where he asks for news of his mother:

§The General of the Five Ways had a frightful disposition,
The bright gleam of his golden armour intersected with the light from his sword;
To his left and his right, there were more than a million men,
And assistants who were continuously flying back and forth. **[724]**
His yelling and shouting was like the terrifying rumble of thunder,
His angry eyes resembled the dazzling flash of lightning.
There were some whose bellies were being rent and whose chests were being opened,
And others whose faces were being skinned alive;

§Although Maudgalyāyana was a holy person,
Even he was completely frightened out of his wits.
Maudgalyāyana wept mournfully as he thought of his dear mother,
He exercised his supernatural powers with the speed of the windborn clouds;
If you ask which is the most crucial place on the infernal paths,
None exceeds that of the great General of the Five Ways.
To the left and the right, a concentration of spears blocks the way,
To the east and west, there are more than ten thousand men with staves erect;
All together, they raise their eyes and gaze toward the southwest,
What they see is the imposing Spirit of the Five Ways.
He has been guarding this road for numerous aeons,
He fixes the type of punishment for thousands and ten thousands;
Starting with the very first one, each of them follows his own karmic conditions.
'The dear mother of this poor monk deviated from the practice of almsgiving
So that her souls were sent drifting along these infernal roads;
Whenever I ask which of the three mires leading to hell is the most painful place,
Everyone says that it is the devils' barrier of the Five Ways.
Men mill everywhere about the evil way to rebirth as an animal,
But the good way to the heavenly mansions is vacant morning and night;
All of those who are sinners must pass along this way,
It is my humble wish that you, General, will make a check of them.'
The General brought his palms together in salutation and said to the exemplar,
'You must not weep so mournfully that you do harm to your appearance.
The crowds on this road are usually as numberless as the sands of the Ganges,
But you have, on the spur of the moment, asked me if I know who Nīladhi is.
In Mount T'ai's regency, there are many sections dealing with names,
Investigations include heaven's bureaux and earth's offices;
Each of the overseers of documents also has these names, [**725**]
And all warrants which come down pass through this place.
Today, it just so happens that I, your disciple, am the officer of names,
I shall spend a few moments trying to check up on this for you, oh Teacher;

§If we are so fortunate as to come across her name,
§It will not be very difficult to locate her whereabouts.

'Have you seen a Lady Nīladhi or not?' the General asked his attendants to the left and right.

On the left side there was an officer-in-charge who informed the General: 'Three years ago, there was a Lady Nīladhi who was summoned away by a warrant sent up from the Avīci Hell. She is at this very moment in the Avīci Hell undergoing torture.'

When Maudgalyāyana heard these words, he spoke to the General who replied to him: 'Reverend sir, all sinners receive their sentences from the King and only then do they descend farther into hell.'

'Why didn't my mother see the King face to face?' Maudgalyāyana importuned him.

'Reverend sir,' replied the General, 'there are two kinds of people in the world who do not get to see the King's face. The first are those people who, during their lifetimes, cultivate the ten virtues and the five commandments. After they die, their souls are reborn in heaven. The second are those people who, during their lifetimes, do not cultivate good karma but commit a large number of sins. After their lives come to the end, they enter hell forthwith and they, too, do not get to see the King's face. Only those people who are half-good and half-bad are taken into the presence of the King to be sentenced. Then they are reincarnated, receiving their retribution in accordance with conditioning causes.'

This is the place where Maudgalyāyana, when he hears these words, goes forthwith to the various hells in search of his mother:

§Maudgalyāyana's tears fell, his thoughts wandered aimlessly,
The karmic retribution of sentient beings is like being tossed on the wind;
His dear mother had sunk into a realm of suffering,
Her souls had already by that time long since dissipated.
Iron discs continuously plunged into her body from out of the air,
Fierce fires, at all times, were burning beneath her feet;
Every place on her chest and belly had been stripped to shreds,
Every inch of her bones and flesh had charred to a pulp.
Bronze-coloured crows pecked at her heart ten thousand times over,
Molten iron poured on the top of her head a thousand repetitions;
One might ask whether the tree of knives up ahead were the most painful,
But can it compare with the cleaving mill which chops men's waists in two?

§Beyond description
Is the congealed fat and ground flesh so like a broad ferry-crossing;
There are wild mountains all around for several hundred miles, [**726**]
Which, from their jagged peaks, plummet downwards for a league.
Ten thousand iron lances are installed at the bottom,
A thousand layers of smoke and fire obscure the four gates;
Should one ask what sort of crimes are being punished herein,
§It is just for those who have killed others in the world of men.

After Maudgalyāyana had finished speaking, he went forward again. Before long, he came to another hell. 'Is there a Lady Nīladhi in this hell?' he asked the warden. 'It is because she is my mother that I have come hunting for her.'

'Everyone in this hell is a man, reverend sir,' replied the warden. 'There are no women at all. If you go on ahead and ask whether she is in the hell with the hill made of knives, I am sure that, through your inquiry, you will get to see her.'

Maudgalyāyana went forward and again he came to another hell. The left side of it was named Knife Hill and the right was named Sword Forest. Inside the hell, spear tips and swords were pointed from opposite sides and blood flowed copiously. He saw the warden driving countless sinners into this hell.

'What is the name of this hell?' Maudgalyāyana asked.

'This is the Knife Hill and Sword Forest Hell,' answered an ogre.

'What sinful karma did the sinners who are in this hell produce that they should have fallen into *this* hell?' Maudgalyāyana asked.

'While they were alive,' the warden informed him, 'the sinners who are in this hell trespassed upon and damaged the perpetual property of the assembly of monks. They befouled the monastery gardens, were given to eating the fruit of the orchards held in perpetuity by the monasteries, and stole firewood from the forests held in perpetuity by the monasteries.'

Here is the place where they are now being made to climb up the trees of swords with their hands causing them to be stripped bare of every limb and joint.

§The white bones on Knife Hill were strewn chaotically every which way,
The human heads in Sword Forest numbered in the thousands and ten
thousands;
Those who wish to avoid clambering up the hill of knives,
Should never pass by the monastery holdings without adding good
earth.

§Propagate fruit trees and present them to the monastery orchards,
Contribute seeds to increase the crops from the fields held in perpetuity.
Oh, you sinners! it is absolutely indescribable,
How you will endure punishment through aeons as numerous as the sands of the Ganges.
Even when the Buddhas achieve nirvāṇa, you still will not get out.
This hell stretches for hundreds of miles from the east to the west,
The sinners race through it wildly, bumping against each others' shoulders;
The winds of karma blow upon the fire which advances as it burns,
The gaolers holding pitchforks jab at them from behind.
Their bodies and heads are all like so many broken tiles, [**727**]
Their hands and feet immediately become like powder and froth;
Boiling iron, light leaping from its surface, is poured into their mouths,
Whomever it touches is pierced to the left and penetrated to the right.
Bronze arrows fly beside them and shoot into their eyes,
Wheels of swords come straight down, cutting them in mid-air;
It is said that it will be a thousand years before they are reborn as men,
§With iron rakes they are scraped together and revivified.

When Maudgalyāyana heard these words, he wept mournfully and sighed with grief. He went forward and asked the warden: 'Is there a Lady Nīladhi inside this hell?'

'What relationship has she to you, reverend sir?' the warden answered in reply.

'She is the dear mother of this poor monk,' Maudgalyāyana informed him.

'Reverend sir, there is no Lady Nīladhi inside this hell,' the warden told him. 'Inside those hells which are on ahead, there are some which are all for women. You ought to be able to find her there.'

After Maudgalyāyana had heard these words, he went forward again. He came to a hell which was about a league in depth. Great clouds of black smoke issued from it and malodorous vapours reeked to the heavens. He saw a horse-head ogre standing there arrogantly and holding a pitchfork in his hands.

'What is the name of this hell?' Maudgalyāyana asked him.

To which the ogre answered, 'This is the Copper Pillar and Iron Bed Hell.'

'Of the sinners who are in this hell,' asked Maudgalyāyana, 'what sinful karma did they create while they were alive that they should have fallen into this hell?'

To which the warden answered, 'While they were alive, be it the woman who led on the man or the man who led on the woman, they indulged their sexual passions on their parents' beds. Those who were disciples did so on their masters' beds, and slaves did so on their owners' beds. Thus they were bound to fall into this hell.'

The breadth from east to west was immeasurable and, in it, men and women complemented each other half-and-half.

§Women lay on the iron beds with nails driven through their bodies,
Men embraced the hot copper pillars, causing their chests to rot away;
The iron drills and long scissors were sharp as lance-tips and sword-edges,
The teeth of the ploughs with their sharp metal points were like awls.
When their intestines are empty, they are at once filled with hot iron pellets,
If they cry out that they are thirsty, molten iron is used to irrigate them;
The metal thorns which enter their bellies rend them like knives,
Swords and halberds shoot by wildly like stars in mid-air.
Knives scrape the flesh from their bones, pound by pound it breaks,
Swords cut the liver and intestines, inch by inch they are severed; **[728]**
Indescribable,
How opposite to each other are heaven and hell!
In heaven's mansions, morning and night there is resounding music,
But there is no one who can beg his way out of hell.
Although parents in this present existence may have blessings created for them,
They receive only one-seventh out of the total;
Even though the eastern sea be transformed into mulberry orchards,
§Those who are suffering punishment will still not be released.

After Maudgalyāyana had finished speaking, he again went forward. Before long, he came to another hell. 'Is there a Lady Nīladhi inside this hell or not?' he asked the warden.

To which the warden asked in reply, 'Is Lady Nīladhi your mother, reverend sir?'

'Yes, she is my dear mother,' Maudgalyāyana answered him.

'Three years ago,' the warden informed the venerable monk, 'there was a Lady Nīladhi who arrived in this hell. But she was summoned away by a warrant sent up from the Avīci Hell. She is at this very moment inside the Avīci Hell.'

Stifled with sorrow, Maudgalyāyana collapsed. It was quite a long while before he revived.

This is the place where he slowly goes forward and soon happens upon an ogre who is guarding the road:

§Maudgalyāyana was greatly distressed as he walked along,
The knives and swords by the side of the road were like wild grass;
He inclined his ear to listen for noises of the hells in the distance,
Abruptly, there was the howling sound of a strong wind.
For thinking of his dear mother, his heart was on the verge of breaking,
Walking without stopping along the road in front of him, he soon arrived;
Suddenly, he happened upon a prince of demons.
§Hand resting on his sword, he sat there blocking the main way.

Maudgalyāyana addressed him, saying: 'I am a poor monk,

§A disciple of the Tathāgata, Śākyamuni Buddha,
I have witnessed the three insights and have escaped from the cycle of birth and death.
How pathetic is my dear mother whose name was Nīladhi;
After she passed away, her souls descended into this place.
I have just now come from inspecting in order all the other hells,
Everyone whom I asked all said, "No, this is the wrong place –"
But lately they've been saying that she was taken into Avīci,
Surely, Great General, you are aware of this matter. **[729]**
Do not hesitate to tell me truthfully whether she is here or not,
For the most profound human kindness is that of suckling one's child;
When I hear talk of my mother, it pains me to the marrow of my bones,
Yet there is no one who can readily understand this poor monk's heart.'
Upon hearing these words, the demon's heart started to waver,
He spoke directly and, moreover, without mincing his words:
'Your filial devotion, reverend sir, is rare in all ages,
You have not shirked making a personal search along these infernal paths.
It seems as though there may be a Lady Nīladhi,
But I can't quite put my finger on what sort of appearance she has;
Poured steel has been used to make the outer walls, copper for the inner –
With a thunderous roar, the winds of karma abruptly begin to blow,
Turning the carcasses of those who enter to smithereens.
I advise you, oh Teacher, to return early to your own home,
In vain do you trouble yourself by seeking her in this place;
It would be better to leave early to see the Tathāgata –
§What good is it for you to beat your chest in vexation?'

When Maudgalyāyana heard of the difficulties of this hell, he immediately turned around. Hurling up his begging-bowl, he leaped into space. Before very long, he had arrived at the Teak Tree Grove. Three times he circled around the Buddha, then withdrew and sat off to one side. He looked reverently upon the countenance of the Honoured One, not averting his eyes for even a moment.

This is the place where he speaks to the World-Honoured:

§'For many days have I been negligent in my services to you, oh Tathāgata,
Because I was following my parents' traces to the ends of heaven and earth;
Only my father obtained rebirth in heaven above,
So I was unsuccessful in reuniting myself with my dear mother.
I have heard it said that she is suffering punishment in Avīci,
When I think of it, before I know what has happened, I become deeply aggrieved;
Due to the fierce fires, dragons, and snakes, it was difficult to go forward,
Nor was I able to come up with a suitable plan on the spur of the moment.
Your supernatural strength, oh Tathāgata, can move mountains and seas,
For which you are much admired by all living beings, **[730]**
"Always has it been that a subject in distress unburdens himself to his lord" –
How will I be able to see my dear mother again?'
The World-Honoured called out to him, saying 'Mahāmaudgalyāyana!
Do not be so mournful that you cry yourself heart-broken;
The sins of the world are tied to those who commit them like a string,
They are not stuck on clay-fashion by anyone else.
Quickly I take my metal-ringed staff and give it to you,
It can repel the eight difficulties and the three disasters;
If only you remember diligently to recite my name,
§The hells will certainly open up their doors for you.'

Having received the Buddha's awesome power, Maudgalyāyana flexed his body and went downwards as swiftly as a winged arrow. In an instant, he had arrived at the Avīci Hell. In mid-air, he met fifty ox-headed and horse-faced guards. They were ogres and demons with teeth like knife-trees, mouths similar to blood-basins, voices like the peal of thunder, and eyes like the flash of lightning. They were headed for duty in the Bureau of the Underworld. When they met Maudgalyāyana, they informed him from a distance: 'Don't come any farther, reverend sir! This is not a good way; it is the road to hell. In the middle of the black smoke on the western side are all the poisonous vapours of hell. Should you be sucked up by them, reverend sir, you will turn into ashes and dust.'

This is the place:

'Haven't you heard tell, reverend sir, of the Avīci Hell?

§Even iron and steel, should they pass through it, would be disastrously affected;
If you're wondering where this hell is situated,
It's over there on the west side in the midst of the black smoke.'
Maudgalyāyana repeated the Buddha's name as often as there are sands in the Ganges,
And said to himself, 'The hells are my original home –'
He wiped his tears in mid-air, and shook the metal-ringed staff,
Ghosts and spirits were mowed down on the spot like stalks of hemp.
Streams of cold sweat crisscrossed their bodies, dampening them like rain,
Dazed and unconscious, they groaned in self-pity;
They let go of the three-cornered clubs which were in their hands,
They threw far away the six-tined pitchforks which were on their shoulders.
'The Tathāgata has sent me to visit my mother,
And to rescue her from suffering in the Avīci Hell.'
Not to be stayed, Maudgalyāyana passed by them with a leap,
§The gaolers just looked at each other, not daring to stand in his way. **[731]**

Maudgalyāyana walked forward and came to a hell. When he was something over a hundred paces away from it, he was sucked in by the fiery gasses and nearly tumbled over. It was the Avīci Hell with lofty walls of iron which were so immense that they reached to the clouds. Swords and lances bristled in ranks, knives and spears clustered in rows. Sword-trees reached upward for a thousand fathoms with a clattering flourish as their needle-sharp points brushed together. Knife-mountains soared ten thousand rods in a chaotic jumble of interconnecting cliffs and crags. Fierce fires throbbed, seeming to leap about the entire sky with a thunderous roar. Sword-wheels whirled, seeming to brush the earth with the dust of starry brightness. Iron snakes belched fire, their scales bristling on all sides. Copper dogs breathed smoke, barking impetuously in every direction. Metal thorns descended chaotically from mid-air, piercing the chests of the men. Awls and augers flew by every which way, gouging the backs of the women. Iron rakes flailed at their eyes, causing red blood to flow to the west. Copper pitchforks jabbed at their loins until white fat oozed to the east. Thereupon, they were made to crawl up the knife-mountains and enter the furnace coals. Their skulls were smashed to bits, their bones and flesh decomposed; tendons and skin snapped, liver and gall broke. Ground flesh spurted and splattered beyond the four gates; congealed blood drenched and drooked the pathways which run through the black clods of hell. With wailing voices, they called out to heaven – moan, groan. The roar of thunder shakes the earth – rumble, bumble. Up above are clouds and smoke which tumble-jumble; down below are iron spears which jangle-tangle. Goblins with arrows for feathers chattered-scattered; birds with copper beaks wildly-widely called. There were more than several ten thousands of gaolers and all were ox-headed and horse-faced.

This is the place where, though your heart be made of iron or stone, you too will lose your wits and tremble with fear:

§Staff in hand, Maudgalyāyana went forward, listening,
As he thought about Avīci, he became more and more preoccupied;
Inside all of the other hells, there are periods of rest,
But within this Avīci, they never see a pause.
Crowds as numerous as the sands of the Ganges simultaneously enter,
Together their bodies are transformed into a single shape;
Supposing that, there being no one else, someone entered alone,
His body itself would fill up the surrounding iron walls.
Relentlessly, lamentlessly, iron weapons are flourished;
Querulous, perilous, the cloud-filled sky is turbulent,
Howling, growling, the wind which blasts the ground is terrifying.
There are long snakes which glisten and have three heads that are black,
There are large birds which glare and have pairs of wings that are dark-green;
In ten thousand red-hot ovens, heaped-up coals are fanned,
From a thousand tongues of crimson flames, shooting sparks explode.
On the east and the west, iron augers stab at the muscles of their chests,
To the left and the right, copper scissors puncture the pupils of their eyes;
Iron spears descend chaotically like the wind and the rain, **[732]**
Molten iron from out of mid-air seems to be a baptismal sprinkling.

§Lackaday! Welladay! How difficult it is to bear!
§And to top it all off, long spikes are lowered intc their bellies and backs.

§When Maudgalyāyana saw this, he cried out 'Horrors!'
Steadfastly he invoked the Buddha many thousands of times.
Though one breathe the poisonous vapours borne on the wind at a distance,
§Right while you're watching, his body will become a pile of ashes.

§With one shake of his staff, the bars and locks fell from the black walls,
On the second shake, the double leaves of the main gate flew open;
Before Maudgalyāyana there even had a chance to call out,
The gaolers came right out, carrying pitchforks in their hands.
'About who, reverend sir, do you wish to find information?'
The gates in the walls of this hell were ten thousand leagues wide,
What sort of person could open and close them so easily?
Inside, knives and swords cluttered with a brilliant light,
The people undergoing punishment were remorsefully sad;
Great fires flamed and flared making the entire ground luminous,
Misty fog spread everywhere, filling the sky with blackness.
'Suddenly we saw an exemplar standing here in hell,
And, furthermore, one with whom we have never been acquainted;
From the looks of things, it would appear that there is no one else,
§It must be due to the compassionate power of the Three Jewels.'

'For what reason, reverend sir, did you open the gates of this hell?' the warden asked him.

'If this poor monk didn't open them, who would?' he replied. 'The World-Honoured entrusted me with an object for opening them.'

'What object did he entrust to you for opening them?' asked the warden.

'He entrusted me with his twelve-ringed metal staff to open them,' Maudgalyāyana informed the warden.

'For what purpose have you come here, reverend sir?' a gaoler asked again.

'The name of this poor monk's mother is Lady Nīladhi,' Maudgalyāyana informed him. 'I have come in order to see if I might find her.'

Upon hearing this, the warden went back inside hell and climbed up on a tall tower from which he signalled with a white flag and beat a steel drum.

'Is there a Lady Nīladhi inside the first compartment?' he called out.

There was none in the first compartment, so he went on to the second compartment. The warden signalled with a black flag and beat a steel drum.

'Is there a Lady Nīladhi inside the second compartment?' Neither was there any in the second compartment, so he went on to the third compartment. He signalled with a yellow flag and beat a steel drum.

'Is there a Lady Nīladhi inside the third compartment?' Again there was none. So he went on to the fourth compartment and again there was none. When he reached **[733]** the fifth compartment and asked, the answer there was also 'none'. He went on to the sixth compartment where again the answer was: 'No Lady Nīladhi.' The gaoler walked to the seventh compartment where he signalled with a green flag and beat a steel drum.

'Is there a Lady Nīladhi inside the seventh compartment?'

At that very moment, Lady Nīladhi was inside the seventh compartment. All up and down her body, there were forty-nine long spikes nailing her to a steel bed. She dared not respond.

The warden repeated the question: 'Is there a Lady Nīladhi in the seventh compartment or not?'

'If you're hunting for Lady Nīladhi, this sinful body is she.'

'Why didn't you speak up earlier?'

'I was afraid, warden, that you'd take me away to another place to receive punishment so I didn't dare to respond.'

'There is a Buddhist monk outside the gate,' the warden informed her. 'His hair and beard have been shaved off and he wears a monastic robe. He claims to be your son and that is why he has come to visit you.'

After Lady Nīladhi heard these words, she thought for quite a while and then replied: 'Warden, I don't have any son who left home to become a monk. Isn't there some mistake?'

Upon hearing this, the warden turned around and walked back to the tall tower. 'Reverend sir!' he said. 'Why do you pretend to recognize a sinner in hell as your mother? For what reason do you tell such a lie?'

When Maudgalyāyana heard these words, tears of sadness fell like rain. 'Warden,' he said, 'when I explained things just now, my message was garbled. When I, poor monk, was a child, my name was Turnip. After my father and mother died, I surrendered myself to the Buddha and left home to become a monk. The title given me upon receiving the tonsure was Mahāmaudgalyāyana. Do not be angry, warden. Go and ask her once again.'

After hearing these words, the warden turned around and went to the seventh compartment. 'Sinner!' he announced. 'As a child, the name of the monk outside the gate was Turnip. After his parents died, he surrendered himself to the Buddha and left home to become a monk. The title given him upon receiving the tonsure was Mahāmaudgalyāyana.'

'If the name of the monk outside the gate as a child was Turnip, then he is my son,' said Lady Nīladhi when she heard his words. 'He is the precious darling of this sinful body.'

When the warden heard Lady Nīladhi say this, he helped her up by pulling out the forty-nine long spikes. With steel chains locked about her waist and surrounded by gyves, she was driven outside of the gate.

This is the place where mother and son see each other:

§The interlocking links of the gyves were as numerous as gathering clouds;
A thousand years of punishment is beyond comprehension,
Trickles of blood flowed from the seven openings of her head.
Fierce flames issued from the inside of his mother's mouth,
At every step, metal thorns out of space entered her body;
She clanked and clattered like the sound of five hundred broken-down chariots,
How could her waist and backbone bear up under the strain?
Gaolers carrying pitchforks guarded her to the left and the right,
Ox-headed guards holding chains stood on the east and the west;
Stumbling at every other step, she came forward, **[734]**
Wailing and weeping, Maudgalyāyana embraced his mother.
Crying, he said: 'It was because I am unfilial,
You, dear mother, were innocently caused to drop into the triple mire of hell;
Families which accumulate goodness have a surplus of blessings,
High Heaven does not destroy in this manner those who are blameless.
In the old days, mother, you were handsomer than P'an An,
But now you have suddenly become haggard and worn;
I have heard that in hell there is much suffering,
Now, today, I finally realize, "Ain't it hard, ain't it hard."
Ever since I met with the misfortune of father's and your deaths,
I have not been remiss in sacrificing daily at your graves;
Mother, I wonder whether or not you have been getting any food to eat,
In such a short time, your appearance has become completely haggard.'
Now that Maudgalyāyana's mother had heard his words,
'Alas!' she cried, her tears intertwining as she struck and grabbed at herself:
'Only yesterday, my son, I was separated from you by death,

§Who could have known that today we would be reunited?
While your mother was alive, she did not cultivate blessings,
But she did commit plenty of all the ten evil crimes;
Because I didn't take your advice at that time, my son,
My reward is the vastness of this Avīci Hell.
In the old days, I used to live quite extravagantly,
Surrounded by fine silk draperies and embroidered screens;
How shall I be able to endure these hellish torments,
And then to become a hungry ghost for a thousand years?
A thousand times, they pluck the tongue from out of my mouth,
Hundreds of passes are made over my chest with a steel plough;
My bones, joints, tendons, and skin are everywhere broken,
They need not trouble with knives and swords since I fall to pieces by myself.
In the twinkling of an eye, I die a thousand deaths,
But, each time, they shout at me and I come back to life;
Those who enter this hell all suffer the same hardships, **[735]**
It doesn't matter whether you are rich or poor, lord or servant.
Though you diligently sacrificed to me while you were at home,
It only got you a reputation in the village for being filial;
Granted that you did sprinkle libations of wine upon my grave,
But it would have been better for you to copy a single line of a sūtra.'
Maudgalyāyana choked and sobbed, his tears fell like rain,
Right away, he turned around and petitioned the warden:
'Although I, poor monk, did leave home so that I could take orders,
How can I rescue my mother with my small strength?
One should cover up for the faults of those to whom he has mourning obligations,
This has been the teaching of sages and saints since ancient times;
My only wish, warden, is that you release my mother,
And I myself will bear the endless suffering for her.'
But the warden was a man of unyielding temperament,
He glared silently and vacantly at Maudgalyāyana;
'Although I, your disciple, do serve as a warden,
All of the decisions come from the Impartial King.
If your mother has sinned, she will receive the punishment for it,
And if you, oh Teacher, have sinned, you will bear the punishment for it;
The records of sins on the gold tablets and jade tokens cannot be wiped or washed away,
In the end, there is no one who can readily alter them.

§It is simply that, today, the time has already arrived for her to be punished,
I must lead her back to the hall of punishments and apply the knife and spear;
If, reverend sir, you wish to obtain your mother's release,
You cannot do better than return home and burn precious incense.'
The words of Maudgalyāyana's mother sounded plaintive,
But gaolers holding pitchforks prodded her from both sides;
Just as she was about to reach the front of the hell, she nearly fell over,
§Quickly she called out long and sad, 'Take good care of yourself!'

With one of her hands, Lady Nīladhi held fast to the gate of hell and turned back to gaze at him. 'Take good care of yourself!' she said. [**736**] 'Oh precious darling of this sinful body!'

§'In the old days, your mother behaved avariciously,
I failed to provide myself with grace for the karmic retribution of the next life;
The things which I said deceived heaven and denied hell,
I slaughtered pigs and goats on a grand scale to sacrifice to ghosts and spirits.
My only concern was for the pleasures of the moment,
How could I have known that on these infernal paths they flog lost souls?
Now that I have already suffered the hardships of hell,
I finally learned to awaken to repentance of my own person.
But even though I do repent, what good does it do me?
"There's no use crying over spilt milk", so says the well-known proverb;
When shall I be able to escape from this horrible suffering?
And how can I dare to hope that I'll ever again be a human being?
You, oh Teacher, are a disciple of the Buddha,
And are capable of understanding the kindness of your parents;
If, one day, you should attain the enlightenment of a sage,
Do not forget your mother who suffers so grievously here in hell.'
After Maudgalyāyana had watched his mother depart,
He wished with all his heart that he could destroy himself;
Then, like Mount T'ai collapsing, he fell to the ground and pummelled himself,
Blood splattered from all the seven openings of his head.
'Mother, do not go back in for a while yet!' he said to her,
'Turn back and listen again to a word from your son;

§The affection between a mother and her son is innate,
The kindness of her suckling him is a natural impulse.
Today, mother, you and I shall take leave of each other,
No one can tell for certain when we shall meet again;
How can I bear to listen to this horrible suffering? –
Sharp is the pain in my heart from the anxiety which weighs upon me.
Hell does not allow one to substitute for another,
All I can do is weep and wail and state my grievance loudly;
§Since there is nothing at all I can do to save you, [**737**]
'I too, will follow you, mother, and myself die before the gate of hell.'

Maudgalyāyana watched his mother go back into hell. Grief-stricken and broken-hearted, he sobbed until his voice became hoarse. Then, as though he were five Mount T'ais collapsing, he fell to the ground and pummelled himself. Blood flowed with a gush from all of the seven openings of his head. After quite a long time, he died, and then he revived again. He got up by pressing against the ground with both hands.

This is the place where, having rearranged his clothing, he leaps into space and goes to the World-Honoured.

§Maudgalyāyana's consciousness was all hazy,
It seemed he could not hear people's voices, they were so indistinct;
After quite a long time, he moaned deeply and came to his senses,
Hurling up his begging-bowl, he leaped into space and called upon the World-Honoured.
Facing the Buddha, Maudgalyāyana stated his bitter grievances,
He spoke both of the knife-mountains and of the sword-trees;
'I received supernatural strength from you, oh Buddha, and borrowed your surplus majesty,
Thus was I enabled to visit my dear mother in Avīci.
Smoke and flames flared up from the fires atop the iron walls,
The forests of sword blades were in ranks many ten thousands deep;
Human fat and ground flesh mixed together with molten copper,
The spattering flesh collected in pools of coagulated blood.
How can my dear mother's features endure such harsh treatment?
The whole night long she confronts the assault of knives and swords;
Her white bones climb the sword-trees ten thousand times over,
Her red face ascends the knife-mountains, making hundreds of passes.
In all the world, what is the most important thing?
It is the affection of one's parents and their kindness most profound;

§You, oh Tathāgata, are the compassionate father and mother of all
living beings,
I beseech you to illuminate this ignorant and trifling heart of mine!'
The Tathāgata was by nature of great mercy and compassion,
When he heard these words, he knitted his brows with sorrow:
'All living beings emerge and disappear in the net of transmigration,
Just like chaff-gnats which have rushed against a spider's web.
In times past, many were the sins your mother committed,
As a result, her souls fell headlong into Avīci; **[738]**
For these crimes of hers, an aeon will elapse before she can get out,
An ordinary person, one who is not a Buddha, cannot understand this.'
The Buddha then summoned Ānanda and the company of his followers:
§'I will go to the infernal regions and save her myself!'

The Tathāgata led the eight classes of supernatural beings who surrounded him, front and back.

This is the place where, radiating light and shaking the earth, they rescue the sufferers in hell:

§The Tathāgata in his holy wisdom was, by nature, impartial,
Out of mercy and compassion, he rescued all the beings of hell;
A numberless host composed of spirits of the eight classes,
Following each other, they went forward as a group.
Such pomp and circumstance! –
In heaven above and on earth below, it was an incomparable sight;
Sinking on the left, disappearing on the right,
They were like mountains projecting high above the clouds.
Precipitous – precarious –
Heaven's mansions and hell's halls opened their doors at once;
Like driving rain – like rumbling thunder –
They made as full a circle as the moon rising over the ocean.
Commandingly, he walked by himself with a lion's pace,
Confidently, he moved alone with an elephant king's gait;
Amidst the clouds, there were strains of the 'Willow Branch' tune,
In space, there fluttered 'Plum Blossoms Falling'.
Sovereign Śakra went forward carrying a jade token,
Brahmā followed behind holding a jade tablet;
It was a sight indescribably indescribable! –
The Tathāgata, with supernatural strength, rescued them from the gates
of Hades.
To his left and right, there were deities and the host of the eight spirit
realms,

§To his east and west, there were attendant guards and the generals of the four directions;
Between his brows appeared a tiny hair that had a thousand different forms,
Behind his neck was a halo of five-coloured clouds.
Saturated by the light, hell dissolved completely,
The sword-trees and knife-forests crumbled as though they were dust; **[739]**
Saturated by the light, all of the gaolers fell to their knees,
They joined their palms in heartfelt respect and prostrated themselves at his feet.
This day, the Buddha's mercy and compassion were aroused,
He destroyed hell, leaving it completely in ruins;
The steel pellets were transformed into luminous jewels,
The knife-hills were transformed into sheets of lapis lazuli.
Molten copper was changed into the water of merit and virtue;
Meandering round pools and in currents, it was refreshing and clear,
Mandarin ducks and other waterfowl nestled together like beads on a necklace.
Every night, emerald mists lifted from the red waves,
Every morning, purple clouds rose above the green trees;
All of the sinners obtained rebirth in heaven above,
There was only Maudgalyāyana's mother who became a hungry ghost.
Everything within hell was utterly transformed,
§And it was all because of the might of the holy Śākyamuni Buddha.

Having been granted the awesome power of the Buddha, Maudgalyāyana was enabled to visit his mother. But the roots of her sin were deep and fast; the karmic forces difficult to eliminate. Thus, although she was freed of the torments of hell, she fell upon the path of hungry ghosts. Here the sorrow and suffering were dissimilar, for misery and joy were completely polarized. When placed next to her previous existence, the difference was intensified hundreds, thousands, even ten thousands of times. Her throat was like the eye of a needle, through which a drop of water could not pass. Her head seemed to be Mount T'ai, which the three rivers could hardly fill. She never even heard the words 'broth' or 'water'. Months would accumulate and years would pass while she endured the miseries of hunger and emaciation. She might see in the distance some clear, cool water but, when she came near, it would turn into a river of pus. Even though she obtained delicious food and tasty meals, they would immediately be transformed into fierce flames.

'Mother, now you are so distressed by hunger that your life is as though it were hanging by a thread. If your plight does not arouse in me compassion and mercy, how can I be called a filial son? Once we are separated by the road between life and death, it will be hard to expect that we shall meet again. If I wish to rescue you from this precarious danger, the urgency of the situation demands that I not delay. The way of those who have left home to become monks is to rely upon the donations of the faithful to maintain themselves. Even though you had a constant source of food and drink, I am afraid that it would be difficult for you to digest.

'I shall take leave of you now, mother, and go towards the centre of Rājagṛha. There I will get some rice and then come to see you again.'

Maudgalyāyana took leave of his mother. He hurled up his begging-bowl and leaped into the air. Within an instant, he had already arrived in the centre of Rājagṛha. As he went from house to house begging for rice, he walked up to the gate of a householder.

This is the place where the householder detains and questions Maudgalyāyana when he sees that he is begging for food at the wrong time:

'The morning meal is already over, reverend sir. Since the time for eating has already past, for what purpose do you intend to use this food which you are begging?'

Maudgalyāyana replied to the householder: **[740]**

§'After this humble monk's mother had passed away,
Her souls fell straightaway into the Avīci Hell;
Recently, I obtained her release with the help of the Tathāgata,
Her body was like a bunch of dried bones, her breath was wispy.
This poor monk's heart was rent in many tiny pieces,
How can anyone else understand the pain which afflicts me? –
Even though I realize that it is inappropriate, I am begging out of time.
Because it is to give to my dear mother to feed her.'
When the householder heard these words, he was greatly startled,
Reflecting on the impermanence of things, he began to feel unhappy.
'Her golden countenance is forever deprived of being made up with rouge and mascara,
Her jade-like appearance has no cause for entering the dressing-room.
We sing for a while – we are happy for a while –
Human life is frittered away like a sputtering candle
We seek not the mansions of heaven where we could enjoy happiness,
Even though all we hear of is how numerous are the sinners in hell;

§Sometimes to eat – sometimes to clothe ourselves –
We should not imitate those stupid people who accumulate much.
It would be better to create many good works for the future,
For who can guarantee that his life will be preserved from morning to evening?
While two people are looking at each other, death steals upon them,
After which their riches are certainly no more to be grudged by their bodies.
When, one fine morning, we breathe our last and enter our eternal coffins,
Who knows what good are the libations sprinkled vainly upon our graves?
The wise man uses his money to create many blessings,
The fool spends his gold by purchasing fields and houses.
Throughout our lives, we search laboriously for riches,
But, after we die, it is all divided up by someone else.'
When the householder heard these words, he was suddenly surprised,
It is not often that one has the opportunity to make offerings to a monk;
Hurriedly, he urged his assistants not to delay,
They brought rice from inside the house to give to the examplar. **[741]**
'From the sudden and complete dissolution of hell,
The ineffableness of the Buddhas is clearly perceived' –
The householder held in his hand the rice which he had obtained,
And gave it over to the exemplar while making a grand vow:
'May this serve not only for you to present to your dear parent, reverend sir,
But may it serve, as well, to fill all the sinners in the whole of hell!'
Maudgalyāyana was successful in begging for table-rice;
He picked up his begging-bowl and took it to present to his dear mother.
Thereupon, he walked as far as the deserted outskirts of the city;
§Holding a golden spoon in his hand, he fed her himself.

Although she had undergone the hardships of hell, Lady Nīladhi's avarice had, after all, not been eradicated. When she saw her son bringing the bowl of rice, the mere expectation of his approach excited her greed.

'The monk who is coming is my own son! He has fetched rice for me from the world of men. The whole lot of you others shouldn't get any ideas! I've got to appease my own hunger right now. There won't be enough extra to help anybody else!'

Maudgalyāyana offered up the rice which was in the begging-bowl.

His mother, afraid that it might be snatched away, raised her eyes and looked about continuously on all four sides. She shielded the bowl with her left hand and scooped up the food with her right. But, before it entered her mouth, the food was transformed into a fierce fire. Although the householder's vow was a solemn one, unfortunately the obstructiveness of her greed was even greater.

Seeing his mother like this, Maudgalyāyana felt as though his heart were being sliced with a knife. 'The strength of my doctrinal understanding is still inferior. I am a wretched person of little wisdom. The only thing I can do is address my questions to the World-Honoured. Then I shall surely learn the way to extricate her.'

Look, now, at the place where he gives his mother the rice:

§When the Lady saw the rice, she went forward to receive it,
Because of her avarice, she senselessly bickered before she began to eat:
'My son brought this rice from far away in the world of men,
I intend to take it to cure my own bottomless pit;
If I eat it all by myself, it still looks like it won't be enough to satisfy me,
All you others should give up your ideas of getting any – go slow with your hopes!'
The karmic force of Nīladhi's avarice was strong,
§As the food entered from her mouth into her throat, fierce flames erupted.

When Maudgalyāyana

§Saw the rice his mother was eating become a fierce fire,
He pummelled himself all over and fell to the ground like a mountain collapsing;
Blood began to flow from both his ears and his nostrils,
Tearfully, he cried out to high heaven: 'Oh, my mother!' **[742]**
This rice was given as charity in the world of mortal men,
Above the rice, there was a spirit-light seven feet high;
They took it to be a savoury, flavoursome sustenance,
But before the food entered her mouth, it had already turned into fire.
Her appetite was avaricious and her heart had not changed,
With the result that, year after year, she underwent punishment;
Now he was painfully afflicted that he had no further means to save her,
But karmic retribution did not allow that one substitute for another.
The people of the world should not entertain jealous envy,
For, once they fall into the three mires of hell, the punishment is endless;
Before the savoury rice had even entered her throat,

§Fiery flames began to issue from his mother's mouth.
Though the sins of the mundane world fill the universe,
It is this very sin of avarice which is most frequent;
Unexpectedly, the flames issued from her mouth,
Which shows clearly that karmic retribution does not devolve upon others.
One should always exercise impartiality toward everything,
And should, furthermore, single-mindedly recite the name of Amitābha;
If only one can rid himself of his greedy heart,
The heavenly mansions of the Pure Land will be gained at his pleasure.
'My obedient son,' Nīladhi called out to him,
'I cannot discard this sinful body by myself;
If I am not favoured by *your* exercise of filiality, oh Teacher,
Who would be willing to exert themselves to save your mother?
I saw the rice but, before I could scoop it into my mouth,
It unexpectedly burst into flames and burned me;
Thinking over in my mind this display of avarice,
It simply must be due to the leftover ill-effects of my past.
You, oh Teacher, who are your mother's obedient son,
§Give me some cold water to relieve the hollowness in my stomach.'

Maudgalyāyana listened to his mother's request for water, her breath catching and her voice harsh. While he was considering what to do, he suddenly recalled that, south of the city of Rājagṛha, there was a great river. Its waters were so wide as to be boundless and it was called by the name Ganges. **[743]** Surely it would be sufficient to rescue his mother from the torment of her fiery calamity.

When the living beings of the mortal world saw the river, to them its waters were refreshing and cool. When the various deities saw the river, to them it was a precious pond of greenglass. When fish and turtles saw this river, to them it was either torrent or marsh. But when Nīladhi saw the river, to her it was a stream of pus and fiery flames. She walked up to the water's edge and, without waiting for her son to utter the requisite vows, immediately supported herself against the bank with her left hand in consequence of her selfishness and scooped up the water with her right hand in consequence of her greed. Her avaricious heart was simply not to be restrained. Before the water entered her mouth, it had already become fire.

Maudgalyāyana had seen how the rice his mother started to eat had become a fiery fire and how the water she was drinking became a fiery fire. He beat his chest and struck his breast, moaning sorrowfully and weeping. He came before the Buddha and circled three times around him. Then, standing off to one side, he addressed him with these words: 'Your disciple's mother, oh World-Honoured, did many things which were not good, and so she fell down into the three mires. Having been blessed by your mercy and compassion, I was able to rescue my mother from her suffering there. But now the rice which she eats becomes fire and the water she drinks becomes fire. How can I rescue my mother from the torment of her fiery calamity?'

'Maudgalyāyana!' the World-Honoured called out to him, 'it is true that your mother, up to now, has not been able to eat any food. She will obtain food to eat only if you observe annually, on the fifteenth day of the seventh month, the provision of a purgatorian feast on a large scale.'

Maudgalyāyana looked at his starving mother and then spoke: 'World-Honoured, may it not be held monthly on the thirteenth and fourteenth? Must she wait each year for the fifteenth day of the seventh month before she gets any food to eat?'

'Not only is this the prescribed date on which to provide a purgatorian feast on a large scale for your mother,' the World-Honoured replied to him, 'it is also the day on which those who have been sitting in meditation in the monasteries end their summer retreat, the day on which arhats achieve the fruit of their religious practice, the day on which Devadatta's sins are annihilated, the day on which King Yama rejoices, and the day on which all hungry ghosts everywhere get to eat their fill.'

Having received the Buddha's clear instructions, Maudgalyāyana went to the front of a temple which was near the city of Rājagṛha. There he read aloud the Mahāyana sūtras and performed the good deed of providing a purgatorian feast on a large scale. It was from these basins of food that his mother was finally able to eat a full meal. But after she received the food, he did not see his mother again.

Maudgalyāyana searched for his mother everywhere but could not find her. Tears of sorrow falling like rain, he came before the Buddha and circled three times around him. Then, standing off to one side, he joined his palms in reverent greeting and knelt respectfully. 'World-Honoured,' he addressed him, 'when my mother ate rice, it became fire; when she drank water, it became fire. Having been blessed by your compassion and mercy, I was able to rescue my mother from the torment of her fiery calamity. But, ever since the fifteenth day of the seventh month when she received the meal, we haven't seen each other again. Perhaps she has fallen into hell. Or perhaps she went towards the path of hungry ghosts?'

'Neither has your mother fallen into hell nor is she on the path of hungry ghosts,' the World-Honoured replied. 'Having obtained the merit of your reading the sūtras and the good deed of providing a purgatorian feast, your mother's body as a hungry ghost has been transformed. She has gone into the centre of Rājagṛha where she has taken on the body of a black dog. If you wish to see your mother, go from house to house begging for food, seeing that your mind and actions are impartial and that you do not question whether they are rich or poor. When you walk up to the gate of a certain very wealthy householder, a black dog will come out. It will tug at your cassock and, holding it in its mouth, will make human sounds. That will be your mother.'

Having been granted the Buddha's clear instructions, Maudgalyāyana immediately took up his begging-bowl in one hand and a basin in the other and went in search of his mother. Without asking whether they were for the rich or the poor, he walked a complete circle through the city's wards and alleys, but nowhere did he see his mother. **[744]** He walked up to the gate of a certain householder where he saw a black dog which came out from the house. It tugged at Maudgalyāyana's cassock and, holding it in its mouth, started to make human sounds.

'Oh, obedient son of your mother!' it said, 'if you could rescue your mother from the infernal paths of hell, why do you not rescue her from the torment of having the body of a dog?'

'My dear mother!' Maudgalyāyana addressed her, 'because your son was unfilial, you met with misfortune and fell into the three mires. But wouldn't you prefer to be living here in the form of a dog rather than existing as a hungry ghost?'

'Obedient son!' his mother called out, 'I have received this body of a dog and my dumbness as a due reward. I spend my life walking, standing, sitting, or lying. When I'm hungry, I eat human excrement in the latrines. When I'm thirsty, I drink the water which drips from the eaves to relieve the hollow feeling. In the morning, I hear the householder invoking the Three Treasures. In the evening, I hear his wife reciting the esteemed sūtras. I would rather have the body of a dog and endure the filth of the earth than hear in my ears the name of hell.'

Maudgalyāyana led his mother away to the front of a Buddhist stupa in Rājagṛha. There, for seven days and seven nights, they read aloud the Mahāyana sūtras, confessing and repenting, and reciting the prohibitions. Availing herself of this merit, she was transformed out of her dog-body. She sloughed off her dogskin and hung it on a tree. Then, getting back her body of a woman, she was once again in complete possession of a perfect human form.

'Mother,' Maudgalyāyana said to her, 'it is difficult to obtain a human body, difficult to be born in the Central Kingdom, difficult to hear the Law of the Buddha, and difficult to manifest a good mind. I call upon you, mother, now that you have regained human form, swiftly to cultivate blessings.'

Maudgalyāyana took his mother to the twin Sāl trees. He circled three times around the Buddha and then, standing off to one side, addressed him in these words: 'Oh World-Honoured! Would you look over for me the path of my mother's karma up to the present, examining it from the very beginning to see if she has any other sins?'

The World-Honoured was not opposed to Maudgalyāyana's request. Observing her from the standpoint of the three types of karma, he found that there were no further individual sins.

Seeing that his mother's sins had been annihilated, Maudgalyāyana rejoiced greatly at heart. 'Mother,' he said to her,

§'Let us go back!
The world of mortal men is not fit to remain in;
Birth, life, death –
It wasn't really a place to stay in anyway.
§It is the Kingdom of Buddha in the West which is the finest!'

Deities and dragons were moved to lead the way in front and heavenly maidens came to welcome her. She was received forthwith into the Trayastriṁśā Heaven to enjoy happiness.

In the very beginning, the Buddha uttered the stanzas with which he converted the first five disciples. At the time *(the time this sūtra was preached)* there were 84,000 Bodhisattvas, 84,000 monks, 84,000 laymen, and 84,000 laywomen, all circling around the Buddha and making obeisance to him. They rejoiced in the receptivity and obedience of their faith.

Transformation Text on Mahāmaudgalyāyana, One Scroll

Written on the sixteenth day of the fourth month in the seventh year of the *Chen-ming* reign-period by Hsüeh An-chün, lay student at the Pure Land Monastery.

CHANG PAO-TA's copy

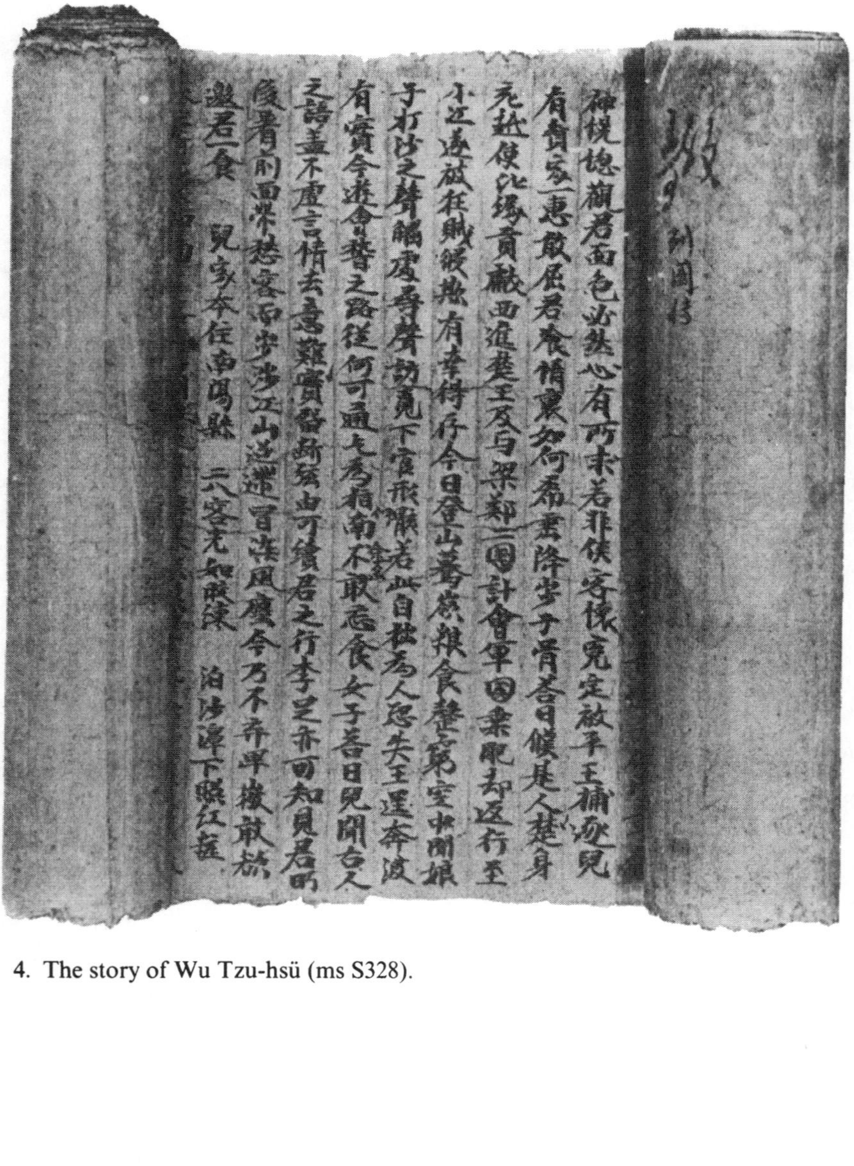

4. The story of Wu Tzu-hsü (ms S328).

3

WU TZU-HSÜ

[The Story of Wu Tzu-hsü]

Of old, when the Chou Dynasty was on its last legs, the six braves began to contest among themselves and the eight barbarians vied with each other in invading the realm.

In the south, there was King P'ing of the Kingdom of Ch'u who, reposing in benevolence, exercised a civilizing influence over his people. There were attendant upon the King's court ten thousand principalities. His charismatic sway spread afar, enabling him to exercise a commanding influence over the sundry states. For external affairs, he sponsored a deliberative body called the 'Bright Terrace' and, for internal matters, he ascended the palace throne. He pacified the area to the south as far as the Gate of Heaven; his northernmost frontier pass was at Huai-hai; his frontiers to the east went as far as the sun and moon; to the west, his borders were the Buddhist kingdoms. He opened up mountains and rivers to correct the earth's axis and adjusted the twelve semitones so as to differentiate *yin* and *yang*. When he mounted the throne, it brought stability to the Imperial Gate; when he shook the Yellow Dragon standard, his assistants came to him. The six dragons sent down from heaven good fortune; the symbols of earth betokened auspicious harvests. Neither did the wind make the branches of trees rustle nor did the rain break up the clods of earth. The avenues, boulevards, streets, and roads, neatly and impressively laid out, were broad and level. Indeed, he had made a name for himself that would last ten thousand generations.

The Prime Minister of Ch'u was surnamed Wu and named Shê. Possessed of literary and military ability, he was dedicated to preserving the altars of Ch'u. He held a three-foot long sword in his hand and entrusted his emotions to his six-foot frame. Ten thousand nations willingly received his commands. He was honest and straightforward in conduct, and faithful and true to ceremonial usages and rules. His opinions were as lofty as the wind and the clouds; his heart was as hard as iron and steel. Of constant purpose and unfailing assiduity, he was attentive both morning and night. Wu Shê served his ruler with dedication as his ideal. Through obedience, he enabled his ruler to be successful. But, if even the monarch were tyrannous, Wu Shê would rebuke him without regard to his superior status.

Now, Wu Shê had two sons who were in the service of their lord. The younger was called Tzu-hsü and the elder, Tzu-shang. The one was serving in the kingdom of Liang and the other in the state of Cheng. Both were loyal and far-seeing men.

The Crown Prince of Ch'u was a grown man but had not yet taken a wife. The King inquired of his officials, 'Who has a daughter worthy of being the Prince's consort? We have heard that, "if a country be without an heir-apparent, half of the land will be barren. Though the flowing springs of the Eastern Sea [2] flood a tree with their plentiful waters, if the tree have no branches, half of it will be dead." The Crown Prince represents half of the majesty of the kingdom, but he has not yet taken a wife. What do you think?'

The Grand Minister Wei Ling addressed the King, saying, 'I have heard that Duke Mu of Ch'in has a daughter aged sixteen who is surpassingly beautiful. Her eyebrows are like the waning moon, her cheeks like concentrated light, her eyes like shooting stars, her face as colourful as a flower. Her hair is seven feet long, her nose is straight and her forehead square, her ears like pendant pearls. Her hands hang below her knees, her ten fingers are slender and long. I would hope that Your Majesty issue directives whereby marriage arrangements be made on behalf of the Prince. If things can be worked out to satisfy Your Majesty's wishes, it would be a splendid event in whose glory all nations could share.'

So the King sent Wei Ling to solicit the Duke of Ch'in's daughter. After Wei Ling had returned with the girl, the King summoned him and said, 'I have troubled you to make this long journey and to brave wind and frost.'

When the King saw how beautiful and charming the girl was, he suddenly became filled with a wolfish, tigerish desire. Wei Ling craftily played upon the King's feelings: 'I would have Your Majesty take her for your own Imperial concubine. We can seek elsewhere for the Crown Prince. There are beautiful girls without number. How could this be an offence against the Ideal?' When the King heard Wei Ling's words, he was happy beyond measure. He forthwith took the girl from Ch'in as his concubine. For three days, he stayed in the inner palace and did not hold court.

Wu Shê was furious when he heard this and, not cowering before the thunder and lightning of the King's majesty, with his hair all dishevelled, he went straight before the palace. Risking the royal displeasure, he straightforwardly reproved the King. The King was startled and apprehensive. 'Has there been an unfavourable omen?' he asked.

'Today I have seen you act so unscrupulously,' answered Wu Shê, 'that I fear for the ruination of the kingdom. If the country should undergo a rebellion and its ministers abandon it, would that not all be attributable to the Duke of Ch'in's daughter? You gave her to your son as a bride but then took her yourself as a concubine. Will not contesting like this with your son for a wife bring you opprobrium before Heaven and Earth? This has made chaos of our laws and overturned the rules of propriety and good custom. I must reprove you for I fear that it is going to be difficult to preserve our country's altars!'

At this, the King's face went pale with shame. Humiliated in the presence of his ministers, he shot back, 'Has the Prime Minister not heard this saying: "Set plans are not to be discussed; spilled water is hard to recover." Things being what they are, do not reprove me again!'

Wu Shê felt that the King, without principle, had taken the Ch'in girl as his own concubine. Not cowering before the thunder and lightning of the King's majesty, he risked the royal displeasure by straightforwardly reproving: 'Your Majesty is the lord of ten thousand men and commander of sundry states. How could you have received so credulously the words of Wei Ling?'

'If your heart of filial piety can indeed swiftly relieve my distress, this soul of mine, suspended above Hades, can avoid having to depart from the world.' When Tzu-shang, far afield, received this summons in his father's letter, he wept grievously and, intending to beg the King of Cheng to save his father, he went to see him. 'My father has been imprisoned by King P'ing,' he said. 'In a letter from afar, I have been ordered to return. I do wish to save my father, but there is really nothing I can do. I hope that you will think of some plan for me.' 'Now,' said the King of Cheng, 'Your father has been severely punished and is being detained in a large prison. A messenger from afar has brought this letter which says that his crimes may be remitted. If you do not save your father from the consequences of his error, how can you be called a filial son? You must depart at once! There is no point in considering the matter further.'

Tzu-shang then bid farewell to the King of Cheng and made a rapid journey through the night [3] to the Kingdom of Liang to see his younger brother, Tzu-hsü. After telling him in detail the content of the letter, Tzu-shang said, 'Now King P'ing has acted without principle. He has received credulously the words of a deceitful minister and imprisoned the person of our father. It being his purpose to be ruthless, I have come this long way to call upon you to go with me. The exigencies of the situation do not permit us to tarry for any length of time. I would hope that you pack your things at once.'

Hearing these words of his brother, Tzu-hsü realized, even though he was far from Ch'u, that his father was being held. From close consideration of the details of the matter, he concluded that the letter was, in all probability, a forgery. So he answered his brother: 'King P'ing, being without principle and believing the words of a treacherous minister, has imprisoned our father and intends to execute him. Inasmuch as we two brothers are abroad, he is tormented by the possibility of revenge later on and so has had this letter written, pretending it is father's. Because we are so far away, he rashly thinks that he can deceive us. Given these circumstances, it is sufficiently clear that, if we go to Ch'u to save our father, then we too will certainly be slaughtered. This express letter and the command it lays upon us are surely but a monstrous pretext intended to bring us brothers back. And, when we get to Ch'u, we will certainly be implicated along with our father. We cannot embark upon this journey. If we do, we shall be like dull-witted birds thrashing about in a net or fish from a fountain swimming in a kettle.'

'Go back, now,' continued Wu Tzu-hsü, 'and relate everything that I have said. As for my roughness toward you just now, please do not take offence at it.'

When the messenger heard these words, he returned at once to Ch'u and, tying himself up with rope, went to see King P'ing. He informed the King, saying:

§'I received your order to act as express messenger;
Day and night I ran, passing through many lands.
South of K'uai-chi Mountain, I caught up with him,
But, pulling out his sword, he thought to behead me.
Your servant cowered before the sword in Tzu-hsü's hand,
Tzu-hsü feared that both of us would end up dead.
Each distrusting the other, neither approached the other,
Word by word across the distance, he explained his case.
"Turn back and report these words of mine to your King P'ing:
§I shall forthwith raise troops and take vengeance for my father!"'

Upon hearing this, the Emperor of Ch'u struck the steps leading to his throne and shouted angrily, 'What an insolent and petty person! How comes it that we endure his existence? "How is an inch-long blade of grass fit for measuring heaven? Can one thin strand of hair hope to withstand the hot coals of a stove?" Tzu-hsü's words are sheer madness and not even worth our notice. They are but wild verbiage thrown upon the wind. There is no necessity for us to pay them any heed.'

The King of Ch'u then called Wu Shê and Tzu-shang out of jail and had them sentenced and punished. When Tzu-shang was about to die, he looked up to heaven and, sighing, said, 'When we were in Liang, I did not follow my brother's advice and so have come all this way only to die with my father. What can I do now? Alas! Nothing! Beyond this, what more know I to say? After I die, may my brother live on and, if a way be opened by heaven, [4] may he avenge our father by slaying Ch'u!' No sooner had he completed these his dying words than they killed him. Father and son were slaughtered at the same instant.

The King of Ch'u issued a proclamation. Accordingly, Tzu-hsü was to be treated in accordance with the terms of the proclamation which read: '*In re* the rebel Tzu-hsü, a servant of the Kingdom of Liang. His father was in service to Your Ruler but, unable to remain loyal and circumspect, he plotted against the altars of our state with cruel rapacity. Tzu-shang, a servant of the Kingdom of Cheng, was executed together with his father at the same time. There only remains Tzu-hsü who has fled and, as of this moment, has not been apprehended. Whoever can capture him and turn him in will be given a reward of a thousand catties of gold and enfeoffed with the income from a thousand households. Whoever gives him shelter will face the usual punishment provided by law, *videlicet*, first the offender will himself be beheaded and this will be followed by the extermination of his entire clan. Should any arresting officer exercise leniency, he will be relieved of his office and brought to prosecution. Your King should be kept constantly informed and the offender escorted, in fetters, to the capital.'

The proclamation having been put in circulation, a water-tight dragnet went into effect. Each province and district was informed and public notices were posted on the highways and roads. Thorough searches were made in every village and ward so that no one dared to shelter Wu Tzu-hsü. Rather, greedy for the rich reward, they vied with one another in their pursuit of him.

Tzu-hsü walked until he came to some wild mountains where, placing his hand on his sword and sighing, he sang this sorrowful song:

§Full of anger, a long, drawn-out sigh escapes me:

§How lamentable for a brave man to be wronged and in peril!
The net of heaven is all-embracing, the road is cut off,
Leaving me afraid and with nowhere to take refuge.
Thirsty, tired, and without food to fill my stomach,
Companionless I wander in this unending wilderness.
Afar, I hear the mighty wind-swept waves of the river-barrier;
The soaring mountains reach to the very heavens.
No boat there is midst the desolate islets of this remote place;
How then shall I get to the southern shore?
If it should happen that High Heaven go against human feeling,
§I'll not escape having difficulties in this place.

His sad song finished, Tzu-hsü resumed his forward progress. Trusting his karma and in accordance with conditioning causes, he reached the River Ying. The wind came to brush against his ears bringing with it the sound of silk being beaten. Wu Tzu-hsü was hesitant to press forward and so stood in hiding.

§I, Tzu-hsü, have come to the side of the River Ying;
Thirsty, tired, and starving, it is difficult to go forward.
Afar, I hear the sounds of the beating of silk in the air,
Cringing and crouching, I come suddenly to a standstill.
I am afraid there may be someone hidden here –
Stealthily, I draw myself into the shade of the trees. [**5**]
Long and sober reflection tells me I need not be afraid;
Ever so stealthily, I peep through the trees.
Beside the river-ford, there are no men –
I see only a nimble, shapely girl beating silk.
A hundred times, she lowers her head and peers into the water;
A thousand passes, her jade wrists dance over the waves.
At once, I want to rush forward and beg food of her;
But my heart is full of doubt and irresolution.
Daring neither to advance nor retreat, I quickly reconsider;
§Though hesitant, I wish to go away meekly at once.

The girl who was beating silk in the water suddenly raised her head and saw a man rushing wildly, his spirits crazed, and with a starved look on his face. Because he was wearing a sword at his waist and running, she knew that it was Wu Tzu-hsü. Full of sympathy, she said to herself: 'I have heard that, "for a single meal given him in the mulberry grove, Ling Che propped up the chariot". "The Yellow Sparrow which was given a salve to heal its wounds requited the donor with a gift of white jade bracelets." Though I have kept myself chaste, pure, and undefiled, it is fortune which has granted me this meeting with a gentleman here by the waterside as I beat my silk. True, our home is not well-provided but why should I grudge him this one meal?'

She walked slowly up the bank, and called out, 'Traveller, won't you stop a while? Where do you come from, my good swordsman? Of what kingdom are you the paragon? You have a spirited appearance and a lofty manner. What urgent business have you to be hurrying on this long journey, companionless, glancing about in fear, and distraught in spirit? Judging from the look on your face, your heart must harbour something for which you are seeking. If you are not a knight-errant who cherishes a grievance, then it must be that you are being pursued by King P'ing. My home, though poor, is hospitable and I make bold to offer you a meal. How would you like that? I hope you will condescend to bend your path this way.'

'I am a man of Ch'u,' replied Wu Tzu-hsü, 'and hold the position of envoy of the Kingdom of Yüeh. Recently, because I was appointed to present tribute from Yüeh, I journeyed westwards to the King of Ch'u. On my way back, I met together and planned defence matters with the two kingdoms of Liang and Cheng. Riding in a chariot drawn by stout horses, I had gone as far as a small river when I was attacked by fierce thieves but was fortunate enough to come out of it alive. Today, climbing mountains and crossing ridges, I have exhausted my provisions. Having heard in the air the sound of your silk-beating, I looked everywhere for its source. Appearing thus, I must present a rather sorry figure. And I am afraid I shall be unable to return within the time set by the King. So I am indeed in a great hurry. Now how can I get through to the road which leads to K'uai-chi? I beg of you only the right direction: I dare not expect any food!'

'I have heard a saying of the ancients,' said the girl, 'which wasn't spoken vainly. "When one's affection is gone, there's no keeping him from his purpose; but a broken bowstring can still be rejoined." It is obvious which way your course leads. Yet seeing you glance behind and look ahead, your anxious face stained by the wind and dust of far-off rivers and mountains which you have had to cross, I am so bold as to hope that you'll not reject my humble offer of a meal:

§From the beginning, I have always lived in Nan-yang District;
Aged sixteen, the glow of my face is like soft, bright silk. **[6]**
As I beat the silk, my red rouge reflects in deep pools;
The lotus flower floating on the water is no match for my beauty.
My guest has come like a boat floating over the sea;
At dusk, the birds return to roost, fearing the close of day.

§Should you not reject this humble offering,
§I pray you try your best to make a meal of it.'

Tzu-hsü wanted to continue on his journey at once but, again and again, she earnestly begged him to stay. It being truly difficult to disregard human kindness, he squatted down right there by the water-side and began to eat. He stopped short after three mouthfuls, thanked the woman, and wanted to set forth at once. Again, he was persuaded by the maiden to eat his fill. Now more deeply indebted than ever, he began to tell her of his cares. He answered her thusly:

§'I am none other than Wu Tzu-hsü;
Escaping from Ch'u, I flee to Wu in the south.
Because I fear pursuit and capture by King P'ing,
I travel at night over desolate roads.
Your gracious gift of a meal is more than enough to fill my hunger;
How will I ever be able to repay you?
My body has regained lightness and strength, my eyes brightness;
And so, taking leave of you, I wish to set out on my long road.
An exile cast out of his native place,
I am this very moment harried by King P'ing.
Be so kind as not to let others know I have been here;
I pray you understand my feelings.'
When Tzu-hsü had finished speaking, he went forward on his way;
The girl cried out bitterly and wept aloud:
'Wanderer so mournful, I truly worry for you,
Crawling in the face of death yet craving life.
You've had a meal from me but that seems not to be enough;
A woman cannot satisfy a hero's heart.
Although you solemnly rejected my offer,
The embarrassment which you have caused me is not light either.'
She paused to restrain her sobbing and wipe her tears:
'Your countenance has suddenly become haggard with care. [7]
If, later on, you are taken by those who pursue you,
You will certainly say, "It was that woman who brought on my troubles."
"Thirty years old, never before having talked to a man",
I live together with my mother in our neighbourhood.
The graceful, charming glow of the face you see before you,
The faith and chasteness of a virtuous woman – all cast away in vain.
My Lord Wu,' she called out, 'do not doubt me!'
Then clasping a stone, she threw herself into the river and died.

§Tzu-hsü turned round and looked from afar;
Having a fond regard for the maiden, he was filled with sorrow.
Far off, seeing her clasp the heavy stone and leap to her death in the river,
Involuntarily, he cried out against this injustice.
As the waters of the Ying relentlessly swallowed up her last traces,
Wu Tzu-hsü wept and, his grief doubled, sighed sadly:
'If, in the future, I should rise to high rank,
§I will certainly give a hundred pieces of gold for her tomb.'

When Tzu-hsü finished weeping, he resumed his forward progress. The wind and dust seared his face; swirling dust darkened the sky. His nerves strained to the breaking point, Wu Tzu-hsü suddenly reached a deep river. Its waters were so deep they seemed to have no bottom and its banks were so far apart it seemed to be endless. He climbed hills and entered valleys, following winding mountain streams to their sources. When dragons and snakes blocked his way, he would draw his sword and rush forward. When his path was full of tigers and wolves, he would draw his bow at once. When hungry, he dined on wild grasses midst reeds: thirsty, he supped from flowing springs neath towering cliffs. A hero incensed and out for vengeance regards death as but a sleep.

Suddenly, he came upon a house which stood in a valley. He quickly knocked at the door and begged for food. There was a woman who came to answer the door. Having recognized from afar the sound of her brother's voice, she knew even at a distance that it was Tzu-hsü. With concerned words and affection, she comforted him and asked what trouble he was in. Tzu-hsü, his lips sealed, spoke not a word. Realizing that her brother had been thirsty and in want for a long time, she took a gourd which she filled with rice and fixed, to go with it, a salad of bitter-tasting endive and chicory. Tzu-hsü was wise enough to apprehend what it was his sister had in mind. Thinking carefully, he explained to himself: 'The gourd filled with rice stands for bitterness within and sweetness without; using chicory and endive for a salad is to match bitterness with bitterness. Taken together, she must mean to send me off at once. I'm to go away at once and cannot tarry longer.'

And so he said goodbye and was about to leave when his sister asked, 'Now that you are setting out again, where do you intend to take recourse?'

'To the Kingdom of Yüeh,' answered Tzu-hsü. 'Our brother and father have been murdered and I must avenge them.' The sister embraced her brother's head and, not daring to cry aloud, choked and sobbed until she was hoarse. 'Alas!' she sighed as she threw herself on the ground and struck her breast. 'How painful! How cruel! What sins we must have committed in former lives to have been thus orphaned and aggrieved! **[8]**

§'Over the vast reaches of time, what sins were there,
That we should now be so ungrateful to our parents?
Although we, in our persons, may be wealthy and honoured,
Father in the south and son in the north, we are scattered.
Suddenly, I recall our father and older brother when they were alive,
And it causes every inch of my vitals to rend.
Today, my younger brother is going away, I know not where,
Leaving me here to bear my grief alone.
Now more than ever I am bereft of a place to devote my love;
Oh, would that I could bring an end to my existence!'
Tzu-hsü took leave of his sister, saying, 'Take good care of yourself.
There's no need to weep and streak your face with tears.
Our father and older brother have been unjustly slaughtered;
In my heart, a raging fire burns with intensity,
Today there is no place for a man of spirit beneath the sun!
The brave man's heart is knotted with deep and bitter resentment.
If the day should come that heaven open a way to me,
I swear I will catch King P'ing of Ch'u alive –
  Wrench out his heart, chop him to bits
  Wipe out his clan to the ninth degree.
  If I do not accomplish all of this,
  §I swear I'll not return to my native place.'

As soon as he had finished with these words, he set out towards the south. He had walked a little more than twenty furlongs when his eyes began to twitch and his ears to tingle, so he immediately drew a diagram on the ground to make a divination and he saw by it that his sister's sons were coming after him. He sprinkled water on his head, inserted a piece of bamboo beneath his waistband, and put his wooden shoes on backwards. He drew the diagrams for 'Earth's Door' and 'Heaven's Gate' and then lay down in the rushes where he chanted the following incantation:

'A plague upon him who catches me;
Death to him who pursues me;
Swiftly, swiftly, *in has leges*.'

Tzu-hsü had two nephews, Tzu-an and Tzu-yung. When they

returned home, they saw where someone had been eating and knew that it must have been their uncle, Tzu-hsü. Disregarding the deep sympathy which their mother held for him and with ill intent, they at once set out in hot pursuit, thinking the while, 'If we gain audience with the Monarch of Ch'u and receive a reward, we'll certainly be able to achieve high rank. The rebel has come to our door today. There shouldn't be any trouble catching him.'

When they had walked about ten furlongs, they rested by the side of the road. Tzu-yung had a slight understanding of *yin-yang* and so drew a diagram on the ground and made a divination. It revealed their uncle had water on his head which certainly meant that he had fallen by the side of the river; there was a piece of bamboo at his waist which meant that his grave was in a wild place; he wore his wooden shoes backwards **[9]** which meant that, wandering aimlessly, he was not making any forward progress.

In accordance with these signs, they felt that he must have died and so did not resume their search. 'There's no more in it for us,' they said. 'Let's go back home.'

Tzu-hsü crouched down to look at his magic markings and saw that his nephews had broken off their pursuit. And so he ran on and on through the starry night without stopping.

In a valley, once more he came upon a house. Its walls were extraordinarily stately. As the farm stood off by itself quite alone, there was no one anywhere around it. Not ashamed of being such a big, husky fellow, he knocked at the gate and begged for food.

§Tzu-hsü knocked at the gate and proceeded to beg for food;
His wife took on a serious expression and came out to answer.
When she saw quite clearly that this was her own husband,
She wanted somehow to express that she recognized him.
But the wife stood there apart and carefully considered;
She dared not go forward – she dared not approach him.
Instead, with all proper civilities, she greeted her husband;
Her tearful voice choked with grief, she asked him politely:
'I dwell here in these wild and desolate confines;
Neighbourless on all four sides, alone I have settled.
From whence have you come, my good man, to this place,
Your face filled with sadness and a look of hunger?
Reduced to nervous trembling you seem frightened of someone;
You cringe and withdraw timidly while begging for food.
Although I have kept myself secluded in the fastness of my rooms,
§You give me the vague impression of being familiar.'

Tzu-hsü replied to his wife, saying:

§'I am a man of Ch'u, sent to fill a distant mission;
Crossing hill after hill and dale after dale, I was returning home.
On the way I became lost and, as though in a stupor,
Wandered about until I unwittingly came to this place.
My native borders are far away at the western end of the sea;
Distant they are and separated by three great rivers.
Just now, I impulsively and rudely barged in on you;
It was really too rash of me, so I turn myself away. **[10]**
'Milady is very forgetful and so has mistaken me;
Nor do I recall having ever met you, good lady, before.
Now I should like to set forth towards the east of the river,
§And hope that you will be so kind as to point the way!'

His wife then composed a poem with the names of medicines its theme and, by means of it, asked him a series of questions:

§'I, Belladonna, am the wife of a man named Wahoo,
Who early became a mandrake in Liang.
Before our matrimonyvine could be consomméted, he had to go back,
Leaving me, his wife, to dwell here ruefully alone.
The mustard has not been cut, the flaxseed bed remains unvisited –
Hemlocked in here without any neighbours, I raised my head and sighed for my Traveller's Joy:
"Parsley, sage, rosemary, and thyme –
I pray that he'll forget me not!"
Gingerly, I hoped, but I recently heard that the King of Ch'u,
Acting without principle and unleashing a bitterroot heart,
Slaughtered my pawpaw and brother-in-law with a jalap! jalap!
Clovered with shame, weak as a wisp of straw,
And arrowhead-swift, my husband fled with fear as a dog would.
Quick as a periwinkle, he became a fungative,
And hid amongst the stinkbushes;
But hiding became a hell-of-a-bore.
He seemed like a jackal pursued by horehounds;
Laudanum almighty, how he hopsed and hyssopped like a jackinthepulpit!
When I think of it, bittersweet tears stain my bleedingheart;
I am arti-choked with antimony.
At nightshade when I sleep, it's hard to endure till the morning's glory;

§I recite his name all day until my tongue curls up like a sliver of cypress.
His voice, begging balm, so ingenuous entered my ears;
Drawn by aniseedent causes, I dillied up to the visitor,
And, seeing it was my long orrised honeysuckle whom I mint at the gate,
Sloed down my steps to a hibiscus pace.
And then I saw your toothwort smile;
It reminded me of my husband's dog's tooth violets.
Borax you don't remember me but, no madder what caper you're up to,
§I'm willing to lay out my scurvy Butter and Eggs.'

Tzu-hsü answered in the same cryptic vein:

§'Potash! Nitre am I this fellow Wahoo whom you speak of,
Nor am I a fungative from injustice.
Listen while I tell you the currant of my travels.
I was born in Castoria and grew up in Betony Wood;
My father was a Scorpio, my mother a true Lily-of-the-valley.
Gathering up all of my goldenrod and silverweed,
This son of theirs became a Robin-Run-Around.
Rose Hips was my low-class companion,
Nelson Rockyfeldspar my uppercrust chum.
Together with them, I waded Wild Ginger Creek,
And caught cold in its squilling, wintergreen waters;
Saffronly, of the three of us, I found myself alone.
Day after day, my lotus-thread hopes dangled tenuously;
My thoughts were willows waving in the wind.
All alone, I climbed Witch Hazel Mountain;
How hard it was to cross the slippery elms and stone roots!
Cliffs towering above me, I clambered over stoneworts and rockweeds;
Often did I encounter wolfsbanes and tiger thistles.
Sometimes I would be thinking of soft spring beauties,
But suddenly would meet up with a bunch of pigsheads;
My thoughts would linger over mid-summer vetches,
Yet I could never see an end to my tormentils.
So I reversed my steps, feeling compelled to spurry back;
Fennelly, I arrived here.
I grow goatsbeard,
Not dog's tooth violets.

§Methinks you've scratched a fenugreek but found no tartar,
§So furze tell me what you mean and don't make such a rhubarb.'

The wife then replied: 'Do not be in such a hurry, for your road is a long and distant one.

§'And even supposing we have never before met,
What harm is there in my mistaken identification?
I am a daughter of the wealthy Kung-sun family;
Fittingly matched with a gentleman, I served him faithfully.
My husband, surnamed Wu, held a high position in government;
As a young man, he travelled a thousand miles to serve his Lord, the King.
From the time he left, he sent no letter, not even a word;
Thinking of him, my heart grows so sad that I nearly expire. **[11]**
The way is long and dark – I feel so isolated and forlorn;
I am not used to being separated for such a long time.
My once rosy cheeks have lost their former hue – how haggard and wan they are;
Fondly I recall him, but the tears, oh when have they ever stopped?
So many years thrown away in vain, keeping watch in these empty rooms,
Who could survive again the beauteousness, the fragrance of Spring?
Day and night, the damsel in her tower feels charm's glow fading;
And it's all because her wandering man is serving in Liang.
Languidly, she goes to the front of the courtyard to gaze at the moon;
Then, full of sorrow, returns to her bed to embrace the marriage pillows.
Even a message by carrier pigeon would still not get through;
The frontiers on the horizon are separated by a long, long road.
She tries to weave at her broken loom but feels too disheartened;
Her painted brows are embarrassed to face the dresser mirror.
She dotes on the chattering magpies in the grape arbour,
And cherishes the pair of swallows which roost in the white jade hall.
You, in not recognizing me, are behaving like Ch'iu Hu;
And I, unwillingly, play the role of his neglected wife.
Seeing in your mouth that set of beautiful teeth,
I feel quite certain that I know from this who you are.
Never would I grudge you a meal, coarse fare though it be;
I hope that you will stop here a moment – be not so hurried.'
Having been recognized, Tzu-hsü declined her offer,

§With deceitful, wily words, he evaded her thusly:
'Don't, my lady, recklessly interfere in my affairs,
There are many men who resemble each other.
Your husband's surname is Wu and he occupies high office.
I come from a poor family and dwell on the grassy plains.
If I should happen to meet your husband, I'll pass on the word,
And, with reason, will exhort him to return to his home.
Now, because I have urgent business, I must go east of the river;
§I cannot tarry here with you another day or night.' [**12**]

His wife realized he was planning some important undertaking and so did not dare further disturb him. According to custom, she gave him provisions and saw him off, as was proper.

Tzu-hsü, having been recognized by his wife, said no more. 'I am a man,' he thought, 'but before I had reached my goal, was recognized by this woman. Yet can I allow such a small matter to defeat me in the performance of this great duty of mine?' And so, hero that he was, Wu Tzu-hsü carried a stone as he walked and, with it, knocked out his teeth.

By day, he was guided by the sun and at night by the stars. He ran on without stopping until he came to the north bank of the River Wu. Afraid that there might be someone concealed there, he slunk stealthily among the reeds. Hand resting on his sword, he sighed as he sang this sad song:

§'Vast are the river's waters – its waves rise up and up,
To the sky they boil – or sink lower and lower.
The flying sand is so dense that it covers up the Milky Way;
The chill wind whips up the waves and howls destructively through
the forest.
White grasses cover the vast expanse of wild fields and plains;
Green willows stand in lines droopingly on both sides of the river.
Crows and magpies intermingle as they peck about for food;
Fishes and dragons jump here and leap there in grand disarray,
Otters sport in the water and hold playful contests of speed.
A thousand times over, I involuntarily sigh;
Suddenly recalling the unjust slaughter of my father and brother,
I at once feel a burning pain in my heart and bowels.
Thinking of my sworn hatred, I gasp with pain and sorrow:
Though we meet today, I would make no renunciation.
My life may well end in the deep waters of this river;
Whether I live or die all depends on what happens tonight.

§I do not shirk the thought that my bones may sink in these waves;
The oath of vengeance for my father and brother must never be broken.
There is always the wind by which the firmament bends the grasses;
§And, still yet, the mighty transforming power of all the deities.'

When his sad song was ended, he walked to the edge of the river and gazed into the distance. All he could see was the broad expanse of its waters; how could he ever get across it? He stretched his neck out from amidst the reeds and, turning his head from side to side, saw that all was silent. His eye met no one out sailing in a boat nor was there anyone on a raft. All he could see were river crows starting out from the banks and egrets contesting in flight, fishes and turtles crisscrossing the surface, cormorants and wild swans gliding about in profusion. He saw, too, long islands here and there on the vast breadth of the river, waves spreading across its coves, dark mists rising, [**13**] black clouds descending. Trees pressed close upon the worn banks, the moon shone upon a solitary peak. Dragons trembled and turtles were startled; globe-fish stirred up ripples.

If one has strayed from his native place, he climbs a high mountain and thinks of home; a traveller on a raft guides himself by Orion and Lucifer. Wu Tzu-hsü spent one night on Min Mountain seeming as a tiger or wolf prowling around. The river rushed by, sounding like drums beating and horns blaring, but there was not a single boat in which to cross it. He had passed two further nights there hiding amidst the reeds when, at last, he saw someone on the waves. He was singing a ballad as he plied his oars. In his hand, he held a reel and hook and was evidently a fisherman. Wu Tzu-hsü emerged from the reeds and called out to him: 'You there in the boat, sir, holding the fishing hook! May I trouble you for a moment to come to the bank so that I may have a word with you? Please do not turn from this trouble. I would be most grateful if you would be so kind as to pay me some heed.'

The fisherman, hearing him call, right away tried to find where the voice was coming from. Suddenly, a man appeared out of the reeds and so he at once rowed his boat to the shore. He reeled in his line and – no longer paddling or poling – let the boat drift along on the current. As he rocked to and fro, the fisherman sang 'Soothing Breezes', using it to ask a series of questions:

§'Where is it you wish to go today, my good man?
On the distant shores and inlets of this river,
I see no other travellers in boats;

§Nor do you have any companions, so lonely you are.
Perhaps you are like drifting tumbleweed,
Stranded here alone on these desolate islets and shores?
If you're hunting for a boat or ferry,
You won't find any at all in this place.
But if you're not put off by my rudeness,
§I request that you tell me fully what's on your mind.'

'I have heard,' answered Wu Tzu-hsü, 'that "men may know each other through virtue and learning just as fish look towards each other in the rivers and lakes." Your humble servant is a traveller. Dare I vainly think up words of deception? Because of a small matter which must be attended to promptly, I need to make my way south of the river. As a person, I am rather inept but I do hope, sir, that I will have the good fortune to receive your understanding. If you will be so kind as to ferry me across the river, my gratitude would be so great that I would even give my life for you. If you cannot agree to this, I will naturally give up the idea altogether.'

'Just now,' said the fisherman, 'as I scrutinized your face and examined your appearance, I observed that you were different from the ordinary sort of person. I can tell what is on your mind; you need not further clarify yourself. I have heard that "he who can distinguish between good and bad men is himself not base and he who can distinguish between good and bad jade shall not be wanting"; "Duke Mu of Ch'in prompted gratitude with his gift of wine"; "the one who was eloquent gained sole command of the three armies"; "he who presented an empty cage received a bounteous reward". I see that you have been distressed for many days and that you have been thirsty and in want for a long time. You cannot cross the river on an empty stomach. Allow me to fix a meal for you. The trip from here to my house and back is a little over ten furlongs. It may take me a while to return, so please don't be suspicious.'

'All that I seek,' said Wu Tzu-hsü, 'is a boat to ferry me across the river. I wouldn't dare expect any food!'

'I have heard,' replied the fisherman, 'that "the unicorn, when it gets food, can travel a thousand miles in a day; the phoenix, when it gets food, can soar across the four seas".' He had scarcely finished these words when he beached his boat and set out towards his house to get some food. Tzu-hsü had heard what the fisherman said and so watched the boat for him. But he reflected to himself, 'This man told me that he was going home to get some food but I wonder whether he might well not have gone to call someone to come and arrest me.' So he abandoned the boat, went over to the reeds, and hid among them.

In no time at all, the fisherman returned to where the boat was. He brought with him a jug of fine wine, five catties of fish, ten thin pancakes, and was carrying a container of rice. When he got to where the boat was, the gentleman of the reeds was nowhere to be seen. There was only the empty boat which had been drawn up on the shore. The affectionate regard in which he held Wu Tzu-hsü caused the fisherman to feel deep disappointment at this and so he called with a song:

§'Oh, gentleman of the reeds!
Why have you gone into hiding?
Come out here so I can have a look at you;
After all, I don't have any bad intentions.
There's no need to doubt or worry;
Don't make things doubly difficult.
I have brought back a meal expressly for you;
§Why don't you come over here and eat it?'

When Wu Tzu-hsü **[14]** heard the boatman speak these words, he knew that he was not ill-intentioned and so came out from the reeds. He was embarrassed by the trouble he had put the man to in going to get the food, so he went forward to meet him and offered his humble apologies. Thereupon, they spread out the meal, and the two of them ate together. The fisherman then struck up the oars at once and rowed out as far as the middle of the river. Tzu-hsü, having had his fill, thought to himself: '"Whoever receives one meal from another, is indebted to him to that extent; whoever receives two meals from another must exert himself on his behalf."' So he presented the jade disc which he carried in his bosom to the boatman. The latter, worried that dusk was coming on and anxious to go forward, would not accept the gift. Tzu-hsü was worried that the fisherman may have considered this token of his gratitude as being too little and so took off his precious sword and offered it, too, as recompense.

The fisherman stopped rowing and, turning around, answered him: 'Don't be so rash! You really ought to think it over carefully. How could the small favour of a single meal be worth so much? Men in trouble, though they be as different as fish are from turtles, flock together; when the going is rough, people as different as dragons are from snakes willingly cohabit. The King of Ch'u is out to get you and the one who succeeds in capturing you will be rewarded with a thousand pieces of gold. Anyone who harbours you will be executed and his family annihilated.

In the first place, I am not greedy for the heavy reward the Sovereign is offering. And, in the second place, I do not run from the possibility of being sentenced and executed. You wish to present your precious sword to me, but how could even it be a match for what King P'ing has to offer? Keep your precious Excalibur to protect yourself, and your jade disc from Ching which will serve to fulfil what you hold dear. Later on, if you should rise to high place and attain great wealth, do not forget that we once met. I rebuke myself for having grown old so early and for having met you so late. As for the matter of the sword and jade disc, please do not again try to leave them with me. If you wish to vindicate my sentiments, it will not be necessary for me to refuse your offer again.'

When Tzu-hsü saw that the man would not accept his gifts, he began to feel increasingly uncomfortable. 'I am afraid,' he thought to himself, 'that the boatman belittles these tokens of my gratitude because they are too poor and too few. And that, even though they are precious things worthy of a lord or king. What more can I do?' Then he threw the sword into the river. It shot forth a spirit-like glow, sparkling brightly as it thrice sank and thrice came to the surface with a great gush and then hovered above the water. The god of the river far off heard the sword's roar and, tremulously, he roiled the waters in a great and frothing frenzy. The fish and turtles were thrown into a panic and burrowed into the mud. Dragons raced along the waves and leaped out of the water. The river god held up the sword in his hand and, frightened, told Wu Tzu-hsü to take it back.

After the sword had left the water, the fish and turtles began to skitter about again. All was as bright and pure as the rays of the sun and moon; the mountains and forests glistened. The clouds parted, and the river fog lifted; mists scattered, and the vapours rolled back. The trees along the bank seemed to have lined up to welcome a visitor, the river wind to be seeing off a guest. One could see, far off, egrets standing beside sand bars in the fading evening light, and making ready to return to their nests in the forest. Along the river banks, there were no boats for hire to be seen. Out on the water, there were no companions for our two passengers. All that was visible was a solitary mountain across a vast expanse of water.

Wu Tzu-hsü turned back to gaze at his homeland and, wiping away the tears which dampened his shirt, felt deeply disturbed at heart. They had crossed the better part of the river and were about to reach the south bank so Wu Tzu-hsü inquired of the boatman: 'What is your surname and name? In what province and district is your native village?'

'I have neither surname nor name,' answered the fisherman, 'and have long lived here with the river my only companion. I pole across the quiet shores and tie up my boat in deep pools. Today, two outlaws meet – what need is there to speak of names? You, sir, are the Gentleman of the Reeds and I the Man in the Boat – that is all we need know about each other. When you become wealthy and honoured, you must not forget me.'

'There will never be a time when I shall forget this aid which I have received from you,' said Wu Tzu-hsü. '"Even a wounded snake which is treated with medicine can repay its benefactor!"'

'When you continue your flight today,' asked the fisherman, 'in which kingdom do you intend to seek refuge?'

'I intend to seek refuge in the Kingdom of Yüeh,' answered Tzu-hsü.

'So you're going to Yüeh –,' the fisherman said. 'The Kingdom of Yüeh and Ch'u get along well with each other and have never been engaged in military conflict. I am afraid that if you go there, they will arrest you and extradite you to Ch'u so the vengeance which you hold in your heart would never be achieved. But if you take refuge in the Kingdom of Wu, the sailing would certainly be much smoother. The King of Wu has constantly [**15**] been at odds with Ch'u. The two kingdoms do not get along well together. Wu has had numerous campaigns against the Kingdom of Ch'u and, furthermore, has no able ministers. Obtaining your services would be extremely important for them.'

'How can I get the Kingdom of Wu to accept my allegiance?' Wu Tzu-hsü asked the boatman.

'When you get to the Kingdom of Wu,' said the boatman, 'enter the market place of the capital, daub your face with mud, and make your hair dishevelled like that of a wild man. Then go running swiftly, now to the east now to the west, and cry loudly three times.'

'Please be so kind,' said Tzu-hsü, 'as to explain all this.'

'Daubing mud on your face,' said the boatman, 'means that, though you are defiled without, you are pure within. Crying loudly three times and running swiftly east and west means that you seek an enlightened ruler. Standing in the market place with your hair dishevelled then makes sense, does it not? Though not a sage, I have had a lot of experience.'

Tzu-hsü received his instructions and bowed gratefully to the fisherman. Fearing that he might meet up with the Ch'u envoys, he could not remain there any longer but set out as soon as they reached the shore. After they parted, he sobbed until he was hoarse. It was like 'the four fledglings each flying their own way' or 'the three thorns being separated'. Thus he left the fisherman and went towards the south. But, because of his tender regard for the fisherman, Wu Tzu-hsü's grief was unceasing. As he turned his head to look back across the distance, he suddenly saw the fisherman overturn his boat and die. Conscience-stricken by this final favour of the fisherman, Wu Tzu-hsü sobbed and wept mournfully without cease and then sang this sad lament:

§'The great river's waters, oh, they stretch on and on without end;
The clouds and waters, oh, they seem to join together!
How painful! How very painful! 'Tis difficult to endure.
How bitter! How very bitter! Injustice upon injustice!
From of old, leavetaking has been a part of human existence;
Life, death, wealth, and honour are all dependent on heaven.
What have I done to make my teacher hold such resentment against me,
That he should capsize his boat in the middle of the river?
His boat bobs up and down on the waves and then sinks beneath them;
I sing of the wrong he suffers – how keen and deep the pain is!
It is as though my sad heart were being sliced in pieces by a sword:
As I go on my way, I cannot suppress the tears which stain my collar.
I look towards Wu but, alas, I cannot reach there;
I think of my native kingdom and my heart is filled with grief.
But if I meet a wise ruler, garnering rank and success,
§I will display to the full this hero's heart of mine!'

His sad song finished, Wu Tzu-hsü once again resumed his forward journey, all the while sick at heart. Now that our hero was isolated, how greatly did he falter! He had served his ruler faithfully and truly for nine years. He had been lax neither in the morning nor at night. In paying his morning respects, he was never remiss. Now that he had encountered such ill-luck, he knew of no words further to express his feelings. The anger in his heart which speech could not convey welled up in his throat. Such was his karma, such his fate – and both depended on heaven.

Wu Tzu-hsü climbed mountains and sprang over ridges, crossed rivers and followed streams. **[16]** He sought to go forward, but often his way was blocked. And going back, of course, was out of the question. Hungered by his exertions, he felt his life in a whirl. 'King P'ing,' he cried out, aggrieved, 'you are too cruel!'

His sword in hand, Wu Tzu-hsü walked on and on until he came to some wild and desolate mountains. There, the rock walls shot ten thousand feet into the sky. A tangled mass of bamboos and creepers interpenetrated the earth. Far off, he saw dodder hanging from the pines on the mountains with their dark, steep cliffs. Wolves and tigers came and went, and hundreds of birds filled the air with chirping. Thinking of his native land, Wu Tzu-hsü sang this song:

§'What weighs on my mind is how long, oh, how long the road is;
Crossing rivers and lakes, I shall enter the domain of Wu.
My father and brother among the shades, I know not where;
Alone, and plagued by anxiety, I have been chased away.
A wandering hero am I who follows his karmic fate;
Life and death, riches and honour – all of these are inconstant.
King P'ing perversely accepted the words of Wei Ling,
Trusted a slanderous flatterer, struck down the honest and true.
Thoughts of my homeland, oh, bring grief which is hard to forestall;
Facing rivers or climbing mountains, my passions are without let.
The ruler of Ch'u has a penchant for buxom grace and narrow waists;
Inside his palaces, many beauties are starving to death.
The daughter of Duke Mu of Ch'in has a face that is like jade;
Sweet sixteen she is – her face glows soft as a peach, bright as a plum.
When he beheld her beauty, he took her in as his concubine;
Is this any way for a lord and ruler of men to behave?
Since fleeing, I have felt constant sorrow in my heart;
I have been left alone and without any recourse.
To travel by day would be like seeking a way to ghosthood,
So I step in shadows or hide: but I range the whole night long.
When shall my deeds be inscribed in stone on Mount Yen?
Until then, my temples greying, I forge through dust and brambles.
I fear nor east nor west nor to resist great cold –
Only thirst, fatigue, and the passage of wild places.
Would that I could safely attain the goal which lies ahead;
May my path be not impeded but flow freely as a brook. [**17**]
If, in the Kingdom of Wu, I meet a wise ruler,
§I shall raise an army and, posthaste, behead Wei Ling.'

His sad song finished and his heart filled with heroic passion, he turned his back on the Ch'u passes to the north and began climbing south towards K'uai-chi Mountain in Wu. It so happened that he came upon a day when the sky was dark, full of clouds black as pitch. He strayed from the road and went running back and forth trying to find it, but the mountain forests compelled him to halt. Flocks of strange birds milled about, wolf packs and bands of tigers prowled everywhere. The birds cried raucously and the beasts roared angrily. Suddenly, the fear in his heart clearly evident, he pulled out his sword and went forward.

§From out of its sheath, light springs forth;
Filling the wild with a spirit-glow.
It holds within the moon and sun,
The Dipper and its seven stars.
The hero's heart burns with sorrow;
A thousand soldiers he shall not fear!
Should King P'ing ever capture me –
My mission not yet brought to rest –
Or if I should be arrested,
A hundred to one I shall die.
Stealthy my steps, cautious my tread –
I hold my breath and keep silence.
The wind blows and stirs the grasses,
§Swiftly I go into hiding.

His sword song completed, Wu Tzu-hsü again went forward. North, he crossed Kuang-ling and south he climbed K'uai-chi. The passes and fords were closely watched. The provinces and districts increased their surveillance. Militiamen were everywhere and there were continual replacements of guards. Keeping himself carefully hidden, he went forward a step at a time.

Before many days had gone by, he reached the Kingdom of Wu. In exact accordance with the instructions of the fisherman, he dishevelled his hair and entered the market place, daubed mud on his face, cried wildly three loud shouts, and went running swiftly east and west. At that moment, a minister of the Kingdom of Wu happened to be riding through the marketplace on horseback. He noticed Wu Tzu-hsü's extraordinary appearance and unusual gifts as well as his six-foot frame and, knowing that he would make a worthy minister, went running to inform the King of Wu. 'Just after leaving your august presence,' he said, 'I was passing through the market and there I saw a gentleman from another land. His face was smeared with mud and he appeared wild; his hair was dishevelled and he cried out pitifully as he ran back and forth from east to west. I looked on from the side, examining him closely. From my scrutiny of his appearance, I am convinced of his worth. I should hope that Your Majesty inquire into the matter thoroughly and have him detained. He must certainly be a knight-errant who harbours an injustice.'

When the King of Wu heard these words, he was pleased and, gathering together his ministers, opened his pearl curtains, and spoke of his dream: 'Last night at the third watch, I dreamed that I saw a worthy man entering my realm upon which my body grew light and my person grew strong so that I could not prevent myself jumping about with joy. Would you, my ministers, carefully discuss this and explain for me whether it portends ill or good?'

When the hundred officials heard these words of the King, they danced and laughed gleefully all at the same time. 'Peace!' they sang out together. 'Long live the King!' they exclaimed with one voice. 'The dream shows that the six-foot gentleman in the market place is superbly fitted to your heart. All of your ministers who are present are overcome with joy.'

The King of Wu forthwith ordered an express messenger to go into the market place and summon this worthy minister-to-be.

'Inform him on my behalf,' said the King, 'that although I have not previously been acquainted with him, I do wish to meet him and that, when he sees me face-to-face, he may express his ambitions.'

As soon as the messenger received these verbal orders, he galloped directly into the market place. There he saw Wu Tzu-hsü and repeated to him entirely the verbal orders of the King of Wu. Tzu-hsü respectfully received the King's mandate and, not daring disobediently to delay, immediately followed the messenger. When they reached the King of Wu's palace, Wu Tzu-hsü went down with his face to the ground. He sobbed and moaned until his voice became hoarse and it was long before he rose. The King of Wu knew that it was Tzu-hsü and sympathetically inquired of him: 'The King of Ch'u did not accept loyal admonishment but perversely listened to the words of a sycophantic minister. He unjustly murdered your father and brother. How could he be so bitterly cruel? The sorrow which he caused is beyond description. Such awful pain! Who could have borne it? For you to have crossed mountain walls and river barriers and to have plodded long distances through wind and cloud to come so far to such a small and narrow kingdom as my own must have caused you great suffering.'

Tzu-hsü waited for quite a while and then, smoothing down his hair, spoke: 'Your servant's father and brother were not attentive in the service of their lord and so they were executed by the monarch of Ch'u. And I, instead of continuing the family traditions, abandoned my father and left my ruler **[18]** to flee as fast as I could run. I have heard that, "when a kingdom is about to perish, calamities and disasters occur in great profusion just as when a tree is on the verge of snapping, wind and frost press upon it". He who is destitute finds it difficult to stand firm. Faced with such distressing circumstances, I was unable to distinguish black from white; snake and dragon became hopelessly confused. I wished to cut my throat and die but was ashamed to see my ancestors in the nether world. Therefore, I have placed myself in the hands of a wise ruler like yourself in the hopes that you might understand the workings of my heart. Having grown up in a humble house and dwelling in the grassy wild, I am incapable of serving or supporting a ruler. It would be my great fortune to be accepted on your rolls!'

'My kingdom,' replied the King of Wu, 'is of narrow compass and is lacking loyal and honest men. In wishing to establish you as a minister, I realize that this is to compromise your integrity. But I hope you will not feel that it is something disgraceful.'

'I am a small person,' said Tzu-hsü, 'an unworthy recipient of your great favour. To be accepted on your rolls is already an exceptional act of kindness bestowed upon me. But further to be raised to office is something I dare not, in the end, accept. To do so would be to incur the death penalty for my presumption!'

'What do you think?' the King of Wu asked those to his left and right.

All of the ranks of ministers sang out their approval, saying, 'Your Majesty has such great influence that even this man from another land has placed himself at your disposal. Make him your helpmate and Minister of State and the entire country will exclaim together: "Long live the King!"'

As a minister, Tzu-hsü showed determination and moral fortitude. Never was he lax in his thinking. Morning and night he strove, single-mindedly serving his ruler all the while. His speech was not offensive; his words were informed with agreeableness. Men came to him in great numbers from far and near, talented officials appeared in abundance. Heaven's soldiers were not mobilized, and the war horses' whips were stayed. Those on the four borders all showed their allegiance, all the eight directions were settled and submissive. No man-made disasters occurred, no natural calamities arose. The people were joyful and sang songs along every road just as in the time of Yao and Shun. Everyone proclaimed: 'Our ruler is possessed of a benign influence. Lofty is the sacred sun, revivified are heaven and earth!'

After Tzu-hsü had governed the country for one year, the wind blew so softly that it scarcely rustled the branches and the rain fell so gently that it broke not the clods of earth. After he had governed the country for two years, the granaries over-flowed with abundance. All under heaven was peace and prosperity. Clerks gave up their greed for pelf, officials left off their tyrannous ways. When he had ruled the country for three years, the six barbarians expressed friendliness, and the ten thousand principalities all threw in their lot with Wu. After he had governed the country for four years, the Dragon of Good Prospect visited the land in answer to the auspiciousness of the day and the Red Sparrow came carrying in its beak a letter. Spirit-fungi grew side by side while portentous grain grew multiple spikes. Ploughmen gave way over questions regarding where to lay the boundary lines between fields. And no one picked up articles which had been lost by others on the highways. The three teachings flourished side by side and the city-gates never had to be closed. There were no more summonses or forced labour: people worked for themselves. When Tzu-hsü had governed the country for five years, the sun and moon doubled their brilliance. In the markets, there were fixed prices. Cats and mice lived together in the same holes. Rice and wheat were carefully weighed out to the last hundredth of an ounce and the jails had no prisoners. Everyone vied to proclaim the harmony of ideals between the King and his minister. Their praise spread far and near.

Indebted to the Minister Wu Tzu-hsü for his achievements, the common people all visited his gate and announced: 'We wish, on behalf of Minister Wu, to wage war upon Ch'u.'

Seeing all of these brave men voluntarily enlist, Tzu-hsü did not dare to make them his private preserve. Instead, he informed the King of Wu: 'I am but a small person who has been the recipient of your bountiful favours. Before I have established any merit, how dare I let ambition stir my heart? I consider that I am of no ability and so, when all is said and done, dare not be presumptuous.'

'I have heard,' replied the King of Wu, 'that "one prepares for old age by bringing up a child and anticipates the time when one will be decrepit by accumulating good deeds". Last year I had thought to commission you to carry out your vengeance but was concerned that the spirit of vengeance had not yet sufficiently developed in you. The peace and prosperity of these years are all a result of your efforts. If you do not now avenge the wrong done to your father and brother, how can you be called a filial son? The time is perfect for our kingdom to raise troops and attack Ch'u.'

And so the King issued a mandate which called for all the brave men in the land to help Minister Wu wreak his vengeance. The text of the mandate read as follows: 'Whereas the father and brother of Minister Wu were wilfully slaughtered by King P'ing, it is our desire today **[19]** to levy an army which has heaven on its side for the purpose of punishing Ch'u and we do thereby call upon our devoted subjects to enlist in this venture. If there be among you any who will risk his life by following the army into battle, he should come to enlist with the greatest urgency. We shall, at the outset, present heavy rewards. The decorations and emoluments conferred will not be light. If there are any such brave and valiant men, come quickly and present your responses to this our plea!'

Once the mandate had been issued and made known to all those far and near, they came severally to sign up, competing with one another to be the first to respond to the call. The War Office selected, screened, picked, tested, examined, and measured until it had come up with a superior fighting force that could decisively conquer at a distance of a thousand miles. Among its men, there were those capable of bending the bar of a door, tossing timber about, picking up huge square beams with their hands, jumping high in the air while clasping heavy stones, and shooting an arrow through seven layers of armour.

After the proclamation had been displayed for seven days, 900,000 crack troops were enlisted. Rewards of crimson silk and inducements of green silk were made, each being presented in lots of one thousand bolts. The recruiting officials led them outside the city-wall where the ranks were made to stand as straight as a formation of wild geese. The King of Wu then saw his soldiers lined up south of the city and proceeded at once to entertain and cheer these brave warriors. 'Today,' he inquired of Wu Tzu-hsü, 'we wish to attack Ch'u. How many soldiers should we use?'

'For the present, we'll need ten thousand soldiers,' was Tzu-hsü's answer.

'Won't ten thousand soldiers be too few?' asked the King.

'I have heard,' replied Tzu-hsü, 'that "when a man is determined to die, a hundred others are no match for him. And, if one hundred work together with one mind, they range at will anywhere under heaven."'

'I feel otherwise,' said the King of Wu. 'Only if you lead 900,000 men will you be able to attack Ch'u.'

The King of Wu then established Wu Tzu-hsü as the Generalissimo and Commander of the Army, as well as Chief of Mobilization. In accordance with the precepts of the Son of Heaven, he was to avenge his father by wiping clean the injustice he had suffered.

Thereupon, there was a mass slaughter of cattle and sheep and a feast was set up south of the city. There were a thousand casks of wine and ten thousand catties of meat. It was all divided equally, there being no rank when it came to eating.

The King of Wu went outside the city-wall to send Wu Tzu-hsü off. 'Sir, you need only do your best,' said the King, 'and be cautious on your forward march. With heaven's mercy, you will certainly be able to carry out the vengeance you hold in your heart. Furthermore, I have nothing to worry about in my kingdom. So you, sir, should not fail the souls of your father and brother in Hades. Return promptly as soon as your business is completed. Do not give me cause for concern.'

'Today,' Wu Tzu-hsü replied to the King of Wu, 'as I lead this army on a punitive expedition against Ch'u, there is no doubt but that the result will be a gratifying one. I should hope that Your Majesty will not worry and fret over me on my distant journey. I expect that, before much time has passed, the affair will be completed and I shall return with the army. For this, I shall be grateful unto death!'

When Wu Tzu-hsü had finished his farewell to the King, he launched the troops at once. The sound of forty-two large drums rumbled across the sky, the strident blare of thirty-six horns swept the earth. For a hundred furlongs to the side, the mountain forests shook with the creaking and rumbling of heavy carts and horses. The vanguard, whose role was to take prisoners alive, was the first to take to the road. Like clouds, the formation spread out in all four directions, making a sound which carried across the whole of the wild, open plains. The powerful cavalry charged ahead pell-mell; the brave soldiers leaped forward ferociously. By leaps and bounds, they had soon gone a thousand furlongs, looking like so many scales on a fish. Rank after rank they came, like the wings of wild geese. Lined up shoulder to shoulder, their long lances stood as erect as a forest of trees piercing through heaven. Restlessly, they strung their bows – palm next to palm – and bent them till they arched like crescent moons. White banners fluttered like falling snow and the battle swords glistened like frost. When their crossbows were released, thunder raced across the sky. When they pulled out their swords, the blades howled in the air.

The General of the Army issued orders so all-embracing that not even a drop of water could have slipped through them. The Commanding Officer-in-Charge's directives were so strict that even a bird would have had trouble flying around them.

There was such an overwhelming sea of soldiers and horses that they stretched out every which way for several hundred furlongs. With clanking golden armour and flashing silver saddles, bounding over hill and forest, they rushed forward tumultuously. Foxes and rabbits raced away in fear. Startled, dragons and snakes outdid each other in scurrying out of sight.

§Mounted on his horse, the general boasts a brilliant red flag;
Each and every soldier is lined up according to order. [**20**]

§The vanguard takes to the road – it rushes like the wind –
And soon reaches the northeast bank of the Yellow River.
The vanguard leads the way as it goes bounding forward;
In boats lined up evenly, the army crosses the river.
Those in charge of the crossing man the craft which they have built;
§The water's spray flies . . .

When the army reached the side of the river, a feast had to be prepared for the soldiers. As soon as the officers had finished eating, they forthwith crossed the river. The wind was with them and the waves were still. The mountain forests glistened; the sun and moon shone pure and bright. Mists rolled back on a blue sky and the clouds drifted out over the broad ocean.

For the simple reason that there were many men, there was a multitude of helping hands and so they reached the west side of the river by dawn. Wu Tzu-hsü issued orders to the soldiers of his army, telling them they must be ready to take prisoners as guides for they were now within King P'ing's territory and unfamiliar with its rivers and mountains. First they had to thread their way through dangerous defiles. The far-roving lookouts and long-ranging major-generals exercised their intricate strategy every which way. The guards stealthily advanced and, after more than a month on patrol, their march drew to a close as they approached the capital of Ch'u.

Unfortunately, the King of Ch'u had died some time before. The Crown Prince had been established as King Chao and was now in overall command of his country's forces. When King Chao heard that Wu Tzu-hsü's army was soon to arrive, he proceeded to levy troops, selecting and screening the bravest of the warriors versed in the use of the five weapons. He rewarded them handsomely with silks and made ample provisions for those who achieved merit. The territory of the Kingdom of Ch'u was extensive and its population dense so that, in no time at all, it raised a million troops. The Ch'u army's banners and streamers blocked out the sun, its uniforms and armour spread across the sky. Formations were deployed in all directions for the purpose of joining battle with Wu Tzu-hsü. Battle redoubts were constructed on top of the city-wall. At each and every gate, ballista were set up. In addition, red-hot, molten bronze was prepared. On all four sides of the city, wooden structures with stones which could be rained down on the attackers were erected. Its forces thus fully prepared, the might of the army of Ch'u was a match for ten thousand men.

King Chao commanded his brave troops in the attack upon the Wu army. Tzu-hsü had deployed his troops in a formation that was every bit as tight as the scales of a fish. Cymbals and gongs resounded with a mighty roar. Three beats were struck on the big drums and, with a great hue and cry, they were off.

A thousand troops were posted at strategic passes leading to Ch'u, and a detachment of ten thousand posted along the city moat. Before long, the two armies had crossed weapons in battle. The drawn swords made a swishing sound as they cut through the air, lances were smeared with sweat and blood, and arrows fell about wildly. Dust covered the sky and cavalry horses whinnied until their throats cracked. Sustaining enormous losses in their forward push, they advanced only with great effort. But each man had his mind set on death and refused to entertain even the thought of retreat.

The army on the west was badly defeated, its corpses lay strewn across the plains. Their shields and spears no more to see action, the bodies of the men and horses pressed upon each other, layer after layer.

During the campaign, Wu Tzu-hsü fought ten battles and gained nine victories without the loss of a single soldier. When King Chao saw that his troops were being slaughtered, he ran frightened back inside the city walls with Wu Tzu-hsü hot in pursuit, looking for all the world like wind-blown tumbleweed rushing upon a fire. The Wu army followed after him trying to catch up, appearing like so many clouds blown headlong. They fell upon and utterly exterminated the Ch'u army as easily as though one were splashing boiling water upon snow.

Tzu-hsü shook his whip and declared to King Chao: 'Your father, King P'ing, must be considered as being highly unprincipled. He picked out a bride for his son but then took her as his own concubine. A faithful minister remonstrated against this and was slaughtered whereas, when a deceitful minister engaged in reckless flattery, he was presented with a fief. Your father murdered my father and brother! Dying so unjustly, they suffered great bitterness. Today, I have come to avenge the punishment meted out to my father – that alone can bring joy to my heart! I want, now, to devour your heart! But that, in itself, will not be enough. Even though ten thousand armed men come against me, they will not be a match for my solitary person.

'Today, I am going to take your father's bones and your own living body as a sacrifice to the souls of my father and brother! **[21]** Only then shall I be content!'

Fearful at heart, King Chao at once displayed a white flag and surrendered. The Wu army let out a great cry and straightway entered the capital of Ch'u. They hunted for King Chao and burned his palace. King Chao abandoned the city and fled but was captured by Prime Minister Wu who had his hands bound behind his back.

'King Chao! Where, now, is your father's tumulus?'

'My father, King P'ing,' replied King Chao to Tzu-hsü, 'has already gone the way of all living things. He bears the guilt of having committed a crime against you and has been condemned to dwell in Hades. Since the matter is one of *quid pro quo*, I myself shall submit to dismemberment. Father's guilt thus borne by his son, what use have you for his corpse? To satisfy your desire for revenge, please feel free to use your battle-axe and halberd.'

King Chao was tortured and, not being able to bear up under the suffering nor endure the pain, he revealed the location of his father's grave.

Tzu-hsü captured Wei Ling and had him dismembered. He wrenched out his heart and liver and hacked his body into a thousand pieces. Then he executed all the nine degrees of Wei Ling's kindred.

Tzu-hsü unceremoniously called King Chao and said to him: 'My father was murdered and cast into the deep river.' Whereupon, ceasing all else, he had the current blocked. Having recovered the bones of King P'ing, he took them together with the hearts and livers of Wei Ling and Emperor Chao to the river side. With them, he sacrificed to the souls of his father and brother, saying: 'I, Tzu-hsü, deeply and humbly recognize how unfilial I have been. How sharply painful it was when you, my father and brother, were unjustly slaughtered! But what could I do? At that time, my power had not yet grown sufficiently and so year after year slipped by. Today, however, I have slain the father and son who were so unjust and shall cast them into the deep river in respectful sacrifice to my father and brother. May your souls accept my offering.'

When he had finished the sacrifice, Tzu-hsü broke out into loud crying which moved the sun and the moon to stop their light, the rivers to churn and seethe. All of a sudden, the clouds and mists darkened, the earth trembled and the hills shook. The multitude of soldiers fought to hold back their tears; all mankind was grief-stricken. Fish and dragons swallowed their tears, the river waters forgot to tide. Mountain streams were exhausted and fountains dried up. The dust-laden winds blew cruelly.

When Tzu-hsü had finished his sacrifice, the deep hatred which gripped his heart caused him to take out his sword and again hack at the white bones of King P'ing. At the stroke of the sword, blood flowed from the bones just as when a lamb is being slaughtered. A fire was made and the bones burned. When the wind blew, the fine ashes of the bones soared aloft on it.

Again, Wu Tzu-hsü grasped his sword and hacked King Chao into one hundred sections. These he threw into the river where the fish and turtles ate them. 'Now you have ended up the same as my father,' he thought.

Wu Tzu-hsü searched for his father's and brother's bones but could not find them. In their stead, he erected a totem which can be seen today at a place forty-odd miles southeast of Po-chou. In later ages, people were unaware of the significance of this place which is the present-day Ch'eng-fu District.

Tzu-hsü regrouped his forces and made ready to return, intending to attack the two countries of Liang and Cheng. 'King P'ing of Ch'u was a man without principle,' he wrote in a letter to the King of Cheng. 'He unjustly executed my father and brother. Tzu-shang was a minister of yours. Why did you not think of some way to help him? Instead, treating him as a petty servant, you sent him to his death at the hands of the King of Ch'u. Vengeance has compelled me to destroy the King of Ch'u and now I shall turn my troops against Cheng!'

When the King of Cheng received this letter, he was flustered and frightened beyond measure. He had no idea at all what course he should take. He wanted to raise troops to resist the enemy but was fearful that his soldiers would not win. So he issued a summons for someone who could devise a secret strategy: 'Whoever can stop the army of Wu will be given a part of my kingdom to rule over in consort with me and a gift of one thousand catties of gold in addition.'

There was a fisherman's son who answered the summons by volunteering his services. 'I can stop the army of Wu without need for so much as "an inch of soldier or a foot of sword". All I shall need is a small boat, an oar or punting-pole, a pair of salted fish, a bowl of wheat gruel, and a wooden cup full of fine wine. The boat, along with all of these things, should be placed in the water at the east of the city-wall. Naturally, I have a way for putting them to use.'

The King of Cheng, in accordance with what he had said, had a boat and all the rest sought out and placed in the water. The fisherman got in the boat and, plying his oar and singing a long ballad, cruised about on the moat. The [**22**] King of Cheng closed the western gate of the city and, from atop the city-wall, looked in the distance to see what sort of plan he had devised that could turn back the army of Wu.

When Wu Tzu-hsü's forces were just over ten miles away from the capital of the Kingdom of Cheng, he sent several able-bodied men ahead to see how many soldiers and horses the Kingdom of Cheng could put against him. When they reached the capital of Cheng, they found the four city-gates tightly closed. Again, when they walked over to the area outside the eastern gate, they discovered in the moat a solitary figure aboard a boat with a tattered top who now spoke and now sang: 'Man in the reeds, are you not a gentleman in distress? I have a cup of good wine, five catties of fish, ten biscuits, and a pot of gruel. Please come to my boat and eat them!

§'Ill-fate please take in natural stride;
Good luck, you know, is what I wish you.
If you but serve a virtuous king,
Glory, riches, and honour will be yours.
Should the matter be handled equitably,
§I pray you not allow yourself to abandon me.'

Having heard these words of the boatman, the leader of the party returned at once. When he reached Wu Tzu-hsü's side, he told him in full the words of the boatman. Upon hearing them, Tzu-hsü knew right away that he was the son of the boatman and was pleased.

'When I bore enmity that absolutely had to be wiped clean, it was due to him that I was able to live through it. How could I possibly be ungrateful? He who, when wealthy and honoured, forgets the days of his penury, High Heaven does not assist. "To receive a kindness but not repay it – can such a one be called a man? But he who repays a kindness which he has received is both genteel and elegant."'

Tzu-hsü reined in his horse, put his whip in its case, and went down to the water's edge where he clasped the young man in his embrace. Patting him on the back, Wu Tzu-hsü cried mournfully as he offered his condolences: 'How bitter it was for your father to have drowned in that deep river! But what could I do? Oh what could I do? I hope you do not harbour any animosity against me for that.'

The King of Cheng had grown frightened and came out from within the city-walls to welcome Wu Tzu-hsü. Stepping forward, he said: 'General, I have heard that your vengeance has been achieved and am happy to congratulate you on this great joy! Today, though I deserve a punishment worse than death, I beg you to preserve this wisp of a life.'

'My brother,' said Wu Tzu-hsü to King Cheng, 'was in your service. You should have given him shelter but, instead, you perversely played up to King P'ing and so sent him to his death. Inasmuch as my brother died, you must pay with your life!'

'A messenger from afar came bearing a letter,' replied the King of Cheng, 'in which it was stated that your father's crime would be remitted. I myself was not clear about the details and so sent your brother to go and have a look, saying that he should come back within a month. I never imagined that King P'ing would execute him. Now, I know that I deserve death for this and am content to die without a murmur. But that you, great General, have been able to wreak your vengeance and destroy the ancestral temples of your enemy makes me so happy I could skip and jump. I cannot congratulate you enough! I humbly pray you to be generous and beg that you will spare my life.'

'Great General!' the boatman spoke up. 'The reason I was enlisted by the King of Cheng was because the armies of Wu were coming to attack him. He proclaimed that anyone who could repulse the forces of Wu would be awarded a thousand catties of gold and a fief of ten thousand households. I am desirous of getting that generous reward. How do you feel about this?'

'You have not claimed my life,' said Wu Tzu-hsü. 'If your wishes are to halt my troops and to claim the reward, how dare I go against them?'

Being thus persuaded by the fisherman, Wu Tzu-hsü at once set free the King of Cheng. The King was delighted and so he assembled a mountain of wine and food. For three days and three nights, he feasted the entire army of Wu.

Wu Tzu-hsü proceeded to appoint the fisherman's son Emperor of Ch'u and the two countries of Ch'u and Cheng [**23**] lived together in peace.

Before long, he had again set out with his righteous army, this time to attack the Emperor of Liang. When the King of Liang heard that the arrival of the army of Wu was imminent, he proceeded to slaughter a thousand head of cattle and to stew ten thousand sheep. Food and drinks were piled high as hills and mountains. Lined up along the sides of the road, canopies were set up and mats spread.

Upon the arrival of the army of Wu, the King of Liang, crawling on his elbows and knees, prostrated himself before Wu Tzu-hsü and respectfully addressed him: 'It is my humble desire that you will show me generosity – I beg that you will spare my life. Recently, we heard that you, oh General, have punished Ch'u at which we were overcome with rejoicing. Though at a distance, we celebrated your joy so profoundly that we skipped and jumped.'

'Because it was an urgent matter,' Wu Tzu-hsü replied, 'and because you did not arrange some plan for retaining me, I bear a grudge against you and so have come to punish you.'

Tzu-hsü saw the wine and food lined up south of the city-wall and asked the King of Liang what it was for. 'This wine and food,' replied the King of Liang to the great General, 'may be used to provide for your troops.'

Hearing these words, Tzu-hsü at once ordered all of his troops to eat their fill which, to be sure, they proceeded to do. One of the soldiers who had stuffed himself on the food and was feeling rather ebullient reminded Wu Tzu-hsü: '"Whoever receives one meal from another is indebted to him to that extent; whoever receives two meals from another cannot thank him enough."' Upon which the other soldiers and generals all joined in: 'These words, great General, are well spoken! Let us not attack the King of Liang.'

'If I bear another enmity,' Wu Tzu-hsü reflected in his heart, 'then I will be intent upon obliterating him. But if another enables me to live, how can I be ungrateful?' Whereupon he absolved the King of Liang of all guilt. His words scarcely finished, he prepared to march. His troops having been recalled, they went as far as the shores of the River Ying where Wu Tzu-hsü looked toward the sky and sighed: 'When formerly I came to this place during my flight, I sought food from a maiden here. Not only did she accede to my request but, clasping a stone, threw herself into the river and died. Today I have nothing other than this to repay the kindness of the maiden.' And, in complete accord with the promise he had kept alive, he proceeded to take out one hundred pieces of gold and throw them into the River Ying. Then he addressed her soul:

§'When formerly I was fleeing towards Wu in the south,
We met by the roadside and there I begged food of you.
I was indebted to you for the noonday meal you gave me,
But you clasped a stone and leaped to your death in the river.
Many years have passed since the time when we parted;
Yet day and night I have remembered you all this time –
I think of your spirit tossed on the waves,
Of your wandering soul drifting through briars and thorns.'
His address finished, he held back his tears and spoke these words:
'May your soul in Hades know what I hold within my heart.
Having cast your body so chaste to its fluvial death,
May you never in the Land of Shades heave a lonely sigh! **[24]**
The road to Hades is cut off – I know not what you feel;
Life and Death, since eternity, have gone their separate ways.
Since there is nothing else for me to present to you,
§I can but take these hundred gold pieces as a mortuary requital.'

When Tzu-hsü had finished his service to the dead, he turned his troops around and marched to his sister's house. There he caught hold of his two nephews, Tzu-an and Tzu-yung. He shaved off all the hair on their heads, cut off their ears, and knocked out their incisors. 'Years ago, during my flight, I begged for food from your mother. You wished to capture me and turn me over to King P'ing of Ch'u. Today, I have avenged myself. May you be slaves forever!'

The heaven-protected army, being under a time limitation, could not linger there long and so, horses racing fast as a stroke of lightning or a meteorite, it marched to the dwelling of Tzu-hsü's wife. He intended to meet his wife there and return with her to the Kingdom of Wu. He knocked on the door at once and called out but his wife stayed hidden in the courtyard behind the locked gate. Separated by the courtyard wall, she answered him from afar saying that she would not admit him.

'When, years ago, I met with trouble in Ch'u,' replied Wu Tzu-hsü to his wife, 'I was beholden to you for having come out to welcome me. Now I have avenged myself upon Ch'u and, returning with my troops, have come to see you. I had hoped that things would be as they were in days gone by. Why do you withdraw from me behind closed doors, so that I can not see your face? Or is it that you have some other affection? What makes you so shy that you'll not receive me? Since that time when we parted, I have often thought of your kindness. My indebtedness to you was, indeed, not light and so I refrained from calling upon you.'

'When, years ago, you met with trouble in Ch'u,' replied his wife, 'the road which you took passed by here. You knocked on my gate and, when I saw your face, I knew right away that you had been wronged and were in danger. And so I eagerly responded as I always had done. But you resisted me as though I were taboo and refused to recognize me which pained me so greatly I could not bear it. The bond between husband and wife is a weighty one and I had hoped that you would live and die together with me. It was you who first gave me no slight insult. Subsequently, I developed an aversion to you and will not now receive you. When you were poor and without position, you paid me no notice. Now that you are rich and honoured, why make a pretence of lifting me up? I covet neither wealth nor splendour and would hope that you understand my feelings!'

Tzu-hsü then admitted he had committed a sin punishable by death. Separated by the gate, he prostrated himself and, begging forgiveness, kowtowed to his wife. His wife, seeing how courteous he was being, proceeded to open the door and admit him. Their kindness and love restored to what it was in days of old and their lives rejoined, they made ready to return to Wu.

Tzu-hsü issued orders to the three armies that they were to join up in units in a single line. On this day, all under heaven was clear and peaceful. The sun by day and the moon by night shone pure and bright. Jade whip tapping a steady rhythm against silver saddle, he sang this song:

§'Ah, nothing can match my heaven-protected army!
Thousands and ten thousands of units fill river and plain.
With one sweep, they erase ten thousand miles of dust and dirt;
The Ch'u armies crumbled before their onslaught like bits of tile.
Brave men in communication with great principles,
Taking up sword and gathering armour, they went to distant war.
My warriors are courageous as tigers and leopards;
My cavalrymen are ferocious as real dragons. **[25]**
Deployed, they are a low-hanging cloud spread across the land,
A heavenly host, this flock of cranes ascends to the sky.
They go wherever they please without opposition;
They shall rule the ten thousand lands who one and all revert to them.
Happy, oh happy, yes how happy we are today;
Joyful, oh joyful, yes how joyful we are today!
My golden whip taps the rhythm, our voices join together;
§We follow the road and, before long, shall enter Wu.'

The war horses mingled all together in noisy profusion and the stallions of the cavalry neighed and whinnied. The great armies were vast in number. Amidst tall, green pines and short, tawny grasses, jade whips sounded refreshingly clear and golden saddles sparkled with exquisite fineness. Day and night, they continued on their long journey and, before long, reached Wu.

The King of Wu heard that Tzu-hsü had gained the victory and so, with a mounted escort, came out to greet him. When Tzu-hsü saw that the King of Wu had come out to welcome him, he got down from his horse and, prostrating himself, paid obeisance to the King. In a loud voice, he inquired about his health and then proclaimed: 'Since parting from Your Dragon Countenance, your humble servant has ever remembered not to be lax. I was granted by you the use of an army to attack Ch'u. The troops and myself were of one mind so that there was no resistance to my commandership – together, we exerted ourselves in perfect unity.

'The army eventually reached the northern side of the river and camped there in the southern part of Ch'u. Unfortunately, King P'ing had already died. The Crown Prince had been established as King Chao and was ruling over his country and its military. When he heard that I had arrived with my army, he came out to oppose me and so our two armies clashed. I sent my bravest soldiers to cut off his rear and despatched fierce generals in a frontal attack. Directly we destroyed the Ch'u army. Its men and horses, layer after layer, pressed upon each other. Their bodies were strewn across the plain; their blood stained the hills and streams. It was as though a falcon had swooped down on a crow or a goose; it was like a leopard attacking a fox or a rabbit. There is a common saying which goes: "If you lift up the Koulkun mountains and set them down on an egg, how could the egg possibly not be destroyed? If you pick up a torch and burn a hair with it, how could the hair not be utterly consumed?"

'When King Chao saw that his forces were being routed, he immediately ran back inside the city-walls and hid there. I followed him in swift pursuit and quickly captured him within the city-walls. The hatred which I bore him was especially deep and so I sliced King Chao into one hundred pieces. The decayed bones of King P'ing I hacked with my sword and blood flowed out of them. When I beheld the aftermath, my thirst for vengeance came to rest.

'All was well with the warriors of Wu. But the corpses of the slain Ch'u soldiers were strewn across the entire plain. It was because of your might, oh King, that my desire for vengeance was satisfied. I am deeply beholden to you, great King, and endlessly look up to heaven.

'We lost not a horse nor a soldier; uniforms and armour are all intact. Among all the others, there are some especially valiant men. I pray that you reward them for their achievements and efforts.'

'Since saying goodbye to you, sir,' said the King of Wu, 'I have thought of you affectionately. You were never out of my mind. I was worried that the Ch'u troops might be too numerous and that you would not be able to carry out the vengeance which you bore in your heart. But heaven has assisted you, allowing you to destroy Ch'u and return to Wu. As to all those who performed worthy service, I shall make especially liberal provision for them.'

Following the Emperor, and along with the various troop units, Wu Tzu-hsü entered the city. Shields and spears were inspected and collected; rewards were granted for achievement and effort. Among the others, the fierce generals of the vanguard were each awarded scarlet silks and presented with the Order of the Gold Fish. The flag-carriers and standard-bearers were all given suitable positions. The remainder of the soldiers were each presented with a decoration known as 'Pillar of the State'. Before long, there was dancing and laughter while everyone proclaimed the suasive influence of the King. Seeing that Wu Tzu-hsü had the makings of a great man, the King proceeded to establish him as Grand [**26**] Minister of the Kingdom.

Afterwards, the King of Yüeh, Kou-chien, having raised troops and mobilized his hosts, came to attack the armies of Wu. A wise minister of

Yüeh, Fan Li, remonstrated with the King of Yüeh, saying: 'The Kingdom of Wu has a wise minister called Wu Tzu-hsü. Above, he is learned in astrology; below, he is learned in geomancy. He has established himself through mastery of literature and command of the military arts. He has an unusual countenance and a remarkable spirit. Grand Minister of the Kingdom of Wu, he is at the head of the State. If, today, you attack Wu, you will certainly bring ruin upon yourself.'

'My plans,' replied the King of Yüeh, 'are already formulated. I cannot stop in midcourse.' So he raised troops and mobilized his hosts and went to attack the armies of Wu.

When the troops of Yüeh came in attack, the King of Wu sent his Minister of State, Wu Tzu-hsü, at the head of his troops to go in counter-attack. Tzu-hsü led the soldiers to join in battle with the troops from Yüeh. He slew so many of the soldiers of Yüeh that their corpses lay strewn across the entire plain. The blood was 'enough to set a pestle afloat'.

Seeing that his troops were being slaughtered, the King of Yüeh together with Fan Li sought refuge on K'uai-chi Mountain to escape disaster. There, the King of Yüeh and Fan Li sent word to Minister Wu, saying: 'Seeing that you, Minister of State, had taken vengeance on behalf of your father, we came to pay a visit. We had no intention of coming to make an attack.'

'If it weren't that I accede to the words of the wise minister, Fan Li,' Tzu-hsü said upon hearing this, 'the King of Yüeh along with his whole kingdom would perish.'

After the King of Yüeh had withdrawn his troops and returned to his own land, then the King of Wu became ill. When he was on the point of death, he enjoined the Crown Prince, Fu-ch'a, saying: 'In future, when you are pacifying the country and ruling the people, in everything follow the words of the State Minister, Wu Tzu-hsü.' After the King of Wu died, the Crown Prince Fu-ch'a became the new ruler of Wu.

At that time, the new King of Wu had a dream during the night in which he saw a mysterious glow in the upper part of his hall. In a second dream, he saw dense greenery atop the city-walls. In a third dream, he saw beneath the southern wall of his room a coffer and beneath the northern wall a pannier. In a fourth dream, he saw soldiers joined in battle at the city-gate. And, in a fifth dream, he saw blood flowing to the southeast. The King of Wu immediately sent for the Premier P'i to explain the dreams. 'The dream in which you saw a mysterious glow in the upper part of your hall,' said Premier P'i, 'means happiness and wealth in abundance. Dense greenery atop the city-walls means richness descending like hoar-frost. The coffer beneath the southern wall of your room and the pannier beneath the northern wall mean that you, King, will have long life. Soldiers joined in battle at the city-gate mean that your defences will be tightly interwoven. Blood flowing to the southeast means that the armies of Yüeh will perish.'

The King of Wu then sent for Wu Tzu-hsü to explain his dreams. Tzu-hsü, above, was learned in astrology, below, was learned in geomancy and, in between, understood human emotions. He was versed in literature and had a command of the military arts. And he was in communication with every sort of ghost and spirit in all their transformations. The King of Wu then sent for him to explain his dreams. 'My interpretation of these dreams,' said Wu Tzu-hsü, 'is that they presage great ill-omen. If you, oh King, follow these words of Premier P'i, the Kingdom of Wu will certainly perish.'

'How is this?' the King asked.

Wu Tzu-hsü straightforwardly explained the dreams: 'The dream in which you saw a mysterious glow in the upper part of the hall means that an important person will come. Dense greenery atop the city-walls means that thorns and briars will be everywhere. The coffer beneath the southern wall of your room and the pannier beneath the northern wall mean that you, King, will lose your throne. The soldiers joined in battle at the city-gate mean that the armies of Yüeh will arrive. Blood flowing to the southeast means that corpses will be everywhere. The armies and Kingdom of Wu shall be destroyed and all because of the words of Premier P'i.'

When the King heard these words of Wu Tzu-hsü, he rolled his eyeballs and glared in anger. Striking the steps which led to his throne, he ranted loudly: 'Disputatious old minister. All you do is curse our land.'

Having completed his explanations of the dreams, Wu Tzu-hsü saw that the King was angry with him and so tucked up his skirt and went down from the hall.

'Why, sir, do you tuck up your skirt and go down from the hall?' the King of Wu asked Wu Tzu-hsü.

'Thorns and briars,' replied Wu Tzu-hsü, **[27]** 'have sprung up in your hall and they are pricking my feet. That is why I tuck up my skirt and go down from the hall.'

The King presented Tzu-hsü with the sword 'Illuminating Jade', commanding him to go and commit suicide. When Tzu-hsü received the King's sword, he made a statement to all of the hundred officials: 'After I am dead, cut off my head, take it and place it so that it hangs above the eastern gate of the city-wall. In this way, I shall see the armies of Yüeh when they come to attack the Kingdom of Wu!'

After Wu Tzu-hsü was executed, Yüeh requested a loan of 4,000,000 piculs of grain from Wu which the King of Wu proceeded to give to the King of Yüeh. The stipulated amount of grain was delivered in instalments. Subsequently, the King of Yüeh had the grain steamed and returned to Wu and wrote a letter in which he reported to the King of Wu: 'This grain is excellent. You may give it to your people to plant.' The grain which was used to repay Wu had been steamed and, when it was sown in the earth, not a single grain germinated. The people having lost their livelihood, there was one year of dearth and five years of famine.

Thereupon, the King of Yüeh consulted with Fan Li: 'The Kingdom of Wu, in pacifying the land and ruling over the people, mostly takes the advice of Premier P'i. What stratagem shall you and I design, sir, whereby we can attack the armies of Wu?'

'The King of Wu,' Fan Li informed the King, 'ordered the wise Minister of the Kingdom of Wu, Wu Tzu-hsü, to commit suicide. When a house is without a strong beam, it will necessarily collapse. If a wall is not made of good earth, before long it will crumble. If a kingdom is without loyal ministers, how can it but degenerate? Now, there is this flattering minister, Premier P'i, who can certainly be won by bribery.'

'But what should we use to bribe him?' asked the King.

'Premier P'i delights in gold and jewels,' Fan Li informed the King, 'and likes beautiful girls. If he can obtain these things, he will certainly open a way for us. Of that you can rest assured.'

When the King of Yü heard these words of Fan Li, he then dispatched emissaries to the Li River to get yellow gold, to Ching Mountain to seek for white jade, to the Eastern Sea to gather lustrous pearls, and to the Southern Kingdoms to solicit beautiful girls. After the King of Yüeh had procured these things, he sent valiant men to take them to the Kingdom of Wu and present them to Premier P'i. P'i saw that, among these things, the beautiful girls were nimble and shapely, the lustrous pearls shone brilliantly, the yellow gold flashed and sparkled, and the white jade was without blemish.

Yüeh made the presentation to Premier P'i and he joyfully accepted it. The King of Yüeh, seeing that this obsequious minister had accepted the bribe, made demands upon him.

'When the King of Wu had Wu Tzu-hsü killed,' the King again inquired of Fan Li, 'did not the Kingdom of Wu go two years without a harvest? The people have, up to this day, experienced five years of dearth and famine.'

The King of Yüeh called Fan Li to him and asked, 'Today, I wish to attack the Kingdom of Wu. What do you think of this matter?'

'If you attack Wu now,' Fan Li answered the King, 'it is the best possible of times.'

Whereupon the King of Yüeh organized troops and mobilized his hosts to the number of 400,000 men. When they had reached the halfway point in their march, he was afraid that the soldiers might be at variance with him. Along the way, he came across an angry frog which was croaking vociferously beside the road. He dismounted and gathered it up in his arms.

'For what reason, oh King,' his assistants asked, 'do you embrace this angry frog?'

'All my life, I have been fond of valiant men,' the King answered. 'This angry frog was croaking vociferously by the road so I dismounted and gathered it up in my arms.'

Each soldier among his hosts reflected to himself: 'The King, upon seeing an angry frog, will even go so far as to dismount from his horse and gather it up in his arms. We, too, must strive to be robust and strong. Then, when the King sees us, he will consider us even as he does the angry frog.'

Thus, to a man, the soldiers took on courage and shouted vociferously three times. Seeing that his troops were at such a pitch, the King presented them all with generous rewards.

They marched until they reached a place where a small river opened into a larger one. They paused on the banks of the smaller river before crossing it. Someone gave the King a gourd full of wine. The King drank from it but could not finish it and so poured it out into the river, saying: 'Soldiers! Drink together with me!' **[28]** The soldiers all prepared to drink the river's waters. Without exception, they smelled the vapours of wine in the water. The soldiers drank the river water and all got drunk. When the King heard report of this, he was greatly pleased.

'A single portion of unstrained wine tossed in the river,
And the three armies are reported drunk.'

The King of Yüeh led his armies north across the mouth of the river intending to go on to the Kingdom of Wu. The King of Wu heard that Yüeh was coming to attack him but, seeing as his people were hungry and their strength flagged, had no one to put against its armies.

That night, the King of Wu saw in a dream the loyal minister, Wu Tzu-hsü, who spoke a word with him: 'Yüeh is leading troops to come in attack. King, you may well ponder it.'

The King of Wu at once sent for his hundred ministers and took counsel with them: 'I saw in a dream the loyal minister, Wu Tzu-hsü, who spoke to me these words: "Yüeh is leading troops to come in attack. King, you may well ponder it."'

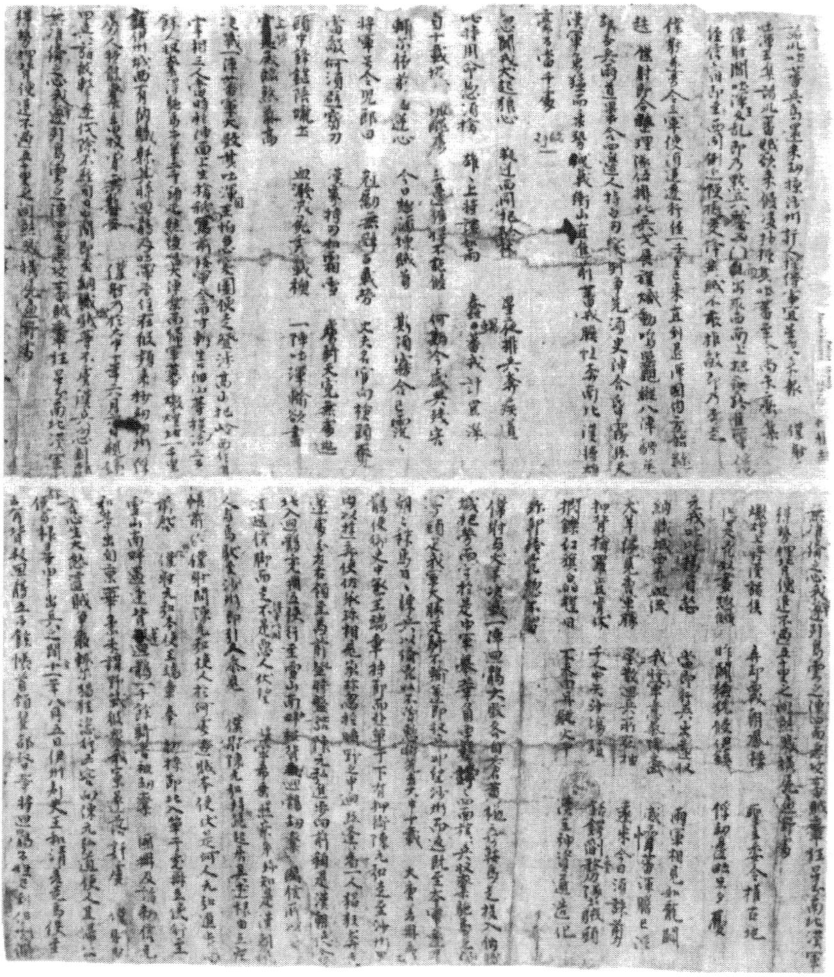

5. Chang I-ch'ao transformation text (ms P2962).

4

CHANG I-CH'AO

[Transformation Text on Chang I-ch'ao]

... The mounted troops of the Tibetans from the Szechwan area were returning to sack Sha-chou. Spies who had obtained information about their movements, without stopping to rest at night, came to report to the Secretary for State Affairs: 'The King of the Tuyughun is gathering together the barbarian bandits from the Szechwan area and is intent upon coming here to invade and pillage. As of today, however, the Tibetans have not yet all assembled.'

When the Secretary for State Affairs heard that the King of the Tuyughun had rebelled, he immediately mustered his troops. The army went out of the city through the gate of death, then advanced via forced march towards the southwest.

After having spent but two nights on the road, they soon arrived in the vicinity of West Paulownia, where they intended to join battle with the enemy. The bandits ran away immediately, not daring to put up any resistance. The Secretary for State Affairs then signalled his three armies that they must pursue them. After a march of more than three hundred and fifty miles which took them all the way to the Kingdom of the Tuyughun, they finally caught up with the bandits. The Secretary for State Affairs immediately ordered his troops to dress their ranks and make ready their weapons. They unfurled their flags and pennants, they beat their lizard-skin drums. The eight formations were executed, brave heroes went galloping by. The troops were divided into two striking-forces so as to envelop the enemy on all four sides. The men grasped their naked swords, the sallying cavalry vied to be first. Within moments, the formation closed like a dark mist spreading over the sky. The Chinese armies valiantly took the initiative. Dragging their spears behind them, they rushed over the hills and advanced directly.

This is the place where the cowardly barbarian tribes flee north and south and where one hundred men of the heroic Chinese General stand against a thousand of the enemy:

§Suddenly, it was heard that the barbarian dogs had begun to show their savagery,
That they had revolted at West Paulownia and held a strategic forest.
Troops were deployed to hurry there on a beeline through the starry night,
They were under orders that this time, no matter how, they must apprehend the foe;
The heroic Field Marshal had plans plentiful as raindrops,
Against them, to what would the schemes of the stupid barbarian tribes amount?
For ten years, lançes raised, they had kept the vile rogues at bay,
On the three frontiers, the fierce and the violent were unable to invade;
Who would have thought that this year they would wreak any havoc? –
Abruptly, and according to precedent, their rebelliousness began to show itself.
Now it was necessary, no matter how, to display the thieves' heads on high poles,
Swiftly, the mist-like armies closed in, wave upon dense wave;
With these words, the General issued orders to his men:
'Persevere! Do not shirk the toil of a hundred battles! **[115]**
The reputation and rank of men of spirit are to be found in the tip of a spear,
In confronting the enemy, you must not flee from his sword!'
The Chinese grasped their swords which glinted like frost and snow,
The savage horsemen had nowhere to flee under the broad heavens;
Heads struck by sword and lance tips were piled up on mounds of earth,
Blood splattered from the barbarian corpses soaked through battle tunics.
After one skirmish, the Tuyughun were almost entirely defeated,
§The Field Marshal approached sternly and with rising fury.

In this one decisive battle, the barbarian armies suffered a great defeat. The King of the Tuyughun was terror-stricken. Breaking through the encirclement, he fled. He ascended a high mountain and took control of a dangerous defile. His three chief ministers, at.that very moment, were being captured alive at the head of the formation. They were unceremoniously executed in front of the horses according to the military code. More than three hundred captives, including women and children, were taken alive. Two thousand head of camels, horses, cattle, and sheep were seized. Then they returned to their camp singing 'Big Battle Music'.

Three hundred and fifty miles north of Tun-huang was Lapchuk

District Town, a strategically important location west of the walled city of Hami. At that time, the Uighurs and the Tuyughun had settled there and frequently came to Hami to pillage. They captured the people and their belongings, forcibly seized their herds, and left them without a moment's peace. On July 11, 856, the Secretary for State Affairs personally organized armoured troops and went there to attack and drive them away. In less than ten days, they reached the town of Lapchuk. The bandits had not expected that the Chinese troops would arrive so suddenly and were totally unprepared. Our armies proceeded to line up in a 'black-cloud formation', swiftly striking from all four sides. The barbarian bandits were panic-stricken. Like stars they splintered, north and south. The Chinese armies having gained the advantage, they pursued them, pressing close at their backs. Within fifteen miles, they caught up with them.

This is the place where their slain corpses were strewn everywhere across the plain:

§The Field Marshal from Tun-huang was a Chinese feudal lord,
He cast out the western barbarians and paid court at the Phoenix Tower;
The Divine Ruler had commissioned him to govern the land in the west,
But the Turkish tribes were utterly antagonistic.
He had recently heard that the Huns were invading the town of Hami,
They plundered and captured the frontier people making them anxious day and night;
The Commander-in-Chief shouted angrily and arched his eyebrows in indignation,
Right away, he marched his soldiers off on a distant mission of retrieval.
When the two armies saw each other, it was like dragons fighting,
The blood even flowed west of the town of Lapchuk; **[116]**
Our general's triumphant manner embodied grace and martial prowess,
He so intimidated the barbarian louts that they lost all courage;
No sooner had the dog barbarians seen that the T'ang armies were victorious,
Than their retreating troops scattered like stars as they deserted their posts.
Having come so far, today the Chinese troops would have to slaughter the foe,
They pressed close at their backs and seized them, unwilling to desist;
A thousand men were struck by arrows and perished on the battlefield,
With razor-sharp blades, they slashed and sliced, lopping off the heads of the bandits.

§Fluttering red flags gleamed as brightly as the sun,
And would not have been shamed by T'ien Tan when he let loose his fiery cattle;
The divine aid of the ruler of China prevailed throughout,
§They exterminated the desperadoes, sparing none at all.

In this decisive battle between the Secretary for State Affairs and the dog barbarians, the Uighurs were badly beatern. Flustered, each of them abandoned his saddled horse and ran inside the city wall of Lapchuk which they held securely. Thereupon, the central armies raised their decorated horns and, with a great clashing sound, made a series of attacks. Troops were set in ambush on all four sides. They seized ten thousand head of camels, horses, and the like. Our armies gained a great victory, not having lost a single mount. They proceeded at once to regroup and, heading for Sha-chou, they returned. After they arrived at their base, they fed their horses every morning and drilled their troops every day. In order to be prepared for the Huns, there was never even a moment's respite.

Previously, in the tenth year of the Ta-chung reign-period (856), the Great T'ang government had deputed the Secretary of the Board of Censors, Wang Jui-chang, as an ambassador to confer recognition upon the Uighurs. Bearing his credentials, he had journeyed to the Khanate. Below him was the peon, Ch'en Yüan-hung. Now, as he ran inside the boundary of Sha-chou, he was spotted by the border-guard, Tso Ch'eng-chen. Suddenly, in the middle of the wilderness, Ch'eng-chen unexpectedly encountered a man who was racing along wildly. So he charged his assistants to bring the man in front of his horse and began immediately to interrogate him. Ch'en Yüan-hung stepped forward in front of him and declared: 'While serving on a mission to confer recognition, I was ordered by the Chinese court to go north and enter Uighur territory. We had gone as far as the southern slopes of the Snowy Mountains when our State documents were wrested from us by mutinous Uighurs. So each of us fled, running wherever his feet led him. Thus have I come to this place – I am not an unfriendly person. I humbly look to you, General, and hope that you will extend your kind consideration.'

Having learned that he was an envoy of the Chinese court, Ch'eng-chen gave him a horse to carry him to Sha-chou. There he was conducted in to an interview with the Secretary for State Affairs. Ch'en Yüan-hung kneeled to him in obeisance and paid his respects. Standing in front of the tent, he stated in full the reasons for his being there.

The Secretary for State Affairs asked Ch'en Yüan-hung: 'Where did you meet the bandits? And who was the chief of your mission?'

Ch'en Yüan-hung stepped forward and addressed the Secretary for State Affairs: 'The chief of my mission was Wang Jui-chang. He had received imperial orders to go north and enter the Khanate bearing his credentials as an envoy to confer recognition. We had gone as far as the southern slopes of the Snowy Mountains when we came across a thousand and more rebellious Uighur horsemen. We were at once robbed of our state documents of appointment and various letters patent. The others and I had come out from the capital, never having had any familiarity with field operations. **[117]** They were many and we were few. As a result, we succumbed to their villainous trickery.'

When the Secretary for State Affairs heard this, his heart was filled with a great rage. 'How dare these bandits be so brazenly seditious that they recklessly engage in wanton destruction!' Then he turned to Ch'en Yüan-hung and told him: 'You may go back to the public hostel where you will be provided with rations.'

In the interval before the troops set out, on August 27, 857, the Prefect of Hami, Wang Ho-ch'ing, dispatched a messenger on horseback. When he arrived at Sha-chou, he said: 'There are five hundred and more tent-units of Uighurs whose leaders are the Military-Governor Ti and others. The Uighur people whom they lead have already reached the vicinity of Hami . . .'

USAGES AND SYMBOLS

While every effort has been made to ensure the accuracy of the translations, they have been designed to be readable for the intelligent layman without having recourse to frequent annotations.* A large number of the notes that have been provided deal with textual problems. Another portion is to identify Sanskrit equivalents for Buddhist technical terms. These are seldom defined since the necessary adjustments are usually made in the translation itself. The Sanskrit equivalents are intended primarily for students of Buddhism. I also hold the faint hope that the Central Asian deserts may someday yield to scholars manuscripts of the forerunners of the Tun-huang narratives. Since they will probably be full of holes if they ever are found, my notes may be of some assistance to Indologists who would reconstruct them.

Variants from the texts as established by *Tun-huang pien-wen chi* (hereafter T) are mentioned only when significant. In general, I have cited them in two situations: when they represent a superior reading and when they are of assistance in understanding a difficult passage.

All emendations given by T are accepted unless noted otherwise. I have also made many additional emendations of my own. When I have done so, this is by no means intended as a recommendation that future editions actually print the emendations instead of the original errors. Quite the contrary, I firmly believe that printed editions should attempt to duplicate the exact orthography of the manuscripts as closely as possible.

It is my practice to put all types of notes in a single series. This is to avoid having the reader flip madly through the pages trying to find in which appendix or set of notes a certain type of information is given.

All notes are keyed to the line numbers of the translated texts, e.g. line 37n. In cases where there are two or more notes per line, they will be distinguished, for purposes of cross referencing, by further numbering, hence line 37n1, line 37n2 etc. mean 'the first note to line 37', 'the second note to line 37', and so forth. Reference to notes in the other texts are preceded by 'Śāriputra', 'Maudgalyāyana', 'Wu' or 'Chang'. The words in bold type are intended to assist the reader in identifying the element of a line that is being commented upon or annotated.

The bold numbers appearing in brackets in the translation indicate the pages of T. The sign § marks the beginning and end of a passage in rhymed verse.

* In general, my attitude toward notes is the same as that of Eugene A. Nida, *Toward a Science of Translating* (Leiden, 1964), pp. 238–9.

The basic texts and manuscripts used as sources are given at the head of the notes section to each text, with the primary manuscript used for the translations given first. For notes on these manuscripts, see 'Inventory'.

For all abbreviated citations, see the References.

I have found it convenient in making the annotations to employ the following symbols:

[ ]	'understood', 'supply'	
→	'should be emended to'	
*	'unattested', 'incorrect reading'	
/	'or'; if this sign passes through another sign, it negates the meaning of the latter, e.g. ↛ 'do not emend'	
=	'equivalent to', 'interchangeable with'	
≡	'similar to', 'stands for', 'is a pun for'	
+	'the following, not in the original, has been added to the translation'	
<	'derived from'	
>	'whence derived'	
√	'root'	
(?)	'this remark is doubtful/made with reservation'	
got...	'*got* is my reconstructed translation' (three dots are approximately equivalent to one missing character in the text)	
r	*recto*	of Tun-huang mss
v	*verso*	
P.	Pāli	
Skt.	Sanskrit	
BHS.	Buddhist Hybrid Sanskrit or Prakrit	

I have also used several other Arbitrary Signs and Symbols for which see the latest edition of *Webster's New Collegiate Dictionary* and the stylesheet of the *Harvard Journal of Asiatic Studies*.

Chinese terms are used for accuracy in the references, thus *chüan* (scroll, roll, fascicle, chapter), *ts'e* (volume, tome), *t'ao* (case), *t'uan* (section), *yin* (section).

NOTES ON THE TEXTS

ŚĀRIPUTRA

MS formerly in the possession of Dr Hu Shih
MS formerly in the possession of Lo Chen-yü
T361–389
S5511
S4398v
P4524v
P4615
Translated in Iriya 25–53

1 **Subduing of Demons** 降魔, *mārajit*; *māra-jaya*; *māra-vijaya*; *māra-bhañjaka*; *māra-abhibhu*. This title would seem more appropriate to describe the content of the preceding piece in T which treats of Buddha's successful stand against the onslaught of Māra's legions (破魔, *māra[-sainya]-pramardana*) at Uruvelā beneath the Tree of Wisdom. The two characters, *hsiáng-mo*, are usually employed in canonical literature to refer to that specific event.

4 **sands of the Ganges** Or 恆伽沙, *Gaṅgā-nadī-vālukā*. + 'To people.'

7 **Deer Park** *Mṛgadāva* (at Śāraṅganātha, northeast of Vārāṇaśi).

8 **converts** *Kauṇḍinya*, also written 拘隣、俱隣, etc. The names of these five early companions of Śākyamuni are Ājñāta-Kauṇḍinya, Aśvajit, Bhadrika, Daśabala-Kāśyapa, and Mahānāma-Kulika. The term is derived from the name of the first disciple who is said to have understood the Buddha's Law.

9 **twin trees** The pair of *śāla* trees under which Buddha entered nirvāṇa.

10 **Brāhman students** *Brahmacārin*. This term was used by other religious organizations contemporaneous with Buddhism and meant one who lived the ideal spiritual life prescribed by each of them. Indeed, both Śāriputra and Maudgalyāyana, before being converted to Buddhism, were *brahmacārya* under the Paribbajāka chief Sañjaya. See *Majjhima Nikāya*, ed. V. Trenckner, R. Chalmers, and Mrs Rhys Davids for the Pali Text Society (1888–1925), vol. II, p. 155. I have been unable to determine precisely who the ten Brahmin students referred to here are. One suggestion is that they may somehow be related to the Jātaka story number 495, 'Daśa-brāhmaṇa-jātaka'. There, ten evil types of Brahmins – who do not really deserve the name – are contrasted with the 500 Pacceka Buddhas dwelling in the Himalayas. See *The Jātaka*, ed. E. B. Cowell (London, 1957), vol. III, pp. 227–31. In the final analysis, however, I am inclined to believe that 十梵志 has somehow arisen by confusion with Subhadra 須/蘇跋陀(羅), a Brahman of Kusinārā 120 years old, who was the *last* (cf. line 8n) disciple converted by the Buddha himself just before passing away.

12 **Wisdom** *Prajñā*.
affliction *Kleśa*.

13 **true origin** 眞原 (or 源 as on S4398v), 'absolute origin'.
three points of Alpha This is a skewed translation for the Devanāgarī letter इ (*i-*[*kara*]). This letter was written ∴ in the Brāhmī script (Aśokan) of the third century B.I.E. and in the Indian cave-temples of the first and second centuries of our era while later, in Tocharian, it was written $^{c\,c}_{c}$. See Hans Jensen, *Sign, Symbol and Script*, tr. George Unwin (New York, 1969), pp. 371–6. As might be expected of the 'writing of the gods', these three little dots are fraught with symbolic meaning. They may represent fire or water or the three eyes of Śiva or the *dharmakāya* 法身, *prajñā*, and *vimokṣa* 解脫 (as in the *Nirvāṇa Sūtra*, ch. 2). Being triangular in shape, this letter is considered to have no beginning, middle, nor end.

14 **mankind** Chou 214.2 and Hsieh 91.1 would prefer to read 人 as 八, hence 'the eight realms'. Cf. T362.5 and see line 121n.
six impurities of sense The six *guṇas* of sight, sound, smell, touch, taste, and ideation. Cf. *ṣaḍ viṣayāḥ*, the six objects of cognition: *rūpa*, *śabda*, *gandha*, *rasa*, *spraṣṭavya*, and *dharma*.

17 **saved** *Pāramitā*, 波羅蜜.

18 **elder** 長者. Technically, this term should be translated as 'householder', [*agrakuliko*] *gṛha-patiḥ* or *śreṣṭhin* so as not to be confused with *sthavira* which means 'Elder [of the Hīnayāna Church]'.
Anāthapiṇḍada 給孤(獨) literally means 'to give to orphans and widows, i.e. the unprotected'. This notion is also expressed by the name of the elder mentioned here, 阿那他賓低.

21 **alms-bowl** *Pātra*.

23 **noon meal** In Buddhist usage, 食 *āhāra* refers to the principal meal of the day which was at noon; *āhāra-sthitika*.

25 **extended** Begging for food is one of the twelve prescribed forms of behaviour (*dhūta*) of a monk; *upapadyamānakāla*/*piṇḍa-cārika*/*bhaikṣya*.
blessed virtue 福德 together stand for *puṇya*, the blessing which derives from good deeds.

26 **various levels** 次第, *kramaśas*, the concept of graduated teaching by the Buddha according to the ability of the recipient. This line is grammatically parallel to the preceding and succeeding lines. Literally, 'his graduated teachings manifested . . .'.
impartial 平等, *sama*/*samatā*.

27 **going barefoot** 洗 → 跣 (Hsü 115).
rules 'Commandment, precept, prohibition'; *śīla-vrata*.

28 **mat** Interpreting 坐 as meaning 坐具 *niṣīdana*/*saṃstarah*.
meditation *Dhyāna*.
calmed his thoughts 靜慮, an alternate translation for *dhyāna*.

30 **deities** *Deva*.
venerated T has 曉. 瞻 is the preferred reading (Chou 214.5). Literally, 'looked up at him in admiration'.

32 **Subhūti** Name of one of the ten chief disciples, an authority on *Śūnya*. As indicated by the English arrangement of the text, the appearance of this name is regarded as an abrupt departure from the otherwise consistently hexasyllabic prose rhythm of this passage. His appearance here, however, is not so unusual when we consider that he is the most frequent interlocutor of the Buddha in many of the Mahāyāna sūtras dealing with transcendent wisdom.

34 **sincere** 誠 seems the better reading (Chou 214.6), also see T363.16.

35 **formlessness** *Animitta*; *nirābhāsa*; *alakṣana*.

41 **opened** 擗 = 闢 (Hsü 37).

42 **fund of meaning** 'Storehouse of Buddhist doctrine.' This is not a usual Buddhist expression despite the superficial resemblance.

44 **Correctly oriented** Compare the Buddhist concept of 無倒 which signifies having

the correct (not upside-down) view of things; *aviparyāsa*.
quadruple hearts Kindness *maitrī*, pity *karuṇā*, joy *muditā*, indiscrimination *upekṣa* = 四無量(心), *catvāri apramāṇani*, the four infinite Buddha states of mind.

45 **quintuple eyes** Five types of vision: human, deva, Hināyāna wisdom, Boddhisattva truth, Buddha-vision.

46 **four fruits** Four grades of sainthood: *srota-āpanna-phala*, *sakradāgāmi-phala*, *anāgāmi-phala*, *arhat-phala*.
banished The punctuation of Chou 214.8 (after 人) is preferred.
illusions regarding the ego Of which there are four, 我人四相 (SH 238a). However, since this is repeated immediately below, I am inclined to believe that the present instance may be a corruption (by inversion) of 人我, the false view that everyone has a personality or soul. When this erroneous view is disposed of, the condition of *asattva-ātman-kathā* 無人我 obtains.

47 **three virtues** Moral qualities of a Boddhisattva: ten stages of wisdom 十住, ten activities 十行, ten goals or directions 十迴向.
eightfold noble path *Āryamārga* 八正道(分).

48 **essential nature** *Atmakatva*; *dharmatā*.
four mental states . . . 我人四想 = 我人四相. The same miswriting occurs on T361.8, see T390n6. Also cf. line 1355n below.

49 **vacuous** T390n5 informs us that everything above this line was brought over from S5511 while Chou 214n1 notes that what follows has been supplemented by reference to S4398v.

50 **six types of sensations** This translation is arrived at through a rather complicated process: 六類有情 (*sattva*, sentient being) means 六衆生, the six creatures. The six senses are then likened to wild animals (dog, bird, snake, hyena, crocodile, monkey) in captivity struggling to escape. Thus, 六衆生 serves as a metaphor for 六情, 六根(*indriya*), 六依, 六入, and so on, all of these latter expressions being different ways of referring to the six senses.
annihilated *Nirvāṇa*.

51 **presentation** 布施 usually stands for *dāna*, 'alms', but may also refer to the Buddha's 'gift' of the Law, that is 法施, *dharma-dāna*.
by stages 初中後, *ādi-madhya-anta*.

52 **portion** *Asaṃtuṣṭa*.

53 **space** *Akāsa*. S4398v has only 虛.

55 **distinguishing marks** *Lakṣaṇa*.

56 **Dharma-body** *Dharmakāya*.

57 **life** *Jāti*.

58 **levelling** *Samatā*.

60 **treasures** *Sapta ratna*, of which there are various lists. See below, line 1693n2 for one.
great chiliacosm 大千(世界), strange to say, means the same as 三千大千世界 *tri-sahasra-mahā-sahasra-loka-dhātu*, a great chiliacosm which consists of 1,000,000,000 small worlds, i.e. $1,000^3$.

61 **terms** 勿 → 句 (unmistakably clear on the Hu Shih ms and on S4398v). There are several enumerations of the four phrases or sentences; *cātuṣ-koṭi*[*kā*]. They deal largely with phenomenal existence (e.g. (1) is, (2) is not, (3) both is and is not, (4) neither is nor is not). Thus they are applicable in the present context whereas the 四勿 are decidedly not because of their clear Confucian associations. *Analects*, 'Yen Yüan' 論語, 顏 , Legge, I.250: 'The Master replied: "Look not at what is contrary to propriety; listen not to what is contrary to propriety; speak not what is contrary to propriety; make no movement which is contrary to propriety."' 子曰: 非禮勿視, 非禮勿聽, 非禮勿言, 非禮勿動.

62 **all living beings** This is *sattva* considered horizontally through time and not, as it

usually is, vertically at a given moment.
five periods of decay *Pañca-kaṣāya*, five turbidities or impurities. They represent stages in the deterioration of human life over enormous stretches of time.

63 **transcendence** One of the last three words in this sentence (*vikrama, jina, visaya*) is superfluous as can be deduced from the parallel structure. Which of these words is unnecessary I am, however, not prepared to say since the meaning remains the same in any case.
as I have not used 等, which was added from S4398v (it actually occurs there after 衆), because it destroys the 6–6–6–6 rhythm. + 'The Law'(?).

64 **renounce** *Upekṣā*.
itself 却 is an adversative.

65 **raft of attachment** This is very nearly a direct quotation from the *Vajracchedikā-sūtra*, 金剛般若經, Ta8.749b: 'Those who understand my simile of the Law as a raft ought to relinquish even the Law itself. How much more should they relinquish what is not the Law!' 知我說法, 如筏喻者, 法尚應捨, 何况非法.

66 **unreality** This will surely be difficult for the average reader to understand. I have added the word 'recognition' to make the sentence slightly more palatable than a full-strength dosage of this most difficult concept would have allowed. To expand somewhat: after one has realized that everything is but illusion, he must then proceed to destroy the abstract notion of illusion itself!

67 **supranoumenal** 妙有 *sat*, 'the incomprehensible entity'.
sphere Here a mental state.

68 **perfect wisdom** *Bodhi*.

69 **comprehension** *Vijñāna*, here nearly synonymous with the six *guṇas* mentioned in the previous sentence.
forms All phenomena; all creation.

70 **wisdom** Again *prajñā*.

71 **... future** Kāśyapa, Śākyamuni, and Maitreya.

72 **this sūtra** By which the *Diamond Sūtra*, *Vajracchedikā-prajñā-pāramitā-sūtra* (T362.2) is intended.

73 **supremely perfect** *Pravaraḥ*; *upacāruḥ*; *viśiṣṭaḥ*.

78 **more** This is a very strange position for 餘 to occur. Surely we are not to interpret this as 'in a little over a year, there were several hundred [translations]'.
several On the variant 四 in S4398v, see the discussion on dating in the Introduction.
Although 雖則, 'in spite of the fact that', cf. T383.15 and T759.1.

81 **holy mind** The Buddha-mind.

82 **central way** That between 有 and 無, realism and nihilism.

84 **Court** The manuscript unmistakably has the character 朝 after 漢, as does S4398v.

87 **... Way** This title is discussed in the Introduction under the section on dating. It is set off from the rest of the text as is indicated by the format of the translation. For felicity's sake, however, 皇帝陛下 is made part of the formal title while it is not so included in the set-off title on the ms.

90 **Five Classics** The *Books* of *Poetry*, *Changes*, and *History*, the *Ritual*, and the *Spring and Autumn Annals*. *History of the Later Han*, 'Biography of Chu Fu' 朱浮傳 (*PNP*) 63(33).6a: 'The Five Classics record the governance of the realm.' 五典紀國家之政. The commentary lists the works at the beginning of this note.

91 **Nine Barbarians** Specifically, all nine tribes of the Eastern Barbarians.

92 **eight directions** 八表 is another way of expressing 八荒. S4398v has 八方.
effortless The Taoist inaction or nonaction of Lao-tzu. Since the tenor of this portion of the text is quite unsectarian and since the subject is briefly about governance rather than Buddhist philosophy, 無爲 should not here be interpreted as *asaṁskṛta*.

93 **every quarter** S4398v has 四海 '[within] the four oceans'.
Yao and Shun Ancient legendary emperors.

95 **Three Teachings** Confucianism, Taoism, and Buddhism.

97 **... sources** Clearly derived from *The Book of Changes*, 'Remarks on the Trigrams', 說卦, Legge (Sung), 338–9: 'They (thus) made an exhaustive discrimination of what was right, and effected the complete development of (every) nature, till they arrived (in the Yi) at what was appointed for it (by Heaven).' 窮理盡性, 以至於命.

99 **perception** 相° (LSY).

100 **Imperial** The placement of 'The Imperial' is to indicate that 聖 and 恩 are separated on the ms.

101 **... ocean** This sounds awkward as does the original to me. I know of a 海潮(音) *jala-dhara-garjita* which refers to the Buddha's voice or to the sound of an assembled body of monks chanting. There is also the expression 涌泉 which may stand for the sūtras or for the bountiful wisdom of the Buddha himself (Ta83.599c). S4398v drops 泉.

102 **Heavenly Vision** 天開 → 天眼, *divyacakṣus*. I believe that the writing in the text may have occurred because of confusion with 天開眼 which is a popular expression for 'Zodiacal Light' 黃道光, a nebulous light which appears in the west after sunset and in the east before dawn. Since it is considered to be auspicious, it may have been used to refer to the emperor in some fashion or other. But this seems too far-fetched to receive serious consideration here. Another reading which was tried and rejected is * 開天, i.e. 開元天寶. The principal grounds against such an emendation are the fact that Hsüan-tsung's reign periods were already mentioned just above and that it destroys the parallelism with 聖恩.

sun and moon The T editors are correct in following S4398v because the reading is superior in terms of prosody and meaning. They are incorrect, however, in stating (collation note 10) that the Hu Shih ms originally read 譬月; it reads 譬日 as Cheng, *Popular*, would have it.

104 **Buddhist Law** I follow S4398v which reads 仏法因慈重曜. Sense can here be made of 'the Buddha-sun' (佛日 *Buddha-sūrya*) only with difficulty.

105 **monasteries** Considering the parallel relationship to 'gardens' below and the probability of phonetic confusion, 之 (*tśi*) should be emended to 寺 (*zi*), *saṅghārāma*. Visual or etymological confusion may also have been involved since 之 and 寺 are related morphemes. Also see the following note.

precious groves This expression, which refers to the avenues of trees in the Pure Land, has been a favourite name for Buddhist monasteries. The most famous of these was the monastery of Hui-neng 慧能 (737–820) who was the sixth patriarch of the Dhyāna sect. It was located in Tian-chiang District, Shao-chou 韶州典江縣 (Kwang-tung Province).

106 **palms** 見葉 → 貝葉 (Hsü 116) are leaves (*pattra*) of the Palmyra palm (*Borassus flabelliformus*) which were favoured by the Indian Buddhists as writing material. Despite the fact that I have accepted Hsü's emendation for the purposes of translation (cf. line 108n), it is necessary to point out that 喜見 (*priyadarśana*) 葉, 'pleasant-seeming leaves' does make sense here and that it seems better rhythmically than having a single syllable adjective dangling at the beginning of the clause.

107 **gardens** *Vihāra*.

esotericism 總持, *dhāraṇī*.

108 **copious** 派 → 沛 (Hsü 116). 派 is certainly wrong. Cheng, *Popular*, 226 and the Hu Shih ms as well as S4398v all have 泒 (= 泋 = 流), 'flowing'(?). 法雲 is *dharmamegha*.

109 ***prajñā*** Interestingly, the ms originally had *jo-po* 若般√, the tiny checkmark after the 般 indicating that the order should be reversed.

110 ***Vajra(cchedikā)*** 能斷 'capable of cutting' is omitted from the following exegesis.

111 ***pāra ...*** This explanation, though frequent, is incorrect. *Pāra* means 'highest'. *Pāragata*, 'gone to the other shore' 到彼岸 (Chou's reading 215.7 the correct one

(although the ms clearly reads 彼到岸!)) is actually another standard translation of the entire word *pāramitā*, Tib. *pha rol tu phyin pa*, which is itself a false etymological reading, **pāram* + $\sqrt{i}$. *Mi* may not be separated from *pāra* since the word *pāramita* is derived from *parama*, 'mastery, supremacy' (see Franklin Edgerton, *Buddhist Hybrid Sanskrit Dictionary* (New Haven, 1953), 341–2). *Ta* by itself serves only a grammatical function, that of indicating a participially derived noun.

112 **[*pāra*]*mita*** Here I am following LSY's suggestion to punctuate after 多. This way, the following definition is correct for 經. *-mita* is totally unintelligible as a qualifier of *sūtra* as it is made to function by the T editors. It should also be noted that the original punctuation marks on the ms (by whose hand it is unknown) separate 多 and 經.

113 **'threaded together'** This is the meaning of *sūtra* alone. Clearly, as explained in the preceding two notes, *-mitā* belongs with *pāra-*.
uprightness 政 = 正. It would be awkward to translate without making this observation, *'hallmark of good government'. Sun 69 has 國 instead of 儀, hence 'country with good government'(?).

115 **World-Honoured One** *Bhagavat*.

116 **Jetavana** Translating out Anāthapiṇḍika here would be too cumbersome.

117 **esoteric** 蜜 → 密

118 **four orders** Four *varga*, that is *bhikṣu*, *bhikṣuṇī*, *upāsaka*, *upāsikā* – 'monks, nuns, male and female devotees'.

119 **immortals** *Ṛṣi*.

120 **four divine flowers** *Mandāra* (*Erythrina Indica*(?) – India Coralbean), *mahāmandāra*, *mañjūṣaka*, *mahāmañjūṣaka* (the latter three are known only to be 'celestial flowers'). Or, possibly, red, white, blue, and yellow lotuses – *padma*, *puṇḍarīka*, *utpala*, and *kumuda*.

121 **eight regions** Presumably the same as 八方 or 八到, the four quarters and the four half-quarters.

122 **power** *Bala*.

123 **Sudatta** 'Well-given, beneficent', an epithet of Anāthapiṇḍika (i.e. Anāthapiṇḍada).

124 **actions** Karmic deeds arising from (in this case, good) causes.

125 **Benefactor** It is possible and, perhaps, preferable rhythmically to punctuate as indicated by the marks on the ms, i.e., after 名 and before 給. Hence, the rhythm of the prose would be divided 6–6–6–6–4–4–6.

126 **gold** See T370.11 *et seq*.

127 **monastery garden** *Saṅghārāma*.

128 **company of monks** 僧 in its original sense of *saṅgha*.

130 **trees** T371.8.

132 **subject** The ms reverses the order of 輕 and 標 but corrects itself with a checkmark.

133 **... to him** This sentence has been slightly modified in translation for purposes of clarity. The full name of the park was 祇樹給孤獨園.
details 委被 → 委備.

135 **southern** Either the author's geographical knowledge is lacking (the kingdom referred to was more than a hundred miles northwest of Kapilavastu which was itself about one hundred miles due north of Benares and northwest of present Gorakhpur) or he meant 'India which is in the south'. If the latter possibility was intended, it must be considered an unusual interpretation of the phrase.

136 **Śrāvastī** Both the name of the kingdom and its major city.

137 **... whole world** The usual form is 威震(鎮)九州. Since the latter segment is obviously related to the Chinese empire, the author had to 'change idioms in mid-stream' (so to speak). 九重 *ch'ung* refers to the heavens. *Huai-nan-tzu*, 'Discourse on Astrology', 淮南子, 天文訓 (*SPPY*) 3.16a: 'Heaven has nine layers.' 天有九重. The *SPTK* edn (13.15a) has 地 instead of 有 but this is an inferior reading and one

which is rejected by most other recensions of the *Huai-nan-tzu*.

139 **three borders** Cf. T54.9, T104.2, *Ch'ü* no. 14 and see Jen, *Prelim*, 423–4.

140 **... were clear** There was no dust nor waves, i.e. no disturbances nor rebellions.

143 **mind** 胷衿 = 胸襟, cf. Chou 215.13.
secret The ms and S4398v both have 秘 instead of 幾 which is an incorrect reading by the T editors. For a high minister to perfect *secret* policy is not necessarily treasonable. It more likely means that he had the complete confidence of the ruler. Cf. 祕計, 祕謀, etc.

144 **... instant** Comparable to 即時? LSY has suggested that 代 → 世 (?) which is a T'ang taboo word (see line 739n2). 即 ≡ 近 / 今 (?), P'ei Hsüeh-hai 605.

145 **Pillar** 柱石 'plinth', literally.

146 **salt and pepper** Literally, 'salt and plum – salty and sour'. This is a long-established comparison applied to highly valued ministers. *Book of History*, Legge III.260: 'Be to me ... as the salt and prunes in making agreeable soup.' 若作和羹, 爾惟鹽梅.

148 **Three Precious Ones** *Triratna* or *ratnatraya* – Buddha, Dharma, and Saṅgha.

152 **all of a sudden** 忽自, cf. T137.6.

153 **Our ... now** 今家 is specifically Buddhist terminology, meaning 'our sect/school'. *Chih-kuan ta-i* 止觀大意, Ta46.459a: 'Our school's doctrine takes Nāgārjuna as its founder.' 今家教門, 以龍樹爲始祖. As such, it is quite out of place in the present context.
lacks 之 → 乏 (LSY).

155 **... married** It would appear from the unusual expression 婚冠 that maturity (capping) and marriage went together. There is strong confirmation for this view in the 'Lecture on the *Vimalakīrti-sūtra*', T538.8: 'When a young man is capped and when a girl reaches the age when she wears her hair pinned up, it is only right that marriage should be arranged for them in complete conformity with [established] procedure.' 男及弱冠, 女及笄[年], [理][須]騁(聘)婚姻, 盡皆次第.
... right Literally, 'reason requires'. Cf. T368.8 and, for a related expression, 道理須 'by all rights should', T89.16.

158 **servants** I interpret as 家衆 rather than as 家內 'wife' or 'members of his family'. Japanese *kachū* 'retainer' rather than *iejū* or *uchijū*.

167 **... night** Cf. T44.13, T45.8, T114.1.

172 **promised** 唯諾. 'The emissary' and 'to fulfil his duty' are added to the translation.

174 **... way** 奔波 and 日夜奔波 occur frequently in Tun-huang popular literature (T3.9, T5.13, T112.14, T579.4) but always with the meaning 'hasten [on one's way]', i.e. modern 奔跑.

177 **... attentive** The usual expression is 注目. In fact, I have never seen 注耳 and it sounds very strange. The visual similarity warrants emendation. Similarly, one would expect in the following member 傾耳 instead of 傾心, the latter generally conveying admiration rather than attentiveness. The grounds for emendation are good here, too, since one could hardly repeat 耳 once one had written it for 目. A plausible reading could, however, be extracted from 傾心, 'alert mind'(?).

178 **walking** 行李, in T'ang popular literature, usually means 'direction of travel' (T5.14, T13.8, T595.2). Here it has a less specific denotation.

180 **Sudatta** This identification by the translator of the emissary as Sudatta himself is to prepare the reader for some textual difficulties which occur below (see line 255n).

182 **staff** *Khakkara*.

184 **Humi** On T405.12, he is called 護勒彌. In the *Hsien-yü ching*, he is called 護彌. It is not mentioned there that he is prime minister.
family 家 is an interlinear addition on the ms.
ten commandments *Daśa kuśala-karma paṭāḥ*, 十善戒 observed by the laity.

185 **cordial** For 親延, 'personally to invite', see *PWYF* 708a. But this is read by Chou 216.7 as 親近, 'to be friendly with, to be affectionate or close to', leading one to

suspect either a typographical or collating error on the part of the T editors since the entire clause 親近於佛僧 occurs on T363.11. Examination of the ms proves that Chou's reading is certainly the correct one. Note, however, that the clause 請佛延僧 occurs on T363.10, also in reference to Humi.

186 **Three Precious Ones** See above, line 148n.

191 **... reverence** Wang Ch'ing-shu (T391n12) is mistaken in saying that 五輪 is inexplicable. The original expression in Sanskrit is *pañcamaṇḍala-namaskāreṇa vandate*, to prostrate oneself making five circular impressions with the forehead, the two palms, and two kneecaps. Cf. Susumu W. Nakamura, 'Pradakshiṇā, A Buddhist Form of Obeisance', *Semitic and Oriental Studies: A Volume Presented to William Popper* (Berkeley, 1951), pp. 345–54.

194 **Śākyamuni** The one who is 'capable in kindness'.

196 **profile** Nowhere else have I encountered the expression 影塩 nor the single character 塩. My hunch is that it means 輪廓.

198 **Hsi-shih** A famous beauty from the kingdom of Yüeh during the fifth century B.I.E.

199 **Luo-p'u** 洛浦 'Banks of the River Lo' would seem to constitute a metastasis of two unrelated classical allusions to famous beauties. The author or scribe was probably, at one and the same time, thinking both of the Goddess of the River Lo (with the sound of the final character of the title of Ts'ao Chih's well-known *fu* perhaps triggering the metastasis, 曹植, 洛神賦, *WH* 19.7b–10b) and of the exemplary Luo-fu 羅敷 of the Kingdom of Chao during the Warring States period (Giles, *BD* no. 1386). The simplest explanation, suggested to me by Prof. Hightower, is that 洛浦 means '[goddess met on the] bank of the River Lo', i.e. 洛神.

201 **So** 遂即.

205 **spears** Chou 216.11 has 戟 for 鐵 but one can safely assume that they mean the same thing. The emendation of 之 to 与 results in a common phrase which makes perfect sense in this context. The mechanical repetition of 之 in the same position of the two parallel lines may very well have been due to negligence on the part of the copyist.

207 **... like** For 菀似, read 宛似 with Chou (216.11) to parallel 稍異 below.

208 **... terraces** This line vividly calls to mind the numerous wall-paintings of Buddhist paradises in the caves at Tun-huang in which the area in front of the central iconographical figure consists of the very elements mentioned here.

209 **quite** 稍 (LSY).

210 **Haven't** 可不. This construction occurs frequently in popular Buddhist literature and with a consistent function – 'Haven't you?/do you mean to say you haven't?/wouldn't that be . . . ?' It is completely the equivalent of 豈不. See T2.9 and 10, T43.6, T90.1, etc. The emendation to 何不 of the T editors is unnecessary.

212 **daily** 日 → 月 (?), 'monthly'.

219 **encountered** The ms has 遇會.

224 **tarry a while** 淹遛 for 淹留.

225 **briefly** 蹔(?) = 暫.

229 **given away** Hsü 37 insists that 仕 is interchangeable with 事, 'in attendance upon'. While this is, indeed, correct for other occurrences, the climate of discussion here is decidedly matrimonial. As such, the substitution by the T editors of a homophone relating specifically to marriage (適, '[bride] to go away to wed') is, in my opinion, adequately justified in spite of Hsü's protestation against it.

231 **pleasant** ⿰女殊 = 姝 (Hsü 37).

233 **deportment** ⿰車范(?) = 範 (Hsü 37).

236 **relieved** 'Comforted, contented, etc.', cf. 欣慰.

240 **paid his respects** Literally, '[asked how the premier's] daily life [was]'.

242 **exchanging pleasantries** They talked about the weather, so to speak.

248 **great** I had translated this as 'put young and old to hustling and bustling' but stand

corrected by LSY who reads 大小 ≡ 多少 'quite'. Note T362.15, 小大 for 'young and old'. At any rate, what with all the activity going on in the next few lines, Humi certainly must have been helped by others in his household.

251 **plaster** 'Mud' would be more accurate but is not an aesthetic word and so unacceptable in this context. An even more unaesthetic word (in our culture) but, perhaps, even more accurate than mud would be 'cow-pat'. Called *gomaya* in Sanskrit, I know from personal experience that it is used weekly to coat the floors and part of the walls in Hindu homes made of mud-brick. From personal experience, I also know that it is highly fragrant. I was told that it keeps the air fresh by slow release of ozone as it dries. See also *Hsien-yü ching*, Ta4.421a: 'Use fine sandalwood to make a fragrant paste.' 以妙旃檀，用爲香泥 (also Ta50.66a).
spread Not necessarily 'decorate' although that meaning is implicit here as seen from the following line. The basic meaning of 飾 (餙 being its vulgar variant) is 'to spread'. See *Shuo-wen chieh-tzu tuan-chu* 說文解字，段注 (Shanghai, 1936), p. 121b. The ms has 餙.

252 **extraordinarily** Chiang 179 says that 異種 has the same meaning as 異樣. But this leaves the clause without a. verb. Cf. T363.9 where 精華 is preceded by a verb. + 'Making.'

253 **Around** For 牆匝 'around the walls'(?), the ms unmistakably has 礚 (here = 磕)迊 (= 匝 or 帀). Cf. 匼匝, 軩匝, 鉿匝, 磕帀, etc.

255 **Sudatta** + 'Sudatta.' N.B. the 'emissary' of T363.7 and before has now become the 'elder' and, by T363.11, is specifically named as Sudatta.

258 **... it all** 所以 here has the classical Chinese meaning of the 'wherefore' of a given situation. Elsewhere in T'ang colloquial texts, it usually means 'so, therefore'.

259 **ceremony** 'Assembly, gathering, meeting.' 娶 I consider an error for 聚. The grounds are: (1) 娶會, though sense can be forced from it ('marriage meeting'), is awkward; (2) in the succeeding line, 聚會 is used as the corresponding answer to the first segment of the choice question (since 帝王 is retained both in the question and in the corresponding segment of the answer, it would be logical that the first segment of the choice question remain the same as in the answer); (3) in writing of marriage, a scribe or typographer would be extremely liable to make such an error unconsciously. In fact, in Humi's answer, he seems to have written 聚 over 娶, hence [illegible]!

260 **... because** The same grammatical pattern (爲當 ... 爲復) recurs on T373.3, T609.14, and T743.13. It constitutes a choice question between whole sentences. Chiang 175–6 discusses this and related constructions.
request 延屈 ≡ 延請. For the meaning of 屈, see line 773nl.

266 **intention** Cf. T330.7 and 9.

267 **offerings** *Pūjā*; or *upa-*$\sqrt{}$*sthā*, 'to stand near in order to wait upon'.

269 **Now ...** Hsieh 92.13 would prefer to interpret this as 'but had not [adding 不] come close to a Buddhist monk'. While such an interpretation is logically more straightforward, it destroys the prose rhythm.

270 **uttered** The 說 is an interlinear addition, undoubtedly for rhythmic purposes.

271 **profuse** 陌目 = 霢霂 (Chiang 146).

273 **manifestations** Literally, 'differences; distinctions'.

275 **... makes me** The literal translation of this line is '[When] I am made to hear their names'.

278 **particulars** 委由 is probably an error for 委曲, 'the inside story', 'the ins and outs of', etc. At least it seems to require such an interpretation in this context.

279 **followed** Chou 217.10 seemed puzzled by this and emended it to 適 which, to my mind, is less satisfactory than 仕. 仕 simply means 事, 'to serve/practise [erroneous/heterodox doctrines]'.

280 **correct** 政 = 正.

281 **desire** BHS. *[adhy]āśaya*.
longing BHS. *abhinandana*; *tarṣa*.
282 **origin** 根源.
284 **Śuddhodana** 淨飯王.
286 **kingship** 金輪, *cakra*, the emblem of sovereignty.
287 **numerous** 弈 is undoubtedly an error for 奕.
. . . full of Everything in this line before these words constitutes a skewed translation of 'abundant leaves'.
288 **descendants** 嫡 is misused here. Although both are genealogical terms, the proper word is 裔 (or 裔 or 裔). Perhaps the author or scribe was attempting to express 'direct' descent.
290 **startled** The ms reads 驚駭心神, with an ambiguous mark (ˡ) beside 心 that probably means its position should be reversed with that of 駭. The translation, in any event, is not affected.
293 **reveal** Following LSY's suggestion, 亦 → 示. This is, indeed, what the ms gives, although the character is blotted on the bottom left side. 'Humi' and 'Buddha' are added to the translation. For 方所, see T364.7 where the expression 佛所 does occur. If we emend 方 to 訪, we may render 'He wished, *too*, that he could visit the Buddha', literally, 'go to the place [where the Buddha was staying]'(?).
296 **Vulture Peak** Gṛdhrakūta near Rājagṛha.
297 **. . . realms** Eight classes of supernatural beings enumerated in the *Lotus sūtra*. Two of these are 龍 *nāga* and 天 *deva*. The others are *yakṣa*, *gandharva*, *asura*, *garuḍa*, *kinnara*, and *mahoraga*.
principles *Siddhānta*, 'aim, end, purpose'.
. . . nirvāṇa Amplified translation of *triyāna*, the three vehicles by which living beings cross *saṁsāra*. There are various explanations according to the different schools, the most frequently mentioned being that generally accepted by Mahayanists: Hīnayāna (Śrāvaka), Madhyamayāna (Pratyekabuddha), and Mahāyāna (Bodhisattva).
302 **sincerity** Cf. line 34n.
303 **compassionate** This epithet 慈 is usually applied to Maitreya but is here clearly intended to indicate Śākyamuni.
304 **give recognition to** I interpret as 表揚.
single-mindedness Of purpose in wishing to advance in the Buddhist Way.
305 **radiant beams** 'Beams of light; light radiating in all directions' – from between the brows of the Buddha.
306 **flooded with light** 洞曉 is nearly always used abstractly with reference to mental clarity. Here, I believe, a more literal interpretation of the phrase is required.
307 **brilliance** Although a case can be made for 暉盈, 'bright-fulness > refulgence', the scribe may have had in mind 暉映, which is a far more likely expression. It should be noted, however, that he does use 暉盈 consistently (e.g. T371.5, T377.8, T398.8, etc.).
312 **thus** 然 in the sense of 是, 乃, 故. See P'ei Hsüeh-hai 568, 571–2 and Yang Shu-ta 5.94–5. Also see Chiang 163–4.
strength *Prabhāva*.
317 **high buildings** There are at least two reasons why, I believe, the expression 高峻 may not be interpreted as 'lofty peaks' or some such. First, Sudatta is obviously still inside the city-walls. Secondly, these two characters most likely carry the meaning of the first half of the expression 高峻諸門 'higher [than] all [the other] gates'. I have not employed the word 'gates' in the translation at this particular point because it has been 'post-empted' (so to speak) by the last word of the line. Cf. T731.1.
318 **morning mist** My translation combines the meanings of the expression given, 'fine

clouds on the horizon', and the homophone which I believe was intended, 淸曉, 'early morning light'.

319 **earnestly** The ms clearly has 渴. Thus the 謁 given by the T editors may be considered only as an emendation, an emendation which I reject because it requires a forced interpretation of 容: 'I think of visiting the Honoured One's presence'(?).' It should be noted that the usual reference to the Buddha's countenance in this text is 尊顏 rather than 尊容.

320 **Fretting** Chou's (218.4) reading, although it is an unannounced emendation, 躊躇, is preferable. What this amounts to is, essentially, an inversion of the T reading because 蹰 (vulgar for 躕) means nearly the same idea as 躊. The ms, though indistinct, appears to have 躇蹰. The implication, in any case, is clear: Sudatta is hesitating.

322 **wisdom-club** I.e., the *vajravara* or 'diamond club'.

323 **compassionate** See line 303n.

326 **celestial ear** *Divyaśrota.*

327 **... intuitively** *Paracittajñāna.*

334 **... energy** BHS. *asthī-kṛtya.*

336 **place** The translation of *ch'u* 處 as 'place' is justified in *Transformations*. Literally, '[as for] the place' or '[in regard to] the place'. In terms of the historical development of these texts, however, it is shown in *Transformations* that the syntactical addition of 'This is' or 'Here is' is not unwarranted.

... go The T editors have added 說. There is a mark (乛\) on the ms between 陳 and 須 which indicates the separation between verse-introductory formula and the verse itself. This is the usual verse-introductory formula for *pien-wen*. For a discussion, see the Introduction.

337 **suddenly** Supply 頓. There is no lacuna in the text here but the scribe has copied the line imperfectly.

340 **All day long** 終朝 is a frequent Tun-huang expression (T590.3, T702.6, T703.6, *passim*) but 終日 also occurs (T709.13).

King of Devils *Māra-rāja; pāpīyān.*

341 **Celestial Teacher** This title seems more appropriate to the Taoist 'Pope' than to Śākyamuni Buddha. *Śāstṛ*(?).

342 **... influence** The ms (cf. Chou 218.10) has 降神. The unjustified and unacceptable reading of the T editors would require some such interpretation as 'Bestow your blessings upon Śrāvastī ...'

bridge Technical Buddhist term, used by a person who wishes to place himself in an inferior position, that is, to announce that he is willing to be trod upon by all (Ta38.391a).

343 **roots of goodness** *Kuśala-mūla.*

... mature This is remarkably similar to T395.11.

344 **easy to train** LSY suggests that 異 → 易 and that 。調 be read in the second tone. If we do not emend 異, perhaps we may understand 'into a different mode' 調°. Iriya 30a interprets this line as meaning that Sudatta had been educated away from his previous heterodox views. There is, on the ms, a mark (丶) next to 化 which indicates that some early reader of the text, perhaps the scribe himself, recognized that a problem existed here. Cf. line 290n above.

345 **responded** Since having Buddha 'respond to an order' is clearly inappropriate, I suggest that 應命 may be a visual error for 應答 or simply the *lapsus calami* of a negligent copyist.

346 **request** 啟請, technical term.

he It is interesting to note that 他 on the ms was originally written 地 and subsequently corrected.

348 **... realms** *Trailokya* or *triloka.*

349 **All-conquering** *Jina*, *vijaya*; *parama*.
350 **self-composed** 安詳, *smṛtimān*/*saṃprajānas*, is equivalent to modern Chinese 安祥 (Iriya, *Index*, 28). But this expression was by no means peculiar to Tun-huang literature nor may it even be considered a vernacularism since it appears frequently in canonical texts and was borrowed by the Buddhists from an identical phrase which already existed in the language but which had a slightly different meaning, 'attentive to details'. The same phrase occurs on T382.10 and T383.9.
351 **. . . dragons** *Devas* and *nāgas*.
352 **Brahmā** The supreme post-Vedic Hindu deity. He was standing on the left side 左 of the Buddha so as to assist him 佐.
353 **Indra** The greatest of the Vedic gods.
354 **Immortals** *Deva-ṛṣi*.
crowd 'Pack, fill', etc. (Chiang 132). The identical phrase, in a different orthography (惻塞虛空), appears in this narrative on T379.10 and T388.15. There are numerous other orthographies as well, for which see Chiang's note. The occurrence of this phrase on T377.13 presents special problems and will be discussed in a lengthy note (line 1246n). Also see line 1933n2.
355 **four orders** See line 118n.
356 **must** Iriya, *Index*, 22 ('the situation requires that').
357 **towers** *Stūpa*, 'tope, pagoda'.
360 **. . . too** Chou 218.13, for 延小, has 無令過小. The ms actually has 無令延小. Syntactically, 無令 is quite unusual in this position; the T editors' aversion to it is understandable. However, as shown in the translation, a reading may be forced from it. 過 is adopted in the translation as an emendation for 延. It should be noted that the scribe makes no distinction between 廴 and 辶. Furthermore, his calligraphy of 延 is consistently 延 which might conceivably have been confused with some vulgar writing of 過 (过, 過, etc.). With difficulty, a reading may be extracted from 延 in the sense of 'spread out, scattered, distant, elongated'; hence, 'should not be made sparse and few'.
362 **. . . doctrine** *Para-pravādin*; [*anya*-]*tīrthya*.
363 **. . . precepts** *Vidhi-bhraṣṭa*.
364 **Take** Compare modern Chinese 把. Cf. T733.4.
365 **regulations** 法式 *paurāṇaṃ cihnavṛttam*; P. *dhammika*, 'model, pattern' is certainly readable here. But a nearly homonymous expression 法事 *saṃghakaraṇīva*, has a specifically Buddhist meaning, one which fits very well in this sentence: 'religious affairs, e.g. discipline and ritual'.
367 **saintly being** *Ārya*.
369 **. . . boxes** Caxton, *Myrrour of the World*, tr. 1481 (E.E.T.S. 1913), II.vi.75: 'An olyphaunt bereth wel a *tour* of woode vpon his backe'(!).
373 **selecting** Everything which precedes this word in this line constitutes an amplified translation of 按行 *àn-háng*, literally, 'to arrange by rank' > 'to put in serial order'. Cf. 案行 with its glosses of 察案, 巡察, and 案次第以爲行隊. But notice below the translation of this phrase in line 900. Such an interpretation could also be used here: 'went from one monastery park to the next'.
378 **took hold** Understandable when interpreted as 捛取. See Morohashi 12105.
379 **monk** *Upādhyāya*.
380 **or not** Sentence-final 不 read as 否, cf. T291.12.
382 **Although** 須 need not be emended to 雖. Cf. T42.14, T735.4, etc. See Chang Hsiang 36–7. Waley, 'Notes', 176 performs a neat trick by translating as: 'The garden is certainly nice, but . . .'.
quite Hsü 37 states that 即 stands for 則. This is a good solution, if we admit that 須 is grammatically the exact equivalent of 雖. Another possibility is that 即 stands for 極 (Chou 219.3). Both interpretations have worked their way into the trans-

lation but this is not to say that I am ambivalent as to which of the two is more likely to be correct. Since 即 and 則 are commonly interchanged while such is not the case with 即 and 極, economy of effort prompts me to opt for the former. Note that this line reappears *in toto* on T365.3.

383 **onion** Variant orthography for 葱.

384 **reeks** 勳 → 熏 or 熏.

387 **back** 却 is not simply an adversative conjunction here. It has full co-verbal function, cf. 却去, 却行, 却回, 却走, 却背, etc.

390 **serious** T prints 歛 *hàn* where it should print 斂 *lièn*. This is a very common orthographical error in Chinese, e.g. Liang Shih-ch'iu 梁實秋, *A New Practical Chinese Dictionary* 最新實用漢英辭典 (Taipei, 1971), p. 548, entry 2677. The ms has 歛. The same is true of the other occurrences of 歛 on this page, T365.8 and 9.

crossed his fingers Gesture of respect. In pre-Buddhist Chinese texts, 叉手 meant 'to cross the arms' (cf. 拱手). In Buddhist texts, the expression actually represents the second half of a four-character phrase, 合掌叉手, *añjaliṃ praṇamya*. This signifies bringing the palms together and interlacing the fingers, which is the Indian monk's style of salutation.

395 **horse market** The horse market doubled as an execution ground. Cf. 'Transformation Text on Li Ling', T94.2: 'Li Ling's old mother, and his wife and children were taken to the horse market where their heads met with [the provisions of] the law. Blood flowed over the whole market.'

399 **Reining in** Hsü 37 correctly identifies 諠 (轞 on the ms) with 轡.

cart I find it intriguing that, in these lines, Sudatta is sometimes riding an elephant (T394.16), sometimes seems to be on a horse (T364.15), and here is in a cart.

406 **... quite** See line 382nn1 and 2 above.

407 **rambling** 芙疏 should be emended to 扶疏 which was, I believe, unconsciously avoided because of its specifically Buddhist meanings: 'Supporting commentary' hence '*Nirvāṇa Sūtra*' which was considered by the T'ien-t'ai sect to be an elaboration of the *Lotus Sūtra*. It is curious that the ms has 蔬 (*shù* or *sū*, 'vegetable food'(?)), the grass radical having been added by a different hand in a distinguishable ink.

408 **bawdy** 猖 = 倡/娼.

409 **... minds** Literally, 'to intensify the dullness'.

sentient beings *Sattva*. The character 衆 appears twice on the ms; in the first instance it has been blotted out.

410 **root** The ms has 原 instead of 源; the meaning is unchanged. Cf. T368.10.

ocean of misery *Duḥkha-arṇava*.

415 **affinity** *Pratyaya*.

416 **Or** See line 260n1.

karmic hindrances *Karmāvaraṇa*.

417 **... ease** Except for 'Sudatta', this line occurs *in toto* on T766.10.

418 **altogether** *Feī-fèn*, 'without measure, unduly', therefore, 'quite'.

perplexed 仿偟 → 傍偟/徬徨/旁皇/徬徨/彷徨. The last example is probably the intended orthography.

420 **selection process** Consult line 373n.

422 **gazed** The meaning of 顯望 is not immediately comprehensible to me. I suspect that it may be an orthographic error for 顧望. Cf. T366.1.

428 **flourish** 翁 → 蓊, cf. T365.5. 欝 → 蔚/鬱, cf. T383.1, T386.4. Cf. *Pei pieh-tzu*, 5.9b.

429 **lush** 靑靑. This is not simply the trick or foible of the translator. While the two characters do, indeed, mean 'green, green' and may so be interpreted in regard to vegetation, they may also be understood in the sense of 菁菁.

430 **brilliant** Chou 219.11 has 灼灼 which must be understood as an unannounced emendation. It is a tempting reading for two reasons: (1) It has a well-recognized

connotation of flowers 'blooming' where 照灼 has only the more general meaning of 'shining brightly'; (2) The suggestion offered by the parallel structure that, in this position, there should be a single character repeated. This latter suggestion, however, is only of partial value in determining the correct reading for, in this very line, and under similar circumstances, we find that the parallel phrasing (芬芬) is only partially maintained (噪咶). Also see T367.10.

434 **Chattering** Comparable to 噪聒.

...harmoniously I suppose that this is comparable to 和鳴.

435 **Three Jewels** *Trīṇi ratāni.*

441 **gardens** 圃 is slightly suspicious because, although in isolated instances it is synonymous with 園, it usually signifies 'vegetable garden'. This seems out-of-place in the present context, except for the mention of 'fruits and herbs'. Another visually similar character, 囿, which has the general meaning of 'enclosed [park (for keeping animals)]', may have been intended. This would not be a hunting-park such as Ssu-ma Hsiang-ju loved to write about, but something like the Deer Park (Mṛgadāva) in Sārnāth (Śāraṅganātha) northeast of Vārāṇaśi.

450 **...achievements** 小果. This term is also used in Mahāyāna texts to refer to Hīnayāna spiritual achievements.

451 **doctrinal strength** 道力.

452 **meditation** *Prayoga.*

453 **Then** Meaning 然後. Cf. T4.4, T377.15, and T378.8. Also see line 312n1.

455 **Collected** Cf. 受定, *samādhi-lābhitā* and 受心行時, P. *citta-saṃkhāra-paṭisaṃvedin.*

456 **gathered** See line 390n1.

moment 須臾 is the Chinese translation of Sanskrit *muhūrta.*

458 **inauspicious** BHS. *ādīnava.*

462 **Countless** 頗 = 叵 which means 不可. 筭 is a vulgar form of 算 (Chiang 156).

464 **body and soul** *Kāya-citta.*

465 **...grin** The same clause occurs on T371.10 and T379.10.

467 **age** *Yuga*, one thousandth part of a *kalpa* (see next note).

469 **millennium** *Bhadrakalpa* is the time-period during which one thousand Buddhas appear. In the present *kalpa*, Śākyamuni is the fourth Buddha, to be followed by Maitreya and 995 others.

477 **protection** 加護 is a technical term and has the following synonyms in Chinese: 加備, 加被, 加祐. The Sanskrit original is *adhitiṣṭhante.*

478 **instantly** The ms clearly has 頓 rather than 盡 'completely'.

479 **seminary** *Bodhimaṇḍala*(?).

480 **four terms** See line 61n.

482 **waver** I.e., 猶豫.

488 **unparalleled** Cf. T385.11 and T387.5 (Chiang 82).

494 **encounter** 過 is a misreading by the T editors for 遇 (Hsü 116, Chou 220.10). The following three rhymes (具, 數, 處) give certain credence to this correction.

495 **Holy bells** **Aryaghantā*(?).

echo each other Admittedly, 應現 is a perfectly good and usable term. More exactly, it is a perfectly good and usable Buddhist term meaning 'responsive manifestation' (cf. 應化), *abhyarhitaṃ*(?). As this particular concept refers specifically to the revelation of the Absolute (Buddha) Body – *dharmakāya* – in accordance with the nature and needs of individual beings as the Incarnate (Buddha) Body – *nirmāṇakāya* – it is out of place where bells are the subject. One would have expected here something like 應聲 or 應響. Since this probably represents neither an orthographical nor a phonological error, it is best attributed to negligence and the ubiquitous fund of doctrinal terminology which quite naturally tends to plug up any holes which appear in men's minds or writings.

496 **immortals** See line 354n1.

498 **countless billions** The astronomical numbers in the mind of the scribe must have been enough to make him giddy. 無億數, though I have tried to make sense of it, is not immediately obvious. Perhaps 無量數 'infinite (*apramāṇa*, *amita*, *ananta*) numbers' or 無量億 'infinite billions' was intended.

499 **wisdom** 明 *vidyā* 知 *vidyā* ($\sqrt{vid}$ > 智 *vi*$\sqrt{jñā}$; *vijñāna* or sometimes *jñāna*). It is possible to interpret as 'clearly to know (*vijñā*)' hence 'it is obvious that'. I prefer the interpretation in the translation because it is syntactically and prosodically less jarring.

ineffable *Acintya.*

500 **... place** This is not the formula for pointing out a scene. It is a literal reference to a place within the narrative verse itself.

501 **astonished** Given the frame of mind Sudatta is in at this juncture, I doubt that he will evince much scepticism concerning anything Śāriputra tells him. 驚疑 most probably should be emended to the near-homonym 驚異.

506 **... sell** Iriya 53an26 believes this line to be untranslatable. He suggests that 不惜 may have been intended for 不賣.

508 **... whirl** 心裏迴惶 appears verbatim on T718.7.

510 **who** 阿誰, cf. T93.16, T351.14.

513 **... respect** See line 390n2.

disclosed This is an unusual meaning for (cf. *PWYF* 144b, 'disperse'). I believe that it is similar to 分擘 in *Ch'ü* no. 650.

514 **ordinary** 隨宜(疑), 'mediocre, common' (Chiang 123).

520 **son** His name was Virūḍhaka.

521 **... monk** Hsü's (116) comments regarding the punctuation of this passage are helpful. However, it seems to me of little consequence whether the terms of address following 言 be included in the quotation as vocatives or outside as the T editors have printed them. The punctuator of the original ms places them outside where Hsü would have them.

524 **a** The second 此 in this sentence is superfluous. 處, following it, also seems unnecessary.

Original Teacher An epithet of Śākyamuni Buddha.

528 **defilements** *Mala.*

529 **pure and clean** 清淨 *pariśuddhi*; *viśuddhi.*

532 **... fragrance** Logically and grammatically, this should be translated as 'exotic incense and heavenly flowers', especially on the analogy of the preceding four-syllable line. But incense smoke, being insubstantial, can 'compete' only in a very special sense, is not liable to '*descend* in disorder', and is not properly described as 'fluttering' or 'a riot [of colours, shapes, etc.]'.

536 **... probe** This is a most difficult line to translate at all, let alone accurately. Chou 221.6 has 著著 for 看了 which is altogether different and even less open to scrutiny. Is this perhaps intended to be 著莫 = 捉摸 'to fathom, to test, to explore, i.e. to feel one out'? This is how I am tentatively reading it. As for 拔探, the T editors emend to 投探 which assumes an orthographical error. If we accept the T reading in its entirety, then we may, with great effort, translate as 'gained audience (看了) through protocol (以禮) and presentation (投) of credentials (探)'(?). If only the first part of the T reading is accepted (i.e. 投), we may, again with some effort, interpret as in the translation. I would myself prefer an emendation to 抉探 or 搜探. Nothing, however, that I have seen or considered regarding this line appears to me to be an entirely satisfactory solution.

537 **determine** 之 → 知 'know; learn'(?).

539 **haggle** 爭.

540 **... refusing** My explanation of this line is derived as follows. 死 is an adverb; 署 is simply a different orthography for 腰; 楔 is a homonymous error for 脅. The result

is a common expression for extortion and threat (usually written 要脅 but originally derived from 腰 and 脅), i.e. 'threaten [us with refusal]'. For another instance in which 楔 is involved in a miswriting, see Wu line 184n.

541 **out of convenience** The English idiom, fortunately, has all the ambivalence of the Chinese original. It is unnecessary to interpret 方便 as 'to deceive' which Chiang 113 does. In Sudatta's mind, he is simply planning to use any means which are appropriate to the situation, just as the Buddha employed 'expedient or partial method' in communicating his principles to individuals who were incapable of absorbing more direct exposure. This is, indeed, what the notion of *upāya* is about. Later (T368.13, T369.8), when the Crown Prince, who is yet ignorant of Buddhist doctrine, rebukes him for employing such tactics, we see the uninformed recipient of expediency lashing out against it. Cf. Paul Demiéville, 'À Propos du Concile de Vaiśālī', *TP*, 40(1951), 271n2 where 方便 is shown to be the equivalent of *prayoga*, 'design, contrivance, plan' and *upāya*, 'way, stratagem, artifice'. The expression occurs with the same meaning in *Yu-hsien k'u*, p. 23.
just have Cf. T519.4 (眞 is an error for 直), T521.3, T557.2, T574.15, *passim*.
ruse Chiang 67 glosses 下脱 as 'deception'. This seems too strong a word. 'Artifice, subterfuge, wile, etc.' are probably closer to the tone intended.

552 **official** Not being able to make much sense of 所有, I have emended to 所由 which, in T'ang colloquial, means 'government servant' or 'civil officer' (Chiang 17).

553 **urgent** 慈 → 急.

556 **put in words** Compare Mandarin 開口 'to open the mouth', i.e. 'to begin to speak'.

565 **...withered** There is nothing unusual in modifying 池 with 枯 or with 涸. The problem is how to interpret 亭 in such a way that it may be modified by one of these adjectives. Another solution than that offered in the translation is to render 'pavilioned ponds dried up', imagining that the pavilions are constructed alongside and even above the water (as in the Tun-huang wall-paintings).

566 **faded** 彫 need not be emended to 凋 inasmuch as these are interchangeable characters.

570 **exceedingly** Chiang 162.

572 **kept** 久淹 may be glossed as 久留. The idea is that many years have accumulated since the time the prince bought the park.

573 **soft** 耎 = 耎 = 輭 (Hsü 37) or 煗 [煖 = 暖] (Chou 221.12).

574 **greenness** 翠, as printed in Chou 221.12. For the orthography given here, see *Pei pieh-tzu*, 4.5a.

575 **cherry-apples** 名花 may mean 海棠 (the Siberian Crab-apple, *Malus baccata*), as I have rendered it. It may also designate the peony 牡丹 or it may simply signify any well-known flower. I have chosen a particular type to match the willows above. 'Famous beauties', of course, is not to be considered in this context.

580 **...nonsense** Hsü 116 and Chou 221.13, 223.7 are correct in reading 狂 as 誑.

583 **Crown Prince** There are two marks next to (⺀) and below (⺄) the character 子 on the right side which may indicate the repetition of 太子 called for by the T editors.

587 **...accusations** 誣罔 is the same as 誣罔, according to Hsü 37. Compare the radical form of the second character with double crosses 网. Note that *Pei pieh-tzu*, 1.19a has 誙 = 誣. Also note the phrase 誣謅 'to malign' (Morohashi 35542.44), which is a variant of the phrase suggested by Hsü. Chou 222.1 inexplicably has 矯罔 [枉(?)], 'to dissemble'.

589 **prevarication** Chou's (222.1) reading of 池 is superior. 馳 is attributable to a scribe who made one of two errors: (1) homonymous confusion, (2) semantic confusion (差understood as *ch'ai* because of its occurrence in connection with the speech of a government servant may have influenced misreading the succeeding character as a related concept – 'courier'). 差 should be pronounced as *tz'u*. Cf. line 1103n and line 1861n2 below.

590 **... head** Literally, 'to keep my waist and neck intact', i.e. to avoid execution.
597 **hyperbole** 謞 is an unattested vulgar writing for 譑 'garrulousness'.
599 **suppress** Meaning 壓 and pronounced *ya* as well.
exorcise 攘 reads perfectly well. The emendation of the T editors is superfluous.
603 **city-gates** Not the entrances to the park (see top of T367.16).
605 **... metal** This is a proverb of high antiquity which stresses the weight of public opinion. If everyone says something is so, that is how it will be. In this case, if the prince proclaims often enough and conspicuously enough that he is selling, the ghosts will take it in earnest and flee the premises. See *Kuo-yü*, 'Discourses of Chou', 國語, 周語 (*SPTK*) 3.19b.
606 **evil** 灾 is a variant form of 災.
615 **notices** The character on the ms is actually the synonymous 牓. The same is true for 榜 just below and on T370.3 and 4 as well as T372.7.
620 **tore** Chou 222.6 prints 坼. The ms has 圻.
notices 'And took them (將來).'
622 **Crown Prince** See line 583n above.
623 **could not reconcile himself** Iriya, *Index*, 5 notes three occurrences of this expression (不忿), all in this text: T367.16, T368.10, and T386.2. Although it would appear to mean 'not to be angry/resentful' (which is precisely the opposite of what the Prince must have really felt at this point), this expression does have a long-attested history as signifying 'unwillingness' or 'disagreement'. I suspect that, somewhere early along the line, it developed as a corruption of 不忍. The range of meanings it carries in this transformation text is: 'not to tolerate/condone/suffer/countenance/accept/yield to/put up with/swallow/stomach/endure'. Iriya 33a simply renders as 'was angered', seeming to have dropped the 不. See *CWTTT* 24.557. Morohashi lists this expression but does not give a satisfactory explanation. Cf. *Ko-t'eng*, 200a. Chang Hsiang 420–2 discusses 不分 together with 不憤 and 不忿. 分 should be read in the falling tone and expresses willingness. Thus 不分 ≡ 不滿, 不平, 不服氣. Chang's earliest reference is to Po Chü-i.
625 **... himself** Cf. T367.12, 躬駕親觀. The awkward English is a conscious attempt to convey the quality of this fractured line.
627 **very park** 'Place where the park was', i.e. 'park-site'(?). I suspect that 所 may originally have been 亭.
632 **person** An attempt to render 之者. See Chiang 5.
oversaw the garden *Mālī*.
633 **developments** The more usual expression is 更張. 改張 (cf. T264.13, T370.10, T556.10, *passim*) is a collapsed form of 改弦更張 'to retune the strings' and, as used in Tun-huang popular texts, simply means 'to change'.
634 **angry** Here 忿 has its usual meaning. Cf. line 623n.
635 **reproached** Literally, 'elegantly rebuked'. In the Tun-huang texts, it seems to mean no more than 'reprimand, upbraid' (Chiang 80). The expression also occurs on T368.10.
638 **create dissension** 扇, here and in classical texts, is customarily written without the fire radical but is interchangeable with 煽 and used in that sense ('incite, inflame, arouse') in the phrase 構扇.
639 **father and son** The ms has 子父.
641 **Shall** Chou 222.9 prints 應亦 'should also' in reverse order.
652 **... credibility** I have been able to provide a plausible rendering with little difficulty but should like, nevertheless, to mention that 虧心 'unconscionable' may have been intended.
655 **inform** Causative *wèn*, 'to make hear'.
659 **... poorly** Cryptic paraphrase of 'Facing each other – one thousand miles apart', which is a collapsed form of the proverb 'Though facing each other, two people

may be strangers; though a thousand miles apart, they may, on the other hand, be of like mind.' 對面不相識，千里卻同風. Cf. *Records of the Transmission of the Lamp* 景德傳燈錄 (*SPTK*) 20.8b. Also see *History of the T'ang Dynasty*, 'Biography of Fang Hsüan-ling' 房玄齡傳 (*PNP*) 66(16).2a: 千里之外猶對面語.

660 **covets** 叨 = 饕.
... position 斑 → 班. I have not located the precise source, but am convinced that the author viewed this line as an allusion. Cf. *History of the Chin Dynasty*, 'Annals of Emperor Hui' 晉書，惠帝紀 (*PNP*) 4.4b: 'Covet the seizure of the throne.' 饕據天位. For an expanded version of this line, see T374.11.

661 **... work** This quotation is from the *History of the Later Han*, 'Treatise on the Five Elements' 五行志 (*PNP*) 13.10a.

663 **throne** The emendation of the T editors ('heavenly court') makes good sense but it is not impossible to construe 天斑 'heavenly sceptre' as a metonymy for the king.

665 **... circumstances** Or 'without regard for each other's feelings'. Cf. 違境.
constitutions Dharma has dozens of meanings, one of which stresses the notion of an entity with distinctive attributes.

669 **Heavenly King** *Mahāraja-deva.*
Śūdra I do not know of a deva king of this name. Śūdra is the appellation of the lowest of the four castes, the peasants. The name is repeated on T368.15 as it is given here. In both cases, it should probably be emended to 首陀衞 *śuddha-āvāsa-deva*, which is the name of Śākyamuni's 'guardian angel'.

673 **good work** P. *kusalā-dhammā.*
... difficulty 留難 is a technical term which indicates the obstruction of the performance of good works.

674 **form** *Pratirūpa*; *pratirūpaka.*
invisible *Tirobhāvaḥ.*

675 **... old man** Note the similarity of this passage to another in the story of Shun-tzu, T131.7: 'Shun-tzu was a good little boy and the Sovereign Śakra [Indra] who was up in heaven knew that. So he transformed himself into an old man and went down to earth to give aid to Shun-tzu.'

676 **hoary** The T editors are correct in not emending to 皓, for 鵠 itself is often used metaphorically to describe grey hair, i.e. 'snow-goose white'.
temple 鬢.
moustache 髭. Here we find 'moustache' in combination with 'temple-locks' whereas it usually is found together with 鬚 or 髯 meaning whiskers in general.

677 **Holding** 筞 is a vulgar form of 策.

679 **... called out ...** The punctuation of this passage is no easy matter. Chou 223.1 begins Śūdra's speech from 向前. This results in the old man's offering seemingly contradictory orders ('go forward and stop!'(?)) and so I find it unacceptable. The punctuation of the T editors results in 'went forward then stopped. "Prince ..."'. Although this is plausible, I have declined to accept it because it makes the old man appear to be doing a jig: first he rushes in front of the horse, then he shouts, then he goes forward again, then he stops. Furthermore, the T punctuation destroys the prose rhythm. The difficulty with my own interpretation is that 住 is seldom used transitively except in closely bound phrases (住手, 住船). Also, I am puzzled by 且住 which ought to be understood as a polite imperative (e.g. T5.8 and T11.11). Thus, a final possibility is to punctuate 'in a loud voice called out as he went forward. "Stop for a moment, Crown Prince!"' Grammatically, this makes the best sense but prosodically it is terribly awkward (前 at the end of two successive lines and too many verbal features in the second line). My conclusion, after all this, is that the text is corrupt.

681 **principles** *Siddhānta.*
good and evil *Śubha-aśubha.* Cf. the frequent definition of 善 as 'in accord with

principle' 順理 and 惡 as 'contrary to principle' 違理.

682 **... quarrelling** Chou 223.2 has for this line 何容喧爭. 'How endure this clamorous contention?'

685 **block** 闌 = 攔.

686 **vehemently** 賁 → 憤 (Hsü 116, Chou 223.3).

688 **Making sure** See line 155n2.

689 **Even** 由 = 猶.

Three Old Ones Legge, *The Lî Kî* (Oxford, 1885), vol. I, p. 360: 'Proceeding to the school on the east, he [the Son of Heaven] unfolded and set forth the offerings to the aged of former times, and immediately afterwards arranged the mats and places for the three (classes of the) old, and the five (classes of the) experienced, for all the aged (indeed who were present).' *Record of Rites*, 'Wen-wang shih-tzu' 禮記, 文王世子 (*Thirteen Classics*) 20.19b: 適東序釋奠於先老, 遂設三老五更羣老之席位焉. Some commentators have insisted that 'three olds' and 'five gerontions' are two different individuals! I find this hard to credit, especially since the expression is immediately followed by 'all the aged'. K'ung Ying-ta's 孔穎達 (574–648) sub-commentary to this passage (20.21a) cites Ts'ai Yung's 蔡邕 (133–192) gloss of the troublesome 更 as 叟 which seems to me an excellent attempt to deal with a difficult problem. Derk Bodde offers an exhaustive treatment of these 'Thrice Venerable Quintuply Experienced' ones in his *Festivals in Classical China* (Princeton and Hong Kong, 1975), pp. 372–9. S1722 mentions a 'Picture of Five Old Ones' 五老之圖. For readers who are wondering what happened to these five old gentlemen, be patient! They will appear on T370.5.

690 **begged their advice** Legge, *The Lî Kî*, vol. I, p. 347: 'All the rules about sacrificial offerings and the nourishing of the old begging them to speak (their wise counsels) and the conversations at general reunions were taught by the lower directors of Music in the eastern school.' 'Wen-wang shih-tzu' (*Thirteen Classics*), 20.14b: 凡祭與養老乞言合語之禮, 皆小樂正詔之於東序. Legge's note: 'This asking the old men to speak was a part of the festal nourishment of them.'

693 **I** '[This] old body.'

694 **can only hope** Literally, 'must expect'.

696 **... countenance** See line 623n.

698 **... and so on** 言曰. What the prince actually says has been deleted from the text.

700 **upbraided** See line 635n.

701 **disobedience** 僫 is a vulgar form of 愆. Cf. Jen, *Prelim*, 448.

702 **instanced** If 'cited' and 'instanced' seem imperfect renderings of 將 and 豎, I can only say that no better solution has come to mind. Iriya 33b–34a interprets them in the sense of 'commit [offence, error]'. This is, indeed, a possible rendering. However, the break in the narrative necessitated by this switch to direct discourse ('You have committed', etc.) seems to me unwarranted.

704 **scolded** 訶 = 呵.

709 **deception** See line 580n.

710 **indulging** The character 行 is smudged heavily over another, indistinguishable character.

711 **convenience** See line 541n1.

tricked See line 541n3.

718 **... elder** Literally, 'staff of marvellous, millenary longevity'. The 椐 (樻, 柜) tree, because it had swellings at its joints, seemed to the Chinese an appropriate staff for the aged. It was for this reason that it very early came to be known as 靈壽木 and is also called 扶老杖. See Read, *Chinese Medicine Plants*, p. 287, no. 882 and *CKYHTTT*, p. 1958.

719 **shaky** 棹 → 掉.

721 **... himself** *The Chronicle of Tso*, 'Ninth Year of Duke Hsi', Legge, V.154:

'Heaven's majesty . . . is not far from me – not a cubic, not 8 inches.' 天威不違顔咫尺. A more modern expression, which probably derives from this, is 咫尺天顔. It refers to the intimate advisers of a king or emperor.

722 **cordial** 合 → 和(?).

. . . issue The meaning of this line is less than transparent. Chou 223.10 reads 開 'opens' hence 'expresses'(?) for 閂. Though indistinct, the character does appear to be an unusual orthography of 闢. See the chart of special Tun-huang forms of characters in Nogami Shunjo 野上俊青, ed., [*Ancient Copies of Buddhist Scriptures Discovered in the Tun-huang Caves, Now Preserved in the Otani University*] (大谷大学所藏)敦煌古写経 (Kyoto, 1965).

723 **vociferousness** Chou 223.10 incorrectly has 喧.

726 **. . . in greeting** See line 390n2 above.

727 **. . . clear** The T editors (336.1) emend 雪 to 說. On T40.14 分 has been misread as 交 (Iriya, *Index*, 7). The expression occurs frequently enough in T'ang popular literature to arrive at a workable definition: 'to clarify [usually a viewpoint or state of affairs]'.

729 **half a regiment** Half an 儀仗 which are 'les emblèmes et armes d'apparat' belonging to the Crown Prince (Rotours, *Fonctionnaires*, 606–7). If this explanation is not accepted, perhaps we may understand 半 → 伴 (LSY), hence 'a guard'. See, however, below, lines 959 and 983, where it is clear that the Crown Prince does have an escort but that it consists of too few soldiers (ten).

733 **conveniently** See line 541n1.

carry out For 興, Chou 223.12 has 與 which does not appreciably improve our chances of being able to read the line.

737 **used** Cf. Chiang 143.

738 **sixes and sevens** Literally, 'twos and threes', i.e. it is inconsistent.

. . . standard There are numerous other interpretations of this and the next line. The main problem is whether the accusation begins here or two lines below with 何須. There is also the question of how to read the sixth character in this line. S4398v has 唯; P4615, which the T editors follow, has 准, and Chou 223.14 reads 雖. The ms has 雄 which is a Tun-huang orthography for 惟 (see the chart mentioned in line 722n2). The latter reading, understood in the sense of 以 or 爲, yields the following sense: 'nothing which *serves as* a standard'. Chang Hsiang 485: 的 ≡ 準 or 確.

739 **ordering** 理 replaces the T'ang taboo-word 治 in Kao-tsung's 高宗 personal name, Li Chih 李治.

people 人 is for 民, also a taboo-word in the T'ang because of T'ai-tsung's 太宗 personal name, Li Shih-min 李世民.

mockery See Wu line 946n1. When used by an individual in reference to himself, 虛霑 is an expression of humility. Since this is the only occurrence I have noted where it is employed in reference to a third person, the nuance is less easy to grasp.

743 **pulverized** Make *paramāṇu-raja*(*s*) ('molecules') of you.

745 **. . . go back on it** Literally, 'should not be of two minds' (二 in the sense of 二心 or 二價). *Wu Yüeh ch'un-ch'iu* 吳越春秋 (*SPTK*) B23a: 'I have heard that a gentleman, once he has said something, does not go back on it' 吾聞君子一言不再.

750 **. . . together** 可 → 合(?).

751 **supporting** Meaning 拯 not 蒸(烝) as given by Chou 224.2.

753 **. . . itself** Compare the modern Chinese proverbs 一個巴掌拍不響 and 孤掌難鳴. The source of this notion in China, in written records, is *Han-fei-tzu*, 'Meritorious Renown' 韓非子, 功名. Liang Ch'i-hsiung 梁啓雄, *Han-tzu ch'ien-chieh* 韓子淺解 (Peking, 1960), p. 223: 'A single hand clapping alone, although done with verve, will not sound.' 一手獨拍, 雖疾無聲.

755 **. . . country** It appears that Sudatta has decided to speak in proverbs and allusions. This one is from the *Analects*, 'Tzu-lu' 論語, 子路, Legge, I.269: 'Is there a single

sentence which can ruin a country?' 一言而喪邦, 有諸? For 一言 meaning 一句, see Legge, I.146.

756 **... hairbreadth** This one is from the historian's personal preface to *Records of the Grand Historian* 太史公自序, *Shiki*, 130.24: 失之毫釐, 差以千里. 厘 is a variant form of the more complicated character in the quotation.

758 **... unwavering** This and the previous line taken together are equivalent to the saying 一言千金 which is ultimately derived from *Yüeh chüeh shu*, 'Yüeh chüeh wai-chuan, chi-tz'u k'ao' 越絕書, 越絕外傳, 紀策考 (*SPTK*) 6.49ab: 'There is no action without a reaction. What virtuous deed goes unrequited? One word of the fisherman was worth a thousand pieces of gold.' 無往不復, 何德不報, 漁者一言, 千金歸焉.

759 **... palm** In our continuing spate of proverbial expressions, this is one that has been especially popular in the world of drama, e.g. Chang Nan-chuang 張南莊, *Ho-tien* 何典 (Shanghai, 1933), 2.14: 'The old troupe-leader said, "If you want a new play, it's as easy as turning over the palm."' 老戲頭道:「要新戲易如反掌」. Ultimately, this is derived from *History of the Han Dynasty*, 'Biography of Mei Ch'eng' 漢書, 枚乘傳 (*PNP*) 51.22a: 'Easier than turning over the palm; more secure than Mount T'ai.' 易如反掌, 安於泰山. The latter half of this allusion may have been operative in the formation of the next line.

765 **make a deal** See Wu line 55n. In the Tun-huang popular texts, 平章 most often may be translated as 'to deliberate/consult'. However in its two occurrences on this page (T370.4, 9) it must be understood as 'discuss terms', hence 'make a transaction'.

771 **... dismay** Compare this line with the following from the 'Biography of Wang Su' in the *History of the Wei Dynasty* 魏書王肅傳 (*PNP*) 63.3a: 'Your subjects are dismayed and have lost their composure.' 臣庶惶惶, 無復情地.

773 **invited** In very polite language, 屈 may be glossed as 請, 'to humble' hence 'to invite'. 遂屈 in this line functions precisely as 即屈 on T371.13. My interpretation of 屈 as 'invite' is supported by an analogous line on T376.15 where 喚 – addressed to a person of lower status – occurs in this position. Cf. T13.4, *Ch'ü* nos. 505 and 684, *Tsu-t'ang chi* I.139.9, II.1.11, II.20.8, II.25.14, II.84.2, IV.80.14. Also see Lev Nikolaevich Men'shikov, *Bian'ven o vozdaianii za milosti; rukopis' iz Dun'-khuanskogo fonda Instituta vostokovedeniia* (Moscow, 1972), vol. I, p. 281n121 who fails to explain fully 屈喚 (occurs in line 665 of the ms he is explicating) when he renders it simply as *zvali*, 'called'.

Crown Prince P4615 has 太子.

... forward Admittedly, this passage is not easy to understand. But I do not believe that the following speech should be construed as Sudatta's (Iriya 35a) both because of the emphasis in it on age as a justification of authority and the overall tone of persuasion and conciliation. Also, the line of argument and, indeed, the very language of T368.9 used by the old man is taken up again here. Finally, at the end of the speech, the Crown Prince is persuaded by the old man and *then turns* to Sudatta and negotiates in accordance with his directions.

775 **Nevertheless** *Pi̯əu: nâ* (should be written 不䢵, see T102.4, Chou 224.8 and 225.1) usually acts as an adversative conjunction, most likely borrowed from another language. This expression also occurs in T370.11, and T38.16, T379.10 and T102.4. See also *Ch'ü* no. 480. Men'shikov, *Bian'ven o vozdaianii za milosti*, vol. I, p. 252n27 and p. 278n89 links 不那 with 兀那 which he labels a 'demonstrative pronoun'. It is difficult for me to accept this connection.

... truth Standard cliché taken from *Analects*, Legge, I.147: 'At sixty, my ear was an obedient organ for the reception of truth.' 六十而耳順.

776 **attended** 由仕 = 猶事 (Hsü 37).

Five Gerontions At last! See line 689n2.

777 **...temple** *Analects*, Legge, I.160: 'The Master, when he entered the grand temple, asked about everything.' 子入太廟, 每事問.

780 **...water** Derived from *Hsün-tzu*, 'The Rule of Kings' 荀子, 王制 (*SPTK*) 9.4b and 31.22a: 'A ruler is a boat and the people are his water – the water may support the boat but it can also capsize the boat.' 君者舟也, 庶人者水也, 水則載舟, 水則覆舟.

781 **...them** Derived from the *Chronicle of Tso*, 'Fifth Year of Duke Hsi' and 'Eighth Year of Duke Ai' 左傳, 僖五 and 哀八, Legge, V.143.13, 815.8: 'When the lips are gone, the teeth will be cold.' 脣亡齒寒.

790 **park** Surely 國 must be emended to 園.

792 **entire** Judging from T367.15 where this same line appears, except that 遍 replaces 與, the latter character is either a misreading of or a typographical error for 具 (Chou 224.11 correctly interprets the ms). Also see T370.14, 16 and T371.8 where the necessity of spreading the gold *everywhere* is stressed.

795 **buy it** I suppose that the T editors meant by 置 'to put down [the money]', hence 'to purchase'. The ms, however, clearly has 買.

796 **...agreement** Cf. Chiang 94, 'transaction, business'. See also *Ch'ü* no. 595.

804 **...terms** See line 765n.

805 **at once** Chiang 139.

808 **change his mind** See line 633n.

811 **...gold** 紫磨(金), also called 鏐 *liu*, is twenty-four carat gold. This term appears frequently in Tun-huang texts (T92.14, T341.8, T346.10 and *passim*).

814 **Unexpectedly** See line 775n1.
assisted *Adhitiṣṭhante*. Cf. T381.13, T388.14, T796.14 and 15, T798.5. This expression is similar to 加佑 (e.g. T78.15) and 加護 (e.g. T796.5). It is equivalent to 加備 (T380.15 and T800.3).

815 **...edges** Even with the unexpected assistance of the Buddha, these events have transpired much too quickly. My suspicions are increased by the unusual expression 向周, 'toward the circumference'(?). Or, perhaps, we may understand 周 as 滿 'filled up'.

816 **some** This is not the 已(以)來 which means 'since, after'. It is, rather, an expression of indeterminate quantity, 'about, around, approximately'. Cf. T40.11, T114.4, T160.5, T227.7, T325.12, etc.

820 **quickly** 知 is an auxiliary particle (Chiang 192).

823 **transported** Iriya 35b interprets 致 as 'spread, pave' 敷. I am somewhat dubious, for this requires understanding 峻嶺 (領 on the ms) 高岑 literally as topographical features of the park. It is unlikely that there would be such in the park since mountainous terrain of any sort has not been mentioned at all in the preceding descriptions of it. In support of my translation, we know from T364.14 that elephants carry 樓 on their backs and from line two of the same page that 崇 and 高峻 may be used attributively of 樓. If it is objected that even an elephant could not carry so much gold, my rejoinder is that they were transporting foil and not bullion. I regard 致 as the causative of 至 which is a common grammatical explanation of the word. If, however, 致 is considered as an error for 置, then the case for Iriya's interpretation is very strong, in spite of the topography.

824 **thickly** Chou 225.4 is correct in reading 洽恰(= 狎恰) (Chiang 128).

825 **household** Sudatta's, I presume.

826 **Great Wisdom** *Mahāprajñā*.

827 **instant** *Kṣaṇa*.

831 **contemplated** The ms has 扌寸(= 刌 = 忖).

838 **embarked** 下手 'to engage in/begin [an enterprise]'. Cf. T38.5, T39.6, 905.14 and *Layman P'ang*, 75, 77.

845 **Buddha-age** Technical term for 'period when a Buddha appears in the world'.

846 **eternity** Endless *kalpa*.

847 **earnest** There is no doubting the correctness of Hsü's (37) surmise that 懇＝懇.

857 **Yesterday** Sudatta passed one restless night on T363.

858 **meet** There is a problem with redundancy in the original. Cf. T363.4 where 幸 and 會 occur in adjoining clauses.
Great Sage *Mahā-muni*; *mahā-ṛṣayah*.

859 **Śuddhodana** Literally, 'Pure Rice [King]'.

860 **was** I switch to past tense because Śākyamuni's mother, Mahāmāyā, died seven days after he was born 'from her right side' (Caesarean section?). His foster-mother was Mahāprajāpati, sister of Mahāmāyā.

861 **self-enlightenment** *Atma-saṃvid*.

862 **neither** 無師 *svayam adhigamya*; adv. *anācāryakam*.

863 **precocity** 'Remarkably, outstandingly.' This is often the force of 穎 in such expressions as 穎悟, 穎異, 穎敏, 穎慧, etc.
achieved 稱 → 成 (?). Without emending, perhaps we may read '[because of] his precociousness, he was acclaimed "individually aware"'(?).
self-awareness In these lines, 自悟, 無師, and 獨覺 (*Pratyeka*[*-buddha*]) are different ways of referring to the same phenomenon – Śākyamuni's self-attained enlightenment.

864 **transformation-body** [*Nirmāṇa-*]*kāya* (化)身.
sixteen feet According to Chinese sources, this is a common attribute of a Buddha while on earth. Images of Buddha were often made to this prescription.

866 **bright** See line 306n2.
as 由＝猶.
. . . suns This identical line occurs on T363.16.

867 **quite** See line 209n.
approach 化 → 比. The responsibility for this error rests with the T editors. Cf. Chou 225.12.

868 **overwhelming** The emendation is unnecessary. See the *History of the Han Dynasty*, 'Biography of Ku Yung' 谷永傳 (*PNP*) 85(55).12a, where 頃動 means 傾動.

871 **actualizing** In the sense of 現實. In modern Chinese pronounced *chiào*, this is actually a causative of *chüéh*, i.e., 'to cause to be perceived'.
form *Nimitta*.

879 **aeons** *Kalpa*.

882 **mighty** Emendation unnecessary, 盛 and 晟 are interchangeable.

883 **. . . worship** 頂禮 is a technical Buddhist term; *vandanīya*.

888 **. . . harmonize** *History of the Han Dynasty*, 'Biography of Ssu-ma Ch'ien' 司馬遷傳 (*PNP*) 62.3a, which has this line and a paraphrase immediately succeeding it; i.e. 'the ruler takes the lead and his subjects follow'.

890 **. . . him** *Analects*, Legge, I.170: 'The Master said, "When we see men of worth, we should think of equalling them; when we see men of a contrary character, we should turn inwards and examine ourselves."' 子曰：「見賢思齊焉, 見不賢而內自省也.」

891 **sages** Supply 聖.

893 **monastery garden** See line 127n.

895 **. . . other** Cf. line 780n.

896 **. . . another** As the text stands, a forced translation would be: '[Where the water is] contiguous with the vessel, there is mutual assistance' (隣 is a vulgar form of 鄰) or 'Neighbouring vessels aid one another.' Clearly, there is a problem with the first character in the line. I have been unable to discover an appropriate replacement which either looks or sounds like 隣. My conclusion is that 隣 ('adjoining') has crept in due to semantic confusion with 同 ('same'). The translation thus assumes such an emendation which results in a common saying derived from *Huai-nan-tzu*, 'Discourse on Military Strategy' 淮南子, 兵略訓 (*SPTK*) 15.4a.

900 **tour** Cf. line 373n. Here I read as *àn* (in the sense of 行)-*hsíng*. Cf. Ta23.3b, 'to go on an inspection tour from house to house'.
901 **ants** Mole-crickets, actually.
905 **... grin** Same as on T365.11.
906 **antecedent causes** Technical Buddhist term.
907 **Jetā** Or Jetṛ.
910 **invited** See above, line 773n1.
911 **measured** Equivalent to 較量.
915 **bad karma** *Pāpa-karma*; *duścarita*; *saṃdoṣa*.
916 **Vipaśyin** First in the series of Buddhas, Śākyamuni being the seventh. 波 = 婆.
appeared in the world The more usual expression is 出世 which, I believe, was avoided because of the phonetic similarity to 時 following.
918 **Śākyamuni** The line indicating a proper name in T should extend down to 文. There are various ways of writing 'holy man of the Śākya [clan]': 釋迦牟尼, 釋迦茂泥, 釋迦摩尼, etc., or 釋迦文(尼) as here.
919 **evil circumstances** Which lead to the production of bad karma.
920 **grant** 受 = 授 or, if taken in its basic sense, we may translate literally 'he will grant and they will receive'.
ten commandments *Śikṣāpada*.
... refuge *Triśaraṇa* or *śaraṇa-gamana*:

> To the Buddha for refuge I go.
> To the Dharma for refuge I go.
> To the Sangha for refuge I go.

(Edward Conze, *Buddhism: Its Essence and Development* (New York, 1965), 86)

> *Buddhaṃ saraṇaṃ gacchāmi.*
> *Dharmaṃ saraṇaṃ gacchāmi.*
> *Sanghaṃ saraṇaṃ gacchāmi.*

921 **sweet dew** *Amṛta*.
perfect wisdom *Bodhi*.
923 **... deities** Not 'in the heavens'. Buddhist usage requires 'among the devas'.
925 **courts** *Ārāma*. Includes the monks' quarters.
temples For (廟)宇 *caitya*(?).
complete 被 → 備.
926 **Tuṣita** Derived from √*tuṣ* 'contented'.
929 **urgency** 火急 occurs frequently in the Tun-huang texts, cf. Iriya, *Index*, 14. Cf. *Ko-t'eng*, 289b.
932 **triple gate** *Trividha-dvāra*, metonymy for monastery.
sculptured The emendation by the T editors is basically sound. The only quibble I might note is that I would have preferred 塐 (a variant of 塑) for its visual closeness to the original character. The error probably occurred through confusion with 素嚩哩拏 *suvarṇa* ('of a good or beautiful colour') which is both an attribute of and a figure of speech for 金 'gold', the succeeding character.
thunderbolts *Vajra*.
933 **icons** *Pratirūpa*; *pratirūpaka*.
934 **side-rooms** There is some difficulty with the first character in this line: T has 俠, Chou 226.10 has 使, and Iriya 37a declines to print anything in this position. I presume that it is to be considered the equivalent of 挾 and understood in the sense of 'on both sides of'.
spirit chambers 'Rooms for pure/spiritual cultivation' (abode of the celibate), hence a monastery. 精室, five lines below, has the same meaning. *Vihāra*; *ārāma*.
935 **delusions** *Varaṇa*; *āvaraṇa*.

937 **loud and clear** It is possible that a less radical emendation than that of the T editors' 嘹亮 (which I follow in the translation) may be in order, i.e. 聊浪 'unrestrainedly'.

939 **chimes** Cf. T652.14.

940 **seat** *Āsana* (= 座). For a note on 高座, see Donald Holzman, 'À propos de l'origine de la chaise en Chine', *TP*, 53(1967), 289.

lectures on the Law 說法 *dhārmī kathā*; *dharma-deśanā*; *vyavsthāna*.

adorned 座嚴 → 莊嚴 *alaṁkāraka*. This is the reading given by Chou 226.12 and I find it much superior to the T version with its two awkward *tso* so close to each other. The ms has 庄 which is a standard Tun-huang form for 莊.

941 **Ox-head sandal-wood** *Gośīrṣa-candana*, also called red sandal-wood 赤栴檀.

942 **nine classes** 九品往生. 'The nine grades, or rewards, of the Pure Land, corresponding to the nine grades of development in the previous life, upon which depends, in the next life, one's distance from Amitābha, the consequent aeons that are needed to approach him, and whether one's lotus will open early or late.' SH 16. The T editors have mistakenly inverted the last two characters of this line.

... vows Since a translation of sorts is possible with the text as given, I have not made an emendation. However, it is virtually certain that 隨緣 *yathā-pratyaya* or *saṃnīpatita*, 'in accordance with conditioning causes' was intended.

943 **cuckoos** *Kalaviṅka*. 'Sweetly singing' is derived from the translated name of the bird, 妙音鳥.

944 **spirit rooms** See above, line 934n2.

947 **germ** Hsü 116 is correct in identifying 牙 with 芽.

951 **Six Heretical Masters** *Tīrthika* or *tīrthya*. They are: Pūraṇa-Kāśyapa, Maskari-Gośālīputra, Sañjaya-Vairāṭīputra, Ajita-Keśakambala, Kakuda-Kātyāyana, and Nirgrantha-Jñātṛputra. See SH 134 and 184. It should be noted that this text employs the term 六師 both in its generic sense (as it does here) and as a specific designation for a particular individual, Raudrākṣa (see line 1458n).

952 **details** This is the sole instance of the occurrence of this expression (委的 *ti*) which I have come across in these texts. The discovery of its meaning, however, presents no particular problem. First of all, it must be taken as cognate with the single character 委 whose meaning, in Tun-huang popular literature, is 'to know' (T155.3 (transcribed incorrectly as 季), T157.13, T218.11, T290.2, T376.15, T623.16, T624.3, T776.13) and 委知 whose meaning is also, of course, 'to know' (T22.12, T601.12). Secondly, on T376.15, the entire line in which 委 is found (尙未委其根由) is analogous to the present line. It is of singular interest to note that in every instance which I have cited, these expressions are preceded or accompanied by a word which has negative meaning (不 once, 難 once, and 未 in every other case). This indicates that, in spite of the enormous number of errors to be found in these texts, there were strong grammatical constraints operative. To return to the situation at hand, 委 means 'to know' and 的 means 'details' as in 的細.

953 **caught a glimpse** Or, trying to duplicate the Chinese more exactly, perhaps we might say 'caught wind of'(!).

955 **half a regiment** See line 729n. This is precisely what the Crown Prince said of himself on T369.6 – before his conversion.

960 **Granted** The ms clearly has 雖.

961 **unhewn** Hsü's (38) suggestion of 斲 is preferable to 琢 (refers to the cutting of gemstones) which was offered as an emendation for 卓 by the T editors. I question, however, that it was ever 'equivalent' 同, as he says, to 卓.

... house This saying occurs in many early texts. Our author probably picked it up from the *Han-shih wai-chuan*, Hightower, pp. 266–7: 'My prince has a throne room with three tiers of earthen steps. The grass thatch is untrimmed, the unpainted rafters are not finished, and still he feared those who built it would be overworked and he who dwells in it [too much] exalted.' 韓詩外傳 (*SPTK*) 8.8b: 吾君有治位之坐土階三等茅茨不翦．樸椽不斲者猶以謂爲之者勞居之者泰. But compare *History of the Han Dynasty*, 'Biography of Ssu-ma Ch'ien' (*PNP*) 62(32).4a: 'The Mohists also followed the way of Yao and Shun. Speaking of their virtuous behaviour, it may be said: their halls are three yards[?] high with three tiers of earthen steps. The grass thatch is untrimmed and the oak rafters unfinished.' 墨者亦上堯舜，言其德行曰：堂高三尺土階三等茅茨不翦採椽不斲. Yen Shih-ku's commentary says that 採 = 柞木 'oak'(?).

963 **mutton** Or any rank-smelling foods.

cooking-pot 餶(= 膾 'minced meat') → 甑 as read by Chou 227.3. *Han-shih wai-chuan*, Hightower, p. 75: 'Tradition tells us that, of old, because Shun's pots and pans did not smell of cooking, those below him did not offend by leaving [food uneaten].' (*SPTK*) 3.1a: 傳曰昔者舜甑盆無膻(羶)而下不以餘獲罪 N.B. the two references to *Han-shih wai-chuan* were pointed out by Iriya 37b.

964 **eliminating** I interpret 約除 as 約儉而除弊.

966 **tassels** Used to tie the ceremonial hat.

970 **ancient** Literally, *The Classic of Odes* and *The Book of History*.

971 **arrogant assumptions** Literally, 'usurpatory/presumptuous mind/opinions'.

973 **go** Cf. line 178n and Wu line 263n.

974 **horseback** And not in a chariot. 單騎 has two meanings: (1) 'one man per horse', (2) 'to go riding alone'. Clearly the first is indicated here.

976 **Or** See line 260n1.

977 **imperative** See line 356n.

978 **must solicit** Literally, 'absolutely take'.

982 **adequate preparation** Chiang 62; Iriya, *Index*, 21.

984 **loose** 聳 → 鬆 or, perhaps as Hsieh 94.33 suggests, 縱.

. . . unequipped It is possible to extract a translation from the text as emended by the T editors and myself (up to this point – more will be proposed in this note), i.e. 'loose your reins on a journey that brings you to here'. It may, however, well be that *all* of the first four characters require emendation. Chiang 62 changes 途 to 徒, hence 'loose your reins on a journey without chariot'(?). See *Shuo-wen t'ung-hsün ting-sheng* 說文通訓定聲 in *Shuo-wen chieh-tzu ku-lin*, 737aa: 'To go without chariot.' 無車而行. Chiang's emendation opens up the possibility that 呈 means 逞 rather than 程. It is on the basis of this final emendation of my own that the translation has been made.

985 **Try to tell** It is interesting to note that in modern colloquial Chinese this would be 說說看. Cf. T378.8. A prose restatement of this entire line may be seen on T377.1.

986 **. . . anything** More literally, 'perpetrate evasion'. Cf. T24.8.

989 **come** One 來 has been omitted through haplology and also for prosodic reasons.

990 **. . . Buddha** The translation does not accurately reflect the grammatical structure of the original. But, in truth, the structure of this line is problematical. If 所 is understood as a relative, the following caesura is so weakened that the rhythm of the line is destroyed. On the other hand, if the rhythmic proportions of the line are preserved by scanning 情所 as a unit, the result is an expression so unusual ('seat of the emotions' therefore 'emotions'(?)) that it may be unacceptable.

992 **returning** The series of three characters 還却歸, all of which seem to mean 'return', merits some discussion. Chiang 194 views 却 as an enclitic and presents convincing evidence to support his claim. Nevertheless, in the prose equivalent of this line (T372.16), 却 functions on a semantic rather than a phonetic level and there too it appears in close association with 歸. Furthermore, it is acceptable in this line (T373.10) to understand 還 as a conjunction ('yet') or as an adverb indicating continuation or process. It is impossible to determine precisely how the word is meant to function here. + 'To the palace.'

994 **... mind** This phrase, with the terms reversed (披肝露[瀝]膽 'to open the liver and expose [empty] the gall-bladder'), is very popular in later Chinese fiction as an expression of utter candour and forthrightness. It appears in a *fu* by Li Yüan 李遠, a T'ang dynasty poet (*chin-shih* 831) from Shu, in the order given here. 'Rhyme-prose on Locust Skins' 蟬蛻賦, *Ch'üan T'ang-wen* 全唐文 (Taipei, 1961), 31, p. 10051 (765.1b).

996 **Gautama's** Śākyamuni's family name.
incomparable While this would be highest praise in the mouth of a Buddhist, coming from the 'Confucian' Masters, it indicates contempt.

997 **swindle** For a brilliant expositon of 和, see Chiang 66. 斷 serves as an intensifier.

998 **died** See line 860n.

999 **... towers** Note how the syntax is wrenched in this line to maintain the (2–2)–3 rhythm. Literally, 'cannot [in] jade halls sit [in] agate towers'.

1002 **boasts** 嘆(歎 on the ms) → 譚 (?). This is only a suggestion for a possible reading. 歎 may mean 'to praise', hence 'praises himself'.
... gold Also referred to as 金軀.

1003 **... people** For a modified restatement of this line in prose, see T374.14.

1004 **adopt** Literally, 'trod and take'. 刾 must be a vulgar writing of 朿刂 which is itself a vulgar form of 刺, one of whose meanings is 取. + 'These perfidious ways.'

1006 **reported** 誠 → 呈. This is suggested as a possible emendation even though 誠 itself may be glossed as 審[陳], '[to state a case] in detail', because it actually seems a less cumbersome way of arriving at a meaningful reading. LSY suggests that the final two characters of the line be transposed.

1007 **impulsively** 輙 = 輒.

1012 **puffed up** 悵 → 脹 (Chiang 119).
jowls 腁 → 腮 (Chiang 119). I have accepted Chiang's emendation rather than that of the T editors (嘶高 'voices became shrill') for several reasons: experience in reading these texts has shown that, where there are orthographical errors, the radical component tends to be more stable than the phonetic-signific; the fact that the other indications of anger in this passage are expressed as physical changes; internal parallel resemblance to 頰脹; proof in T374.9 that the scribe knew how to write 嘶.

1013 **abruptly** The emendation by the T editors and the note by Iriya (*Index*, 8) to the effect that 斗 → 陡 are correct. By way of supplement, I should only like to add that 阧 is a variant form of 陡.

1014 **bared** I am unable to make with confidence a literal translation for this particular character because I am uncertain of the correct reading. The main text has 衝牙 but I am sceptical because this phrase has been pre-empted as the name of a type of insignia used in Chou and Han times. P4615 has 銜牙 but it is difficult to visualize what this might mean ('chomp the bit'(?)). Surely, something like 'gnashed [the teeth] and gnarled the teeth' must have been intended. Moreover, there does exist an expression 咬牙切齒 which has been much used by writers of popular literature to describe extreme anger and which, it is worth noting, has three of the four characters of the phrase in our text. There is one final possibility and that is that 衝冠 may have been intended or operative in the author's mind. The meaning fits perfectly and there is some visual resemblance between 冠 and 牙 (㸦 and 㸦). I hesitate, however, to propose this seriously as an emendation because it usually occurs in combination as 怒髮衝冠 'to be so enraged that the hair stands on end and pushes the cap up'.

1015 **irate** Chiang 119. 醋 is a variant of 酢.

1016 **rather** Chiang 154.
give our lives Not to be confused with 絕命 'cut short one's life; die'. 'For a worthy cause' is implicit in 決命 (cf. 校命).

1017 **live twice** To *continue* living.

1018 **away** 將 is a directional complement (Chiang 201).

1020 **ridiculed** 陵 may be glossed as 淩.

1021 **reviled** Chiang 89 makes a rather tenuous phonological connection between (陵)藉 and 祖. Supporting his argument by contextual evidence, he arrives at 'insulted' as the meaning of 作祖 although he does not account for 作. Iriya, *Index*, 25 interprets as 作詛 which seems somewhat more convincing. In this regard, I should like to point out that 作 itself is interchangeable with 詛. What we have in the present case, I believe, is a seriously corrupted form of 作(= 詛)祝. This also occurs on T251.14 and on T251.12 in an even more seriously corrupted form (竈(=竈 (?))祖). To say the least, it is puzzling: Chou 228.2 reads 作阻 and Cheng, *Popular*, 228 has 作袓(?)!

1027 **Bounded** 麁 on the ms = 麄, a vulgar form of 麤, the primary meaning of which is given in the translation.

1030 **representative** 所司 'attendant in charge'.

1044 **. . . songs** Literally, 'are not attentive to the folk-songs'.

1045 **He** From what follows, it is clear who most disturbs the Masters.
prime minister Cf. line 660n2.

1047 **Six Kingdoms** Ch'i 齊, Ch'u 楚, Yen 燕, Chao 趙, Han 韓, Wei 魏 of the Warring States period. All these kingdoms were east of the Han-ku Pass 函谷關 and were absorbed by a seventh kingdom, Ch'in 秦, which was west of it.

1048 **six relations** There are so many possibilities that it would be otiose to catalogue them all.

1051 **inform** *Wèn.*
throne See line 663n.

1052 **foreign** Serindian. Note that the argument in this and the following lines is precisely the sort of anti-Buddhist propaganda that was employed in China.

1056 **. . . kindness** Literally, 'By consistently acting contrary [to the dictum that one should show his] gratitude [by being attentive to] his appearance as he cares for [his parents].' *Analects*, Legge, I.148: 'Tsze-hsiâ asked what filial piety was. The Master said, "The difficulty is with the countenance."' 子夏問孝, 子曰 : 色難. This is often taken to mean that a filial child does not just go through the motions of caring for his parents. He must not mechanically do his duty to them with a scowl on his face. I have not emended 恆 because it does read. However, it is worth noting that from 不孝 down to 禮, there is almost perfect parallelism and that, by emending 恆 to 橫, there would be even more.

1059 **production** Making a living.

1060 **shave the head** Perform the tonsure.

1062 **no one** *Niṣpudgala.*
. . . verified This is only a tentative translation. I am particularly uncertain about the meaning of 的見. Literally, 'views that no one [can] substantiate'(?) (cf. 的知). For 的 used in this sense, see 的實 on T377.15 and cf. T379.9. Another interpretation (less likely because it weakens the parallel grammatical relationship to the preceding line) is 'When [the statements] are pursued, no one can, indeed, see them [heaven and hell].'

1063 **. . . place** Cf. T373.16

1065 **. . . minds** Cf. T373.11 and see line 994n.

1070 **ringleader** 頭首. Lo, *Studies*, 684 states that nouns in Tun-huang popular texts formed from two different characters which have the same or nearly the same meaning occur with greater frequency than in classical Chinese (including canonical Buddhist texts), with slightly less frequency than in modern Chinese, and with about the same frequency as in the records of the sayings of Zen masters.

1071 **. . . government** The translation makes sense but it is not necessarily what the author intended. Cf. 'Clarifying the Basic' in *Pao-p'u-tzu*, tr. by James R. Ware as

Alchemy, Medicine, Religion in the China of A.D. 320: The Nei P'ien of Ko Hung (Cambridge, Mass., 1966), p. 170: 'With lack of faith, delight was taken in slandering God (the True and Correct) as being a mere deception.' 抱朴子，明本 (*SPTK*) 10.4a: 既不信道好爲訕毁謂眞正爲妖訛. On this basis, we might wish to consider an alternative interpretation: 'His illicit provocation (= 煽) and seductive swindles throw truth and genuineness into chaos.' In support of this second interpretation, it may be noted that, in these texts, 政 is frequently written for 正 (e.g. T376.4 twice, T389.4). Also, the rhyme here has required the order *cheng chen* instead of the other way around as in *Pao-p'u-tzu.*

1073 **... Ruler** This line is poorly conceived. 孝 is meant to refer in a general way to the performance of one's duties to his parents. This is evident not only from the meaning of the word itself but also from the subsequent line which develops from the present one and where both ruler and parents are mentioned.

1074 **nor** The force of 不 carries through the second verb.

1075 **belittles** Though the two are interchangeable, the ms has 陵 rather than 凌.

1076 **wish** Though the meaning remains approximately the same, the ms clearly has 願 rather than 望 'expectation'.

mirror Symbol for penetrating intelligence. Cf. *ādarśana-jñāna* 大圓鏡智, wisdom of the great, circular mirror, one of the five types of wisdom 五智.

1079 **... lowered** 'Hunched spines and bent bodies.'

1080 **possess** 護 → 獲.

1083 **... skill** Or, as in P4615, 'knows that we are foremost (首)'.

1087 **... protection** 'Receive [our plea for] protection.'

1093 **apparitions** 孽 (?) = 孽.

1094 **government** Hsieh 95.32 would prefer to understand 政 as 正 'correct'. Cf. lines 1071n and 1120n.

1096 **despicable** Collation note 26 of the T editors (that P4615 has 猥) is unnecessary since the Hu Shih ms clearly also has 猥.

1098 **monks** It is noteworthy that the King consistently refers to the Six Masters as 和尙 (e.g. T378.3,6).

1099 **... carefully** This sentence is virtually unreadable as printed. It may be rectified simply by the following emendation: 聰 → 聴 (as on ms) = 聽. Literally, 'Just examine/be careful about (= 愼) [the evidence] you have gathered from hearing.'

1101 **inquire** 委 in these texts may often be interpreted as 'to know, to learn of'.

1103 **irregularities** 'Mistakes', see line 589n. Pronounced *tz'u-ch'ih* (池), cf. 參差 *ts'en-tz'u.*

1105 **representatives** See line 1030n.

1109 **gyves** 生杖 (cf. T42.8 and T733.12) must be a penal device. Lo, *Studies*, 848 has solved the problem well by identifying this instrument with the 'green thorn-cane' 生荊之杖 which is mentioned in the 'Legal Treatise' 刑法志 of the *Sui* and *Old T'ang Histories*. Note that the term 荊杖 occurs twice on T131.4.

1110 **immediately** See line 805n.

1113 **impulsively** See line 1007n.

turned 將作 'to take as'. Cf. T742.2.

1117 **omitting nothing** 'Without bothering to be evasive.' Cf. line 986n.

1118 **mine** 眹(?) = 朕, as printed in Chou 229.8. But LSY suggests that it may be similar to 視/眎 'view as' in expressions of comparisons. From this point on, the appellation 'Six Master(s)' is sometimes used to refer to the heretics as a group but oddly often just to their leader, Raudrākṣa.

1119 **... models** Derived from *Analects*, Legge, I.202: 'The Master said, "When I walk along with two others, they may serve me as my teachers. I will select their good qualities and follow them, their bad qualities and avoid them."' 子曰：三人行，必有我師焉．擇其善者而從之，其不善者而改之．

1120 **crystal** *Vaidūrya*. To sit in state is to 'occupy the principal seat'. 政 = 正 (see line 1071n).

1121 **...folded** Picture of effortless government. *The Book of History*, Legge, III.316: 'Then he had only to let his robes fall down, and fold his hands, and the empire was orderly ruled.' 垂拱而天下治.

...palace 勾陳 = 鉤陳

directly See line 1071n.

1122 **...men** *Records of the Grand Historian*, 'Biographies of Confucians' 儒林傳, *Shiki* 121.12: 'From that time on, the ministers, doctors, and officials were largely splendid literary men.' 則公卿大夫士吏, 斌斌多文學之士矣.

...problems 'Order *yin* and *yang*.'

1123 **Gallant** 糾糾 → 赳赳 (cf. Chou 229.10).

soldiers *Book of Odes*, Legge, IV.13: 'That stalwart, martial man/ might be shield and wall to his prince.' 赳赳武夫, 公侯干城.

...breeze 'Provide a cooling breeze' is filler to lengthen the English line.

1130 **poured out** 頃 = 傾.

1134 **Buddha-body** *Buddhakāya*.

sixteen feet See line 864n2.

1135 **While** 還 is an adverb.

1137 **five-coloured** *Pañca-varna*: blue, yellow, red, white, black. In Buddhist scriptures, these five primary colours and a corresponding set of five compound colours are assigned various symbolic meanings.

divine light 神光, cf. T14.8.

1138 **...Kings** *Catur-mahārājā*: Dhrtarāṣtra, Virūḍhaka, Virūpākṣa, and Dhanada (or Vaiśravaṇa).

1139 **...realms** See line 297n1.

1140 **toad** Read *há* (= 蛤) · *ma* (= 蟆).

1141 **great** *Mahā-ārya*.

unicorn Or 'horse which can travel 1,000 *li* per day'. It matters little that these two characters (*ch'i-lin*) have different radicals, for 騏 and 麒 are interchangeable as are 驎 and 麟.

1143 **ignorant** 委 ('to know, to learn') is invariably preceded by a negative (almost always 未, occasionally 不 or 莫), cf. T155.3 (季 → 委), T157.13, T218.11, T290.2, T379.16, T623.16, T624.3.

1144 **call** Consult line 773n1.

1147 **...fall** Cf. T368.4–5 above.

1152 **flippancy** Chiang 122, cf. 因循.

1157 **What** Chiang 183, cf. T433.7.

1162 **In the event** 忽然 = 惑然 (Chiang 148).

1166 **universal kings** *Cakravartin*.

1171 **grandsons splendid** 玄孫 ('great-great-grandson') = 炫孫 ('brilliant grandsons'(?)).

1174 **eight** I know of no particular significance attached to this number. Perhaps we may simply understand as 'the kingdoms of [all] the eight directions' 八方之國.

1175 **was** See line 860n.

1176 **India** 竺. Iriya 40b supplies 人: 'She was situated in a [position of] peerlessness among gods and men (*devamanuṣya*).' This is, of course, possible but I prefer the reading I have given for two reasons: (1) there is strict parallelism operative in these lines and we should expect a geographical or political entity to match 八國 above; (2) 天人 is, perhaps, too grandiose a claim for Māyā's matchlessness.

1178 **south** See line 135n.

1185 **...experience** 'Nothing' in the last two lines is literally 'nowhere' 無所.

1187 **Siddhārtha** 'Realization of all aims.'

1192 **tree of wisdom** *Bodhitaru/Bodhivṛkṣa/Bodhidruma*; the pipal tree, *Ficus religiosa*.

6. 'Fasting Siddhārtha', dating from the Kuchān era (second to third century, I.E.), from Sīkri, now kept in the Lahore Museum. After [Osamu Takata and Teruo Ueno] 高田修, 上野照夫, [*The Art of India*] インド美術 (Tokyo, 1965), vol. II, pl. 315.

1195 **... emaciation** In the following lines we have a verbal description of the condition of the Buddha depicted by the Gandhāran sculptor so stunningly well.

1196 **sesame** Or, perhaps, hemp-seed.
grain *Yava*, probably barley.

1198 **Crows** The ms clearly has 烏. Cf. Chou 230.9.

1205 **hungry ghost** *Preta*.

1208 **sixteen feet** See line 864nn1 and 2.

1209 **radiant light** See line 307n.

1210 **swastika** *Śrīvatsa-lakṣaṇa*, an attribute of Vishnu and the Buddha. Actually, it is a sauvastika 卍 and not a swastika 卐.

1212 **... tongue** *Prabhūta-tanu-jihvā-lakṣaṇa*, another attribute of the Buddha.

1213 **appearance** 能 = 態(?). Or 'he has a calm manner'(?). 能 may also be glossed as 'so', hence 'so flat'(?).

1214 **breast** This is as the text appears in T. Chou 230.11 has 臆(?). 臆 seems out of place for several reasons. In the immediately surrounding lines, the description centres on the physical appearance of the Buddha, in particular of his head. 臆 usually refers to the breast only in the sense of the feelings contained therein. Even if we assume that it is fully equivalent to 胸, it is still out of place here for the reason mentioned above and also because 胸 itself has already been mentioned in this passage. 頤 *i*, 'cheeks, jaws, chin', would seem more appropriate, both because it deals with the appearance of the head, and because it is a distinctive attribute of a Lion King. Note that the Lion King *is* the Buddha.
Lion King *Siṃha-rāja*.

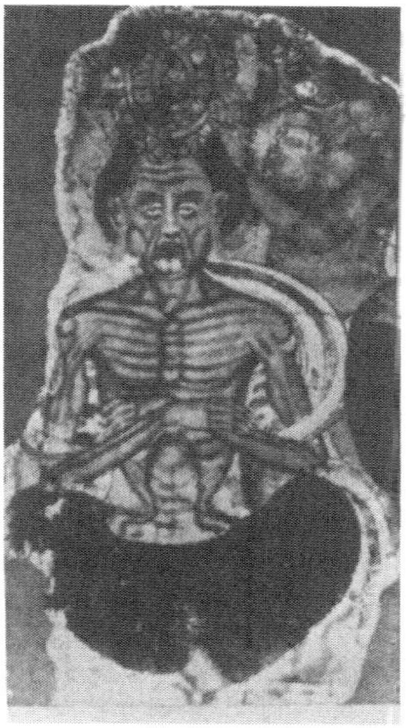

7. From a wall-painting in the Shiffahrtshöhle at Qyzil in Central Asia, now kept at the Museum für Völkerkunde. After A. von le Coq, *Bilderatlas zur Kunst und Kulturgeschichte Mittel-Asiens* (Berlin, 1925), fig. 166.

1215 **conch shells** Iriya 41b is incorrect in placing the hair on the breast of the Buddha. 螺髮 or 螺髻 is a distinctive trait of both Brahmā and the Buddha.

1216 **at-nir** This curiosity which has been inflicted upon the Sanskrit word *nirvāṇa* somehow deserves preservation as a specimen of the incredible absorptive power of the Chinese language. LSY has told me a joke whose *punch*-line is dependent on an identical linguistic trick: 你喝葡, 我飲萄 'You drink the gray, I'll have the pee.'

1218 **muddied** *Kaṣāya*.

1219 **settle** Pronounced *tèng*.

clear *Amala*.

1221 **illuminate** The original is nearly unreadable: 'Darken him and right away he becomes bright.' Iriya's (41b) suggestion that 闇 → 闡 is excellent and, I believe, correct. Cf. the common expression 闡幽 'elucidate the obscure'.

1226 **kumiss** 蘇 → 酥 (Chou 230.13). But this emendation is not really necessary within the context of T'ang colloquial since the same orthography occurs in *Tsu-t'ang chi*, IV.65.10.

1230 **cut through** 斫 *chó*, though I have attempted to translate it, should probably be emended to 鑿 *tsò* 'drill a hole through [the bottom and let the water out]'.

1234 **great body** Another way of referring to the Buddha's 化身 *nirmāṇakāya*, 'transformation-body'.

1236 **minor body** I have not been able to discover that this expression has any particular significance.

1240 **jocular** Chiang 115.

1244 **isolated** Literally, 'is not anxious [about his lonely condition]'. Cf. 悽悽 *ch'i-ch'i*.

1245 **two hearts** *Dvicitta*, the 'original mind' 眞心 *anākula* and the 'deluded mind' 妄心 (≡ 妄念), or the 'meditative mind' 定心 *akṣubhita-citta* or *samāhita-citta* and the 'distracted mind' 散心 *vikṣiptacitta*. The translation has been amplified to make it self-explanatory.

rudiment *Vīja*, 'seed, germ'. This probably means they contain all germinal possibilities, *sarva-bījaka/ākāra/prakāram*.

1246 **close** Chiang 132, though confident (and, I believe, correct) in his identification of 惻塞 and 閦塞 as 'to pack, to fill, to crowd' (T364.12, T379.10, and T388.15 – see line 354n2) feels that the strange character 閦 remains inexplicable here. He has good cause for maintaining a cautious attitude because the same graph has not been identified elsewhere. The problem is, indeed, so perplexing that Iriya 41b forthrightly considers the character as unreadable. However, if a translation is possible for T364.12, we may extrapolate from the graph's assumed meaning there, adverbialize it because of the 然 which follows, and thus obtain 'closely, thickly, densely, in crowds' and so forth which are not impossible meanings in this context.

I should like now to offer several observations as a supplement to Chiang's helpful exposition. *Shuo-wen t'ung-hsün ting-sheng* (*Shuo-wen chieh-tzu ku-lin*), 3539b: '惻 is a phonetic loan for 側.' (惻叚借)爲側. *Shih-ming*, 'Explanation of Appearances' 釋名, 釋姿容 (*SPTK*) 3.1a(17a): '側 means 逼 ("to crowd, to press").' 側, 逼也. *Hsün-tzu*, 'Explication of the Obscure', 荀子, 解蔽 (*SPTK*) 15.11a, commentary of Yang Chiang 揚倞 on the words 滿側: '側 is to say "close in, press upon" which means the same as "to fill completely".' 側謂逼側亦充滿之義.

As to the most difficult problem of the identification of 閦, one likely possibility is that the character is actually meant to be 闕 (*tś'i̯wät*), that this is phonetically similar to 側 (*tṣi̯ək*) and 惻 (*tṣ'i̯ək*), and that it is therefore eligible to be employed in all the situations where these two characters are considered interchangeable with other characters (whether through meaning or through sound). Thus, (1) 闕塞 ↔ 惻塞 ↔ 逼塞; (2) 闕然 ↔ (*側然) ↔ 迫然. Another possibility is that 閦 is related to 閃 (to the fourth power!?) (cf. Chou 218.12 and 231.2), 'shimmering', hence 'pullulating', hence 'teeming or crowded'. Also, compare 閦 *ch'ù*, 'crowded'. On D1502v, we find the name of the Buddha Akṣobhya written [阿]閦 (= 閦).

1251 **. . . men** *Devamanuṣya-śāstṛ*.

1252 **all wisdom** *Sarvajña*.

1253 **. . . born** *Catur-yoni*. This method of release employed by *pratyeka-buddhas* would seem to be inappropriate in reference to Śākyamuni who was concerned with saving others.

triple-world *Triloka* or *trailokya*. Cf. the Brahmanic *bhuvanatraya* of earth, atmosphere, and heaven; *bhūr*, *bhuvaḥ*, and *svar*.

1254 **all-conquering** *Jina* or *vijaya*.

1260 **moral powers** Understand 此德能(?).

1261 **. . . fashion** 'Have not displayed the actuality.' For 的, cf. line 1062n2 above.

1262 **trial** 'Verification', according to Hsü 38 who believes that 諫 should be emended to 譣 (= [証]驗). Hsieh's 96.46 emendation to 練 more readily yields the translation given.

1263 **Then** Chiang 164.

1267 **thousand-pound** The force required to set the bow. The actual weight mentioned here is one thousand catties ($1\frac{1}{3}$ pounds) times thirty.

1268 **not** The T editors are faithful to the ms in omitting 不. However, this reading does not make sense. The addition of 不 is necessary; cf. Chou 231.6; Cheng, *Popular*, 228; and Hsü 116.

launched Its trigger cannot be set off.

. . . mouse *Ch'uan-teng lu* (*SPTK*) 12.8b differs only in the addition of 而 before 發. Cf. T187.1–2.

1273 **stand up against** Both Chou 231.7 and Cheng, *Popular*, 228 read 抵敵. This is certainly the meaning required by the context. Yet it is necessary to point out that 祇敵 appears consistently in similar contexts on T379.11 and T386.8. It remains to observe that, in all three places, the mss consistently have 袛敵 which must, therefore, be considered as the standard Tun-huang orthography for this expression.

1283 **nephew** Or 夘甥 = 外甥.

1284 **... monk** *Pravraj.*

1285 **... Law** 學法.

is Hsieh 96.49 suggests that 有 → 猶 '[is] still'.

1290 **Yen Ying** A famous statesman of the Warring States period who served as prime minister of the State of Ch'i. See Giles, *BD* no. 2483. *Shiki*, 62.9: 'Although Yen-tzu was not a full six feet in height, he acted as the Prime Minister of Ch'i and his name was pre-eminent among the feudal lords.' 晏子長不滿六尺. 身相齊國, 名顯諸侯.

1294 **Fabricating** 搆 = 構.

1301 **proclaiming** Iriya 41a emends 頒下 to 班下. While the syntax of the original is slightly awkward, it is possible to make sense of the text as given and so I leave as is.

1310 **religious arena** *Bodhimaṇḍala.*

1313 **converted** Literally, 'turn to and serve'.

1317 **extremely** Chiang 163.

1319 **... cheeks** Although I have made a translation of sorts for 蹙頰, this phrase strikes me as being so unusual that I am compelled to mention that 蹙頞/額 'contracted/wrinkled the forehead' would read much more smoothly.

1322 **changed** From what they usually were (常). The same expression occurs in the next line. Cf. line 633n on 改張 above.

1333 **demonstrate** 逞, glossed as 肆, 盡, or 申. Cf. 出 on T379.1.

1341 **sagacity** The sage individual 聖人 and the unenlightened man 凡人(夫) are frequently contrasted in Buddhist literature.

1342 **predicament** See line 1353n.

1343 **... power** This sentence is difficult to comprehend. To make matters even more complicated, the punctuation on the ms falls between 悲 and 進. Hence, 'May you be so kind as to show compassion; in my predicament, I hope ...' 垂委實 may be a telescoped form of 垂委委實. This still presents serious difficulties because 垂委 is seldom used figuratively and 委實 is restricted to adverbial functions (cf. 確實). If forced, perhaps we may understand 'confer[?] upon me substantial[?] [aid]'. A second possibility is to take 委 in the sense of 'to know' (but see line 1143n above), hence 'extend [to me] understanding of the actual [situation]'. The third possibility, which I have adopted for the translation, is to emend 委實 to 威勢. Aside from the phonological resemblance, there are at least three reasons for doing so: it makes sense and, from the discussion above on telescoping, it is easy to see how the line could have been corrupted by erroneous associations of each succeeding character. Finally, partial confirmation for this emendation is found on T380.15 and T381.3 where 威 occurs in similar contexts. It remains problematical whether Sudatta is hoping for assistance from the Buddha or from Śāriputra. I have opted for the latter because of what is mentioned in line 1341n, because Sudatta is with Śāriputra and speaking to him, and because it forms a nice hierarchy (Sudatta – Śāriputra/ Śāriputra – Buddha) when Śāriputra makes the same requests of the Buddha on T381.

1345 **comfort** Cf. glosses of 適 as 快, 悅, etc. 'Sudatta' is added to the translation.

1353 **predicament** Iriya 42ab, both here and above (T378.15), understands 進退 somewhat differently than I do. His interpretation is 'course of action, approach'. Although such an interpretation works very well in the present instance, I have not adopted it because it can be used in the former instance only with effort: 'be so compassionate [as to bestow] a course of action'(?). On another level, however, our differing viewpoints may be reconciled by the observation that a 'course of action' is, indeed, what one takes to get out of a 'predicament'. They are two aspects of the same concept: with the one, there is embarrassment, with the other, an attempt at disembarrassment. Both represent a state of 'advance-retreat'.

1355 **notions** *Parikalpitā*; *vikalpana*; *vibhāvanā*. 相 and 想 are constantly confused in these texts. Apart from the natural tendency for this to occur because of the visual and phonological resemblance between the two characters, there is the added complication which results from the interplay in Indian thought between cognition and object of cognition.

1357 **otter** 獺. This is a fairly definite reconstruction. In the first instance, there is an affinity between fish and otters. The drawing of the otter in the *San-ts'ai t'u-hui* 三才圖會 (Taipei, 1970), p. 2231 – 'Birds and Animals' 鳥獸, 3.25a, shows it holding what comes most naturally in its forepaws – a fish. Secondly, there is a long-standing literary connection between the two in China. Legge, *The Lî Kî*, I.251: 'The east winds resolve the cold. Creatures that have been torpid during the winter begin to move. The fishes rise up to the ice. Otters sacrifice fish.' 禮記 (*Thirteen Classics*) 14.4a: 東風解凍, 蟄蟲始振, 魚上冰, 獺祭魚. Presumably this expression, which occurs frequently in literary texts, derives from the otter's gluttonous habit of spreading more fish on the bank than it can eat. It later came to have the extended meaning of writing an essay by piling up a large number of quotations and allusions. Thirdly, and what to me is the most convincing evidence, it fits perfectly in the rhyme scheme for this section: 達 (*d'ât*), 割 (*kât*), 獺 (*t'ât*), 撮 (*ts'uât*), 末 (*muât*), 掇 (*tuât*), 薩 (**sât*). It is for this reason that Lo's (*Studies*, 813) reconstruction of 龍 'dragon' is unacceptable.

1359 **pecks** 斗. Cf. the very popular saying 海水不可斗量. This is included in the *T'ung-su pien*, 'Geography' 通俗編, 地理 (Peking, 1958), 2.30 where *Huai-nan-tzu* 淮南子 (*SPTK*) 20.2a is cited: 江海不可斗斛也. There is a character (扶(?) = 摸 'to grope for') in this space but it is written heavily over another character which is illegible.

1364 **Certainly** Cf. line 1062n2.

1365 **have** 建 'to establish' is a problem character. Chou 232.10 has 遺 'to grant'. My own reading of the ms is that it has a variant of 遣. This reading is confirmed by the recurrence of the character which is written in exactly the same way on the ms at the points indicated in lines 1485n2 and 1676n1 as well as at T387.12 and T388.6.

1368 **minor sage** This expression, 小聖, generally refers to an arhat or a Bodhisattva.

1369 **Nevertheless** See line 775n1.
high places The Buddha. Grammatically, we must understand either 處高者 or 高處.

1370 **. . . of** Literally, 'only like'.
correct 政 = 正.

1372 **Scourge of Heaven** Deva Māra.

1373 **crowd** See line 354n2 and line 1246n.

1376 **stand against** See line 1273n.

1378 **Accumulating** 佇 glossed as 積.
practising my artifice Cited by Chiang 208 as awaiting explanation. My translation assumes an emendation to 機練. This is not at all far-fetched since Buddhist thought places great emphasis on 'potentiality' and what becomes of it through 'response' 感 or 應 to the Buddha and his teachings 教 or to conditions 緣 in general. Considering what Śāriputra has in store for the heretics ('a bag full of tricks' 機變百出!), I have decided to make my translation correspondingly playful. Finally, the orthographical error, 譏練, probably occurred because of: (1) visual resemblance, (2) phonological resemblance, (3) mistaken analogy with 譏諫. Hsieh

98.74 suggests 譏 → 試, hence 'practice training'. Cf. line 1262n and T377.15 which has 試諫.

1383 **hole** 突 → 竇 (Waley, 'Notes', 176). 莵 → 兔. *Yu-hsien k'u*, p. 16: 'Don't make excuses, milady. The rabbit has entered the dog's hole. What are you going to do about it?' 娘子莫分疎; 兔入狗突裏, 知復欲何如!

1384 **... table** Literally, 'the food is cooked'. I am indebted to Iriya for my understanding of these two lines.

1385 **... road** 'Do our stuff; show our tricks.' Iriya's note 42 on 53b is instructive.

1390 **daybreak** 齊 → 啟.

1395 **supply** As elsewhere, 祗 (祗 on ms) 抵, 'make good'.

1399 **returned** To his home.

1405 **agreed** I.e., 'agreed to the engagement'. The syntax of this line is slightly warped; see T380.4 for the correct order.

contest of skill 鬪聖 does have the meaning given in the translation and need not be rendered 'contest to see who is the more holy' (LSY).

1406 **pulled foot** This expression only occurs once in T but its meaning is clear enough from the context: 'used his feet'. I have employed a slang expression in the translation to match what I believe is the level of diction of 使脚.

1407 **... hopeless** 襟 → 禁, i.e. '[the situation] is beyond his control'. This and the succeeding line are very difficult to understand.

1408 **... way** 'Is not a fitting response/recompense.'

1409 **Law** Dharma.

1410 **be content** 分 'accept my lot'.

1411 **Crown Prince** 'The person of the Crown Prince.'

1412 **... crime** 'What crime [has he committed that he should] receive execution?' Although there is no serious difficulty with this reading, 何故 'why? for what reason?' should perhaps be considered as a possible emendation.

1413 **Hurriedly** 蒼 → 倉 (from confusion with 蒼茫 'vast expanse').

1416 **knew** See line 952n.

1417 **At last** 'Because.'

nine Chou 233.5 and Lo Chen-yü both take the liberty of changing 九 to 牧 'to tend cattle'. This is unjustified since the two characters have neither graphic nor phonetic similarity. Why 'nine'? A good question, but probably attributable mostly to euphony. Cf. the expressions 九牛草, 九牛二虎, 九牛一毛. It certainly is not meant to be a precise number with any particular significance. Indeed, it could just as well be rendered 'several head of cattle'.

1422 **Grandpa** The punctuation in T, which follows that on the ms, seems incorrect. Surely 阿翁 is a vocative. The herdboy uses the same term of address near the end of his speech.

1431 **knew** Iriya, *Index*, 30 lists 委是 as a special form. This is an oversight, for 知 and 委 must go together as a unit. See T131.7, T156.15, and T611.15. Cf. Chiang 85–86. Iriya himself (*Index*, 19) lists 知委. Also refer to line 952n.

1433 **one** See line 632n1.

1436 **banyan tree** 尼拘陀 *Nyag-rodha*, *Ficus Indica*, the banyan or Indian fig-tree.

1437 **Motioning aside** 併 glossed as 屏 or 摒.

1438 **... fingers** See line 390n2.

1443 **agreed** See line 1405n1.

1447 **actually** Not in the original.

1453 **... greeting** See line 390n2.

spiritual master *Acārya* (阿)闍梨.

1454 **ignorant** 凡愚 *bāla* is a technical term which refers to those who have not yet been converted.

unenlightened Chou 233.13 has 未 instead of 不.

1456 **treating** 捉 is a pretransitive (Chiang 174–5), cf. Mandarin 把.
1457 **instructions** Or 'decision' as to how to behave.
1458 **Raudrākṣa** This is the first time that Śāriputra's chief opponent is mentioned by name (= Six Master).
1459 **predicament** See line 1353n.
1462 **... meditation** *Samādhi.*
1464 **... views** This is the simplest explanation. By analogy with 妄念, however, one could also interpret 非 as 非想, i.e. 非有想非無想處 *naivasaṃjñānāsaṃjñāyatana*, which is an advanced stage of meditation (beyond thinking and not-thinking, a state in which there is neither perception nor non-perception) but which is itself yet an imperfect form of existence. This may, however, be assuming far too great a sophistication on the part of the author with the principles of meditation.
1465 **... senses** *Caura*, cf. line 11n2.
1466 **ineffability** *Acintya.*
mind-control *Samādhibala*, the power derived from ecstatic meditation.
1467 **acquired** *Śrāvaka*, literally 'hearer', a disciple of the Buddha who has *heard* his message; one who has awakened to the unreality of the phenomenal.
1471 **Vulture Mountain** See line 296n.
1474 **World-Honoured** *Lokajyeṣṭha* or *Lokanātha.*
1477 **bestowed** See line 814n2.
1478 **King of the Law** *Dharmarāja.*
1479 **monks'** *Saṅgha*, the monastic order of monks.
1480 **decoration** See line 251n2.
1481 **quite** See line 209n.
insufferably Mandarin *nán tāng.*
1482 **spiritual powers** *Ṛddhy-abhisaṃskāra*; *anubhāva*; *abhijñāna.*
1484 **subduing** 降伏 *abhicāraka* is an exorcist or subjugator of demons.
readily 一時, 'swiftly, at once'. Cf. T86.3, T205.3, and T341.13.
1485 **redeemed** *Pāramitā*; *uttāraṇa*; *nayati.*
made 'Sent'(?). But see lines 1365n and 1676n1 for the character as it is written on the ms.
ranks It is interesting to note that 行 on the ms is interlinear, having been written next to the original character which was 房 'quarters'.
1487 **acquired** Cf. T380.14 and line 1467n.
1488 **summoned** Cf. T715.16.
come close by Cf. T114.3 (側近).
1489 **patch-robe** *Saṅghāṭī.* 'Of our monastic order' is filler to complete the English line.
1490 **Through** 暦 = 歷.
aeons of time *Kalpa.*
you The Buddha seems here to be addressing the patch-robe. But, judging from the next line, it would seem that he is referring to a person, most likely Śāriputra; in the final four lines of verse, he is probably addressing Śāriputra directly again. Ānanda's role may have been no more than to take the robe from the rack and give it to Śāriputra. Indeed, Prof. Nagatomi has provided me with solid textual evidence to substantiate this particular function of Ānanda – that is, as transmitter of the robe on behalf of the Buddha. See *Madhyamāgama-sūtra* 中阿含經, Ta1.511b: 'Thereupon, the World-Honoured turned around and spoke, saying: "Ānanda! You are to bring the cassock made of golden thread (*suvarṇa-sutratantu*) for I wish, today, to give it to the *bhikṣu*, Maitreya." At that time, the honoured one, Ānanda, received the World-Honoured's instructions. He brought the cassock made of golden thread and handed it over to the World-Honoured. Thereupon, when the World-Honoured had received the cassock made of golden thread from the honoured one, Ānanda, he spoke: "Maitreya! You are to take this cassock made of

golden thread from the Tathāgata . . .”' It is clear from what follows in this account that the robe is valuable in the subduing of demons (*Māra-pāpīyān*), just as it is in the Śāriputra transformation text. Cf. *Gayāśīrṣa-sūtra* 伽耶山頂經, Ta14.433b. The robe also figured as a symbol of the transmission of authority in the Zen sect, e.g. *The Platform Sutra of the Sixth Patriarch*, tr. Philip B. Yampolsky (New York, 1967), p. 133: 'I make you the Sixth Patriarch. The robe is the proof and is to be handed down from generation to generation.'

1491 **. . . wisdom** 惠 = 慧. *Jñāna* and *prajñā*. + 'With this.'

1492 **gold-embroidered** 蘭 → 襴.

cassock *Kaṣāya*.

1493 **Infinite** *Apramāṇa*.

beneficent deities 善神 are spirits which protect believers in Buddhism.

. . . you Literally, 'guard and protect it', hence *you* who are wearing it.

1494 **all** There should only be one; this implies his followers as well.

kings *Māraḥ pāpīyān*; *pāpīyas*.

1495 **undefiled** *Pariśuddhi*; *viśuddhi*.

underlying nature *Dharmatā* = *bhūtatathatā* (眞如).

unconditionalness In the philosophical sense of *asaṁkṛta*.

1500 **. . . realms** See line 297n1.

1501 **supported** May be glossed as 擁持. Cf. line 1570n below.

1503 **Titans** *Asura*.

1505 **. . . musicians** *Kinnara*. 郍 = 那.

1506 **. . . spears** It would appear that our author was only superficially learned in Indian mythology! Also note that the ms has 鎗 rather than 槍.

1509 **. . . master** I suspect that these titles refer to the Maruts, the ancient Indian spirits of the storm, who controlled *vāyu* and *varṣa*, wind and rain.

1512 **kings of spirits** Unidentifiable as specific divinities.

1513 **Diamond deities** Probably *vajra-deva*.

thunderbolts *Vajra*.

1514 **selected** 蕳 → 簡.

1517 **Conches . . .** *Dharma-śaṅkha*.

1518 **Drums . . .** *Dharma-bherī*.

1520 **. . . majesty** In esoteric Buddhism, 威怒王 is the form the Buddha takes when dealing with people who are difficult to transform.

1524 **elephant king** *Gajapati*. One of the Buddha's attributes is that 'his progress is like that of the king of elephants'.

1525 **lion . . .** This is Mañjuśrī's mount; or the Buddha in a previous incarnation. In the lines which follow, the description seems not to include the elephant. Indeed, the picture presented (and even the language) is very close to that found in Po Chü-i's 'Entertainers from West Liang' 西涼伎, *Po-shih ch'ang-ch'ing chi* 白氏長慶集 (*SPTK*) 4.3b: 'The Entertainers from West Liang are masked Serindians. They use carved wood as the head of their lion, silk threads for its mane, gilt gold for its eyes, and silver foil for its teeth. The hair of its coat bristles and it wags its ears.' Yang Hsien-i 楊憲益, *Ling-mo hsin-chien* 零墨新箋 (Shanghai, 1947), pp. 45–8, offers a fascinating record of the modern survival of the West Liang Lion Dance.

1527 **. . . jaws** Literally, 'displayed its teeth'.

1528 **bristled** 'Strained.' *Vijṛmbhita*; *siṃha-vikrīdita*.

coat One wonders whether the use of the word 衣 does not indicate that the author's knowledge of lions was restricted to lion dances. Cf. line 1525n above.

1529 **wagged** 擗 = 擺 (Chou 234.14, Hsü 38).

1530 **weapons** 扙 → 仗.

reflected In comparable descriptions of armies, the usual word in this position signifies 'screen' or 'block out', e.g. 蔽, 隱, 遮. Judging from the parallel word in the succeeding line, which also has to do with 'covering', it is safe to say that the probability of corruption is very high for 映.

1532 **matched** 諍 = 爭.
demonstrate 逞 → 呈.

1533 **... majesty** 威神力, *prabhāva*.
bestow See line 814n2.

1535 **... hosts** In this line, 而 is both supernumerary and ungrammatical; it may safely be dropped.

1537 **Heavenly King** *Maharāja-deva*.
Virūpākṣa Deva King of the West. This may also refer, however, to Virūḍhaka, Deva King of the South.

1538 **Dhṛtarāṣṭra** Guardian of the East.

1540 **vast profusion** 論 → 淪.

1541 **... Deity** King of *yakṣas* who protects Buddhism.

1542 **Fire** 火 (printed correctly in Chou 235.3) misread by the T editors as 大.
... Deity Ucchuṣma(?). In charge of sewers(!).
unceasingly 慜(?) → 歇.

1544 **glistening** 晈 = 皎.

1545 **... immortals** *Deva-ṛṣi*.
beautiful Literally, 'famous', but see line 575n above.

1546 **continuous** Chiang 23.
hymns *Pāṭha*; *pāṭhaka*.

1548 **sword** More often 刃, 'blade'.
wisdom See line 1491n.
glimmered Literally, 'arose'.

1550 **flags** Chiang 208 and Iriya 45a consider this character to be inexplicable. Chou 235.5 has 幢 where T has 憧. This is certainly a superior reading, especially when one considers the verbs at the end of this line. Lo, *Studies*, 839–40, forces an interpretation from the erroneous reading of the T editors in this fashion: 邪 ≡ 不正, 憧 ≡ 惷, hence the heretics(?). N.B. 忄 is standard Tun-huang orthography for 巾! Cf. T382.10 where the ms has the identical radical.
heterodoxy **Mithyādhvaja*(?); **mithyāketu*(?).

1552 **royal** Although I have translated this literally, it may actually be preferable to consider 皇 = 隍 'dry moat outside city-wall'. I offer this suggestion because the contest-ground is *outside* the city-wall and it is clear below that Śāriputra does not enter the city, which he would have to do to 'arrive at the royal city' (the 'forbidden city').

1559 **commoners** Cheng, *Popular*, 229 reads 應 'correspondingly [to the King's position]'. But see T384.4.

1560 **possibilities** 'Paths.'
... defeat This refers to each round of the overall contest.

1563 **tally** *Śalākā*. Lo, *Studies*, 831ff, and elsewhere through his book, compares the contest between Śāriputra and Raudrākṣa to a polo match.

1565 **score** 尙字 means 上字, i.e. 'the word "[came out on] top"'. See Chiang 38.

1567 **... pleases** The same line occurs at the end of the next paragraph.

1568 **self-composed** See line 350n.
platform *Siṃhāsana*.

1569 **... curtains** *Ratnadhvaja*.

1570 **supported** See line 1501n. 'By his followers' is not in the original.

1571 **... platform** *Ratnāsana*.
Speaking 'Emitting.'

1572 **... sides** Literally, 'the four orders'. See line 118n. Below, this expression will be translated as 'those assembled, the assembly', or as it is here. In this non-Buddhist

kingdom, there is no justification to translate as 'the four orders'.
Now 然 is an introductory particle (Chiang 189).
1573 **mind** *Hṛdaya.*
... identity That is, there is no ego or human soul, *ātman.*
1574 **... false** Cf. T379.10 and line 1370n2.
1575 **establish** 'To settle the thoughts; to settle something.' *Upacāra; prajñapayati; vijñapti.*
transformations Discussed in *Transformations*. Although *pien-hsien* here functions as a compound noun, it means more than simply 'transformation'. It also carries with it the idea that the transformation is manifestable, which idea I have tried to work into the translation as explained in the following note. Cf. Skt. *prātihārya.*
come up with Literally, 'has [in his bag of tricks to manifest]', i.e. 'can perform'.
1579 **leagues** *Yojana.*
1583 **grasses** 薪 ('fire-wood') glossed as 草.
1585 **Orion and Lucifer** The constellations 參 and 辰.
1588 **... plants** I have chosen to translate the characters 籐(藤) and 蘿 individually rather than as a compound word, 'wistaria'.
1593 **none** Translating the rhetorical interrogative as a negative.
present Line 1572n1.
1597 **Diamond Deity** 金剛(手), *vajrapāṇi*, 'one who holds the *vajra'* (i.e. diamond club or thunderbolt). Cf. above, T382.2.
... Deity This question represents a highly significant element of the written *pien-wen*. For a discussion, see the Introduction.
1601 **pedestal** 鉆 should probably be emended. I propose 坫, but with some reservations, for I have not seen it attested as a pedestal for a person. It is usually described as a platform for placing drinking cups or food. The most compelling reasons for its acceptance are its phonetic and orthographic similarity to 鉆 and the fact that it serves as a suitable parallel to 蓋 above. 站 is a less likely possibility because of its late appearance in Chinese lexicons.
bushy 欝 (欝 on the ms) must be a variant of 欝 which is a vulgar form of 鬱. The original actually says 'as bushy and purplish blue'. Hence 翠 → 萃 or 蔡.
twin I am following the reading of the T editors because it seems to make more sense than the 'rainy'(?) of the ms. 兩 and 雨 are distinguished on the ms by having the vertical, central line pass through the top, horizontal line in the former case (兩) and having it stop abruptly in the latter case (雨). The two characters are also distinguished on the ms by the marks within the enclosure.
wooded Literally, 'blue-green'.
1602 **opened wide** Chou 236.3 reads the onomatopoetic binome as 吒吒(＝咤咤), 'shouting angrily', but this is unacceptable for, by analogy with the preceding sentence and because of the inherent, logical consistency required of the simile expressed in the sentence under discussion, the binome must reinforce the meaning of 廣闊. For this reason, 嘏嘏 (glossed as 咽咽) is also unacceptable. Actually, both the T editors and Chou are incorrect for the ms clearly has 吒嘏. I believe that a cognate word, 挓挱 (also written 觰沙, 扎煞), was intended and that a 口 radical was substituted simply because the mouth was being described.
1605 **pointed** 擬 glossed as 向. Cf. T383.11 and especially T384.11 where there are complicating factors. An acceptable rendering may also be arrived at by using the basic meaning of the word: 'intimated [that he was about to strike it]'.
1607 **fell** 'Were carried away by the wind'.
1608 **disappeared** Literally, 'nobody knew where they were'.
1615 **all of** 'About, around.'
leagues *Yojana.*
1619 **... Ling-wei** Taoist immortals, Giles, *BD*, nos. 2240 and 1938.

1621 **continuously** Although all of the texts are in agreement that this reading, 往往, is correct, I would be more comfortable if there were some justification for rendering this 'went back and forth' 往來.
beautiful See line 1545n2.

1623 **introduced** 來入 'came forth into'(?). P4524v has 來在 'came to be/exist' hence 'materialized'(?). Whether 入 or 在, the character is both supernumerary and superfluous. Vandier-Nicolas, p. 14, takes an entirely different view of the matter by interpreting the final three characters as referring to Śāriputra's entrance into the assembly. I object to this interpretation because: (1) He is already seated on his platform (T382.10) and was told to remain there throughout the contest by the King (T382.11); (2) grammatically, the transitive verb's need for an object has destroyed the caesura. This makes it highly unlikely that Śāriputra could serve as the subject of both clauses. The correct grammatical interpretation is thus that the entire final clause is the object of 見. Vandier-Nicolas was, however, dealing only with P4524v in which 弗 is missing. As such, the second argument I have just outlined does not obtain *for that particular text*. Iriya 45b translates as I do.
assembly *Nikāya*.

1624 **meditation** *Samādhi*.

1626 **... muscles** Literally, 'body which was lumpy'. Those who have studied the statuary of the Mo-kao Caves will appreciate the accuracy of this description. 礨 is a vulgar form of 磊. The T editors (see their collation note 31) have misread P4524v as 旋. It should be 碨 which rhymes with and means virtually the same as 磊.

1627 **diamond** 'Adamantine', not 'metal' or 'golden'. 剛 has been elided for prosodic reasons.

1628 **pointed** See line 1605n.

1635 **... be** Literally, 'Since [Raudrākṣa] was not equal to the other this time, no[one] knew what additional miraculous transformation (神變) [he would offer].'

1638 **score marker** See line 1565n.

1641 **Now** See line 1572n2.

1642 **... transformations** 神通變現 'supernatural transformative manifestations'.
first round This is an *ad hoc* translation of 一般. The phrase occurs frequently in the Tun-huang texts. Except for the present instance, it has two broad areas of meaning, just as it does in Mandarin: (1) 'altogether; common; general' (T336.13, T401.12, T510.2, T535.15, T700.1, T790.9) and (2) 'the same' (T444.3, T502.13, T504.11, T511.14, T514.15, T515.2, T541.9, T601.15).

1646 **Damascus** Literally, 'Dragon Fountain Swords'. See Wu line 699n2.
dewlap I am quite confident that 斛 must be emended to 胡, the basic meaning of which is as I have given in the translation. Since 垂胡 is a very common designation for the fold of loose skin hanging from the throat of cattle (and, by extension, other animals), the homonym 垂斛 would be easily understood. The choice of a measure word (ten pecks) as a euphemism is most appropriate. Cf. *Erh-ya chu-shu*, 'Notes on Birds', commentary on Pelican 爾雅注疏, 釋鳥, 鵜鴮鸅, 疏 (*SPPY*) 10.1b–2a: 'The dewlap beneath its neck is as large as a bag which could hold several pecks.'

1651 **remained** Although the ms has 菀, the meaning intended is that of the character which the T editors print.

1654 **gorge** 谽谺 = 谽谺 → 谽豁.

1663 **seized** 㩶 → 攝. Cf. T384.13 and T386.13. Pronounced *ché*, 'to tear crookedly' (cf. 折) or, pronounced *niéh*, 'to grasp'.

1668 **taken aback** 恾 ≠ 忙 ≠ 茫 ('vague, uncertain' as printed in Chou 237.3). 恾然 may be glossed as 'flustered' 失據 or 失措.

1671 **... enraged** P4524v has 六師不忿又爭先, 'Six Master would not give up [see line 623n] and, again, struggled to take the lead.'

1672 **impressive** Literally, 'lovely'.

1676 **transmit** This assumes a gloss of 令 or 發 for 遣. But I am not wholly confident that the translation given is the correct one. Cf. Iriya 47a: '"Our doctrine is made popular among the people," [they boasted].' This makes very good sense but it is not obvious how it was arrived at. An alternative translation which I had considered is 'Our doctrine may be banished, but the citizens will transmit it.' Vandier-Nicolas's interpretation (p. 14) is much the same as my alternative translation and she notes in support of it that the copy formerly in Hu Shih's possession had 違 'repudiated' instead of 遣. However, that such a reading is incorrect is borne out by the recurrence on the Hu Shih ms of the identical character (遣) on lines 1365 and 1485. This represents the grammatical structure of the line better than does Vandier-Nicolas's rendering and my alternative translation which logically require the inversion of 乃 and 遣. One final note is that Cheng, *Popular*, 230 does indeed print 違. This is either a mistranscription or typographical error and was probably the source of Vandier-Nicolas's knowledge of the Hu Shih ms.

our doctrine Since 我法 is spoken here by the heretics, it cannot mean *ātma-dharma*, 'ego and objects'.

1680 **imperatorial** 威稜 = 威靈.

1682 **tapered** 'Slender.' Or, if we understand 纖 = 殲 (glossed as 刺 or 尖), simply 'sharp'.

pointed claws 'Quick claws' 迅抓(→ 爪) according to T, but I follow P4524v which has 峻爪. Note, however, Chiang's (122) proof that 迅 = 峻 in the compound 嚴迅. The same is probably true here with the result that, except for the orthographies, the two texts are identical. 'Cut' is added to this line.

1684 **seized** See line 1605n above which would tend to indicate some such translation as 'aiming directly at the water-buffalo, injured it'. But note that P4524v has 捉 which, I believe, is a superior reading, especially when compared with the equivalent prose passage (T384.3).

1685 **ripping** Although Vandier-Nicolas forces a translation from the text as given ('subdued and vanquished'), the evidence I have presented in lines 1663n above and 1802n below adequately justifies the emendation to 攝 which my translation assumes. This and the following line are missing in the Hu Shih ms.

slashing 剉 glossed as 折傷. See the preceding note.

1688 **. . . plan** P4524v has 傪酢口燋黃 'were chagrined [Chiang 119] and parched in the mouth'.

1693 **adorned** *Alaṁkāraka.*

. . . jewels *Sapta ratna*, of which one list is the following: *suvarṇa* gold, *rūpya* silver, *vaiḍūrya* lapis lazuli, *sphaṭika* crystal, *musāragalva* agate, *rohita-mukta* rubies or red pearls, *aśma-garbha* cornelian. SH 12. It is, obviously, not the same list as that known to the author of this text (see T385.4).

1694 **golden sand** *Kāñcanavālukā*, cf. chapter ten of the *Nirvāna sūtra*.

1695 **leaves** More often referred to as 枼 or 葉.

1697 **lotuses . . .** Not hibiscus, in spite of the fact that they encircle the pond. See the corresponding verse passage (T385.6) and line 1727n below.

1700 **. . . alarm** Literally, 'gasp in alarm'.

1701 **. . . king** *Pāṇḍara-gaja-(pota) rāja.*

1704 **six tusks** See Lao Kan, 'Six-Tusked Elephants on a Han Bas-Relief', *HJAS*, 17 (1954), 366–9.

1705 **seven** Cf. 七華 'the seven flowers [of enlightenment]', i.e. *Sapta-bodhyaṅga*. 枝 is a numerary adjunct (not 'a seven-stemmed lotus blossom').

1707 **Holding** T has *ch'ōu* 搊 'plucking, strumming' but this is suspicious with 'strings and *winds*', unless the character is given the unusual (in this context) reading *chǒu* which may be glossed 持. There is no objection to the character when it occurs below in the verse section, however, for only stringed instruments are mentioned.

P4524v there has 扫 which is a variant of 搊. In both instances, Chou (237.12 and 238.4) inexplicably gives 擎 'to hold, to grasp'. The Hu Shih ms, in both places, has 擿 which must be another form of 扫. It would appear that the scribe was being sloppy in his usage and can be rescued only by the suggestion offered in the first sentence of this note.

1715 **... water** In the verse section (T385.15), this line is written exactly as it is here, including 已 = 以.

1725 **... way** No one has as yet been able to make any sense of 衡冠 (e.g. Chiang 208; Vandier-Nicolas, p. 15, 'se heurtaient à l'envi'(?); Iriya 47b 'wearing cross-caps'(?)). A very simple and, I believe, incontestably correct solution is to emend both characters with the homonyms 橫貫.

1726 **... chaos** Although both T and Chou have 穀竄, I am sceptical because this is impossible to read and because P4524v seems to have 頭竇(?). That, too, is unacceptable both because it does not make much sense and because it does not fit the rhyme pattern. Even if 竄 is retained, 穀 must be emended. One possibility is 鷇 used as a homonymous euphemism for 胡 (cf. line 1646n2) which results in an expression comparable to 亂竄 'to run away in disorder'. My translation is based chiefly on this understanding. Also, compare with the expressions 四竄 'scrambled away in all four directions' and 競竄 'compete to scramble away' (T19.15). Another possibility is 殼 of which there are two applicable renderings: (1) understood in the sense of reptilian shells and skins; (2) understood as an onomatope, 'the sound of striking something dead-centre from above', in this instance, 'kerplunk', i.e., 'competed in scurrying away with a "kerplunk" sound'. A final possibility is that 頭 in P4524v be emended to 投 which gives 投竄, a reading which fits well here (cf. T4.8). 穀 might also be accounted for in this fashion because of its partial visual resemblance to 投. See Wu line 194n. Ideally, the word in this position should have had some such meaning as 豎 to match 橫 in the parallel position of the preceding line.

1727 **lotus blossoms** Note that the 芙蓉 are now *in* the water. See line 1697n.

1729 **... self-satisfaction** Cf. P4524v which has 誇.

1730 **... round** Playful adaptation of 'Watch our [side] compete (爭) to be the stronger [not] the weaker this time.'

1731 **south** There must be a special reason for the direction being specified as the south. Śāriputra was sitting on the east and would have been facing the west. Some likely explanations are: (1) India was in the south and 'looking to the south' may have been the equivalent for Chinese Buddhists of 'facing Mecca'; (2) a possible reference to the Southern Pure Land 南(方)無垢(世界); (3) elephants came from south of China; (4) the audience was in the south (T382.8), i.e. Śāriputra was 'grandstanding'; (5) there may have been a ritual governing elephants that required Śāriputra to look towards the south such as in esoteric Buddhism, where there was a rigid prescription for the placement of a censer in the shape of an elephant – the head had to point south (see Mochizuki 1065b).

1732 **... fragrance** *Gandhahastī.*

1735 **sharply** 嚵 → 巉.

1736 **hundred** For 一百, P4524v has 數十 'several tens of', which seems slightly more credible, even for a transformation.

1738 **incomparable** Cf. Chiang 82.

1752 **parched** 㙯 → 燥.

1755 **fierce wolf** I.e. 'a tough cookie'.

1756 **fend off** 襟 → 禁.

1758 **... expert** Literally, 'he is showing off in front of Lu Pan'. Lu Pan is the name of a famous carpenter of the state of Lu during the Warring States period who was later deified as the god of craftsmen. See Giles, *BD* no. 1424. Cf. the well-known proverb

班門弄斧, 'wielding an ax at the gate of Lu Pan', i.e. 'showing off in front of an expert'.

1759 **If** 忽若, see Chiang 149.

1760 **. . . before** Chiang (149 and 208) says that the meaning of this sentence is unclear. 打破 ('break [my string of bad luck]') presents no problems, nor does 承前 ('carrying on from', i.e. 'including the previous'). The difficulty is how to deal with the final character [氵彗]. I am convinced that it must be a vulgar form of 雪 which, when pronounced in the fourth tone (glossed 洗), is commonly used to convey the ideas of 'avenge an insult' and 'wipe out a disgrace'. This is surely what Raudrākṣa means to say here. As for the form of the character itself, I believe it must be a corruption of the archaic form of the phonetic element in 雪, that is 彗(→彗) with a water radical added to reinforce the notion of cleansing. The basic etymological meaning of 彗 is 'sweep away, broom'. 'Snow', by the way, is 'rain that can be swept away'. Lo, *Studies*, 840 has noted the series of rhyming words beginning on T385.16: 惱, 倒, 燥, 攪, 咬, 巧, and the mystery character, which he suggests is a vulgar form of 掃. This fits in well with my etymological discussion and leads to the conclusion that 雪 'wipe clean' is related to 掃 'to sweep'.

1761 **. . . endure** See line 623n.

1762 **. . . dragon** Śākyamuni in a previous incarnation had been a poisonous dragon but escaped from that form by accepting the commandments (*Mahāprajña-pāramitā sūtra* 智度論 14, Ta25.162a and following).

1765 **blinked** 眴 → 瞬, cf. T387.2.

1768 **Ominous** The English word indicates something bad almost as often as the Chinese original (祥) indicates something good. This, fortunately, allows the translator to evade the question of why 'auspicious clouds' would be imputed to Raudrākṣa. The answer is probably just force of habit – 祥 is a standard epithet for clouds. Consider, however, an emendation to 翔 'soaring'.

1773 **bejewelled platform** *Ratnāsana*.

1775 **. . . Birds** *Garuḍa*. This is also a symbol of the Buddha.

1776 **rare** *Āścarya*; *adbhuta*.

unusual *Pṛthak*.

1777 **wings** 翅 → 翌 = 翼.

1779 **claws** 抓 → 爪. Hsü 38 says the two characters are interchangeable. I have not seen this claim attested elsewhere. 抓 'to scratch, to claw, to clutch' is the verbalized form of 爪.

spurs 距 does have the meaning given in the translation. It is not to be rendered as 'large'.

. . . slender Or 'long and sharp' 殲. Compare line 1682n1 above.

1780 **. . . Toledo** The original Chinese is Feng which is the name of a city where famous swords were made. See Wu line 699n2.

1784 **attacked** Hsü's (116) suggestion that 接 → 擊 seems well-taken. 'Prey' is implicit in 搏. On the ms, the latter character more nearly resembles 愽 (cf. Chou's 238.13 搏) than it does 博. The meaning intended, in any event, is that indicated by the T editors.

1786 **. . . snack** Literally, 'stop up/choke/quell my hunger'

pecked 啅 = 啄.

1787 **legs** 'Uprights', 'stumps' (in modern parlance). T386.6 prints the vulgar form 竪 as on the ms, Cheng, *Popular*, 231 the correct form 豎.

1788 **left** Chiang's lengthy note (104–5) on this meaning of 殘 is unnecessary for this was used in the sense of 餘 as early as the Han Dynasty.

1789 **muddle** The text is certainly defective at this point. The first ten lines of the verse passage have been added from P4524v.

1790 **frustrated** 冒惨 = 毷氉 (Chiang 120).

1791 **not** P4524v has 冈 = 罔, a negative particle. See line 687n.
turn The proposed reconstruction of this word is almost certainly correct. I have arrived at the reading 無控告 in the following way. First, the T editors are mistaken in placing the lacuna in the middle. The rhyme scheme works against such a reading. And, from an examination of P4524v, it is clear that the missing character comes at the end of the line. There is, in fact, a small dot in the position where we would expect the missing character. Compare the following line, for example, where 敵 occurs in this position. As for choosing 告 to complete the line, it is both a perfect rhyme and means exactly what is needed. 控告 'to accuse; *to make a plaint*'. Hence, literally, 'nowhere to [or no one to whom he could] complain'.

1792 **forced** Iriya, *Index*, 7 lists only this occurrence of 打强, but compare 强打 on T386.16.
... resistance See line 1273n.

1793 **premonition** 懸 glossed as 預.

1795 **full of ire** 操暴 = 暴躁 (Chiang 116–17).

1797 **claps and peals** 磞礫 = 霹靂.

1799 **... another** Cf. *History of the Later Han Dynasty*, 'Biography of Chou Chia' 周嘉傳 (*PNP*) 81(71).13a: 'Thereupon the gang of bandits looked at each other in groups of twos.' 羣賊於是兩兩相視 ...

1802 **... tail** Vandier-Nicolas's translation is impossible: 'De la tête à la queue, il inspirait la crainte et l'effroi, et il paraissait invincible.' The most objectionable part is 'inspirait ... l'effroi' for 㪷. See lines 1685nn1 and 2 above for an explanation of 懾㪷.

1804 **muscles** Misreading by the T editors of 𦬕 = 筋 (cf. Chou 239.2; Cheng, *Popular*, 231 (𥮊 is vulgar for 筋); Umezu Jirō 33).

1806 **... power** 威神力, *prabhāva*.
Three Precious Ones See line 148n.
unfathomable 測 is an unannounced, though acceptable, emendation for 惻 on the ms.

1807 **King of Demons** *Māra-rāja*.
vexation *Kleśa*.

1809 **Monk** It seems odd that the King would call Six Master a 和尚.
behind the scenes 猥地 'in an out-of-the-way place; with the back turned'. Cf. Wu line 199n2.

1815 **pluck** Cf. line 1792n1 above.

1817 **our doctrine** Cf. T384.7.

1818 **after all** For 卒 (平 on the ms), Chou 239.5 erroneously has 本.
... exhausted Cf. T383.15.

1822 **contorted** This translation is highly problematical unless somewhat complicated emendation is accepted. Hsieh 98.68 suggests 拐憎 but the meaning intended is not clear. I am rather disinclined to accept the T editors' reading of 拐 because most of its commonly accepted meanings ('kidnap, swindle, turn [a corner]') are late accretions while the original meaning ('support oneself with a staff') is not applicable here. Furthermore, I have elsewhere found no such compound as 拐曾. Cheng, *Popular*, 231 reads 揚薈 'display a dense tangle' which makes little sense. Chou 239.6 gives 楞曾 (the ms has 拐首) which, although it is itself unreadable, has served as the basis of my translation. The process by which it has been reached may be outlined thus: 楞曾 → 崚嶒(層). This expression refers to the layers and levels of a high mountain. The meaning fits well and it is homonymous with the characters given in Chou. It is also easy to understand how the error might have arisen. 楞(伽) is the Buddhist Chinese word for Laṅkā (Ceylon); it would certainly have been present in the mind of the scribe who copied this manuscript. And the dropping of a radical for the second character is a small error frequently committed.

1824 **. . . rubies** Literally, 'comparable to vermilion but still redder'. Cf. 赤珠 (< 朱 (?)), 'red pearl, ruby', *rohita-mukta*.

1828 **. . . whirlwinds** Iriya 49a says 'like a bird flying'(?). Parallelism, however, would seem to call for a meteorological phenomenon.

1829 **. . . eyes** Cf. line 1765n above.

1831 **. . . pimples** Literally, 'downy hair stood erect'.

1833 **Before long** Not in the original.

Vaiśravaṇa See line 1138n.

1836 **weapons** 技 → 仗. The same error is mentioned above at line 1530n1.

1837 **Earth deities** *Pṛthivī*. Vaiśrāvaṇa is always depicted thus in sculpture.

1841 **incomparable** 般 = 班 (Chiang 82).

1842 **yellow-headed** The *Hsien-yü ching* says that they had flaming heads. One explanation that comes to mind as to why the monsters should be described as having yellow heads is by suggestion from one of the many names for the tailor bird. This is a small bird but an extremely vicious one and is often kept for fighting. It is also called 'Yellow Throat' 黃脰. Note too the yellow-haired monsters described on T347.16. In Sanskrit, 黃頭 is *kapila* which is the name of a legendary figure after whom the city of Kapilavastu (Buddha's birthplace) is supposed to have been named.

1843 **strange sort** Chiang 179.

carcasses 屍骸 is a contemptuous term for a live body (cf. Chiang 25).

1845 **pondered** Cf. 舉 glossed as 謀.

1847 **rage** 震 glossed as 怒.

1848 **. . . ground** It seems obvious that 擗地 ought to be interpreted as 伏地. However, there is no justification for such an emendation. It is possible to understand 擗(闢) = 辟 which, glossed 著, can be rendered as in the translation. Although there can be no certainty in this matter, I believe that the author must have begun to write 擗 (or 辟 = 闢) 踊 (or 踴), 'beat their chests and stomped the ground', but that he was forced to adopt a different second character because of the rhyme.

In place of the preceding eight lines, P4524v has the following sixteen lines, the Chinese text of which may be found on T393:

§So many times had Six Master shown himself the weaker that his breast was filled with shame,
In the midst of the gathering, he conjured up yellow-headed ghosts;
Their appearance was of a strange sort and their carcasses were ugly,
They looked toward the people on the four sides, filling them with dread.
But Śāriputra was as amiable and as happy as could be,
He knew for sure that he would certainly[1] do better than the other side;
'Even if[2] you have a hundred or a thousand different transformations,
You cannot avoid giving yourself up and becoming a disciple.'
In the middle of the arena, he conjured up a great Heavenly King,
Majestic and splendid he was, and of an extraordinary spirit.
He wore on his body golden armour which was as dazzling as the Three Gods,[3]
From the precious sword at his waist, a frosty glitter emanated;
The gem-encrusted pagoda[4] in his hand emitted a divine light,
His long halberd pulsated[5] with a bluish-green glimmer.
With an angry look, the Heavenly King briefly rolled his eyes,
§Which so stupefied the two monsters that they fell to the ground.[6]

[1] Hopefully, I have made the English as poor as the Chinese.
[2] 遮莫 means 儘管, 'even though, no matter, despite' (Chiang 155).
[3] *Trimūrti*: Śiva, Viṣṇu and Brahmā.
[4] *Ratna-naya-stūpa*.

[5] 森森 when used of lances and other weapons generally refers to their vast numbers. My translation is based on the gloss 戰栗貌, 'aspect of trembling'. It may be, however, that the author or scribe has confused this expression with 森槮 which is descriptive of tall objects and which would be an appropriate modifier for Vaiśravaṇa's lance.

[6] See the beginning of this note.

1850 **shaken** For the first time in this piece, 慴 'faint-hearted' need not be emended.

1851 **Compassionate One** The Buddha, of course. I am indebted to Iriya 49b for my understanding of this line.

1852 **patience** 耏 = 耐.

1854 **. . . dragon** From context, it is clear that Dragon Scale must be the name of a superb horse. Cf. Liu Tsung-yüan 柳宗元, 'Preface to a Eulogy on a Picture of a Dragon Horse' 龍馬圖贊序 *T'ang Liu hsien-sheng wen-chi* 唐柳先生文集 (*SPTK*) 19.5ab: 'I once heard that, when Hsüan-tsung was on the throne, a strange horse was found by the river at Ling-ch'ang *chün* . . . In appearance, it had the scales of a dragon and the tail of a lizard.' 始吾聞明皇在位, 靈昌郡得異馬於河 . . . 其狀龍鱗虺尾.

P4524v has twelve quite different lines which serve as its ending and which come immediately after 'scale of a dragon'. Portions which are of assistance in understanding the Hu Shih ms are cited in the notes.

1855 **by-way** 逕 = 徑.

1856 **gate of Buddhism** *Mahādharmaparyāya*, the doctrines or methods of Buddhism.

1859 **Let's** Note 看看 for the optative.

1860 **. . . errors** This line may be of assistance in attempting to understand the difficult line at line 1760n above.

1861 **In the event** See line 1162n.

mistake 使 (馳 on the ms) → 池. See lines 589n and 1103n.

1862 **bow down** 啟首 means 稽首 (cf. Hsü 38), i.e. 'to kowtow'. My translation is based on the Sanskrit equivalent, *vandana*; *vandi*.

1865 **great tree** *Mahāvṛkṣa*.

1866 **dense** 婆娑 has many meanings, several others of which are applicable here: 'sway to and fro; spreading; dancing', etc. but not 'withered'.

1868 **spreading** Although the text has 芳, I believe we should avoid translating as 'fragrant' or 'flowery'. Parallelism and common sense go against such an interpretation. Cf. the next line in T where 芳 *does* have such meanings. The same character occurs in the Maudgalyāyana transformation with the same meaning (T731.2). See Maudgalyāyana line 673n. Cf. Chiang 210 who is unsure what it means in either case. I have assumed an emendation to 放 which may be glossed as 縱, 出, 開, 散, 射, 肆, etc.

1870 **fowl** 擒 in T is probably a typographical error. Cheng, *Popular*, 231 and Chou 240.2 both give 禽. The ms has 獖, a corrupt form of the latter.

. . . omen Our author has become carried away with himself. Surely the heretics could not produce such wonderful things!

1872 **green** Or 翠 (the ms has 䔺) → 萃, 'dense'.

1873 **Abruptly** The character on the ms is 廾. Cheng, *Popular*, 231 gives 升 and Chou 240.2 has 廿. The T editors are correct in interpreting 廾 as 斗 (see the chart of special Tun-huang characters in Nogami Shunjo, 1965 – cf. line 722n2). Their emendation to 阧 (陡) is also good and has been adopted for this translation. Another possible interpretation, however, is that 廾 has a graphic similarity to 共 and matches perfectly 和 in the parallel unit above. If 共 were considered as an emendation on graphic grounds, it would yield the following translation: 'Made everything dark for several miles around.'

1876 **God of Wind** *Vāyu-deva*(?). See below, line 1884n.

1877 **. . . greeting** See line 390n2.

1879 **chiliacosm** See line 60n2.

1884 **bag of wind** This detail has enabled me to solve a problem in Tun-huang iconography that, to the best of my knowledge, has not hitherto been discussed by art historians. In many of the wall-paintings at Tun-huang that depict the scene in which Śāriputra blows down Raudrākṣa's tree or pavilion (caves 8, 138, 74, 63, 118f, 52, 167, 149 and Wan-fo hsia 萬佛峽 cave 2, southeast wall), two little creatures appear in the left and right bottom corners holding bags. I now feel confident in stating that they hold bags of wind. They must have evolved from the Spirit King of the Wind which was one of a group of ten spirit kings current in the sixth century. Chavannes, 'Une Sculpture Bouddhique de l'Année 543', *Ars Asiatica* 2 (Aug. 1915) was probably the first to notice their existence on the E. Wei stele in the Isabella Stewart Gardner Museum. Emmy C. Bunker, 'The Spirit Kings in Sixth Century Chinese Buddhist Sculpture', *Archives of the Chinese Art Society of America*, 18 (1964), 26–37, is a valuable study of these strange figures. She suggests that the wind-bag derives ultimately from Aeolus. J. Leroy Davidson, in *The Lotus Sutra in Chinese Art* (New Haven, 1954), p. 91 and plates 36 and 37, discusses the wall-paintings at Tun-huang which depict the wind scene in the contest between Śāriputra and Raudrākṣa but does not mention the funny little men with the bags. Illustrations of the Japanese descendant of these little men, called Fūjin, may be found in Jacques de Langre, *The Second Book of Dō-in* (Magalia, Calif., 1974), p. 49 and Juliet Piggott, *Japanese Mythology* (London, 1969), p. 40. The wind-bag is not mentioned in the *Hsien-yü ching* which says only that Śāriputra used his supernatural powers to stir up the wind.

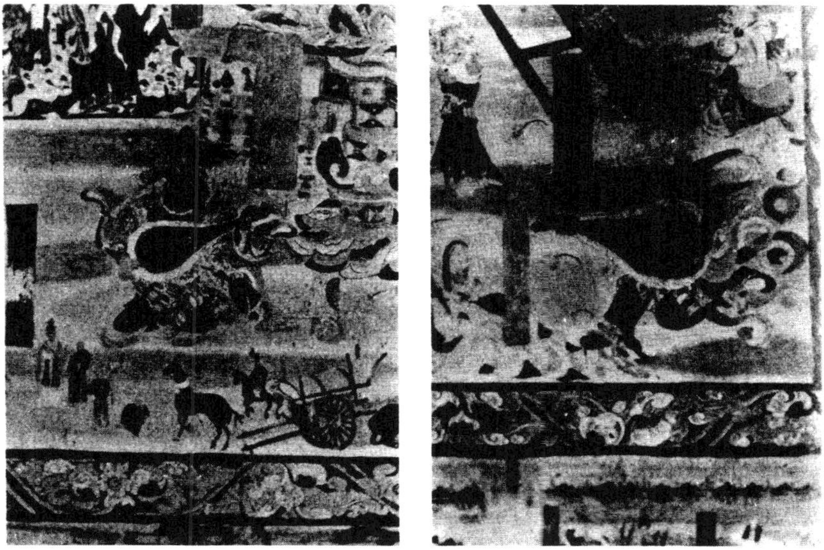

8. Details from the left and right sides of the back wall of cave 8 at Tun-huang. Magnified reproductions from Paul Pelliot, *Les Grottes de Touen-houang* (Paris, 1914–24), vol. I, pl. 27.

1885 **like a carpet** Literally, 'like cotton/floss silk'.
1886 **... dust** The grammatical structure of this sentence should be understood as 石碎同塵, 'rocks broke [into particles fine] as dust'.
1888 **... trunk** Literally, 'no one knew where the stalk and trunk were'.
1891 **again** The probability that the missing character is 頻 is nearly one hundred per cent. Cf. T385.16 for an almost identical sentence.
1893 **... bottom** 高下 occurs with the same meaning ('height') in P4524v at the beginning of the description of the mountain. Cf. 高低.
leagues See line 1579n.
1894 **luxuriant** See line 428n for a list of variant orthographies of this expression.
1895 **doctrinal power** See line 451n.
beyond conception See line 499n2.
1899 **spirit king** I.e. 風神, God of Wind.
thunder Literally 'lightning'.
1900 **leaving** Chiang 104.
1904 **thurible** The 寶子, according to a Sung Dynasty authority, was a small platform for burning incense inside a particular type of censer associated with Kāśyapas (disciples of Buddha). See Chiang 42 and Morohashi 7376.135.
1905 **... platform** See line 1571n1.
1907 **... twos** Cf. line 1799n.
judged See line 765n. 'Everyone' is not in the original.
1908 **How can** Hsü 116 notes that the emendation 可 → 何 is unnecessary.
mustard seed *Sarṣapa*.
1910 **... day** 比 read *pì*, 'in succession; every; recently'.
1914 **worthless** 濫 glossed as 浮華 or 失實. It may also be argued that 濫 → 爛 'glittering'.
1920 **must** 總須 also means 'must in any event' (see Chang line 35n) or simply 'certainly must' (T658.2, T660.6, and T780.3).
head Literally, 'heart'.
1922 **ego ...** Two types of illusion discussed in the *Diamond Sūtra* (*catvāri lakṣaṇāni*). In the final portion of P4524v (see T394n51), it is said that the Six Heretics unjustifiably advocate 我仁 'our [principle of] humanity'. One comes more and more to feel that these heretics are, indeed, Confucians in disguise.
1930 **assistance** See line 814n2.
1931 **palmyra** *Tāla*, the fan-palm (*Borassus flabelliformis*). Its great height (70–80 feet) came to be established as a unit of measure. Thus we could translate as 'seven chains' or the like.
1933 **major body** See line 1234n.
packed See lines 354n2 and 1246n. To supplement the information given there, it should be noted that 惻塞 is analogous to 遍 in the third line of the following verse section.
1935 **eighteen** Kenneth K. S. Ch'en, 'A Study of the Svāgata Story in the Divyāvadāna in Its Sanskrit, Pāli, Tibetan, and Chinese Versions', *HJAS*, 9(1947), 298–9n233 presents a list of these eighteen different types of transformations. *Aṣṭādaśa* was a very popular number with Buddhists. For several lists of things that come in eighteens, see SH 45–6. It is interesting to note that eighteen is also the traditional number of martial arts (十八般武藝) in later popular literature (e.g. *Water Margin*, tr. J. H. Jackson (Shanghai, 1937), chapter 2, pp. 11–12).
1940 **universe** *Dharmadhātu*.
1943 **theirs** I.e., 'not mine', hence 'the Buddhists'', hence 'yours [Śāriputra's]'.
1944 **you** Śāriputra? His cohorts? More likely the former considering what Raudrākṣa says in the next line and also considering the fact that he is facing Śāriputra with his palms joined in reverence.

correct 政 = 正 (cf. line 1071n).
path *Aryamārga* or *samyaṅ-mārga*.
1948 **Three Jewels** See line 148n.
1949 **fiery** Influence of Zoroastrianism (拜火教)?
dragon I am not certain of the precise identification of this divinity. In the final passage of P4524v, it is said that the heretics had spent the whole day scurrying about in service of 大神 which would seem to mean 大神王 Mahākāla, i.e. Śiva.
1951 **emptiness** I.e. 'illusion', *śūnyatā*.
1955 **pray** Chiang 194. N.B. both Chou 243.9 and Cheng 233 correctly have 着 instead of 著.

MAUDGALYĀYANA

S2614
T714–744
P2319. This abbreviated version is translated by Eugene Eoyang in Y. W. Ma and Joseph S. M. Lau, eds., *Traditional Chinese Stories* (New York, 1978), pp. 443–55
P3485
P3107
P4988v
S3704
PK876
PK4085
PK3789
MS formerly in the possession of a certain Li of Te-hua 德化李氏
Translated in Iriya 54–81
Partial translation in Waley 217–34

2 **With Pictures** The pictures have not been preserved. Indeed, the two characters 幷圖 of the title have been blotted out on the ms.
4 **day** On S2614, there is a small 日 written between 五 and 看. On P3107 and P3485, it is written in the line of characters.
heavens The *devasabhā* or *devaprāsāda* which are located between the earth and the realms of form (*Brahmaloka* 梵世界).
5 **hells** *Naraka*.
mires The three *gati* (途 paths) to the hells of fire, blood, and swords (*asipattra*).
dissipate Because of the otherwise strictly parallel relationship between this and the following line, I am somewhat perplexed by the penultimate character in each of the two lines. 業消 '*karma* dissipates' is given by T and Chou 150.2. Cheng has 棄消 from which I can make little sense unless 棄 be glossed as 散. Ta1307a has 棄消 which is awkward. P2319 has 消業. I believe that the structural problem (there is no difficulty in understanding the meaning) arose because of one or both of the following reasons: (1) 業 is quite likely the correct reading but it pre-empted a second use in the natural position after 十善 below; (2) one of the usual expressions 十善業 (or 道, 位, 王, 戒) 'karma [etc.] of the ten good characteristics' was intended but the closely bound unit 增長 displaced one character from the rhythmic four-beat line.
6 **ten virtues** *Daśakuśala*, i.e. avoidance of the ten evils, 十惡 *daśākuśala*.
7 **summer retreat** 咨下 → 恣夏 which is a shortened form of 自恣解夏 *pravāraṇa*. Cf. Iriya 54b, 77n2.
confers All of the published texts give 會福之神 'deities who assemble/gather blessings', but this is suspicious because unheard of elsewhere that I know of. I believe we should understand 曾 (= 增) 福之[財] 神, i.e. Kuvera or Kubera

(Vaiśravaṇa), the god of wealth, 'confer blessings' (*puṇya-udaya*) being a stock epithet of this deity.

8 **. . . beings** See Śāriputra line 297n1.

convey 敎 = 交 glossed as 給.

9 **make offerings** *Pūjā.*

10 **supply of blessings** 福(德)資(糧), *puṇya saṃbhāra.*

reborn *Jātiparivartaḥ.*

11 **. . . place** *Abhibhv-āyatanāni.*

purgatorian The problem of the meaning of *yü-lan-p'en* 盂蘭盆 is far too complicated to discuss in detail here. Two thorough investigations of early references to the expression in Chinese texts are: Kenneth K. S. Ch'en, *The Chinese Transformation of Buddhism* (Princeton, 1973), pp. 61–4 and M. W. deVisser, *Ancient Buddhism in Japan* (Leiden, 1935), vol. I, pp. 59–68. I am hesitant to accept either the standard reconstruction of Skt. *avalambana* (BHS. *ullambana*) – 'hanging down/on; depending upon' – or the folk etymological explanation of this term (see line 14n). Recently, Japanese scholars have been suggesting a possible connection with Iranian *urvan*, 'soul'. Iwamoto Yutaka 岩本裕, *Mokuren densetsu to urabon* 目連傳説と盂蘭盆 (Kyoto, 1968), pp. 225–44; Sawada Mizuho 澤田瑞穗, *Jigokuhen* 地獄變 (Kyoto, 1968), pp. 131–3. Thus, *yü-lan-p'en* would mean a sacrifice for departed souls. This is attractive because of the strong salvationist tendencies in the popular versions of the Mu-lien story and possible Manichaean influence (Iwamoto Yutaka, *Mokuren densetsu to urabon*, pp. 190ff). However, David Utz, a Middle Iranian specialist, has pointed out to me in conversation a number of phonological difficulties in the direct identification of *yü-lan* and *urvan* (Sogdian *arwān*; Parthian and Middle Parthian *'rw'n/rw'n*).

12 **Three Honoured Ones** There are several lists but the most common and most appropriate in this context is that consisting of Amitābha, Avalokiteśvara, and Mahāsthāmaprāpta who *receive* (來迎 *pratyudyāna*) into the Western Paradise those who invoke the name of Amitābha.

welcoming Into the Pure Land (see the previous note).

13 **great assembly** *Mahāsaṅgha.*

put a priority *Hsièn* 先 is, however, elided from Chou 150.3.

14 **. . . limbo** Literally, 'hanging upside down' which is the folk etymological explanation of *yü-lan*, *p'en* being explained as a basin filled with food.

16 **Maudgalyāyana** Derived from *mudga* (胡豆 'Serindian bean'). See line 17n2.

17 **. . . monk** *Pravraj.*

Turnip 羅卜 (*lâ puk*) = 蘿蔔 (*lâ biuk*), 蘿菔, 萊菔, 蘆菔. I am able to say with full confidence that 羅卜 does indeed mean 'Turnip'. Previously scholars have only noted the resemblance in sound between Mu-lien's name as a child and the Chinese word for turnip, e.g. Wolfram Eberhard, ed., *Folktales of China* (Toronto, 1965), p. 201: 'The connection of Mu-lien with the radish (or carrot) probably comes from a pun: Mu-lien's personal name in Chinese popular tradition is Lo Pu; this is close to lo-p'u, the radish.' Indeed, for modern Chinese, the connection between 羅卜 and 蘿蔔 is that of a pun. In the local Shao-hsing 紹興 plays, however, Mu-lien is directly referred to as 'Turnip' Fu 富蘿蔔; see Sawada Mizuho 澤田瑞穗, *Jigokuhen* 地獄變 (Kyoto, 1968), p. 138. Historically, I am now able to prove that Maudgalyāyana's nickname in Chinese was created by a mistranslation of his Sanskrit name. This occurred in the *Wen-shu-shih-li wen ching* 文殊師利問經, *chüan* A (Ta14.492c) which I was able to locate by a reference in the Sung Dynasty *Fan-i ming-i chi* 翻譯名義集 (*SPTK*) 1.17b: 'Mahāmaudgalyāyana. (This means turnip-root. His father liked to chew this vegetable and that is how he got his name.)' 大目揵(犍)連(此言羅茯根.其父好噉此物因以爲名). But this is to misinterpret the derivation of Maudgalyāyana which is: *mudga* (*Phaseolus mungo*, the mungo bean) [> *maudga*, 'relating to beans, consisting of beans'] > *mudgala*, 'name of an ancient sage' > *maudgalya*, 'descended from Mudgala' > Maudgalyāyana, 'patronymic for son of Mudgala'. I might further suggest that the mistake may have occurred because of a resemblance in sound between Mu-lien and *Mūram* or *Mūlam* which is the real Sanskrit word for turnip (Prakrit *mūlī*, *mūliā*). This, then, is the story of how an Indian bean became a Chinese turnip. Those who are interested in how the turnip itself got to China may begin by considering that the word for turnip in Greek is ῥάπυς, in Latin is *rāpa*, *rāpum*, Old Norse *rofa*, Slavic *repa*, etc. See Victor Hehn, *Cultivated Plants and Domesticated Animals*, ed. James Stallybrass (London, 1891), p. 440.

In addition to accounting for the connection between Mu-lien and the turnip, the reference I have cited to the *Wen-shu-shih-li wen ching* (written 518) has pushed back by nearly one hundred and fifty years the earliest previously known reference to our hero as Luo-pu. That was in the *Ching-t'u yü-lan-p'en ching* 淨土盂蘭盆經 (P2185) which was written in the mid seventh century. See Iwamoto Yutaka, *Mokuren densetsu to urabon*, p. 44.

18 **Three Precious Ones** See Śāriputra line 148n.
regard Although 敬重 is synonymous with 重敬, the latter order would have been more appropriate here to contrast with 深信 above.
Salvationism *Mahayāna*, the Greater Vehicle.

19 **... trade** Chiang 93.
disposed 支分 glossed as 分割 'divide up'. See *Ch'ü* nos. 603, 614. For a more precise description of how he divided it, see the 'Maudgalyāyana Retribution Story', T701.4.

20 **vegetarian food** 齋[食] or 齋[席].

21 **provided** See line 9n.
Trinity Buddha, *dharma*, *saṅgha*. One wonders, however, whether the author meant by this 'many monks of the Buddhist persuasion'.
and In P2319, 及 is added in a smaller hand to the right of the line.

22 **numerous** Ta1037b reads 詵 'droves of' or 'clamorous'. P3107 has 訖ト諸, the small mark beside the first character indicating that it is an error. P3485 has 諸.
But P2319 lacks 及.

23 **stingy** I suspect that 怯 (忲 on P3485) is a vulgar form of 恡, which is itself a variant of 悋 (= 吝). S2614 has 怪 and P3107 has 惜.

25 **months** Probably 'ten months', for that is just about the right amount of time necessary for a merchant to complete his business and for the mother to waste all the money in the manner described later. However, such formulas in popular literature are not to be taken seriously as precise indications of time. The 'Maudgalyāyana Retribution Story' T701.7 has 旬日 'ten days' but 日 and 月 are frequently confused in these texts. Waley 217, 'before very long'; Iriya 54b, 'before a month had passed'. See Chang line 70n.

26 **charged** Chou 150.6 has 咐.

27 **vegetarian feasts** See line 20n.
blessings *Puṇyakriyā*. Cf. 作善 *sukṛtakarma*, 'to do good; to bestow alms'. Such activities serve to build up good karma which ensures that one will receive blessings in the future.

28 **... saints** The profane and the sacred, i.e. 'everyone'.

29 **Avīci** The deepest of the eight hot hells.
suffering *Duḥkha*.

30 **three full years** Although there is a 三周 in Buddhist doctrine (referring to stages in the Buddha's lectures on the Law – see the *Lotus Sūtra*, ch. 8, section 28), it is curious that the term is here decidedly Confucian.

32 **... lives** 宿 [善 or 福] *pūrva* [*kuśala* or *puṇya*], good karma from previous existences.

33 **inherent causes** *Sabhāga-hetu.*
... Law *Śravaṇam agrayānasya*; *śruta ... dharma.*
34 **arhatship** Literally, 'the fruit (*phala*) of saintly discipline'.
... six paths Indicates that Maudgalyāyana was hunting for his mother among sentient beings.
35 **transmigration** *Saṃsara.* The usual expression, 六道四聖, which sounds somewhat the same, would indicate that he thought she may have been born among the ranks of the holy (as a *śrāvaka*, *pratyeka-buddha*, *bodhisattva*, or *buddha*). Another nearly homonymous expression frequently encountered is 六道四生 (*catur-yoni*), the four modes of the six rebirths: *jarāyuja*, viviparous; *aṇḍaja*, oviparous; *saṃsvedaja*, icthyic or entomoid; *aupapāduka*, metamorphic. P3485 reverses the order 死生.
... vision *Divyena cakṣuṣā.*
37 **enjoying** Note the seemingly superfluous objective marker 於 which is frequent in T'ang colloquial texts.
38 **World-Honoured** *Lokajyeṣṭha* or *Lokanātha.*
40 **now** Chou 150.9 and Cheng 4347.6.
41 **fruit ...** I.e. *bodhi* obtained through discipline leading to arhatship.
42 **knowledge** *Vidyā.*
will 欲 is certainly not *rajas*, 'passion' or *kāma*, 'desire, love'.
only if 'Only if' is to render the grammatical structure 若非…乃.
43 **assembly** Implies 'assembly of monks'. Read 僧衆 as it appears on the ms.
44 **... monks** *Saṃgha.*
... directions Up, down, and the eight points of the compass.
disband Cf. 解脫 *mukti*, 'setting free, release'. Contrary to what the T editors say (746n12), P2319 does not add 勝. P3485 has it but indicates with a mark that it should be removed.
... retreat See line 7n1
46 **... method** *Upāya.*
story *Artha*, 'matter'. On the ms, 事 is written small and to the right of 也.
... offerings See line 11n2.
47 **founded** Neither P3107, P3485, nor P2319 has 用.
49 **sorrow** S2164 has 垃 (cf. Cheng 4347.8; Ta1037b reads as 拉). P3107 has 畢 but with a small 泣 written in as a correction beside it. P3485 has simply 泣.
50 **... happy** *Analects*, Legge, I.328: 'A superior man, during the whole period of mourning, does not enjoy pleasant food which he may eat, nor derive pleasure from music which he may hear.' 夫君子之居喪, 食旨不甘, 聞樂不樂. The ms has an unnecessary 道 after the first 樂.
51 **foods** Often written 指 when used now as a proverb.
pleasure Same as line 50n.
... bones Literally, 'injured his flesh and bones'.
52 **Deer Park** *Mṛgadāva.* See Śāriputra line 7n.
53 **comforted** P3107 and P3485 have 憮.
... deities *Sarva manuṣyadeva*, also written 一切天人 *sarva devamanuṣya* (e.g. P2319).
54 **Tathāgata** Should be 'seek the Tathāgata to study the Way'.
55 **twin trees** See Śāriputra line 9n.
visit 問 glossed as 訪問, 'to call upon' or, more simply 'to inquire of'. P3485 gives the more readable 'heard the Buddha's words' 聞仏聲.
Buddha P2319 has after this 'and so on and so forth', 云 𠄌, then skips to T716.6. A discussion of the significance this has for understanding the nature of transformation texts may be found in *Transformations.*
56 **came** See the following note.
immediately The classical meaning of 逡巡 is 'to waver; to shrink back'. In T'ang

colloquial (of which there are many instances in T), it may be rendered 'in an instant' (Chiang 137; Iriya, *Index*, 17). Since neither of these interpretations seems applicable here, the only other way to force a meaning from the text as given would be to resort to a literal translation of the individual characters (逡 glossed as 往來 and 巡 as 行). Hence, 'the Buddha himself was out taking a stroll'. But this does not seem justifiable in view of the regularity of meaning which this expression has throughout the rest of the corpus of Tun-huang popular literature. As such, I have felt compelled to look elsewhere in the line for a possible error. 自 seems to be the most likely candidate for at least two reasons: (1) it leaves the portion of the line before the caesura without a verb (*indeed it leaves the entire line without a verb* if we accept that 逡巡 has its constant colloquial meaning); (2) it juxtaposes two function words (自, 便 – reflexive, conjunction) across the caesura which strikes me as extremely awkward and even impossible. Therefore, I have decided to emend this character but it has been difficult to decide upon an appropriate replacement. If we assume a phonological error, perhaps 至 (*tśi-*) 'came/arrived [to receive him]' may be considered close enough to 自 (*dz'i-*). If an orthographical error, perhaps 見 (= 現) 'appeared [to receive him]' is similar enough to be considered. P3485 has 在 instead of 自, yielding 'the Buddha was present'. As a final note, two additional reasons why I have resisted tampering with 逡巡 are that it often occurs as the last segment in a heptasyllabic line (e.g. T51.8, T58.11, T347.5) and because it is the correct rhyme (巡, 尊…門, 津, 親). + 'To receive him.'

57 **monk** *Vandya*(?), 'reverend'; *upādhyāya*.
prostrated himself *Vandana*, *vandi*. I have assumed an inversion of the first two pairs of characters in the line (→ 和尙稽首). Another possible solution is that 和尙 → 合掌, hence, 'prostrated himself and brought his palms together in salutation'. See Śāriputra line 390n2. Even so, we would normally expect these gestures to occur in the opposite order.
most honoured ... Literally, 'most honoured among bipeds'; *dvi-pada-uttama*.

58 **mighty** *Mahā*.
... hosts (帝)釋梵(天) and (梵)衆(天), *brahmakāyika* or *brahmapāriṣadya*.

59 **generals** Iriya's 77n7 comment that these are probably the 四天王 *catur-mahārājā* (*lokapāla*), Indra's generals, is well-taken.
other *Viprakṛī*, i.e. 'scattered about > diverse'. There are many difficulties in the interpretation of this and the preceding line. Note how badly P3485 mangles the latter: 東西散大將散諸神. Syntactical parallelism indicates that 釋 should be construed as 'spread out' but this leaves 摩訶 hanging. 散支 on S2614 and P3107 probably is a result of confusion with the name Pañcika, variously a general of Vaiśravaṇa or one of his demon-escorts.

60 **sauvastika** The Buddha's *śrīvatsa*, lucky mark. See Śāriputra line 1210n.
crystalline P3485 has 波利 (*pari*, 'around') which must be emended to 頗黎. The latter has the same meaning as 玻璃 *sphāṭika*, 'rock crystal'. In spite of collation note 16 to the contrary, P3107 is the same as T(S2614).

61 **... moon** Chou 151.5, however, gives 日輪. If we follow 倫 on P3485, we may render simply 'like the moon'.

62 **... know** I view 欲知 as a parenthetic expletive comparable to 君不見 in classical texts.
... throne Cf. T649.14 (*grâce à* Iriya 77n8).

63 **five-coloured** *Pañca-varṇa*. The five primary colours blue, yellow, red, white, and black.

64 **... desires** Literally, 'dwells in the five desires', *kāma* (of which there are various lists, e.g. property, sexual love, eating and drinking, fame, sleep).

65 **renounce** *Parityāga*; *prahāṇa*; *vinivṛtta*; *upekṣā*.
desire and anger Two of the three poisons, 三毒 *tri-doṣāpaha*, that is 貪瞋(=嗔)

痴, *rāgadveṣamoha*, 'desire, anger, ignorance'. Cf. T342.2.

66 **sinful karma** *Aśukla-karma*; *karma-āvaraṇa*.

67 **extended** 入 → 及. The other printed versions are unanimous in correctly reading 及.

68 **impermanence** *Anitya*, i.e. 'death'. That is to say, Maudgalyāyana is concerned that his mother will remain in limbo instead of being reborn.

69 **ocean of misery** *Dukha-arṇava*.
ford *Tīram*; *gartaḥ*; *bhaiṣajyam*.
births and deaths *Saṃsāra*; *jāti-maraṇa*.

71 **concentrate** P. *sallīna*.

74 **doctrine** I follow P3107 and P3485 which have 法 'law'. 去 can make sense as an abstract directional complement, i.e. 'explained away'.
Four Noble Truths *Catvāri ārya-satyāni*: (1) Misery, (2) origination of misery, (3) stopping of misery, (4) eightfold path that leads to the stopping of misery.

75 **. . . acts** Means the same as 沒遮七逆罪 'avoid non-confession/concealment of the seven deadly sins; shedding a Buddha's blood, killing one's father, a monk, teacher, or arhat, disrupting religious organizations'.

76 **towers** S2614 and P3107 have 陵 instead of 凌.

77 **. . . good** In terms of the blessings (hence, suitable rebirth) that will accrue to oneself.
urgently Iriya 55b renders 蹔 = 暫, 'momentarily'. This is a possible reading but I prefer the primary sense of the character given.
persuade 交 = 教.

78 **. . . log** *Nirvāṇa-sūtra*, Ta12.372c. Also in *Yogācārya-bhūmi śāstra* Ta30.844c as well as *Lotus Sūtra*, Ta9.60ab and Ta9.193c. For another example in Tun-huang popular literature, see T843.1.

79 **. . . water** Both this and the preceding line are metaphorical expressions of the improbability of a man being reborn as a man or meeting with a Buddha and his teaching. The implication is that one should accumulate as much good karma as possible to better his chances of a happy rebirth. In this line, for the character after 大, T and Cheng 4348.6 both have 火 while Ta1307b and Chou 151.14 have 水. The latter reading is the correct one, so far as the ms is concerned. The *locus classicus* of this expression (*Vimalakīrtinirdeśa-sūtra*, Ta14.550b), however, does indeed read 火. If we so emend, the translation would be 'like a lotus blossom issuing from a great fire'.

80 **. . . flames** This is the famous parable of the burning house in the *Lotus Sūtra*. See line 83n.

81 **. . . misery** See line 69n1.
shores 邊 → 涯 (Hsü 43). Although Hsü does not justify this emendation, it is clear from the rhyme that 邊 is an error (cf. Lo, *Studies*, 465).

83 **. . . nirvāṇa** The 三車 are the three carts offered by the father to lure his children – who are oblivious to their danger – from the burning house (see line 80n): (1) goat carts (*śrāvaka*), (2) deer carts (*pratyekabuddha*), (3) bullock carts (*bodhisattva*). These correspond to Hīnayāna, Madhyamayāna, Mahāyāna.

84 **summoned** Cf. T381.6.

85 **then** The other printed texts are unanimous in reading, with S2614, P3485 and P4988v, 便 instead of 變.
cassock *Kaṣāya*.

86 **sainthood** Arhatship. Here and in line seven of this page (T716), there seems to be some confusion between Ānanda and arhatship. Because of his past errors, Ānanda was required to attain arhatship before being permitted to attend the First Buddhist Council at Rājagṛha. See Tsukamoto Keishō 塚本啓祥, [*A History of the Early Buddhist Order*] 初期佛教教團史の研究 (Tokyo, 1966), pp. 203–6. This, plus the

similarity between the Chinese transcriptions *A-nan* and *A-lo-han*, may account for the confusion. P2319 correctly reads 先得阿羅漢果.

87 **commandments ...** *Prātimokṣa*, not *pratimokṣa*, 'emancipation'.

89 **... in wreaths** Onomatopoetic, probably means '[rose in] puffs' or 'copiously'.

90 **... earth** The English, though poor, is not as bad as the Chinese. Cheng 4348.9 has 又 instead of 六 but this only makes matters worse. P3485 simply drops 林 but this is no help either. Iriya 77n12 suggests, on the evidence of the parallel relationship to the line below, that a verb should occur in the position where we find 瓊林. Hsü 122 suggests that 標樣 → 標映 and that 葉 is an error, which Iriya also indicates. While I do not accept all of their suggestions (see the next few notes), it is clear that there are many difficulties in these lines. Indeed, I feel that this and the following three lines were poorly conceived and are evidence that their author was not in full command of the classical style which he was attempting. Certainly the author had somewhere in the back of his mind 六種震動 *ṣaḍ-vikāram prakampitam ... samprakṣubhitam*, 'the six earth-shakings', which are auspicious signs of the Buddha's power. At the same time, however, I do not believe we are free to substitute this phrase for 'the fabulous forest' because the latter was often paired with 'elegant brocades' which occurs two lines below (e.g. *P'i-p'a chi* 10, 'Spring Banquet in the Apricot Orchard' 琵琶記, 春宴杏園 (Peking, 1954), p. 73). Furthermore, 花 and 林 match in this couplet as do 錦繡 and 珠幡 in the next. All in all, these four lines are meant to convey the atmosphere of something momentous happening. That event, of course, is the acceptance of Maudgalyāyana as a disciple of the Buddha which is mentioned in the final couplet.

91 **... flowers** See Śāriputra line 120n.
wafted ... 標樣 → 飄揚.
scattered 葉 may be glossed as 散. Cf. 散花(華), *puṣpaiḥ samavakirati*, 'to scatter flowers [in honour of a Buddha]'. P4988v seems to have 葉.

93 **banners** *Patākā*. Instead of 'pearled', P3485 has 'extraordinary' 殊.

95 **Mighty ...** Mahāmaudgalyāyana.

96 **sainthood** The fruit (*phala*) of discipline leading to arhatship.

97 **twin trees** See Śāriputra line 9n.
How ... That Maudgalyāyana first attained the fruit of arhatship and then studied the Way (see below).
Lotus Sūtra *Saddharmapuṇḍarīka-sūtra*.

98 **prodigal son** *Daridra-puruṣa*, see the *Lotus Sūtra*, Ta9.16b. 品 is *varga* 'class, type; section'.
worth PK876 and P4988v have 位, 'position'.

100 **sainthood** P4988v, P2319 and P3485 read precisely as the collation note 22 on T742 recommends, 阿羅漢.

101 **meditating** *Dhyāna*.

106 **contemplated** *Vipaśyanā*; *vidarśanā*.
unreality *Śūnyatā*.
and Instead of 而坐, P4988v has 'practised sitting' 學坐.
meditation P2319 has after this 'and so on and so forth', then skips to T717.4. Cf. line 55n3.

107 **... unreality** Saw through to the unreality of all things.
good and evil *Śubha-aśubha*.

108 **mind** *Citta* rather than *hṛd*.
settled ... *Cittasthiti*(?).
adhered A state in which the mind is no longer attached to anything.

109 **mirror** *Ādarśa*. Cf. the famous pair of poems by Shen-hsiu 神秀 and Hui-neng 惠能 in *The Platform Scripture*, tr. Wing-tsit Chan (New York, 1963), pp. 35, 41:

> The body is the tree of perfect wisdom (*bodhi*)
> The mind is the stand of a bright mirror.
> At all times diligently wipe it.
> Do not allow it to become dusty.
>
> Fundamentally perfect wisdom has no tree.
> Nor has the bright mirror any stand.
> Buddha-nature is forever clear and pure.
> Where is there any dust?

Another verse says:

> The mind is the tree of perfect wisdom.
> The body is the stand of a bright mirror.
> The bright mirror is originally clear and pure.
> Where has it been defiled by any dust?

These poems appear on pp. 130 and 132 of *The Platform Sutra of the Sixth Patriarch*, tr. Philip B. Yampolsky (New York, 1967).

its The mind's.

unwavering *Acala*; *niścala*; *dhruva*. That is to say, the transient had been stifled.

110 **right** Ta1037c has 右 . . . 右 (?); Chou 152.13 has 右 . . . 左. Cheng 4348.14 has the same as T. These are Zen postures for meditation, *nyaṣīdat paryaṅkam ābhujya* (結跏趺坐). Right foot on left thigh is called 'sitting posture for overcoming evil spirits' 降魔坐. Left foot on right thigh is 'sitting posture for good fortune' 吉祥坐.

111 **. . . rock** To symbolize solidity; *parvatopama*. There are, however, many expressions beginning with 盤 which signify 'sitting with legs crossed [in the manner of an ascetic in meditation]', e.g. 盤坐, 盤足, 盤腿, 盤膝, 盤脚. One cannot help but wonder whether such may not have been what the author was really trying to express. Cf. *paryaṅkabandha* or *utkuṭukāsana*. P4988v has a full heptasyllabic line: 端身坐著盤石上.

112 **. . . mouth** Ta3.766b.

113 **. . . empty** This is the ninth and final stage of meditation on the decomposition of a corpse (*vidagdhakasaṃjñā*) to curb desire (*navasaṃjñā*).

114 **. . . intertwined** That is, exhalation and inhalation were discrete. This he achieved by counting his breaths (數息) to calm body and mind for meditation, i.e. *ānāpāna*, 'controlled breathing'.

115 **stopped** P3485 has 正 which would serve to emphasize 當時.

drink 吟 → 飲 (?). The chief justifications for this emendation are phonetic similarity (*ngi̯əm* → *·i̯əm*) and the content of the following line. If the emendation is considered unacceptable, perhaps we may translate 'barking in the woods' or 'in the rustling woods'(?).

116 **waters** Although ponds in parks as well as some of the great Central Asian lakes are sometimes called 海, 海頭 'seaside' is unlikely. Perhaps 波頭, 'ripples', which has a slight visual resemblance, was intended and may have been unconsciously avoided because of its partial identity with 波頭摩 *padma*, 'lotus'. See line 119n1 below and cf. T717.7.

117 **listened** P4988v has 看 'watched [with his all-seeing eye(?)]'. See the next note.

religious discourses 'Buddha's message or doctrine.' For this meaning of 法眼 *dharma-cakṣus*, see Ta50.303b. Emendation to 法言 or 法語 is unnecessary.

118 **sat meditating** All of the printed editions have 坐唯禪 except Chou 153.3 who gives 唯坐禪 'only sat in *dhyāna*'. Although this makes sense, it is impossible because 禪 cannot rhyme with 頭, 樓 . . . 由. 唯 in its original position may have been thought of simply as a 'padding' word (metrical filler). Perhaps we should understand 坐禪蒲 'sat on a meditation mat'(?) which is a partial rhyme. 禪樓 'meditation hall'

is a perfect rhyme but is used in the next line.

119 **lake** Or ‘ocean’ (see line 116n). One reason for the difficulty in finding an appropriate translation for 海 is that one is never quite certain of the landscape which the author is imagining (India? China? Central Asia?).
. . . clouds Cheng 4348.17 has 無叚椶(?); Chou 153.4 無暇換. Since neither of these readings makes much sense nor is that in T (following S2614) and Ta1307c any better, we must seek elsewhere. P4988v has 如霞喚 which begins to be understandable. I suggest as a final solution 如霞煥 or 煥 (more likely the latter) which is the basis of my translation.

120 **frontier** One could hardly translate ‘beyond Kansu’.

121 **centre** P4988v has ‘courtyard’ 庭.

123 **reposefully** 宴 = 晏.
incorporeality ‘Realm of nothingness/bliss/nirvāṇa.’

124 **. . . mind** *Adhigamāvahṛd*(?), ‘mind of spiritual realization’. Cheng 4348.18 has a blank for 心. P4988v has 澄 ‘cleansed’ instead of 證.

125 **discipleship** [*Mahā-*]*śrāvaka*, ‘[personal] disciple of the Buddha’.

126 **mountains** In Buddhist parlance, ‘mountain’ often stands for monastery.

127 **. . . meditation** *Samādhi.*

130 **wind** P2319 skips to T717.8.

131 **Wild** ‘Ocean’, ‘lake’ (see line 119n1 above).
darts 繒 (= 矰) 徹 or 徹 (S2614, P4988v, P3485, Chou 153.9, Cheng 4348.20) (→ 繳), ‘arrow with attached cord’.

132 **Grey** The text reads ‘cranes and hawks’ but I have followed Iriya 56b 鶬鷹 → 蒼鷹.

133 **greenish** ‘Pea-soup fog’(!).

134 **. . . red** A paraphrase emphasizing the popular Buddhist connotations of 紅(塵) might be ‘The pure sky was far from the red dust of the mundane world.’ Cf. 遠塵離垢 ‘distant from the dust and defilement of the mundane world’.

135 **supernatural power** All the other printed editions correctly have 神通.
freedom *Īśvara.*

136 **begging-bowl** *Pātra.*
. . . space Cf. T729.10. This curious line may also be found in canonical texts, e.g. Ta15.662b.

137 **instantaneously** Chiang 136. Cf. 一晌.

138 **. . . Brahmā** *Brahmadeva*; *brahmaloka*. P2319 skips to T718.14.

139 **. . . instant** It is possible to render 一向 as ‘headlong; straight ahead’.

141 **Red towers** Means ‘splendid home/mansion’. See T557.2, *Ch’ü* nos. 10 and 627.
faintly reflected ‘Half reflected.’

142 **profusion** Both Chou 153.14 and Ta1308a follow S2614, P4988v, and P3485 in giving 論 which would, nevertheless, have to be emended to 淪.
walls Iriya’s 57a emendation (成 → 城) is undoubtedly correct.

143 **. . . staff** *Khakkara.*

144 **crisscrossing** P3485 and P4988v have 交盈 (cf. 盈盈 ‘copious; overflowing’). Chou 153.13 gives 交溋.

145 **to** P4988v has 而 instead of 如.

146 **. . . palms together** In salutation (see Śāriputra line 390n2).
sincere 中 → 忠 (Chou 153.14) or 衷.

148 **I** ‘[One who follows] the Way of Poverty’ or, an interpretation which I prefer, ‘[I who am of] minor [achievements in the] Way.’
Jambūdvīpa The southern of the four continents around Mount Meru; the world of men.

150 **lacking** 小 = 少, as on P4988v. These two characters are frequently exchanged in T’ang colloquial.

151 **orphaned** Hsieh 144–5.25 suggests that 孤惸 was intended.
152 **Nīladhi** How I concocted this name from 青提 I leave for curious readers to puzzle out. Cf. Alfons Hilka, *Beiträge zur Kenntnis der indischen Namengebung: Die altindischen Personennamen*, Indische Forschungen (Breslau, 1910), pp. 97, 99, 107, 127, 149ff. S2614 has 清 instead of 青.
153 **Śūlakṣaṇa** Arrived at by the same method as Nīladhi. Hint: only half of each name *sounds* the same as the Chinese. Note: P3485 has 輸 instead of 輔. There is no evidence in the canonical Buddhist texts that the name of Maudgalyāyana's father meant 'prime minister'.
154 **... works** Literally, 'creating causes (*hetu*) for fields of blessedness'. P. *puññakkhetta*.
159 **strummed** P4988v has 'harps and lutes' 瑟琴.
loud and clear 遼亮 = 嘹喨.
162 **peaceful** Waley 218 seems to have emended 安和 → 安知: 'would that I might know'.
well Cf. T718.15.
since P4988v has 久 'long' for 後.
163 **now** Waley 219 has 來 do double duty: 'have come now'.
164 **seemed** 以 → 似 (cf. Chou 154.9 and Cheng 4349.8). Literally, 'his feelings seemed sympathetic'. Or, with LSY 以 → 已 'already'.
165 **in a whirl** 迴惶 = 佪惶.
167 **aware** LSY regards 省 as 曾, a past indicator (cf. Chang Hsiang 514 and Iriya, Review, 180).
169 **types of people** 人倫 glossed as 人類. It is also possible to translate in the more commonly used sense of 'human relationships'.
170 **first** P4988v has 迮.
took Iriya 78n18 and *Index*, 16 notes that 將爲 = 將謂. Cf. 將作.
... stranger Waley 219: 'When I suddenly heard what you have told me I was very much surprised.' Iriya 78n18 emends 異 to 是 but this is somewhat difficult to justify. Admittedly, however, it does read ('thought you were he') and merits consideration because of the visual resemblance.
171 **reflect upon it** 'Gather my spirits.'
somewhat 似 is a particle which usually follows an adverb. See Chiang 191 and cf. T556.14. ≠ 'seemed'. For 稍 'quite', see Śāriputra line 209n.
173 **... similar** Cf. T435.6.
174 **disposition** I follow P4988v 大性, 'general character', *svabhāva*, *pradhāna*, *prakṛti*.
176 **Teacher** *Ācārya*.
seeking 來 → 求 (Waley, 'Notes', 176).
177 **Please** Cf. T377.1.
186 **... well** Cf. T718.5.
188 **asked** I have added 問 from P4988v.
189 **enjoying** 於 is an objective case marker frequent in T'ang colloquial texts.
190 **activities** *Karma*.
191 **ten virtues** See Śāriputra line 184n3.
192 **five commandments** *Pañca veramaṇī*: no killing, stealing, adultery, lying, or liquor.
my soul Cf. T725.7 and see Wu line 1370n. Cheng 4349.14 reads 識 as do Chou 155.6 and P2319.
193 **number** P2319 has 之 instead of 諸. The meaning is exactly the same (Chiang 132).
198 **vanished** 頓 → 遁(遯).
200 **aimlessly** *Book of Odes*, commentary on the Wei ode, 'Shih mou chih chien' 魏風, 十畝之間 (*Thirteen Classics*) 5.3.10b: 'Men and women going and coming without distinction.' 閑閑然, 男女無別往來之貌. However, Legge's (IV. 169) translation of 閑閑然 as 'stand idly about' is the correct one. See Bernhard Karlgren, 'Glosses

on the Kuo Feng Odes', *Bulletin of the Museum of Far Eastern Antiquities*, 14 (Stockholm, 1942), 198 (p. 116).

204 **reverence** *Vandana*; *namas-kāra*.

205 **good friends** *Āyuṣmat*.

206 **all** If possible, 都 should be translated as an adverb.

208 **around** Not '*come* to roam'. 來 often serves as a past or present continuative particle in final position (e.g. T721.9, T724.8).

walls 墎 is a vulgar form of 郭 'outer wall of a city'.

209 **. . . today** For 此間, cf. T363.5, T376.1 and T380.5. For 今朝, cf. T702.1 and T710.16.

210 **really** 只手, 'truly' (Chiang 169). 手, 首 (or, even more rarely, 守) is an adverbial postposition.

215 **homes** 'We were judged' and 'to our homes' are amplifications not in the Chinese text.

217 **flung** Chou 156.1 reads 抛 and Cheng 4349.20, following S2614 and P3485, 拋.

219 **crows** 鵶 = 鴉.

222 **wandering ghosts** They may be *pretas* (cf. T719.16).

223 **. . . verdict** 'Additional report'(?).

224 **Today** The order of 今而 is reversed from what it should be (Hsü 122).

cut off This would be fine – if they were now in heaven.

births and deaths *Saṃsāra*.

225 **never** Notice the reversed order of 不再 on P3485.

229 **folded** 攬 (same in Ta; Chou 156.7 and Cheng 4350.3 have 欖) → 㩹.

paper money Chinese still present such offerings to the dead.

230 **sons and daughters** *Not* 'men and women' (Chiang 12).

telling Of the more than a dozen occurrences of 男女 listed in Iriya, *Index*, 11, this is the only instance where it is followed by 道 and so I have discounted the possibility that the latter is some sort of nounal suffix.

231 **. . . deeds** 'Cultivate blessedness [for us by doing good deeds]'.

240 **cudgels** P2319, as well as all the other printed editions, has 棒 instead of 捧.

247 **was** 被 ↛ 披. It is a passive signifier.

taken 得 → 將 (Ta1308b, Chiang 17, P2319, and S2614), cf. 引 just below.

248 **functionaries** These 所由 (Chiang 17) are the 門官 of the very next line.

252 **quickly** Chiang 137.

. . . salutation See Śāriputra line 390n2.

253 **What** 沒 means 甚麼.

is 又 → 有 (P3485).

254 **bowed** Cheng 4350.8 reads 祗色; Ta1308b and Chou 157.1 read 祇色. P3485 has 邑 for the latter character and P2319 has 挹. Hsü 43 says that all of these are incorrect and should be emended to 揖, 'bow'. N.B. 挹 = 揖!

respectfully 祇! S2614 and P3485 have 祗.

behind P3485 has 上 'on'.

table For pictures of the sort of table in question, see Matsumoto Eiichi 松本栄一, *Tonkō-ga no kenkyū* 燉煌画の研究 (Tokyo, 1937), vol. II, plates 115, 116, 117, 118.

255 **Exemplar** *Ācārya*.

257 **flog** 栲 → 拷 (cf. Chou 157.2).

260 **either** See Śāriputra line 260n1. The normal structure for this grammatical pattern would require 爲當 or 爲復 before 別有 below. The choice, of course, constitutes a question.

262 **Mount T'ai's** This is 泰山府君, the Taoist counterpart of Yama. Ku Yen-wu 顧炎武, *Jih-chih lu chi-shih* 日知錄集釋 (edition of 1892) 30.30b–31b and 31.45ab, has shown that the Commandant of Mount T'ai (T721.11) was originally the name of an official in the Han Dynasty. In this section of the transformation text, one

almost begins to feel that we are dealing with a Taoist underworld such as that described in *Tung-yü ta-sheng pao-ch'an* (*Tao-tsang* 道藏, 東嶽大生寶懺, *ts'e* 296), 13b. This is but one example of the strongly eclectic nature of these texts. Cf. Osabe Kazuo 長部和雄, 'Le Roi Yama et le T'ai-chan fou-kiun dans le tantrisme des T'ang', in *Études Taoïstes* 道教研究, ed. Yoshioka Yoshitoyo 吉岡義豊 and Michel Soymié, vol. IV (Tokyo, 1971), pp. 1–28.

in the end Chou 157.4 and Cheng 4350.10 both have 本 for 卒.

263 **heaven's** P3485 drops 天.

264 **conditional causation** *Pratītya-samutpāda.*

265 **... moment** 造此 (Chiang 134).

266 **Long Night** Of transmigration (*saṃsāra*) – that is to say, a long, long time full of darkness; *dīrgha-rātram.*

270 **... could** I have been unable to determine precisely what is wrong with this sentence. Cf. 不得意. The meaning is fairly clear – he *spoke* but *expressed* himself with difficulty.

271 **... King** Compare line 283 below in the English translation.

272 **... alive** This line displays obvious structural weaknesses. N.B. Maudgalyāyana is not dead.

273 **laws of abstinence** *Upavasatha*, the last of the eight prohibitions, i.e. not to eat out of regulation hours.

... noon The other printed editions have all correctly read 短 (homonymous with 斷 *uccheda*). See Śāriputra line 23n.

275 **Pure Land** *Sukhāvatī.*

279 **High Heaven** 'Yellow Sky' was the title assumed by Chang Chüeh 張角, leader of the Yellow Turbans at the close of the Eastern Han. In spite of what I said in line 262n1, such a reading would make no sense here. My translation is based on 黃 → 皇.

280 **... earth** Though there are several problems with this line, the overall meaning is fairly clear. 放 → 訪. Iriya 78n25 suggests 放 → 尋 (?). He also emends 縱 → 蹤. Cf. T725.3 and T732.14. For 蹤由 see Wang I *et al.*, comp., *Gwoyeu Tsyrdean* (Shanghai, 1937), p. 3455b.

286 **Kṣitigarbha ...** Overlord of Yama, he is guardian of the earth.

obeisance *Vandana.*

287 **come** 來 may also be considered as a functional particle. Cf. the translation of Maudgalyāyana's reply which could also be rendered 'I have come in search of'.

290 **number** See line 193n.

limitless *Apramāṇa.*

boundless *Ananta.*

291 **come** See the following note.

duty-officers 當(直), see T730.7. Iriya has the King telling Maudgalyāyana to go on ahead and saying that he will follow soon after. Such an interpretation is unacceptable for several reasons: (1) Maudgalyāyana does not leave until T721.12. (2) 即至 refers to the functionaries (see T721.8 where this is clear). (3) The King stays where he is. (4) It would be illogical for the King (or for anyone) to say 'I must come right away.' Waley resorts to three dots.

294 **book-keeper** I trust that the translation sufficiently conveys the duties of these officials. The last-mentioned kept the 'karma accounts' 業簿.

299 **Commandant** 都尉, cf. Rotours, *Fonctionnaires*, 1045.

300 **Mount T'ai** See line 262n1.

Recorder Rotours, *Fonctionnaires*, 401 (錄事史).

Bureau ... 天曹 is taken over from Taoist cosmology. See 'Biography of Wang Yüan' 王遠傳, *Shen-hsien chuan* 神仙傳 (*Han-wei ts'ung-shu* 漢魏叢書, 1791, *ts'e* 40) 2.6b–7a. Cf. T218.1,2, T225.2.

301 **Boys** *Kumāra*. Lo, *Studies*, 252 says that they are mentioned in S1164 which consists of prayers for the dead. I have spotted them in the Tun-huang story about Tung Yung 董永, T109.3: 'All things, good and bad, are recorded; the Good and Evil Boys copy everything down.' 好事惡事皆抄錄/善惡童子每抄將. Also note T211.16.

305 **. . . Five Ways** The *Pañcagati* General (*senāpatih*) who is the keeper of the book of life.

309 **Wathellwedo River** The Styx of the Chinese Buddhist underworld. My translation is a crude attempt to convey the sense of the pun (奈河 ≡ 奈何). Iriya 78n28 suggests that the Sanskrit word for hell, *naraka* (捺落迦·奈落) may be the basis of the expression.

310 **. . . trees** Lo, *Studies*, 277, 282 astutely suggests that the particular choice of scenes in hell in the Maudgalyāyana transformation text may have been influenced by the requirement that they be paintable. On p. 299, he notes the *visual* impact of the hanging of the skin on a tree. Cf. T744.6.

312 **apprehensive** 迴惶 = 佪惶.

315 **. . . west** Iriya (78–9n30) has discovered a fascinating parallel to this line in the Recorded Sayings 語錄 of the Zen Master Chao-chou 趙州 (778–897), *Jōshū zenji goroku* 趙州禪師語錄, tr. Akizuki Ryōmin 秋月龍珉 (Tokyo, 1964), p. 42 (no. 213): 'It was asked, "During the twelve hours, in what way does cleansing take place?" To which the Master replied: "The waters of the Wathellwedo River are muddy. The western waters flow swiftly."' 問「十二時中如何淘汰.」師云「奈河水濁, 西水流急」 Also see Akizuki Ryōmin, *Jōshū roku* 趙州錄 (Tokyo, 1972), note on p. 198.

316 **road . . .** The last three characters of this line on P3485 read 人行路.

318 **Pursued** 趁 glossed as 逐.

allowed 交 = 叫.

moment 向 → 晌. Cf. line 137n.

319 **called out** Hsü suggests 問 → 聞 '*hear* them calling out the names'. Chou 158.11 and Cheng 4351.2 both have 眞 instead of 點, i.e. 'their *true* names'.

323 **I** Cf. 我家.

in thrall Chou 158.12 has 爭 'strove for'.

. . . possessions The translation of this line is not to be taken as authoritative.

324 **golden** 今 → 金 (Iriya 60, also as written on P3485), an emendation which is preferable to Hsü's (43) 今 → 高.

crimson Or 'with pearl inlaid wheels'. But 珠 = 朱.

325 **change** 千 → 迁 = 遷 (cf. Hsü 43).

328 **buried** This is actually an unannounced emendation by the T editors (following P3485), for all the other printed texts and S2614 read 理.

331 **inexpressible** *Anabhilāpya*; *nirabhilāpya*.

334 **who** Note 之者 here and just below in line 344.

335 **circumstantial** *Pratyaya*.

336 **later on** For 迴(= 回), P3485 has 會 and Chou 159 5 has 海(?).

338 **look longingly** Literally, 'get their fill of looking at each other', i.e. take a good, last look.

341 **ox-head guards** *Gośīrṣa*.

342 **hell's gaolers** *Naraka-pāla*.

343 **filled with distress** Ta1309a and Cheng 4351.8 both correctly read 盻盻.

345 **sink** 別後 is an error for 到沒 which P3485, S2614, P2319, and all of the other printed editions give. Cf. T725.11. Chiang's (185) explanation of 沒 as 'such a' is criticized by Iriya 79n32 for its improper treatment of the word as a colloquial expression.

346 **. . . do** The beginning phrases of the translations of this and the previous line are

amplifications.

not Logically, 不 negates 生.

done good works 'Cultivate fields of blessedness', see line 154n.

349 **Heaven's Mansions** See line 4n2.

insubstantial *Abhūta*.

350 **punishes** P2319 and P3485 both have 罰. This line is miscopied by a student on S2614v as 行惡不論天所造. See the entry in my 'Inventory'.

351 **minions ...** 冥零 is troublesome. The meaning intended must be something like 冥府 or 冥官. I would suggest 冥靈 'spirits of the underworld' as a homonymous emendation but am dubious because the expression has been pre-empted by the mythical sea-turtle in the first chapter of the *Chuang-tzu*. 冥界, 'Hades', has a slight visual resemblance but not enough to convince me fully. Iriya 79n34 *cautiously* suggests 螟蛉 'moth caterpillar', i.e. '[even such a small creature as] the moth caterpillar would join in'. I should like to offer several additional observations which may be of value in unravelling this troublesome passage. P3485 has 遷 (according to T collation note 55; my reading of the microfilm is 逦) instead of 冥. It is obvious that there is something amiss with the first line of the previous couplet. Except for that line, there are no major deviations in the prosody of this extended verse section (56 lines). I would tentatively like to suggest that it read 目連問言樹下人. The next two lines should remain as given. And the final line of the quatrain would be 應時奈河 (or some other word for hell beginning with 奈) 亦共誅. However, once the dislocation had occurred, subsequent copyists would have attempted to remedy it and, I suppose, this accounts for 冥. A final remark is that, in the sixteenth-century eclectic account of hell known as *San-pao t'ai-chien hsia hsi-yang chi* 三寶太監下西洋記, there is a 'Hell of the Dark-Cold' 溟冷之府獄. Perhaps it may have some connection with the 冥零 here. See J. J. L. Duyvendak, 'A Chinese "Divina Commedia"', *TP*, 41(1952), 304–5.

353 **three mires** See line 5n2.

354 **taken** 將 'take' and 來 (non-directional complement).

355 **... ask** Chou 159.14 and Cheng 4351.10 both have 促曰, 'urgently I say to you'.

356 **teacher** *Upādhyāya*.

358 **that** (以)來 'since'.

359 **we** Note 等 as pluralizing suffix.

361 **suffering** S2614, P2319, P3485, Ta1039a, and Cheng 4351.12 all have 辛苦 '[to know such] hardship'.

362 **... has** 縱令 is a suppositional phrase, comparable to 即使.

367 **spent** For 勞, P3107 and P3485 have 浪 'wasted'.

368 **avail** Cf. T719.16.

370 **wish** For 欲得, see the entries in Iriya, *Index*, 31.

obliterate 沒 glossed as 滅. P2319 has 不 ('not to') instead of 沒.

372 **back** Cf. T372.16.

373 **Instruct them** 教令, as printed in Chou 160.9.

374 **We wish ...** From here down to 慈親普降, there are huge differences among the editors of the four printed texts as regards punctuation and meaning of individual characters. Clearly, this section is garbled beyond any reasonable hope of repair. The translation should thus be considered only as a crude approximation of what may have been intended.

375 **you** It may be argued that 和尚 is simply a vocative and that the statements which follow regarding perfect wisdom are not made with particular reference to Maudgalyāyana. The final sentence of this paragraph, as well as the grammatical context of 和尚 itself (subject of clause which is subordinate to 願), however, indicate otherwise.

... nirvāṇa **Bodhinirvāṇa*(?).

376 **. . . concealed** 尋常, literally, 'distance of eight or sixteen feet'. See the next note. 不沒, literally, 'is not submerged, does not sink', hence 'is not checked' *anirudhyamāna*, hence 'is manifest'. This cryptic clause cannot, I believe, be fully understood apart from the information given in the next note.

377 **conveyance** The 'conveyance' here is, of course, to ferry people across the ocean of *saṃsāra*. I offer the following from the *Chuang-tzu* (p. 116), 'Heaven's Cycles' 天運 because it has several intriguing similarities to the present clause: 'The capability of a boat is to move through the water. If you seek to push it on the land, the world would end before you'd get eight or sixteen feet.' 以舟之可行於水也, 而求推之於陸則沒世不行尋常. The sub-commentary (疏) on this passage uses the words 運載.

all living beings *Sarvasattva.*

blade 鈕 → 鈏(?) = 刃, cf. 智慧劍 which severs the cycle of *saṃsāra* by cutting through passion.

knowledge 惠 → 慧, *jñāna.*

378 **not** 不 by itself may mean 無 'there be no'. For purposes of a smoother rendering, I have assumed a word such as 染 or 障 after 不, hence 'unsullied, unobstructed by'. The happiest solution would be to emend 不 to a word meaning 'chop down' but I have been unable to think of any which are justifiable

forest Masatoshi Nagatomi has explained in conversation an interesting folk etymology for *nirvāṇa* that might account for 不煩惱林: 不 means *nir* and 煩惱 sounds like *vana* which is the Sanskrit word for 林!

affliction *Kleśa.*

379 **awe-inspiring** *Prabhāva.*

mind *Citta*(?). I have exchanged the positions of 行 and 心.

active 行 (see previous note).

380 **realize** I have added 成 after 而. A neater solution and one to which I am more inclined upon reflection is 諸 → 著 'make manifest [the great vow of the Buddha]'.

vow To save all living beings.

381 **joyless place** *Niraya*, i.e. hell.

382 **compassionate regard** 慈親 → 慈觀, *kṛpana-locana*; *maitra-locana.*

383 **heard** 問 → 聞.

384 **short** 時餉, see line 318n3.

387 **disposition** 令 → 分 or, perhaps, 靈 or 命, hence *jivita-saṃskārāḥ*(?).

388 **gleam** Chou 160.13 and Cheng 4351.18 both have 晶 which is a slightly superior reading. The line would be much improved if the character were dropped altogether, 'golden armour and gleaming sword'. Iriya 61b breaks the line into two smaller units.

390 **flying** I am suspicious of 飛 (Chou 160.14 and Cheng 4351.18 both have 長). The author must have been trying to express some such notion as 接踵(而至) '[arrive] in quick succession'.

391 **yelling** 叫 is a vulgar form of 叫.

shouting Chou 161.1 prints 噉 'to eat' which is inappropriate here. The T editors' emendation to 喊 is unnecessary for 譀 itself may mean 'angry shouting'.

392 **resembled** Chou 161.1 alone prints 如. All the other printed editions have 得; it is probable that this represents a special type of colloquial usage ('got' therefore 'had about it' therefore 'was like').

dazzling flash 輝霍 (P2319) is the correct reading.

393 **chests** 心 may be glossed as 胸.

395 **holy person** *Ārya-jana.*

396 **Even** The first character in this line is difficult to read – T has 亦, Chou 161.3 has 嚇 'terrified' and Cheng 4351.20 has 煞 'struck by the violence of it'. Cf. *Ch'i-hsia wu-i* 七俠五義 (Taipei, 1975) 5.13b: 吳良嚇的魂飛膽裂. Also *Hua-yüeh hen*

花月痕 (1888) 1.30b (chapter 4): 弄得箇箇魂驚膽戰.
... wits If we accept the T reading for the first character, 得 may be said to function as a reflexive particle. If we accept the reading of either Chou or Cheng, it functions as a particle for the complement of degree. The latter seems much the more likely possibility.

398 **... powers** *Ṛddhi[-sampad]*; *abhijñā[na]*.
... speed of 'As speedily as.' + 'He exercised his.'

399 **ask** 聞 → 問. Cf. line 10 on this page of T and my line 410n1.
most crucial 刑要 → 形要. I have tried to make the least radical emendation. Cf. 險要處. Given the fact that 要處 itself means the same thing as 險要處 and considering the specific location involved (e.g. see below, line 8 in T on this page), it is easy to see how 形 would have been mistakenly written 刑. Note the *strategic* value of this place in the following lines in terms of funnelling the sinners into hell.

401 **concentration** S2614 has 積.

403 **All together** 縱 → 總 (?). This still requires understanding 總然 in a special sense for it generally means approximately the same as 縱然.

404 **imposing** 俄俄 → 峨峨, 'towering' (Iriya 62a).

405 **... guarding** For 來, cf. line 358n.
aeons *Kalpa*.

406 **... ten thousands** As the text stands, 'with troops by the thousands and hosts in the ten thousands'. I believe, however, that Iriya 62a is correct in understanding 千群萬衆, cf. T722.11.

407 **very first one** This expression (從頭) also may be rendered as 'right from the top', 'from the very beginning'. Cf. T33.11, T43.1, T85.6, T110.6, T330.15, T520.14, T595.1, and T790.12. The last occurrence, in particular, resembles the present one.
each Both Chou 161.9 and Cheng 4352.3 have 自各.

408 **deviated** 傍行 usually stands for *pīṭhasarpiḥ* ('boa') which makes no sense here. The translation represents an exceptional understanding of the expression.
almsgiving *Dāna*.

409 **souls** Celestial and terrestrial; 心身.

410 **ask** 向 → 问(問). Cf. Wang Meng-ou 王夢鷗, *Han-chien wen-tzu lei-pien* 漢簡文字類編 (Taipei, 1974), p. 113a.
three mires See line 5n2.

412 **everywhere** 偏 → 徧 = 遍 as printed in Chou 161.11 and Cheng 4352.4.
rebirth ... *Tiryagyoni*.

416 **exemplar** *Ācārya*.

418 **numberless ...** See Śāriputra line 4n.

419 **spur of the moment** 卒 (*ts'u*) = 猝.

420 **Mount T'ai's** See line 262n1.
regency Waley 226 translates 都要 (*·i̯äu*) as 'all told'. Others who have read this, in desperation, have proposed such interpretations as 'is all-important' and 'altogether needs'. I believe, however, that by analogy with the lines below, it must be an administrative term. Cf. 都御 (*ngi̯wo*), 都吏, 都校 (*kau-*), to choose only a few which bear some phonetic or orthographic resemblance to 都要. The correct emendation, however, is to 都尉, cf. T721.11 and line 299n. N.B. From line 420 to line 427, there are several equally vexatious problems where my translation differs from those of Waley and Iriya. I shall not bother to point out such differences in every case.
sections Or 名簿 (?) 'name books'.

421 **... offices** Bureaux for the underworld and offices for hell.

422 **overseers** 知司 → 直司 (?).
... names Literally, 'each has names'(?).

423 **warrants** 符弔 → 符书 = 符書.

425 **a few moments** 蹔 = 暫 (Ta1309b and Chou 162.4).
trying 看.
Teacher *Ācārya.*
426 **If** 可中 (Chiang 148).
fortunate 果報, P. *mahapphala*. 'Retribution [lit. fruit] [for one's deeds]', i.e. if it's in the cards.
427 **whereabouts** See line 280n above.
430 **officer-in-charge** 都官, bureau in charge of officials in the capital. Rotours, *Fonctionnaires*, 117–20, 906n.
431 **was . . . by** To translate 被.
432 **away** 將 as a postposition (to verbs) meaning 'out' or 'away' is frequent in these texts. Cf. Śāriputra line 1018n and the entries in Iriya, *Index*, 16.
Avīci *Lowest* of the eight hot hells.
. . . Hell The entire clause recurs on T728.7.
is I.e., 現[存], cf. T728.2 and 7, T729.14.
434 **General . . .** The text as established by the T editors down to 王面 cannot be read, especially since it has Maudgalyāyana referring to himself by his own name and is extremely awkward from the beginning with its two 'generals' coming one after the other. It is incorrect to state, as the T editors do in collation note 62, that P2319 repeats 將軍. The marks next to 將軍 on the ms do not signify repetition since they occur two lines later in a context where repetition is clearly ruled out. My own impression is that something has dropped out of the text at the point marked by this note.
435 **from . . .** Literally, 'from the King's side', but 邊 in this position has little force (see T191.2, T292.9, T855.5, and T709.15 (a bit stronger)); cf. the modern Chinese localizers 那儿 and 這儿. See Samuel Cheung, 'The Language of the Tun-huang *Pien-wen*' (Ph.D. dissertation, Berkeley, 1974), pp. 201–2.
436 **King** Yama.
only then See line 447n below.
. . . hell 'Farther into hell' is added to the translation. 來 is a directional complement.
438 **importuned** 貧道 → 頻道 as given in all of the other printed editions. But this is still not an entirely satisfactory explanation because the latter form is frequently used interchangeably with the first.
439 **are** P2319 has 有 after 間.
441 **cultivate** For 於, see line 189n. P2319 lacks this character.
ten virtues See line 6n and Śāriputra line 184n3.
442 **five commandments** See line 192n1.
souls See line 192n2.
. . . in heaven P2319 adds '[so they] do not get to see the King's face' 不見王面.
444 **good karma** *Sucarita*; *śubham karma*.
a large number See line 193n.
of 諸 would be a preferable reading to 之.
446 **bad** The positions of 善 and 惡 are reversed in P2319.
447 **Then** Cf. Chiang 164.
448 **retribution** 報.
. . . causes *Pratyaya*.
451 **wandered . . .** 'Were far off.' 遙遙 (P2319) is correct
453 **sunk** Chiang 185 notwithstanding (cf. line 345n).
454 **souls** See line 409n.
455 **Iron discs** *Cakravāla*; *cakravāḍa*.
. . . air Cf. T727.3.
458 **Every inch** 尋時 → 尋尺 or even 寸尺 rather than 瞬時 as suggested by Iriya 63a.

459 **crows** 鳥 → 烏 (cf. Cheng 4352.15).
pecked 擮 → 啄.
461 **tree of knives** In the *asipattra* hell.
463 **Beyond description** Cf. T728.1.
464 **broad** 津 is the rhyme word. I have supplied 廣 (?) just before it.
465 **wild mountains** See Wu line 189n.
... miles To comprehend this passage, it is essential to spot the rhymed lines so as to know which lines are paired. This line, being unrhymed, goes with the following one.
466 **league** *Yojana* (a day's march).
467 **thousand** 釼 (? probably a form of 刃) is a classifier (numerary adjunct) for 'lances'. It is not to be translated as 'swords' (劍) which Hsü 43 suggested. This is clear both from the obvious parallel relationship to 重 below and from the awkward relationship between 鐵 and 萬 which would result if it were made parallel to 鎗.
lances 鏘 → 鎗 = 槍.
469 **ask** The emendation indicated by the T editors is unnecessary since S2614 already has 問.
470 **world of men** 閻浮 inadvertently transposed in T. *Jambūdvīpa*.
471 **... speaking** The preceding verse passage is thus, apparently, a descriptive monologue.
again All of the other printed versions and S2614 have 更 before 向. P2319 has 更往.
476 **ask** P2319 lacks 問, hence, 'If you go on ahead to the hell with the hill made of knives'.
481 **Sword Forest** See line 461n above.
482 **copiously** 涓涓, 'aspect of water bubbling up from a stream; a trickle of water'.
485 **ogre** *Rākṣasa*.
489 **perpetual property ...** 常住([僧]物), P. *avissajjiya sanghika*, i.e. the monasteries with their dormitories, fields, and orchards.
490 **befouled** 游泥 → 淤泥 = 汚泥, 'defile'. Cf. T563.3 and Ta84.52b.
gardens *Saṅghārāma*.
491 **in perpetuity** 常住 *nitya*; *śāśvata*; *kūṭastha*.
494 **made** 交 = 叫.
497 **white bones** The 白骨觀, *vidagdhaka-saṃjñā*, is the last of the nine reflections upon the decomposition of the human body.
500 **monastery** *Vihāra*.
holdings 寺家 refers to the legal entity of the monastery in regard to the land and tax structure. Popularly, it simply means 'Buddhist monks'. *New History of the T'ang Dynasty*, 'Treatise on Foodstuffs and Currency' 食貨志 (*PNP*) 52.7b: 'Middle and lower-class fields are given to the able-bodied monastery tenants ...' 中下田給寺家奴婢丁壯者…
without The sense requires understanding 不塡好土.
good earth 'Fertilizer', that is.
501 **Propagate** I follow P2319 which has 插 instead of S2614's 椄(=接) 'graft'.
503 **you** 箇 is enclitic so this is still effectively heptasyllabic. Cf. the more usual 阿你 on T249.9, T250.4, T267.9 and 12, T268.14. P2319 has just 你箇.
absolutely Added in the translation.
indescribable 不可說 is a technical term.
504 **... Ganges** See Śāriputra line 4n.
505 **Even** 從 = 縱.
507 **bumping** 桵 → 挼 glossed as 刺 'to pierce' hence 'to poke' (cf. Chou 164.8).
509 **holding** 杷 = 把 (cf. Chou 164.9, Cheng 4353.5). See T727.8.
jab Cheng 4353.6 and Chou 164.9 both have 押 'escort'.

510 **bodies and heads** 身手 → 身首 (cf. Iriya 64a).
all Chiang 180 cites numerous examples where 應是 means this (see also the entries in Iriya, *Index*, 30). However, Iriya's 64a translation as 'instantly' (probably assumes an emendation to 應時) deserves serious consideration because of the parallel phrase in the following line. See also Iriya, 'Review', 179. I would have accepted it without hesitation were it not for the repetition of 時. Curiously, on S2614, 是 is written interlinearly to replace an original 時.

511 **powder and froth** Though I have translated 粉沫 (Chou's 164.10 reading of 粉沫 is even worse), I must declare that it sounds awful – and perhaps even wrong. I believe that it should have been 粉落 'crumbling dust' or simply, as LSY suggests, 粉末 'dust'.

512 **surface** + 'From its surface.'
poured 傾 ≠ 傾 → 傾 (Hsü 122). Chou 164.10 and Cheng 4353.6, who must have used a different manuscript, both have 澆.

513 **and** 如 = 而.

515 **. . . mid-air** Cf. T725.12.

516 **is** P2319 has 唯 'only' instead of 爲.
. . . as men Literally, 'will not be men'.

517 **rakes** 把 = 杷, as on P2319 and S2614.
scraped Certainly, 樓 → 摟 which itself may be glossed as 聚.
revivified This does not constitute genuine rebirth. It is only part of the torture process. 交 is the sign of the causative.

526 **ahead** In the sense of deeper penetration into hell.

528 **words** P2319 has 語 instead of 以(已).

529 **about** 可, a particle indicating approximation.
league See line 466n.
depth 'Height.' For 高下, cf. T726.1.

530 **issued** The translation represents a combination of two glosses for 蓬勃:雲盛貌 and 氣出貌.
malodorous Both S2614 and P2319 have the vulgar character 臰.

531 **. . . heavens** A nearly identical clause with the same orthographical error (勳 → 燻) is to be found on T364.16, see Śāriputra line 384n.
ogre See line 485n.

537 **create** 'Have.'

541 **sexual passions** *Kāma*; *maithuna*. P2319 has 婬浴.

542 **masters'** 'Senior', *mahallaka*; 'teacher', *ācārya/upādhyāya*.
owners' Iriya 79n38 has also discovered this term (曹主) on a certificate from Tunhuang granting freedom to a slave. I have been unable to verify his reference.

544 **immeasurable** 笇 = 算 (as given in all of the other published versions). 'Breadth' is added to the English translation.

545 **complemented** 合 is probably an unannounced emendation; all of the other published versions have 和, as does P2319.
half-and-half Naturally, since this type of sin requires two to commit it.

546 **driven** P2319 has 釘其身 'nails in their bodies'. Note that, for 釘釘, the translation has noun–verb.

547 **hot** 'Hot' is added in the translation.
. . . rot away 胸 (P2319) must be accepted in any case, but there are serious questions regarding the reading of the next character. T and Cheng 4353.14 have 懷, Chou 165.8 and Ta1310a.28 have 壞, as does P2319. Although neither of the possibilities reads particularly well, it is a curiosity that the translation is not substantially affected no matter which of the two is used.

548 **scissors** 交 → 鉸. Iriya 64b seems to have emended 長 to 常 and to have understood 交 as a causative marker for the verb in the second part of the line.

549 **ploughs** 饞 → 鑱 (as written on S2614 and printed in Chou).
metal points 似 → 耜 (= 耛 or 梠) which is glossed as 耒頭金. If my emendation is not acceptable, we may opt for the following intentionally awkward rendering: 'The teeth of the ploughs were as pointed as though they were like[?!] awls.'
550 **... empty** I.e. 'when they are hungry'.
hot Again, 'hot' is added in the English translation. This is, after all, the hell for those who gave in to their fires of passion.
551 **thirsty** 喝 → 渴 as it appears on S2614 and as read by Ta1310b.1 and Cheng 4353.15.
irrigate In the medical sense, of course. For 還將: more literally, 'even/yet take'.
552 **metal thorns** 蒺蘺 → 蒺藜 (or 蔾), *Tribulus terrestris*, 'Puncture-vine'. The shape of the plant was used as a model for a primitive sort of barbed wire which was employed as an obstacle against enemy cavalry.
rend Or 劈 or 闢.
554 **pound by pound** Obviously, these two characters are difficult to decipher. On S2614, they appear to be 斥ノ. Cheng 4353.16 has 仟仟 which means 'dense growth' while the T reading of 斥斥 means 'extensive'. Because of the parallel relationship to the line below, I have followed Chou 165.12 who has 斤斤. There would naturally be a strong resistance on the part of any literate listener (or reader) to accept this as meaning 'pound by pound' because of the well-established meaning of 'penetrating intelligence'. *The Book of Odes*, Legge, IV.579: 'How penetrating was their intelligence!' 斤斤其明. For the latter meaning, however, this character must be pronounced in the falling (去) tone. Thus, by pronouncing 斤 in the level tone, the meaning required here could be conveyed.
556 **Indescribable** Cf. T725.16.
557 **opposite** 疋 = 匹. Literally, 'how they match/correspond to each other'.
559 **who** This translation assumes 相 to have weak force (compare, for example, T729.8).
560 **present existence** I.e., 'in hell' (see the following notes). 見存 is awkward even if we understand as 現在 (e.g. Lo, *Studies*, 302n12). Cf. line 432n4. *Pratyautpanna*; *vartamāna*.
blessings ... BHS. *puṇyakriyā*.
561 **one-seventh** Cf. T665.14 and *Ch'ü* no. 602. This is the folk-Buddhist concept of 七分全得. If one 'pursues the departed with rites for their happiness' 追福, he will receive a full complement of blessings while those for whom the ceremony is held will receive one-seventh of the total.
562 **Even though** 縱令 expresses supposition.
eastern sea ... I.e., 'a long, long time'. Ko Hung 葛洪 (234–305), *Biographies of Immortals* 神仙傳 (*Han-wei ts'ung-shu* edn), 7.4a. The meaning of the latter part of this verse passage seems to be that there are very few people who are able to accumulate enough good karma while they are alive to avoid being sent to hell. And, once they are in hell, their chances of getting out are very slim.
564 **... speaking** Cf. line 471n1.
565 **... hell** See lines 431n and 432nn1, 2 and 3.
574 **collapsed** None of the other published texts print 倒 nor do the T editors indicate its origin. P2319 has 僻地 'fell to the ground'. 僻 = 辟 (glossed as 傾 or 側), 'tilted' hence 'slumped'.
575 **revived** 'Breath circulated.'
580 **ear** All of the other published versions correctly have 耳 instead of 身.
hells Cheng 4354.2 and Chou 166.8 both have 後獄 'next hell' instead of 地獄. 'Noises' is added to the English translation. 間 means 'inside'.
583 **without stopping** My translation is based on 婁 → 遱 (glossed as 行步不絕之貌) and takes 不 as a particle to fill out the line (cf. Chiang 190). Cf. line 1173n below.

For those who insist on maintaining 不 as a negative, I offer the following (forced) readings. 婁 → 僂. Confusion may have arisen because 僂 may also be glossed as 疾 and it would simply be incorrect to speak of Maudgalyāyana as being 'un-hurried'. Perhaps 婁 = 屢(= 數), 'did not amount to much'(?). Iriya 65a has made a tentative emendation to 久, 'was not long'.
arrived In the vicinity of the Avīci Hell.
584 **prince of demons** *Yakṣa-adhipati.*
585 **sat** 地 is a particle which appears after intransitive verbs, not necessarily indicating continuousness.
588 **witnessed** 'Experientially perceived.'
three insights Three types of knowledge of an arhat: (1) Memory of past lives, 宿命明 *pūrva-nivāsa*; (2) supernatural insight into the future, 天眼明 *divyaṃ cakṣuḥ*; (3) knowledge of present mortal sufferings which allows for the extinction of all outflows (of passion and temptation), 漏盡明 *kṣīna-āsrava*; *āsrava-kṣaya*. Not to be confused with the *Trividyā* (*anitya*, *duḥkha*, *anātman*).
cycle ... *Saṃsāra.*
595 **hesitate** 沈吟 glossed as 遲疑不決.
598 **readily** See line 265n.
599 **waver** An emendation on phonetic grounds, 逷逷 → 惕惕 ('sympathetic, alarmed') is preferable to one on orthographic grounds, 逷逷 → 逿逿 = 盪盪 ('agitated'(?)).
600 **moreover** Chou 167.4 and Cheng 4354.7 both have 然 instead of 亦. In either case, it sounds awkward.
mincing his words Chiang 70.
603 **as though** Chiang 202.
604 **on** 的 in T'ang colloquial texts functions adverbially (cf. 底, 地) and means 'clearly, evidently, truly'. Examples may be found on T374.13, T369.11, T372.16, and T379.9. Also see Lo, *Studies*, 762–3.
appearance 影向 (as given on P2319 and S2614 and printed in all the other published versions) is a technical term which usually refers to the manifestation of a Buddha in the world (like a reflection of the moon upon the surface of the water). I suspect, however, that what was really intended here was 影像, not in its technical sense of *pratibimba*, 'shadows without independent existence or nature', but rather in its more frequent meaning of 'resemblance, likeness'.
606 **winds of karma** *Karma-vāyu.*
607 **Turning** 'Seem like.'
carcasses All the other published versions and S2614 have 身骸, cf. Śāriputra line 1843n2.
611 **it** 知 is a particle.
beat your chest See Wu line 352n.
612 **heard** 見說 ≡ 聽見說 (Ōta, *Kōgobun*, 143n1).
613 **turned around** P2319 has 迴身.
begging-bowl *Pātra.*
614 **... space** Cf. line 136n2.
Teak 娑 → 娑 hence Śālavana, the grove of sāl (*Shorea robusta*) trees near Kuśinagara where Buddha is said to have died.
615 **Three times** *Pradakṣiṇāṃ kṛtvā.*
617 **averting** 舍 = 捨, as on P2319.
620 **following** For the solution to this and other problems in the present line, see line 280n.
623 **is** 見 = 現 'now'.
624 **... aggrieved** Literally, 'unconsciously, my liver and intestines break'.
625 **fires** I follow T in spite of the fact that S2614 has 大 instead of 火.
... snakes 龍蛇, in Buddhist parlance, usually mean 'the common and the holy'.

626 **. . . able** 'Had not the wherewithal.'
suitable plan *Upāya*.
. . . moment See line 265n.

627 **supernatural strength** *Ṛddhy-abhisaṃskāra*.

628 **. . . admired** The other printed texts and S2614 all have 多受戀. See also Hsieh 148.81. But 戀 could be used to refer to the Buddha's love for all living beings only in a very exceptional sense. I believe we should read as 多愛戀 (the basis for my translation) but am not wholly satisfied with this solution.
all living beings *Sarvasattva*.

629 **Always . . .** 由來, glossed as 向來.
subject I have interpreted this in an impersonal vein because 臣 and 君 would be unusual forms of address for a disciple to use with the Buddha.
. . . lord *Ch'ao-yeh ch'ien-tsai* 朝野僉載 (*TSCC*, *ts'e* 2830, *chüan* 4), 51: 'A subject in distress unburdens himself to his lord, a son in distress unburdens himself to his father.' 臣急告君，子急告父 (Ōta, *Kōgobun*, 143n19). For 解 in the sense of 會 'can; able to', see Chiang 129.

632 **heart-broken** I have followed Chou 168.4 who indicates more clearly than T that there are two characters missing. The reconstruction I am tentatively proposing is 傷懷. 懷 is one of the most popular members of the *-ai* group rhymes in the level tone and often appears in combination with several of the same characters as it does here (e.g. T564.7, T565.13, T568.9, T597.10, T623.8, T629.13, *passim*, for only a very small sample).

633 **commit them** 'Tied to those who commit them' is added in the English translation.

634 **stuck on . . .** 尼碾 → 䵒 (or perhaps 泥) 黏.

635 **Quickly** 火急 'urgently', see Iriya, *Index*, 14.
take 將 may also be understood simply as a pre-transitive.
. . . staff See Śāriputra line 182n.
. . . you The structure of this line is not entirely clear and it is also possible that it may be rendered 'Quickly take my metal-ringed staff which I give to you.' The happiest solution would be to take 與 as some sort of imperative particle but I have not seen it so attested. The most natural word to appear in the final position would be 去. And, indeed, P'ei Hsüeh-hai, p. 7, says that 與 may mean 去, but that is a classical usage and so I still have my doubts.

636 **eight difficulties** *Aṣṭa akṣaṇāni*, situations in which it is difficult to see a Buddha or hear his Dharma: in hell; as a hungry ghost; as an animal; in the comfortable northern continent of *uttarakuru*; in the long-life heavens; as someone deaf, blind, and dumb; as a worldly philosopher; in the interim between a Buddha and his successor.
three disasters *Saṃvartany[aḥ tirso]*. Major: fire, water, and wind. Minor: war, pestilence, famine.

639 **awesome power** *Prabhāva*.

640 **winged arrow** Ōta, *Kōgobun*, 143n28 explains as 'the wind or an arrow'. My translation is based on the gloss 風 || 羽. The gloss 風 || 速 'swift' is also acceptable here.

641 **ox-headed** *Gośīrṣa*.

642 **horse-faced** Literally, 'horse-brained', but cf. *aśvamukha* and *aśvaśīrṣa*. 腦 'brain' is generally interpreted as meaning 面 'face'.
ogres and demons *Rākṣasa* and *yakṣa*.

643 **blood-basins** Cf. T679.11, 12, 15, and T699.1, 2. There is a *Blood-Basin Sūtra* 血盆経, first mentioned in 1194, describing the hell in which women who die in childbirth are tortured by having to bathe in an enormous pool of blood. *Dainihon zoku zōkyō* 大日本続蔵経 (*t'ao* 84, *ts'e* 4) 299a. There are two longer Taoist texts, called *Blood Lake Scriptures* 血湖経 (1223), mentioned by Michel Soymié in 'Étude documentaire sur le sûtra du *hiue-pen king*' 血盆経の資料的研究, in *Études Taoïstes* 道教研究, vol. I (Tokyo, 1965), pp. 109–66.

644 **duty** See line 291n2.
645 **Bureau ...** Literally, 'Celestial Bureau' which, in this context, means the 'Celestial Bureau in charge of Underworld Affairs'.
646 **This** 此間 simply means 此地 and so we would expect the sentence to end 無好道.
648 **vapours** 炁 = 氣 (emendation unnecessary). Similar black gasses are also mentioned by Dante in Canto V of the *Inferno*.
hell 獄中, in spite of the T editors' collation note 73, also appears on S2614.
649 **sucked up ...** Where T has 着, all the other editions as well as the mss S2614 and P2319 have 吸著. Note that 著 is probably already functioning as a resultative complement here (rather than literally meaning 'touch, contact'). See T731.1 where it is clear that the vapours do the sucking which is why I have not translated this as 'should you inhale them'.
650 **place** Such a vast difference of opinion exists among the various editors of the published versions regarding the punctuation of the dozen or so characters on lines 649–51 that there is no point in trying to reconcile them.
653 **wondering** 爲言 seems to have very weak force, amounting to little more than an enclitic.
654 **over there** I am not convinced by the elaborate and somewhat arcane orthographic connections which lead to the gloss of 'abundant and thick' for 怒那 (Chiang 133–4). I prefer Iriya's (79n41) contextual interpretation. The resemblance to T101.16 is unmistakable: 祁雍更能何處在/只應弩郁白雲邊. There is a Pāli indeclinable word, *nūna*, meaning 'indeed, surely, certainly' which might be considered, especially since it parallels 爲言 (discussed in line 653n).
655 **... Ganges** See Śāriputra line 4n.
656 **And said to himself** Added in the translation.
... home Iriya 79n42 cites the Buddhist precept of 'not abiding in nirvāṇa' 無住處涅盤, the converse of which is the present line. The Bodhisattva ideal of not allowing oneself to enter nirvāṇa until all other beings (including those in hell) have been saved is the source of such precepts.
659 **... sweat** The first four characters of this line occur in *Chan-kuo ts'e*, 'Ch'u-ts'e' 戰國策, 楚策 (*SPTK*) 5.44b and the commentary there gives the following note: 'White sweat means "to perspire when there is no summer heat."' 白汗, 不緣暑而汗也. 'Their bodies' is added in the translation.
661 **three-cornered** I follow Chou's 169.3 reading of 楞 which is popularly confused with 稜. Cheng 4355.4, P2319 and S2614 have 楞 (= 槾 'thorn-bush')(?).
664 **suffering** The term 波吒 always occurs in contexts which indicate suffering (T344.9, T660.3, T709.7, T764.8) and even occurs in combination with 苦 (T736.6 and 14). See also *Ch'ü* nos. 564, 583, and 597. There is thus no difficulty in understanding what the expression means but there is a question as to its origin. I had been uncertain of the Sanskrit, thinking it to be perhaps *baddha/bandha*, 'bound, fettered' or *pātaka*, 'a sin which causes one to fall into purgatory'. The explanation of 波吒 as an abbreviation of 波波吒吒 (see Morohashi 17308.82) merits consideration. The name of one of the major Buddhist hells is Ababa 阿波波 where it is so cold that the tongue is frozen with the result that the only sound one can utter is this. Another hell is Aṭaṭa 阿吒吒 where the lips freeze and only the tongue moves. Supposedly, taken together they are meant to represent the general suffering of hell. Avīci, however, is the deepest of the eight hot hells whereas the hells which I have just mentioned are two of the eight cold hells. Also, in the usual listings of these cold hells Aṭaṭa comes before Ababa instead of the other way around. See Daigan and Alicia Matsunaga, *The Buddhist Concept of Hell* (New York, 1972). Professor Nagatomi has suggested that the origin of 波吒 may be found in the Sanskrit word *puttra*, 'preserving from the hell called *put* [which was supposedly for the childless]'. This word seems to have been invented to provide an etymology for

the word *putra*, 'son'. A son, according to this etymology, is one who saves from the sufferings of hell.

665 **stayed** 往 → 住 (cf. Chou 169.5, Cheng 4355.5 and P2319).

669 **tumbled over** Literally, 'fell looking upwards'. Since Maudgalyāyana has been caught up in the gasses which are still *ahead* of him, we would expect him to fall face-forward. Note, however, that on T731.3 吸 seems to mean 'exhale'.

670 **walls of iron** *Ayaḥ-prākāra*.
immense Cf. Wu line 189n.
clouds P2319, stating that 'the evil things in here cannot be told in their entirety', adroitly leaps from this point to 'all were ox-headed and horse-faced' just before the next verse section.

671 **ranks** See line 929n.

672 **thousand** The reader should be alerted to the enormous disagreement among the various editors regarding the punctuation and reading of characters from 千尋 down to 模地. For a sampling, Chou 169.7 and Cheng 4355.7 have 蒡 instead of 芳. Chou and Ta1311a.5 have 刺 for 刾. Hsü 122 suggests that 楷 be emended to 偕 and that there is a character missing before 横. Subsequent notes will provide additional information on their readings but not on the punctuation which is hopelessly confused. My own interpretation of the passage is reflected in the translation and in the following notes.
with Leave 以 unemended. Cf. line 674n.

673 **flourish** 芳 → 放, see Śāriputra line 1868n. 放撥 is provided with three citations in *PWYF* 3722c, all of which have to do with the strumming of stringed instruments. I would concede, however, that the author may have understood 撥 in its more basic meaning of 'spread, scatter'. 'Reached' in the translation derives partly from the context and partly from 放撥 in precisely the same fashion as 'soar' is derived in the next sentence. LSY suggests 芳 → 旁 'at the side'.
points 刾 is a vulgar writing of 刺.
brushed 楷 → 揩. Otherwise leave unemended and gloss as 直 to match 倒 below.

674 **in** Add 以 before 横.

675 **Fierce fires** Cheng and Chou (see line 672n for approximate locations) have 猛犬掣淆(?). Ta has 猛大犁淡(?!).
throbbed Since there is no consensus whatsoever on how to read the word after 掣 (S2614 has 汐(?)), and since there are no combinations of 掣 followed by a character which has a water radical that I know of, it would seem best to understand 掣掣 by analogy with 簇簇 below.
leap about 咷踉 → 跳踉 (cf. Hsü's 123 inadvertent emendation).

676 **thunderous** 雲 → 震 (as printed by both Chou and Cheng).
Sword-wheels Cf. T727.3.
whirled Note that the English word 'whirl' also means 'bustle, commotion'. S2614 has 族く.
brush 模 = 摸(= 摹 = 撫).

678 **breathed** See line 669n.

679 **every** 'Three' and 'four' have become 'all' and 'every' in the translation.
direction See Śāriputra line 139n.
Metal thorns See line 552n1.

681 **every which way** We must, with Iriya 67a, understand 旁 in the sense of 横. Cf. 旁射 which means 'to shoot in all directions'.
flailed 踔 → 戟. This emendation which shows both graphic and phonetic relationship is probably better than the following alternative (phonetic similarity only) which I am also mentioning because the meaning is so appropriate: 戳 'to poke with a sharp instrument'. Hsieh 148.88 suggests the less appropriate 啅(= 啄)'peck'.

682 **jabbed** 'Lacerate; file.'

683 **white** Because bloodless.
oozed 'Is channelled off.'

684 **to crawl up** Hsü's(43) suggestion that there is a character missing here is excellent. I have tentatively supplied 匍. Note the preponderance of *-an* rhymes in these trisyllabic clauses.
coals Chou 169.11 and Cheng 4355.8 both have 灰 'ashes' instead of 炭 (vulgar for 炭). But consider the latter part of the previous note.

686 **liver** This is a difficult character to read: Cheng 4355.9 has 丰 *chiè* which is impossible to make sense of. 手, given by the T editors, reads poorly, even though that is what S2614 seems to have. Surely what must have been intended is 干, perhaps with a very hastily written 'flesh' radical mistakenly running into the vertical stroke. Hence Chou's 169.11 reading of 肝 is basically correct.

688 **clods . . .** A quite different rendering is also possible: 'the sides of the hovels[?]/cauldrons[?] in hell'.

689 **. . . groan** 岌岌 may mean 'urgent, harried' which could be applied here. But 汗汗 is usually explained as descriptive of a great expanse of water which makes no sense in this context. Therefore, I have felt free to consider them as onomatopoeic binomes to which an appropriate meaning can be assigned on an *ad hoc* basis. There are more than half-a-dozen such binomes which end in *-an* in the next few sentences and this presents the translator with a task that is even more impossible than that of interpreting a Han dynasty *fu*. Matters are further complicated by the horrendously poor punctuation of the text given in T. To indicate what I consider a more rational ordering (mostly, but not always, following Chou and/or Hsü and/or Cheng), the translation will be kept painfully literal.
roar A small piece of S2614 is torn away here. Hsü 123 thinks there should be two additional characters above 雷; Ta1311a.13 indicates that there should be one extra after it. By analogy with the second clause above, it would seem that Chou is correct in leaving two spaces. Thus I have made the following tentative reconstruction: 雷鳴震地.

691 **spears** 鏘 → 鎗 (Iryia 67a). I am also suspicious of 鐵 but have not changed it because it reads passably well.

692 **chattered** All of the other printed texts incorrectly have three 嘍's.
birds . . . *Tāmra-tuṇḍāḥ . . . vāyasāḥ*. Apparently, pictures were drawn of these creatures. *Hsüan-ho hua-p'u* 宣和畫譜, ed. Yü Chien-hua 兪劍华 (Peking, 1964) 17.279, 18.281: 'T'ang Chung-tso, one painting of copper-beaked [bird(s)] with thorny bush; Chao Ch'ang, one painting of copper-beaked [bird(s)] with hibiscus.' 唐忠祚柘枝銅嘴圖一; 趙昌芙蓉銅嘴圖一. I have been unable to determine either the popular or the scientific name of this bird. D2106 mentions copper-drinking iron dogs and birds.

694 **ox-headed** See line 641n.
horse-faced See line 642n1.

695 **though** The borrowing of 饒 for 任 was common in the T'ang period.

696 **too** Chou 169.14 and Cheng 4355.10 have 急. Several times below, the same discrepancy occurs.

699 **periods** Added in the English.

700 **see** As in English, 見 means 得 'get'.

702 **shape** 刑 = 形.

703 **Supposing that** Chiang 148.

704 **itself** Literally, 'also'. Compare line 696n above.

705 **. . . flourished** There is no agreement at all among the editors of the published texts on how to read this and the following line. Clearly, the text is defective for the rhyme (primarily even tone *-ing*) in this section begins by running along the bottom half of the page as would be expected but, after this troublesome spot, it skips to the

top. We may deduce, therefore, that a line is missing, probably above this one, and that it would be parallel in structure and meaning to it. My understanding of this line itself, and one with which I am reasonably comfortable, is 案難案難振鐵[兵].

706 **turbulent** My understanding of this line, one with which I am not comfortable, is: 吸[吸]岌[岌]雲空[沸](?). The first binome which I posit is expressive both of the movement of clouds and of sadness. The second is commonly used to express height, urgency, and danger.

707 **blasts** Chou 170.6 has 括. Iriya's 67a suggestion, 栝 → 聒 'cacophonous, uproarious', merits consideration. We may further say in defence of it that 地 was already employed as a sign of adverbial modification in the T'ang. However, my own preference is to emend 栝 → 刮. The expression 刮地 is frequently used to describe a harsh wind blowing across the earth.

708 **three heads** This is a perplexing problem (see Chiang 113 who declares it unsolved). I had tried 三層 'three layers' but could not force it to mean 'three *layers [of scales]' or 'three *parts of the snake [head, body, tail]'. The best possible solution I can think of is that 三曾 → 三首. There is graphic similarity and, by analogy with the following line, the difficult word must be an anatomical feature. There are many references in Chinese literature to three-headed monsters such as those mentioned in *Shan-hai ching* 山海經 (*SPTK*) II.38a and II.55b. The source of this notion here, however, is likely to be Indian. One type of *asura* (titanic demon) was said to have three heads and eight arms 三頭八臂. Mahākāla, whose face, by the way, was exceedingly black, had three faces 三面大黑. As Sanskrit equivalents, I offer *trimūrdha* 'three-headed' and *trimūrdhan* 'name of a three-headed *rakṣas*'.

709 **glare** Iriya 79n44 and Chiang 113 each note one of the more than half a dozen variants of 睚眦. See *Tz'u-t'ung* 1898–9.

710 **ten thousand** 道 is a numerary adjunct.

712 **stab** 讒 → 劖 (Hsü 123) or 鑱 (Hsieh 149.93).
muscles 觔 = 筋. Presumably on grounds of visual similarity, Hsieh 149.93 suggests 肋 'ribs'.
chests 凶 → 胸 (Hsü 123).

713 **puncture** 石 glossed as 砭; or 石 → 射 (cf. Hsieh 149.93 and T727.2).
eyes 精 = 睛.

714 **spears** See line 691n.

715 **sprinkling** In spite of the fact that all the published versions have 灌傾 and that a translation of sorts could be extracted from it, Iriya's 67b emendation to 灌頂 deserves acceptance. Skt. *abhiṣecana*; *mūrdhābhiṣikta*.

717 **are** 交 is incorporated into the English verb as a causative.

721 **watching** 著 is a continuative (cf. Chiang 103 and the entries in Iriya, *Index*, 21).

722 **locks** 鏁 = 鎖.

723 **main** The 明門 is the first in a set of triple gates (Lo, *Customs*, 55).

724 **Before** Iriya 79n46 suggests 伋 → 及. But 伋 means 急 and it is also possible to render the phrase with that understanding. All the other texts have 未 for 来.
there 那邊 is highly colloquial and I have tried to show this in the translation. In these texts, it has about the same range of usages as in modern Chinese (T444.8, T498.4, T563.2, T698.16).

726 **who** Ungrammatical English to indicate colloquial 阿誰.

727 **gates** Cheng 4355.18 correctly has 廣闊. Chou 171.2 and Ta1311b.3 have 闊廣.
leagues *Yojana*.

728 **What** 沒.
open Chou and Ta correctly give 開閉; S2614 has 閑沢.
easily 卒倉 must be understood in the reverse order as Chou 171.2 prints it.

729 **. . . swords** Unless by 刀釼 ('knife blunt'(!)) the scribe or author meant 刀刃 ('knife-edge'), we would be well-advised to read as 刀劒 (cf. Chou 171.3 and Ta1311b.4 who give 刀劍). The same situation recurs below. + 'Inside.'

cluttered Cheng 4355.19 and Chou 171.3 have 呵 which I emend to 砢.
brilliant The reading given in Chou and Cheng, 晶光 'crystalline light', is also acceptable.

730 **remorsefully** Chou 171.3 and Cheng 4355.19 have 懺悔(?) but I follow T and Ta1311b.4 because the concept of *kṣamayati* is so pervasive in Mahāyana Buddhism.

731 **flared** The sound of 終融 is equally as important as its meaning, 'totally fuse'.

732 **everywhere** 滿滿 can, of course, be understood ('filled completely') but, as Hsü 123 suggests, 漫漫 is far more suitable in the present context.
filling 悵 → 漲/張.

733 **exemplar** *Ācārya*.
here Since the texts read 此 instead of 彼, we are compelled to render this as direct discourse. I imagine this to be the gaolers reporting to the warden but do not rule out the possibility that they are speaking to Maudgalyāyana himself.

735 **From the looks . . .** 縱由 → 蹤由. Cf. line 280n.
appear 當 (read in the fourth tone) is a particle which occurs after transitive verbs (Chiang 199).

736 **must be** 應是 as indicating strong supposition (Ōta, *Kōgobun*, 145n58). Chiang's 179 explication of this phrase as meaning 'all' is not applicable in this particular instance.
compassionate *Maitreyakaruṇa*.
Three Jewels See Śāriputra line 148n.

737 **For what reason** 'On account of what business?' P2319 has 緣有何事. As will be seen from Maudgalyāyana's illogical answer, he understood the warden to ask 'How did you open . . .?' P2319 lacks the first sentence of Maudgalyāyana's reply (cf. Ōta, *Kōgobun*, 144). This leads me to believe that the question was inserted in S2614 as a sort of commentary by the scribe.

741 **What** 沒 in S2614 means precisely the same as 甚.

743 **. . . staff** *Khakkhara*.

745 **gaoler** It is odd that the ms reads 獄卒 rather than 獄主.

746 **asked again** Back to the original question (see line 737n).

749 **might find her** P2319 lacks 看.

751 **from** The Chinese sentence is ungrammatical.
signalled 迢 → 招.
flag All the other published editions have 幡, as do P2319 and PK876.

753 **compartment** *Utsada*, section of a larger hell.

755 **flag** S2614, PK876, and the other published editions all have 幡 which is interchangeable with 旛.

757 **Neither** For all of the 亦 in this section, Cheng prints 應 'the response was'. S2614 erroneously adds an extra 已否 before 亦無.

769 **forty-nine** 道 is a numerary adjunct. Iriya 79n48 offers interesting information about the history of such beds as this for handling criminals. As to the significance of the number forty-nine, I am convinced that it suggested itself to the author because forty-nine days is the length of the funeral service (7 × 7). As to the placement of these nails in her body, the *Mokuren sonja jigoku meguri* 目連尊者地獄巡り, which is kept in the library of the Japanese Literature Department at Kyoto University, says that there are three in the head, two in the eyes, six in the wrists, fourteen in the chest and stomach, and twenty-four from the waist down to the feet. Cf. Iwamoto Yutaka, *Mokuren densetsu to urabon*, p. 154.

770 **respond** Cheng 4356.6 and Chou 172.1 have 獄主 only once, Ta1311.25 not at all. The two characters do occur on the ms with small marks beside them which may indicate repetition. In that case, it would be necessary to translate 'respond to the warden'.

776 **respond** Same as the preceding note.

777 **Buddhist monk** See Śāriputra line 148n. The expression here, however, refers to a single monk. Cf. line 1063n below.

778 **monastic robe** *Vastra*; *kāṣāya*.

782 **... monk** See line 17n1.

... mistake Double negative amounting to conjectural interrogative or strong supposition ('There must be some mistake'). Cf. 莫非錯了. P2319 lacks 不是.

784 **... recognize** This is more simply given in P2319 as 緣何錯認.

785 **what** 沒 means 什麼.

787 **explained** 解 glossed as 解說 or 講. 來 (also on S2614) is a complemental particle.

788 **name** S2614 has 自 (→ 字), cf. T733.8 and 9.

789 **... Buddha** Cf. T714.7.

792 **once** 迴 (Cheng 4356.10 has 廻) = 回.

799 **said** We must understand 報言 or the like here.

800 **precious darling** 'Son so beloved that it breaks my heart in tiny pieces.' The same expression recurs on T736.1.

... body There are marked differences among the four published versions of the passage that corresponds to this and the following paragraph of the translation. Except where noted, I have followed T.

802 **pulling out** All of the other texts have 却 after the two problem characters. Contrary to T750n81, PK876 has 拔 (? blacked over) 升㖧却. Neither 升𡁱 (S2614) nor 毋瘦 (Chou 172.11 and Cheng 4356.11) makes good sense. Ta1311c.9 has □□. My translation assumes a reading of 拔却. I would suggest that 提 may have been displaced from Nīladhi just above.

chains See line 722n.

803 **gyves** See Śāriputra line 1109n.

804 **... other** There is one line of verse missing from the manuscript (Iriya 79n49).

805 **... links** 'Fish-scale' is a fixed designation for a particular type of cloud pattern. Compare English 'mackerel sky'. 'Numerous' has been added to the translation.

gyves See Śāriputra line 1109n.

806 **thousand years** See T734.13.

807 **Trickles** 血汁 sounds wrong although all of the published editions print it. Iriya 69a emends to 血汗 'blood and sweat'. Or consider 血汙 'foul blood'.

... head The 七竅 of the head: eyes, ears, nose, and mouth. Cf. S5466 and S5975.

808 **issued** All of the other published versions correctly give 出. Cf. T742.6 where this exact same line recurs.

809 **metal thorns** See line 552n1. 'Body' is added to the translation.

810 **like** 由如 = 猶如. 'Clanked and clattered' is added to the English translation.

... chariots I find this a most extraordinary and striking simile. See also T704.16 and T761.3.

811 **... strain** Literally, 'how could they [maintain] control/jurisdiction?' I have arrived at this interpretation by the following process: 管拾 → 管括 = 管轄 (cf. *Tz'u-t'ung* 2430). The waist and backbone are *central* to the anatomy in Chinese medicine. For 於, cf. line 37n.

813 **Ox-headed guards** See line 641n.

816 **because** Understanding 由如 as 由於 (?) and not as in line 810n1. Ōta, *Kōgobun*, 149n79 says that this line is somewhat unclear.

unfilial Iriya 80n51 observes that, from this line down to 'the vastness of this Avīci Hell', the rhyme changes with every quatrain which creates an effect of heightened tension.

817 **innocently** This is the implication of 殃及 'disaster extends to'.

triple mire See line 5n2.

819 **in this manner** Chiang 185.

820 **P'an An** P'an An-jen 潘安仁 (P'an Yüeh 潘岳), Giles, *BD* no. 1607. The story goes

that the ladies of Lo-yang were so taken by his beauty that they tossed fruit at him when he went out on the street.

821 **haggard** 燋悴 = 憔悴.
worn 摧濺 → 摧殘.

823 **ain't it hard** 'Difficult Is the Road We Walk On' is the title of a *yüeh-fu* tune (originally expressing how hard life in the world is) to which many Six Dynasties and T'ang poets wrote words. See *Yüeh-fu shih-chi* 樂府詩集, *chüan* 70 and 71.

824 **father's** All of the other published editions give 取 instead of 耶. 'Misfortune of having you taken[?] away by death.'

825 **remiss** Literally, 'frequently'.

827 **. . . time** 一過 means 一過目.
haggard See line 821n1 above.

829 **struck** 怕 → 拍(?).
grabbed Chou 173.10 and Cheng 4356.19 have 搦 but that reads even less well than 搦. 'She cried' and 'at herself' are added to the translation.

830 **by death** Literally, 'life and death'.

833 **ten evil** *Daśākuśala.*

836 **extravagantly** For 芬榮, see *PWYF* 1118b.

837 **Surrounded** Literally, 'in my coming and going'.
screens I.e. 行障.

838 **How shall I be** Cf. T736.14.

839 **hungry ghost** *Preta.* 行 is *saṃskāra* 'form, operation', i.e. 作 . . . 行 'to exist in a given mode'. Does not mean 'roaming'.

841 **are made** 耕 'to plough'.

844 **. . . eye** '[Every] moment and instant'.

845 **each time** Added to the translation.

854 **Although** See Śāriputra line 382n1. PK4085 (*Tsa-lu* 34a.2) has 雖.
. . . orders PK4085 (*Tsa-lu* 34a.2) has 出家.

856 **. . . faults** *Book of History*, Legge, III.393: 'You must deal speedily with such parties according to the penal laws of King Wăn, punishing them severely and not pardoning.' *Thirteen Classics*, 14.23a: 乃其速由文王作罰, 刑茲無赦. The subcommentary (by K'ung Ying-ta) to this passage states: 'What the "Charge to K'ang" is talking about here is covering up for the faults of one's blood relatives.' 康誥所云, 以骨肉之親得相容隱. There is also the famous illustration in *Analects*, Legge, I.270, where Confucius boldly claims that it is proper for a son to protect his father, even though he be a criminal: 'The father conceals the misconduct of the son, and the son conceals the misconduct of the father. Uprightness is to be found in this.' 父爲子隱, 子爲父隱, 直在其中矣.
. . . obligations I.e., his relatives, primarily the parents. The copyist of PK4085 obviously did not understand this line because he writes 'five eyes' 五眼 (cf. Śāriputra line 45n) instead of 五服.

857 **sages and saints** 賢聖 as on S2614, PK4085, and PK876.
since ancient times In Chinese tradition! See line 856n1 above.

861 **glared** 嗔 = 瞋.
silently 點點 → 默默 as given in PK876, PK4085, and in all the other published editions.

863 **Impartial King** I.e. Yama, because he treats everyone the same (*samatā*).

865 **have** 受 → 遶 (PK876) → 有, following the suggestion of T751n87. However, a reading which is even more to be preferred is that of 造 'make, commit', correctly given by both Hiang 63 and *Tsa-lu* 34a.8 for PK4085.
. . . for it Cf. T660.3, T703.6 and 11.

866 **. . . tokens** *Feng-su t'ung* 風俗通 (*Pai-tzu ch'üan-shu* edn 百子全書), 2.1b. According to a Taoist cult whose beliefs centred on Mount T'ai, the lengths of

men's lives are recorded on 金篋玉策 (Iriya 80n54). + 'Records of sins.'

867 **end** 卒 may be first person for the warden but he refers to himself in T735.8b as 'your disciple'.

alter See Śāriputra line 633n.

868 **already** 以 = 已.

869 **hall** Since the published texts are unanimous in giving 刑殿 and since a crude translation is possible with that reading, I have retained it. Iriya's 70a emendation to 刑典 'criminal code', however, is excellent and deserves our consideration.

874 **front** 門, brought over from PK4085, is unnecessary.

875 **out** + 'She called out.'

876 **Nīladhi** There are serious defects in the structure of this and the second and third lines below. These defective lines come at the very centre of an extraordinarily long section of verse. The rhymes preceding them are in the *-ang* group and those following in the *-en* group. Furthermore, the repetition of 'Take good care of yourself!' in such close proximity means that one occurrence probably properly belongs to a section of verse and one to a section of prose. Hence, I do not follow the T editors in printing all of these lines as verse. This understanding is clinched by Hsieh 155.164 who correctly quotes PK4085 as follows: '*The place where* Lady Nīladhi, with one of her hands, held fast to the gate of hell and turned back to gaze at him, saying, "Take good care of yourself, oh precious darling of this sinful body!"' 青提夫人一個手託着獄門迴顧盻[→盼]言好住來罪身一寸腹嬌子處. Cf. also the format of PK876 which indicates that these lines should not be verse.

held fast 託住 = 托住. PK4085 (*Tsa-lu* 34b.2) has 託着.

877 **... yourself** Cf. *Ch'ü* nos. 169–82, 'Take Care Mother' 好住娘 (S1497, S4634v, S5892, P2581v, P2713, D278, D109, D3903). Here, although the injunction is to the son, we may still see the insertion of a trisyllabic line into a series of heptasyllabic lines.

878 **precious ...** 長 is probably a gloss added to the text (Hsü 43). Cf. T733.10. This line is either out of place or has been inaccurately transmitted as can clearly be seen by the surrounding rhymes.

879 **avariciously** *Mātsarya.*

880 **grace** I find 恩 rather awkward here. PK4085 (*Tsa-lu* 34b.3 and Hiang 64) has 因 'reason, cause', *hetu.*

karmic retribution *Karma-vipāka.*

881 **deceived** 作 → 詐(?). Compare the usage of 作 in the expression 作祖 'insult' (see Śāriputra line 1021n). Yet the meaning of this line is less than obvious. One could stubbornly force some such interpretation as 'I said "I'll make heaven's mansions – there'll be no hell [for me],"' But this just does not ring true considering the irreligious disdain for heaven of Maudgalyāyana's mother. 作 may have some colloquial meaning such as 'what about' and, paired with interrogative 沒 (cf. line 728n1), might possibly be an expression of dismissal. We may not emend to 怎 because this word was not used until the Sung. Furthermore, I have examined dozens of instances of 沒 in the third position from the end of a seven-syllable verse line (Iriya, *Index*, 6) and have found that it almost invariably functions as a negative and is often coupled with a word of negative meaning in the first part of the line. N.B. I have expanded the first part of the English line for prosodic reasons.

883 **... moment** This is not a literal translation but it does represent the meaning of the entire line.

886 **learned** PK4085 has 反 for 及 after 知. In either case, the character is supernumerary and adds little to the essential meaning of the line so I have not made a special effort to represent it in the translation.

887 **... repent** Cheng 4357.13 has 然 instead of 亦. In either case, x 時 x 亦/然 is a fixed grammatical pattern meaning 'x yes, but ...'. Compare Mandarin x 是 x.

. . . me ‘Knowing this, what [can] I say?’ ‘What [more] can I say?’ ‘I don’t know what to say.’

888 **. . . milk** Literally, ‘Spilt water is difficult to recover.’

. . . proverb S2614 has 㑌(?). Iriya 80n55 wishes to emend to 太公. As indicated by the translation, I prefer to follow the reading established by the T editors on the basis of PK4085. Standard dictionaries and collections of proverbs almost invariably cite the *Shih-i chi* 拾遺記 of Wang Chia 王嘉 (Chin 晉) as the ultimate source for this saying. This attribution cannot be verified from existing recensions. Others (e.g. *T’ung-su pien*, p. 32) cite *Ho-kuan-tzu chu* 鶡冠子注. Neither can this attribution be verified from existing recensions. The earliest reference I have been able to find connecting this saying to the ‘Grand Duke’ is in the *Kuang po-wu chih* 廣博物志 (Taipei, 1973, reprint of 1607 edn), vol. III, p. 1625 (19.9b–10a). In popular literature, the saying has also been firmly attached to the story of Chu Mai-ch’en 朱買臣 (d. 116 B.I.E., Giles, *BD* no. 465) since at least the Yüan Dynasty but does not occur in his biography in the *History of the Former Han* (*PNP*) 64.11a–13b. A painting of this scene is listed in Chang Yen-yüan 張彥遠 (fl. 847–874), *Li-tai ming-hua chi* 歷代名畫記; see William Acker, tr. and annot., *Some T’ang and Pre-T’ang Texts on Chinese Painting* (Leiden, 1974), II.i.196 and II.ii, ch. 8, p. 98 (Chinese text), cf. also II.i.155 and II.ii, ch. 7, p. 86. It does, however, occur several times in the *History of the Later Han* (*PNP*) 1.18b, 69.15a related to other individuals. Li Po used this saying in a memorable line from the poem ‘How Frail Her Life’ 妾薄命, *Fen-lei pu-chu Li T’ai-po shih* 分類補註李太白詩 (*SPTK*) 4.33b: ‘Rain which has fallen does not go back up to the sky; water which has been spilled is difficult to gather again.’ See also *Tsu-t’ang chi*, III.50 and cf. Sarah Allen, ‘The Identities of Taigong Wang 太公望 in Zhou and Han Literature’, *Monumenta Serica*, 30 (1972–3), 57–99.

889 **horrible** 波吒 = 波吒, see line 664n above.

890 **hope** 承聖 → 承望 (Chou 175.13, Chiang 63, PK4085 (*Tsa-lu* 34b.8)).

891 **are** Cheng 4357.14 and Chou 175.14 both omit 是 which has been brought over from PK4085 to replace 子 of S2614. PK876 has 阿師子是.

892 **understanding** ‘Comprehending and being aware of’. 之 seems to function here as a particle which serves to connect the verb to its object.

893 **If** See line 703n.

894 **. . . hell** To reduce this line to seven syllables, 地獄 could very easily be dropped without affecting the basic meaning.

896 **. . . himself** Literally, ‘Hated that he did not take his body and destroy it himself.’

897 **. . . himself** 擧身 means 五體[投地] *pañca-maṇḍala-namaskāra*.

898 **. . . head** See line 807n2.

901 **innate** ‘Heaven-born; natural.’ Hsü 43, Chou 176.5, *Tsa-lu* 35a.1 and Hiang 64 (following PK4085) have 天性.

905 **horrible** See line 664n.

906 **Sharp** *Tsa-lu* 35a.3 (misreading PK4085’s 楚) has 悲, ‘sad, sorrowful’.

908 **All I can do** ‘I know only to . . .’

weep and wail The text says clearly 號叫 ‘to call out; to command’ but context indicates that the author must have been thinking of 號咷.

909 **Since** 隔是, cf. 格是. See *T’ung-su pien*, p. 733. Iriya, Review, 179 says that it means 已是.

910 **mother** This line could easily be reduced to seven syllables by dropping 隨孃孃. PK4085 drops 兒亦.

913 **as though** 由如 = 猶如.

five Mount T’ais This is what the text says even though it sounds strange. Chou 176.10, Hiang 65, and *Tsa-lu* 35a.6 (following PK4085) have 大 for 太 (‘five huge mountains’) which does not improve matters significantly. Cf. T741.15b, where

PK3789 has ‘like Five Mount T’ai’s (→ Five Terraces Mountain) collapsing’ 由(= 猶)如五太(→ 臺)山崩(= 崩). I believe that the numeral has crept in because of confusion with Five Terraces Mountain (Wu-t’ai shan 五臺山). This mountain, which was the most famous pilgrimage site for Chinese Buddhists during the T’ang Dynasty, was well known to the inhabitants of Tun-huang. The wall-paintings of the Caves of the Thousand Buddhas include detailed panoramas in which it is depicted.

914 **... himself** See line 897n.

916 **... again** One would have expected that he *revived* after a long time or that he was dead for quite a long time and then revived. This is stated more clearly on T705.3. Also see T190.13 where the expression is as it should be: ‘After quite a long time, he revived.’ PK4085 has 兒 instead of 而.

920 **consciousness** Cf. 心地 (?). Lo, *Studies*, 768 explains this as 情然 but I do not know how to construe such a gloss.

922 **... senses** 性悟 → 惺 (or 醒) 悟.

923 **called upon** 問 glossed as 訪. Cheng 4358.2 has 向 which also makes sense. Written quickly, 問 is virtually indistinguishable from 向.

926 **majesty** *Prabhāva*.

928 **iron walls** See line 670n1.

929 **forests** *Tsa-lu* 35a.12, Hsü 123, and Chou 177.3 read 森森, following PK4085, but, as on T731.2, 森林 itself seems to have meant ‘in numerous ranks’.

931 **collected** 含 = 函 = 涵 = 浛 ‘water and mud’.

932 **features** 容皃 on S2614. *Not* ‘how could I stand [to look at]?’. + ‘Such harsh treatment.’

933 **confronts** 他 is a particle which appears between a verb and its object.
knives and swords See line 377n3.

934 **sword** See line 377n3. *Tsa-lu* 35b.1–2 prints 劍 for this and the previous note.

939 **ignorant** *Saṃmoha*.

940 **... compassion** *Mahā-kāruṇika*; *mahāmaitrī-mahākaruṇā*.

941 **knitted** 斂 → 歛 (as printed in Ta1312b.22), cf. Śāriputra line 390n1.
with sorrow Cf. 慘然 on T42.13.

942 **net ...** 輪(廻之)網, **saṃsāra jala*(?).

943 **chaff-gnats** 蠊蝨 → 糠蟁 (or 蟁 = 糠蚊 (?)). This is listed in Chiang 210 as a problem which awaits solution. To the best of my knowledge, there is no such word as ‘chaff-gnat’ in English but the translation should be clear enough nonetheless.
rushed against 兎 → 突.
spider’s web 望絲 → 網絲.

944 **In times past** The syntax here seems somewhat out of joint. I believe that the correct grammatical order should be 昔時多造罪 as it is given in PK4085 (Hiang 65, *Tsa-lu* 35b.7).

945 **As a result** Added in the translation.

947 **... person** *Bālaprthagjana*.

949 **... myself** N.B. PK4085 (Hiang 66 and *Tsa-lu* 35b.10) follows this after a blank space equal to the width of three lines with the words ‘the second scroll’ 卷第二! Since the scroll on which the text is written remains the same, it is possible that this refers to the second in a series of lost picture scrolls which the text was meant to match.

950 **eight classes ...** They are *deva*, *nāga*, *yakṣa*, *gandharva*, *asura*, *garuḍa*, *kinnara*, *mahoraga*.

951 **surrounded** 遶 = 繞, as printed in Chou 177.14 and Cheng 4358.10. See line 1268n2.

952 **... earth** Cf. line 90n.

953 **sufferers** The following verse passage explains why I have not specified this as ‘*her* sufferings’.

954 **holy wisdom** *Ārya-jñāna*.
955 **beings** *Sattva* which, because of the location, cannot be rendered in English by the standard translation, 'all living beings'.
956 **eight classes** See line 950n. + 'Composed.'
958 **pomp** 隱隱 glossed as 盛貌 or 衆多貌. Cf. Wu line 1442n.
circumstance 逸逸 glossed as 往來有次序. It is clear from the rhymes that this and the following few lines are defective.
959 **sight** Added to the translation.
961 **projecting high** 岌岌 glossed as 高貌.
963 **... at once** 'Halls' and 'doors' have been added to the translation.
965 **circle** Although I agree with the emendation given in T (cf. PK4085), I find this a rather odd simile.
966 **Commandingly** 俄俄 → 峨峨.
lion's *Siṃha*.
967 **Confidently** 偘偘 = 侃侃.
moved alone 虎行 → 狐行 as printed in Chou 178.5 and PK4085 (*Tsa-lu* 36a.3 and Hiang 66).
elephant king's *Gajapati*.
gait In Sanskrit literature, the elephant's gait is often noticed e.g. *gajagati*, *gaja-vraja*. The notion of 'circular' (迴) gait is probably best seen in the word *gajagāminī*, 'woman with an elephant-like walk'.
968 **... tune** 楊柳枝詞. See *Tz'u-p'u* 詞譜 (1715 edn) 1.30b: 'Name of a tune in the T'ang Music Academy.' 唐教坊曲名. Incidentally, the example cited in the *Tz'u-p'u* by Wen T'ing-yün 溫庭筠 is a heptasyllabic quatrain 七言絕句 (cf. the Introduction, pp. 22–3). Also see *Yüeh-fu tsa-lu* 樂府雜錄 (Shanghai, 1957), p. 41. 'Tune' is added in the translation.
969 **fluttered** 鑌芬 → 繽紛. This may well refer to the movements of a dance.
Plum Blossoms Falling *Yüeh-fu tsa-lu*, p. 34: 'The transverse flute is a barbarian musical [instrument]. Of old, there was a tune [for it called] "Plum Blossoms Falling."' 笛者,羌樂也,古有落梅花曲.
970 **Śakra** Or Indra.
token I prefer the reading of 諫 → 簡 (PK4085, T751n99) for 寶. Compare T735.10.
971 **tablet** After PK4085, see T collation note 99.
972 **... indescribable** *Anabhilāpyānabhilāpyaparivarta*. The translation reflects the meaning and diction but not the grammar of the original line. + 'It was a sight.'
973 **rescued** Or 救 → 就 'arrived at'.
974 **deities** Not deities and men (*devamanuṣya*).
... realms See line 950n.
975 **attendant** 持 → 侍 (cf. Chou 178.9, PK4085 (*Tsa-lu* 36a.7), PK876 and P2319).
generals ... I am interpreting as 四方大將, Saṃjñeya *et al.* (SH 176). In the *Mahābhārata*, the 四方神 are Indra, Yama, Varuṇa, and Vaiśravaṇa (= Kubera) but they are probably not intended here.
976 **appeared** Non-grammatical translation of 相 *lakṣaṇa*, 'mark, sign'.
hair *Ūrṇā-keśa*, one of the thirty-two attributes of a Buddha.
forms *Rūpa*.
977 **halo** *Vyomakaṃ*.
980 **fell ...** Etymologically, 'knelt Serindian (踯胡) fashion'. Cf. *Fei pieh-tzu* 1.21a.
981 **... palms** See Śāriputra line 390n2.
... feet *Vandanīya*... 'Respect' and 'feet' are added to the translation.
984 **jewels** 摩尼 *maṇi*, probably a pearl.
985 **lapis lazuli** *Vaiḍūrya*.
986 **water ...** *Aṣṭāṅga-upeta-ambhaḥ*. This refers to the eight lakes of meritorious deeds

in Paradise.

988 **nestled** This character is difficult to read. Cheng 4358.19 and Chou 179.2 have 狀. I prefer the reading in T, Ta1312c. 16, and PK4085 (misread in *Tsa-lu* 36b.1 as 快). It is possible, however, that 扶 should be emended to 浮, 'bob; float'.
beads ... 淚淚 → 纍纍(?).

990 **rose** 氣 → 起 (Hsü 123).

992 **hungry ghost** *Preta.*

1001 **... existence** In Avīci. 'The difference was intensified' is added to the English translation. The message that the author is attempting to convey here is that, in hell, the suffering is unmitigated while, as a hungry ghost, there is present the contrast between gratification and deprivation. It is this contrast which makes being a hungry ghost such a miserable proposition.

1003 **head** Iriya 72b emends 頭 → 腹(?). Certainly the hungry ghost is depicted in paintings as having a grossly distended abdomen. See, for example, the second section of the eighth scroll in the *Kita no tenjin engi* 北野天神縁起 published in Mushakōji Minoru 武者小路穣, *Emaki* 絵巻 (Tokyo, 1963), opposite p. 243. See also Ta4.223b and *Dainihon bukkyō zensho* 大日本佛教全書 (Tokyo, 1912, *ts'e* 148), p. 37b where hungry ghosts are expressly described as having a 'belly like a big mountain'. However, since Tsung Mi's 宗密 (780–841) commentary to the *Yü-lan-p'en sūtra* 盂蘭盆經疏, *chüan* B, does have 'head' instead of 'abdomen', I have not emended. Ta39.509a: '"Needle-throated ghost" is to say that it has a head big as a mountain and a throat like the eye of a needle.' This detail, I believe, lends credence to Lo's (*Studies*, 306ff) assertion that Tsung Mi's commentary was a principal source for the Tun-huang stories on Mu-lien.

1004 **three rivers** There are at least a dozen possibilities as to which 'three rivers' the author had in mind. It is likely that he had no specific group in mind but meant only 'an enormous amount of water'. For those who are interested in pursuing the Szechwan connection, Shu had its 'three rivers': the Min, the Fu, and the T'o 岷江, 涪江, 沱江.

1007 **clear** There is no need for emendation. S2614 and P2319 both have 涼 which is a variant orthography for 涼. PK4085 (*Tsa-lu* 36b.6) simply has 淸涼(= 涼)水. Cf. T739.4 and T743.1. + 'Some.'

1008 **river of pus** *Pūya-nadī.*

1011 **Mother** PK4085 (*Tsa-lu* 36b.7 and Hiang 67) does not have the character 見.

1012 **plight** Added to the translation.

1016 **urgency** 亦 → 急 as printed in Chou 179.9 and Cheng 4359.3.

1018 **donations ...** 信施 usually means the gifts of the lay believers to the *saṇgha* (community of monks).
maintain ... 安存, cf. *Ch'ü* nos. 59 and 608.

1019 **constant source** See line 491n.

1021 **mother** I would prefer not to replace 孃 with 阿 (PK4085).

1022 **and** This sentence is awkward. One would expect that 與 mean 'to give to' but one's hopes are dashed by the final two characters. 'There ... then come ... again' are added to the translation.

1023 **hurled up** 擲 glossed as 振 or 播, *prakṣepa*. Note that this word, in Sanskrit, also has the meaning 'launch'!

1026 **householder** *Gṛhapati.*

1027 **place** This is an exceptional occurrence of *ch'u* 處, cf. Wu line 168n.

1029 **... wrong time** That is, after noon (cf. line 273nn1 and 2 and Śāriputra line 25n). Begging for food at the proper time is called *upapadyamānakāla*.

1031 **use** PK4085 (*Tsa-lu* 36b.10) has 欲 'want, wish' instead of 用.

1035 **souls** Cf. 魂 (*yang* element) 魄 (*yin* element).

1036 **help** Added to the translation.

1041 **give** 以 = 與 which is as Chou 180.3 prints it and as written on PK4085.
1043 **impermanence** *Anitya.*
1044 **countenance** This line is unintelligible without a modicum of emendation. I have tentatively proposed the following: 金鞍 (*·ân*) → 金顏 (*ngan*) (which may have caused some confusion because it commonly was used to refer to a special type of fragrance or to the emperor's cap); 晶 (actually 皛 'white' on S2614, PK876, and PK4085) → 靚 (note the verb in the corresponding position in the parallel line); 珠心 → 朱玄(?), cf. 朱顏, 玄眉. N.B. Maudgalyāyana continues to speak (see T740.15).
1045 **appearance** P2319 has 白(?) instead of 貌.
1046 **a while** Chou 180.6 and Cheng 4359.9 both have 促且 .. 促且, 'we busy ourselves with'.
1047 **frittered** 由由 → 悠悠 (Chou 180.6).
sputtering ... Literally, 'revolving candle'. This is a favourite Buddhist metaphor for the ephemerality of human phenomena. A burning candle gives the illusion of a continuous flame but it is actually only a series of discrete moments of combustion.
1048 **seek not** 何覓, rhetorical question transposed into a negative statement. P2319 and Chou 180.7 give 不見, 'we see not'. Cheng 4359.10 (following PK4085) has 何不見, 'why do we not see?'(?). 'Even though' is added to the translation at the head of the next line.
1051 **stupid people** *Moha-puruṣa*; *abuddha.*
accumulate ... T reverses the order of 財多 on S2614.
1052 **... works** Literally, 'broadly to create causes (*hetu*)'.
future *Anāgata.*
1054 **two people** See Śāriputra line 1799n.
1055 The grammar of this line is somewhat problematical. *Tsa-lu* 37a.8 misreads 魚(?) for 莫 on PK4085. +'After which.'
bodies *Kāya*; *tanu*; *deha.*
1056 **breathe our last** I have translated 擗手 with a phrase that approximates its supposed level of diction. I have not encountered the expression elsewhere but believe that it is comparable to 撒手 in 撒手西歸, 撒手人間, 撒手長辭, etc. +'Fine.'
1057 **Who** Added in the translation. The force of 知 is very weak. P2319 simply has 有 instead of 知.
1058 **wise man** *Paṇḍita*; *prajñā-yukta*; *manīśin*, etc.
1063 **... monk** Literally, 'It is hard to encounter [a member of] the *ratnatraya* [here *saṅgha* alone] [engaged in] the field of blessedness [i.e. poverty] [P. *puññakkhetta*].' This interpretation is somewhat awkward. Since 'three' is a common number for lists of types of *puññakkheta* (e.g. showing (1) respect to monks, (2) gratitude to parents, (3) compassion to the poor), I am inclined to think that the appearance of 寶 in this line is rather gratuitous.
1064 **to** 交 is a sign of the imperative which, because of indirect discourse, has not been made evident in the translation.
1065 **give** 以 (S2614) will do just as well as 與 (P2319). Cf. line 1069n1. The two characters were used interchangeably in this sense.
exemplar *Ācārya.*
1067 **ineffableness** Chiang 72.
1069 **gave** PK4085 (*Tsa-lu* 37b.2) has 與 instead of 以.
grand vow *Mahā[bodhi-]praṇidhāna.*
1072 **begging** *Piṇḍāya carati*; *piṇḍa-pāta.*
table 'Ordinary; non-glutinous.' Hsieh's 153.140 emendations to 秔粮 are preferable to those given by the T editors.
1077 **after all** *Uttara.*

1080 **own** 卽 ‘very; none other than’. This character is missing in PK3789 (*Tsa-lu* 38a.1).

1081 **whole lot** Lo, *Studies*, 293 suggests 令 → 衆(?). S2614 does not have 心.

1082 **. . . hunger** PK3789 (*Tsa-lu* 38a.2) has 我今自救無蕣.
won’t I have transposed the rhetorical force of 況 into a negative.

1084 **offered** 將 is pre-transitive.
was in ‘Together with.’

1085 **raised** PK3789 lacks 擧.

1086 **sides** 伴 = 畔 (Hsü 43 and PK3789 (*Tsa-lu* 38a.3)). Cf. T293.2.
shielded P2319 has 將 ‘took’, S2614, PK876, and PK3789 have 鄣.

1087 **scooped** Having learned to eat Indian-style, I can verify that one does, indeed, make a ball of the rice in the palm by shaping it with the thumb (primarily) and a cradling effect of the fingers.

1089 **unfortunately** For 不那, see Śāriputra line 775n1.

1090 **obstructiveness** 鄣 (as given in PK3789 (*Tsa-lu* 38a.3)) = 障. *Varaṇa*, *āvaraṇa*. P2319 and PK876 have 部(?).

1093 **. . . understanding** *Śrāvaka*.
still ‘Now.’
wisdom *Jñāna*.

1094 **can** P2319 has 須 ‘must’ instead of 有 ‘there is’.

1100 **. . . pit** Literally, ‘hunger hole’, i.e. ‘hollow hunger; aching void’. This is an unusual expression, but compare Lu T’ung 盧仝 ‘Lunar Eclipse’ 月蝕詩 in *Yü-ch’uan-tzu chi* 玉川子集 (*SPTK*) 1.2a: ‘Not only does it fill up the hollow hunger, it also unwraps the sorrow encircling the heart.’ 不獨塡飢坑, 亦解堯心憂.

1102 **go slow . . .** Chiang 64. Chang Hsiang 228–9 explains 慢 together with 漫 and 謾 as meaning ‘vainly/simply/just/worthlessly’. P2319 has 謾, S2614 has 㥟. PK3789 (*Tsa-lu* 38a.8) has 滿承亡(?). ‘Getting any’ is added to the translation. LSY has pointed out that 忘承 would make for a better rhyme.

1106 **eating** P2319 lacks 喫飯 which reduces the line to seven syllables.

1107 **fell to the ground** Chiang 48; also see Wu line 352n.

1109 **. . . mother** In PK3789, the preceding four lines are divided into six prose sentences and are quite different in wording (cf. Iriya 80n61). In particular, the last part says ‘cried out tearfully to his mother’ 哭言阿孃 which would indicate that the next few lines (Iriya has the quotation extend eight lines) are addressed to his mother. I have not construed them to be so in the translation because S2614 is ambivalent on this point, because many of the comments in these lines elsewhere belong to the narrator and, most important, because having Maudgalyāyana verbally chastise his mother seems imprudent and improbable. I would, however, agree to rearrange the next four lines as being spoken by Maudgalyāyana. In my estimation, from this point all the way down to where the mother speaks is a generalized sermonizing intended to edify the audience directly, particularly from ‘The people of the world . . .’ on. There is a messy problem with tense in the translation because the narrator keeps skipping back to descriptions of the mother.

1110 **world . . .** *Jambūdvīpa*.

1111 **seven feet** 往 is supernumerary, cf. PK3789 which does not have it. I am uncertain as to the precise significance of ‘seven feet’ in regard to the ‘spirit-light’. Whether in Buddhist or non-Buddhist texts, it generally is the height of a man of spirit.

1112 **took it to be** Cf. 將爲, 將謂 (Iriya, *Index*, 16) and Mandarin 以爲.

1116 **Now** PK3789 (*Tsa-lu* 38b.2) has ‘Now, the son’ 兒今 instead of 如今.

1118 **people of the world** *Manuṣya*; P. *nara*.
envy 姤 → 妬 = 妒(!).

1119 **three mires** See line 5n2.

1122 **mundane world** *Laukika*.
universe *Sahā*.

1125 **. . . others** Literally, 'it is clearly known [that it is her own] karmic retribution [and is] not due to other causes [or people]'.

1126 **impartiality** *Samatābhiprāya*.

everything *Sarva*.

1127 **single** 壽 → 專 (as printed in Chou 182.12 and PK3789 (*Tsa-lu* 38b.7)).

1128 **. . . one** PK3789 (*Tsa-lu* 38b.8) has 慳貪心.

greedy *Rāga*.

1129 **Pure Land** *Sukhāvatī*, presided over by Amitābha.

1132 **. . . Teacher** This line appears to be defective. S2614 has 阿行邪.

1133 **. . . mother** 耶 → 阿 (as printed in Chou 183.1, Cheng 4360.8 and PK3789 (*Tsa-lu* 38b.10)).

1135 **flames** PK3789 (*Tsa-lu* 38b.11) has 大火 instead of 見火.

burned me T has 損傷 'wounded [me]' which makes perfectly good sense. PK3789 has 腸 instead of 傷, hence 'scorched my innards'.

1136 **display** The manuscripts and published editions differ somewhat in the reading of this and the following line. Here, with Chou 183.3 and Cheng 4360.9, I read 去 'get rid of' → 表. PK3789 has 'how could I?' 豈得.

1137 **. . . past** I follow PK3789 for this line: 只應過去有餘央(→ 殃), cf. Chou 183.3.

1140 **her** Iriya 75b imputes these conditions to Maudgalyāyana.

1143 **river . . .** PK3789 has twenty-nine additional characters inserted here which serve mainly to enhance Maudgalyāyana's filiality by having him carry his mother to the Ganges on his back.

wide 澖 = 闊 as printed in all the other published editions.

1144 **Ganges** *Gaṇgā*. The translation does not accurately reflect the grammar.

1147 **cool** But note that all the other printed editions, following PK876, PK3789, P2319 and S2614, have 冷 instead of 之.

1148 **greenglass** *Vaiḍūrya*.

1149 **torrent** PK3789 (*Tsa-lu* 39a.4), 潤澤 'fertile swamp', is to be preferred.

1151 **waiting** Literally, 'looking [out for]'. PK3789 (*Tsa-lu* 39a.4), however, has 及 which gives a superior reading. + 'Requisite.'

1152 **immediately** 便 rather than 更, following PK876, PK3789 and P2319.

1161 **. . . side** PK3789 (*Tsa-lu* 39a.6–7) adds 跚跪合掌, 'he joined his palms in reverent greeting and knelt respectfully'. Cf. T743.11 and see line 1193n1 and 2.

1163 **. . . not good** *Aśubham* [*karma*].

1166 **drinks** PK3789 (*Tsa-lu* 39a.8) has 飲.

1167 **. . . calamity** This must have seemed awkward to the various editors for they all give different readings.

1169 **. . . food** The position of the last two characters is reversed in Chou 183.11 and Cheng 4360.15. + 'It is true that.'

1170 **only** I parse as 無過 . . . 始得. LSY has mentioned that 無過 may mean 'there is no better [way] than to', hence 'the best thing is to . . .'.

1171 **. . . feast** See line 11n2.

1173 **not** Chiang 191 wishes to treat 不 as a particle without negative meaning, hence 'may it be held?'.

1176 **prescribed** PK3789 (*Tsa-lu* 39a.11) drops 須.

1179 **. . . meditation** P. *nisajjā*; P. *paṭisallīyati*; P. *viveka*.

monasteries 'Hill' stands for 'monastery'.

end . . . 戒下 → 解夏.

1180 **achieve . . .** Literally, 'attain the Way'.

1181 **Devadatta's** The son of King Droṇodana and a cousin of Śākyamuni with whom he competed by cultivating supernatural powers. He was said to have been swallowed up in hell for his evil behaviour towards the Buddha. Later, however, a tradition grew up in which it was predicted that he would be a future Buddha known as Devarāja.

1182 **rejoices** I suppose because he is free of the complaints of a large number of his charges on this day. 歡喜日 is a synonym for 解夏日 (see line 7n1), while 歡喜會 is a synonym for the *Ullambana Festival.
day P2319 and PK876 both have 日 at the end of the Chinese sentence.

1186 **read aloud** 轉 in this expression is generally explained as describing the action of unrolling the scrolls.
good deed *Kuśala-mūla*. '[Planted] good roots' would be a more accurate translation.

1188 **basins of food** To interpret 盆 as a vessel filled with offerings of food, clothing, and money, as the Chinese have constantly done, is quite likely a literalization of a phonetic symbol used to transliterate the foreign word designating the festival which is held on the fifteenth day of the seventh month. See line 11n2.

1189 **mother** Iriya 75b suggests 子 → 姿(?), hence 'did not see any signs of his mother again'. Neither Ta1313c.23 nor Cheng 4360.18 have 相 but the text as given in T makes perfectly good sense. Cf. T743.12.

1192 **circled . . .** *Pradakṣiṇāṃ kṛtvā.*

1193 **. . . greeting** See Śāriputra line 390n2.
knelt respectfully 'After the Serindian 胡 fashion.'

1197 **fiery** Cf. T743.5.

1199 **Or** See Śāriputra line 260n.

1204 **body . . .** PK3789 (*Tsa-lu* 39b.4–5), PK876, S2614, P2319, and S3704 all have 餓鬼之身.
transformed *Vartana*; *pravartana*; *vṛtti*. PK3789 makes clearer the fact that Nīladhi has been transformed *out* of her body as a hungry ghost by writing 轉却.

1206 **dog** PK3789 specifies here and throughout this section that it is a bitch 母狗.
. . . mother PK3789 (*Tsa-lu* 39b.5) drops 者.

1209 **gate** PK876 drops 家 here and on T744.1.
a All the other published texts as well as P2319 and S2614 have 一 after 有. 'Certain' has been added to the translation.

1210 **cassock** *Kaṣāya.*

1212 **clear instructions** Instead of 勅, which sounds too imperial, I follow PK3789 and PK876 which have 明教. Cf. T743.9.

1215 **. . . circle** There are nearly as many variations of this clause as there are manuscripts and printed editions. S2614 has 逦 instead of 匝 given by T. My interpretation, which reconciles several of the variants, is as follows: 行依匝合. Note that 衣 → 依 ('following; according to') = 於, the latter character appearing in this position in several of the texts. 匝合, though intelligible, is unusual. 匝洽, the meaning of which is not applicable here ('thoroughly to imbue') may have been its inspiration. Cf. 迨匝 on T547.4.

1220 **if** Cf. Chiang 148–52.

1221 **infernal paths** 冥路 is missing from PK3789 (*Tsa-lu* 39b.9).

1224 **three mires** See line 5n2.

1225 **rather** The ms (S2614) has 寧卜你作 instead of 你作. 寧 . . . 寧 (as on PK3789) is a common form of disjunctive question in Tun-huang colloquial.

1228 **dumbness** 音 → 暗. Dogs are, of course, normally dumb. That the dog is able to speak to Maudgalyāyana in this particular case is due to a special dispensation of the Buddha.

1229 **. . . lying** *Catur-vidha īryā-pathaḥ*; *gate sthite niṣaṇṇe śayite*; *caṇkramati, tiṣṭhati, niṣīdati, śayyāṃ kalpayati. Ta-ch'eng pen-sheng hsin-ti-kuan ching* 大乘本生心地觀經, Ta3.297a: 'Whether walking, standing, sitting, or lying, to endure all sorts of torments.' 行住坐臥, 受諸苦惱.
excrement *Aśuddha.*

1230 **. . . eaves** 長流 could be rendered as 'long currents' but it does not make sense in the present context unless we somehow understand it to mean 'ditches' or 'gutters'. I have tentatively emended to 長霤.

1232 **Three Treasures** See Śāriputra line 148n.

evening Cheng 4361.5 and Chou 184.14 have a very different understanding of this passage. The correctness of T is borne out by P2319 and PK876 which have 夜 instead of 莫.

1235 **away** S2614, S3704, P2319, and PK876 all have 往 instead of 住.

1237 **repenting** *Kṣama*; BHS. *deśanā karaṇīyā*.

1238 **prohibitions** *Śīla*.

1240 **once again** Added to the translation.

1241 **perfect** *Sampūrṇa*.

1243 **Central** 衆 → 中 (P2319, PK876, and added as a note on S2614). The 'Central Kingdom' here refers to India, not China. Cf. S4654.

1244 **Law ...** *Buddhadharma*.

good mind Technical expression.

1246 **cultivate blessings** See line 27n2.

1247 **... trees** See Śāriputra line 9n.

1250 **path ...** 業道 *karma-patha*.

examining Although it is possible to render 觀占 ('behold-divine'), the connotations of the latter member are inappropriate to the Buddha. I suggest the cognate 覘 which may be glossed as 視 or 觀.

1253 **... karma** *Trividha-dvāra*. Literally, 'inspecting from the way of the three karmas'.

1254 **... sins** It is obvious that, with or without the 人 which the T editors (in spite of collation note 145) could not have found in PK3789 because the ms ends before this point, this clause is corrupt and requires fundamental emendation. Waley's (233) translation 'I do not find a scrap of sin left' is so imprecise and lacking in justification that his suggestion (264n164) that 私 → 絲 (or 緦?) is suspect. My translation follows the text as given in T with a single emendation, 率 → 無, which I justify on the ground of orthographic similarity and by the clear contrast with 有 at the top of the same line.

1257 **... back** Iriya 80n66 has identified Maudgalyāyana's speech here as having the form of a 'Hymn on the Theme "Let Us Go Back!"' 歸去來讚. In addition to his reference to P2066 (Ta85.1261), see also *Ch'ü* nos. 190–203 and *Tsa-lu*, A82ab, a series of calls to leave the mundane world, which is no place to dwell, and go to the Pure Land. The calls are preceded by the refrain 'Let Us Return' (*kuei-ch'ü-lai*). The sentiment and the style are precisely the same as in Maudgalyāyana's speech. There are two articles by Yoshioka Gihō 吉岡義豊 on the Buddhist origins of the 'Let Us Return' theme in Chinese literature: 關于歸去來辭 ['On T'ao Yüan-ming's Kuei-ch'ü-lai-tz'u'], [*Journal of Chinese Literature*] 中國文學報 6(April, 1957), 25–44 where he says that the expression is a translation of the Sanskrit word *namaḥ* and 帰去来の辞与佛教 ['Kuei-ch'ü-lai-tz'u and Buddhism'], [*Oriental Studies in Honour of Juntaro Ishihama on the Occasion of His Seventieth Birthday*] 石濱古稀紀念東洋學論叢 (Osaka, 1958), pp. 610–22. Chow Tse-tsung 周策縱, 釋"無以"與"來" ['A Study of the Chinese Function Words *wu-i* and *lai*'], (Madison, Wisc., 1965 – mimeographed copy deposited in the Harvard-Yenching Library: R5143/1373.3), 36ff is an extremely elaborate analysis of the grammatical properties of the component elements in the expression *Kuei-ch'ü-lai*.

1258 **... remain in** For this line, cf. T482.5.

1259 **Birth ...** Cf. 生住滅 *utpāda-sthiti-bhaṅga/nirodha/vikāra*. The more usual formula is 生住異滅, 'birth, dwelling, decay (*anityatā/vyaya*), death'.

1260 **... place to stay** *Apratiṣṭhita*.

1261 **finest** *Śivaḥ*.

1262 **lead** All of the other published editions as well as PK876, P2319, and S2614 have

行 → 引 which is preferable, even though 奉行 'to carry out [the Buddha's teachings]' is a common Buddhist expression (see the last line of this text).

1263 **heavenly maidens** *Devakanyā*; *apsaras*.

1265 **... beginning** Of the transmission of the Law of the Buddha after his enlightenment. + 'The Buddha.'
stanzas *Gāthā*.

1266 **... disciples** [五]俱輪, see Śāriputra line 8n.

1267 **... preached** This no doubt refers to the present 'sūtra', i.e. transformation text loosely based on the **Avalambana Sūtra*. I have given the parenthetical expression in italics because, on P2319, it is clear that it has been added to the text as an explanatory note. 'Was preached' is added to the translation. Hsieh 155.165 makes the suggestion that 時 should be emended to 說, hence 'When this sūtra was preached.'
84,000 八萬 stands for 八萬四(千) which is the supposed number of atoms in the human body. As such, it was a frequently used figure for a large number of various phenomena or objects.
laymen *Upāsaka*.

1268 **laywomen** *Upāsikā*; 姨 → 夷.
circling around *Anvāhiṇḍya*; *samantataḥ*. 'The Buddha' and 'to him' are added to the translation.
making obeisance 作禮(而去) is a standard formula at the end of a sūtra.

1269 **receptivity** *Abhyupagamana*; *saṃpratyaya*; *abhiśraddhāna*.

1270 **... faith** Standard formula for the closing of a sūtra.

1272 **Written** I.e. 'copied'.

1273 **... period** May 26, 921.
Hsüeh An-chün Independently of Iriya 80n69, I have spotted this name on P2054r 'Songs of the Hours' 十二時曲 where he is also the copyist: 'Copied by the student, Hsüeh An-chün, on June 21, 924.' 同光貳年 甲申歲, 蕤賓之月 蓂彫二葉 學子薛安俊書. I have also noticed his name on several other documents from Tun-huang. It appears twice in an inscription on PK8668, 'Text Exhorting One to Keep the Commandments' 勸戒文, which is dated February 13, 920. S2614v has a register of monks belonging to the Pure Land Monastery. Hsüeh's name is not included. There are at least three possible reasons why this might have happened: the register and the transformation text are from different times; Hsüeh was still a novice; he was only temporarily dwelling in the monastery as a student. It is most unfortunate that another line which follows the colophon of S2614 has been torn off and is only barely visible.

1275 **Chang Pao-ta** As may be seen from the photograph of the ms published by Keiki Yabuki, this name appears in lighter ink and seems to be by a different hand.

WU TZU-HSÜ

S328
T1–28
P3213
P2794v
S6331
Partial translation in Waley 25–52
Translated in Iriya 135–65

2 **six braves** Han 韓, Chao 趙, Wei 魏, Yen 燕, Ch'i 齊, and Ch'u 楚.

3 **eight barbarians** 八□. We may tentatively supply 狄 or 方. The geography section 釋地 of the *Erh-ya* 爾雅 (*SPTK*) B.11b lists of barbarians state that there were eight *ti* tribes in the north. If 八方, this would mean 'in the eight directions [i.e. compass points]'.

6 **over his people** Added to the translation.

10 **Bright Terrace** Cf. *Kuan-tzu*, 'Questions of Duke Huan' 管子, 桓公問 (*SPTK*) 18.3b: 'The Yellow Emperor initiated discussions at "Bright Terrace".' 黃帝立明臺之議者.

... matters 'Affairs' and 'matters' are added to the translation.

12 **Gate of Heaven** 天門. The location of this place is as enigmatic as its name. There are a number of mountains in China (including several in Chekiang, Anhwei, and Hunan) with this name, the most southerly of which is that located thirty *li* to the south of Ta-yung 大庸 District Town in Hunan.

Huai-hai 淮海. The outlet and channel of the Huai River which drains part of Hunan and northern Anhwei (cf. 'Contribution of Yü' 禹貢 in the *Book of History*, Legge, III.108).

13 **sun and moon** The shore of the ocean to the east, whence the sun and moon rise. I would prefer, however, to emend to 日本 'Japan' which would parallel the 'Buddhist kingdoms' on the west.

15 **correct** The ms (P3213), which is certainly corrupt, has 開山 ⸢而⸣ 川 (→ 川而□) 地軸. Emendation is based on marks beside and below 而. I have tentatively supplied 正 for the missing character.

16 **differentiate** 辯 → 辨, cf. *To-so* 57.4, 辨.

throne 紫極 means the seat of the emperor.

17 **Imperial Gate** I.e. the capital – not the Dipper in Ursa Major. *To-so* 57.5 prints 闕 instead of 闕.

18 **assistants** Iriya's (135a) emendation 負 → 輔 is correct. Both were pronounced in the rising (上) tone.

six dragons The six lines of the diagram *ch'ien* 乾, ☰, representing heaven, which is the first of the sixty-four diagrams in *The Book of Changes*. See Confucius's commentary in the *t'uan* 彖, Legge (Sung), p. 3: '(The sages) grandly understand (the connexion between) the end and the beginning, and how (the indications of) the six lines (in the hexagram) are accomplished, (each) in its season. (Accordingly) they mount (the carriage) drawn by those six dragons at the proper times, and drive through the sky.' 大明終始, 六位時成. 時乘六龍以御天.

19 **harvests** 和 → 禾 (Iriya 135a).

21 **... earth** I.e., the wind and rain were gentle.

22 **neatly and impressively** Cf. 蹌蹌濟濟.

Indeed Though uncertain of its precise meaning, I believe that 然 should be considered as a sentence-initial particle (cf. Chiang 189).

27 **emotions** Hsü 32 casts doubt on 清 → * 請 given by the T editors. I tentatively propose 清 → 情 instead.

nations Probably the same as the 'principalities' mentioned near the beginning of the second paragraph of the piece. 'Willingly' has been added to the translation.

32 **with** I have tentatively supplied 以 for the missing character in the text. The resulting 以致 is not to be taken in its usual sense of 'with the result that'. I consider 致 as a gerund and give 誠 as a possible gloss.

34 **tyrannous** 僭 'cunning/crafty' is an error for 僣 which is a vulgar form of 僭.

41 **... wife** Cf. T405.9.

44 **Eastern Sea** 東海 is the ocean area south of the mouth of the Yangtze and north of the Taiwan straits.

flood It is nearly impossible to relate this clause to the surrounding text. I have done so only at the cost of having to add 'a tree with their plentiful waters ...' to the translation. The proverb would be much better off without it.

49 **sixteen** 二八, cf. T5.16.

50 **... moon** Cf. *Ch'ü* no. 3, 'eyebrows like the new moon' 眉如初月!

53 **... pearls** Cf. T139.11. On P3213 璫 is written as 㯗 (hanging, split, or swept clean). Cf. T139.11 which has 'ears like hanging pearls'. 耳如懸珠.

54 **... knees** This may sound grotesque to the reader, yet it is precisely what the author meant to say. In ancient India, *dīrgabāhu* ('long-armed') was an honorific and a sign of high qualities. This also accounts for one of the most noticeable features of the heroes in the Indonesian shadow plays. The strange, initial description of Liu Pei 劉備 in *San-kuo chih yen-i* 三國志演義, however, may be traced back to his biography in the 'Treatise on Shu' 蜀志 (*PNP*) 2.1b: 垂手下膝. In C. H. Brewitt-Taylor's translation, *Romance of the Three Kingdoms*, vol. I (of two) (Rutland, Vermont, 1959), p. 4, part of the description reads: 'His ears were long, the lobes touching his shoulders, and his hands hung down below his knees.' Cf. 'The Biography of Liu Yao' 劉曜, *History of Chin* (*PNP*) 103.1a: 垂手過膝. Whether Indian influence was operative in these two instances remains a moot question.
ten 拾 = 十, cf. T640.3, T789.6.
slender Cf. 纖手 in *Yu-hsien k'u*, p. 3.

55 **arrangements** 平章. This term also occurs on pp. 27 and 28 of this story and half-a-dozen other times in T. In the *Book of History* (*Thirteen Classics*, 2.6b), these two characters mean 'distinguish/differentiate clearly'. During the T'ang, they were also used as the name of an official position. In T'ang popular literature, however, the phrase usually means 'to plan, to deliberate'. In certain instances, it also had the connotation of 'to make marriage arrangements' as in *Yu-hsien k'u*, p. 27 and *T'ai-p'ing kuang-chi* 太平廣記 (Peking, 1959), 281 (no. 10), 2242–3: 'The aunt said, "I have a niece surnamed Cheng who was orphaned when she was still young and who was left with my sister to be brought up. She is very good-looking and quite well-mannered. I ought to make her a proposal of marriage for you."' 姑曰. 吾有一外甥女子姓鄭. 早孤. 遺吾妹鞠養. 甚有容質. 頗有令淑. 當爲兒平章.

60 **... girl** The storyteller does not supply us with this information. Note also the clumsy use of the demonstrative 其 which recurs at the beginning of the next line in the printed text. Cf. I. T. Zogrof's remarks on this particle in Lev N. Men'shikov, *Bian'ven o vozdaianii za milosti* (Moscow, 1972), vol. II, pp. 37–8.

69 **beyond measure** For 昇 = 勝, see Chiang 48.

78 **If** 忽若(爾) = 或若. See Chiang 148–51. Also compare p. 3, last line (not mentioned by Chiang).

81 **Will not** 可不 = 豈不, Chiang 166.

84 **reprove** 諫交 = 諫教.

87 **shot back** There is no quotative verb in the text.
Has ... not The T editors emend 可不 to 何不 but this is unnecessary. In the previous line (for which see line 81n) and on T43.6, there are similar usages. Also note T90.1 which duplicates exactly the present line: 可不聞道.

89 **... recover** See Maudgalyāyana line 888n2.

95 **Wei Ling** P3213 breaks off here. What follows after the gap is S6331. One would expect that, in the large gap which occurs here, there would be an angry reaction by the King to Wu Shê's remonstrance. Then he would have him imprisoned. Reminded by Wei Ling of the danger of the existence of Wu Shê's two sons, the King would have him write letters to them. The letters would say that, if the sons returned to the capital, the father would be set free. The following, much-mutilated passage begins with Tzu-shang, who is in the Kingdom of Cheng, reading his father's letter.

96 **swiftly** Enough of the missing character is visible to determine that it has the 辶 radical. There are many words (e.g. 速, 适, etc.) with this radical and the meaning 'swift' (which is appropriate here). Another possibility is the disjunctive particle *nai* 迺 which would serve to reinforce the meaning of 果. In that case 'swiftly' could simply be dropped from the translation.

98 **world** A crude attempt at reconstruction of the ten missing characters here might be 挂之魂, 即可免脫與世相(?).

100 **... has been** 乞鄭王救父，乃見王曰，父被(?). My crude reconstruction here and just below is based chiefly on what transpires in lines eleven and twelve on T22.

102 **to return** Added to the translation.

104 **... Cheng** 臣實無方. 願王與臣設計. 鄭(?).

106 **If you do not** 於大窂(→牢)遠使將書, 云捨慈父之罪. 不(?). N.B. except for several of the initial words that are partially visible, none of the reconstructions given in lines 98–106n, 129n and 132n make any pretence whatever to being the actual missing words. A modest claim of accuracy regarding content can, however, be made because of internal parallels within the present version of the story and because of external parallels in other versions.

115 **ruthless** Compare 嚴迅 and 嚴訊(迅), T59.5 and 14.

116 **exigencies** Hsü 110 suggests that 意 → 急. The translation hovers between the two possibilities.

120 **close** 迸委 → 詳委. The final character means 'to know'. Cf. line 1301n.

127 **rashly thinks** 妄相 → 妄想.

deceive 下脫, cf. T367.6 and T368, fourth line from end.

129 **... will certainly be** 二, 如往楚救父, 則必見(?).

132 **... father** 我兄弟, 至楚則必與父同陷罪網(?).

133 **like** 由 = 猶.

134 **thrashing about** 盪 in the sense of 'to move' 動 or 'to shake' 搖.

fountain But see T7.0 where 泉 means little more than 'a body of water'.

... in a kettle 游鑊 or 釜 seems plausible. This is the end of S6331. In the lengthy lacuna which follows, the two brothers would agree that Wu Tzu-shang return to Ch'u and to his death as a demonstration of filial piety and that Wu Tzu-hsü remain alive to carry out revenge. When the latter does not appear in Ch'u with Wu Tzu-shang, the King becomes anxious and dispatches a messenger to bring him back. The messenger pursues Wu Tzu-hsü but the latter shoots arrows at him and succeeds in capturing him. What follows must be the conclusion of Wu Tzu-hsü's instructions to the messenger.

135 The following is from S328 (with some additions and corrections coming from P2794v – between T7.4 and T12.14).

137 **... at it** I am indebted to Iriya 136b for my understanding of this sentence. S328 has 麁 instead of 麤.

139 **rope** This detail occurs neither in the *Wu Yüeh ch'un-ch'iu* nor in the *Yüeh chüeh shu.*

143 **K'uai-chi Mountain** Southeast of modern Shao-hsing 紹興 in Chekiang Province.

146 **both of us** 惣 = 摠 = 總.

147 **distrusting** 擬 → 疑 (?). It is possible that, without emending, we may understand 擬 as 'take aim at' or 'draw a bead on'. See Śāriputra line 1605n.

149 **your** N.B. 你.

151 **Emperor** 帝 (!) occurs indiscriminately.

struck ... Cf. T45.2, T53.12, and T295.10.

152 **insolent** 勃逆 = 悖逆.

159 **punished** This would seem to be a misuse of the term 徒刑. Wu Shê and Tzu-shang are clearly about to be executed whereas 徒刑 only refers to a particular statute which specified detainment for various periods of time and forced labour. See *Tz'u-hai, yin* 258.

160 **When ...** 當 = 從前, see Chiang 142. Waley 26 manages to convey the sense of this passage but wrenches the grammar of the Chinese in doing so: '"Had I but listened to my younger brother's advice, I would not have come all this way only to share in my father's execution."' 不 is taken by Waley to govern 遠來 instead of 用.

163 **know ...** 知 presents problems. Waley 26: 'But now it is too late to repent'(?). I believe that this sentence means approximately the same as 知復何言 which occurs

on T14.8 and T15.16, that is, literally, 'what more do I know to say' hence 'I don't know what to do about it' hence 'there is nothing I can do about it'.

if See line 78n. This clause may be literally translated as 'if the Way of Heaven be opened [after having been blocked]'.

168 **. . . proclamation** Waley 28: 'The King of Ch'u issued a proclamation ordering[?] the arrest of Wu Tzu-hsü. How does this passage go?' and has a note, p. 254, which says this is a cue for a fresh performer. I have found no evidence to justify this interpretation. Although it bears a superficial resemblance to the formula which occurs before verse passages in the transformation texts, 處 meaning 'place', hence 'situation, case, time', is also found apart from the formula on T623.11 and T739.15 but there without the 若爲 following it. The meaning of 處 itself is discussed at greater length in the Introduction, its appendix, and in *Transformations*. For the present, we may say that in every other case where 處 occurs as part of the verse-introductory formula, it is preceded by a sentence which describes an action or series of actions which has already been narrated in the prose or (less often) will be narrated in the verse. Waley's translation is thus impossible because: (1) Wu Tzu-hsü is not captured, (2) the addition of 'ordering' is unjustified. Neither 勅 nor 曰 ever occurs after the verse-introductory formula. I view the occurrence of 若爲 here as an anomaly which has been inserted (clumsily albeit) into the narrative under the influence of genuine *pien-wen* style. Note that 若爲 on T4.11 occurs apart from the formula (see the appendix for other citations). Chou 302.9 punctuates '. . . 子胥. 處若爲勅曰:'. It *is* tempting to translate 捉 as 'capture' or 'arrest' for it occurs frequently in the 'Transformation on Han General Wang Ling' with that meaning. But see Chiang 174–5 where it is given as a T'ang colloquial equivalent of the pre-transitive 把. In attempting to translate this passage, it must also be reiterated that Wu Tzu-hsü does avoid capture. As such, 遂捉 could hardly mean 'then arrested'. The sentence in our text is quite similar to a line from the first 'Rhapsody on the Swallow' 鷰子賦, T250.13, where 捉我支配 = 把我支配. 處, following this interpretation, would be read in the rising tone instead of in the falling tone as it is in the verse-introductory formula. Admittedly, the two 勅 in such close proximity come out rather awkwardly in translation. I would venture to say only that the author was not a master of syntax. T18.6 has 勅召曰 preceding the proclamation of a king. This is more like what we would expect. To add to our worries, in the very next line, we have an equally annoying construction, 戶封千邑戶, which surely must mean 封邑千戶 (Chiang 17) or 邑封千戶 (Hsü 32).

171 **plotted . . .** Waley 28 translates 徒(圖)謀社稷 as 'when he should have been planning the welfare of the realm', probably considering it somehow parallel to 父事於君. I prefer a different translation for the following reasons: (1) 圖謀 is generally pejorative; (2) the sense of the preceding and succeeding clauses would seem to operate against such a translation; (3) it is difficult to justify the insertion of 'when he should have' on the basis of the Chinese.

cruel 暴虎 (乕 on S328) → 暴虐 (Hsü 32).

176 **thousand households** Chiang 9. S328 actually has 千 (crossed out) 邑万戶.

179 **followed** T unnecessarily adds 後 after 然 which, of itself, means 後. See Chiang 17.

entire clan 九族. Four generations above and below the present generation as explained in the commentary 傳 to the 'Canon of Yao' 堯典 in the *Book of History* (*Thirteen Classics*) 2.6b: 'From great-great-grandfather to great-great-grandson.' 上自高祖下至玄孫.

180 **arresting officer** 所由, see Chiang 17 and J. J. L. Duyvendak, Review of Rotours, *Fonctionnaires*, *TP* 38 (1948), 299. E. Pulleyblank, in a note to H. W. Bailey, tr. and ed., *Indo-Scythian Studies: Khotanese Texts*, vol. IV, *Saka Texts from Khotan in the Hedin Collection* (Cambridge, 1961), p. 137, translates the term as 'those responsible'. On T219.11, it is made clear that one of their duties was to perform arrests:

捕賊官及捉事所由等.

brought ... In spite of Chiang's elaborate defence, the T editors' emendation * 科徵 → 科徵 'collect taxes according to statute' is wrong. It should be 科懲.

181 **constantly** Waley 28 and Iriya 137b (with hesitation) both interpret 盡日 as 'at once'. The usual gloss, however, is 終日 'the whole day long'. + 'The offender.'

182 **... capital** The text is unclear as to what the King is to be informed of and who is to be escorted in fetters to the capital. I have assumed that this refers to the careless officials but Wu Tzu-hsü may have been intended.

183 **circulation** A small mark to the right of 行 on S328 indicates that it should be elided.

184 **... effect** Waley 28 is certainly mistaken in translating 水楔不通 as 'the waterways were wedged with ships'. The phrase occurs later in this story (T19, last line but three) where the T editors correctly mark the 楔 as being a homophonous exchange for 泄. The result is a very common saying. Cf. T39.7 and see *Su-yü k'ao-yüan* 10b. The translation is intentionally a little bit odd to indicate the defective Chinese. One further minor note concerning Waley's translation of this sentence is that 既 does not equal 卽 and so cannot be translated as 'no sooner than'.

189 **wild** The T editors indicate that *mang-tang* 莽蕩 is the name of a particular mountain. Perhaps they were thinking of 芒碭山 in Kiangsu southeast of Tang-shan District 碭山. From other occurrences of the expression (T16.1, T731.1), it is possible to determine its approximate meaning which is 'enormous, wild, vast [mountains/walls]'. Chou 302.14 is correct in not indicating that it is a proper name. Cf. line 811n below. As for the geography of this story, it would be well to advise the reader that it is impossible to understand precisely where things are supposed to be happening. For the real geography of the period, see Albert Hermann, *An Historical Atlas of China* (Chicago, 1961), pp. 6–7 and the end papers of Lin Han-ta 林漢達, *Revised Romance of the Eastern Chou Kingdoms* 東周列國志新編 (Peking, 1956) which, by the way, has a fresh look at Wu Tzu-hsü in chapters 80–90.

192 **in peril** 屈厄 means approximately the same as 困厄 'predicament'.

193 **... all-embracing** This is the first half of what might be called a *hsieh-hou-yü* 歇後語: 'The net of Heaven stretches everywhere, its meshes are wide, but nothing escapes them.' 天網恢恢疏而不漏. The saying occurs in its original form in *Lao-tzu* (*SPTK*) 2.18a: 天網恢恢疏而不失.

194 **take refuge** 投竄. Literally, 'to escape and hide' 逃匿.

196 **... wilderness** 逈 is vulgar for 迥 so 逈 must be even more vulgar. 連翩 means 'to fly about continuously and urgently'. One might possibly describe Wu Tzu-hsü in such a manner. But perhaps 連綿 'unbroken' was intended.

197 **river-barrier** Also written 天塹. This expression may refer to any natural depression in the earth's surface which presents an obstacle to free travel. It is most often used with reference to the Yangtze.

198 **very heavens** 雲漢. Literally, 'Milky Way'.

199 **boat** 舩 is vulgar for 船.

remote place 隈際 ≡ 猥地, see Chiang 145, *Ch'ü* no. 506.

201 **High Heaven** T has 下倉(蒼) from which I can make no sense. S328 and Chou 303.3 have 上蒼. See also Chiang 149 and Hsü 32.

202 **difficulties** 留難 sounds strange enough for Iriya 137b to be prompted to consider the first character as unreadable. Most likely, it is a carry-over from the Buddhist concept of 'obstruction of the performance of good works'. There is also the question of how to understand 逆 in the preceding line. It is possible that we should render 'If High Heaven *understands* [see line 339n2] my heart' (cf. T3.16–4.1 and T8.9), in which case there may be some error in this line, e.g. 可免 'can avoid ...'. Another possibility is that the meaning intended is 'my life will be hard to preserve' 生難留 and that the syntax has been warped to accommodate the *-an* rhyme.

204 **... causes** The text sounds as suspiciously Buddhist as my translation.
207 **press forward** 前邉. Cf. T7.10, 邉前. Also see T37.6.
in hiding 隈形 ≡ 猥身 'stay out of sight', Chiang 146.
213 **shade** The original character on the manuscript 暯 (which may be glossed as 冥) seems preferable to the emendation (映) given by the T editors. Cf. T112.13.
214 **reflection** Depending on how one glosses 審, there are several possible interpretations of this line. The translation assumes the most common meaning of the word. If glossed as 安定, we may understand 'when things had settled down [穩 itself may be understood as 安] for quite a while'. I reject this as less appropriate than the translation given because the girl does continue to beat the silk and so things never really do completely 'settle down'. Glossing 審 as 聽, however, is somewhat more attractive and results in '[after] listening quietly for quite some time'.
225 **wildly** 獐狂 'like a frightened deer'(?). Hsü 32 states that this expression should everywhere be understood as 張皇. Note how the time sequence of the prose narrative and the song are somewhat out of joint. Wu Tzu-hsü in the verse section was last seen going away meekly.
crazed 怳惚 = 恍惚, 惚恍, 怳忽, 慌惚, etc. Also see T5.9.
227 **knew** Because of the widespread publication of his supposed crimes. + 'Because he was.'
to herself The reason for adding 'to herself' to the translation will become obvious at the beginning of the next paragraph.
229 **Ling Che** 靈輒爲之扶輪. This allusion represents one possible indication of positive Tun-huang literary influence on drama. It is related to an incident which occurs in the Yüan drama, *The Orphan of Chao* 趙氏孤兒. In the wedge before act one and in the fourth act (Tsang Chin-shu 臧晉叔, ed., *Yüan-ch'ü hsüan* 元曲選 (Peking, 1961) – this incident does not occur in the Yüan edition of the play), T'u An-ku 屠岸賈 plans to harm Chao Tun 趙盾 by removing one of his chariot wheels and two of his team of four horses. From nowhere, Ling Che 靈輒 appears and supports the chariot, thus allowing Chao Tun to make good his escape. In the *Chronicle of Tso* (Hsüan 宣 2), Ling Che assists Chao Tun by using his spear to ward off a party of attackers (the story is repeated, somewhat confusedly, in the *Records of the Grand Historian* (*Shiki* 39.70–1)) but there is no mention of his supporting a chariot. The two characters 扶輪 here in the Tun-huang story of Wu Tzu-hsü might readily have been confused for 扶輔 which means 'poles attached to a cart to keep it from upsetting' and hence 'to help' in which sense it is synonymous with 扶助. Perhaps the original story merely said 'helped' but, sometime during the process of transmission, 'prop up the chariot' was written down and later accepted as a pseudo-historical fact by the Ming editors of *The Orphan of Chao*. Cf. line 315n. This incident is also recorded in several Tun-huang encyclopaedias (D970, D6116, P2524, S2588). It occurs in some of these encyclopaedias under the heading 'Paying back Kindness' 報恩 together with the anecdotes about a wounded snake (see line 743n) and jade bracelets (line 231n). This indicates that the author or copyist of the Wu Tzu-hsü story was a reader of such encyclopaedias (or vice versa).
231 **... bracelets** When Yang Pao 楊寶 of the Later Han period was nine years old, he travelled to the north of Hua-yin Mountain 華陰山. There he saw a yellow sparrow that had been injured by an owl and had fallen to the ground where it was being tormented by ants. Yang Pao nursed it until it could fly. That night, a child in yellow clothing came to Yang Pao in a dream and, wishing him a prosperous life, presented him with four white jade bracelets. See *History of the Later Han*, 'Biography of Yang Pao' (*PNP*) 54.1a, in commentary, citing *Hsü ch'i-hsieh chi* 續齊諧記. Also in *Sou-shen chi* 搜神記 (Shanghai, 1957, 3rd printing), vol. XX, pp. 151–2.
233 **well-provided** Waley, 'Notes', 172 is correct in his interpretation of this occurrence

of 被 = 備 but I am unable to trace his reference to a similar usage on T26.10 (彼 → 話).

238 **... lofty** An alternate translation might be 'Your face looks alert and your manner agitated (悚汗(?)).' But I feel that this sentence has greater affinity with the preceding question than with the succeeding ones. 聳幹 'scaring trunk' (see the entries in *PWYF* 2977–8 under 竦幹) thus is considered as being used in an exceptionally metaphorical sense. But noble men have frequently been compared to trees in Chinese literature (e.g. 玉樹).

239 **... in fear** 周章 'bewildered' = 惆悵, 輈張, 輈章, etc.

241 **... seeking** 心有所求. Waley 29, 'you are on some quest'. 'Quest' seems too strong, too positive a word for the defensive posture that Wu Tzu-hsü presents here. Similar objections may be offered against 'vendetta' for 懷冤 in the next sentence.

243 **offer** See Śāriputra line 773n1.

247 **Recently** 比, in Tun-huang colloquial, includes a broad range of temporal meanings, ≡ 本來, 從前, 近來. The latter seems most appropriate here. Chiang 144–6.

249 **... planned** Waley 29, 'After having also collected contribution for military purposes in the lands of Liang and Cheng ...' 計會 T174, third line from end, T190, last line, 'make an accounting of'(?) and T223.1, 'convened'. 計會 may, indeed, mean 會計 but, as here, it may also mean simply 'to meet together with and plan'.

defence matters 軍國 usually means 'military affairs and state government'. Consider also the common idiom 軍國大事 which has the same meaning.

251 **stout horses** Cf. *Analects*, Legge, I.185: 乘肥馬衣輕裘. This cannot be explained as 'mounted on a plump charger and wearing a light, but warm, gown' because the clothing worn by officials during the time of Confucius would simply not allow such a posture. Legge is quite correct to say 'had fat horses to his carriage and wore light furs'. There are no references in the ancient classics to horse riding 騎馬. This art was not learned until the Warring States Period (403–221 B.I.E). Waley 29 has 'richly laden'(?). Iriya 138b translates as 'straining'(?).

255 **I** See line 282n.

262 **... purpose** S328 clearly shows a √ beside 實 which indicates that it should be deleted. Cf. Iriya 160n8. The purest statement of this expression is probably on T193.4, 情意難留 'his feelings were such that it would be difficult to detain him' – i.e. his mind was set on going.

still 由 = 猶 as given by Chou 304.

... rejoined This is a difficult passage, which is evidenced by the fact that neither Chou nor the T editors attempt to provide it with rational punctuation. The first problem is where does the 'saying' end? It may well end at 留, though I read it as continuing down to 續 and it is not impossible, though highly unlikely, that it continues to 知. The next question is, to what purpose does the girl quote the proverb? Is she simply saying that Wu Tzu-hsü is not to be detained? This is the view of Waley and of the alternate interpretation which I offer here: '"One whose mind is set on going is harder to detain than a broken bowstring is likely to be rejoined."' Even though this sounds plausible, I have my doubts. The girl, I think, is not taken in by Wu Tzu-hsü's long-winded fabrication in answer to the questions she had put to him. She had observed earlier that he was either a knight with a grievance or someone fleeing from King P'ing. She must still believe that he is desperately in need of assistance. Wu Tzu-hsü, himself, does not make strenuous refusals of the girl's hospitality but only says politely, 'I dare not expect any food.' For the girl to quote the proverb as an acquiesence in his supposed determination to leave at once fits neither with what has gone before nor with what follows for she immediately repeats her offer of a meal.

Another view, which is partially reflected in the translation as I have given it in the text, is more subtle. In this view, the girl is saying that she understands Wu Tzu-hsü's estrangement from his native land and suggests, by way of encouragement, that he can remedy the situation by seeking succour elsewhere (thus presaging Wu). She goes on to say that Wu Tzu-hsü's future course is thus fairly well mapped out for him.

Other problems include the fact that 弦 does not necessarily mean 'bowstring'. Cf. *Li-chi*, "Records of Music" 禮記, 樂記 (*Thirteen Classics*) 38.6b: 'Shun made the five-stringed lute to sing the southern style.' 舜作五弦之琴以歌南風 where 弦 equals 絃. This further complicates matters because of the well-known idiom in which a broken guitar string symbolizes a wife who has passed away and the mended guitar string the woman who replaces her. If the idiom applies here, the translation would have to be revised to 'though a wife's been lost, she can always be replaced'. Again, though at this point we are unaware of the fact, Wu Tzu-hsü is carrying a bow (see T7.10) which may influence the girl to make the illustration she does. This notion evolved from an anecdote in *Hai-nei shih-chou chi* 海內十洲記 (*Pai-tzu ch'üan-shu* edn, *ts'e* 90) 3b, under the heading 'Feng-lin chou' 鳳麟洲, which is said to be in the central part of the western sea. There, a fabulous glue made of phoenix beaks and *lin* horns is described. It is known as 'glue for rejoining bowstrings' 續弦膠 because Han Wu-ti used it for this purpose with astounding success when he was hunting in that area.

A fourth possibility reflected in the saying is that the young lady may be hinting, ever so indirectly, that Wu Tzu-hsü simply does not hold any affection for her. Yet, in spite of this, she feels that the 'broken bowstring' (which was, indeed, never whole) may yet be rejoined. She will repeat her offer of hospitality.

The final irony of this analysis is that, in the next prose passage (T6.4), it is clear that Wu Tzu-hsü was, indeed, determined to leave, that the young lady repeatedly begged him to stay, and that he did so only in deference to her wishes. But, where the 'saying' occurs, we are not given the evidence to make such assumptions. Failure to provide the reader with sufficient evidence to interpret the 'saying' – at the point in the story where it occurs – may simply have been a lapse on the part of the narrator. The fact remains that we are presented with difficulties and ambiguities which border on the insuperable. I have tried, in my translation, to include as many as possible of the ambiguities which the Chinese text contains without total loss of intelligibility to the English reader.

263 **course** 行李 cannot possibly be rendered 'baggage'. It means 'course/path/direction'. Cf. T13.8.

267 **I** *Not* 'my home'. 兒家 is a first-person pronoun used by women, cf. T11.1. **Nan-yang District** 南陽 in modern Honan north of Hsin-yeh District 新野 (?). There are other possibilities.

268 **is** It might have been best to translate in the past tense because the girl's age is below revealed to be thirty, but see line 306n. Also, it seems somewhat odd that she would be praising herself so lavishly in the present tense but, again, see T7.3 where it is clear that she is capable of it. The remainder of her recitation here is definitely a commentary on the present situation and, furthermore, there is no transitional particle or time marker to indicate a time-shift. The age discrepancy seems rather to be attributed to narrative neglect which was probably brought on by a too casual application of conventional epithets. 二八 is a conventional expression of feminine beauty, see Lo, *Customs*, 45. 二 on the manuscript is written in such a fashion that it might be a careless 三 (the bottom line having been positioned on top of the middle line), thus making her 24.

271 **like** Chou again has 猶 for 由.

272 **return** 皈 = 歸. This usage is a Buddhist predilection.

274 **... a meal of it** 努力當餐飯. Cf. the first of the nineteen ancient poems 古詩十九首, *WH*, 29.1a: 'When I think of you, it makes me old; the years and

months quickly grow late. I'll speak not again of my rejection but make an effort to eat some more.' 思君令人老，歲月忽已晚.棄捐勿復道，努力加餐飯. Some commentators treat this quite differently, interpreting it as showing concern for someone and hoping that this person will take care to eat well.

277 **disregard** 通 → 違(?) (Hsü 110). However, LSY has assured me that 難通 reads well enough as it is: 'difficult to pass' hence 'won't do'.

... kindness Also see T630, fourth line from end and T633.3.

278 **thanked** 媿賀(荷), cf. T14.1, T15.6, T18 last line but four, and T25.12.

282 **I** 下官. Waley 30 translates as 'Your humble servant' but in T'ang colloquial the term generally indicates the first person regardless of sex or position. See Chiang 4 and compare *Yu-hsien k'u*, p. 10.

286 **more** S328 has 甚 rather than 堪.

287 **... ever** I suspect that 未審 = 未省, 不省, 何省 (cf. Chiang 152) all of which amount to 未曾, 沒有, 何曾.

289 **road** Lo, *Studies*, 580 and Hsü 110 are in agreement that 路 should be replaced by 道 to meet the requirements of the rhyme.

295 **bitterly** 咷 = 啕.

wept aloud Lo, *Studies*, 498 and Hsü 110 both agree that the rhyme in this line would be better served by 哭聲 than as it is given by the T editors. Note that Wu Tzu-hsü has already left the girl in the previous line of the translation. What follows is the girl's monologue which continues down to 'all cast away in vain' (T7.3).

301 **... either** Because, on one level, he does not trust her and, on another, her contact with a man has sullied her honour (cf. T7.2). 慚 is 慙 on S328.

305 **troubles** 帶累 'involve, implicate'. Also see T131.2 and 11.

306 **... man** Another proverb. *Wu Yüeh ch'un-ch'iu* (*SPTK*), 3.1b: 'I lived together alone with my mother for thirty years without having married.' 妾獨與母居三十未家. That she lived with her mother till the age of thirty is repeated just below the sentence here cited. Therefore, we are not permitted to emend 三十 to 二十 even though she is 'sweet sixteen' on T5.16 (see line 268n).

310 **do not doubt me** Cf. *Wu Yüan Plays the Pipes* (*Yüan-ch'ü hsüan*) 元曲選 (Peking, 1955), Act IV, p. 653, last line but 4; p. 654.4–5; and during the singing of the aria 'Shepherd's Pass' 牧羊關 where the girl repeatedly tells Wu Tzu-hsü to put his mind at rest.

312 **and** 聊 which I take to be equivalent to 且. It may also be interpreted as 'could only'. P2794v has *keng* 耿, 'disquietly'(?).

314 **... death** Waley 32 interprets as 'disappear'. Chiang 51 and Hsü 32 point out that 透, during the T'ang, also meant 跳 and need not have been emended to 投 by the T editors.

... river This passage is alluded to in Tung Chieh-yüan 董解元, *Hsi-hsiang chi chu-kung-tiao* 西廂記諸宮調; see Lili Chen, *Master Tung's Western Chamber Romance* (Cambridge, 1976), p. 234: 'In antiquity, a chaste laundress/Weighted herself with stones and drowned.'

315 **... injustice** Literally, 'he let forth a cry, exclaiming, "How unjust!"' Waley 32 is mistaken in this and the following lines when he has the girl continue to speak. The narrator has had the poor girl throw herself in the water twice by this time and there is little likelihood of even 'a last outraged cry', let alone a plea for a hundred pieces of gold to build a tomb. To make his translation work, Waley has had to make a major rearrangement of the lines. Though he may have felt justified in doing so, it would seem to be ruled out as a possibility by the first sentence in the succeeding prose passage which indicates that the grief and tears were Wu Tzu-hsü's and not the girl's. That my assertion is correct is, I believe, borne out by a similar passage in the Yüan drama, *Wu Yüan Plays the Pipes* 伍員吹簫. There Wu Tzu-hsü uses almost the same words: 'If, on another day, I attain my ambition, I ought to

build a temple for you beside this river to publish the chastity which you maintained to the death and to repay the kind favour of the meal you gave me, 異日得志, 我當在此水上與你修蓋祠堂, 表揚眞烈. 報答一飯之恩便了 (*Yüan-ch'ü hsüan*, p. 654). Other Yüan dramas which, at least in part, resemble the Tun-huang story of Wu Tzu-hsü are Kao Wen-hsiu's 高文秀 *Wu Tzu-hsü Abandons His Family and Flees to Fan City* 伍子胥棄子走樊城, Cheng T'ing-yü's 鄭廷玉 *The Fisherman Refuses a Sword at Coloured Stone Creek* 采石渡漁父辭劍, and Wu Ch'ang-ling's 吳昌齡 *The Silk Washing Girl Embraces a Stone and Throws Herself into the River* 浣紗女抱石投江. See Fu Hsi-hua 傅惜華, *Yüan-tai tsa-chü ch'üan-mu* 元代雜劇全目 (Peking, 1957), pp. 126, 106, and 179. See also line 229n. I am not, of course, claiming that any of the Yüan dramas were based wholly or even largely on Tun-huang popular narratives. But I do suggest that studies are necessary to demonstrate specific instances of probable influence.

316 **relentlessly** Cf. T369.8, T394.4, T580 last line, T742.8. In the latter case, 無端 means 'abruptly/suddenly/unexpectedly' which meanings could be used here. In most cases, however, the phrase means 'arbitrarily/without reason' but a river can hardly be that.

318 **in the future** P2794v has 一日 'one day' instead of 在後(?).

319 **will certainly** I prefer the reading of 准 from P2794v (*To-so* 61.1, but the ms could also be read as 唯) to 唯 'the only thing I can do is'(?).

321 **darkened** 暎. Chou 305.6 has 映 which I adopt and gloss as 蔽 or 陰.

322 **... point** P2794v has 神情抱亂.

330 **regards** 將 ≡ 以爲; 由 = 猶, Chiang 159.

... sleep Cf. *Ch'ü* nos. 553, 629, 1019. This is a Buddhist concept.

333 **recognized** Waley, 'Notes', 173 addresses himself unsuccessfully to the problem of what to do with 蔭 (→ 音 (?)). Iriya 140a hesitantly suggests that it means 察 (?). My suspicion is that 蔭 → 認. The two characters are homophonous in some dialects and the proposed emendation perfectly suits the required meaning.

334 **was** 'Her brother' is dropped from the translation. The following lines on P2794v are somewhat garbled but provide additional information that is helpful in understanding this passage.

338 **salad** Though there is very little difference one way or the other, my preference is to follow the editors who keep 蕣 here and in the next line rather than emend to 蕽 as Hsü 32 suggests.

339 **chicory** Chou 305.10–11 has two additional lines inserted here: 'which she gave to her brother to eat. His heart seemed set on going away quickly.' 與弟食之, 心由速去.

apprehend 逆知 'to anticipate, to know beforehand'. P2794v has 逆即知.

342 **... without** Both T and Chou 305.12 have 內苦外甘 but Waley 32 translates as 'bitterness without and sweetness within'. Wishful thínking. Perhaps we may interpret: 乾 *kân* 'dry' (the gourd) stands for 甘 *kâm* 'sweet' and 飯 *b'iwɒn-* 'rice', its 'opposite' 反 *pi̯wɒn:*, is a 'grain' 穀 *kuk* which sounds a little like 'bitter' 苦 *k'uo:* (in archaic pronunciation *k'âg*).

343 **mean** Cheng, *Popular*, 254 has 含 instead of 合, hence 'the meaning which it embodied was...'.

344 **at once** On P2794v 速去 is not repeated.

345 **... leave** S328 reads 便辞即去.

348 **To** 'I intend to take recourse' has been elided from the translation.

350 **head** P2794v omits 頭.

352 **... breast** Grammatically, there is no justification for taking this clause out of the discourse. But, as Iriya 160n12 rightly claims, it could not really have been spoken by the sister either. Chou 306.1, Chiang 49, Cheng 255, and the T editors differ so greatly in their readings of the four characters in question that it is necessary to

review them here briefly. According to T collation note 11 on p. 29, S328 has 自摸塊搥 but Chou reads this as 自模魂搥 (misquoted by Chiang as 自摸魂塠). Based on the frequent occurrences of similar clauses throughout T'ang popular religious literature (see the Introduction), a normative reading is as follows: 自摸 (→ 撲) 魂 (→ 渾) 搥 'to throw oneself to the ground and pummel the entire body'. P2794v, which is adopted by the T editors, makes more immediate sense but means nearly the same thing. This is a curious motif in Tun-huang popular literature. It occurs often (T46.4, T91.8, T140.14, T190.8, 13, T251.9, T299.3,9, T337.10, T580.4, T707.8, T729.9, T736.10, T737.2, T741.15, T743.4, T759.1–2, T796.16) and serves to express a condition of extreme grief. This practice has been described in detail in two articles by Lien-sheng Yang, 'Tao-chiao chih tzu-po yü fo-chiao chih tzu-p'u' 道教之自搏與佛教之自撲, *Tsukamoto hakase shojū kinen bukkyōshigaku ronshū* 塚本博士頌壽紀念佛教史學論集 (Kyoto, 1961), pp. 962–9; ['Additional Note on the Tzu-po of Taoism and the Tzu-p'u of Buddhism as a Penance'] 道教之自搏與佛教之自撲補論, *CYYY*, 34, Dr Hu Shih Memorial Volume, pt I (1962), 275–89 (includes the earlier article).

353 **former** P2794v omits 前.

356 **ungrateful** 孤負 = 辜負.

parents Cheng, *Popular*, 255 has 前 'deceased' instead of 阿.

358 **... scattered** Which is nonsense since the father is in the north and is already dead. For this meaning of 分張, cf. T719.12 and T756.10. This expression may also mean 'distinguish/differentiate' (T659, last line).

359 **when** Following P2794v which has 處 instead of 哭.

alive An abbreviated form of 行住坐臥 (see Maudgalyāyana line 1229n1).

360 **... rend** Cf. T96.2.

363 **ever** P2794v has 身 'my person' instead of 更.

365 **... yourself** See Maudgalyāyana line 877n.

367 **have been** For 被刑 'received sentence', see *PWYF* 121b. P2794v has instead 'by Ch'u' 被楚.

368 **raging** 寫 glossed as 吐, cf. 瀉.

369 **... sun** Unless he destroys his enemies. Waley 33 has 'Only a coward would consent to live under the same sun!'(?) I believe the author is trying to make Wu Tzu-hsü say that, although today his time (read 分 in the falling tone, i.e. 份 'lot') has not yet come, he will wait – filled with a desire for vengeance – until the proper moment. P2794v (*To-so* 62.9) has 天地 'in the world' for 天日.

371 **... me** Cf. T3.16–4.1.

374 **... ninth degree** See line 179n2 above.

379 **... tingle** 眼瞤耳熱, cf. T45.4, T205, last line but one, T250.3, *Yu-hsien k'u*, p. 10. From reading this text alone, it is obvious that these signs are omens of impending danger. It is significant that, in early and pre-T'ang literature (see Iriya 160n13 for examples), these signs were considered to be good omens, while in Yüan and Ming fiction and drama, they were considered to be omens of death. The change in meaning seems to have occurred at about the same time as the appearance of the present text. Cf. the following passage from H. W. Bailey, tr. and ed., *Indo-Scythian Studies: Khotanese Texts*, vol. IV (Cambridge, 1961), pp. 113–14: 'Whose nostrils twitch, one must know there will be good talk with kinsmen and friends. Whose left eyebrow twitches, one must know: I shall win in court. Whose left ... twitches, one must know: I shall win from enemies. Whose left side of the eye twitches, strain ...'

381 **sprinkled** Hsü 110 proposes an emendation to 禳 'sacrifice for exorcism'.

383 **... backwards** Although I have no idea how these strange practices originated, it is clear enough that Wu Tzu-hsü is performing them to make himself invisible or to throw the nephews off course (the inverted *getas* would be particularly effective for this purpose!).

... Gate 地戶天門. The *Yüeh chüeh shu* would seem to have been instrumental in the choice of language here. The terms occur several times in the 'Outer Chapters' 外傳.

388 ***... leges*** 急急如律令 was a standard documentary expression in Han times used at the close of communications from higher officials to lower ones. It meant that the recipient should 'act upon this matter swiftly, as though it had the force of law'. Around the end of the Han Dynasty or the Period of the Three Kingdoms, the expression began to be used frequently by Taoists at the end of curses and meant something like 'Do this immediately, as I command you' and was addressed to the spirit which was being asked to carry out the curse. It also occurs on PK2095, S5666, and P2723. For other examples of this formula, see Morohashi 10475.15. Ho Ch'ang-ch'ün 賀昌羣, *Wei-chin ch'ing-t'an szu-hsiang ch'u-pien* 魏晉清談思想初編 (Shanghai, 1947), pp. 4 and 21n4 also discusses it in some detail (Iriya 161n15). Also see Nishino Teiji 西野貞治, 'Tonkō zoku bungaku no sozai to sono tenkai' 敦煌俗文学の素材とその展開, *Jimbun kenkyū* 人文研究, 10.11 (November 1959), 1154 and Miu T'ien-hua 繆天華, *Ch'eng-yü tien* 成語典 (Taipei, 1971), p. 302c. The Latin in my translation is sheer hocus-pocus (= upon these terms) from Livy.

393 **gain** The T editors have inadvertently dropped the future signifier 將.

399 **divination** Cheng, *Popular*, 255 punctuates after 占.

402 **... place** Waley 34, 'his body had not been recovered and a cenotaph had been built'(?).

406 **... us** The meaning of 廢我 is not entirely clear. It probably means something like 'we're wasting our time'.

409 **... pursuit** Cf. T408.10. The 不 given by the T editors is an unannounced emendation (which I follow) for S328 clearly has 來.

413 **around** Although the meaning is almost certainly 'on all four sides', 四迴 is a doubtful reading. T repeats it below (9.8). But Chou 306.14 gives 廻 here and 307.3 gives 迴.

423 **I** Cf. T10.4, T101.5.

confines 側 '[narrow] confines'(?). Cf. 'Tale of the Capture of Chi Pu' 捉季布傳文, T57.2: 'Today I find myself in straits between the narrow confines of Heaven and Earth. To whom can I turn for recourse?' 今受困厄天地窄, 更向何邊投莽人? S5439 has 側 for 窄. The two words were pronounced the same and were used interchangeably.

427 **Reduced** For 落草 Waley 35 has 'cowering in the bushes' which is too literal a translation. The actual meaning is more like 'fallen so low'. See *Pi-yen lu* 碧巖錄 (Tokyo, 1969), vol. I, p. 70: 'Because of this, you have become vile.' 自是儞落草. In later colloquial usage, the term means 'to join with a band of thieves'. Cf. P2794v which has 落藿.

428 **withdraw timidly** 攢刑 → 攢形 (as printed in Chou 307.4). Waley, 'Notes', 173 thinks this a scribal error for 潛形. However, since the expression as given in Chou also occurs on T4.16, we may accept it without further emendation.

435 **Wandered** 行由 → 行遊 (Hsü 110).

436 **far away** 迢遰 means 'high and far away'. Chou 307.6 prints 迢遞 which means precisely the same thing. P2794v has 迢递.

western ... 海西 appears in the *History of the Later Han*, 'Account of the Southern Barbarians' 南蠻傳 (*PNP*) 86.27b with the meaning of the Roman Empire or perhaps Syria.

437 **three great rivers** See Maudgalyāyana line 1004n.

438 **... in on you** Waley skips this and the following line which, I concede, are not easy. For 專輒, see the *History of the Chin Dynasty* 晉書, 'Biography of Liu Hung' 劉弘傳 (*PNP*) 66.1b: 'I willingly receive the punishment for my impetuosity.'

甘受專輒之罪. 忓 (*not* 忤 as Chou 307.6 reads it) means 干 and so 相忓 may be rendered as 'intervened in your affairs'. Cf. T11.13.

439 **rash** 造次, cf. T729.2 and the second line from the end, T720.14 where this phrase occurs in head position and would seem to mean 'in the end/after all'. But, on T187.4, where it occurs in terminal position as here, it changes its meaning as I have indicated in my translation.

turn ... Cheng, *Popular*, 256 has 惻. Although I have forced a translation from 側, a possible emendation to 測 'fathom, measure' should be considered.

440 **forgetful** *Not* 'is very full of hope' since 多望 → 多忘 (Iriya 161n16 and *Index*, 13). Compare the set phrase 貴人多忘事 of Yüan and later periods.

442 **east ...** 江東 'the lower reaches of the Yangtze River'.

445 **by means of it** Added to the translation.

... questions I hasten to concur with Waley 36 that 'this passage is of course untranslatable'. But, unlike Waley, I have attempted to reproduce the plays on words in English. Since there is at least one medicine name in each clause, I have decided to reduce all of the identifications to a single note in order to avoid cluttering these pages with line numbers. A few of the puns were found to be directly translatable into English in which case they may not be discussed below. I had planned to give brief accounts of the medicinal properties, dosages, preparations, and prescriptions of each of the drugs identified and my own notes on these matters are extensive. In most cases, however, I have decided not to do so in order to keep this note within manageable proportions. Furthermore, this information is readily available in the reference works mentioned below. My main tasks have been to identify the medicines and the puns involved. Where I have mentioned specific applications, it is either because the treatment itself is interesting or because the plant, animal, or mineral under discussion would seem, to the uninitiated, to have no likelihood at all of being a medicine. The principal reference tools used are: Read, *Chinese Medicinal Plants*; *Chung-kuo yao-hsüeh ta tz'u-tien* 中國藥學大辭典 (Peking, 1956), referred to as *CKYHTTT*; *Chung-yao ta tz'u-tien* 中藥大辭典 (Hong Kong, 1977); Shiu-ying Hu, comp., *An Enumeration of Chinese Materia Medica* (Hong Kong, 1980); *Tz'u-hai*; *Mathews' Dictionary*; *A Barefoot Doctor's Manual* (U.S. Department of Health, Education and Welfare, 1974) and its Chinese original, *Nung-ts'un i-sheng shou-ts'e* 農村醫生手册 (Peking, 1971, rev. edn), both kindly loaned to me by Katherine Lazarus; F. Porter Smith and G. A. Stuart, *Chinese Materia Medica: Vegetable Kingdom* (Shanghai, 1911); L. H. Bailey, *Manual of Cultivated Plants*, revised edn (New York, 1949); Harlan P. Kelsey and William A. Dayton, *Standardized Plant Names* (Harrisburg, Pa., 1942); Henry A. Gleason, *The New Britton and Brown Illustrated Flora of the Northeastern United States and Adjacent Canada*, 5th edn (New York, 1974), 3 vols.; Siri von Reis Altschul, *Drugs and Foods from Little-Known Plants: Notes in Harvard University Herbaria* (Cambridge, 1973); Ben Charles Harris, *The Compleat Herbal* (Barre, Massachusetts, 1972); Margaret B. Kreig, *Green Medicine: The Search for Plants that Heal* (Chicago, 1966); Alexander Nelson, *Medical Botany* (Edinburgh, 1951); Ono Ranzan 小野蘭山, *Honzō kōmoku keimō* 本草綱目啓蒙, ed. [Sugimoto Tsutomu] 杉本つとむ (Tokyo, 1974); [Junpei Sato] 佐藤潤平, [*On the Japanese Medical Plants*] 漢薬の原植物 (Tokyo, 1959); Isabella Beeton, *The Book of Household Management* (London, 1861); and John Lust, *The Herb Book* (Sini Valley, California, 1974). In cases where I give only the scientific name of a plant, the reader may use the genus name as the common name, e.g. *Angelica polymorpha*, 'a species of angelica'.

(i) 仵茄 is a pun for 伍家 'The Wu Family'. The second character means 'egg-plant' or 'brinjal' which is rich in vitamins. However, the pun goes two ways here for what is actually involved is 五加(皮) *Acanthopanax sessiflorus* or *gracilistylus*, 'carambola root/ginseng bark/prickly ginseng' from which a very expensive

medicinal wine is prepared.
(ii) 細辛, *Asarum sieboldi* or *heterotropoides*, a type of wild ginger. Perhaps we may say that Wu Tzu-hsü's wife's name was Prudence 細心. A serving maid in *Yu-hsien k'u*, p. 11, has that name.
(iii) 於 is for 榆(?), 'elm', the bark of which is used as an expectorant.
(iv) 梁 = 粱, *Setaria italica*, 'spiked millet'.
(v) 當歸, *Ligusticum acutilobum*, used to prepare fumenol extract.
(vi) 獨活, *Angelica polyclada* or *pubescens*, 'Chinese angelica tree'.
(vii) 膏 (?) 茛 ≡ 薯茛, a dark brown dye for silk but also used as a stimulant (see *CKYHTTT*, p. 1809). But perhaps this stands for 高粱, 'great millet, broomcorn'. This is not too likely, however, since we have just seen 'spiked millet' above. Other possibilities are that it means 高良薑, *Alpinia kumatake* or *officinarum*, 'lesser galangal' or 藁茇/本, *Ligusticum sinense*, 'Chinese lovage'. Whatever the medicine, I believe that the pun may be for 告(?)郎 'told my man'.
(viii) 薑, 'ginger'.
(ix) 芥, 'mustard', can be used as a rubefacient or counter-irritant.
(x) 澤瀉, *Alisma plantago-aquatica*, var. *orientale*, 'water plantain'.
(xi) 檳榔, 'betel nut', kills worms, relieves stoppages, aids diuresis and conversion of moisture. The Chinese borrowed both the plant and its name from the Malayans who called it *Pinang*. Without the wood radical, the characters mean 'honoured guest' (from the custom of placing a container filled with betel before visitors). This is also the long-standing Chinese folk etymological explanation of the term and the pun operative here.
(xii) 遠志, *Polygala tenuifolia*, 'Japanese senega'. The translation assumes 遠至 'arrive from afar' to be the pun but 'when will his *far-reaching aspirations* [be fulfilled]' also deserves consideration.
(xiii) 無道 stands for 烏頭 'Chinese aconite (monkshood, crow's head)' – also called 烏獨 – or, perhaps, 烏豆, 'black soybean'.
(xiv) 材狐 → 柴胡, *Bupleurum falcatum*, 'sickle-leaved hare's ear', a species of thoroughwax. The pun is for 豺虎, 'cruel'.
(xv) 芒消, 'Glauber's salt', a laxative. The pun is undoubtedly for 亡消, 'annihilate'.
(xvi) 苜蓫 = 苜蓿 (?), *Medicago sativa*, 'alfalfa, lucerne'. The pun is probably for 默縮, 'silently to withdraw'. P2794v has 潛.
(xvii) 葳蕤 = 萎蕤, *Polygonatum officinale*, 'Solomon's seal', used to treat conjunctivitis. The pun may be for 畏惴 (?), 'panicky', or 畏縮, 'cringing'.
(xviii) 石膽 ≡ 石礶, 'sulphate of copper' (especially from salt-wells in Szechwan). The pun is achieved by literally interpreting as 'bladder [i.e. nerve] of stone'.
(xix) 逃人 ≡ 桃仁, *Prunus persica*, 'peach kernal'. The literal pun is obvious.
(xx) 茱萸, *Cornus officinalis*, 'dogwood'. The pun is for 須臾, 'a moment'.
(xxi) 菌草 → 茵[蔯]草, *Artemisia capillaris*, 'absinthin'. The pun is for 蔭草 'hiding in the grasses'.
(xxii) 藜蘆, *Veratrum nigrum*, 'black false hellebore; Cape jasmine'. Iriya 161n34 suggests that the pun might be for 離閭, 'away from his village'.
(xxiii) 野干, *śṛgāla*, an Indian jackal, stands for 射干, *Belamcanda chinensis*, 'blackberry lily'.
(xxiv) 莨菪, *Hyoscyamus niger*, 'a type of black henbane'. The pun is for 浪蕩, 'to hang around'.
(xxv) 赤石, aluminum-bearing red clay, see *CKYHTTT*, pp. 651–2. The pun is for 澈濕, 'thoroughly soaked'.
(xxvi) 青箱(子), *Celosia argentea*, 'prince's feather'. The pun is for 情想.
(xxvii) 決明, *Cassia tora*, 'foetid cassia', 'sickle senna'. The pun, which is

obvious, can be translated as 'till the break of dawn'.
(xxviii) 卷柏, *Selaginella tamariscina*. The translation is fairly literal but Iriya 162n40 suggests that there is a pun for 卷剝, 'peel off in a curl'.
(xxix) 厚朴, *Magnolia officinalis*, a type of magnolia having a thick bark which is used for medicinal purposes, especially that from Szechwan. The pun is for (敦)厚(淳)朴, 'honest and simple'.
(xxx) 躑躅. (1) 花 = 羊躑躅, *Rhododendron sinense*, 'azalea' – when ingested by sheep, it makes them tipsy. Hence the name. (2) 茶 = 山茶花, *Thea japonica*, 'camelia' or 'tea oil tree', Jp. *tsubaki*. The pun is obvious.
(xxxi) 夫㚕 → 夫婿 or 夫壻 as it is written in Chou 307.12. There is a plant known as 夫須 in ancient texts, but more commonly known as 香附子, *Cyperus rotundus*, 'nutgrass flatsedge'. See *CKYHTTT*, pp. 935–40.
(xxxii) 麥門(冬), *Liriope spicata*, 'black leek'. The pun may be for 驀門, 'suddenly arrived at my gate'.
(xxxiii) 蓯蓉 = 肉蓯蓉, *Boschniakia glabra*, 'broomrape'. The pun is obviously for 從容.
(xxxiv) 龍齒, dragon (i.e. fossil) teeth, used in curing those who are possessed of spirits or fevers, see *CKYHTTT*, p. 1763.
(xxxv) 狼牙 ≡ 狼子, *Potentilla cryptotaeniae*, 'cinquefoil', a poisonous plant which has medicinal applications, e.g. relief of itching. 狼 is a pun for 郎, 'the gentlemen's', i.e. 'your'. The significance of the teeth will become clear to those who are unfamiliar with the folklore of Wu Tzu-hsü in line T12.4 below.
(xxxvi) 桔梗 (not to be confused with 桔子, Mandarin orange), a root from which cough medicine is made, *Platycodon grandiflorum*, 'Balloon-Flower'. The pun may be for 究竟, 'after all'.
(xxxvii) 枳殼. The 枳, *Citrus poncirus* or *trifoliata*, 'thorny limebush; trifoliate orange; hardy orange'. This is a variety of orange with a very thick peel which, when dried, is called 枳殼. Perhaps the pun is for 粗穀, 'course grain'. Cf. T11.11.
(xxxviii) 仵茄, see (i).
(xxxix) 之子, see (xlviii).
(xl) 逃人, see (xix).
(xli) 行李 ≡ 杏李, 'apricot (almond) and plum'. The pun is for the meaning of the words given in line 263n.
(xlii) 巴蜀 ≡ 巴菽 = 巴豆, *Croton tiglium*, 'croton-oil bean' which is mentioned in Tso Szu's 左思 '*Fu* on the Capital of Szechwan' 蜀都賦, *WH*, 4.11a together with 巴戟 (see (lxiii) below). The pun is for the literal meaning of the two characters, 'the Szechwan area'.
(xliii) 藿鄉 ≡ 藿香, *Lophanthus rugosus*, 'betony'. The pun is probably for 霍縣, the name of a district in what is now Shansi.
(xliv) 蜈公 is half pun (伍公) and half centipede (蜈蚣) which is used in a decoction for the treatment of infantile convulsions, cramps, spasms, lockjaw, and snakebite. In Taiwan, one may purchase a preparation of centipede soaked in acetic acid that is remarkably effective in curing advanced cases of 'Hong Kong foot'. It may be, however, that the author meant to refer to 'centipede grass', 蜈蚣草, a type of *Lythrum*.
(xlv) 貝母 = 莔, *Fritillaria verticillata*, var. *Thunbergii*, an herb of the lily family. Since Wu Tzu-hsü has already told us where he was born and where he grew up, I am disinclined to view 貝母 as a pun for a place-name. I feel that the literal meaning of 母 is the main element in the pun. Perhaps 陪母 'in company with my mother' or 悲母 'with my sympathetic mother' was intended.
(xlvi) 金牙(石), also referred to in ancient texts as 黃牙石 and most commonly found in the hills of Szechwan and Shensi. The pun may be from the literal

meaning of the two characters, 'broker's fee in gold' or 'gold [in the shape of] teeth' (cf. 玉牙).
(xlvii) 採寶 literally says 'took up my valuables' which is what merchants in Chinese fiction invariably do when they start on a journey. This is so immediately obvious that we need not understand as 財寶 'wealth'. The pun is probably for 菜伯, 'Chinese small onion' or 'ciboule'.
(xlviii) 支子 ↛ 之子 but rather 支子 ≡ 之子. 支子 is another name for 山梔子, *Fructus gardeniae* (*Gardenia florida*), 'Chinese yellow berry'. The pun 之子 is from *The Book of Odes*, Legge, IV.41b: 'This man [King Yu 幽] is sending me away.' 之子之遠.
(xlix) 劉寄奴, the second *tzu* of Liu Yü 裕 who was Kao-tsu 高祖 of the Sung Dynasty during the epoch of division between the North and the South. He had effectively used a certain grass (*Senecio palmatus*, a type of groundsel) to dress sword wounds, and the grass came to be called by his name.
(l) 賤朋 ≡ 硼砂, borax, a slightly *alkaline borate* of sodium ($Na_2B_4O_7$) which has antiseptic and cleansing qualities. Or perhaps the pun is for 鹼(鹽)蓬 which is described in *CKYHTTT*, p. 1936 and p. 1966, as a 'miscellaneous grass'.
(li) 徐長卿, *Pycnostelma chinense*, a species from the milkweed family. It was given this name after a man who used it to treat epilepsy. Von Reis Altschul, *Drugs and Foods*, p. 231, no. 3428: 'Use as a drug. If this plant is in the house there will be no entering of snakes. It has the widest use – so-called "Drug King."' Also known as 鬼督郵.
(lii) 貴友 may be a pun for 桂油 'cinnamon bark oil' or 鬼油麻, *Siphonostegia chinensis* (see von Reis Altschul, *Drugs and Foods*, p. 274, no. 4083).
(liii) 蘘河 ≡ 蘘荷, a variety of wild ginger, *Zingiber mioga*. The pun is for the name of a river.
(liv) 寒水(石), calcareous spar, can be used to decrease appetite in case of fever.
(lv) 傷身 is a pun for 桑葚, mulberry achenes, from which a liquor with tonic properties may be fermented.
(lvi) 芒消, see (xv).
(lvii) 獨活, see (vi).
(lviii) 斷續 → 續斷, *Sonchus asper*, 'prickly sowthistle' or *Lamium album*, 'white nettle'. The pun is from the literal meaning of the two characters, 'breaking and binding'.
(lix) 飄颻 ≡ 漂搖草, the ancient name for 薨搖, *Astragalus sinicus*, a type of milk vetch. The pun is most appropriate for the stem of this plant is quite flexible.
(lx) 恒山 is, apparently, a reference to the northernmost of the five sacred mountains which is in Shansi and Hopei. Another name for 恆山 is 常山 which latter is, as well, the name of a plant, *Orixa Japonica*, 'Japanese orixa'. It is produced in the Wan District of Szechwan and has numerous medicinal applications. Another name is Szechwan varnish 蜀漆.
(lxi) 石膏, gypsum, plaster of Paris. The pun may be for 'rocks were high' 高.
(lxii) 難渡 ≡男犢 (?), *Lyonia ovafolia*.
(lxiii) 巴戟(天), *Bacopa moniera*, 'water hyssop'. Another item for the Szechwan connection. See (xlii) above. The pun may be for 爬脊 'climb [mountain] ridges'.
(lxiv) 狼胡 sounds like 狼毒, *Aconitum lycoctonum*, 'wolfbane monkshood'. P2794v has 柴胡 which repeats pun (xiv) above.
(lxv) 款冬, also written 款東 and 款凍, is coltsfoot. Its Chinese names are derived from the fact that it is considered a harbinger of spring because it comes up through the ice in watery places. The pun comes from interpreting the name literally.
(lxvi) 鍾(鐘)乳(石), stalactite, of which the powder was believed to stimulate the production of a mother's milk. The pun may be for 衆豬 'group of wild boar'

or 衆狙 'monkey crowd'.
(lxvii) 半夏, *Pinellia tuberifera* or *ternata*. The pun is for the literal meaning of the two characters.
(lxviii) 鬱金 or 川鬱金 (because grown in Szechwan), *Curcuma longa*, 'common turmeric'.
(lxix) 當歸, see (v).
(lxx) 芎窮(藭), also called 胡藭, 川藭, etc. *Cnidium officinale*, 'drug selinum'. The pun may be for 躬窮, '[my] body exhausted'.
(lxxi) 羊齒, ferns and bracken (pteridophytes), used against tape-worms and other parasites. The pun is obvious.
(lxxii) 狼牙, see (xxxv).
(lxxiii) 桔梗, see (xxxvi).
(lxxiv) 其意 ≡ 七(葉)一(枝花) *Paris polyphylla*, 'seven-leaves-to-a-flower'. A decoction of the roots is used to reduce fevers; resolves bruises, reduces swelling, detoxifies. If this is not acceptable (there are phonological problems in this identification), perhaps we may see 遠志 ((xii) above) in 願知. At any rate, there is sure to be a medicine name lurking somewhere within these four characters.

All in all, this 'medicine poem' is a most extraordinary and ingenious *tour de force*. Examples of such puns on medicine names can be found from the Six Dynasties through the Ming and were most popular in the Sung. The last section in *chüan* 2 of *Shih-jen yü-hsieh* 詩人玉屑, citing the *Man-sou shih-hua* 漫叟詩話 (Shanghai, 1958), pp. 42–3, deals with such poems. And, in the section on 'Poetic Forms' 詩體 of *Ts'ang-lang shih-hua* 滄浪詩話, 'medicine poems' are discussed under the heading 'Plays on Words' 字謎. But the poem found in the Tun-huang story of Wu Tzu-hsü is far and away the longest and most complicated specimen known to me. It is quite likely, however, that the three persons mentioned under the heading 'Medicine Storytellers' 說藥 near the end of the sixth *chüan* of *Wu-lin chiu-shih* 武林舊事 could have carried this sort of exercise to even greater lengths.

For a discussion of the influence which this 'medicine poem' may have had upon later drama and fiction, see Liu Ts'un-yan 柳存仁, *Buddhist and Taoist Influences on Chinese Novels* (Wiesbaden, 1952), vol. I, pp. 197–8.

446 **Wahoo** Wahoo bark, *Eunonymus atropurpureus*.

451 **neighbours** 憐 → 隣 (Iriya 161n22), as on P2794v. In the same note, Iriya suggests that 澤瀉 is a pun for 托借 'dependent upon others'(?).

456 **brother-in-law** The translation goes against the probable 2-2-2 structure of the line by dividing it 3-3 but I can think of no other solution.

474 **caper** The young flower-buds, known as capers, have astringent and diuretic properties.

475 **scurvy** The English word has at least four meanings, two or three of which I hope register with my reader: 'contemptible' and the name of a grass (esp. *Cochlearia officianalis*) which is used in the treatment of scurvy.

476 **... vein** 'In the same cryptic vein' is implicit in 答.

485 **Rockyfeldspar** For the medicinal properties of feldspar, see B. E. Read and C. Pak, *A Compendium of Minerals and Stones Used in Chinese Medicine*, second edn, (Peking, 1936), no. 58.

488 **three** P2794v has 二伴 '[my] two companions'.

502 **... violets** Cf. line 473 in the wife's part of the 'medicine poem'.

503 **... tartar** This line and the next are modified in the translation for fun and to clarify what is happening. Literally, they probably mean 'what, after all, your feelings are' and 'I'd like to know what you're thinking'.

505 **... hurry** P2794v and Cheng 256 omit 急即. Even though the line as it is found in T has eight syllables, it appears in S328 as a part of the verse.

509 **Kung-sun** This would seem a not altogether arbitrary choice for a surname inasmuch as this was the designation of grandsons of feudal lords during the Spring and Autumn period and later became a double surname. 鍾鼎 sounds like a name and the T editors have taken it so. This may have been the intention of the author of the story but 鍾鼎 means 鐘鼎, extended form 鐘鳴鼎食, 'bells ringing and eating out of fine brass ware', which Wang Po 王勃 uses to describe wealthy families in 'Preface to "Feast of Departing at the Pavilion of King T'eng"' 滕王閣餞別序, *Wang Tzu-an chi* 王子安集 (*SPTK*) 5.2a.

510 **Fittingly** 疋配 = 匹配, 'married'.
faithfully 貞艮 = 貞亮. Cheng 256 and P2794v have 賢 for the latter character.

512 **young man** The 'hair bound' designates maturity.

516 **... time** It is grammatically impossible to construe the line as given. It seems that 欲 has been used by example of the penultimate character in the preceding rhymed line. The logical emendation is 離 (Iriya 143b). For 兒家, cf. *Yu-hsien k'u*, p. 2.

518 **when** P2794v has 曾無 'have never' instead of 何曾.

520 **again** 'Again' is added to the translation. P2794v has 痊對 ('make up for'(?)) instead of 渡得.

521 **tower** 青樓. Cf. Ts'ao Chih 曹植, 'On Beauteous Women' 美人篇, *Ts'ao Tzu-chien chi* 曹子建集 (*SPTK*) 6.5b: 'Her green tower is next to the main road. It has high gates and double-thick doors.' 青樓臨大路, 高門結重關.

524 **marriage pillows** Literally, 'mandarin duck [quilt/coverlet]'. See the eighteenth of the nineteen old poems in *WH*, 29.5b, for this figure.

525 **carrier pigeon** The Chinese actually says 雁 'wild goose' which is an allusion to the means by which Su Wu 蘇武 (cf. his biography in the *History of the Han Dynasty* (*PNP*) 54.20a) had a letter sent back to the Son of Heaven while he was in captivity among the Hsiung-nu.

527 **weave** 識 → 織 (Hsü 32).

529 **grape arbour** 蒲桃 which I assume is a variant for 葡萄, also written 蒲陶.

531 **Ch'iu Hu** *Biographies of Virtuous Women* 列女傳 (*SPTK*) 5.17ab – paraphrase: Ch'iu Hu of Lu had taken a wife but five days later was called to an official position in Ch'en 陳 where he spent five years before returning. As he neared his home, he saw beside the road a woman picking mulberry leaves and was pleased with her. He got down from his chariot and said to her, 'Toiling in the fields is not as good as enjoying a bountiful year, and working on the mulberry trees is not as good as meeting a minister. Now, I have some money and I am willing to give it to you.' The wife replied, 'I work hard at picking the mulberry to make a living and to support my parents. I don't want your money.' Ch'iu Hu reached home, gave money to his mother, and sent someone to call his wife. When she appeared, he discovered it was the woman who, just a moment before, had been picking mulberry leaves. Feeling his actions vile, she left him and went to the east where she committed suicide by throwing herself into the river.

There is also a T'ang colloquial version of this story, see T154–9.

533 **beautiful teeth** 板齒 does not mean 'protruding teeth' (Waley 36). The term is equivalent to 門牙/齒 and means simply 'incisors/front teeth'. It appears in Tu Fu's 'Poem in Jest to a Friend' 戲贈友詩, *Tu-shih ching-ch'üan* 杜詩鏡銓 (*Ssu-pu chi-yao* 四部集要, Taipei, 1962) 9.6a: 'One morning he was kicked by a horse; His lip was split and he lost his front teeth.' 一朝被馬踏, 脣裂板齒無. Cf. T139.11–12 for another hero in Tun-huang popular literature whose beautiful front teeth were knocked out.

The legend about Wu Tzu-hsü's teeth is not that they were protruding but that they were beautiful. 'Wu Tzu-hsü had beautiful teeth. During his flight from Ch'u, he came to Protect Tooth Mountain. Fearing that he would be recognized by others, he knocked out his teeth with a stone upon which the mountain spirit rumbled. And that is why it is called Protect Tooth Mountain. At the foot of it, there is a temple to Wu Tzu-hsü.' 伍子胥美齒牙. 避楚至護牙山. 恐爲人所識. 以石擊毀其牙. 山神爲震. 因名護牙. 下有子胥廟. From *T'u-shu chi-ch'eng* 圖書集成 (Shanghai, 1884), typeset edn, 'Affairs of Men' 人事, *tien* 15, quoting *T'ai-p'ing ch'ing-hua* 太平清話 by Ch'en Chi-ju 陳繼儒 (1558–1639).

536 **moment** P2794v has 且 instead of 旦. S328 is ambiguous.

538 **evaded** For 方便, see Śāriputra line 541n1. The text would seem to say that Wu Tzu-hsü wrote a note to his wife in an irregular style of calligraphy 帖寫 but I am sceptical. I follow Chiang 114 who says that 寫 and 卸 are interchangeable and, therefore, that 帖寫 must stand for 推卸 or 脫卸. P2794v has 相 instead of 而.

539 **affairs** P2794v (*To-so* 66.7) has 謗錯相忏; Cheng, *Popular*, 256–7 reads 謗惜錯忏.

540 **each other** Cf. T435.6 and T718.9ff.

541 **Your** 娘子 is supernumerary. Cheng 257 and P2794v drop 姓仵 'surname is Wu'.

542 **grassy plains** 草野 is often used simply to refer to 'poor/common folks' but, in this line 'cold door' 寒門 has already given us that meaning. More specifically, the term refers to the dwelling of a man out of office which, in contradistinction to the husband holding high office in the previous line, fits very well. Cf. the following line by Po Chü-i, 'Dwelling in a Hermitage (*araṇya*) 蘭若寓居, *Po-shih ch'ang-ch'ing chi* (*SPTK*) 6.5a: 'The famous minister was old and so sought repose; retiring, he settled on the grassy plains.' 名宦老慵求, 退身安草野.

543 **husband** 夫聟. See the notes to the medicine poem above, line 445n2 (xxxi). 聟 = 壻.

547 **he** Cheng 257 and P2794v add 胥.

551 **...goal** 未達於前, cf. T362.13, 即達前所. A less likely translation of this would be 'before I had even walked up to her'.

553 **hero** For 列, Chou 309.1 prints 烈 which reads better.

561 **...lower** The prosody of this line is unusual in the original. The first 或 is probably an error for a word similar in meaning to 沸.

562 **Milky Way** Chou 309.3 prints 雲漢 which is certainly correct. It is also the wording of P2794v (*To-so* 67.2).

563 **chill** With all that sand aloft, I doubt that the wind would be very 'clear/gentle/refreshing' 清 which is as the text has it. The whole impression one gets from reading this particular poem is somewhat surrealistic. Note, for example, the colours in the next line and the images of the lines succeeding it. The author is trying, successfully, I think, to make an expressionistic statement of the state of mind Wu Tzu-hsü is in at this stage of his flight.
howls 喻 (*i̯u-*) → 吁 (*xi̯u*)(?), 'whistles, blows'. 喻 cannot be made to mean 'as if; as though'.

564 **White** 白 seems necessary for the parallelism but is a strange modifier for grass unless we accept it in the surrealistic vein mentioned in the preceding note. Prof. Hanan has suggested to me that it might mean 'withered'.

566 **Crows and magpies** Both the T editors and Chou print 鳥鵲 but I think 烏鵲 seems more reasonable.

568 **Otters** 水猫 → 水狗 (?), 'common otter'. *Mao* and *pao* both beginning with labials, I suspect, however, that 水豹 may have been intended.

573 **...renunciation** Is this declaration made to the river? To his enemies? To his wife? The latter would appear unlikely inasmuch as Wu Tzu-hsü has been running, at the least, one day and one night since he left his wife whereas this line speaks of 'today'. However, there is a common proverb which might indicate the need for an emendation of 捨 to 識. See *Hua-yüeh hen*, 2.43b: 'They met but did not recognize each other.' 相逢不相識 (cf. also T10.13a). If such be the case, 今日 could either be taken as a narrative lapse or simply a vague reference to the recent past. Or he might be saying 'if we should meet *again* today...'. Without emendation and taking

不 as a mild intensifying particle (Chiang 190–1), we might render this as 'though we met today, we forsook each other'. Even so, I cannot quite understand why Wu Tzu-hsü should be thinking of his wife – with whom he had to employ every artifice to free himself – in these circumstances. From the following lines, it is clear that he is extremely worried about his chances of getting across the river. Not to cross it might be considered a sort of 'renunciation'. My translation hedges somewhat to preserve the ambiguities but tends to indicate he is thinking of his enemies who are the objects of his vengeful hatred in the preceding line.

578 **... grasses** This line means that no one escapes the will of heaven, just as all grasses are swayed by the wind. Wu Tzu-hsü is saying that, no matter what happens to him, he must follow his fate.

579 **... deities** This line has a suspiciously Buddhist ring to it.

586 **egrets** 白鷺 *Egretta gurzetta*. The emendation of the T editors is good, 白露 being a solar term. Bernard Read, *Chinese Materia Medica* (*Avian Drugs*) (Peking, 1932), p. 22, says that the egret comes when the dews 露 are thick and hence the name. The construction of this sentence seems faulty yet the difficulty may be partially alleviated by recalling that the *Pen-ts'ao* lists 白鳥 as another name for the egret. Thus 白 might be considered as governing both 鷺 and 鳥, the three characters together being an extended cognomen for 'egret'.

587 **gliding** Various notes in the *WH* interpret 紛泊 as the 'aspect of flying about'. See *CWTTT* 27919.14.

592 **... ripples** This sentence seems to say 'the *turbid* waters[?] of the river crested in waves'. But parallelism demands that we emend 江沌 → 江魨, 'the Yangtze porpoise', *Spheroides vermicularis*.

594 **guides** My translation shows that I do not accept the emendation of the T editors. Literally, 'points to Orion and Lucifer for the right [direction]'.

595 **Min Mountain** Here, again, a geographical feature of Szechwan (Sung-p'an District 松潘) which would have been rather far out of Wu Tzu-hsü's way.

596 **... around** The justification for this translation is T42.6.

rushed Iriya 145a attributes the sounds in this line to the roaring of the (real) tigers and wolves in the previous sentence. I do not accept this interpretation primarily because it does not fully express the function of 似 and because it necessitates taking 濆濆 in an unusual sense. This expression is not attested elsewhere but it is unusual to find 濆 by itself referring to anything other than water (usually means *surging*). Finally, I believe it must be considered in conjunction with the following clause rather than the preceding one.

599 **saw** Or 'there appeared'.

ballad (棹)謳 is, specifically, a song sung by an oarsman while he rows.

600 **reel** This is the most immediate and obvious explanation. But 輪 is sometimes used for 綸 which may mean 'fishing-line'. Also see T13.5 just below where 輪 may be construed as a parallel equivalent to 索.

evidently 欲以(似) ≡ 似, 欲 being genuinely an 'empty word', Chiang 189.

602 **You** 仕 = 士 (Hsü 32).

trouble 屈, see Śāriputra line 773n1.

603 **... you** Literally, 'see [= meet] you'.

604 **this** See Waley's good explanation in 'Notes', 173, where he takes 之 as meaning 這.

607 **appeared** 見. Waley translates this passage as 'suddenly [he] noticed that there was someone among the reeds'. Iriya's (145a) translation is similar. This is certainly possible but I prefer to take 見 as 現 because, by this time, Wu Tzu-hsü has already emerged from the reeds as is evident from a clause in the previous line, 即出蘆中.

611 **... questions** 'Using it' and 'a series of questions' have been added to the translation. Unlike the rest of the verse in the story, this passage is neither regularly rhymed nor does it retain the seven (4–3) beat pattern characteristic elsewhere.

Though there are six beats to a line, the poet is permissive as to where he lets the caesura fall (3–3, of course, would be the expected pattern). The rhymes, if they can be called that, consist of *e* and *an* sounds.

The interpretation of 歌淸風 presents some difficulties. Does it mean 'sang briskly' or 'sang in the clear breezes'? Or might it mean, as my translation rashly assumes, that he sang the tune 'Soothing Breezes'? If so, as in the dramatic *ch'ü* or *tz'u* (see Introduction pp. 22–3), any suitable words could be used to fill in the fixed tune pattern. Note that 淸和風 is an alternate title for the well-known tune 'Washing in the Sandy Brook' 浣溪沙. Wen Ju-hsien 聞汝賢. *Tz'u-p'ai hui-shih* 詞牌彙釋 (Taipei, 1963), p. 381.

613 **distant** 䖍 = 逈 which is vulgar for 迥 'far'. Because of the rather peculiar grammar, it would seem that this word must technically be treated as an adverb. Iriya 145a renders it as 'hiding'(?). If we are to emend, 窘 'in straits' might be considered. All in all, these lines do not read smoothly.

616 **Perhaps** 爲當 ≡ 還當, see Chiang 176.

. . . tumbleweed Perhaps 'the appearance of floating duckweed' (if we take 漂蓬 → 漂萍(?)). Chiang 176 has 飄蓬 which expresses well the sense of lonely drifting about, 蓬 being a component in many plant names, one of which has woolly seeds that fly about.

617 **desolate** See Chiang 145. 旅 is given correctly in Chou 310.3 as 㭹 which is a graphical error for 梖, cf. T8.6.

islets 舟 → 洲 (Hsü 110).

620 **rudeness** Literally, 'Not ashamed of my lowliness and stupidity.' There is a conventional expression, 不恥下問, which refers to the readiness of a superior to ask instructions of those beneath him. I do not think, however, that this expression has any direct bearing on the present occurrence of 不恥 for in the succeeding clause it is the (humble) fisherman who is doing the asking. Nor is it likely that we may interpret as 'do not be ashamed that I am a' for such an interpretation is simply too awkward. 下末 refers to someone in an inferior position. *Shih-ming* 釋名 (*SPTK*) 7.52b: 'The ornament for someone who is in a lower position is called *pei*. *Pei* means *pei* (inferior) and is an expression of subordination.' 下末之飾曰琕. 琕卑也, 在下之言也.

623 **virtue and learning** Not 'Taoist magic'. By a change in the wording, the meaning of this saying has been changed drastically from what it meant in its ultimate source, *Chuang-tzu*, 'A Great and Seminal Teacher' 大宗師, p. 50: 'When the springs go dry, fish have to share the land. They blow moisture on each other and they moisten each other with froth. But it would be better if they could forget each other in the rivers and lakes.' 泉涸, 魚相與處於陸. 相呴以濕. 相濡以沫. 不如相忘於江湖. + 'Just as.'

624 **humble servant** 下奏(走), cf. T251.7.

625 **vainly think up** 虛相 → 虛想(?).

626 **make my way** See Śāriputra line 178n.

628 **understanding** 知委. Chiang 85 treats this term along with 委 and 委知, saying that all three mean 'to know'. I am inclined to feel, however, that, in some cases, there is a little bit more involved. See, for example, T22.12: 'I didn't know the details of the situation.' 臣不細委知; T156.15: 'I had no way of knowing what the situation in my home was.' 家內無由知委; and T611.14: 'I am aware of that fact.' 我以知委. In a translation into English, at least, more than a simple 'to know' is often needed. Cf. also the phrase 原委 which means 'the ins and outs/beginning and end/ details/ circumstances [of a case/story]'. Here, 'understanding [of my situation]' is called for.

635 **clarify** 分雪, cf. T250.1, 'be explicit'; T369.5, 'state one's case'; and T336.1 where the editors have → 分說.

distinguish 別 I take as 別白, 'discriminate/distinguish clearly'

636 **... not base** Waley 38 gives the wrong impression by translating this as 'will always rise in the world'. The fisherman is talking about himself and I suspect, from what transpires below, that he is really not much interested in 'rising in the world'. In these lines and in the following three difficult allusions, he is explaining why it would be proper for him to assist Wu Tzu-hsü.

637 **... wanting** Iriya 145b translates this proverb as 'Do not despise others; do not covet others' jade.' He has either misread or emended 貧 to be 貪 which is unacceptable because of its parallel relationship to 賤 above. I am also opposed to Iriya's translation on the grounds that it simply does not fit with the rest of the fisherman's speech. I object to Waley's translation on the grounds that it requires an undue amount of amplification and transposition and because of the criticism mentioned in the preceding note. I regret that I have been unable to identify the source of the proverb and that my own translation has twice added to the original: 'can ... between good and bad'.

638 **... wine** 'Now Duke Mu had gone hunting on Liang Mountain and, having lost several fine horses during the night, sent a party of officials in search of them. They traced them to the foot of Mount Ch'i where there was a group of more than three hundred savages gathered together eating the horse flesh. The officials were afraid to provoke them and so hurried back to report to Duke Mu. "If you send off soldiers to arrest them at once," they said, "you will be able to take them all." Duke Mu sighed and said, "The horses are already dead. If I should proceed on that account to slaughter human beings, the people will say that I put more value upon animals than I do upon men." And so he had ten great urns of fine wine brought out from the army's supplies and sent over to the foot of Mount Ch'i. When the messengers arrived, they proclaimed the Duke's wishes and presented the wine, saying, "Our Lord has said that eating fine horseflesh unaccompanied by wine is injurious. And so he has presented you with this fine wine." The savages kowtowed to express their deep gratitude and then divided up the wine. "Not only did he refrain from punishing us for our thievery of the horses," they sighed, "but he was even concerned for our health and so presented us with this wine. The Duke's benevolence is great indeed! How can we repay him?"' This rendition is translated from the thirtieth chapter of *Tung-chou lieh-kuo chih* 東周列國志 (Peking, 1962), vol. I, p. 255.

639 **... armies** *Faute de mieux*, I hazard that this may be a reference to Sun Shu-ao 孫叔敖 (Giles, *BD* no. 1818) who was a great statesman of the Spring and Autumn period and who is described in the *Chronicle of Tso*, Hsüan 宣 12, Legge, V.318ff, as being at the head of the Ch'u 楚 army in the Battle of Pi 邲. The 'three armies' refer to the armies of the great feudal states during the Chou Dynasty in contrast to the 'six armies' of the Emperor. Sun Shu-ao was supposed to have been thrice appointed prime minister, which did not make him happy, and thrice relieved of his duties, which did not make him sad. In a biographical notice (*Shiki* 119.2–4) of about two hundred words, the character for 'three' occurs five times. The Grand Historian remarks that Sun Shu-ao wisely instructed and guided the people. In particular, once when the market of the Ch'u capital, Ying, was in disorder, Sun Shu-ao said but one word and things returned to normal. 太史公曰:孫叔敖出一言郢市復. This would qualify him for the epithet 能言. This epithet is appropriate for a subject or minister in contrast to 'knows how to listen' 能聽 which is descriptive of a ruler. See *Jen-wu chih* 人物志 (*SPTK*) B.4ab under 'Abilities' 材能. I am also attracted to the identification with Sun Shu-ao because he is from the same general historical period as the other two allusions in this series. 正 = 政 glossed as 治.

640 **... reward** *Shiki* 66.25: 'Of old, the King of Ch'i sent Ch'un-yü K'un 淳于髡 as an ambassador to present a snow-goose to the Kingdom of Ch'u. After he went out of the city-gates, the snow-goose flew off along the way and he was left vainly holding

an empty cage. But he made up a story which he told the King of Ch'u when he went to call on him: "The King of Ch'i sent me here as an ambassador to present a snow-goose to you. As I was crossing the river, I could not bear to see how thirsty the snow-goose was, so I let it out to have a drink whereupon it flew away from me. I wanted to commit hara-kiri or strangle myself and die. Yet I feared that people would criticize my King as having ordered the suicide of an official because of a bird. The snow-goose is a feathered creature and there are many like it. I wanted to buy another to replace it but I would have been dishonest and deceitful to you, oh King, to have done so. I wanted to flee to another land, but was vexed that to do so would have caused the failure of this embassy between my two Kings. Therefore, I have come to confess my faults. I kowtow to you, Great King, and will submit to whatever punishment you mete out."

'The King of Ch'u replied: "It's marvellous that Ch'i has such honest officials as this." He rewarded Ch'un-yü K'un liberally with gifts that were double the amount he would have received had he brought the snow-goose.'

Without seeing the manuscript, LSY has pointed out to me that 重貴 reads awkwardly here. He suggests that a more natural reading would be 重賞. S328 does, indeed, read thus.

I am indebted to Iriya 163–4n78 for the identification of the source of this allusion.

655 **... not** 'I wonder whether he might well not' is derived from the pattern 不多 ... 以否 which amounts to something like 'chances are good'. 以否 (also appears as 已不/已否/以不) is the T'ang colloquial equivalent of 與否. See Chiang 178. Cf. T186.7.

657 **... all** 逡巡, see Chiang 137 and Maudgalyāyana line 56n2.

658 **ten** For 番 as a numerary adjunct, cf. T549.1. The character is actually written 翻 on S328.

663 **song** This song is untitled. Like 'Soothing Breezes' above, it departs from the usual metrical scheme of the prosimetric narrative. The prosody here is (4–4–6–6) × 2.

664 **gentleman** 仕 = 士.

669 **... difficult** Iriya 146a translates as 'Don't be worried about betrayal'(?). The meaning of 二難 adopted in my translation is derived from the tertiary definition of the two characters.

678 **river** Waley has them eating in the middle of the river. Though there is some problem in unravelling the sequence here, the syntax (especially 便即) would seem to indicate that they ate first and *then* rowed. The middle of the river is mentioned because it is here that Wu Tzu-hsü, having had a good chance to ruminate on his full stomach, decides to offer the fisherman a gift.

680 **... extent** The T editors' collation note is somewhat confusing, inasmuch as they offer both 飽 and 報 as possible emendations for 包. Iriya 164n79 states that 報 simply does not read. Waley 39 has 'a look of gratitude is enough' which he arrived at, no doubt, by taking 包 as 色. This is, indeed what S328 gives. The succeeding clause is pure hypothesis on Wu Tzu-hsü's part. He has received one meal and, feeling indebted, makes an offer of a gift as repayment. I do not think he intends 'to exert himself' for the fisherman – at least, not yet. A proverb, after all, does not really have to be taken literally. Waley translates 食 as 'dish' but this is difficult to justify. See below, T23.5. Compare also T868.7: 凡喫人一食, 斬人一色, 喫人兩食, 与人著力. 色, according to T891n25, was originally 邑 but the two characters are very difficult to distinguish in Tun-huang manuscripts.

682 **... boatman** The syntax is 以懷中璧玉, 贈船人.

684 **gratitude** It appears that 信 is not really necessary, other than to preserve the 4–6 prose rhythm (cf. 於 just below). However, it is clear from T14.8 that 信 stands for 信物 which is the basis for my translation.

688 **really ought** 大須 cf. T20.5.

692 **... cohabit** Waley's ellipsis is an indication of the difficulty of these lines. I am confident that I have understood their meaning but have had to amplify in English slightly to make the translation comprehensible.

696 **possibility** Literally, 'offence, error'.

699 **... offer** Waley 39 interprets this incorrectly as meaning that the sword belongs to the King.

Excalibur 龍泉 'Dragon Spring' was the name of a fabulous sword. There is a story concerning it which is quite similar to the last mention of King Arthur's famous weapon in Malory's *Morte D'Arthur*. The details are given in the 'Biography of Chang Hua' in the *History of the Chin Dynasty* 晉書, 張華傳 (*PNP*) 36.12b–13a. Here I present a brief sketch: Dragon Spring and another sword, T'ai O 太阿, were located in the foundation of a jail by an astrologer named Lei Huan 雷煥 who had understood the significance of a strange purple light 紫氣 sighted in the heavens. When he died, the sword which he kept for himself (the other he gave to Chang Hua) was passed on to his son. Once, as he was crossing a river, the sword, of its own power, leapt into the water and was surrounded by two dragons which churned up the water furiously. This was the last it was ever seen. The following episode of the present narrative, in which Wu Tzu-hsü throws the sword into the river, echoes this story. For the connection between astronomical phenomena and treasure swords, see Edward H. Schafer, *Pacing the Void: T'ang Approaches to the Stars* (Berkeley, 1977), pp. 148–60.

700 **... Ching** 荊珍 here is 荊璞 'uncut/crusted jade from Ching Mountain' which, like the sword in the previous note, is mentioned in the *History of the Chin Dynasty*, 'Records of Emperor Ching' 景帝紀 (*PNP*) 2.3a.

702 **met** 朝. Waley 39 has 'day of meeting'. One cannot have it both ways. Either it means 'day' or, as I prefer, 'meeting'.

... early 蒲柳之年. Because the water-willow loses its leaves earlier than the other trees, it is commonly used as a metaphor for rapid ageing in men. This too, be it noted, may be found in the *History of the Chin Dynasty*, 'Biography of Ku Yüeh-chih' 顧悅之傳 (*PNP*) 77.15b: 'Yüeh-chih and Chien-wen were the same age but the former's hair had long since turned grey. The Emperor asked him why and he replied: "The fir and cypress are so constituted that they are luxuriant even after a frost. The water-willow's character causes it to lose its leaves even before autumn comes on."'

704 **... leave** Iriya 146b translates 'forget about the matter of the sword and jade disc', which is probably a transposition from 'don't keep [in mind]'.

vindicate To translate 表 as 'understand' (Waley 39) and 'read [my thoughts]' (Iriya 146b) is acceptable. It is, however, an unusual word in this situation and, I believe, extremely important for understanding the real significance of the fisherman's actions below. Although I am not entirely satisfied with the way the translation of this sentence reads, 'vindicate' does seem to be close to the meaning intended. 'If you wish to' is derived from the subjunctive 'if you would' 子若.

706 **his gifts** Added to the translation.

712 **... surface** I have reversed the order of 'sank' and 'surface' in the translation.

713 **hovered** 偏偏 = 翩翩 (Hsü 32).

714 **tremulously** 戰悼. The T editors' emendation to 踔 is incorrect. It should read 戰掉.

715 **... frenzy** 騰波 may also mean 'leap above the waves' (*CWTTT* 45921.9) which is how Iriya 146b takes it.

burrowed 攢 → 鑽, even though there are few fish which would really 'burrow' into the mud. Perhaps 濽 'splash about'. The etymon 贊, in any case, is certainly correct. The only problem is with the radical element.

716 **mud** 埿 = 泥.
Dragons Literally, 'fish and dragons'.
leaped 透 meaning 'to jump'. See line 314n1.
717 **told ...** My translation is derived from 分付 glossed as 吩付 (not 咐) 'to enjoin; to charge' which is a characteristic T'ang usage of the expression (*Tz'u-t'ung* 1793c).
719 **skitter ...** I.e. they came out of their hiding places. 跳梁 ≡ 跳踉. Much of the following passage is either recondite or repetitive. It is one of the weakest passages in the story. To make it slightly more palatable, I have inserted a number of similes where the original has direct statements.
720 **... moon** Literally, 'the sun and moon [shone] pure and bright'.
721 **clouds** S328 clearly has 雲.
728 **... water** Iriya 146b has rendered 淼漫 as 'hazy' but this is not possible.
731 **the better part of** Added to the translation.
735 **... companion** Waley 40 and Iriya 146b both have reservations about the meaning of this sentence but I cannot see any particular difficulty in understanding it.
736 **... shores** I have had to make two emendations in this clause, 干 → 竿 and 莫 → 漠/寞 (glossed as 靜 or 寂) 'lonely, desolate'.
... boat Literally, 'tie up the line [of my boat]'. 劍 → 綠 (glossed as 索).
740 **not forget me** In the light of what the fisherman says above and does below, this appears an antithetical statement. But, from the standpoint of the Chinese code of honour, his reputation after his death would be considered as important as his material comfort while alive.
742 **Even** 由 = 猶.
743 **... benefactor** Hsü Shen's 許愼 note to 'The Pearl of the Marquis of Sui' 隋侯之珠 in *Huai-nan-tzu* (*SPTK*) 6.3b: 'The Marquis of Sui once saw a large snake which had been cut. He treated it with medicine. Later, the snake repaid him by presenting a large pearl from the river.' 隋侯見大蛇傷斷. 以藥傅之. 後蛇於江中御大珠以報之. Also see *Ch'ü* no. 59.
749 **... go there** This clause added to the translation.
756 **services** Added to the translation. An alternative interpretation based on the emendation 得 → 待 would be: 'treat you very well'(?).
761 **... wild man** Compare line 225n1.
768 **... does it not** By all means! Literally, 'the rationale for ... is like this'. 理合 '[in accord with] reason, [it is] appropriate to', hence 'follows logically'. Or 'the reason *ought* [cf. *Ch'ü* nos. 24, 83, 84] to be like this'. LSY suggests a possible pun of 絲 'threads' and 斯, cf. T2.10. After completing his course of study and deciding to seek a position as an official in the state of Wei 魏, Ch'iu Hu also disarranges his hair and acts deranged in another Tun-huang story (see T155.12). It appears that this odd behaviour was meant to impress the ruler of his supplicant's passionate sincerity.
773 **After they parted** Added to the translation.
774 **... own way** 由如四鳥分飛. This is a common figure of speech that derives from the story related by Yen Hui 顏回 in *K'ung-tzu chia-yü* 孔子家語 (*SPTK*) 5.2ab (section 16) about a mother bird on Huan Mountain 桓山 and her brood. When the four fledglings had grown up, she tearfully sent them off knowing that she would never see them again.
775 **... separated** 狀若三荊離別 is another common trope which occurs frequently in combination with the 'four bird' figure. See, for example, Lu Chi's 陸機 'Yü-chang hsing' 豫章行 in the *WH* 28.3a where Li Shan 李善 explains 三荊 as three thorn-bushes growing together from the same root. Hsü 33 cites the following anecdote which is from *Hsü ch'i-hsieh chi* 續齊諧記 by Wu Chün 吳均 (469–520) (*Han-wei ts'ung-shu* edn, *ts'e* 89) 1b–2a: 'T'ien Chen and his two brothers, who were from the capital, were discussing together the division of their wealth. The livestock and

property were all to be divided equally. Only a purple thorn-bush which grew in front of the hall, they decided together, would have to be broken into three pieces. On the next day when they cut down this tree, it withered and died, its roots having the appearance of flames. Chen went over to look at it and was greatly startled. "The tree, after all," he said to his two younger brothers, "has but a single trunk. It heard that it was about to be split up and, because of that, it became shrivelled. Here is a case where men have not proven themselves the equal of wood."

'As a result, they were disconsolate beyond measure and stopped separating the tree to which the tree responded by becoming exuberant. The brothers were moved by this. They combined their wealth and lived as a filial household.'

The same anecdote, in a slightly different form, occurs in D970 which consists of stories in prose, that about T'ien Chen and his brothers being the first (*Opisanie*, I. 573, no. 1455).

779 **final favour** Like that of the young lady earlier, the fisherman's death was intentional and done to protect Wu Tzu-hsü.

781 **oh** A distinctive feature of this song is the frequent occurrence of the particle 兮. I have not mechanically rendered it as 'oh' in every case.

787 **What** 何勿, which appears on T27.7 of this piece and also on T221.2 and T726.2 as 何物, means simply 何 'what/what reason'.

789 **bobs ...** 浮没 or 浮沉 would not be cause for suspicion but 浮没沉 is. If not an error, it must at least be declared clumsy.

791 **... sword** 一寸愁腸似刀割. Cf. *Shih-shuo hsin-yü* 世說新語 'Dismissal' 黜免, section 28 (*SPTK*) 下. 下. 29a: 'Every inch of his intestines was sundered.' 其腸皆寸寸斷.

798 **Now** Iriya 147b interprets this section (down to 知復何言) as a monologue spoken by Wu Tzu-hsü.

isolated There are numerous meanings for 契闊 (see the interminable note in *Tz'u-t'ung* 2404–6). I have chosen the gloss 睽隔 because it seems to fit the present context best.

800 **in the morning ...** The parallel relation with the following sentence makes one wish that 夙夜 could somehow be made to mean simply 'at night'. That, however, is impossible for the entire four-character expression is taken verbatim from *The Book of Odes*, Legge, IV.543.

801 **morning respects** 晨省 means to ask after one's parents (here, supposedly, his ruler at court) in the morning, in contrast to 昏定 which is to settle them in at eventide. I suspect, however, that 省 is an error for a word meaning evening or night, perhaps 宵 or 昏, both of which bear some orthographic resemblance to 省.

remiss 偿 = 僁 = 愆.

802 **ill-luck** Some modern dictionaries give *t'ò* as the pronunciation of 魄 in this expression. Historically, this is incorrect since it was used interchangeably with 薄 in early texts (*Tz'u-t'ung* 2532c).

... feelings The force of 知 is very weak here, so weak that this sentence could also be rendered 'what more could he say?' or 'there was nothing more for him to say; nothing could be done about it'. Cf. T14.8. P2794v has 伏 instead of 復.

807 **... question** Adapted from 'He sought to retreat but [could] not retreat; he sought to go forward but [could] not go forward.'

811 **desolate mountains** Chou 313.9 does not indicate that 莽蕩 is a proper name. See line 189n above.

812 **bamboos and creepers** 騰竹 (?) 'soaring bamboos'. I think not. 籐(藤) would probably be a better reading.

813 **dodder ...** 松羅 is not a 'blanket/covering of pines' but a mistake for 松蘿. It is also the name of a mountain thirteen *li* northeast of Hsiu-ning District Town 休寧 in Anhwei. Surprisingly, it is within the realm of geographical possibility for this

story. Perhaps the name Dodder Mountain suggested the visual detail presented here.

815 **chirping** 關關 refers specifically to the sound of the osprey. See *The Book of Odes*, Legge, IV.1.

816 **song** Which, to my mind, borders on incoherence.

819 **shades** 莫 I take as 漠. This probably stands for the nether world.

820 **... anxiety** 栖惶 I understand as 栖遑 / 皇. Elsewhere in this story, it is written 恓惶 (T4.8 and 8.4).

824 **and true** Instead of 良, P2794v has 'minister' 臣.

827 **penchant** 怜 = 憐.

828 **death** Iriya 164n83 suggests they are starving themselves to death to suit his taste for tiny waists.

831 **beauty** 姿首 'pretty face and beautiful hair'.

832 **... behave** The basic grammatical pattern of this line reduces to the rhetorical expression 豈有此理.

833 **fleeing** 逃逝 (?), compare 逃世 'escape from the world as a recluse'.
constant 鎮 'frequent; for a long period of time', Chiang 169–70.

836 **step in shadows** 躡影 was the name of a swift horse of the First Emperor which can also be written 躡景 (*ying*). The literal meaning of the expression is 'fleeting shadows'.

837 **Mount Yen** Southeast of Chi 薊 District in Hopei province. Though the geography of this story is often unreal, as I have pointed out, the author does not here intend to place the action in the Yen area. He is making an allusion which is a variation of the proverb 燕然勒石 'to display martial prowess'. The inscription itself is normally referred to as 銘 rather than 勒 or 頌 as here. The source of the allusion, in brief, is as follows: in the time of Emperor Ho 和 of the Han Dynasty, the Hsiung-nu tribes experienced a rebellion, the southern tribes becoming satellites of the Han Empire. The northern tribes, however, continued to make raids on the border areas and, at the request of the southern tribes, the Emperor sent a contingent of troops under the command of Tou Hsien 竇憲 deep into the enemy's territory. It was an entirely successful campaign and, to commemorate it, a stone with an inscription by Pan Ku 班固 was erected on the top of Yen-jan Mountain. See Pan Ku's inscription and preface to it 封燕然山銘並序 in 'Biography of Tou Hsien', *History of the Later Han* (*PNP*) 23.22a *et seq.*

838 **dust and brambles** Iriya's 148b emendation to 風塵 is to be highly commended inasmuch as it is a constant metaphor for the rigours of travel. The resulting translation would be something like 'my temples stained [autumn-]grey by the wind-blown dust which I brave'.

839 **great cold** 天塞 must be an error for 天寒 (see Chou 314.2) which in itself is a perpetuation of the *Chuang-tzu*'s (p. 239) miswriting in 'Abdication' 讓王 of 大寒, as it appears in the *Lü-shih ch'un-ch'iu*, 'Cautious Men' 呂氏春秋, 愼人 (*SPTK*) 3.4a.

847 **K'uai-chi Mountain** 會稽 mountain is southeast of modern Shao-hsing 紹興 in Chekiang Province. I take this as a reference to the mountain because of the verb 登 (cf. T17.5). However, 吳會 might equally well refer to the commanderies of Wu and K'uai-chi which would be anachronistically employed here inasmuch as the former was established during the Eastern Han and the latter during the Ch'ing. The two commanderies together comprised large portions of modern Chekiang and Kiangsu. Iriya 148b understands the expression in the latter sense.
happened 屬 glossed as 適 (?).

849 **trying to find it** Added to the translation.

850 **compelled** 摧 in the sense of 抑壓.

851 **tigers** (大)蟲. + 'milled about' and 'prowled everywhere'.

852 **raucously** 姓姓 onomatopoeia(?). I propose that this may be identical with 悻悻 'angrily' or 惺惺 which is descriptive of the cry of a bird. P2794v has 性子 (?). See line 852n3 below for a possibility of parallelism. Hsü 33, however, wishes to emend to 狌狌 (i.e. 猩猩 chimpanzee) which, although it makes for perfect parallelism with baboon below, still leaves me wondering how a chimpanzee can be considered a fowl (in spite of Hsü's disclaimer to the contrary). LSY, in support of Hsü, has mentioned the expression 人禽 which means 'men and beasts'. My translation shows that I am still not convinced. It should be noted that there is a 生生鳥 (also called 命命鳥), which is a bird of the partridge family. It is known in Sanskrit as the *jīva(m)jīvaka*.

roared 名, in accordance with the notes just above and below, should be emended to 鳴. Cf. line 1141n.

angrily 狒狒 does mean 'baboon' (*Cynocephalus hamadryas*) but I think, for the sake of symmetry, we may emend to 茀茀 which, read as *po* in the entering tone, is descriptive of the angry howl of beasts. This, of course, would be incorrect if it could be discovered that 姓姓 were, in fact, the name of a bird as I have hinted it may be at the end of line 852n1. One final justification for my tentative interpretation outlined here is that the angry animal cries account well for the fear which suddenly grips Wu Tzu-hsü in the next sentence. P2794v has 祓祓(?).

853 **evident** P2794v has 'take' instead of 示.

went forward ... The following rhymed (*-ing* and *-eng*) four-syllable verse, which has been patched together from fragments of P2794v, is yet lacking something of the order of 乃(亭而)歌曰 to preface it. The sentence which follows the song indicates both that this was a sung passage and that Wu Tzu-hsü had probably stopped walking to sing it.

857 **... stars** For a description and a picture of swords decorated thus on the blade, see Schafer, *Pacing the Void*, pp. 157–8.

861 **rest** 消 in the sense of 'completion' 盡(?), 寧 in the sense of 'finish' 息 (?), together amounting to 'settled'.

865 **... silence** The same expression occurs on T601.1.

868 **sword song** 劍歌.

869 **Kuang-ling** 廣陵 name of an ancient city founded by King Huai of Ch'u (reigned 327–293 B.I.E.) which was located southeast of modern Chiang-tu District 江都 in Kiangsu Province.

870 **closely** 忽 → 急 (orthographical or typographical error). There were tight (i.e. *urgent*) security precautions at strategic points.

871 **Militiamen** 勒捕. Compare 勒率 'officers who pursue and arrest criminals'.

872 **replacements ...** 'Replacements of guards' is an attempt to render 鎮代 which strikes me as a rather peculiar expression. It is so peculiar, in fact, that an emendation to 鎮戍 (orthographic resemblance) might be considered. This would result in a translation something like 'there was a continuous [series/string] of guards/garrisons'.

874 **days** Neither 'a full month' nor 'ten months' will work here. This is a standard phrase for the passage of time in Tun-huang colloquial narratives. See Chang line 70n.

876 **and** P2794v has 'directly' 直 instead of 遂.

on his face The addition of 而行 'and went running' from P2794v is unnecessary inasmuch as it does not directly tally with the instructions of the fisherman. As far as the prose rhythm is concerned, however, a four-beat line is probably less preferable than a six-beat one.

878 **At that moment** To translate 正 below.

a minister ... 'Who was good at spotting talented men' (P2794v has 吳臣善別君子).

883 **market** 纏 = 廛.
884 **face** S328 adds 面 before 而.
886 **. . . closely** 的 (*ti*) 審. 的 in the sense of 'clearly' 明/'truly' 眞實/'accurate' 明確; 審 in the sense of 'clearly' 明/'in detail, closely' 詳/'thoroughly examining' 熟究. I follow Hsü 33 in punctuating after 審.
887 **. . . worth** Literally, 'one can know [that he is no ordinary fellow]'.
889 **detained** 遛 = 留.
891 **words** Following P2794v, I omit 相 only because it allows for a neater English rendering. T17.11 has 王 in the same position.
892 **. . . curtains** Cf. T792.5.
899 **laughed gleefully** Cf. T336.2, 笑呵呵.
901 **The dream shows** Added to the translation.
907 **I do wish** T723.10, T735.12.
908 **. . . ambitions** Waley 42 interprets this as meaning that the King wishes to tell Wu Tzu-hsü of his own ambitions. But 懷抱 is used several times in this story, all indirectly or directly in reference to Wu Tzu-hsü and it must here be very close to the 懷寃 which the minister who first spotted Wu Tzu-hsü mentioned in his report to the King. My chief objection to Waley's translation, however, is that, in the Chinese context, kings seldom express their 'ambitions' to a subject. As for the grammatical justification of my interpretation, 'and have him express his ambitions to me personally' more nearly conveys the grammar than does the translation I have given. Furthermore, 申 is generally restricted to persons of inferior status notifying or reporting to a superior. Finally, the motivation for Wu Tzu-hsü's outlandish behaviour is manifestly to draw the King's attention to him. It is he who has something on his mind and not the King. This is explicitly stated on T18.2: 'Therefore, I have placed myself in the hands of a wise ruler like yourself in the hopes that you might understand the workings of my heart.' Indeed, in the interview below, it is primarily Wu Tzu-hsü who says what is on his mind, not the King.
916 **sympathetically** 悲 in the sense of 悲憫. 予 has the force of 'confer' or 'grant'. In effect, the King was *granting* Wu Tzu-hsü his sympathy.
920 **bitterly cruel** For this meaning of 荼毒, see *The Book of Odes*, Legge, IV.525.
924 **. . . suffering** 'Taxed you, sir, to come here from so far'.
925 **smoothing down his hair** I assume that he does so to signal that he has found the 'wise king' 明主 he spoke of in the penultimate line of his last major song. No longer need his hair be dishevelled to symbolize his deranged state of mind. Waley 43 says that he 'clutched' his hair and Iriya 149b that he 'thrashed' it. My understanding of 攬, however, is that it primarily signifies gathering together a number of separate items, e.g. 攬統, 攬綴, 攬載, etc. In fairness to opposing interpretations, I should note that Chou 315.6 reads 攪 'to ruffle'.
928 **traditions** Added to the translation. Perhaps just 'carrying on the family' would be an adequate rendering.
929 **to flee . . .** 'Ran away; escaped; fled.'
934 **snake and dragon** This expression is probably due to Buddhist influence for it is constantly used by Buddhists to mean 'sacred and profane' or 'holy and common'.
935 **my ancestors** Or 'my late father'.
939 **supporting** '[Helping] to establish.'
943 **compromise your integrity** Because it is not your own land. Chou 315.11 has 乏少忠良列卿. 今欲爲臣屈節. Also see Hsü 110 for another view on the order and punctuation of this sentence which is awkward, to say the least. S328 has 命 rather than 今 so I have not translated 'In wishing to establish you *today* . . .'
946 **great favour** 大造 usually means 'great merit/achievement' and, in the sense of 造化 'creator', may have an even larger connotation. Here, however, I translate as 'favour' but it is the King's merit, of course, which enables him to bestow favours.

The entire sentence 臣是小人，虛沾大造 occurs in the 'Li Ling Transformation Text', T93.1. The words are exactly the same and the circumstances are similar. Li Ling utters these words to the chieftain to whom he has just surrendered and who has taken a liking to him, Wu Tzu-hsü to the King of Wu upon their first meeting.

already Iriya, *Index*, 25, says that 早是 = 既 'already'. Cf. T190.11 and 428, sixth line from end.

947 **raised to office** Hsü 110 punctuates after 立爲臣. The remainder of Wu Tzu-hsü's speech is then 死罪終當不敢 'under penalty of death, I dare not, in the end, [accept]'. My translation is an amplification of this interpretation of the text.

949 **... presumption** 死罪 is a conventional form of humility used in communicating with persons of exalted status.

953 **influence** 敢 → 感 ≡ 感化. Iriya 150a interprets 感 as 感應 or 'response [to your dream]'.

954 **Make** 'Acknowledge; confer; appoint.'

960 **agreeableness** 合光, literally, 'matched the brilliance [of the King]'(?). Perhaps this should be emended to 和光, an expression favoured by Buddhists to indicate the capacity to live with all sorts of people and not be contaminated by them.

962 **Heaven's soldiers** This becomes more familiar to us when we recall that every Christian nation has had 'God on our side' in every war that it fought. But, no matter, what follows is gross and unadulterated hyperbole. The reader must be prepared for anything.

963 **... allegiance** Although 歸臨 is somewhat unusual in this context, the meaning is clear enough. I do not think we may translate, with Iriya 150a, 'the fortresses on the four borders relaxed their guard'.

964 **submissive** 拈 → 帖 *t'ieh* meaning 'settled' or 'submissive' (cf. 妥貼) or, as Hsü 33 suggests, 怗 which is what the character on S328 appears to be.

966 **Yao and Shun** 堯舜, two semi-legendary paragons who ruled China during its golden age.

967 **Lofty** This is possible but an emendation to 煒煒 'shines brightly' might be considered. Cf. Iriya 150a 輝輝.

968 **heaven and earth** 乾川 (not 'dry streams') → 乾巛 = 乾坤. This is Hsü's (33) fine emendation.

972 **granaries** Or 'foodstuffs and granaries'.

over-flowed 益 → 溢.

975 **expressed ...** 送款 would appear to mean 'sent in tribute' but does not. It means 'to convey/express cordiality/friendliness'. 遞送款曲.

977 **Dragon ...** 景龍. See the Introduction pp. 11–12.

979 **Red Sparrow ...** 赤雀銜書. These exact words occur in Ts'ao Chih's rhapsodic eulogy on the red sparrow 赤雀賦贊, *Ts'ao Tzu-chien chi* (*SPTK*) 7.7b.

Spirit-fungi The term 芝草 may be applied to a purplish fungus which, in ancient times, was held to be a divinely efficacious medicine (also called 瑞芝 and 靈芝 or simply 芝). For a photograph of a cultured specimen, see *Jen-min hua-pao* 人民畫報, 4(1973), 25.

981 **... fields** This, alternatively, could mean that, when crossing on the narrow rice-field paths, they ceded the way to each other.

983 **teachings** This is a blatant anachronism for Buddhism did not exist in China at the time of Wu Tzu-hsü and it is problematic that either Taoism or Confucianism were sufficiently organized to be termed 'teachings' or 'religions'.

987 **... fixed prices** 市無二價. Cf. the signs which may be seen in many shops on Taiwan today: 不二價.

... holes (!)

992 **Indebted** 'Embarrassed by their indebtedness ...' See line 278n.

996 **... preserve** Literally, 'to act on his own authority'.
997 **bountiful** Actually, 'an excess of'.
999 **... stir my heart** 興心, alternatively, 'stir up the hearts of the people'.
consider 度 *tò*.
no ability Iriya's (105b) interpretation of this as meaning that Wu Tzu-hsü considers the expediton against Ch'u to be unwarranted is incorrect. 無堪 is a term of introspection, particularly when coupled with 自度 or 內省, etc.
1003 **... good deeds** 養子備老, 積行擬衰. Cf. T696.2, 人家積穀本防飢, 養子還徒(圖)被老時 and 674.3, 積穀防饑, 養子備老. The last occurrence attributes the saying to 'the book' 書. The *History of the Later Han* has 養子爲後 (*PNP*) 6.14b. Cf. *Tsu-t'ang chi*, II. 109.9, which has 養子代老 The usual modern wording of this proverb is 養兒待老, 積穀防飢. The substitution of 行 *saṃskāra* points to Buddhist influence.
1005 **sufficiently ... in you** Added to the translation.
1016 **to enlist in this venture** Added to the translation.
risk 判 need not be emended inasmuch as this was the usual T'ang form of 拚 (Hsü 32).
1017 **with the greatest urgency** 火急, see Śāriputra line 929n and Maudgalyāyana line 635n1.
1019 **valiant** 列 → 烈. In this passage, I have followed the punctuation suggested by Iriya's (150b) translation, i.e. pauses after 賞, 輕, and 夫. + 'Conferred.'
1020 **... plea** This is a free translation of the 'documentese' in the text. 所咨, cf. 所咨呈 which is a formula used in dispatches by high-ranking officials. 陳牒, cf. 呈牒 'to hand in a report'.
1025 **... force** 勇冠三軍 is a cliché, literally, 'champions in bravery in all the three armies'. Cf. *History of the Later Han*, 'Biography of Hsün Yü' 荀彧 (*PNP*) 70.29ab: 'Yen Liang and Wen Ch'ou were champions of the three armies.' 顏良文醜勇冠三軍. This entire passage is marred by excessive hyperbole.
1029 **... armour** Compare 徹七札焉 'pierced the seven layers of his armour'. Literally, I suppose, they were strong enough to bend a bow that could shoot through seven layers of armour.
1032 **... bolts** This is a difficult passage to construe. One requirement is that any decent interpretation cannot allow each one of those 900,000 soldiers to be given a thousand pieces of silk. My translation is based on the understanding that 借 of 借緋 means 獎借 or 推獎 and that 排 → 緋. The 'Monograph on Carriage and Dress' 輿服志 in the *Old T'ang History* (*PNP*) mentions these two colours of silk cloth as being worn by officers of the sixth rank and below. Iriya 164n85 presents an additional reference which lends support to the translation I have given. In the *T'ang hui-yao* (1884 edn), 31.9a, under the heading 'Insignia and Dress of Inner and Outer Officials' 內外官章服, it is recorded that in 716 the practice of special awards to military men of coloured silk not in accord with the regulations began. Tun-huang ms PK9768 (published in *Tsa-lu, hsia* 176a) is a declaration of the award of crimson silk and fish bags to several individuals who had broken up a gang of bandits.
1033 **recruiting officials** 所由 during the T'ang meant officials on patrol in the districts and prefectures, cf. line 180n1 above. Perhaps such a meaning may have been intended here, but these officials were more administrative than military and would hardly have constituted an army or its leaders. Therefore, I have rendered the term as in the translation to emphasize that they were not military officers. It is also worth mentioning in this regard that Wu Tzu-hsü himself was not commissioned inside the city.
led 將 glossed as 領. Cf. T364.13.
1041 **Won't** 以不 = 已不. Cf. T42.4.

1042 **determined** 判 = 拚, see line 1016n2 above. Hence it is incorrect to translate as 'condemned/sentenced to death'.

1048 **Chief** 節度 is actually either a term for a type of quartermaster during the Three Kingdoms (Wu 吳) or the name of a military governor for border areas during the T'ang Dynasty 節度使. Rotours, *Fonctionnaires*, 656 *passim*.

1049 **Son of Heaven** The Chou Emperor.

1050 **wiping clean** 俠 → 雪 (Hsü 110). Another possible emendation is 俠 → 挾 'to bear [a grudge]'. Cf. T25.14. + 'He suffered.'

1058 **carry out** 宂 → 究.

1064 **gratifying** 稱所心. It is possible to read this as '[I must] state what is in my heart.'

1066 **... passed** See line 874n.

1068 **launched** 徵發 usually means 'to requisition supplies and labour service from the people for public use'.

1072 **... horses** 隱隱轟轟. The first binome refers to the rumbling of heavy carts and the second to large numbers of horses and carts. See Chang Heng's 張衡 'Rhapsody on the Western Capital' 西京賦, *WH*, 2.9b and Tso Ssu's 'Rhapsody on the Capital of Shu', *WH*, 4.16a.

1073 **take** 搦 means 捉, cf. T20.5. A less likely interpretation is that they were going out as a challenge party, i.e. 搦戰. In ancient Chinese warfare, it was customary for opposing armies, especially the one on attack, to send out such parties. See the account of the Battle of Pi in the *Chronicle of Tso*, Hsüan 12, Legge, V.319a.

1076 **leaped forward** Chiang 51 says that 競透 does not equal 競進 as the T editors emend it. He is absolutely right but, then again, in defining 競透(跳) as 踊躍向前, he feels the need to preserve the notion of advancing which, I suppose, he derives from 競. To convey the force of 爭 and 競 more clearly, a slightly expanded translation would read: 'The powerful cavalry raced pell-mell, each rider struggling to be in the lead; the brave soldiers advanced ferociously, each man competing to be first.'
ferociously Hsü's (33) suggestion that 生寧 = 生獰 is neater than the emendation given by the T editors though they mean the same.

1079 **shoulder** 肩 is probably a variant orthography for 肩.

1080 **piercing** 刾 is vulgar for 刺
heaven Comma after 豎, semi-colon or period after 天.
Restlessly 屑角 → 屑屑 (?). This emendation also has other suitable meanings ('urgency, hustle-bustle, numerousness').

1082 **... crescent moons** 如寫月, literally, 'like the shape of the moon *written* [i.e. character for moon]' ⺝.
White banners Which, Iriya 151b notes, signify a battle to avenge a person's death.

1087 **... slipped through them** See line 184n.

1092 **clanking** 聆朧 → 玲朧, 'tinkling sound of jade; finely made/wrought; elegant'. The translation could also have been made to emphasize that the armour was well-wrought.

1094 **Startled** We would expect 驚 to come after 虵 (Hsü 110).

1097 **... order** It is rather disconcerting that the army is, somehow, well-ordered at one moment and tumultuous the next.

1099 **... Yellow River** Historically, this is highly improbable.

1101 **lined up evenly** 排批. There are two possible explanations for this phrase, the first and simplest being that the second character stands for 比 which is, indeed, how Chou 318.4 reads it. The second possibility is arrived at by the following process: 批抵 = 排擠(推擠) = 排抵(排詆) = 排批. See *Tz'u-t'ung* 1851 for examples of all but the last which is my own assertion. Cf. T114.4, T191, last line but two, T289.2, T222.9, etc.; *Tsu-t'ang chi* II.111.4 and 126.1, V.2.9 and 15.14.

1102 **in charge** For 所由, see line 1033n1. The more often I see this term, the more am I convinced that, for the author of this story, it signifies paramilitary government workers.

craft 楔 'a ferry'(?), Chiang 204. But 楔 may be an error for 模 (see Chou 318.4) → 塢 (?) 'docks/launching platforms'.

1103 **... flies** This passage is patently defective. 水 is written on the ms immediately after 渡 without a break and probably should be considered as belonging to the line before the one where the T editors place it. It is likely that 風, 騰, and 蓬 ought to be considered as rhymes but that function of the latter is obscured by the fact that the scribe has placed 飛 immediately after it as though they belonged to the same line.

1104 **river** Yangtze?

1105 **officers** More likely 'army and officers' but the term is only exceptionally to be understood in that sense.

1107 **... still** 屬風浪靜. Another reading would be: 'They encountered still wind and waves', where 屬 means 會. If we interpret in this way, Hsü's (33) assertion that there is a character missing before 靜 becomes even more compelling.

1112 **... by dawn** One would expect that, because enormous numbers of men were involved, the river crossing would be described as taking a long time. But the language used here cannot be subverted to that end. If the author had wished to stress the great length of time required, he would have used 手雜 for 手衆 and 方 for 即.

1113 **be ready** 存心 means 'be on the alert; ready; mindful', cf. T40.11 and 15.

take prisoners 捉搦 (as it appears on S328) means 捉拏. + 'As guides.'

1114 **unfamiliar** 識悉 ≡ 熟知 is possible but 習 might give a better reading.

1116 **lookouts** 虞候 (*TCTC* 190.5973, 191.6016, 273.8930) is an official title. In the *Chronicle of Tso*, Chao 昭 20, Legge, V.683, it refers to the keeper of fire-wood in the meres (fens, bogs) and, during the T'ang, to a type of security officer. My translation is based on a literal interpretation of the face value of the two characters. Rotours, *Fonctionnaires*, 647nl. P2708, which contains a list of the members of a layman's religious organization 社 (published in Naba 466), ends with the name Chang Liu-chu 張留住 who had the office of *yü-hou* ('sergeant-at-arms'(?)). See also D2256, D2264, and P2889.

major-generals 子將 (*TCTC* 211.6719, 257.8374) was the title of a military official during the T'ang (means 小將) of which there were eight in an army.

1117 **guards** The T editors are probably mistaken in emending 傔奏 to 傔走 by which, I take it, they intend 'forced march' or 'double time'(?), cf. 兼步, 兼行, 兼程. A more likely emendation is 傔卒 which is the basis of the translation and which may have come to be written as it is in the text by confusion with 奏傔(從). See *Old History of the T'ang Dynasty*, 'Biography of Feng Ch'ang-ch'ing' 封常淸傳 (*PNP*) 140(54).3b.

1118 **on patrol** 遊奕. In *TCTC* 209.6621, there is a 前鋒遊奕使 which Hu San-hsing 胡三省 says is someone who leads roving troops on patrol 巡奕. Compare 游移 and 奕奕 both of which mean 'wavering, undecided, vacillating, hesitating'. 游奕 may mean 'to patrol [esp. of naval vessels]', also written 遊奕 and synonymous with 游弋. By the Sung, the term had become a military designation and meant 'roving troops' or 'guerilla squad' which got its name because it had no set position (i.e. 'undecided/unfixed'). Cf. T40.11. S1153, a miscellaneous list of names (published in *Tun-huang tzu-liao*, vol. I, p. 206) includes 'Patrolman Chu' 朱遊弈.

1119 **capital** 邦 does have the meaning 'city and its environs'.

1122 **command** 知 → 治 (?). See, however, *Chronicle of Tso*, Hsiang 襄 26, where the combination 知政 occurs and is glossed as meaning 'to be in charge of the country's administration' 知國政 (*Thirteen Classics*, 37.7a).

1125 **five weapons** 五戎. This does not mean the 'five barbarians' (五胡) who invaded north China during the fifth century B.I.E., Hsiung-nu 匈奴, Hsien-pei 鮮卑, Chieh 羯, Ti 氐, Ch'iang 羌 nor does it refer to the 'Five *jung* tribes' mentioned in the *Chou li* 周禮 (*Thirteen Classics*, 33.12b). It here refers to five types of weapons: 'bow' 弓 and 'arrow' 矢, 'javelin' 殳, 'lance' 矛, 'spear' 戈, and 'halberd' 戟.

1126 **... merit** More literally, 'established [incentives] for meritorious service'.

1129 **blocked out** Though I accept the T editors' emendation 敝 → 蔽, it is not strictly necessary, for the original character could give a reading of 'were a match for the sun'.

1132 **every** 格 → 各.
ballista 抛車 → 抛車.
set up Punctuate after 車.

1133 **red-hot** 作 (*tsâk*) → 灼 (*ts'i̯ak*). The first character is sometimes used for the second.
... molten bronze The use of ballista and molten bronze is described in *T'ung-tien* 通典 160 (Shanghai, 1935), pp. 845–6, and *T'ai-p'ing yü-lan* 太平御覽 337 (Peking, 1960), p. 1546. Cf. Iriya 164nn87, 88.
prepared 'Concealed, hidden.' If a different punctuation is adopted, 伏 may be considered as referring to 伏道 'underground passage-ways' or perhaps to 'ambuscades'.

1134 **... attackers** 擂 = 檑 = 礌 'piles of stones; to roll or push stones from a high place'.

1136 **... ten thousand men** Strange to say, since Wu's army consisted of 900,000 soldiers and Ch'u's of 1,000,000! By 萬夫, the author certainly intended 'a host/multitude'.

1139 **Cymbals** 跋 → 鈸. The same miswriting is found on T372.11.
gongs 羅 → 鑼.

1141 **... cry** 名 → 鳴. Cf. 揚聲吶喊 'the noise of many persons shouting'.

1143 **city moat** Both Chou and the T editors put a line next to 黃池 indicating that they identify this as a particular place name, probably that mentioned in the *Chronicle of Tso*, Ai 13, Legge, V.830, as the site of a meeting held by Duke Ai of Lu, Duke P'ing of Shan, Duke Ting of Chin, and Fu-ch'a of Wu. 公會單平公, 晉定公, 吳夫差于黃池. The place was located to the southwest of modern Feng-ch'iu District 封丘 in Honan Province. The only possible relevance it might have here is that it was a significant place during the Spring and Autumn period. I would prefer to read the two characters simply as they were used in the 'Seven Stimuli' 七發 of the Han writer, Mei Ch'eng 枚乘, *WH*, 34.4b: 'The city moat twists and turns.' 黃池紆曲. The *WH* commentary is incorrect in saying that 黃 is used for 湟 since the latter is the name of a river (in Kansu). 黃 is actually used for 隍 which means '[dry] moat' (a moat with water being 池) or for 潢 which means 'pond'.

1146 **sweat** But 汗 may be a mistake for 汙 'befouled'.

1149 **mind set on death** More literally, 'acted [with] heart [set on] killing'.

1150 **... retreat** The translation of the last two sentences is fairly free.

1153 **men and horses** 人馬, as given by Chou 319.2. Also see T25.9.

1158 **... fire** As Iriya 164n89 points out, this is an extraordinarily strange simile.

1160 **as easily as** The missing character must be either 似 or 若, more likely the latter (cf. T25.9–10). There is a small but illegible interlinear mark at this point.

1162 **shook** 遙 → 搖. The former reading is possible, but only if forced.
declared 語 is to be read in the falling tone.

1169 **that alone** Cf. T880.11.

1179 **King Chao** The frequent repetition of the Ch'u King's name in English is an accurate representation of the style of the Chinese.

1180 **hands bound ...** 返縛 = 反縛.

1185 ***quid pro quo*** The idea is that King Chao's father being in hell serves to counterbalance or equalize 相當 the murder of Wu Tzu-hsü's father. Cf. 相當 in the sense of 'appropriate' as it appears in the modern juridical terms 相當行為 'appropriate action' and 相當位置 'appropriate position'. The modern usage, which came about through contact with Western jurisprudence, is unrelated to this compensatory sense of justice. An eye for an eye, a tooth for a tooth, a life for a life. See lines 1273n2 and 1315n1 below.

1187 **corpse** 屍骸, Chiang 12.

1189 **tortured** 考 → 拷
bear up 不前. My translation is somewhat forced and derives from taking 前 as an intransitive verb meaning 'persist/go on [forward] with'.
1193 **wrenched out** 捥 → 剜.
1195 **unceremoniously** Implied in 喚.
1196 **ceasing ...** 偃息 in combination (or 偃 alone) refers to the cessation of military activity, e.g. 偃旗息鼓, 偃息武備, and 偃武修文. The progression of events in this passage of the text is described quite sketchily and clumsily.
1198 **together** The original text reads somewhat awkwardly here.
1200 **humbly** To translate 小子.
1203 **At that time** Chiang 142.
1205 **who were so unjust** Added to the translation.
1206 **souls** I do not think that this can be construed as being addressed to the 'gods'.
1211 **hold back** 哈 = 含.
1215 **... finished his sacrifice** Here the actual narrative continues. The preceding paragraph, which also begins with this clause, is a stylized, hyperbolic account of the sacrifice. The effect of this repetition of the same moment (cf. line 315n) is similar to cinematographic time-suspension. The next sentence, 自把劍結恨之深, etc., should read something like 因結恨之深, 自把劍重斬平王, etc.
1217 **blood flowed** !
1226 **totem** 樹(?) = 豎 by itself and in combination with 立 means 'to erect'. Something has to be erected, however, so perhaps we may take 樹 as 木 'piece of wood'. Other possibilities include emending 樹 (*źi̯u:*) to 柱 (*d̂'i̯u:*) 'pillar' or 主 (*tśi̯u:*) 'ancestral tablet'.
1227 **Po-chou** In modern Anhwei.
1229 **... Ch'eng-fu District** Waley 254n36 is in error when he says that 'the place still existed in the ninth century A.D., but is not heard of later'. It was not until the Ming that the district of this name was abolished and there still exists at this place in Anhwei a Ch'eng-fu village.
1230 **made ready** 却 (Jen, *Prelim*, 360).
1244 **... one thousand catties** See T22.14.
1247 **soldier** Or 'weapon'.
1248 **punting-pole** 椑 'oval-shaped pole; handle of an ax'(?).
1254 **long** Quite likely, however, 長 → 唱 'sang' which would obviate the necessity for adding 'singing' to the translation.
1260 **how many** Also on T233.8 and T265.12. Cf. 幾多 T532.1 and 幾許多 T611.16.
1262 **tightly** Waley, 'Notes', 173 says that 穻 is a misreading for 罕 which is an unusual Tun-huang form of 牢. S328 has 窂. Cf. *Pei pieh-tzu*, 2.11b and *Le Concile*, 298n2. For 牢關, cf. *Ko-t'eng*, 297b.
1264 **tattered top** 漏蓋 (?). Waley 47 translates as 'with an awning'. My translation is derived from such comparable expressions as 漏星堂 and 漏屋.
now spoke ... 'Singing a song with his mouth, he spoke.'
1266 **ten** 播 → 番 (?). Cf. T13.14.
1272 **Should** 忽爾. Chiang 148.
1273 **allow** 生 'to cause, create' hence 'to resort to [abandonment]'.
... abandon me Waley 254 says that 'these six lines are intentionally cryptic and I may well have misunderstood them'. He has, indeed, especially the middle two lines:

> Come as an enemy, and you must take the consequences,
> Come as a friend and you will understand what I mean.
> If I can do a service to my wise ruler
> It will gain for me glory, riches and honour.
> If by chance the thing is feasible,
> I appeal to you not to cast me aside.

Admittedly, this is a difficult passage. As I have pointed out above, line 1185n, 相當 may have juridical significance. The same can be said of 遺棄 (e.g. 遺棄兒 which is mentioned in both the T'ang and Ming codes). The fisherman's son (echoing his father on T14.4 – the key to understanding these lines) is, in a sense, making the same plea for compensatory justice that the King of Ch'u did, T21.3.

1278 **... wiped clean** Iriya 154a interprets this differently: 'my life was just on the point of coming to an end'.

1280 **ungrateful** 孤 need not be emended to 辜 for the two characters were considered interchangeable for the meaning 孤負 even during the Western Han. See Li Ling's 'Reply to Su Wu's Letter' 李陵答蘇武書 *Ku-wen kuan-chih* 古文觀止 (Peking, 1956), vol. I, p. 264: 'Although I have been ungrateful, the Han [Royal House] has also been lacking in magnanimity.' 陵雖孤恩, 漢亦負德.

1281 **High Heaven** We would expect 皇 for 黃 as in 皇天后土. 黃天 was the name taken by Chang Chüeh 張角, leader of the Yellow Turbans, at the close of the Han Dynasty.

1283 **... elegant** Waley 254 and 'Notes', 173 says that this is a quotation from *Family Instructions of the Grand Duke* 太公家教, a book of moral aphorisms popular at Tun-huang, S1163. Cf. Lo Chen-yü, ed. 羅振玉, *Manuscripts Recovered from Whistling Sands Cave* 鳴沙石室佚書 (n.p., 1928, *ts'e* 4) 40a: 'If someone gives you a cow, you should return a horse; not to requite someone is impolite. To receive a kindness and repay that kindness is to be genteel and elegant; to receive a kindness and not to repay it is being less than a man.' 得人一牛還人一馬往而不來非成禮也. 知恩報恩風流儒雅. 有恩不報豈成人也. (往↔來 (?).)
Also see *Tsa-lu, hsia* 161a, PK8127 which is similar to this and S3011v.

1301 **clear about** 委知 'to know', Chiang 85.

1305 **wreak** The T editors have 允, Chou has 免. I suggest 充 as making better sense than either, i.e., 'complete/work out'.

1308 **spare my life** 'Preserve my life [-road].' Cf. T23.3.

1310 **... because** + 'Reason ... because.'

1315 **... claimed my life** Wu Tzu-hsü considers that the fisherman's son has that right – always compensatory justice – because he was the cause of the father's death.
If your wishes 由自 is a problem. It occurs frequently in T'ang colloquial texts, most often written 猶自 and with a wide variety of meanings. T27.14, 'and yet/even/and will even go so far as'; T765.4, 'still/after all'; T269.6, 由自不 'far be it from/of course not'; T198.7, 'but still'; T251.12–13, 'went on'; etc. In the present instance, it would seem somehow to be related to the saying 由自爲之 'to his own deserts/as he pleases'. Or we may simply understand 由自與之 as 'yet/would rather/prefer/instead'.

1316 **halt my troops** 'On behalf of Cheng'(?) can probably not be construed from 與之. See the latter part of the preceding note.

1320 **entire army** Including the horses!

1324 **set out** 伐 → 發, as S328 reads.

1328 **piled** 埴 = 堆, cf. T131.16.

1335 **celebrated** The emendation to 祝 is unnecessary (Chiang 98).

1344 **Hearing** 見 glossed as 聞.

1345 **they proceeded to do** Literally, 'the soldiers 兵士 finished eating'.

1346 **stuffed** Literally, 'had drunk [喫, cf. T28.1] and eaten his fill'.

1349 **... not thank him enough** See above, T14.2. 色 is here, too, incorrectly read by the T editors as 包.

1353 **intent** 端 glossed as 專.

1354 **... be ungrateful** Which would seem to make no sense at all. Perhaps the author now intends Wu Tzu-hsü to say that, since he absolutely had to take revenge for his father and brother, the King of Liang as much as gave him life by *not* detaining him. This allowed him to escape to Wu from where he was able to carry out what was more important to him than life – revenge. Or it may simply imply that he is grateful for the food which the King of Liang provided to his army. I have translated as a generalization which may have specific applications. Iriya's (155a) translation is very different from mine: 'I had decided to destroy all those against whom I bore enmity. But, if I allow him alone to live, it will not be an offence against kindness'(?).

1356 **sought food** The apparent discrepancy with lines 256ff is explainable by Wu Tzu-hsü's monumental problem of 'face' (i.e. pride) vis-à-vis women. He wanted and needed the food badly but could not possibly bring himself to ask for it.

1362 **... kept alive** The Chinese says '[which he had made] when [she] was alive'. Since this is not exactly true (see the translation on line 315 above), I have adapted the wording slightly. Waley 48, 'as she had asked him to do when she was still alive', is incorrect.

1367 **death** It is possible to avoid emendation by glossing 極 as 盡

1370 **spirit** Cf. T35n2. Waley, 'Notes', 173 refers us to Ta14.403c and says that 神識 'is not, as might at first sight appear, a new kind of *vijñāna*'. It would be more correct to say that it simply *is* one Chinese translation of *vijñāna*. Cf. *Fa chi-yao sung ching* 法集要頌經, Ta4.777c and Franz Bernhard, ed., *Udānavarga, Sanskrit Texte aus der Turfanfunden* (Göttingen, 1965), vol. I, p. 35. Also see Richard H. Robinson, 'Some Buddhist and Hindu Concepts of Intellect-Will', *Philosophy East and West* 22.3 (1972), 300: '*Vijñāna* is the regular Buddhist term for the fifth *skandha*, the last of the five constituents of the individual. It is usually translated as "consciousness ...". In the Pāli Canon, the term has several meanings, one of which is "continuing psychic element, that which passes over from one life to another". [Mrs Rhys-Davids, *The Birth of Indian Psychology and Its Development in Buddhism* (London, 1936), pp. 245–6.]' Richard Mather, 'The Conflict of Buddhism with Native Chinese Ideologies', *Review of Religion*, 20 (1955–6), 25–37 (p. 28): 'All schools of Indian Buddhism denied the survival of a personal entity or "soul" from one incarnation to the next. Only one component of the pseudo-personality survived, namely consciousness, *vijñāna* (Chinese *shih*). Chinese Buddhists, on the other hand, linked this surviving consciousness to the native concept of the departed spirit, or *shèn*, calling it the "conscious spirit" (*shih-shèn*), or "spirit-consciousness" (*shèn-shih*), and from it developed a purely indigenous doctrine of immortality.' Walter Liebenthal, 'Shih Hui-yüan's Buddhism as Set Forth in His Writings', *JAOS*, 70.4 (October–December 1950), 243–59 (p. 252) refers to (*shen-*)*shih* as 'transmigrational entity'. And Derk Bodde, in a translation of Fung Yu-lan's 'The Philosophy of Chu Hsi', *HJAS*, 7.1 (April 1942), 1–51 (p. 48n1), renders this term as 'Spiritual Intelligence'. *Shen-shih* was adopted by the Taoists as well; see Tai Yüan-ch'ang 戴源長, *Tao-hsüeh tz'u-tien* 道學辭典 (Taipei, 1971), p. 155.

1371 **drifting through** Literally, 'flowing'.

1374 **so** 能, Chiang 188.

1378 **present to you** Waley's addition of 'as you once asked' is superfluous. See line 1362n.

1379 **... mortuary requital** We know from D970 (see line 775n) what happened after this: 'After he had thrown the gold into the river and left, the girl's mother wept and came to the river to recover her corpse and take the gold ...' 投金水中而去後女子之母哭泣而來至水中得屍并獲金.

1385 **capture** 捉 cannot function as a pre-transitive (cf. line 168n) here because it is separated from the main verb by an auxiliary verb.

1399 **Or is it** 爲當, Chiang 176.

1402 **calling upon you** For the meaning of 屈, see Śāriputra line 773n1.

1406 **as I always had done** LSY suggests 仍 → 引 (?). Other possibilities: glossed as 從, '[was ready] to follow you', glossed as 厚, 'treated you well'. The translation I have given takes the path of least resistance by using the most common sense of the word.

1408 **bear it** 能 (*nai*) = 耐

1416 **... punishable by death** See line 949n.

1420 **lives rejoined** Or, perhaps, 'made a covenant'(?).

1425 **steady rhythm** However, 齊 'even', to be more precise, means 'together [in unison]' as on T25.4. I have avoided such a translation because it would have called for too many jade whips and silver saddles.

1428 **dust** 塵 *guṇa* is a popular word with the Buddhists for designating mortal existence.

1430 **Brave men** 大丈夫兒 = 大丈夫.

1431 **gathering** 驟 → 聚.

1435 **heavenly host** T25.1 has 族; Chou 324.2 has 旌. Literally, 'spirit tribe'.
ascends 陵空 → 凌空 'rise into space'.

1437 **shall rule** 將知 must be interpreted as being parallel to 橫行 above. On T20.7 and T25.8, 知 means 'rule/lead'.

1442 **noisy profusion** 隱隱 means 'numerous'; 'the sound of a large number of chariots'; 'loud noise'; etc. 堪 is an unusual character which I have not encountered elsewhere. Hsü 33 says it is used for 填 which, when reduplicated, has as one of its meanings 'the sound of a crowd moving'.

1443 **whinnied** 提撕 'to attend to/manage' works here only with great difficulty; → 嗁嘶(?).

1444 **vast in number** 浩汗 → 浩瀚.
tawny Parallelism demands that 禾 be emended to 褐.
jade whips Cf. the last line of prose before the preceding song and the next but last line of the song itself.

1445 **sparkled** 錫 = 細 or → 熙(?), 'shone brightly'.

1464 **Directly** 一向, Chiang 136 renders as 片刻 'in a flash/no time at all' for other occurrences in T.
destroyed Cf. T20.14.

1467 **as though** 由如 = 猶如.

1469 **... which goes** 俗 → 俗謂(?).

1471 **burn** 熕 = 焚(?).

1478 **aftermath** Literally, 'wound/damage [I had made]'.

1483 **beholden** 賀 → 荷 in falling tone.
... to heaven In gratitude. S328 has 天 rather than 王 as given by T.

1484 **... nor a soldier** Wu Tzu-hsü is probably fudging just a little, see T20.11.

1490 **bore** 俠 (in entering tone) = 挾. As in line 1050n, Hsü 110 here, too, would emend to 雪.

1493 **liberal** 加 → 假(?). Cf. *History of the Later Han*, 'Biography of Liu K'ai' 劉愷 (*PNP*) 39.14b: 'Hsiao-tsung was impressed by his righteousness and so treated him especially well.' 肅宗美其義, 特優假之.

1494 **Emperor** Although I have not used it for the translation, Hsü's 110 suggestion that 帝 → 帶 is worth mentioning, hence 'followed by the troop units'.

1498 **... Fish** 緋 does occur in the *Shuo-wen* but was especially popular during the T'ang (see above, line 1032n). The 金魚 was a gold pendant in the shape of a fish. The 'fish token' 魚符 properly belongs to the T'ang and was an official badge. Early dynasties had employed a 'tiger token' 虎符 for the same purpose. Cf. the T'ang poet Lu Kuei-meng's 陸龜蒙 'To Censor Tung during an Excursion on Mao Mountain' 送董少卿遊茅山詩, *Fu-li hsieng-sheng wen chi* 甫里先生文集 (*SPTK*) 10.40b: 'You wore as a pendant the fish token and administered Red City.' 曾佩魚符管赤城. Also see the *Old T'ang History*, 'Carriage and Costume' (*PNP*) 25.14b where it is noted that, after 721 (K'ai-yüan 9), the fish pouch was generally awarded together with crimson and purple silks. It is, therefore, virtually impossible that this Tun-huang version of the Wu Tzu-hsü story could have been written before the seventh century. Cf. also the specifically T'ang reference to 'military governor' (*chieh-tu* 節度) on T19.7.

1499 **standard-bearers** 旌兵. Elsewhere, this means 'banners and weapons'.
were all given 佔 → 站 as a causative, 'were made [allowed] to stand in/occupy'.
remainder 自餘 also occurs on T85, third line from the end and T817, fifth line from end.

1501 **Pillar of the State** 柱國 known also as 上柱國. A title awarded by Ch'u to favoured military men.

1503 **makings of ...** 大人之相 literally 'appearance/physiognomy/markings of an important personage'. I think a pun has been attempted here with 大相 which follows.

1509 **... below** Heaven above and Earth below.

1510 **command** Both Hsü 110 and Chiang 192 would emend 律 to 緯, which results in a well-known phrase ('literary warp and military woof'). If this emendation is considered unacceptable, we must render 'literature, classics, military arts, and music'.

1512 **head** 垓首 which I interpret as 陔首 'summit/chief rank/degree'. 陔 are literally the steps or degrees in a flight of stairs 階/堦. Still, I am not satisfied, partly because Chou 325.6 reads 城首 (which is indeed what S328 appears to have), the meaning of which escapes me.

1513 **will certainly** 知 is a modal particle (Chiang 192).

1517 **the** 其 (before 'King'), by which a demonstrative is intended. Cf. three lines later, 其越王, and 其子胥 in T26.10 which are similarly crude usages of this pronominal adjective. There are many other such instances which deviate from the structure of the classical language (cf. line 1533n).

1521 **corpses lay strewn** Once more, with blood(!).

1522 **... pestle afloat** *Book of History*, Legge, III.315: 'and the blood flowed till it floated the pestles about'. 血流漂杵.

1524 **sought refuge** 捉西 → 投向 following Wang Ch'ing-shu as given in the forty-sixth collation note of T31. The first part of the emendation is more convincing than the second, hence 'fled to K'uai-chi Mountain towards the west'.

1531 **... would perish** Waley 50 could not translate this sentence (the two troublesome characters are 綠 and 合) and so dropped it. But without this important information, we are mystified as to why Wu Tzu-hsü let Yüeh off scot-free when he clearly could have done with them whatever he pleased. On this point and similar instances (such as giving up a score of lines from the end), the translator was being more than cavalier. He was being irresponsible. If he wanted to drop this sentence gracefully, Waley should have excluded everything beginning with 越王共范蠡 in the previous sentence.

1533 **then** 乃 'then'. I purposefully make this word obtrusive in the English sentence to duplicate the Chinese. 乃 in the sense of 就 normally occurs before verbs, adjectives, and modals such as negatives but rarely before nouns and even less rarely before a noun which is the subject of a sentence (see, for example, T27.10 where it is used properly). Thus, if 乃 must be used, it should come after 吳王, not before. It is not unlike the displacement of 就 in the following, modern Chinese sentence which is an attempted translation of the sentence in the text: 那個越王撤兵回到自己的國家以後, *就吳王生病了.

The present version of the story is not at all clear as to why the King of Wu fell ill. According to Wu Tzu-hsü's *Shih-chi* biography, it was because he had received an injury on the finger (Rudolph, p. 115 – some say toe, Jäger, p. 10) during the battle with Ch'u. I imagine that he was stricken with tetanus. Be that as it may, the story has confused two separate battles (496 B.I.E. and 494 B.I.E.) and two separate Wu kings (Ho-lu 闔廬 and Fu-ch'a 夫差). In the first encounter, Wu was actually defeated by Yüeh. The second occurred because of Fu-ch'a's wish to avenge his father's death. There is no record of Fan Li's fawning words to Wu Tzu-hsü.

1534 **enjoined** 咐囑 of which the normal order is the reverse.

1537 **... ruler of Wu** I have two minor objections to Waley's translation here which I would not normally mention but cannot avoid doing so in this instance because they occur in the same sentence of eleven characters: (1) 後 means 'after', not 'soon'; (2) 'in his stead' is gratuitous but I can well understand why one would be tempted to insert it!

1538 **At that time** 爾時 is equal to classical 此時 or modern 這(那)時候.

1540 **third dream** I follow the T editors' excellent collation note (T31n47) with the slight addition of 四夢 to be added at the end of the ten characters they propose to insert here and the change of 四 below to 五.

1542 **pannier** 匡 may be thought of as 筐 ≡ 莒, which is probably what Waley did when he translated as 'open basket'. 匡, as in the *Shuo-wen*, is defined as a 'receptacle/basket for food'. (The *Shuo-wen chieh-tzu* 說文解字, edition of 1873 (Hong Kong, 1966, photo-reprint), p. 268 (12.20a) wrongly has 飲器.) It is for this reason that one might wish to emend 匣 ('a case/small box'), wherever it occurs in this passage, to 匧 which may be translated as 'clothes hamper' according to ancient definitions of the term. This would, perhaps, account for Minister P'i's deduction below that the two types of containers together (*viz*. food and clothing) presaged long life for the King. I disagree with Waley 254n39 that P'i's interpretation is meant to sound absurd. Cryptic it is, but it is at least as logical as that of Wu Tzu-hsü below in which, for example, Wu claims that the two containers beneath the north and south walls mean that the King will lose his throne. Yet Wu Tzu-hsü's interpretation was certainly not considered nonsensical, at least by the King, for it drew from him an immediate and obvious response.

A further note is that, in the *Shuo-wen chieh-tzu ku-lin* (*pu-i*) 詁林補遺, vol. XXII, p. 847, *Kuang-i chiao-ting* 廣義校定, we read that, being square, the *kuang* is therefore straight and, by extension, upright which might help to account for P'i's favourable interpretation. If I, however, were interpreting the dream, I would draw the same conclusion as Wu Tzu-hsü and justify myself by saying that 匡 means 尪 'crippled' (cf. *Shuo-wen t'ung-hsün ting-sheng* in *Ku-lin*, 5731b and 'Discussion of Rectitude' in *Hsün-tzu* 荀子正論 (*SPTK*) 11.5b) and 匣/匧 is a near homophone of 瞎 'blind'. My free translation of 匡 and 匣/匧 attempts to allow for both a favourable and an unfavourable interpretation: 'coffer' (of riches) sounds like 'coffin' and 'pannier' (L. *panis*, bread!) sounds a bit like 'pain'.

1548 **... hoar-frost** I take 露 *luo-* in the sense of 潤. Also compare Li Po's first 'Ch'ing-p'ing tiao' 清平調 *yüeh-fu-shih* 樂府詩 in which the beauty of Yang kuei-fei 楊貴妃 is compared to thick dew 露華濃 from which we may derive 'splendour'. *Fen-lei pu-chu Li T'ai-po shih* 分類補註李太白詩 (*SPTK*) 5.19a. Iriya 165n99 provides additional information which is helpful in illuminating this sentence. He cites the *Book of Odes*, Legge, III.195: 'The reeds and rushes are deeply green,/And the white dew is turned into hoarfrost.' 蒹葭蒼蒼. 白露爲霜. The Mao commentary to these lines (*Thirteen Classics*) 6.4.22a explains that the dew congeals into frost at the time of the completion of the harvest and is thus considered a good sign. Also in P3105, which is a handbook for explaining dreams 解夢書, there is the following dictum: 'If one dreams of trees and grass growing within his doors, it is an omen of wealth and honour.' 夢見門中生草樹富貴. But 'one who dreams of a mulberry tree at the top of his hall worries about trouble from his officials.' 夢見桑木在堂上憂官事 (see *To-so*, *ts'e* 4, no. 91, pp. 389–90). S2222 has a similar prediction. Cf. also S620, P2829, P3105, P3685v, P3908, and P3990v. For references to other dream interpretation manuals discovered at Tun-huang, see Kazuo Enoki, 'Appendix: Chinese Manuscript Fragments', in Louis de La Vallée Poussin, *Catalogue of the Tibetan Manuscripts from Tun-huang in the India Office Library* (Oxford, 1962), p. 264 and Giles, nos. 6978–80.

1549 **northern wall ...** 者 is missing from this sentence. In each of these sentences except the first in Premier P'i's augury, there occurs an ellipsis of 夢見 which results in the recurring structure 夢見 ... 者 'the dream in which you saw ... [means/presages]'.

1550 **in battle** On the basis of what appears in the King's dream and in Wu Tzu-hsü's interpretation, 鬥戰 or simply 戰 must be inserted here.

1551 **defences** 手備 → 守備.

southeast ... 行 should be dropped from the text. It occurs neither in the description of the King's dream nor in Wu Tzu-hsü's interpretation and, furthermore, destroys the symmetry of the grammatical structure.

1555 **... human emotions** This is the usual order of the 'Three Powers' 天, 地, 理. For 天文 and 地理, Waley again (cf. T26.1–2) has 'astronomy' and 'geography' which, especially in this context, would seem inappropriate. See line 1509n.

1556 **... military arts** See above, line 1510n.

1557 **he was in communication** Added to the translation.

1561 **will certainly** Chiang 192.

perish 除喪, in the only sense in which I am aware that it exists, means 'to remove mourning garments at the end of the mourning period'. The author of this story has thought of each character in its individual sense, 'to pass away' and 'to die', therefore 'to perish'.

1565 **important person** Kou-chien(?). Fan Li(?).

1566 **everywhere** 備 in the sense of 'complete'.

1574 **in anger** 努 → 怒.

Striking ... See line 151n2.

1575 **Disputatious** Waley 51, in translating as 'a flood', has mistaken (or emended) 監監 for 濫濫. The characters, admittedly, make little sense as they stand ('inspecting closely/not interacting'). But if they must be emended, it should be done in such a way that they remain attributes of 老臣 since 光 would seem to block off their influence adverbially upon 呪. My suggestion is that an emendation to 翦翦 would allow for four interesting possibilities, all of which would make excellent sense here and three of which may be derived from glosses to *Chuang-tzu*, 'Letting It Be' 在宥, p. 83: 'You have the petty heart of a sycophant.' 而佞人之心翦翦者. (1) Kuo Hsiang 郭象 says that 翦翦 means 'good at disputing' 善辯; (2) Ch'eng Hsüan-ying 成玄英, 'narrow-minded and base' 狹劣; (3) Chu Chün-sheng 朱駿聲, borrowed for 諓(諓) which means 'clever/artful/sweet/plausible words'; (4) 諓諓 in the *Kung-yang chuan* 公羊傳, twelfth year of Duke Wen 文 (*Thirteen Classics*) 10.23a is glossed as 'shallow' or 'superficial' 淺薄.

All I would prefer to translate 光 as 'blatantly' or 'openly' but do not feel confident that such renderings are justifiable.

1585 **Illuminating Jade** 燭 in the sense of 爥 'to illuminate'. The sword is named 'Shu-lu' 屬鏤 in *Shih-chi* 66.

1587 **... officials** S328 has 諸臣百官.

1588 **place** 安 may mean 'to put in place/position' 位置之. Irya, *Index*, 28 says that 安 = 在. In the *Shih-chi*, the notion of *seeing* the Yüeh army come is made even more vivid by Wu Tzu-hsü's request to have his eyes plucked out and hung atop the city-wall.

1594 **Subsequently** 將後. My translation obtains from any of the following possible uses of 將: a future indicator, 其, 乃.

1601 **people** 人 is used during the T'ang for the taboo-word 民 in Li Shih-min's (Emperor T'ai-tsung) name.

1602 **... Premier P'i** 吳國安化治人. I would have preferred to translate as: 'The King of Wu, in pacifying the Kingdom, mostly follows the advice of Premier P'i.' First, see T26.7 where we have the dying Ho-lu enjoin the King-to-be, Fu-ch'a: 汝後安國治人, 一取國相子胥之語. The dictates of symmetry and irony require a similar statement in the present instance, i.e. 吳王安國治人, 多取宰彼之言. Secondly, we would normally expect that 取 be an action done by a 王 and not by a 國. Thirdly, 安化 was the name of a district during the T'ang Dynasty. It was in Kansu and may thus have been operative in the sloppy scribe's mind when he wrote down this section.

1613 **... rest assured** Literally, 'There is nothing more [= at all] to be apprehensive about.'

1615 **Li River** 麗水, also called 麗江 and 'River of Golden Sands' 金沙江, is a river in Yunnan. 'Gold is produced in the Li River.' 金生麗水. Francis W. Parr, ed., *The Thousand Character Classic* 千字文 (New York, 1963), p. 48.
Ching Mountain 荊山. There are at least four different mountains with this name. The one in question being famous for its jade must be that in modern Hupei, west of South Chang District 南漳, anciently a part of Ch'u.

1617 **solicit** 娉 = 聘 'to invite with presents; to engage/betroth'. The English translation has been made with the full awareness of all the connotations of the word.
... girls The 'Southern Kingdoms' were indeed noted for their beautiful young ladies but, alas, Ch'u, Yüeh, and Wu were these 'Southern Kingdoms'.

1625 **... upon him** Iriya 159a translates differently: 'The King [of Wu] seeing that this crafty courtier had gotten his hands on these treasures, wished that he himself could have them.' There are several difficulties in the next lines as well, the chief being the unrelated, consecutive questions of the King to Fan Li without a response from the latter. I suspect that, at the least, something is missing which describes the demands made upon Premier P'i and, perhaps, his assent to them.

1636 **at variance ...** Compare 心不齊 'not of one mind'.

1637 **angry frog** 怒蛙. Of all creatures to be upset. But it makes, perhaps, a teeny bit more sense than the original (before emendation) which was a 'striving/hard-working snail' 努蝸! Cf. *Wu Yüeh ch'un-ch'iu* (*SPTK*), B56b–57a.

1645 **reflected** 'Deliberated, discussed, weighed.' See line 55n.

1646 **will even ...** See 1315n2.

1647 **strive** This is a pun ('strive' *nu*) on the anger (*nu*) of the frog (Iriya 165n102).

1653 **small river ...** The arrangement of the rivers here and below is hopelessly confused. For anyone who feels compelled to attempt to make some sense of the riverine geography of the region in question, see A. Tschepe, 'Die drei Kiang des Chouking. Ihre Geschicte von ehedem bis jetzt', *Mitteilungen des Seminars für Orientalische Sprachen*, vol. VIII, pt 1(1905), pp. 139–81. 江口, 'confluence of a smaller river with a larger [not necessarily the Yangtze 江]'. This may refer to a particular place since there are several geographical entities known by this name in Szechwan and elsewhere.

1655 **a** The character 一 has been added interlineally to S328 at this point.

1657 **prepared** This word is not in the Chinese.

1658 **Without exception** 例 glossed as 皆.

1662 **are reported** 告 is more likely to be glossed as 示 'show [themselves]' but the basic meaning of the character works well here and so I have employed it in the translation.
... drunk Taken verbatim from 'Discussion of Tea and Wine', T267.6 (I am indebted to Iriya 165n103 for this reference).

1670 **The King** Crudely reconstructed: 吳王便卽遣百官.

1672 **to come ...** Although the text breaks off here, it is actually not a bad ending. I would imagine, however, that there was yet a scene in which the Yüeh armies invaded the capital of Wu. This would, of course, be witnessed by Wu Tzu-hsü's head hanging on the city-wall (as in *Wu Yüeh ch'un-ch'iu* 10). There would probably be a gory description of the corpses *strewn across the plain*. And then there would be platitudinous vindication of our hero, perhaps in verse. The final element might be an attribution which would intend to establish the pedigree of the story. Some of the details of Tun-huang lore about Wu Tzu-hsü may be filled in by reference to the following translation from P2721 (in Naba, p. 230, lines 84–8), a sort of 'textbook for children': 'Who, when he died, had a cloth put over his face? Because of whom? Of old, the King of Wu did not accept the straightforward remonstrances of his loyal minister but adopted instead the calumnious advice of the flattering minister, Premier Hsi [喜 *sic*], and so wrongly killed the loyal minister, Wu Tzu-hsü. Later, when he was executed by the Yüeh armies, facing death, the King of Wu told his officials: "I followed the slanderous advice of the flattering minister, Premier Ḥṣi, and wrongly killed my loyal minister, Wu Tzu-hsü. Now, after I die, I will certainly see Tzu-hsü beneath the ground which would shame me endlessly. From this day on, please cover my face forever with a piece of silk."'

CHANG I-CH'AO
P2962
T114–117

2 **Tibetans** 吐蕃. They had originally taken control of Tun-huang in 781 but were expelled by Chang I-ch'ao in 848. By the tenth month of the year 857, Chang I-ch'ao had brought all eleven *chou* 州 of the Kansu corridor under the control of the Chinese government. See *New T'ang History*, 'Basic Annals of Hsüan-tsung' (*PNP*) 8.12b; also reported in 'Account of the Tibetans', 216B.9a. In 851, Chang had already gone to Ch'ang-an to express his allegiance. See *TCTC*, 248.8044–5, 8048–9; cf. Ts'en Chung-mien 岑仲勉, *Sui T'ang shih* 隋唐史 (Hong Kong, 1950), p. 426n5. After Chang's death in 872 (cf. *TCTC*, 252.8164), many of the territories were lost back to the 'barbarians' from whom he had captured them. See also Édouard Chavannes, *Dix inscriptions chinoises* (Paris, 1902), pp. 77–96, for an inscription of 894 from Tun-huang that gives a long account of Chang I-ch'ao's family, their attachment to Buddhism, and his contributions to the T'ang Dynasty for settling the area.
Szechwan area 諸川, also occurs near the bottom of the present line in T. Does this mean something like 三江 (see Maudgalyāyana line 1004n) or 四川 where there were large concentrations of Tibetans during the T'ang Dynasty? Other editors have emended to 諸州 (e.g. Chin, Fujieda) by which expression I suppose they mean the various administrative areas established by the T'ang government in the Kansu corridor.
3 **Sha-chou** The prefecture of which, during the T'ang, Tun-huang was a part.
Spies 奸 = 奸 = 姦. Cf. 奸細 *chien-hsi*, 'spy; stool pigeon' and 間諜 *chien-tieh*, 'spy; secret agent'. 奸人 means 'a scout; a reconaissance man'.
4 **movements** 事宜, 'manner of undertaking an enterprise'.
without stopping ... 星夜, 'starry night'. See T2.16.
5 **Secretary ...** Rotours, *Fonctionnaires*, 4 and 27: 'vice-président du département des affaires d'État', an official of the second degree, second class. This is, of course, Chang I-ch'ao. The title was awarded him in 857 and is thus anachronistically employed here.
Tuyughun 吐渾 is a shortened form of 吐谷渾, * *Tuyuγun* or * *Tuyuγ-γun*, a proto-mongolian grouping of nomadic tribes. See Paul Pelliot, 'Note sur les T'ou-yu-houen et les Sou-p'i', *TP* 20(1921), 322. This association of desert nomads is often equated with the Tibetan name *'A-ža*. See Paul Pelliot, 'Les Noms Tibétains des T'ou-yu-houen et les Ouigours', *JA* 2(1912), 520–3. Also see Denis Sinor, *Introduction à l'Étude de l'Eurasie Centrale* (Wiesbaden, 1963), p. 234.
6 **barbarian** 蕃(番) refers in a general way to all people who were looked upon by the Chinese as uncivilized. Here the term has the more specific denotation of 'barbarians from the southwest [i.e. Tibetans]'.

11 **through** 塹 → 鏨 (Hsü 35), see the following note.
gate of death This means that they left from the northern gate (which was decorated with white hangings like that of a family holding a funeral ceremony) to signify their willingness to die on their mission. Cf. *Huai-nan-tzu*, 'Discourse on Military Strategy' 淮南子, 兵略訓 (*SPTK*) 15.6a, *Yen-shih chia-hsün*, 'Feng-ts'ao' 顏氏家訓, 風操 (*SPTK*) A6.20a, and T125.13, all of which have exactly the same phrase as here: 鑿凶門而出.
via 把. This is a most peculiar usage and the English rendering is intended to reflect that. See the following note.

12 **towards** 上 understood as a directional word. Literally, 'took a southwest course and advanced the army by way of a quick road'.

14 **West Paulownia** 西同 → 西桐, cf. T125.14 and T126.2. This place was a marshy land west of Sha-chou and not far from Tun-huang.

16 **his three armies** I.e. his combined armies.

17 **more than** 已來 (cf. modern Chinese 以來) occurs in Tun-huang popular literature almost equally divided between temporal ('since; from . . . on', e.g. T40.11, T352.12) and spatial ('as far as; as much as; as many as', e.g. T160.5, T227.7, T370.11) usages.

18 **. . . miles** Literally, '1,000 *li*'. This is not simply an indeterminate large number and so I have provided a crude equivalent in English miles.

19 **Tuyughun** 退渾 is another shortened transcription of * *Tuyuyun*. Supposedly, their base was at Boukhaïn-gol, about five miles from Kokonor. See Louis Hambis, 'Note sur les * *Tuyuyun*', *JA* 234(1948), 241.
caught up with Chiang 58. + 'The bandits.'

21 **make ready** Cf. 排備, 'to line up [in preparation]'. See Chiang 59 and *Ch'ü* no. 1020.

22 **lizard-skin drums** Although I have not seen such drums referred to elsewhere as 'booming[?] lizards', I am confident of this interpretation for at least three reasons: drums were customarily beaten while staging an attack (鳴鼓而攻); the skin of this particular lizard was especially suitable for making drums; there was some confusion regarding the sound of this lizard and that of the drum made from its skin.

23 **went galloping by** To taunt the enemy – an ancient practice of Chinese warfare. See Wu line 1073n.

24 **striking-forces** Literally, 'routes'.
envelop 褁 and 裏 (Chou 400.6) → 裹.

25 **Within moments** 叟 → 臾 (Hsü 35, Chou 400.7).

26 **dark mist . . .** Cf. 霧合, 'mist gathering', which is a constant metaphor for great masses of troops. See also T114.12 and T115.10.

27 **Dragging** 拽 → 曳 as it appears on the ms since the radical has been smudged out intentionally (cf. Chou 400.7, *To-so* 77.9 and specifically noted by Naba 447). In any event, this is an unusual description of attacking soldiers, given the famous parable in *Mencius* where the word is used to describe *fleeing* soldiers. Legge, IV.130: 'they throw away their coats of mail, trail their arms behind them, and run'. 棄甲曳兵而走.

29 **cowardly** Naba 447 notes that this is written 瞻怯 on the manuscript.

31 **thousand** The Chinese seems to say that there are one hundred heroic generals. 'Of the enemy' is added to the translation.

32 **barbarian dogs** T has 'dog barbarians' which is what we would expect. However, both Naba 447 and Sun 491 give the two characters in the opposite order, which is as the ms reads.
show their savagery Literally, 'wolf-hearts [i.e. voracity, savagery] had been aroused'.

35 **. . . must** Cf. Śāriputra line 1920n1. + 'The foe.'

36 **heroic** 雄雄 does not mean 'heroic, brave, commanding'. But judging from the parallel expression in the next line and the fact that there should not be *numerous* (which is what it does mean) field marshals in an army (cf. line 53n and T115.12), the author or scribe may well have intended such a meaning. It is unlikely that this adjective is meant to modify 'plans'. See, however, the following note.

37 **stupid** There are two possible interpretations of these two characters. If we assume that the author or scribe misunderstood 雄雄 in the preceding line as 'heroic', we may emend as follows: 蠢蝺 (蝸 Chou's 400.9 incorrect reading) → 蠢愚, 'stupid, doltish'. If, however, we credit him with understanding 雄雄, then we must emend 蠢蝺 to 蠢蠢, 'squirming', which is actually what was originally written on the ms. The mark for repetition has been blotted out and 蝺 is written to the side. This indicates that at least one person who made revisions on this ms understood the text less well than the copyist. 蠢, in various combinations, is often used to describe the busy movements of *many* troops in preparation for action (e.g. 蠢蠢欲動).
+ 'Against them.' Literally, 'How deep would ... be?'

38 **For** My inclination is to elide 自 for the following reasons: (1) it is supernumerary; (2) the parallel structure indicates that this line should begin with a numeral; (3) Chou 400.9, *To-so* 78.1, and Sun 491 delete it. On the ms, moisture has completely obliterated any writing in the space where the T editors give 戈, even though that is a plausible reconstruction and something like it seems necessary for the line to make sense.

39 **three frontiers** See Śāriputra line 139n.
violent 猂 is a vulgar form of 悍 (cf. Chou 400.9 and *To-so* 78.1). Naba 447 reads 獷捍, 'fiercely defend'. Although this reading agrees more closely with the parallel 'lances raised' above, I have rejected it because 獷 is nearly always used pejoratively of the rude, the uncivilized and the savage.

42 **... no matter how** See line 35n.
... high poles 摽 → 標 (Chou 400.12, Naba 447). Sometimes, however, the two characters are used interchangeably.

43 **closed in** See line 26n. + '-like armies.'
... dense wave 霃霃 = 沈沈 (cf. 沆沆(漭漭)), 'a vast expanse of'.

45 **Persevere** The translation is my guess at what the author intended. 尅勵 means 'to repress or overcome one's personal desire'.

46 **rank** 宧 is a vulgar form of 宦. Naba 447 prints '官 *sic*', which is as the character actually appears on the ms and, I suppose, may be considered a vulgar form of 官. 名宧 is the more probable expression. The translation employs a secondary interpretation of this expression, not the more common 'distinguished officials'.
... spear There is at least one supernumerary character in this line (Naba 447 reads 不見 instead of 覔). While it makes sense as given in T, the confusion regarding the reading of the final element of the line and the fact that it is still understandable when that element is elided (向 'face/go toward') lead me to observe that 不見 (or 覔) is an interpolation.

50 **struck** 中° is used precisely in the same way as a passive verb on T116.4.
piled up 陪 glossed as 加, 益, 滿, 重土. Or 伴, 'consigned to'.

53 **Field Marshal** Chang I-ch'ao. Cf. line 36n. See Rotours, *Fonctionnaires*, 502.

55 **King** *To-so* 78.7 has 國 after 王. It actually appears, written small to the side of the line, *before* it.

56 **ascended** 涉 → 陟. The former is possible if we assume 'high mountains [and streams]'. Cf. T5.9 and 15.
took control Cf. T114.7.

57 **dangerous ...** 嶮 = 險.

59 **unceremoniously** This character is obviously difficult to read. Although I have followed T's 祇 ('only, simply'), it should be noted that Chou 401.2 reads 抵, Naba

447 reads 秖, and *To-so* 78.8 reads 秪. The ms actually has 秖.
executed 'Cut up in inch-size chunks.'

60 **captives** 生口 in these texts means either 'captives' (T126.13) or 'slaves' (T176.7,8,11), *not* 'livestock'.
... children The translation is a bit of a guess. The ms unmistakably has 佃小. But the problem is complicated because 佃 ('farmer') can sometimes be used for 細. 細小 commonly means 'tiny; petty' which is inappropriate here. Another possibility is that the expression as used here may be related to some such term as 細崽, 'servant' (cf. 細婢, 細人, etc.). For 等 as a pluralizing suffix, cf. T27.1

61 **head** Note the doubled numerary adjunct. This frequently occurs in T'ang colloquial, cf. T175.14.
camels 駞 = 駝.

62 **Big Battle Music** Tune title.

63 **Lapchuk** This is the name of a district established by the T'ang government. It was located southwest of Hami in Sinkiang Province. Only by coincidence do the characters used in this name mean 'offer tribute'. Lapchuk is an approximation of the sound of a non-Chinese (夷) word for Shan-shan 鄯善 i.e. Charklik (anciently called Lou-lan 樓蘭, i.e. Kroraina, known as Navappa 納縛波 to Hsüan-tsang), the people who originally built the town. *Serindia*, 1156–7. Here and below (T115.9 and 16, T116.7) the T editors have made an unannounced emendation from 軄 to 職.

65 **Hami** 伊(吾廬).

68 **July 11, 856** 大中十年六月六日.

70 **less than ten days** (前後)不經/遠旬日/月(之/中間), with slight variations, is a standard formula in Tun-huang narrative texts for the passage of time (cf. T19.10, T37.9, T42.2, T44.8, 16, T45.4, T62.11, T115.9, T155.7, T204.4, T205.12, 15, T218.9, T224.6, T227.7, T289.1, T701.7, T714.5). It may simply be rendered 'before many days/months had passed'. Cf. T217.3 行經數日.

72 **totally** 都 is to be translated as an adverb! In T'ang colloquial, the adjective for inclusion in this position is 總.

73 **... formation** See line 26n.

74 **panic-stricken** Cf. 傽偟, 慞惶, 張惶, etc. Supposedly the roebuck got its name from being so skittish.
splintered Cf. T116.2, T91.7, and T121.2. Users of the Taiwan reprint of T should be warned that the knife radicle in 分 has dropped out of some of the copies.

77 **they caught up with them** Added to the translation.

80 **Field Marshal** See line 53n.

81 **cast out** Sun 492 has 擊却, 'repulsed'.
Phoenix Tower I.e. 'building within the royal precincts' hence 'the Court'.

82 **Divine Ruler** Emperor Hsüan-tsung 宣宗.

83 **Turkish tribes** 兇奴 → 匈奴, Huns.

84 **Huns** *Hsien-yün* was the Chou Dynasty appellation for the Hsiung-nu.

86 **Commander-in-Chief** Chang I-ch'ao.

87 **retrieval** Or, glossed as 止, 'to put a stop to it'. Hsü's (112) suggestion (收 → 搜) is unjustified, even though the two characters are phonetically similar (*śi̯ə̯u* and *sə̯u*), since much more than reconnaissance is involved.

89 **west** Chou 401.1 has 南 'south'.

90 **Our** One of the first two characters in this line, probably the first, is supernumerary. If the second, we may render 'our army's' but this is unlikely.

91 **intimidated** 愶 = 脅, 脅, or 協.
louts I have used 渾 as the basis of my translation but the homonymous and nearly synonymous 混 (or 昆) was more frequently used in names denoting the western tribes.
lost all courage Literally, 'their bladders floated'(!).

92 **dog barbarians** 犬羊 (*i̯ang*) → 犬戎 (*ńźi̯ung*), cf. line 32n1. Without emendation, we must render 'as soon as the dogs and sheep [i.e. domestic animals?] saw ...'. But this sounds rather improbable and, furthermore, it requires a forced translation of the next line (抽 'were divided up'?). It is also clear from the equivalent prose passage (T115.10) that 'scattered like stars' *must* refer to the enemy troops in retreat. Finally, T116.7 clinches this interpretation.

93 **... deserted their posts** See the preceding note.

94 **slaughter** 剪 is a vulgar substitute for 翦.

... the foe Because they would neither be able adequately to garrison the place nor to take the enemy back to Tun-huang as captives. + 'The Chinese troops' and 'the foe'.

96 **battlefield** 沙場 may also mean 'desert' which would be equally applicable here.

97 **slashed** 剖, which is marked on the manuscript 七彫反 (**ts'i̯au*), may mean approximately the same as 勦 (**dz'i̯äu*), 'cut'. P2717 (*To-so*, *ts'e* 5, 566) also has this character 剖 but gives the phonetic reading 乃(? → 及) 彫反.

sliced *Faute de mieux*, 務 → 瞀.

98 **Fluttering** 撊 means 'rapidly moving', 鑠 (which is interchangeable with 爍) means 'shining, lustrous'. The two characters together were probably intended to convey the same meaning as 閃爍, 'flashing, twinkling'.

brightly Chou 401.13 and *To-so* 79.10 correctly read 晶 which does not require a different translation.

99 **... fiery cattle** *Shiki*, 82.5 describes how T'ien Tan raised the siege of Chi-mo 卽墨: 'Thereupon, T'ien Tan gathered together more than a thousand cattle from within the city. He dressed them in clothes of red silk with multi-coloured dragon designs drawn on them. Swords and knives were tied to their horns. Bunches of reeds dipped in fat were tied to their tails and the tips of the reeds were set on fire. Several dozen holes were bored through the city-wall and the cattle were let out through them during the night, five thousand stout warriors following behind them. The tails of the cattle being on fire, they ran wildly at the Yen armies. The bright flashing of the torches on the tails of the cattle in the night greatly startled the Yen armies. Everywhere, the Yen armies saw the dragon designs which killed or wounded whomever was touched.'

100 **prevailed** Emphasizing the latter part of the standard gloss 創造化育, 'create and sustain', i.e. 'influence'.

101 **exterminated** 殄 = 殄.

desperadoes 凶 = 兇, as it is actually written on the ms. 殘兇 may also be interpreted as 'remaining villains'.

103 **dog barbarians** See line 92n.

Flustered 蒼黃 = 倉惶 or 倉皇 as printed by Chou 402.2 and *To-so* 79.4.

105 **central** It is likely that this means 中原之軍, 'armies of China' rather than the middle army in the left, centre, right division of the three-part army. The horn and drum signals did, however, originate from the middle army.

raised 'Blew.'

107 **set in ambush** The ms has 方実 which appears to have been written over another character that has been erased. Supply 伏 (?). So as to capture those who flee.

108 **head** See above, line 61n1.

109 **single** 疋 is a vulgar writing of 匹.

110 **Sha-chou** See line 3n1.

112 **Huns** See line 83n.

114 **Previously** 先去 (?).

115 **Secretary** 御史中丞. Rotours, *Fonctionnaires*, 281: 'vice-président du tribunal des censeurs', an official of the fourth degree, second class.

116 **Jui** 瑞 → 端. For details regarding him, see line 139n.

117 **Khanate** 單于 refers both to the ruler of the Huns and to the area under his jurisdiction. With regard to the preparation of this ms, it is interesting to note that the character 單 has been written on a tiny square of paper and pasted over another character.

118 **peon** 押衙. Rotours, *Fonctionnaires*, 225n2.
Now This word is added in the English translation to mark off the new narrative from the background exposition that precedes it in this paragraph.

119 **border-guard** 遊弈使, see Wu line 1118n.

120 **unexpectedly** Chou 402.6 correctly gives 逈 which is a vulgar form of 迥 *chiung* ('different; unusual' hence 'unexpected').

126 **slopes** A very small character written to the side of 畔 seems to be 面 'face'.
Snowy Mountains Not the Himalayas which are also rendered in Chinese as 雪山. The mountains here referred to are the Karlik-tāgh, part of the Richthofen Range. They lie north of Tāsh-Bulak which is near Hami. Cf. *Le Concile*, 298n2. The Ch'i-lien ṣḥan 祈連[山] of T127.10 are the same mountains.

127 **mutinous** *To-so* 80.8 gives 叛亂. 亂 is actually written in very faintly over a blotted out 叛. Hence the ms originally read 背叛. Cf. T116.16 near top (逆 is written to the side of a blotted out 叛) and T117.2 bottom (where the reviser permits it to remain as is).
So Note 所以.

128 **fled** 波 means 跑 or 奔. Cf. T121.2 and see Śārīputra line 174n.
... led him 'Trusting to his feet, he ran', i.e. 'running about aimlessly'.

129 **unfriendly** 'Evil.'

130 **General** Tso Ch'eng-chen's military *rank*(?). His *title* is mentioned in line 119n.
kind Literally, 'illuminating'.

132 **gave** Lo, *Studies*, 814–15 analyses 與 as a preposition here and on T117.2. It would appear, however, that it functions in both instances as a full verb.
carry *To-so* 80.10 has 馱. I do not think this can be understood as 'camel' because of the orthography used on T115.6.

134 **paid his respects** '[Asked how] his rising and resting [were].'

135 **in full** The ms has 具.

137 **And** 伏 → 復 as suggested by T120n5.
chief of your mission This is an *ad hoc* translation for 本使.

139 **Wang Jui-chang** We know from the *Old History of the T'ang Dynasty* (*PNP*, 18B.17a), *TCTC* (249.8066), and *T'ang ta chao-ling chi* 唐大詔令集 ((Peking, 1959), *chüan* 128, p. 693 and *chüan* 129, p. 698) that Wang Jui-chang had been sent by Hsüan-tsung 宣宗 to confer the recognition of the T'ang court upon the nephew of the Uighur Khan. We further know from these official sources that the nephew's name was P'ang-t'e-le 龐特勒 (i.e. 厖歷 Mänlig(?), see Hamilton, *Ouighours*, pp. 7 and 147; cf. Francis Woodman Cleaves, 'The "Fifteen 'Palace Poems'" by K'o Chiu-ssu', *HJAS*, 20, 3 and 4 (December 1957), 440n42) and that Wang Jui-chang was banished for his failure to carry out the mission successfully. But the events related in the latter part of the transformation text on Chang I-ch'ao regarding this mission make the events seem so much more real and vivid that one regrets only the dearth of such materials.

143 **rebellious** See line 127n1.

147 **villainous** 姧 = 奸 = 姦.
trickery 虞 glossed as 欺 or 逆.

149 **How** 争 is comparable to 怎. Cf. early colloquial 争得 and modern colloquial 怎得.

151 **hostel** This character is written faintly to the side of the line and is not fully legible.

152 **... rations** There are many problems with the printed editions of the text before and after the point marked by this note. Chou has 便與根尋由末. I can imagine forced

translations of both the T and Chou versions but neither of them would be satisfactory. My translation is based on the following reading: 便與粮 (= 糧, cf. Naba 448)餉 (*śįang-*, 尋 *zįəm*). 由 (= 猶) 未出兵之間 . . .

153 **on** Sun 493 does not print 至. It is written very small to the right of 十.

August 27, 857 [大中] 十一年八月五日.

154 **Prefect** Rotours, *Fonctionnaires*, 721: 'préfet', an official of the third degree, second class.

Wang Ho-ch'ing I have not been able to find other references to this person.

155 **at Sha-chou** Added to the translation.

156 **Military-Governor** Rotours, *Fonctionnaires*, 707.

Ti This would seem to be the same person as Ti baɣa 翟毛哥 who is mentioned in the *Old History of the Five Dynasties* (*SPTK*) 138.5b. Baɣa was a Turkish title much used by the Uighurs, cf. Hamilton, *Ouighours*, pp. 85–6, 147.

158 **Hami . . .** For 將, see Wu line 1033n2. The text breaks off here. There is much additional information about Chang I-ch'ao in the Tun-huang mss (see, for example, D5870, S6342, S6973 (records that he died at age 74 in Ch'ang-an), PK5259, etc.).

REFERENCES

This list is not a bibliography for the study of Tun-huang popular literature. Fuller bibliographic references will be provided in *Transformations*.

Chang Hsiang
Chang Hsiang 張相. *Shih tz'u ch'ü yü tz'u-hui shih* 詩詞曲語辭滙釋, 2 vols. Shanghai, 1954.

Cheng
Cheng Chen-to 鄭振鐸. *Library of World Literature* 世界文庫. Shanghai, 1935.

Cheng, *Popular*
Cheng Chen-to 鄭振鐸. *Chung-kuo su-wen-hsüeh shih* 中國俗文學史, 2 vols. Peking, 1954.

Chiang
Chiang Li-hung 蔣禮鴻, *Tun-huang pien-wen tzu-i t'ung-shih* 敦煌變文字義通釋, rev. and enl. edn. Peking, 1962. Available in Taiwan reprint from Ku-t'ing Bookshop 古亭書屋, Taipei, 1975.

Chin
Chin Ch'i-tsung 金啟綜. 'T'ang-mo Sha-chou (Tun-huang) Chang I-ch'ao te ch'i-i – Tun-huang hsieh-pen "Chang I-ch'ao pien-wen"' 唐末沙州(敦煌)張議潮的起義—敦煌寫本張議潮變文, *Li-shih chiao-hsüeh* 歷史教學, 38 (Feb. 1954), 31–5.

Chou
Chou Shao-liang 周紹良. *Tun-huang pien-wen hui-lu* 敦煌變文彙錄, rev. and enl. edn. Shanghai, 1955.

Ch'ü
Jen Erh-pei 任二北. *Tun-huang ch'ü chiao-lu* 敦煌曲校錄. Shanghai, 1955.

Chuang-tzu
Chuang-tzu tsuan-chien 莊子纂箋, Ch'ien Mu 錢穆 ed. Taipei, 1974.

CKYHTTT
Chung-kuo yao-hsüeh ta tz'u-tien 中國藥學大辭典. Peking, 1956.

Le Concile
Demiéville, Paul. *Le Concile de Lhasa: Une Controverse sur le Quiétisme entre Bouddhistes de l'Inde et de la Chine au VIIIe Siècle de l'Ère Chrétienne*, vol. I. Paris, 1952.

CWTTT
Chung-wen ta tz'u-tien 中文大辭典. Taipei, 1962–8.

D, F

Tun-huang mss in the library of the Leningrad branch of the Institute of Asian Peoples, Academy of Sciences, U.S.S.R.

Fujieda

Fujieda Akira 藤枝晃. 'An Account of the Sha-chou *kuei-i chün* Military Governorship' 沙州歸義軍節度使始末 (2), [*The Tōhō Gakuhō, Journal of Oriental Studies*] 東方學報, Kyoto, 12.4(1942), 494–527.

Giles

Giles, Lionel. *Descriptive Catalogue of the Chinese Manuscripts from Tunhuang in the British Museum*. London, 1957.

Giles, *BD*

Giles, Herbert A. *A Chinese Biographical Dictionary*. Taipei, 1964 reprint of 1898 edn.

Hamilton, *Ouighours*

Hamilton, James Russell. *Les Ouighours à l'Époque des Cinq Dynasties*. Paris, 1955.

Hiang

Hiang Ta 向達. '[A Selection of Tun-huang Mss. Preserved in the National Library of Peiping]' 敦煌叢抄, *Journal of the Peiping National Library* 國立北平圖書館館刋, 5.6(1931), 53–80.

Hightower

Han Ying (fl. 179–140 B.I.E.). *Han shih wai chuan: Han Ying's Illustrations of the Didactic Application of the 'Classic of Songs'*, tr. and annot. James R. Hightower. Cambridge, Massachusetts, 1952.

HJAS

Harvard Journal of Asiatic Studies.

Hsieh

Hsieh Ch'un-p'ing 謝春聘. *Tun-huang chiang-ching pien-wen chien* 敦煌講經變文箋. Taipei. 1975.

Hsien-yü ching

Hsien-yü ching 賢愚經, *chüan* 10, section 40, Ta4.418b–421b.

Hsü

Hsü Chen-o 徐震堮. 'Tun-huang pien-wen chi chiao-chi pu-cheng' 敦煌變文集校記補正, *Hua-tung shih-ta hsüeh-pao* 華東師大學報, 1 (January 15, 1958), 32–46.

Hsü Chen-o 徐震堮. 'Tun-huang pien-wen chi chiao-chi tsai-pu' 敦煌變文集校記再補, *Hua-tung shih-ta hsüeh-pao*, 2 (April 15, 1958), 110–26.

'Inventory'

Mair, Victor H. 'Lay Students and the Making of Written Vernacular Narrative: An Inventory of Tun-huang Manuscripts', *Chinoperl Papers*, 10(1981), 5–96.

Iriya

Iriya Yoshitaka 入矢義高, assisted by Matsuo Yoshiki 松尾良樹 and Mizutani Kazuo 水谷和郎. *Bukkyō bungaku shū* 仏教文学集. Tokyo, 1975. (*Chūgoku koten bungaku taikei* 中国古典文学大系, vol. LX.)

Iriya, *Index*

Iriya Yoshitaka 入矢義高. '*Tonkō hembun shū' kōgo goi sakuin* 敦煌変文集口語語彙索引. Kyoto, 1961.

Iriya, Review
Iriya Yoshitaka 入矢義高. Review of Chiang. [*The Journal of Chinese Literature*] 中國文學報, 11(1959), 175–80.
JA
Journal Asiatique
Jäger
Jäger, F. 'Das Biographie des Wu Tzu-hsü (Das 66. Kapitel des Shih-chi)', ed. Yong-Oon Tai, *Oriens Extremis*, 7(1960), 2–16.
Iwamoto Yutaka
Iwamoto Yutaka 岩本裕, *Mokuren densetsu to urabon* 目連傳説と盂蘭盆. Kyoto, 1968.
Jen, *Prelim*
Jen Erh-pei. *Tun-huang ch'ü ch'u-t'an* 敦煌曲初探. Shanghai, 1954.
Ko-t'eng
Dōchū 道忠. *Kattō gosen* 葛藤語箋, 1739. Tokyo, 1959.
Layman P'ang
Iriya Yoshitaka, ed. *Hō Koji goroku* 龐居士語錄. Tokyo, 1973.
Legge
Legge, James. *The Chinese Classics*. vol. I, *Confucian Analects*; vol. II, *The Works of Mencius*; vol. III, *The Shoo King*; vol. IV, *The She King*; vol. V, *The Ch'un Ts'ew, with the Tso Chuen*. Hong Kong, 1960.
Legge (Sung)
Legge, James (tr.) and Z. D. Sung (ed.), *The Text of Yi King (and Its Appendixes): Chinese Original with English Translation*. Shanghai, 1935.
Lo, *Customs*
Lo Tsung-t'ao 羅宗濤. *Tun-huang pien-wen she-hui feng-su shih-wu k'ao* 敦煌變文社會風俗事物考. Taipei, 1974.
Lo, *Studies*
Lo Tsung-t'ao 羅宗濤. *Tun-huang chiang-ching pien-wen yen-chiu* 敦煌講經變文研究. Taipei, 1972.
LSY
Conversations with Lien-sheng Yang.
Mochizuki
Mochizuki Shinkō 望月信亨. *Bukkyō daijiten* 佛教大辭典. Tokyo, 1931–63.
Morohashi
Morohashi Tetsuji 諸橋轍次. *Dai Kan-wa jiten* 大漢和辭典. Tokyo, 1955–60.
Naba
[Toshisada Naba] 那波利貞. [*Historical Studies on the Society and Culture of T'ang China*] 唐代社會文化史研究. Tokyo, 1974.
Opisanie
Men'shikov, Lev Nikolaevich, *et al. Opisanie kitaiskikh rukopisei Dun'-khuanskogo fonda Instituta Narodov Azii*, 2 vols. Moscow, 1963, 1967.
Ōta, *Kōgobun*
Ōta Tatsuo 太田辰夫. *Chūgoku rekidai kōgobun* 中国歴代口語文. Tokyo, 1957.
P
Pelliot mss in the Bibliothèque Nationale, Paris.

Pei pieh-tzu
Lo Chen-yü 羅振玉. *Tseng-ting pei pieh-tzu* 增訂碑別字, rev. and enl. edn. N.p., 1928.
P'ei Hsüeh-hai
P'ei Hsüeh-hai 裴學海. *Ku-shu hsü-tzu chi-shih* 古書虛字集釋. Shanghai, 1954.
PK
Tun-huang mss in the Peking National Library (numbered according to the system described in 'Inventory', appendix 2).
PNP
Po-na pen 百衲本 edition of the dynastic histories.
PWYF
P'ei-wen yün-fu 佩文韻府, 7 vols. Shanghai, 1937.
Read, *Chinese Medicinal Plants*
Read, Bernard E. *Chinese Medicinal Plants from the Pen Ts'ao Kang Mu* 本草綱目 *A.D. 1956*, third edn. Peking, 1936.
Rotours, *Fonctionnaires*
des Rotours, Robert. *Traité des Fonctionnaires et Traité de l'Armée*. Leyden. 1947.
Rudolph
Rudolph, R. C. 'The *Shih-chi* Biography of Wu Tzu-hsü', *Oriens Extremis*, 9(1962), 106–20. For another English translation, cf. Burton Watson, *Records of the Historian: Chapters from the 'Shih chi' of Ssu-ma Ch'ien* (Columbia, 1969), pp. 16–29.
S
Stein mss in the British Library.
Serindia
Stein, Mark Aurel. *Serindia: A Detailed Report of Explorations in Central Asia and Westernmost China*, 5 vols. Oxford, 1921.
SH
Soothill, William Edward and Lewis Hodous. *A Dictionary of Chinese Buddhist Terms*. London, 1937.
Shiki
Takikawa Kametarō 瀧川龜太郎. *Shiki kaichū kōshō* 史記會注考証, 10 vols. Tokyo, 1932–4.
Shuo-wen chieh-tzu ku-lin
Ting Fu-pao 丁福保, comp. *Shuo-wen chieh-tzu ku-lin chi pu-i* 說文解字詁林及補遺, 12 vols. Taipei, 1959.
SPPY
Ssu-pu pei-yao 四部備要, typeset edition of Chinese classical texts.
SPTK
Ssu-pu ts'ung-k'an 四部叢刊, photolithographic edition of Chinese classical texts.
Sun
Sun K'ai-ti 孫楷第. *Ts'ang-chou chi* 滄州集. Peking, 1965.
Su-yü k'ao-yüan
Tu Yüan-ch'ing 杜元清. 俗語考原. N.p. 1937.

T
Wang Chung-min 王重民 *et al. Tun-huang pien-wen chi* 敦煌變文集, 2 vols. Peking, 1957. Bracketed numbers in the translation refer to this, the standard edition. Available in Taiwan reprint (World Book Company 世界書局, Taipei, 1973, Library of Chinese Popular Literature 中國俗文學叢刊, series I, vols. 2 and 3).

Ta
Taishō shinshū daizōkyō 大正新修大藏經. Tokyo, 1924–32.

TCTC
Ssu-ma Kuang 司馬光. *Tzu-chih t'ung-chien* 資治通鑑, 4 vols. Peking, 1957.

Thirteen Classics
Juan Yüan, ed. 阮元. *Shih-san ching chu-shu* 十三經注疏, 32 *ts'e*. 1887 lithograph.

To-so
Liu Fu, comp. 劉復. *Tun-huang to-so* 燉煌掇瑣. Nanking, 1925.

TP
T'oung Pao

Transformations
Refers to a work by the present writer that will be published under the title *T'ang Transformations: Contributions to the Study of the Origins of Fiction and Drama in China*. The contents include theoretical discussions on Tun-huang popular narratives, their origins, influence on later popular literature in China, and analogues in other Asian countries.

Tsa-lu
Hsü Kuo-lin 許國霖. *Tun-huang shih-shih hsieh-ching t'i-chi yü Tun-huang tsa-lu* 敦煌石室寫經題記與敦煌雜錄. Shanghai, 1937.

TSCC
Ts'ung-shu chi-ch'eng 叢書集成. Shanghai, 1935–40.

Tsu-t'ang chi
祖堂集 (compiled 952), hand-copied by Yanagida Seizan 柳田聖山 from the ms of 1245 kept in Hae-in sa 海印寺. Kyoto, 1972. This edition indexed by Ota Tatsuo. '*Sodō shū*' *kōgo goi sakuin*「祖堂集」口語語彙索引. N.p., 1962. Another edition, a facsimile of the 1245 ms with an introduction by Minn Yong-gyu 閔泳珪, may be found in *Pulgyo sahak nonch'ong* 佛教史學論叢 *Buddhistic Studies Presented to Dr Joh Myong-gi on His Sixtieth Birthday*. Seoul, 1965, pp. 1–129 (separate pagination).

T'ung-su pien
Chai Hao 翟灝 (1736–1788). 通俗編. Peking, 1958.

Tun-huang tzu-liao
敦煌資料, vol. I. Peking, 1961.

Tz'u-hai
辭海. Numerous editions available.

Tz'u-t'ung
Chu Ch'i-feng 朱起鳳. 辭通. Shanghai, 1934.

Umezu Jirō
Umezu Jirō 梅津次郎. 'Hen to hembun' 変と変文, *Emakimono sōkō* 絵巻物叢考. Tokyo, 1968.

Vandier-Nicolas

Vandier-Nicolas, Nicole. *Śāriputra et les Six Maîtres d'Erreur* (Mission Pelliot en Asie Centrale: Fac-similé du Manuscrit Chinois 4524 de la Bibliothèque Nationale). Paris, 1954.

Waley

Waley, Arthur. *Ballads and Stories from Tun-huang*. New York, 1960.

Waley, 'Notes'

Waley, Arthur. 'Notes on the *Tun-huang pien-wen-chi*', *Studia Serica Bernhard Karlgren Dedicata*, ed. Søren Egerod and Else Glahn. Copenhagen, 1959, pp. 172–7.

WH

Wen-hsüan 文選. I-wen 藝文 reprint of 1809 recutting of the Sung, Ch'un-hsi 淳熙 (1174–1189) edition.

Yabuki

Yabuki Keiki 矢吹慶輝. [*Rare and Unknown Chinese Manuscript Remains of Buddhist Literature Discovered in Tun-huang*] 鳴沙余韻. Tokyo, 1930.

Yang Shu-ta

Yang Shu-ta 楊樹達 [*A Study of Chinese Characters in Relation to Their Parts of Speech*] 詞詮, ed. Fang I 方毅. Shanghai, 1931.

Yu-hsien k'u

Chang Wen-ch'eng (Tsu) 張文成(鷟). 游山窟. Shanghai, 1955.

Other works of interest

Brown, William. 'From Sutra to *Pien-wen*: A Study of "Sudatta Erects a Monastery" and the *Hsiang-mo Pien-wen*', *Tamkang Review*, 9.1 (1978), 67–101.

Catalogue des Manuscrits Chinois de Touen-Houang (Fond Pelliot Chinois), vol. I, nos. 2001–500. Paris, 1970.

Eichhorn, Werner. *Heldensagen aus dem unteren Yangtse-Tal* (*Wu-Yüeh ch'un-ch'iu*). Abhandlungen für die Kunde des Morgenlandes, 38.2. Wiesbaden, 1969.

Johnson, David. 'The Wu Tzu-hsü *Pien-wen* and Its Sources: Part I', *HJAS*, 40.1 (June 1980), 93–156 and Part II, *HJAS*, 40.2 (December 1980), 465–505.

Kanaoka Shōkō 金岡照光. [*Classified Catalogue of Literary and Popular Works in Chinese in Tun-huang Documents – From Stein and Pelliot Collections*] 敦煌出土文学文献分類目録附解説ースタイン本・ペリオ本. The Toyo Bunko 東洋文庫, 1971.

Lagerwey, John. 'A Translation of the *Annals of Wu and Yüeh*, Part I, with a Study of Its Sources.' Ph.D. dissertation. Harvard University, 1975.

Lévi, Sylvain. 'Le Sūtra du Sage et du Fou dans la Littérature de l'Asie Centrale', *JA*, 207 (July–September 1925), 305–32. Study of *Hsien-yü ching*.

Schmidt, J. *Der Weise und der Thor*. St Petersburg, 1843. Study of *Hsien-yü ching*.

Schüssler, Axel. *Das 'Yüe-chüe shu' als hanzeitliche Quelle zur Geschichte der Chan-kuo-Zeit*. Inaugural-Dissertation zur Erlangung des Doktorgrades der Philosophischen Fakultät der Ludwig-Maximilians-Universität zu München. Leuterhausen bei Weinheim, 1966.

Tschepe, Albert. *Histoire du Royaume de Ou (1122–473 av. J-C.)*. Variétés sinologiques, 10. Shanghai, 1896.

Tun-huang i-shu tsung-mu so-yin 敦煌遺書總目索引. Peking, 1962.

Yanagida Seizan 柳田聖山. 'Sodō shū hombun kenkyū (I)' 「祖堂集」の本文研究(一), *Zengaku kenkyū* 禅学研究, 54 (July, 1964), 11–87. Study of *Tsu-t'ang chi*.

Yanagida Seizan 柳田聖山. 'Sodō shū no shiryō kachi (I)' 「祖堂集」の資料価値(一), *Zengaku kenkyū*, 44 (October, 1953), 31–80. Study of *Tsu-t'ang chi*.

INDEX

This index is primarily designed to allow easy access to the Introduction and to representative information of general significance in the Notes on the Texts.

Ababa hell 245
abstinence 234
ācārya 232, 239
acting 20
adornment 198, 215
Aeolus 221
affliction 174, 237
Akizuki Ryōmin 235
Allahabad Stone Pillar 15
Allen, Sarah 253
allusion 193, 268, 285, 289
alms 176, 225
alms-bowl 175
almsgiving 238
Amitābha 224, 259
Analects 176, 193ff, 201f, 226, 251, 269
Ānanda 210, 228
Anāthapiṇḍada 175
Anāthapiṇḍika 179
Anhwei 12
anti-Buddhist polemics 27, 201
Aoki Masaru 18n
aphorisms 298
arhatship 226, 228
Arthaśāstra 20
Arthur, King 286
Aśvaghoṣa 15
Aṭaṭa 245
authorship 10
avadāna 6
avalambana 224
Avalokitésvara 224
avarice 252
Avīci 239, 243, 245, 256

bad karma 197
Bailey, H. W. 273
ballad 282
banyan tree 209
batō 17
Baxter, Glen William 23
begging 175, 257
begging at the wrong time 256
begging-bowl 231, 243
Bernhard, Franz 299
betel nut 276
Bhagavat 179
Bharata 19
Bibliothèque Nationale ix
blessings 224f, 242
Blood-Basin Sūtra 224
Bodde, Derk 192, 299
bodhi 177, 197, 226, 230
bodhimaṇḍala 207
Bodhisattva 3, 183
Bodhisattva ideal 245
boundlessness 234
Brahmā 19, 185, 205, 219, 231
'The Brahman' 27
Brāhman students 174
Brāhmī 175
'Briar Branch Lyric' 21
British Library ix
Buddha 3, 19
Buddha, attributes of 204, 255
Buddha-body 203
Buddha-mind 177
Buddhism 14, 172
Buddhism at Tun-huang 305
Buddhism in China 24
Buddhist concept 267
Buddhist establishment 9
Buddhist imagery 25
Buddhist influence 268, 272, 282, 293
Buddhist narrative 22
Buddhist storytelling 26
Buddhist technical terms 172
Buddhist thought 208
Buddhist translations 24
Buddhist usage 270
bugaku 16
Bunker, Emmy C. 221

campū 15

cassock 210f, 228, 260
causation 239
causes 257
Central Asia 5, 17, 25, 172 205
Central Kingdom (India) 261
central way 177
Chan, Wing-tsit 229
Chan-kuo ts'e 245
Chandragupta 20
Chang Chan 19
Chang Chüeh 234, 298
Chang Heng 16, 294
Chang Hua 286
Chang I-ch'ao manuscript ix
Chang I-ch'ao transformation text 1, 7, 166ff
Chang I-ch'ao transformation text, date of 11
Chang Liu-chu 295
Chang Nan-chuang 194
Chang Pao-ta 262
Chang-tsung 21
Chang Yen-yüan 253
Ch'ang-an 25
ch'ang-ching-tz'u 23
ch'ang-chuan 23
ch'ang-po pu-tuan 23
ch'ang-shua-ling 23
Changes, Book of 178, 263
chantefable 1
Chao-chou 235
Chao, King 296
Chao Ling-chih 21
Chao Tun 268
Ch'ao-yeh ch'ien-tsai 244
chastity 272
Chavannes, Édouard 221, 305
Chekiang 12, 20
Chen, Lili 271
Ch'en Ju-heng 15n
Ch'en, Kenneth K. S. 222, 224
Ch'en Yüan-hung 170
Cheng-Chen-to 10
Cheng Ch'ien 22n
Ch'eng-fu District 12, 297
Ch'eng I-chung 15
Ch'eng-tu 25
Cheung, Samuel 239
chi 6
Chi Hsien-lin (Dschi Hiän-lin) 19n
Chi Pu 7
Chi Pu, tale of the capture of 274
Ch'i 285
Ch'i-hsia wu-i 237
Ch'i-lien shan 310
chiang-ching-wen 6ff, 14
chiliacosm 176
Chin period 4, 19, 21
Chin-shu 191, 264, 274, 286
Ch'in period 15
ching 6
Ching Mountain 304
Chiu T'ang-shu 17n, 202, 293, 295, 310
Chiu Wu-tai shih 311
Ch'iu Hu 7, 280, 287
Chou Emperor 294
Chou I-po 18n
Chou period 284
Chow Tse-tsung 261
chu-kung-tiao 21, 23
Chu Mai-ch'en 253
Ch'u 16, 265, 284f, 296, 301
Ch'u, King of 298
Ch'u-tz'u 16
chuan 6
chuan-pien 9
ch'uan-ch'i 22
Ch'uan-teng lu 191, 206
Chuang-tzu 236f, 283, 289, 303
Ch'un-yü K'un 284
Chung-tsung 11
ch'ü 22, 25, 283
ch'ü(-tzu-tz'u) 6
chüeh-chü 23
cinematography 297
citrakār 5
cītrakathī 5
Cleaves, Francis Woodman 310
cliché 194
colloquial language 1, 5, 24, 227, 231f, 266, 271, 290, 298
colophons 9f
community of monks 256
compartment of hell 249
compassion 237, 249, 254
compensatory justice 296, 298
concentration 228
conches 211
conditional causation 234
confession 17
Confucianism 176, 200, 292
contemplation 229
converts 174
copyist 251, 262
costume 23

dance 16, 21, 23
dancing 20
Dante 245
dating 9
datta 20
Davidson, J. Leroy 221
DeBary, William Theodore 20n
Deer Park 174, 226
delusion 197
Demiéville, Paul 189
desire 183
deva 25, 175, 185

Devadatta 259
Devanāgarī 175
dhāraṇī 178
Dharma-body 176
dharmadhātu 222
Dharmarakṣa 19
Dhṛtarāṣṭra 212
diamond deities 211, 213
Diamond Sūtra 222
disciples 222
discipleship 231
distinguishing marks 176
doctrine 185, 215
dog barbarians 309
donations 256
drama 1, 13ff
dream interpretation 302
Droṇodana 259
drums 211
duty officers 234
Duyvendak, J. J. L. 236, 266

Earth deities 219
Eastern Barbarians 177
Eastern Han period 24
Eastern Sea 263
eating Indian-style 258
Eberhard, Wolfram 224
Edgerton, Franklin 3n, 179
eight barbarians 262
eight classes of supernatural beings 254
eight difficulties 244
eight lakes 255
eight realms 183
eightfold noble path 176
elephant king 211, 215, 255
elephant's gait 255
emendation 172
emptiness 223
Enoki, Kazuo 302
entertainers 8f, 16, 18, 211
Eoyang, Eugene 8n, 223
Erh-ya 262
esoteric Buddhism 178, 211
etoki 5
etymology 217
exemplar 238, 249, 257
evam uktam 27n
evaṃ-vācaka 27n
evaṃ-vādin 27n

Fa chi-yao sung ching 299
face 299
Fan-i ming-i chi 224
Fan Li 301, 304
Feng-su t'ung 251
Feng Yüan-chün 14n
fiction 1, 13
field of blessedness 257
filial piety 259
First Buddhist Council at Rājagṛha 228
fish pouch 12, 293
fish token 300
fixed prices 292
Five Classics 177
five-coloured 227
five colours 203
five commandments 232, 239
five desires 227
Five Dynasties period 2, 4, 6, 9, 22f, 26
five gerontions 192
Five Terraces Moutain 254
five turbidities 177
folk Buddhism 242
folk culture 9
folk entertainment 7
folk etymology 237, 276
folklore 13
folk tales 6
formlessness 175
formula for closing of sūtra 262
four divine flowers 179
four fruits 176
Four Kings 203
four mental states 176
four modes of the six rebirths 226
Four Noble Truths 228
four orders 179, 185
freedom 231
fu 6, 15f, 200, 266, 277, 294
Fu-ch'a 301, 303
Fūjin 221

gadya 15
Gandhāran sculpture 204
Ganges 174, 245, 259
Garfias, Robert 16n
Gargi, Balwant 15n, 20n
garuḍa 217
Gate of Heaven 263
gāthā 22, 26, 262
Gautama 200
General of the Five Ways 235
gesture 23
ghanta 20
Giles, Lionel 12
Gimm, Martin 17n
Gobi desert 4
God of Wind 220, 222
golden sand 215
good and evil 191, 229
Good and Evil Boys 235
good deeds 260, 293
good karma 239
good works 232
Grand Duke 253, 298
Gṛdhrakūta 183
greed 259

Greek 18
Grube, W. 18n
guṇa 300

Hai-nei shih-chou chi 270
halo 255
Hambis, Louis 306
Hami 169, 311
Han 'Catch Tiger' 7
Han-fei-tzu 193
Han P'eng 7
Han period 16, 289
Han-shih wai-chuan 198f
Han-shu 12f, 194, 196, 199, 253, 280
Han Wu-ti 270
Han Yü 27
Hanan, Patrick 8n
Hariṣeṇa 15
Heavenly King 212
heavenly maidens 262
hell 223, 235, 238f, 242
heptasyllabism 7, 22, 240
Hermann, Albert 267
hetupratyaya 6
hexasyllabic prose rhythm 175
Hilka, Alfons 232
Hīnayāna 183
Ho Ch'ang-ch'ün 274
Ho, Emperor 289
Ho-lu 301, 303
holy wisdom 255
Holzman, Donald 198
Horrowitz, E. P. 18n
Hou-Han shu 191, 218, 253, 268, 274, 293, 300
householder 256
Hsi-ching tsa-chi 13
Hsi-hsiang chi chu-kung-tiao 271
hsi-wen 20
hsiang-kung 20
Hsiang Ta 17n
hsieh-hou-yü 267
Hsien, Shaman 16
Hsien-yü ching 180, 182, 219, 221
Hsin T'ang-shu 305
Hsiung-nu 289
Hsü ch'i-hsieh chi 287
Hsüan-ho hua-p'u 247
Hsüan-tsang 308
Hsüan-tsung 9, 11, 310
Hsüeh An-chün 262
Hsün-tzu 195, 302
Hu Chi 14n
Hu San-hsing 295
Hu Shih manuscript 174
Hu Shiu-ying 275
hua 6
Hua-chien chi 23
hua-pen 23
Hua-yüeh hen 237, 281
Huai-hai 263
Huai, King of Ch'u 290
Huai-nan-tzu 179, 196, 208, 287, 306
Hui-neng 178
Hui-yüan 7
hungry ghosts 204, 251, 256
Huns 309
hymns 212

iconography 181, 196f, 221
ignorance 209, 254
illusion 176, 222
immortals 179, 185, 212
Impartial King 251
impartiality 259
impermanence 228, 257
indescribability 255
India 5, 15, 25
Indian drama 15, 20
Indian influence 1
Indic languages 24
Indonesia 5
Indonesian shadow plays 264
Indra 26, 185, 191
ineffability 210, 257
Inferno 245
infinity 211
interpolated words and sounds 23
Iran 25
Iranian 224
Iwamoto Yutaka 224, 249

Jackson, J. H. 222
Jambūdvīpa 231, 240, 258
Japan 4f, 16, 25
Jātaka 19
Jātakamālā 15
Jen Erh-pei 15n
Jen Pan-t'ang 14, 16
Jen-wu chih 284
Jensen, Hans 175
Jetā 197
Jetavana 179
Johnson, David 12
jongleur 8n
Journey to the West 3

Kālidāsa 20
kalpa 26, 187, 196, 210, 238
Kansu corridor 305
Kao Ming-k'ai 24n
Kao-tsung 193
Kapilavastu 219
Karakhoto 21
Karlgren, Bernhard 232
Karlik-tāgh 310
karma 25, 223, 225, 232
karmic hindrances 186

karmic retribution 259
katbu 5
Kauṭiliya 20
Keith, A. Berriedale 15n
Kenney, Don 16n
Khotan 25
Kiangsu 12
killēkyata 5
Kita no tenjin engi 256
King of Demons 218
King of Devils 184
King of the Law 210
kingship 183
knowledge 226, 237
Ko Hung 242
Kokonor 306
Korea 25
körünč 5
Kozlov, Petr Kuz'mich 21
Krebs, E. 18n
Kroraina 308
Kṣitigarbha 234
Ku-wen kuan-chih 298
Ku Yen-wu 233
K'uai-chi Mountain 265, 289
Kuan-tzu 263
Kuang-ling 290
Kuang po-wu chih 253
Kucha 18
kuei-ch'ü-lai 261
Kumārajīva 11
K'ung-tzu chia-yü 287
K'ung Ying-ta 192
Kuo-ch'ing ssu 20
Kuo-yü 190
Kuśinagara 243
Kuvera 223

Lalitavistara 15
Lan Ling 16
de Langre, Jacques 221
Lao Kan 215
Lao-tzu 177, 267
Lapchuk 308
Lau, Joseph S. M. 223
Laufer, Berthold 19n
Law 207, 209
lay students 9
laymen 262
laywomen 262
lectures 198
legends 6, 13
Lei Huan 286
Li-chi 192, 208, 270
Li Chih 193
Li Ling 298
Li Ling, transformation text on 186, 292
Li of Te-hua manuscript 223
Li Po 302
Li River 304
Li Shan 287
Li Shih-min 193, 303
Li-tai ming-hua chi 253
Li Yüan 200
Library of Congress ix
Liebenthal, Walter 299
Lieh-nü chuan 280
Lieh-tzu 19
limitlessness 234
Lin Han-ta 267
Ling Che 268
lion dance 211
Lion King 204
lion platform 212
literary texts 8
Liu Chih-yüan Medley 4, 21
Liu Pei 264
Liu Ts'un-yan 279
Liu Tsung-yüan 220
Liu Wu-chi 26
Liu Yao 264
Liu Yü 18, 278
Liu Yü-hsi 23
Lo Chen-yü 298
Lo Chen-yü manuscript 174
Lo Chin-t'ang 19
Lo, Goddess of the River 181
lokapāla 227
long-armed 264
longing 183
'Lotus Flower Twirl' 21
Lotus Sūtra 89, 183, 186, 228f
Lou-lan 308
Louis, René 8n
Lu Chi 287
Lu Kuei-meng 300
Lu kuei pu 21n
Lu Pan 216
Lu T'ung 258
lun 6
Luo-fu 181
Lü-shih ch'un-ch'iu 289
Lust, John 275

Ma, Y. W. 13n, 223
Madhyamāgama-sūtra 210
Madhyamayāna 183
Mahābhārata 18n, 255
Mahākāla 223, 248
Mahāprajāpati 196
Mahāsthāmaprāpta 224
Mahāyāna 183, 225
Maitreya 187
majesty 212, 254
Mandarin 189
Manichaean influence 224
Mañjuśrī 211
maṇkha 5

Mao Ch'i-ling 20, 21
Mao Tun 9n
Māra 174
marriage 280
masks 16, 18
Maspero, Henri 24n
Mather, Richard 299
Matsumoto Eiichi 3n, 233
Matsunaga, Daigan and Alicia 245
Maudgalyāyana 3
Maudgalyāyana, etymology of 224
Maudgalyāyana manuscript ix
Maudgalyāyana play 22
'Maudgalyāyana Retribution Story' 225
Maudgalyāyana transformation text 1, 7, 28, 86
Maudgalyāyana transformation text, date of 11
māyā 2
Māyā 196
medicine poem 25
medicine storytellers 279
medicines 275ff
meditation 175, 187, 210, 229, 230, 259
meditative mind 205
medleys 21f
Mei Ch'eng 296
Mencius 306
Meng, Entertainer 16
Men'shikov, L. N. 194
metaphor 269, 289
meta-texts 8
metrical filler 230
metrics 24
Milky Way 281
mime 23
mind 213, 229, 237
mind-control 210
Minn Yong-Gyu 25
mirror 202, 229
Mohism 199
Mokuren sonja jigoku meguri 249
monasteries 178f, 196, 231
monastery gardens 240
monastic order 210
Monier-Williams, Monier 15n
monks 8f, 185, 202, 218, 226, 250, 257
Mount Meru 231
Mount T'ai 233f, 238, 251
Mu, Duke 284
mukti 226
mundane world 258
Mushakōji Minoru 256
music 17f, 23
musical notation 23
musicians 211
myth 13

Naba Toshisada 5
nāga 185
Nagatomi Masatoshi 237, 245
Nakamura, Susumu W. 181
namaḥ 261
Nan-yang District 270
Nāṭya Śāstra 19
neo-Confucians 27
Nida, Eugene A. 172n
nidāna 6
Nīladhi 232
nimmāna 3
Nine Barbarians 177
nine classes 198
nineteen old poems 270, 280
nirmāṇa 3
nirmāṇakāya 187, 196
nirvāṇa 174, 176, 205
Nirvāṇa-sūtra 228
Nishino Teiji 274
notes 172
Nogami Shunjo 193
noon meal 175
Northern Chou period 18

obeisance 234
obstruction 258
ocean of misery 186, 228
offerings 182
Ogiwara Unrai (Wogihara Unrai) 27n
oral epic 8
oral literature 9
original mind 205
Orphan of Chao 268
orthography 172
Osabe Kazuo 234

Pa-shiang pien 17
padding words 23
padya 15
painted scrolls 3
Pak, C. 279
Pāli 245
Pan Ku 289
P'an An-jen (P'an Yüeh) 250
P'ang-t'e-le 310
Pāṇini 20
pao-chüan 23
Pao-p'u-tzu 201f
paper money 233
paṛ bhopo 5
parallelism 7, 290
Parr, Francis W. 304
Parthian 224
paṭuā 5
P'ei P'u-hsien 17n
Pelliot, Paul 221, 305
Pen-ts'ao 282
perfection 261
performers 7ff, 13

perpetual property 240
phonology 24
Pi-yen lu 274
P'i, Premier 302ff
picture scrolls 9, 254
picture storytellers 5
picture storytelling 8
pictures 223
pien 1ff
pien-wen 1ff, 7
pien-wen, Buddhist connotations 2
pien-wen, corpus 2, 4, 6
pien-wen manuscripts 9
pien-wen, meaning of 1ff
pien-hsiang 3
Piggott, Juliet 221
pilgrimage 254
p'ing-hua 5, 23
P'ing, King 269
Platform Sutra 211, 229f
Po-chou 297
Po Chü-i 9, 23, 211, 281
po-t'ou 16f
poetry 4
polysyllabism 24
popular Buddhism 24
popular culture 9
popular entertainment 26
popular genres 1
popular literature 27
prabhāva 25
practice characters 25
prajñā 178
Prakrit 20
prātihārya 213
pratimādhāriṇ 5
pratītya-samutpāda 6
pratyaya, 6, 25
Pratyekabuddha 183, 196, 206
precepts 185
principles 191
prodigal son 90, 229
prohibitions 261
promptbooks 8
propriety 176
prose 7
prose rhythm 179, 290
prosimetric form 5, 7, 14ff, 20f, 285
prosimetric narrative 1, 6
prosody 285
prostration 227
proverbs 190, 193f, 196, 216, 253, 263, 269, 271, 281, 284f, 293
Průšek, Jaroslav 13
Pulleyblank, E. 266
puns 224, 235, 275ff, 287
puppet show 18
puppets 19
Pure Land 178, 198, 224, 259, 261
Pure-Land sect 17
purgatorian feast 224

quadruple hearts 176
quid pro quo 153
quintuple eyes 176
Qyzil 205

'Rainbow Skirt and Feathered Blouse' 27
Rājagṛha 183
rākṣasa 240
ranjō 16
Raudrākṣa 198, 202, 210
Read, B. E. 279, 282
realms of form 223
rebirth 224, 238
receptivity 262
redemption 210
regulations 185
release 226
remorse 249
renunciation 177, 227
repartee 23
repentance 261
retribution 239, 252
reverence 233
rhyme 5n, 7, 250, 252, 267, 283, 295
river of pus 256
robe 210, 250
Robinson, Richard H. 299
Russian 18n
ryō-ō 16

Saddharmapuṇḍarika 15
Sage 196
saint 185
sainthood 229
Śakra 191
Śakuntalā 20
Śākyamuni 181, 187
sāl tree grove 243
salutation 186
salvation 175
samādhi 210, 214, 231
saṃsāra 3, 228, 233, 237, 243
Samudragupta 15
San-kuo chih yen-i 264
San-pao t'ai-chien hsia hsi-yang chi 236
saṅgha 179
Sanskrit 20
Sanskrit plays 15
Śāriputra 3
Śāriputra illustrated scroll ixf
Śāriputra manuscript ix
Śāriputra transformation text 1, 7f, 26, 28ff
Śāriputra transformation text, date of 10
Sārnāth 187
Sastri, Gaurinath 15n
śaubhika 5

sauvastika 227
Sawada Mizuho 224
sayings 198, 267, 270, 275, 293
Schafer, Edward H. 286, 290
schoolmaster 13
schools, monastery 9
scribes and copyists 7ff
scripture 6
self-enlightenment 196
sena 20
Serindia 201
Serindians 211
sermonizing 258
seven deadly sins 228
seven treasures 176, 215
sexual passions 241
Sha-chou 305, 309
shadow figures 19
Shan-hai ching 248
Shao Weng 19
Shen-hsien chuan 234
Shen-hsiu 229
Shiffahrtshöhle 205
shih ('poem') 6, 22
Shih-chi 12, 16, 19, 194, 203, 268, 284, 301, 309
Shih-ching 199, 203, 232, 242, 288f, 291, 302
Shih-shuo hsin-yü 288
Shionoya On 18n
shu 6
Shu-ching 199, 203, 251, 264, 301
Shui-hu chuan 222
Shun 26, 177, 199, 270, 292
Shun-tzu 191
Sīkri 204
silk 12, 18, 293, 300
simulated context 8
sin 245
sinful karma 228
singing 20
singing girls 9, 13
Sinor, Denis 305
Śīva 175, 219
Six Dynasties period 2, 7, 24
six earth-shakings 229
Six Heretics 198, 222
six impurities 175
Six Kingdoms 201
six sensations 176
so-yu 294
sociolinguistics 24
Sogdian 224
songs 21, 23, 283, 291
Sou-shen chi 268
soul 238f, 256, 299
sources 12f
Southern Sung period 20
Soymié, Michel 244
spiritual master 209
spiritual powers 210
spiritual realization 231
Spring and Autumn Period 16, 284, 296
Śrāvaka 183, 210
Śrāvastī 31, 179
Ssu-ma Hsiang-ju 187
staff 231, 249
statues 214
Stein, M. A. ix
storytellers 3, 8
storytelling 9, 15
stūpa 185
stupid people 257
Styx 235
su-chiang 7
Su Chung-lang 18
Subhūti 175
subjugation of demons 174, 210
Sudatta 179
Śuddhodana 183, 196
suffering 225
Sui period 18
Sui-shu 18n, 202
Sui Shu-sen 18n
Śūlakṣaṇa 232
summer retreat 223
Sun Ch'i 9n
Sun Shu-ao 16, 284
Sung period 19, 22
Sung *tsa-chü* 23
śūnya 175
śūnyatā 229
supernatural powers 238, 259
supernatural strength 244
sūtra lectures 5n, 6, 8, 15, 20
sūtras 11, 22, 179
swastika 204
swords 214, 254, 286, 290, 303
Szechwan 9, 24f, 200, 256, 277ff, 282, 305

Ta-mien 16
T'a-yao niang 17
taboo-words 193, 303
Tai-mien 16
T'ai-p'ing kuang-chi 264
T'ai-p'ing yü-lan 296
T'ai-tsung 7, 193
Taiwan 9
Takata Osamu 204
t'an-ch'ang yin-yüan 23
t'an-tz'u 23
T'ang and Ming codes 298
T'ang hui yao 10, 293
T'ang Kuei-chang 21n
T'ang period 2, 4, 6, 9ff, 19, 21ff, 26
T'ang-shu 240
T'ang ta chao-ling chi 310
Taoism 177, 233, 251, 273, 292

Taoist curse 274
Taoist immortals 213
Taoist texts 244
Taoist underworld 234
Tathāgata 211, 226
teacher 236
temples 197
ten commandments 180, 197
ten evils 251
ten virtues 223, 232
textbook for children 305
theatricals 19
three carts 228
three disasters 244
Three Honoured Ones 224
three insights 243
Three Jewels 180f, 187, 218, 223, 225, 249, 261
Three Kingdoms 19
three mires 223, 236, 250, 258, 260
three old ones 192
three poisons 227
three realms 184
three rivers 256
Three Teachings 178
three vehicles 183
three virtues 176
thunderbolt 197
Ti baγa 311
Tibet 25
Tibetans 305
T'ien Chen 287f
T'ien Shih-lin 14n
T'ien-t'ai 186
T'ien-t'ai Mountain 20
T'ien Tan 309
Togi, Masataro 16n
tonsure 201
Tou Hsien 289
transformation texts 21
transformations 2, 213f
translation 7
transmigration 226, 234
tree of knives 240
tree of wisdom 203
Trinity 225
Tripiṭaka 12
triple-world 206
tsa-chü 22
tsa-fu 15
Ts'ai Yung 192
tsan 6
Ts'an-chün hsi 18
Ts'ao Chih 181, 280, 292
Tschepe, A. 304
Ts'en Chung-mien 305
Tso Ch'eng-chen 310
Tso-chuan 12, 192, 195, 268, 284, 294ff
Tso Ssu 294
Tsuji Naoshirō 27
Tsukamoto Keishō 228
Tsung Mi 256
Tu Fu 280
T'u An-ku 268
T'u-shu chi-ch'eng 281
Tuan An-chieh 17n
Tun-huang cave shrine 1
Tun-huang manuscripts 2
  D109 252
  D278 252
  D296 11n
  D970 268, 288
  D1502v 206
  D2106 247
  D2256 295
  D2264 295
  D2889 295
  D3903 252
  D5870 311
  D6116 268
  P2094 11n
  P2249v 25
  P2319 223
  P2524 268
  P2581v 252
  P2713 252
  P2721 11, 305
  P2723 274
  P2794v 26, 262
  P2829 302
  P2962 305
  P3105 302
  P3107 223
  P3212 262
  P3485 223
  P3685 302
  P3808 23
  P3908 302
  P3990v 302
  P4524v 174
  P4615 174
  P4988v 223
  PK876 223
  PK2095 274
  PK3789 223
  PK4085 223
  PK5259 311
  PK8668 262
  PK9768 293
  PK9802 11
  S328 12, 262
  S620 302
  S1497 252
  S1722 192
  S2222 302
  S2588 268
  S2614 223
  S2614v 262

S3704 223
S4398v 11, 174
S4634v 252
S5511 174
S5666 274
S5892 252
S6331 12, 262
S6342 311
S6973 311
Tun-huang manuscripts, discovery of 1
Tun-huang popular literature, terminology 4
Tun-huang popular narratives 2, 4, 7
tune 283, 308
Tung Chieh-yüan 21, 271
Tung-Chou lieh-kuo chih 267, 284
Tung-yü ta-sheng pao-ch'an 234
Tung Yung 7, 235
T'ung-su pien 208, 253
T'ung-tien 296
Turkestan 18
Turkish 18n
Turks 308
Tuṣita Heaven 197
Tuyughun 305f
twin *śāla* trees 174
Twin Trees 226
two hearts 205
tzu-pu 17
tzu-p'u 17
tz'u 6, 22f, 25, 283

Ueno Teruo 204
Uighur Khan 310
Uighurs 5
ullambana 224
Umezu Jirō 5
unconditionalness 211
underworld 238
universal king 203
universe 258
unreality 177, 229
upāya 226, 244
urvan 224
Utz, David 224

Vaiśravaṇa 219f
vajra 213
Vajracchedikā 15
Vajracchedikā-prajñā-pāramitā-sūtra 11
Vajracchedikā-sūtra 177
Vārāṇási 187
vegetarian food 87
vernacular literature 1
verse 7
verse-introductory formula 6, 27, 184, 266
vexation 218
vijñāna 177
Vimalakīrtinirdeśa-sūtra 228
Vimalakīrti-sūtra, lecture on 180
Vipaśyin 197
Viṣṇu 219
de Visser, M. W. 224
von le Coq, A. 205
vow 257
Vulture Peak 183, 210

wall-paintings 181, 189, 221, 254
Wan-fo hsia 221
Wang Chao-chün 13
Wang Chi-te 21
Wang Chung-min 23n
Wang Ho-ch'ing 311
Wang Jui-chang 310
Wang Kuo-wei 17, 20
Wang Ling, transformation on the Han General 28, 266
Wang Meng-ou 238
Wang Po 280
Wang Wen-ts'ai 14
Ware, James A. 201
Warring States period 269
Wathellwedo River 235
Way of Heaven 266
wayang bèbèr 5
wedge 20
Wei Chuang 23
Wei Ling 264
Wei-shu 194
Wen-chou 20
Wen Ju-hsien 283
Wen-shu-shih-li wen ching 224f
Wen T'ing-yün 23, 255
'West Chamber Tale' 21
West, Stephen H. 8n
Western Paradise 224
winds of karma 243
Wisdom 174f, 177, 188, 195, 211, 258
wise man 257
World-Honoured 210, 226
worship 196
Wu 296
Wu, Emperor 19
Wu-lin chiu-shih 279
Wu Shê 264f
Wu Tzu-hsü scroll ix
Wu Tzu-hsü, story of 1, 7, 25f, 122ff
Wu Tzu-hsü story, date of 11f
Wu Tzu-shang 264f
Wu Yüan Plays the Pipes 271
Wu Yüeh ch'un-ch'iu 26, 193, 265, 271, 304

ya-tso-wen 6
yakṣa 243
Yama 233f
yamapaṭa 5
Yampolsky, Philip B. 211
Yang Hsien-i 211

Yang kuei-fei 302
Yang Lien-sheng 17, 273
Yang Pao 268
Yang, Shaman 16
Yang-ti 18
Yang Yin-shen 20
Yao 177, 199, 292
Yeh Ching-neng 7
Yellow Turbans 234, 298
Yen Hui 287
Yen, Mount 289
Yen-shih chia-hsün 306
Yen Ying 207
yin 6
Yin Fa-lu 22, 23n
yin-yang 133, 203
yin-yüan 6
Ying-ying chuan 21n
Yogācārya-bhūmi śāstra 228
Yoshioka Gihō 261
yü-hou 295
yü-lan-p'en 224
Yü-lan-p'en sūtra 256
yü-lu 24
yüan 6
Yüan Chen 21n
yüan-ch'i 6
Yüan *ch'ü* 23
Yüan-ch'ü hsüan 263, 271
Yüan drama 15, 223, 268, 271f
yüan-pen 22f
Yüan period 7
yüan-wai 20
Yüeh 301
Yüeh chüeh shu 26, 194, 265, 274
Yüeh-fu shih-chi 251
Yüeh-fu tsa-lu 255
yuga 187

Zen 24, 178, 201, 235
Zen postures 230
Zograf, I. T. 264
Zoroastrianism 223
Zucker, A. E. 18n